Computer Vision and Pattern Recognition with Applications

Computer Vision and Pattern Recognition with Applications

Guest Editor

Teng Li

MDPI

Basel • Beijing • Wuhan • Barcelona • Belgrade • Novi Sad • Cluj • Manchester

Guest Editor
Teng Li
School of Electrical
Engineering and Automation
Anhui University
Hefei
China

Editorial Office
MDPI AG
Grosspeteranlage 5
4052 Basel, Switzerland

This is a reprint of the Special Issue, published open access by the journal *Mathematics* (ISSN 2227-7390), freely accessible at: https://www.mdpi.com/si/mathematics/Computer_Vision_Pattern_Recognition_Applications.

For citation purposes, cite each article independently as indicated on the article page online and as indicated below:

Lastname, A.A.; Lastname, B.B. Article Title. *Journal Name* **Year**, *Volume Number*, Page Range.

ISBN 978-3-7258-5707-4 (Hbk)
ISBN 978-3-7258-5708-1 (PDF)
https://doi.org/10.3390/books978-3-7258-5708-1

Contents

About the Editor vii

Preface ix

Gang Lv, Yushan Xu, Zuchang Ma, Yining Sun and Fudong Nian
Scale and Background Aware Asymmetric Bilateral Network for Unconstrained Image Crowd Counting
Reprinted from: *Mathematics* **2022**, *10*, 1053, https://doi.org/10.3390/math10071053 1

Guo Zhang, Jinzhao Lin, Enling Cao, Yu Pang and Weiwei Sun
A Medical Endoscope Image Enhancement Method Based on Improved Weighted Guided Filtering
Reprinted from: *Mathematics* **2022**, *10*, 1423, https://doi.org/10.3390/math10091423 18

Meng Han, Jilin Zhang, Yan Zeng, Fei Hao and Yongjian Ren
A Novel Method of Chinese Herbal Medicine Classification Based on Mutual Learning
Reprinted from: *Mathematics* **2022**, *10*, 1557, https://doi.org/10.3390/math10091557 35

Xianwei Li, Guolong Chen, Liang Zhao and Bo Wei
Multimedia Applications Processing and Computation Resource Allocation in MEC-Assisted SIoT Systems with DVS
Reprinted from: *Mathematics* **2022**, *10*, 1593, https://doi.org/10.3390/math10091593 48

Szidónia Lefkovits, Simina Emerich and László Lefkovits
Boosting Unsupervised Dorsal Hand Vein Segmentation with U-Net Variants
Reprinted from: *Mathematics* **2022**, *10*, 2620, https://doi.org/10.3390/math10152620 65

Fudong Nian, Ling Ding, Yuxia Hu and Yanhong Gu
Multi-Level Cross-Modal Semantic Alignment Network for Video–Text Retrieval
Reprinted from: *Mathematics* **2022**, *10*, 3346, https://doi.org/10.3390/math10183346 96

Yaming Wang, Minjie Wang, Wenqing Huang, Xiaoping Ye and Mingfeng Jiang
Deep Spatial-Temporal Neural Network for Dense Non-Rigid Structure from Motion
Reprinted from: *Mathematics* **2022**, *10*, 3794, https://doi.org/10.3390/math10203794 115

Young Won Lee, Jung Soo Kim and Kang Ryoung Park
Ocular Biometrics with Low-Resolution Images Based on Ocular Super-Resolution CycleGAN
Reprinted from: *Mathematics* **2022**, *10*, 3818, https://doi.org/10.3390/math10203818 132

Weiwei Sun, Huiqian Wang, Yi Lu, Jiasai Luo, Ting Liu, Jinzhao Lin, et al.
Deep-Learning-Based Complex Scene Text Detection Algorithm for Architectural Images
Reprinted from: *Mathematics* **2022**, *10*, 3914, https://doi.org/10.3390/math10203914 162

Qingxia Li, Dali Gao, Qieshi Zhang, Wenhong Wei and Ziliang Ren
Interactive Learning of a Dual Convolution Neural Network for Multi-Modal Action Recognition
Reprinted from: *Mathematics* **2022**, *10*, 3923, https://doi.org/10.3390/math10213923 184

Ganbayar Batchuluun, Se Hyun Nam and Kang Ryoung Park
Deep Learning-Based Plant Classification Using Nonaligned Thermal and Visible Light Images
Reprinted from: *Mathematics* **2022**, *10*, 4053, https://doi.org/10.3390/math10214053 199

Liqiang Liu, Tiantian Feng, Yanfang Fu, Chao Shen, Zhijuan Hu, Maoyuan Qin, et al.
Learning Adaptive Spatial Regularization and Temporal-Aware Correlation Filters for Visual Object Tracking
Reprinted from: *Mathematics* **2022**, *10*, 4320, https://doi.org/10.3390/math10224320 . . . . **217**

Xiaochen Ju, Xinxin Zhao and Shengsheng Qian
TransMF: Transformer-Based Multi-Scale Fusion Model for Crack Detection
Reprinted from: *Mathematics* **2022**, *10*, 2354, https://doi.org/10.3390/math10132354 . . . . **236**

Satyawant Kumar, Abhishek Kumar and Dong-Gyu Lee
Semantic Segmentation of UAV Images Based on Transformer Framework with Context Information
Reprinted from: *Mathematics* **2022**, *10*, 4735, https://doi.org/10.3390/math10244735 . . . . **254**

Ge Jin, Xu Chen and Long Ying
Deep Multi-Task Learning for an Autoencoder-Regularized Semantic Segmentation of Fundus Retina Images
Reprinted from: *Mathematics* **2022**, *10*, 4798, https://doi.org/10.3390/math10244798 . . . . **271**

Hui Yan and Jianrong Dai
Reconstructing a 3D Medical Image from a Few 2D Projections Using a B-Spline-Based Deformable Transformation
Reprinted from: *Mathematics* **2023**, *11*, 69, https://doi.org/10.3390/math11010069 . . . . **286**

Tingzhang Zhan, Qieshi Zhang, Guangxi Chen and Jun Cheng
VRR-Net: Learning Vehicle–Road Relationships for Vehicle Trajectory Prediction on Highways
Reprinted from: *Mathematics* **2023**, *11*, 1293, https://doi.org/10.3390/math11061293 . . . . **298**

Jaesin Ahn, Jiuk Hong, Jeongwoo Ju and Heechul Jung
Redesigning Embedding Layers for Queries, Keys, and Values in Cross-Covariance Image Transformers
Reprinted from: *Mathematics* **2023**, *11*, 1933, https://doi.org/10.3390/math11081933 . . . . **313**

About the Editor

Teng Li

Teng Li received his B.S. degree from the University of Science and Technology of China (USTC), Hefei, China, in 2001, his M.S. degree from the Institute of Automation, Chinese Academy of Sciences (CASIA), Beijing, China, in 2004, and his Ph.D. from the Korea Advanced Institute of Science and Technology (KAIST), Daejeon, South Korea, in 2010. He has authored 100+ papers, and received the Best Paper Award of *IEEE Transactions on Circuits and Systems* for Video Technology in 2014. He is currently a Professor at Anhui University, Hefei. His research interests include deep learning (artificial intelligence), pattern recognition, and computer vision.

Preface

In the contemporary era, computer vision and pattern recognition have emerged as quintessential instruments in the science and technology sector, playing an increasingly critical role in addressing everyday challenges. Distinct from the approaches rooted in probability theory, these disciplines provide novel methodologies for tackling uncertainties arising from incomplete or complex information. Computer vision employs algorithmic and data-driven techniques to detect and classify visual patterns through the analysis of images and video data.

The theoretical and practical advancements in these fields are continuously progressing. For instance, in medical image analysis, computer vision aids in pinpointing disease markers, enhancing the precision of medical diagnoses. In security monitoring, pattern recognition technologies are utilized to detect potential threats, thus improving public safety. Additionally, these technologies contribute significantly to the development of autonomous vehicles by enabling them to recognize and interpret environmental cues for real-time decision-making.

With the escalation of computational power and the proliferation of big data, the applications of computer vision and pattern recognition are extending across diverse sectors. This includes physical sciences, economic management, and expert systems such as financial planning, diagnostics, meteorology, information retrieval, and control systems, and extends to industrial automation, robotics, decision-making, programming, medicine, biology, the humanities, education, and virtually all human activities. The advancements in these applications have not only yielded significant improvements in efficiency and accuracy but also have demonstrated vast potential in enhancing human cognitive functions. As these technologies advance, it is anticipated that computer vision and pattern recognition will increasingly infiltrate every aspect of our lives, altering how we interact with our world.

The present book contains the 18 articles that were accepted for publication in the Special Issue "Computer Vision and Pattern Recognition with Applications, 2022" of MDPI's *Mathematics* journal. This Special Issue belongs to the section "Mathematics and Computer Science." The 18 articles, that appear in the present book in the series that have been published in Volumes 10 (2022) and 11 (2023) of the journal, cover a wide range of topics connected to the theory and applications of computer vision and pattern recognition. These topics include, among others, image classification; image detection, image segmentation; medical image recognition; medical image enhancement; multi-modal action recognition; text detection; video–text retrieval; dense non-rigid structure from motion; computation resource allocation; crowd counting, etc.

It is hoped that the book will be interesting and useful for those working in the area of computer vision, pattern recognition, and their applications, and for those with the proper mathematical background who are willing to become familiar with recent advances in computer vision and pattern recognition.

As the Guest Editor of the Special Issue, I am grateful to the authors of the papers for their quality contributions, to the reviewers for their valuable comments towards the improvement of the submitted works, and to the administrative staff at MDPI for the support to complete this project. Special thanks are due to the Managing Editor of the Special Issue, Ms. Grace Du, for her excellent collaboration and valuable assistance.

Teng Li
Guest Editor

mathematics

MDPI

Article

Scale and Background Aware Asymmetric Bilateral Network for Unconstrained Image Crowd Counting

Gang Lv [1,2,3], Yushan Xu [3], Zuchang Ma [1,2], Yining Sun [1,2] and Fudong Nian [3,4,*]

1 Hefei Institutes of Physical Science, Chinese Academy of Sciences, Hefei 230031, China; lvgang@hfuu.edu.cn (G.L.); zcma@iim.ac.cn (Z.M.); ynsun@iim.ac.cn (Y.S.)
2 School of Information Science and Technology, University of Science and Technology of China, Hefei 230026, China
3 School of Advanced Manufacturing Engineering, Hefei University, Hefei 230601, China; xuyushan11219@163.com
4 School of Artificial Intelligence, Anhui University, Hefei 230601, China
* Correspondence: nianfd@hfuu.edu.cn

Abstract: This paper attacks the two challenging problems of image-based crowd counting, that is, scale variation and complex background. To that end, we present a novel crowd counting method, called the Scale and Background aware Asymmetric Bilateral Network (SBAB-Net), which is able to handle scale variation and background noise in a unified framework. Specifically, the proposed SBAB-Net contains three main components, a pre-trained backbone convolutional neural network (CNN) as the feature extractor and two asymmetric branches to generate a density map. These two asymmetric branches have different structures and use features from different semantic layers. One branch is densely connected stacked dilated convolution (DCSDC) sub-network with different dilation rates, which relies on one deep feature layer and can handle scale variation. The other branch is parameter-free densely connected stacked pooling (DCSP) sub-network with various pooling kernels and strides, which relies on shallow feature and can fuse features with several receptive fields to reduce the impact of background noise. Two sub-networks are fused by the attention mechanism to generate the final density map. Extensive experimental results on three widely-used benchmark datasets have demonstrated the effectiveness and superiority of our proposed method: (1) We achieve competitive counting performance compared to state-of-the-art methods; (2) Compared with baseline, the MAE and MSE are decreased by at least 6.3% and 11.3%, respectively.

Keywords: crowd counting; asymmetric structure; bilateral network; density estimation

MSC: 68T10

1. Introduction

Crowd counting, a fundamental task in many public safety monitoring systems, aims to estimate the number of people in a still image. There are many studies have been devoted to solve this problem and they have made some progress [1,2]. Conventional methods solve the crowd counting problem by using hand-crafted features to detect each individual person, predict the count of people via regression or density estimation [3–7]. Due to insufficient semantic representation of hand-crafted features, these methods usually have low performance. Recently, benefiting from the powerful feature representation of CNN, CNN-based methods become dominant in crowd counting. In view of different types of network architectures, CNN-based crowd counting models can be divided into two categories: single column based methods [8,9] and multi-column based methods [10,11].

However, there are still several challenges preventing the computer vision community from designing a model capable of performing precise and robust crowd counting, such as occlusion, complex background, scale variation, non-uniform distribution, perspective distortion, rotation, illumination variation and weather changes. In this paper, we make an effort to address two of these challenges: scale variation and background noise. As illustrated in Figure 1, the scales of person vary as the distance from the camera, the background regions may have similar colors or textures with the people.

The scale variation is the primary problem that should be addressed in the crowd counting models. In the era of deep learning, researchers have made efforts to integrate semantic features of different scales to solve this problem. The main algorithm framework can be divided into three categories: (1) Multi-column. Some works [10,12,13] adopted "multi-column" architecture, where each branch has a different filter kernel size to handle a specific scale; (2) Nonstandard convolution. Some nonstandard convolution operations like dilated convolution [14–16] or deformable convolution [17,18], are exploited to model multi-scale information; (3) Feature pyramid networks (FPN). Several works [19–21] assumed features from different levels can capture different scale information and utilized FPN to fuse multi-level features. To eliminate noises caused by cluttered backgrounds, semantic segmentation or visual attention operations [22–25] are two common ways to suppress the response of the background regions. These methods guide the network focus on person instance via a mask image. Moreover, transformers are a new genre of deep neural networks that stack multiple self-attended layers. Unsurprisingly, we see an increasing effort on re-purposing such types of transformer models for crowd counting [26–31]. However, all methods mentioned above usually require millions of extra to-be-learned parameters (e.g., learnable multi-column, learnable segmentation/attention branch, multi-head transformer structure), which results in a higher computational burden.

(a) Scale variation (b) Background noise

Figure 1. Illustrations of the challenges of varying scales of people and cluttered backgrounds.

Recently, there have been some works [32–34] that attempt to model scale and background problems in a unified framework. The structures of these models are basically the same: a backbone to extract the image feature, and two multi-scale fusion branches to predict a density map and a background mask, respectively. These two branches share the image feature in a dual/symmetric way, that is, they utilize one or multiple common layers to learn scale and background aware features respectively. However, the latest research [35] shows that, compared with deep features, shallow features have a better ability to distinguish background and people. In addition, ref. [36] demonstrates the effectiveness of asymmetric module.

In this paper, we propose a new method for unconstrained image crowd counting, termed Scale and Background aware Asymmetric Bilateral Network (SBAB-Net), which is able to handle scale variation and background noise in a unified framework. Specifically, the proposed SBAB-Net contains three main components—a pre-trained backbone CNN as the feature extractor and two asymmetric branches to generate a density map. These two asymmetric branches have different structures and use features from different semantic layers. One branch is a densely connected stacked dilated convolution (DCSDC) sub-network with different dilation rates, which relies on one deep feature layer and can handle scale variation. The other branch is a densely connected stacked pooling (DCSP) sub-network with various pooling kernels and strides, which relies on shallow features and can fuse features with several receptive fields to reduce the impact of background noise. Compared with the existing semantic segmentation or visual attention based background aware methods, the proposed DCSP is learnable, parameters-free. Two sub-networks are fused by an attention mechanism to generate the final density map. Comprehensive experimental results on three widely-used benchmark datasets demonstrate that the proposed method is effective at the crowd counting task.

We note that Huang et al. [37] also apply the stacked pooling structure for crowd counting. The main differences between our method and [37] are three-fold. First, feature fusion strategies are different. We present a densely connected manner to fuse features with several receptive fields while [37] utilizes channel-wise average operation. Second, inspired by [35], we utilize shallow features to suppress the background noise while [37] use deep features to model scale information. Third, we handle scale and background information simultaneously while [37] only considers the scale problem.

Moreover, it should be noted that although there are several existing methods (e.g., CSRNet [16], DSACA [14], ADNet [15], DADNet [38]) that also utilize a dilation convolution structure to model scale variation, the differences between these existing dilation approaches and the proposed approach are three fold—Firstly, the proposed densely connected stacked dilated convolution (DCSDC) sub-network is a new and effective module to handle scale variation. Compared with the most famous dilation solution, CSRNet [16], our DCSDC fuses features from three different convolution layers with different dilation rates (i.e., 1, 2, 3) while CSRNet only stacks six dilated convolution layers with the same dilation rate (i.e., 2). Although ADNet [15] presents an adaptive dilated network in which the dilation rate can be learned online, only a specific dilation rate is estimated for an input feature map. DSACA [14] uses different dilation rates to capture multi-scale information by fusing features from different layers of the backbone. On the contrary, the proposed DCSDC only utilizes the last feature layer of the backbone, and captures multi-scale information by a densely connected stacked dilated convolution sub-network with different dilation rates. The multi-dilation convolution branch in DADNet [38] is a parallel structure while in our DCSDC it is a serial structure. The disadvantage of the parallel structure is that it neglects the small scale visual context when modeling a large scale visual context. Extensive experiments on three widely-used benchmarks demonstrate that the proposed method is better than these existing dilation approaches. Secondly, the scale aware feature f_s is refined by the background aware feature f_b in our framework. Finally, the dual branches in our SBAB-Net are asymmetric while most existing frameworks are symmetric, for example, SFANet [32].

In summary, this paper makes the following contributions.

- We propose a novel asymmetric bilateral network to handle scale variation and background noise in a unified framework. The scale-aware feature is captured by a multi-convolutional branch based on one deep feature layer. The background-aware feature is captured by a multi-pooling branch based on one shallow feature layer. These two features are fused in an attention manner. On the contrary, most existing methods organize scale and background branches in a symmetric/dual structure, that is, share the image feature from one or multiple common layers.
- A new DCSP sub-network is proposed to capture background-aware feature, which can fuse features with several receptive fields by several pooling layers with different strides to reduce the impact of background noise, and without any extra learnable parameters.
- We propose a new DCSDC sub-network to extract multi-scale information based on one deep feature layer, which densely connected several stacked dilated convolution layers with different dilation rates to capture the scale-aware feature. Moreover, the scale-aware feature is refined by the background-aware feature to ensure that the final feature can handle scale and background information simultaneously.

- We conducted extensive experiments on three challenging crowd counting datasets, that is, ShanghaiTech [10], UCF-QNRF [39], NWPU-Crowd [40]. Both quantitative and qualitative results demonstrate the effectiveness of the proposed method.

The remainder of this paper is organized as follows. Section 2 reviews the related work of CNN-based crowd counting methods for addressing scale variation and background noise challenges. Section 3 presents the proposed method in detail. Section 4 conducts comparisons on benchmarks and provides the experimental analysis. Finally, we conclude this paper in Section 5.

2. Related Work

The research on crowd counting can be roughly divided into three different dimensions: detection-based, regression-based and density estimation approaches.

Conventional methods [6,41] count the number of people in an image by using the handcraft feature to detect head or body, which performs worse for high crowd images. Thus, the direct regression methods have been proposed, which aims to predict the number of people directly from the image feature. These regression methods can also be divided into traditional and deep learning algorithms according to the utilization of low-level [4,42] or deep [9,43,44] features. However, direct regression methods ignore the spatial context information, which leads to the results not being robust. Recently, deep learning based density map estimation methods become dominant in crowd counting area. Each value in the density map represents the count of the person which corresponding to the original image region. Apparently, the sum of the density map is the number of people appearing in the whole image.

We shortly review some representative density estimation works related to our framework in the following.

2.1. Handle Scale Variation

Early work [10,11,16] for scale-aware feature extraction is via the multi-column or multi-network structure; each column or sub-network handles specific scale information via different convolution types, which is more complicated for optimization and computation wasting. Thus, single-column architecture becomes more popular. There are three common strategies modeling multi-scale in a single-column CNN: (1) Fuse features extracted from different layers [45], in which they assume that a different layer could capture different object scales; (2) Integrate features via pyramid operation, which may be an image pyramid [46] or a feature pyramid [19,20]; and (3) Learn scale from the annotations' distribution directly [47–49]. Different from the above methods, we propose a novel densely connected stacked dilated convolution sub-network with different dilation rates, which can handle multi-scale variation only based on one deep feature layer.

2.2. Handle Background Noise

Attention structure is widely-used to handle background noise. Liu et al. [22] present a detection module to guide the network counting of the crowd region. Gao et al. [50] introduce spatial-wise and channel-wise attention modules to constrain the network's focus on the head region—a similar idea is reported in [51]. Sindagi et al. [52] propose an inverse attention mechanism which can infuse segmentation information into the counting network efficiently. Shi et al. [53] consider the pixels near to annotations as foreground and design a branch to predict these foreground regions to learn attention factors. Liu et al. [54] propose a recurrent attentive zooming network to detect ambiguous regions recurrently.

2.3. Handle Scale Variation and Background Noise Simultaneously

Recently, some works have attempted to handle scale variation and background noise simultaneously in a unified framework. Zhang et al. [55] propose a cross layer attentional neural field. Guo et al. [38] and Liu et al. [17] use both attention and deformable convolutional structures in a model. All methods with the attention structure mentioned above have a common shortcoming, which is that these attention modules need millions of parameters to be optimized, which makes the model become more complex.

In addition, there are some works that attempt to improve the performance of the counting model by using auxiliary tasks, for example, a classification task is used in [21,56,57], a segmentation task is utilized in [58–60], and a depth estimation task is adopted in [59,61]. These methods improve the performance significantly, which indicates that modeling related tasks simultaneously can improve the crowd counting accuracy. Inspired by this, in this paper, we deem the foreground mask prediction as the auxiliary task, and achieve it efficiently by feeding the shallow feature into the proposed novel parameter-free densely connected stacked pooling sub-network.

3. Methodology

In this section, we introduce the proposed SBAB-Net for crowd counting in detail. Our goal is to estimate the number of persons in a crowd image. To this end, following [62], we formulate the crowd counting task as a density map regression and distribution matching problem. In SBAB-Net, the input is the crowd image and the output is the corresponding density map.

3.1. Framework

As shown in Figure 2, our proposed SBAB-Net is composed of three modules, that is, backbone, densely Connected Stacked Dilated Convolution (DCSDC) and densely Connected Stacked Pooling (DCSP) modules. The backbone is a pre-trained CNN to extract both shallow and deep features of the input image. Let $I \in R^{H\times W\times 3}$ denote the input crowd image of width W and height H. The extracted shallow and deep features are represented as $S_I \in R^{\frac{H}{d_1}\times\frac{W}{d_1}\times c_1}$ and $D_I \in R^{\frac{H}{d_2}\times\frac{W}{d_2}\times c_2}$, respectively, where d_1 and d_2 are output strides, c_1 and c_2 are channels of the feature maps. D_I is fed into the DCSDC module to obtain scale aware feature f_s, and S_I is fed into the DCSP module to obtain background aware feature f_b. We ensure the dimensions of the two features f_s and f_b to be equal by assigning proper convolutional kernel numbers in the DCSDC module. Then we use a foreground mask regression head (a light weight CNN to predict the probability of pedestrians at each location) to distinguish background and person instance based on feature f_b. To handle scale and background information simultaneously, we present an element-wise multiple based attention mechanism which refines the feature f_s based on the feature f_b, formulation is as,

$$f = f_s \otimes f_b. \tag{1}$$

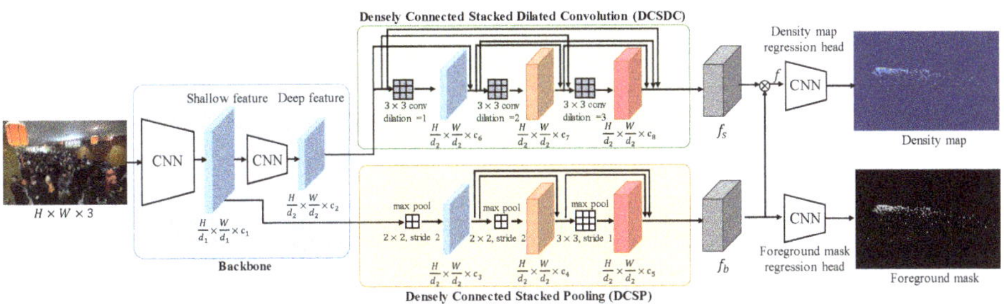

Figure 2. Overview of the proposed SBAB-Net. Backbone: a pre-trained CNN to extract both shallow and deep features of the input image. Densely Connected Stacked Dilated Convolution (DCSDC): a densely connected sub-network with different dilation rates, which relies on one deep feature layer and can get scale aware feature. Densely Connected Stacked Pooling (DCSP): a densely connected sub-network with different pooling kernels, which relies on one shallow feature layer and can get background aware feature. Finally, scale and background features are fused by an attention mechanism to generate density map.

Apparently, according to Equation (1), the features of background regions in f_s will be suppressed. Finally, a density map regression head (a light weight CNN to predict the number of pedestrians at each location) is utilized to predict a person density map based on the refined feature f. Therefore, the sum of the density map is the estimated person numbers of the input image I. The structure of the proposed density map regression head and foreground mask regression head are illustrated in Figure 3; the learnable structures and input-output dimensions of these two sub-networks are the same, while the output semantics are different. In addition, both density map regression head and foreground mask regression head are mapping local features to semantics. Therefore, f_s is sensitive to person scales and f_b is sensitive to regions with pedestrians; the refined feature f is sensitive to scales and background regions simultaneously.

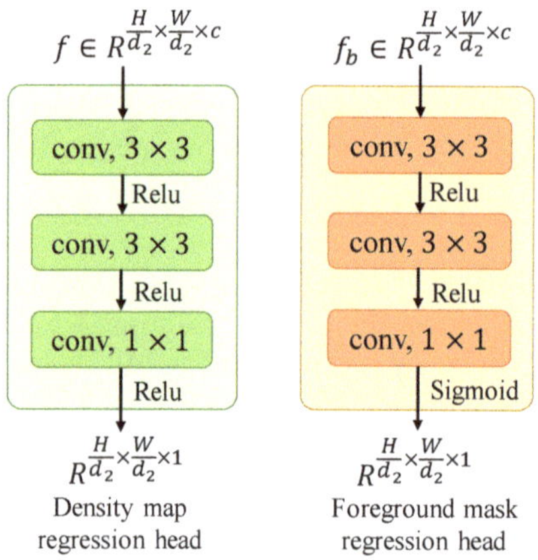

Figure 3. The structure of the proposed density map regression head and foreground mask regression head.

It should be noted that we should predict both foreground mask and density map in training, and only the density map needs to be estimated in the test.

Next, we will introduce the DCSDC and DCSP modules in detail.

3.2. Densely Connected Stacked Dilated Convolution (DCSDC)

The DCSDC implements a non-linear mapping function $H(\cdot)$ which takes the deep feature D_I as input, and produces a scale aware feature f_s, that is,

$$f_s = H(D_I). \tag{2}$$

As shown in Figure 2, DCSDC consists of three dilation convolution layers with different dilation rates, and these layers are connected in a densely connected way. It is able to handle scale variation based on one deep feature layer.

Specifically, all of the three convolution layers have 3×3 kernels, the dilation rates are 1, 2, and 3 respectively. Meanwhile, since the feature dimensions of each convolution layer in the DCSDC shall be consistent, the corresponding padding sizes are also set to 1, 2, and 3 respectively. The non-linear functions of three dilation convolution layers are denoted as $h_1(\cdot)$, $h_2(\cdot)$, and $h_3(\cdot)$ and the output of the first dilation convolution layer H^1 is formulated as,

$$H^1 = [D_I, h_1(D_I)], \tag{3}$$

where $[\cdot]$ represents the feature concatenation operation.

The output of the second dilation convolution layer H^2 is formulated as,

$$H^2 = [D_I, h_2(H^1), H^1]. \tag{4}$$

Consequently, the output of the third dilation convolution layer, that is, f_s, is formulated as,

$$f_s = [D_I, h_3(H^2), H^1, H^2]. \tag{5}$$

3.3. Densely Connected Stacked Pooling (DCSP)

The DCSP implements a non-linear mapping function $G(\cdot)$ which takes the deep feature S_I as input, and produces a background aware feature f_b, that is,

$$f_b = G(S_I). \tag{6}$$

As shown in Figure 2, DCSP consists of three max pooling layers with different pooling kernels, and these layers are connected in a densely connected way. It is able to fuse features with several receptive fields to reduce the impact of background noise via a learnable parameter-free manner.

Specifically, the first two pooling kernels in DCSP are 2×2 max pooling with stride 2, and the third pooling kernel is a 3×3 max pooling with stride 1. The non-linear functions of three pooling layers are denoted as $g_1(\cdot)$, $g_2(\cdot)$, and $g_3(\cdot)$, the output of the first pooling layer G^1 is formulated as,

$$G^1 = g_1(S_I). \tag{7}$$

The output of the second pooling layer G^2 is formulated as,

$$G^2 = [g_2(G^1), G^1]. \tag{8}$$

Consequently, the output of the third pooling layer, that is, f_b, is formulated as:

$$f_b = [g_3(G^2), G^1, G^2]. \tag{9}$$

3.4. Loss Function

In this section, we first introduce the ground-truth generation strategy, then detail the loss function.

To obtain the ground-truth density map D_i^{GT} (here i represents the i-th image), we follow the method of generating density maps in [62], which does not need any Gaussian to preprocess ground truth annotations. The generation of density map D_i^{GT} can be formulated as,

$$D_i^{GT}(x) = \delta(x), \tag{10}$$

where $\delta(x)$ means the annotated person numbers in the position x.

Based on ground-truth density map D_i^{GT}, we compute ground-truth foreground mask F_i^{GT} as follows:

$$F_i^{GT}(x) = \begin{cases} 0 & \delta(x) = 0. \\ 1 & \delta(x) > 0. \end{cases} \tag{11}$$

Equation (11) ensures that position x with person instance will be deemed foreground.

To increase the generalization performance of the proposed model, inspired by [62], counting loss, optimal transport loss and total variation loss are utilized to measure the difference between ground-truth density map D_i^{GT} and predict density map D_i^P.

Counting loss (L_c) is defined as follows:

$$L_c(D_i^P, D_i^{GT}) = |||D_i^P\|_1 - |||D_i^{GT}\|_1||, \tag{12}$$

where $\| * \|_1$ denotes the L_1 norm of a vector.

Optimal transport loss (L_{ot}) is defined as,

$$L_{ot}(D_i^P, D_i^{GT}) = \langle \alpha^*, \frac{D_i^{GT}}{\|D_i^{GT}\|_1} \rangle + \langle \beta^*, \frac{D_i^P}{\|D_i^P\|_1} \rangle, \tag{13}$$

where α^* and β^* are the solutions of Monge-Kantarovich Optimal Transport formulation [63].

Total variation loss (L_{tv}) is defined as,

$$L_{tv}(D_i^P, D_i^{GT}) = \frac{1}{2}\|D_i^{GT}\|_1\|\frac{D_i^{GT}}{\|D_i^{GT}\|_1} - \frac{D_i^P}{\|D_i^P\|_1}\|_1. \quad (14)$$

To measure the difference between the ground-truth foreground mask F_i^{GT} and predicted foreground mask F_i^P, BCE segmentation loss (L_b) is defined as,

$$L_b(F_i^P, F_i^{GT}) = -F_i^{GT}\log F_i^P + (F_i^{GT} - 1)\log(1 - F_i^P). \quad (15)$$

The final loss is the weighted summation of the four loss terms mentioned above,

$$Loss = L_c + \lambda_1 L_{ot} + \lambda_2 L_{tv} + \lambda_3 L_b, \quad (16)$$

where the hyper-parameters λ_1, λ_2 and λ_3 control the contributions of different components.

4. Experiments

In this section, we first introduce the experimental setting and implementation details, and then analyze in detail the effectiveness of each component in our framework through a set of ablation experiments on three public benchmarks. After that, we evaluate our method by comparing to the state-of-the-art methods.

4.1. Experimental Setting

4.1.1. Datasets

The experiments are conducted and evaluated on three common crowd counting benchmarks, including ShanghaiTech [10], UCF-QNRF [39] and NWPU-Crowd [40]; some samples are shown in Figure 4. Each person in a crowd image on these datasets is annotated with one point close to the center of the head.

Figure 4. Some samples from representing crowd counting datasets.

The ShanghaiTech dataset consists of 1198 annotated crowd images and 330,165 annotated people. It is divided into two independent parts: Part-A and Part-B. Part-A contains 482 images which are collected from the Internet, and it is split into train and test subsets consisting of 300 and 182 images, respectively. Part-B contains 716 images which are collected from the busy streets, and it is split into training and test subsets consisting of 400 and 316 images, respectively.

UCF-QNRF is composed of 1535 images (1201 for training and 334 for testing) with more than 1.25 million label instances.

The NWPU-Crowd dataset is a large-scale congested dataset recently introduced in [40], which consists of 5109 images, with a total of 2,133,375 annotated heads with various illumination scenes and density ranges. The dataset is randomly split into training, validation and test subsets, which respectively contain 3109, 500 and 1500 images.

4.1.2. Evaluation Metrics

Follow the existing works [64–67], mean absolute error (MAE) and mean squared error (MSE) are used to evaluate the performance of different crowd counting methods.

The MAE is calculated by,

$$MAE = \frac{1}{N}\sum_{i=1}^{N} \|C_i - C_i^{GT}\|. \tag{17}$$

MSE is formulated as,

$$MSE = \sqrt{\frac{1}{N}\sum_{i=1}^{N} \|C_i - C_i^{GT}\|^2}, \tag{18}$$

where N is the number of images in the test set, C_i and C_i^{GT} are the estimated and ground-truth individuals of i-th image, respectively.

4.2. Implementation Details

We set hyper-parameters following [62]. All empirical studies are conducted on an Nvidia GTX 3070 GPU in PyTorch. During training, the input size is 256 × 256 on ShanghaiTech Part-A, 384 × 384 on NWPU, 512 × 512 on ShanghaiTech Part-B and UCF-QNRF; all of them are randomly cropped from the original image. During testing, the input image of the network maintains the original resolution. The AdamW [68] optimizer is used to train all models, and the learning rate and weight decay are set to 0.00001 and 0.0001 respectively. The output strides d_1 and d_2 are set to 4 and 8, respectively. The hyper-parameters λ_1, λ_2 and λ_3 in loss function are set to 0.1, 0.01 and 1, respectively. There is no augmentation during training and inference.

4.3. Ablation Studies

The purpose of this section is to demonstrate the effectiveness of the proposed solution rather than achieving a state-of-the-art performance in a certain dataset by all manner of means. Therefore, we utilize the light network MobileNetV2 [69] as our backbone.

4.3.1. Convergency

Figure 5 shows the value of the loss function of our method versus the different number of training epochs on the ShanghaiTech Part-A dataset. We can observe that the loss value decreases almost monotonously and converges smoothly during the entire training procedure, which indicates that the proposed framework can be efficiently trained by using the stochastic gradient descent optimization algorithm, AdamW. The model has reached convergence if the value of loss does not decrease in 20 consecutive epochs.

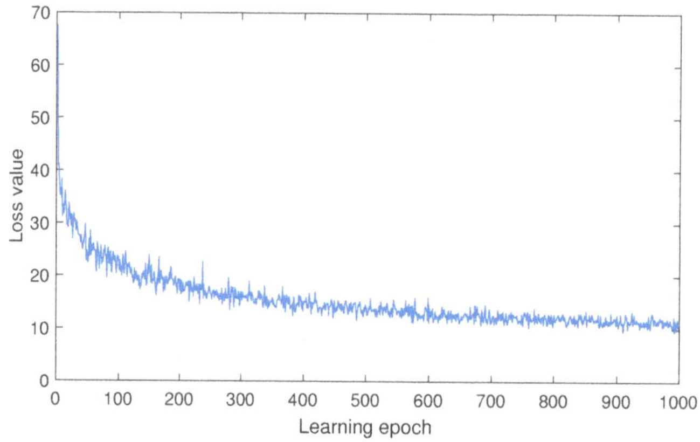

Figure 5. The value of the loss function of SBAB-Net versus the different number of training epochs on the ShanghaiTech Part-A dataset. (The backbone is MobileNetV2.)

4.3.2. Impact of Different Components

Compared with the baseline [62], the proposed SBAB-Net has two novel terms, that is, DCSDC and DCSP. To investigate the impact of these terms on the performance of the proposed method, we developed and evaluated two variations of SBAB-Net: the one is SBAB-Net w/o DCSDC, that is, only backbone and DCSP are used to predict the density map directly. The other is SBAB-Net w/o DCSP, that is, it does not model the background region explicitly. The optimization procedure of these two cases is similar to the proposed SBAB-Net.

Table 1 shows the performance comparisons of SBAB-Net and its two variations on three benchmarks. From the results, we can see that the full SBAB-Net performs best on all datasets, which indicates that all of the two novel terms (DCSDC and DCSP) contribute to the final counting accuracy. We can also see that SBAB-Net w/o DCSP outperforms SBAB-Net w/o DCSDC by a large margin, which indicates that the importance of the DCSDC for the model to learn the scale aware representation.

We qualitatively evaluate the effectiveness of the proposed SBAB-Net by visualizing the density maps, as shown in Figure 6. We can see that there are obvious differences between density maps of the baseline and SBAB-Net on the following two aspects: (1) *Robustness to noises*, as shown in the second and fourth rows; (2) *Robustness to scale variations*, as shown in the first and third rows.

Table 1. Ablation studies. Performance comparison of the proposed SBAB-Net and its three variations in terms of MAE and MSE on benchmarks. The highest score is shown in boldface. (The backbone is MobileNetV2).

Components	ShanghaiTech Part-A		ShanghaiTech Part-B		UCF-QNRF		NWPU	
	MAE	MSE	MAE	MSE	MAE	MSE	MAE	MSE
Baseline	68.92	108.08	8.57	15.38	210.56	393.69	85.29	401.35
SBAB-Net w/o DCSDC	65.06	105.29	8.34	14.88	172.11	255.84	-	-
SBAB-Net w/o DCSP	62.50	100.31	8.17	13.72	-	-	82.87	389.29
SBAB-Net	**60.57**	**95.89**	**8.03**	**12.24**	**108.58**	**185.38**	**69.91**	**237.14**

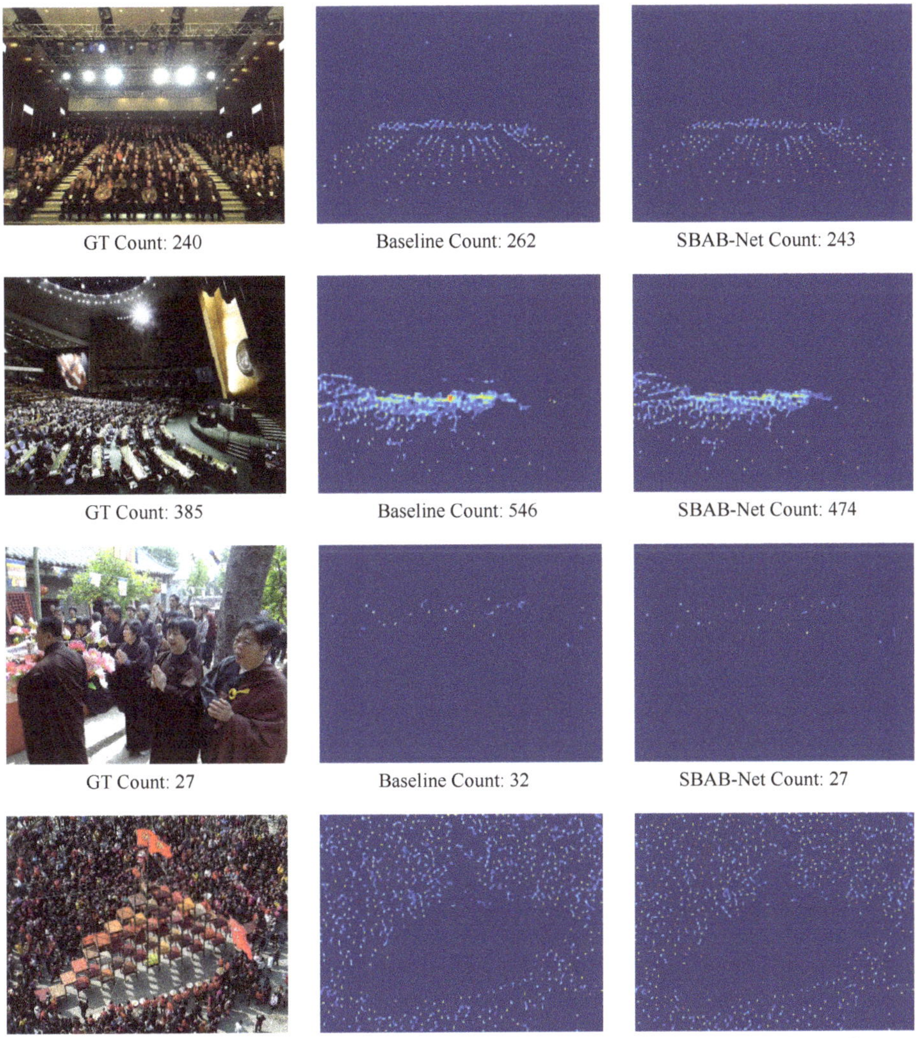

Figure 6. Density maps of NWPU dataset generated by baseline and our SBAB-Net. (The backbone is MobileNetV2).

Both quantitative and qualitative experimental results (Table 1 and Figure 6) demonstrate that utilizing f_b refines f_s by element wise multiple operation can improve the counting performance ("SBAB-Net w/o DCSP" and "SBAB-Net" comparisons on Table 1) and suppress background regions (visualization results in Figure 6).

It should be noted that the major difference between our DCSP and the SP presented in [37] is that features from several different pooling kernels are fused by the densely connected method in our framework. Figure 7 shows the performance comparison of the proposed DCSP and SP in terms of MAE and MSE on the ShanghaiTech Part-A dataset. From this, we can see that DCSP performs better than SP. We think the reason is that channel-wise average operation in original SP loses many details.

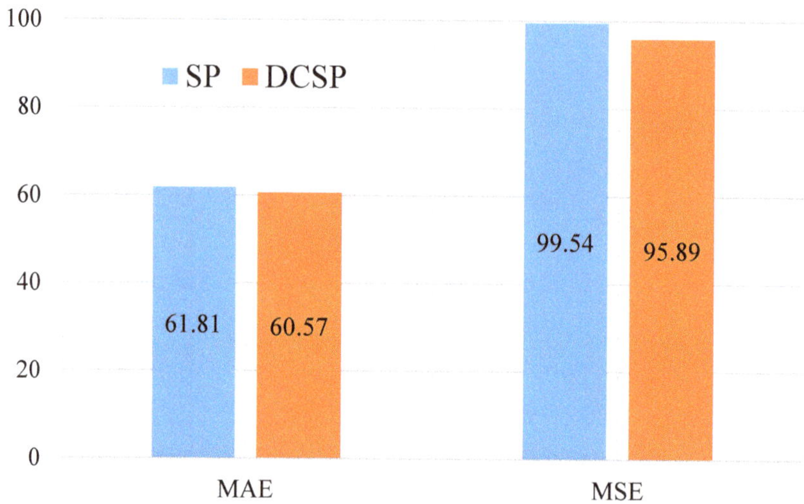

Figure 7. Ablation study. Performance comparison of the proposed DCSP and SP [37] in terms of MAE and MSE on ShanghaiTech Part-A dataset. (The backbone is MobileNetV2.)

4.4. Comparison with State-of-the-Art Methods

To verify the effectiveness of our SBAB-Net, we compare the proposed method with sixteen state-of-the-art methods in the experiments, namely, CSRNet [16], SFCN [70], CAN [71], Bayesian+ [65], S-DCNet [72], SANet + SPANet [73], SDANet [35], ADNet [15], ADSCNet [15], ASNet [74], AMRNet [75], AMSNet [76], DM-Count [62], P2PNet [64], DADNet [38] and SFANet [32]. As with the structure in DM-Count [62], the backbone of the proposed SBAB-Net is the pre-trained VGG-19 [77].

Tables 2–4 report the MAE and MSE of the proposed SBAB-Net and the compared methods (performance numbers directly cited from the original papers) of ShanghaiTech, UCF-QNRF, and NWPU datasets, from which we have the following observations:

- Although the structures of DCSDC and DCSP are simple, the proposed SBAB-Net is able to achieve a competitive counting performance compared to state-of-the-art methods on both small and large datasets. SBAB-Net, especially, significantly outperforms baseline (DM-Count [62]) while using the same backbone as the feature extractor.
- The proposed asymmetric bilateral network performs better than the commonly used dual structure (e.g., SFANet [32]). It is a further proof of the observation in [35], that is, the features of different layers in CNN have different abilities to model background noise.
- Although the same three dilation rates are utilized in the proposed framework and CSRNet [16], we achieve a much better performance, which indicates the advantage of our DCSDC structure.
- Our SBAB-Net is not the best approach. A better multi-task learning framework (e.g., P2PNet [64]), a better CNN structure (e.g., AMSNet [76]) or a better training strategy (e.g., ADSCNet [15]) can obtain a higher crowd counting performance.

Table 2. Performance comparison of the proposed in terms of MAE and MSE on ShanghaiTech Part-A dataset.

Methods	ShanghaiTech Part-A	
	MAE	MSE
CSRNet [16]	68.2	115.0
SFCN [70]	64.8	107.5
CAN [71]	62.3	100.0
Bayesian+ [65]	62.8	101.8
S-DCNet [72]	58.3	95.0
SANet + SPANet [73]	59.4	92.5
SDANet [35]	63.6	101.8
ADSCNet [15]	55.4	97.7
ADNet [15]	61.3	103.9
ASNet [74]	57.78	90.13
AMRNet [75]	61.59	98.36
AMSNet [76]	56.7	93.4
DM-Count [62]	59.7	95.7
DADNet [38]	64.2	99.9
SFANet [32]	63.8	105.2
Ours	57.69	93.77

Table 3. Performance comparison of the proposed in terms of MAE and MSE on the UCF-QNRF dataset.

Methods	UCF-QNRF	
	MAE	MSE
CSRNet [16]	120.3	208.5
SFCN [70]	102	171
CAN [71]	107	183
Bayesian+ [65]	88.7	154.8
S-DCNet [72]	104.4	176.1
ASNet [74]	91.59	159.71
AMRNet [75]	86.6	152.2
AMSNet [76]	101.8	163.2
DM-Count [62]	85.6	148.3
SFANet [32]	100.8	174.5
P2PNet [64]	85.32	154.5
ADNet [15]	90.1	147.1
DADNet [38]	113.2	189.4
Ours	84.81	152.17

Table 4. Performance comparison of the proposed in terms of MAE and MSE on the NWPU validation set.

Methods	NWPU Validation Set	
	MAE	MSE
CSRNet [16]	104.8	433.4
SFCN [70]	95.4	608.3
CAN [71]	93.5	489.9
Bayesian+ [65]	93.6	470.3
DM-Count [62]	70.5	357.6
Ours	63.26	211.75

5. Conclusions

In this paper, we presented a new framework (SBAB-Net) for unconstrained image crowd counting, which can handle scale variation and background noise in a unified framework. SBAB-Net achieved this goal with an asymmetric bilateral network, which consists of two novel branches. One branch is a densely connected stacked dilated convolution (DCSDC) sub-network with different dilation rates, which relies on one deep feature layer and can handle scale variation. The other branch is a parameter-free densely connected stacked pooling (DCSP) sub-network with various pooling kernels and strides, which relies on shallow features and can fuse features with several receptive fields to reduce the impact of background noise. Two sub-networks are fused by an attention mechanism to generate the final density map. Extensive experimental results on three widely-used benchmark datasets have demonstrated the effectiveness and superiority of our proposed method: (1) We achieve competitive counting performance compared to state-of-the-art methods; (2) Compared with baseline, the MAE and MSE are decreased by at least 6.3% and 11.3%, respectively.

Author Contributions: Conception, F.N.; Formal analysis, G.L.; Methodology, G.L.; Project administration, Y.S.; Validation, Y.X.; Writing—original draft, Y.X.; Writing—review & editing, Z.M. All authors have read and agreed to the published version of the manuscript.

Funding: This work was supported by the University Synergy Innovation Program of Anhui Province (No. GXXT-2019-048), the National Natural Science Foundation (NSF) of China (No. 61902104), the National Key R&D Program (No. 2020YFC2005603), the Anhui Provincial Natural Science Foundation (No. 2008085QF295), and the University Natural Sciences Research Project of Anhui Province (No. KJ2020A0651).

Institutional Review Board Statement: Not applicable.

Informed Consent Statement: Not applicable.

Data Availability Statement: Data available in a publicly accessible repository. The data presented in this study are openly available at https://github.com/gjy3035/Awesome-Crowd-Counting, accessed on 12 February 2022.

Conflicts of Interest: The authors declare no conflict of interest.

References

1. Li, T.; Chang, H.; Wang, M.; Ni, B.; Hong, R.; Yan, S. Crowded scene analysis: A survey. *IEEE Trans. Circuits Syst. Video Technol.* **2014**, *25*, 367–386. [CrossRef]
2. Gao, G.; Gao, J.; Liu, Q.; Wang, Q.; Wang, Y. Cnn-based density estimation and crowd counting: A survey. *arXiv* **2020**, arXiv:2003.12783.
3. Ge, W.; Collins, R.T. Marked point processes for crowd counting. In Proceedings of the IEEE/CVF Conference on Computer Vision and Pattern Recognition, Miami, FL, USA, 20–25 June 2009; pp. 2913–2920.
4. Idrees, H.; Saleemi, I.; Seibert, C.; Shah, M. Multi-source multi-scale counting in extremely dense crowd images. In Proceedings of the IEEE/CVF Conference on Computer Vision and Pattern Recognition, Portland, OR, USA, 23–28 June 2013; pp. 2547–2554.
5. Idrees, H.; Soomro, K.; Shah, M. Detecting humans in dense crowds using locally-consistent scale prior and global occlusion reasoning. *IEEE Trans. Pattern Anal. Mach. Intell.* **2015**, *37*, 1986–1998. [CrossRef] [PubMed]
6. Li, M.; Zhang, Z.; Huang, K.; Tan, T. Estimating the number of people in crowded scenes by mid based foreground segmentation and head-shoulder detection. In Proceedings of the International Conference on Pattern Recognition, Tampa, FL, USA, 8–11 December 2008; pp. 1–4.
7. Pham, V.Q.; Kozakaya, T.; Yamaguchi, O.; Okada, R. Count forest: Co-voting uncertain number of targets using random forest for crowd density estimation. In Proceedings of the IEEE/CVF International Conference on Computer Vision, Santiago, Chile, 7–13 December 2015; pp. 3253–3261.
8. Fu, M.; Xu, P.; Li, X.; Liu, Q.; Ye, M.; Zhu, C. Fast crowd density estimation with convolutional neural networks. *Eng. Appl. Artif. Intell.* **2015**, *43*, 81–88. [CrossRef]
9. Hu, Y.; Chang, H.; Nian, F.; Wang, Y.; Li, T. Dense crowd counting from still images with convolutional neural networks. *J. Vis. Commun. Image Represent.* **2016**, *38*, 530–539. [CrossRef]
10. Zhang, Y.; Zhou, D.; Chen, S.; Gao, S.; Ma, Y. Single-image crowd counting via multi-column convolutional neural network. In Proceedings of the IEEE/CVF Conference on Computer Vision and Pattern Recognition, Las Vegas, NV, USA, 26 June–1 July 2016; pp. 589–597.
11. Babu Sam, D.; Surya, S.; Venkatesh Babu, R. Switching convolutional neural network for crowd counting. In Proceedings of the IEEE/CVF Conference on Computer Vision and Pattern Recognition, Honolulu, HI, USA, 22–25 July 2017; pp. 5744–5752.

12. Yang, Y.; Li, G.; Du, D.; Huang, Q.; Sebe, N. Embedding Perspective Analysis Into Multi-Column Convolutional Neural Network for Crowd Counting. *IEEE Trans. Image Process.* **2020**, *30*, 1395–1407. [CrossRef]
13. Cheng, Z.Q.; Li, J.X.; Dai, Q.; Wu, X.; He, J.Y.; Hauptmann, A.G. Improving the learning of multi-column convolutional neural network for crowd counting. In Proceedings of the ACM International Conference on Multimedia, Nice, France, 21–25 October 2019; pp. 1897–1906.
14. Xu, W.; Liang, D.; Zheng, Y.; Xie, J.; Ma, Z. Dilated-Scale-Aware Category-Attention ConvNet for Multi-Class Object Counting. *IEEE Signal Process. Lett.* **2021**, *28*, 1570–1574. [CrossRef]
15. Bai, S.; He, Z.; Qiao, Y.; Hu, H.; Wu, W.; Yan, J. Adaptive dilated network with self-correction supervision for counting. In Proceedings of the IEEE/CVF Conference on Computer Vision and Pattern Recognition, Seattle, WA, USA, 14–19 June 2020; pp. 4594–4603.
16. Li, Y.; Zhang, X.; Chen, D. Csrnet: Dilated convolutional neural networks for understanding the highly congested scenes. In Proceedings of the IEEE/CVF Conference on Computer Vision and Pattern Recognition, Salt Lake City, UT, USA, 18–22 June 2018; pp. 1091–1100.
17. Liu, N.; Long, Y.; Zou, C.; Niu, Q.; Pan, L.; Wu, H. Adcrowdnet: An attention-injective deformable convolutional network for crowd understanding. In Proceedings of the IEEE/CVF Conference on Computer Vision and Pattern Recognition, Long Beach, CA, USA, 15–21 June 2019; pp. 3225–3234.
18. Zou, Z.; Su, X.; Qu, X.; Zhou, P. Da-net: Learning the fine-grained density distribution with deformation aggregation network. *IEEE Access* **2018**, *6*, 60745–60756. [CrossRef]
19. Amirgholipour, S.; He, X.; Jia, W.; Wang, D.; Liu, L. Pdanet: Pyramid density-aware attention net for accurate crowd counting. *arXiv* **2020**, arXiv:2001.05643.
20. Chen, X.; Bin, Y.; Sang, N.; Gao, C. Scale pyramid network for crowd counting. In Proceedings of the IEEE/CVF Winter Conference on Applications of Computer Vision, Waikoloa Village, HI, USA, 7–11 January 2019; pp. 1941–1950.
21. Sindagi, V.A.; Patel, V.M. Generating high-quality crowd density maps using contextual pyramid cnns. In Proceedings of the IEEE/CVF International Conference on Computer Vision, Venice, Italy, 22–29 October 2017; pp. 1861–1870.
22. Liu, J.; Gao, C.; Meng, D.; Hauptmann, A.G. Decidenet: Counting varying density crowds through attention guided detection and density estimation. In Proceedings of the IEEE/CVF Conference on Computer Vision and Pattern Recognition, Salt Lake City, UT, USA, 18–22 June 2018; pp. 5197–5206.
23. Hossain, M.; Hosseinzadeh, M.; Chanda, O.; Wang, Y. Crowd counting using scale-aware attention networks. In Proceedings of the IEEE/CVF Winter Conference on Applications of Computer Vision, Waikoloa Village, HI, USA, 7–11 January 2019; pp. 1280–1288.
24. Liu, L.; Wang, H.; Li, G.; Ouyang, W.; Lin, L. Crowd counting using deep recurrent spatial-aware network. *arXiv* **2018**, arXiv:1807.00601.
25. Chen, J.; Su, W.; Wang, Z. Crowd counting with crowd attention convolutional neural network. *Neurocomputing* **2020**, *382*, 210–220. [CrossRef]
26. Sun, G.; Liu, Y.; Probst, T.; Paudel, D.P.; Popovic, N.; Van Gool, L. Boosting crowd counting with transformers. *arXiv* **2021**, arXiv:2105.10926.
27. Gao, J.; Gong, M.; Li, X. Congested Crowd Instance Localization with Dilated Convolutional Swin Transformer. *arXiv* **2021**, arXiv:2108.00584.
28. Sajid, U.; Chen, X.; Sajid, H.; Kim, T.; Wang, G. Audio-visual transformer based crowd counting. In Proceedings of the IEEE/CVF International Conference on Computer Vision, Montreal, QC, Canada, 11–17 October 2021; pp. 2249–2259.
29. Tian, Y.; Chu, X.; Wang, H. Cctrans: Simplifying and improving crowd counting with transformer. *arXiv* **2021**, arXiv:2109.14483.
30. Liang, D.; Xu, W.; Bai, X. An End-to-End Transformer Model for Crowd Localization. *arXiv* **2022**, arXiv:2202.13065.
31. Wang, F.; Liu, K.; Long, F.; Sang, N.; Xia, X.; Sang, J. Joint CNN and Transformer Network via weakly supervised Learning for efficient crowd counting. *arXiv* **2022**, arXiv:2203.06388.
32. Zhu, L.; Zhao, Z.; Lu, C.; Lin, Y.; Peng, Y.; Yao, T. Dual path multi-scale fusion networks with attention for crowd counting. *arXiv* **2019**, arXiv:1902.01115.
33. Rong, L.; Li, C. A Strong Baseline for Crowd Counting and Unsupervised People Localization. *arXiv* **2020**, arXiv:2011.03725.
34. Modolo, D.; Shuai, B.; Varior, R.R.; Tighe, J. Understanding the impact of mistakes on background regions in crowd counting. In Proceedings of the IEEE/CVF Winter Conference on Applications of Computer Vision, Breckenridge, CO, USA, 5–7 January 2021; pp. 1650–1659.
35. Miao, Y.; Lin, Z.; Ding, G.; Han, J. Shallow feature based dense attention network for crowd counting. In Proceedings of the AAAI Conference on Artificial Intelligence, Hilton New York Midtown, New York, NY, USA, 7–12 February 2020; Volume 34, pp. 11765–11772.
36. Yi, Q.; Liu, Y.; Jiang, A.; Li, J.; Mei, K.; Wang, M. Scale-aware network with regional and semantic attentions for crowd counting under cluttered background. *arXiv* **2021**, arXiv:2101.01479.
37. Huang, S.; Li, X.; Cheng, Z.Q.; Zhang, Z.; Hauptmann, A. Stacked Pooling for Boosting Scale Invariance of Crowd Counting. In Proceedings of the IEEE International Conference on Acoustics, Speech and Signal Processing, Barcelona, Spain, 4–8 May 2020; pp. 2578–2582.

38. Guo, D.; Li, K.; Zha, Z.J.; Wang, M. Dadnet: Dilated-attention-deformable convnet for crowd counting. In Proceedings of the ACM International Conference on Multimedia, Nice, France, 21–25 October 2019; pp. 1823–1832.
39. Idrees, H.; Tayyab, M.; Athrey, K.; Zhang, D.; Al-Maadeed, S.; Rajpoot, N.; Shah, M. Composition loss for counting, density map estimation and localization in dense crowds. In Proceedings of the European Conference on Computer Vision, Munich, Germany, 8–14 September 2018; pp. 532–546.
40. Wang, Q.; Gao, J.; Lin, W.; Li, X. NWPU-crowd: A large-scale benchmark for crowd counting and localization. *IEEE Trans. Pattern Anal. Mach. Intell.* **2020**, *43*, 2141–2149. [CrossRef]
41. Leibe, B.; Seemann, E.; Schiele, B. Pedestrian detection in crowded scenes. In Proceedings of the IEEE/CVF Conference on Computer Vision and Pattern Recognition, San Diego, CA, USA, 20–26 June 2005; Volume 1, pp. 878–885.
42. Chan, A.B.; Liang, Z.S.J.; Vasconcelos, N. Privacy preserving crowd monitoring: Counting people without people models or tracking. In Proceedings of the IEEE/CVF Conference on Computer Vision and Pattern Recognition, Anchorage, AK, USA, 23–28 June 2008; pp. 1–7.
43. Zhang, C.; Li, H.; Wang, X.; Yang, X. Cross-scene crowd counting via deep convolutional neural networks. In Proceedings of the IEEE/CVF Conference on Computer Vision and Pattern Recognition, Boston, MA, USA, 7–12 June 2015; pp. 833–841.
44. Iqbal, M.; Rehman, M.A.; Iqbal, N.; Iqbal, Z. Effect of Laplacian Smoothing Stochastic Gradient Descent with Angular Margin Softmax Loss on Face Recognition. In *International Conference on Intelligent Technologies and Applications*; Springer: Berlin/Heidelberg, Germany, 2019; pp. 549–561.
45. Zeng, L.; Xu, X.; Cai, B.; Qiu, S.; Zhang, T. Multi-scale convolutional neural networks for crowd counting. In Proceedings of the IEEE International Conference on Image Processing, Beijing, China, 17–20 September 2017; pp. 465–469.
46. Kang, D.; Chan, A. Crowd counting by adaptively fusing predictions from an image pyramid. *arXiv* **2018**, arXiv:1805.06115.
47. Xu, C.; Liang, D.; Xu, Y.; Bai, S.; Zhan, W.; Bai, X.; Tomizuka, M. AutoScale: Learning to Scale for Crowd Counting and Localization. *arXiv* **2019**, arXiv:1912.09632.
48. Song, Q.; Wang, C.; Wang, Y.; Tai, Y.; Wang, C.; Li, J.; Wu, J.; Ma, J. To Choose or to Fuse? Scale Selection for Crowd Counting. In Proceedings of the AAAI Conference on Artificial Intelligence, Arlington, VA, USA, 4–6 November 2021; Volume 35, pp. 2576–2583.
49. Ma, Z.; Wei, X.; Hong, X.; Gong, Y. Learning scales from points: A scale-aware probabilistic model for crowd counting. In Proceedings of the ACM International Conference on Multimedia, Singapore, 16–18 December 2020; pp. 220–228.
50. Gao, J.; Wang, Q.; Yuan, Y. SCAR: Spatial-/channel-wise attention regression networks for crowd counting. *Neurocomputing* **2019**, *363*, 1–8. [CrossRef]
51. Sindagi, V.A.; Patel, V.M. Ha-ccn: Hierarchical attention-based crowd counting network. *IEEE Trans. Image Process.* **2019**, *29*, 323–335. [CrossRef] [PubMed]
52. Sindagi, V.A.; Patel, V.M. Inverse attention guided deep crowd counting network. In Proceedings of the IEEE International Conference on Advanced Video and Signal Based Surveillance, Taipei, Taiwan, 18–21 September 2019; pp. 1–8.
53. Shi, Z.; Mettes, P.; Snoek, C.G. Counting with focus for free. In Proceedings of the IEEE/CVF International Conference on Computer Vision, Seoul, Korea, 27 October–2 November 2019; pp. 4200–4209.
54. Liu, C.; Weng, X.; Mu, Y. Recurrent attentive zooming for joint crowd counting and precise localization. In Proceedings of the IEEE/CVF Conference on Computer Vision and Pattern Recognition, Long Beach, CA, USA, 15–21 June 2019; pp. 1217–1226.
55. Zhang, A.; Yue, L.; Shen, J.; Zhu, F.; Zhen, X.; Cao, X.; Shao, L. Attentional neural fields for crowd counting. In Proceedings of the IEEE/CVF International Conference on Computer Vision, Seoul, Korea, 27 October–2 November 2019; pp. 5714–5723.
56. Gao, J.; Wang, Q.; Li, X. Pcc net: Perspective crowd counting via spatial convolutional network. *IEEE Trans. Circuits Syst. Video Technol.* **2019**, *30*, 3486–3498. [CrossRef]
57. Sindagi, V.A.; Patel, V.M. Cnn-based cascaded multi-task learning of high-level prior and density estimation for crowd counting. In Proceedings of the IEEE International Conference on Advanced Video and Signal Based Surveillance, Lecce, Italy, 29 August–1 September 2017; pp. 1–6.
58. Jiang, S.; Lu, X.; Lei, Y.; Liu, L. Mask-aware networks for crowd counting. *IEEE Trans. Circuits Syst. Video Technol.* **2019**, *30*, 3119–3129. [CrossRef]
59. Zhao, M.; Zhang, J.; Zhang, C.; Zhang, W. Leveraging heterogeneous auxiliary tasks to assist crowd counting. In Proceedings of the IEEE/CVF Conference on Computer Vision and Pattern Recognition, Long Beach, CA, USA, 15–21 June 2019; pp. 12736–12745.
60. Huang, S.; Li, X.; Zhang, Z.; Wu, F.; Gao, S.; Ji, R.; Han, J. Body structure aware deep crowd counting. *IEEE Trans. Image Process.* **2017**, *27*, 1049–1059. [CrossRef]
61. Lian, D.; Li, J.; Zheng, J.; Luo, W.; Gao, S. Density map regression guided detection network for rgb-d crowd counting and localization. In Proceedings of the IEEE/CVF Conference on Computer Vision and Pattern Recognition, Long Beach, CA, USA, 15–21 June 2019; pp. 1821–1830.
62. Wang, B.; Liu, H.; Samaras, D.; Nguyen, M.H. Distribution Matching for Crowd Counting. *arXiv* **2020**, arXiv:2009.13077.
63. Villani, C. Optimal transport, old and new. Notes for the 2005 Saint-Flour summer school. In *Grundlehren der Mathematischen Wissenschaften [Fundamental Principles of Mathematical Sciences]*; Springer: Berlin/Heidelberg, Germany, 2008.
64. Song, Q.; Wang, C.; Jiang, Z.; Wang, Y.; Tai, Y.; Wang, C.; Li, J.; Huang, F.; Wu, Y. Rethinking Counting and Localization in Crowds: A Purely Point-Based Framework. In Proceedings of the IEEE/CVF International Conference on Computer Vision, Montreal, QC, Canada, 11–17 October 2021; pp. 3365–3374.

65. Ma, Z.; Wei, X.; Hong, X.; Gong, Y. Bayesian loss for crowd count estimation with point supervision. In Proceedings of the IEEE/CVF International Conference on Computer Vision, Seoul, Korea, 27 October–2 November 2019; pp. 6142–6151.
66. Ranjan, V.; Le, H.; Hoai, M. Iterative crowd counting. In Proceedings of the European Conference on Computer Vision, Munich, Germany, 8–14 September 2018; pp. 270–285.
67. Ranjan, V.; Sharma, U.; Nguyen, T.; Hoai, M. Learning To Count Everything. In Proceedings of the IEEE/CVF Conference on Computer Vision and Pattern Recognition, Nashville, TN, USA, 19–25 June 2021; pp. 3394–3403.
68. Loshchilov, I.; Hutter, F. Decoupled weight decay regularization. *arXiv* **2017**, arXiv:1711.05101.
69. Sandler, M.; Howard, A.; Zhu, M.; Zhmoginov, A.; Chen, L.C. Mobilenetv2: Inverted residuals and linear bottlenecks. In Proceedings of the IEEE Conference on Computer Vision and Pattern Recognition, Salt Lake City, UT, USA, 18–22 June 2018; pp. 4510–4520.
70. Wang, Q.; Gao, J.; Lin, W.; Yuan, Y. Learning from synthetic data for crowd counting in the wild. In Proceedings of the IEEE/CVF Conference on Computer Vision and Pattern Recognition, Long Beach, CA, USA, 15–21 June 2019; pp. 8198–8207.
71. Liu, W.; Salzmann, M.; Fua, P. Context-aware crowd counting. In Proceedings of the IEEE/CVF Conference on Computer Vision and Pattern Recognition, Long Beach, CA, USA, 15–21 June 2019; pp. 5099–5108.
72. Xiong, H.; Lu, H.; Liu, C.; Liu, L.; Cao, Z.; Shen, C. From open set to closed set: Counting objects by spatial divide-and-conquer. In Proceedings of the IEEE/CVF International Conference on Computer Vision, Seoul, Korea, 27 October–2 November 2019; pp. 8362–8371.
73. Cheng, Z.Q.; Li, J.X.; Dai, Q.; Wu, X.; Hauptmann, A.G. Learning spatial awareness to improve crowd counting. In Proceedings of the IEEE/CVF International Conference on Computer Vision, Seoul, Korea, 27 October–2 November 2019; pp. 6152–6161.
74. Jiang, X.; Zhang, L.; Xu, M.; Zhang, T.; Lv, P.; Zhou, B.; Yang, X.; Pang, Y. Attention scaling for crowd counting. In Proceedings of the IEEE/CVF Conference on Computer Vision and Pattern Recognition, Seattle, WA, USA, 14–19 June 2020; pp. 4706–4715.
75. Liu, X.; Yang, J.; Ding, W.; Wang, T.; Wang, Z.; Xiong, J. Adaptive mixture regression network with local counting map for crowd counting. In Proceedings of the European Conference on Computer Vision, Glasgow, UK, 23–28 August 2020; pp. 241–257.
76. Hu, Y.; Jiang, X.; Liu, X.; Zhang, B.; Han, J.; Cao, X.; Doermann, D. Nas-count: Counting-by-density with neural architecture search. In Proceedings of the European Conference on Computer Vision, Glasgow, UK, 23–28 August 2020; pp. 747–766.
77. Simonyan, K.; Zisserman, A. Very deep convolutional networks for large-scale image recognition. *arXiv* **2014**, arXiv:1409.1556.

mathematics

Article

A Medical Endoscope Image Enhancement Method Based on Improved Weighted Guided Filtering

Guo Zhang [1,2], Jinzhao Lin [3], Enling Cao [4], Yu Pang [3,*] and Weiwei Sun [3,*]

1 School of Communication and Information Engineering, Chongqing University of Posts and Telecommunications, Chongqing 400065, China; zhangguo@swmu.edu.cn
2 School of Medical Information and Engineering, Southwest Medical University, Luzhou 646000, China
3 College of Photoelectronic Engineering, Chongqing University of Posts and Telecommunication, Chongqing 400065, China; linjz@cqupt.edu.cn
4 School of Software Engineering, Chongqing University of Posts and Telecommunications, Chongqing 400065, China; 2020215130@stu.cqupt.edu.cn
* Correspondence: pangyu@cqupt.edu.cn (Y.P.); sunww@cqupt.edu.cn (W.S.); Tel.: +86-13372653576 (Y.P.); +86-15201339539 (W.S.)

Abstract: In clinical surgery, the quality of endoscopic images is degraded by noise. Blood, illumination changes, specular reflection, smoke, and other factors contribute to noise, which reduces the quality of an image in an occluded area, affects doctors' judgment, prolongs the operation duration, and increases the operation risk. In this study, we proposed an improved weighted guided filtering algorithm to enhance endoscopic image tissue. An unsharp mask algorithm and an improved weighted guided filter were used to enhance vessel details and contours in endoscopic images. The scheme of the entire endoscopic image processing, which included detail enhancement, contrast enhancement, brightness enhancement, and highlight area removal, is presented. Compared with other algorithms, the proposed algorithm maintained edges and reduced halos efficiently, and its effectiveness was demonstrated using experiments. The peak signal-to-noise ratio and structural similarity of endoscopic images obtained using the proposed algorithm were the highest. The foreground–background detail variance–background variance improved. The proposed algorithm had a strong ability to suppress noise and could maintain the structure of original endoscopic images, which improved the details of tissue blood vessels. The findings of this study can provide guidelines for developing endoscopy devices.

Keywords: contrast enhancement; detail enhancement; endoscopic image; tissue structure; secondary weighted guided filtering

MSC: 68U10

1. Introduction

With the development of science and technology, endoscopy has become a widely employed medical procedure [1]. Through endoscopy, doctors not only directly observe the tissue morphology and lesions of human internal organs but also further process endoscopic images to achieve excellent visual and diagnostic effects. However, owing to the particularity of human tissues and the limitation of imaging conditions, images obtained directly via endoscopy often have low contrast between blood vessels and surrounding tissues; thus, some vascular features are missing. Therefore, it is necessary to enhance endoscopic images [2–4].

Numerous image enhancement (IE) algorithms have been proposed to improve the quality of endoscope images. Retinal vascular enhancement in medical images [5] is achieved using image processing methods, such as the adaptive histogram equalization method, unsharpened mask algorithm [6], morphological method, Hessian matrix method [7], and multiscale filtering method [8–10]. The global and adaptive histogram equalization algorithms [11,12] are histogram-based IE algorithms. Wavelet analysis-based IE algorithms mainly include high-frequency wavelet transformation [13] and adaptive filtering [14]. Homomorphic filtering enhancement is typically used in image denoising [15] and dehazing [16]. Okuhata et al. [17] proposed a homomorphic filtering-based algorithm, wherein images containing brightness layer information are extracted from the original images and gamma correction is used to achieve high contrast. Considering the noise reduction, Gopi et al. [18] proposed a color image noise reduction method based on a dual-density dual-tree complex wavelet transform. Mo-hammed et al. [19] proposed a "tri-scan" IE algorithm that enhances the tissue surface and vascular characteristics. For the mucosal layer, the image R channel is processed using an adaptive sigmoid function to enhance the vascular contrast. Finally, tonal transformation is performed to enhance the structural characteristics of microvessels and tissues.

The quality of endoscopic images may be low due to some reasons; therefore, it is imperative to enhance endoscopic images. The deficiencies of endoscopic images are as follows. First, owing to the poor image quality of conventional photography, improving the image quality of an endoscope and enhancing image details are critical for accurate diagnosis. Second, the background of some tissues and blood vessels captured by an endoscope is red. The overall image contrast is insufficient, making distinguishing microvessels from the tissue background and finding lesions difficult, thereby affecting diagnosis. Third, during the shooting process using a complementary metal–oxide semiconductor (CMOS) camera, endoscopic images may have insufficient brightness because of light source problems or insufficient exposure, affecting the image observation. Finally, during endoscopy, the interior of the human tissue is smooth and some water droplets are present in the tissue, causing specular reflection areas in endoscopic images.

Therefore, in this study, we proposed an improved weighted guided filtering (WGF) algorithm for IE. Compared with the traditional guiding filter algorithm, the defect of noise residual can be overcome using our algorithm. The vascular detail and contour of endoscope images were enhanced by the proposed algorithm. The contrast enhancement of endoscopic images reduced the red component and enhanced the blue and green components so that the contrast between the background and vascular regions of endoscopic images could reach the maximum. A highlighted area in an endoscope image will induce errors in the feature point matching process of three-dimensional (3D) reconstruction; therefore, the detection and removal of the highlighted area are crucial. During the shooting process of a CMOS camera, an endoscope image may be taken with insufficient brightness due to an insufficient light source or exposure; thus, it is imperative to enhance the image brightness of an endoscope image with insufficient brightness. An adaptive and integrated neighborhood-dependent approach for nonlinear enhancement (AINDANE) algorithm [20,21] was employed to enhance the brightness of endoscopic images. Combined with the above algorithms, an endoscope image processing scheme was proposed in this study. The scheme included detail enhancement, contrast enhancement, brightness enhancement, and highlighted area removal, which could effectively improve the quality of endoscope images. The overall flowchart of this process is shown in Figure 1.

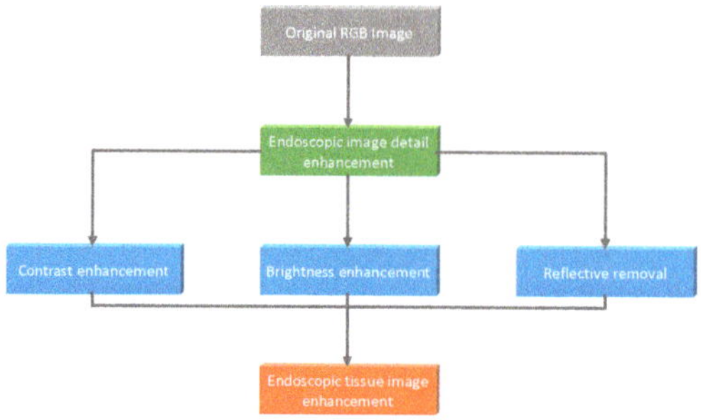

Figure 1. Algorithm flowchart.

2. Methods

2.1. Guided Filtering

Guided image filtering (GIF) is a filtering algorithm proposed by He Kai-ming [22] and can be used for stereo matching, IE, image fusion, defogging, etc. To the best of our knowledge, GIF is the fastest edge-preserving algorithm and its complexity is O (N). The following linear relationship exists between the leading image G and the output image Q:

$$q_i = a_k G_i + b_k, \forall i \in w_k \tag{1}$$

where w_k denotes the filter window and a_k and b_k are constants in the window.

As the gradient between the texture of the output image and that of the guide image is the same, the equation $\nabla Q = a \nabla G$ is satisfied. Therefore, guided image filtering (GIF) can preserve edges to a certain extent. GIF's energy function is defined as follows:

$$E(a_k, b_k) = \sum_{i \in W_k} \left((a_k G_i + b_k - P_i)^2 + \lambda a_k^2 \right) \tag{2}$$

where λ denotes the regularization parameter, whose function is to prevent a_k from becoming too large; P represents the input image. Equation (3) is solved using the least-squares method as follows:

$$a_k = \frac{\frac{1}{|W|} \sum_{i \in W_k} G_i p_i - \overline{P_k} u_k}{\sigma_k^2 + \lambda} \tag{3}$$

$$b_k = \overline{P_k} - a_k u_k \tag{4}$$

2.2. Weighted Guided Filtering

However, the regularization coefficient is fixed in the energy function of GIF and the effect of sharpening the prominent edge while denoising is not good. The λ in GIF is artificial and the differences in image textures between various windows are ignored. Therefore, some researchers have proposed a weighted GIF (WGIF) [23]. Thus, an edge weight factor is introduced in WGIF to adaptively adjust the regularization parameters as follows:

$$\Gamma_G(i) = \frac{1}{N} \sum_{i=1}^{N} \frac{\sigma_{G,1}^2(i) + \varepsilon}{\sigma_{G,1}^2(i^2) + \varepsilon} \tag{5}$$

where i denotes the center pixel of the current window and $\sigma_{G,1}^2(i)$ denotes the variance of the guiding image G in pixel i in the window. Currently, the window size is 3×3, and N denotes the pixel size of the image. In this study, ε is $(0.001 \times L)^2$ and L is the dynamic range of the input image. For 8-bit images, the value of L is 256 and the value of ε is a fixed value of 0.065536. The energy function of Formula (6) can be expressed as follows:

$$E(a_k, b_k) = \sum_{i \in w_k} ((a_k I_i + b_k - p_i)^2 + \frac{\lambda}{\Gamma_I(i')} a_k^2) \tag{6}$$

WGIF outperforms GIF in terms of image sharpening and edge highlighting because of the adjustment of the edge weight factor. Furthermore, the algorithm complexity does not increase in WGIF compared with GIF.

2.3. Detail Enhancement of Endoscopic Images

(1) Determine parameter α

In this study, α is defined as the sharpening factor that controls the sharpening degree of the image. However, the factor is sensitive to noise and should be suppressed to control α. Considering this factor, the following formula is used to calculate α:

$$\alpha = 8 \times \frac{1}{n} \sum_{i=1}^{n} H_c \tag{7}$$

where n denotes the total number of pixels of the grayscale image; I_c denotes the gray image; and C represents the R, G, and B channels of the image.

Endoscope images contain details, such as blood vessel information; therefore, the selected window radius should not be too large. Further, the influence of noise should be considered. Therefore, the window radius in the proposed endoscope IE algorithm was set to 16 and λ was 0.12.

(2) Quadratic improved WGF

The original endoscope image typically has some noise, whereas the noise of the WGF image is partially reduced. However, some residual noise exists in various frequency bands. A quadratic improved WGF algorithm was introduced to suppress the noise to overcome this defect.

First, the original endoscope image was filtered using the improved WGF algorithm to obtain the filtered image $P1$ with a window radius of 16 and $\gamma = 0.12$. Next, the original image was considered as the input image and $P1$ as the guide image. The improved WGF was performed again.

2.4. Endoscopic Image Contrast Enhancement

In this study, an endoscopic blood vessel contrast enhancement algorithm based on spectral transformation was modified. To make the endoscopic image visually distinct, the maximization target of the tonal distance was defined as follows:

$$\max(||B_{en}, V_{en}|| / ||B_{ori}, V_{ori}||) \tag{8}$$

where B_{ori}, V_{ori} represent the background and blood vessel areas of the original endoscopic image, respectively, and B_{en}, V_{en} represent the background and blood vessel areas of the endoscopic image after the detail enhancement algorithm, respectively.

For the R channel component, the model linearly reduces its information using an attenuation factor of α. For the G and B channel components, the model acts to improve the overall information; therefore, it uses a nonlinear function to process the endoscopic image to improve its contrast. The formula is as follows:

$$s = \frac{L}{1 + (m/r)^E} \tag{9}$$

where m can control the degree of translation of the function, E can control the slope of the function, r represents the input image, and s represents the output image.

The model parameters were as follows.

$m = 20$ endoscopic images and $n = 84$ sets of parameters (each set of parameters are α_j, L_j, m_j and r_j, respectively) are selected for training. The steps of training parameters are as follows:

(1) Input the i th image, where the image size is 316×258. If i is greater than m, end the training and skip to *S8*; otherwise, execute *S2*.
(2) Select the vessel and background regions of the endoscopic image.
(3) Enter the j th group of parameters. If j is greater than n, skip to *S7*; otherwise, go to *S4*.
(4) A stretch is performed on each of the three channels using the following formula:

$$\begin{cases} proG_i = \frac{L_j}{1+(m_j/r_i)^{E_j}} \\ proR_i = d_j \times R_i \\ proB_i = \frac{L_j}{1+(m_j/r_i)^{E_j}} \end{cases} \tag{10}$$

(5) Both the original training image and processed image are in the RGB space and now they are converted to CIE space. The conversion formula is as follows:

$$\begin{cases} X = 2.7690 \times R + 1.7518 \times G + 1.1300 \times B \\ Y = 1.0000 \times R + 4.5907 \times G + 0.0601 \times B \\ Z = 0.0000 \times R + 0.0565 \times G + 5.5943 \times B \end{cases} \tag{11}$$

$$\begin{cases} x = \frac{X}{X+Y+Z} \\ y = \frac{Y}{X+Y+Z} \end{cases} \tag{12}$$

(6) Calculate the distance $\|B_{en}, V_{en}\|$ between the original image and blood vessel and the distance $\|B_{ori}, V_{ori}\|$ between the original image and background of the processed image; save the ratio $\|B_{en}, V_{en}\| / \|B_{ori}, V_{ori}\|$ in the array $VecDis$ and go back to *S3*.
(7) According to the maximization objective of Formula (12), a set of optimal parameters α_i, L_i, m_i and E_i of the original image can be obtained, and the optimal parameters of this set are saved in $VecA$, $VecL$, $VecM$ and $VecE$, respectively; finally, go back to *S2*.
(8) Take the average of $VecA$, $VecL$, $VecM$ and $VecE$, and obtain a set of optimal parameters α_{best}, L_{best}, M_{best} and E_{best}; finally, end the training.

After training on 20 images, the final results were $\alpha = 0.75$, $m = 0.525$, $E = 2.15$, and $L = 1.241$.

2.5. Brightness Enhancement of Endoscopic Images

In the shooting process of a CMOS camera, the brightness of an endoscope image may be insufficient due to a light source problem or insufficient exposure. To solve this problem, it is imperative to enhance the brightness of the endoscope image. Li Tao et al. [24] proposed the AINDANE algorithm, which can improve the brightness of an image when the color of the endoscope image is dark due to the shooting equipment or surrounding environment. This function is mainly realized by the adaptive brightness enhancement module.

First, convert RGB images to grayscale images. The calculation process is expressed as follows:

$$I(x,y) = \frac{76.245 I_R(x,y) + 149.685 I_G(x,y) + 29.01 I_B(x,y)}{255} \tag{13}$$

where $I_R(x,y)$, $I_G(x,y)$, and $I_B(x,y)$ represent the values of the R, G, and B channels (x,y), respectively, each of which is 8 bits.

Then, normalize $I(x,y)$ using the following formula:

$$I_n(x,y) = \frac{I(x,y)}{255} \tag{14}$$

The calculation process of the nonlinear transfer function is expressed as follows:

$$I'_n = \frac{I_n^{(0.72z+0.25)} + (1 - I_n)0.4(1 - z) + I_n^{(2-z)}}{2} \tag{15}$$

This process is called dynamic range compression, where the parameter z is related to the histogram of the image as follows:

$$z = \begin{cases} 0 & L \leq 50 \\ \frac{L-50}{100} & 50 < L \leq 150 \\ 1 & L > 150 \end{cases} \tag{16}$$

When the cumulative distribution function value is 0.1, L represents its corresponding gray value.

L is used as an indicator of the brightness of an image. If the image is dark ($L < 50$), brightness enhancement is required; if the image is not so dark ($L \approx 100$), there is less need for brightness enhancement; if the image has sufficient brightness ($L > 150$), no enhancement is required. As such, the algorithm is adaptive. Figure 2 shows the cumulative distribution function of gray values at the gray level L.

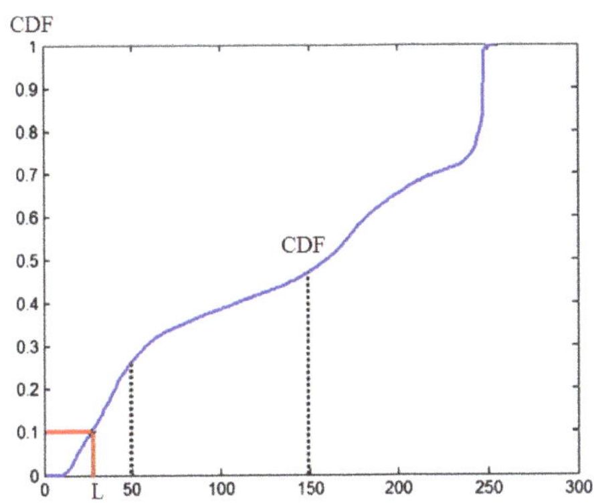

Figure 2. Cumulative distribution function of the gray value: The red line is the cumulative probability; blue line is the CDF curve; gray line is the brightness value.

The transfer function is a combination of three simple functions. In Figure 3, curve 6 ($z = 0$) is compared with the dotted line (line labeled 1), which represents the identity transformation. The first two terms are plotted as curve 2 and line 3, respectively, and their sum is curve 4. By adding the normalized curves 4 and 5 and dividing by 2, the transfer function shown in curve 6 was generated. The results showed that this transformation significantly increased the brightness of the darker regions and reduced the intensity of the brighter regions.

Figure 4 shows the contrast of the brightness enhancement effect. Three original endoscope images with low brightness were enhanced using the proposed algorithm and their brightness was significantly improved.

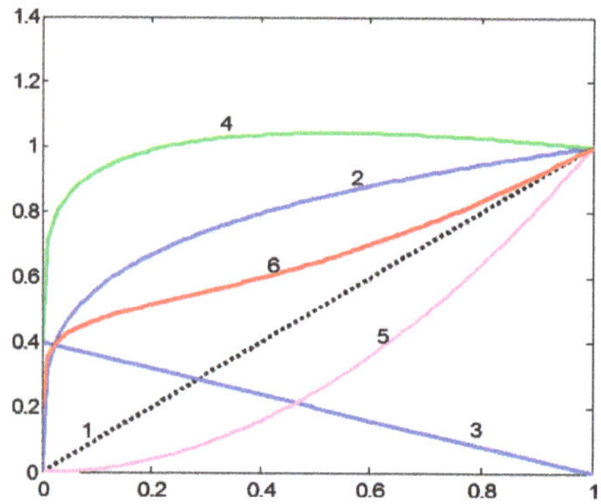

Figure 3. Nonlinear transfer function: Line 1 is the identity transformation; Line 2 is the energy function; Line 3 is the first-order constraint term; Line 4 is the sum of lines 2 and 3; Line 5 is the first-order edge-aware constraint term; Line 6 is the line 4 and 5 phase Add and divide the normalized transfer function by 2.

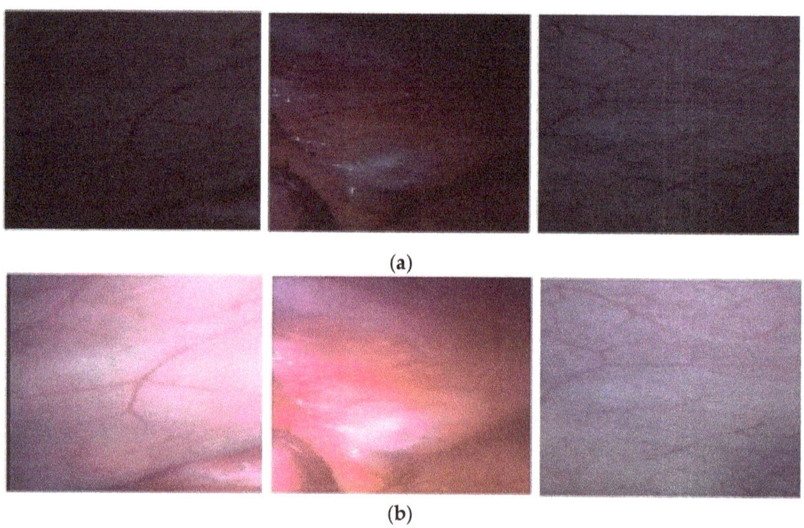

Figure 4. Comparison of brightness enhancement effects: (**a**) original images and (**b**) after brightness enhancement.

2.6. *Removal of Highlights from Endoscopic Images*

(1) Highlight spot detection

First, the original image from the RGB model is converted to the HSV color model. To obtain absolutely bright areas, two thresholds T_s and T_v regarding saturation and lightness, respectively, are employed if the area is a highlighted area as follows:

$$\begin{cases} s(x) < T_s \\ v(x) > T_v \end{cases} \tag{17}$$

However, the disadvantage of this method is that the rapid movement of the endoscope lens causes the misalignment of the color channels; therefore, the detected highlights can appear white or highly saturated R, G, or B.

The G and B channels, namely, c_G and c_B, can be normalized as follows:

$$c_E = 0.2989 \cdot c_R + 0.5870 \cdot c_G + 0.1140 \cdot c_B \tag{18}$$

Then, comparing 95% of the grayscale intensity of c_G and c_B with 95% of the intensity of c_E, we obtain the following:

$$r_{GE} = \frac{P_{95}(c_G)}{P_{95}(c_E)}, r_{BE} = \frac{P_{95}(c_B)}{P_{95}(c_E)} \tag{19}$$

If a pixel x_0 is a highlighted area, it satisfies the following formula:

$$c_G(x_0) > r_{GE} \cdot T_1 \vee c_B > r_{BE} \cdot T_1 \vee c_E(x_0) > T_1 \tag{20}$$

Then, the algorithm detects the parts of the endoscopic image where the highlights are not too intense. Its purpose is to compare each given pixel with a smooth, nonspecial surface color at the pixel location, which is estimated by local image statistics in the endoscopic image. A slightly lower threshold T_2^{rel} is set for the contrast intensity using a method similar to detecting brighter highlighted areas. Owing to the robustness and edge-preserving properties of the original image to outliers, it is essential to perform median filtering on the R, G, and B channels of the original image. Each detected highlighted region is then filled to the centroid of the pixel color within a fixed distance from the region outline. Then, this region of interest is isolated by complete separation of the masks obtained by performing two dilation operations on the masks of possible highlighted locations. For the dilation operation, disk-shaped structuring elements with radii of 2 and 4 pixels are used.

By comparing pixel values in the input image and median-filtered image, highlights are found as color outliers. For this comparison, several distance measures and ratios are possible. An example of such a metric is the Euclidean distance or the infinite norm of the difference in the RGB space. During the evaluation, it was found that the maximum ratio of the three color channel intensities in the original image to the median-filtered image yielded the best results. For each pixel position x, the intensity ratio maximum is calculated as follows:

$$\varepsilon_{\max}(x) = \max\left\{ \frac{c_R(x)}{c_R^*(x)}, \frac{c_G(x)}{c_G^*(x)}, \frac{c_B(x)}{c_B^*(x)} \right\} \tag{21}$$

where $c_R^*(x)$, $c_G^*(x)$, and $c_B^*(x)$ denote the intensities of the median-filtered R, G, and B components, respectively.

Different color balance and contrast can cause this characteristic to vary significantly between images. These changes are compensated for using a contrast factor τ_i, which is calculated for the three color channels of each given image:

$$\tau_i = \left(\frac{\overline{c}_i + s(c_i)}{\overline{c}_i}\right)^{-1}, i \in \{R, G, B\} \tag{22}$$

where $\overline{c}_i$ denotes the sample mean of all pixel intensities in the color channel and $s(c_i)$ denotes the sample standard deviation. Using the coefficients, Equation (22) is modified to obtain a contrast-compensated intensity ratio $\widetilde{\varepsilon}_{\max}(x)$ as follows:

$$\widetilde{\varepsilon}_{\max}(x) = \max\left\{ \tau_R \cdot \frac{c_R(x)}{c_R^*(x)}, \tau_G \cdot \frac{c_G(x)}{c_G^*(x)}, \tau_B \cdot \frac{c_B(x)}{c_B^*(x)} \right\} \tag{23}$$

If this pixel is a highlighted pixel, we have

$$\widetilde{\varepsilon}_{\max}(x) > T_2^{rel} \tag{24}$$

The outputs of the first and second modules are connected using logical disjunctions that generate masks. The two modules complement each other well: the first module uses a global threshold, thus only prominent and bright specular highlights can be detected, whereas the second module detects less obvious highlighted regions by comparing the relative characteristics of surface colors. Owing to the high dynamic range of the image sensor, the second module alone can also achieve good results. However, because the sensor is easily saturated, the relative highlights become less intense such that no given area of the image is bright; thus, the first module still allows for detection in this case. Figure 5 shows the detection of the highlighted area of an endoscope.

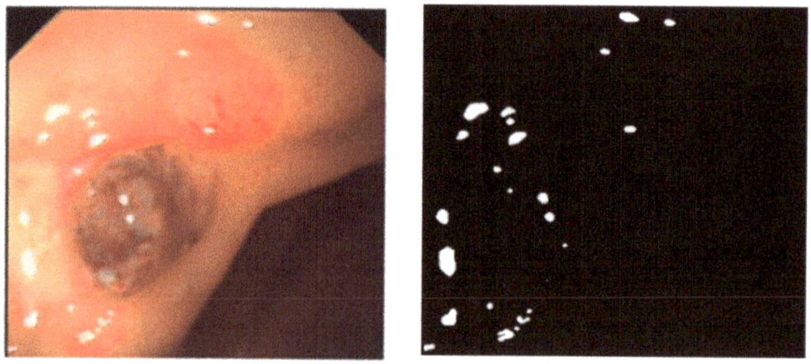

(a) (b)

Figure 5. Detection of highlighted regions in endoscopic images: (**a**) original specular image and (**b**) detected highlighted area.

(2) Repair of highlighted areas

Fill each detected highlight region with pixel color points within the range of the distance profile. Then, the Gaussian function is used to filter the image, which is similar to the median filtering after the image is filled, and, finally, a smooth image is obtained.

The binary mask of the highlighted area in the labeled image is converted to a smooth weighted mask. Smoothing is achieved by adding nonlinear attenuation to the contour of the mirror area. The weight b of the pixels around the highlight in the weighted template is calculated according to the Euclidean distance d from it to the contour of the highlighted area:

$$b(d) = \left[1 + \exp((l_{\max} - l_{\min})\cdot(\frac{d}{d_{\max}})^{c} + l_{\min})\right]^{-1}, d \in [0, d_{\max}] \tag{25}$$

where the logical attenuation function ranges from $l_{\min}$ to $l_{\max}$ in the window, the distance range of the mapping is from 0 to $d_{\max}$, and $c = 0.7$.

The weighted sum between the integer-weighted mask $m(x)$, the original image $c(x)$, and the smooth image $c_{sm}(x)$ after the Gaussian filtering can obtain the repaired image $c_{inp}(x)$. The calculation process is expressed as follows:

$$c_{inp}(x) = m(x)\cdot c_{sm}(x) + (1 - m(x))\cdot c(x) \tag{26}$$

Figure 6 shows the comparison before and after the restoration of the highlighted area of the endoscope image. From the figure, the highlighted area was well repaired after using the proposed algorithm.

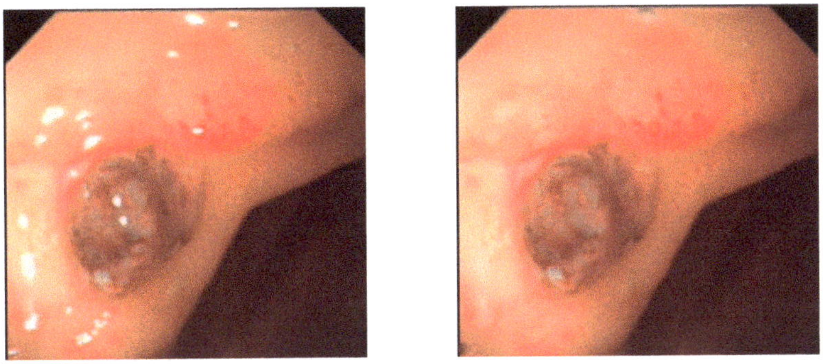

(a) (b)

Figure 6. Comparison of endoscopic image highlights before and after restoration: (**a**) original highlight and (**b**) restored highlight.

2.7. Specific Steps of the Endoscope IE Algorithm

The steps of the IE algorithm are as follows:

(1) Categorize the original endoscope image into R, G, and B channels.
(2) Obtain the base layer image of each channel using the quadratic improved WGF algorithm for the three channels.
(3) Subtract the corresponding base layer images of R, G, and B of the three channels to obtain the images of the detailed layer of the three channels.
(4) Multiply the detailed layer images of the three channels by the coefficient α to obtain the enhanced detailed layer images.
(5) Add the detailed layer images and the corresponding base layer images of the three channels. Finally, merge the three channels to obtain the enhanced endoscope image.

2.8. Evaluation Method

In the endoscopic image evaluation, doctors' subjective evaluation is still the main technique that is used to verify image quality. For laparoscopic endoscopic images, the establishment of a quantitative assessment is challenging because there are no available gold standards. In this study, to verify the performance of tissue vascular, brightness, and color enhancement, we defined the evaluation indexes for verifying IE: (1) peak signal-to-noise ratio (*PSNR*), (2) structural similarity index (*SSIM*), and (3) detail variance–background variance (DV-BV).

We used *PSNR* and *SSIM* to evaluate the image quality. In the experimental results, the higher the values of *PSNR*, the better the image quality. *PSNR* is a measure of image reconstruction quality as follows:

$$MSE = \frac{1}{\mathrm{mn}} \sum_{i=0}^{\mathrm{m}-1} \sum_{j=0}^{n-1} [I(i,j) - K(i,j)]^2 \tag{27}$$

$$PSNR = 10 \times \log_{10}(\frac{MAX_I^2}{MSE}) \tag{28}$$

where MSE denotes the mean square error, MAX_i^2 denotes the maximum possible pixel value of the picture, $I(i,j)$ denotes the original image, and $K(i,j)$ denotes the noise image.

SSIM is used to measure the similarity of two images, where the larger the value, the more similar the two images are.

$$SSIM(x,y) = [l(x,y) \cdot c(x,y) \cdot s(x,y)] \tag{29}$$

$$l(x,y) = \frac{2\mu_x\mu_y + c_1}{\mu_x^2 + \mu_y^2 + c_1} \quad (30)$$

$$c(x,y) = \frac{2\sigma_x\sigma_y + c_2}{\sigma_x^2 + \sigma_y^2 + c_2} \quad (31)$$

$$s(x,y) = \frac{\sigma_{xy} + c_3}{\sigma_x\sigma_y + c_3} \quad (32)$$

where μ denotes the mean, σ denotes the variance, and σ_{xy} represents the covariance of x and y; $c_1 = (k_1L)^2$ and $c_1 = (k_2L)^2$ are two constants, with $k_1 = 0.01$ and $k_2 = 0.03$, and L is the range of image pixels.

The image to be evaluated can be divided into two areas: detail and background. The local variance of the detailed area is obtained and then averaged. The detail variance (DV) can be obtained. The local variance of the background area is obtained and then averaged. The BV can be obtained. The calculation steps of the DV-BV value [25] are as follows:

(1) Compute a histogram of the local variance values in the augmented image (each pixel is within a 5 × 5 field). The given threshold Tv is 5. Pixels that do not exceed this threshold are the detailed areas; otherwise, they are the background areas.
(2) The DV-BV value is estimated as DV/BV. Its value is proportional to the degree of image detail enhancement.

3. Results

The experimental operating system was Windows 10, 64-bit. Matlab R2018b was used. The experimental dataset was provided by the Hamlyn Centre Laparoscopic/Endoscopy Video Dataset (http://hamlyn.doc.ic.ac.uk/vision/ (accessed on 2 September 2021)). with real laparoscopic images. The dataset contained 32,400 pairs of binocular endoscopic images. The size of an image was 384 × 192.

We filtered by inputting a grayscale image with three large difference grayscale values and then drew the corresponding histogram. The histogram distribution can measure the weakening of the halo. As shown in Figure 7, GIF had an obvious halo; EGIF had a small amount of halo; WGIF and GDGIF significantly improved the degree of halo reduction. The proposed algorithm was almost free of halos. Therefore, it was better than the other algorithms regarding the degree of halo reduction.

As shown in Figure 8, GIF, WGIF [26], GDGIF [27], EGIF [28], and the proposed algorithm were used to process the original endoscopic images; six endoscopic images were enhanced by the endoscopic IE algorithm. The results of the endoscopic IE in Figure 7 revealed that although GIF and others enhanced the details of blood vessels, image distortion and noise amplification also occurred, which was attributable to the low edge maintenance ability of GIF and others. The noise retained by an image was amplified by a sharpening factor α; the image detail layer was obtained while retaining the noise. The edge retention capabilities of the proposed algorithm were superior to those of GIF, WGIF, GDGIF, and EGIF. Further, the proposed algorithm was less noisy and enhanced the details of the endoscopic tissue and blood vessels.

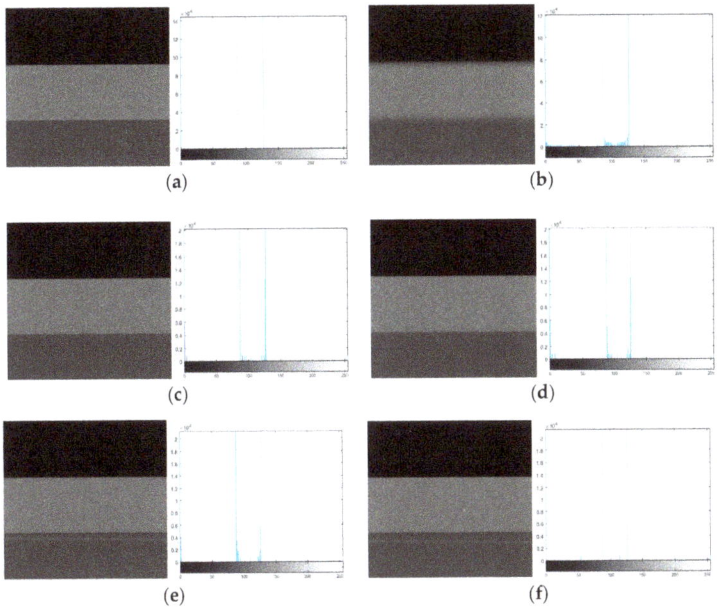

Figure 7. (**a**) Original image (**left**) and histogram (**right**). Image after implementing (**b**) GIF (**left**), with filtered histogram (**right**); (**c**) WGIF (**left**), with filtered histogram (**right**); (**d**) GDGIF (**left**), with filtered histogram (**right**); (**e**) EGIF (**left**), with filtered histogram (**right**); and (**f**) proposed algorithm (**left**), with filtered histogram (**right**). The blue line is the halo distribution of the histogram.

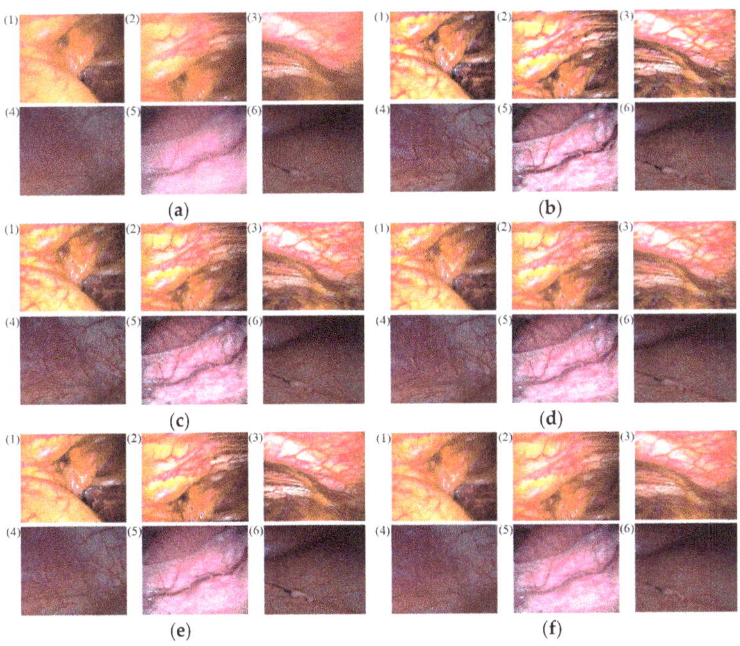

Figure 8. (**a**) Original image, (**b**) GIF renderings, (**c**) WGIF renderings, (**d**) GDGIF renderings, (**e**) EGIF renderings, and (**f**) the proposed algorithm renderings. Subfigures (1)–(6) are randomly selected Hamlin laparoscopic images.

PSNR was used to measure the proportion of noise. Image quality is proportional to PSNR. To validate the proposed algorithm, we selected six images from the Hamlin Center Laparoscopy dataset. As shown in Table 1, the PSNR values of five algorithms were compared. Compared with GIF, WGIF, GDGI, and EGIF, the proposed quadratic WGF algorithm had the highest PSNR value, indicating that our technique made the tissue blood vessels clearer and had a better ability to suppress noise.

Table 1. PSNR calculation results.

Image Number	GIF	WGIF	GDGIF	EGIF	Proposed
(1)	20.9569	24.5021	24.7910	26.6537	29.4090
(2)	19.7178	23.6563	24.0289	25.1088	28.4882
(3)	20.0447	23.3038	23.3767	24.6815	28.0150
(4)	29.5328	31.2070	31.8931	33.8716	37.5925
(5)	21.3806	24.7216	25.1418	29.3361	29.9575
(6)	33.3530	36.4773	37.1277	32.8452	42.1757
Average	24.1643	27.3114	27.7265	28.7495	32.6063

The similarity of two images can be measured using SSIM. The similarity of images is proportional to SSIM. As shown in Table 2, the proposed algorithm had the highest SSIM value compared with GIF, WGIF, GDGI, and EGIF, indicating that the proposed algorithm could better preserve the tissue structure of endoscopic images and had a higher structural similarity.

Table 2. SSIM calculation results.

Image Number	GIF	WGIF	GDGIF	EGIF	Proposed
(1)	0.7531	0.8373	0.8444	0.9156	0.9212
(2)	0.7341	0.8368	0.8458	0.8919	0.9214
(3)	0.7241	0.8105	0.8124	0.8808	0.9071
(4)	0.8778	0.9026	0.9138	0.9417	0.9681
(5)	0.7024	0.7771	0.7904	0.9225	0.9304
(6)	0.9478	0.9644	0.9686	0.9450	0.9868
Average	0.7899	0.8548	0.8626	0.9163	0.9391

As shown in Table 3, the DV-BV value of the proposed algorithm was compared with the original endoscopic image. The DV-BV values of the images processed by the proposed algorithm were much higher than those of the raw endoscopic images, indicating that the proposed algorithm for enhancing image details and highlighting local information considerably improved the contrast. The enhancement effect was obvious.

Table 3. DV-BV calculation results.

Image Number	Original Value	Proposed
(1)	17.1937	26.9770
(2)	22.8585	45.6375
(3)	32.8440	68.8868
(4)	7.8341	10.0505
(5)	12.5660	24.4680
(6)	9.5032	17.3654
Average	17.1333	32.2309

As shown in Tables 1–3, the average values obtained from the proposed improved quadratic WGF algorithm for the PSNR and SSIM were 32.6063 dB and 0.9391, respectively. The average DV-BV was 32.2309, which was 88% higher than that of the original image. We compared recent endoscopic IE algorithms, such as Sato et al.'s [29] endoscopic IE algorithm based on texture and color enhancement imaging (average SSIM = 0.9256), Wang et al.'s [30] vessel enhancement algorithm of nonlinear contrast stretching in multicolor space (DV-BV = 4.64, which was 54% higher than that of the original image), Qayyum et al.'s [31] single-shot deep image prior-based approach for retinal IE (*PSNR* = 22.47 dB and SSIM = 0.897), Fang et al.'s [32] endoscopic enhancement algorithm based on nonlinear unsharp mask and CLAHE (average PSNR = 24.5967 dB), and Gómez et al.'s [33] low-light IE algorithm based on convolutional neural networks (PSNR = 23.79 dB and SSIM = 0.88). Clearly, the proposed algorithm was superior to the comparison algorithms, which demonstrated the effectiveness of our technique.

4. Discussion

Because there are no corresponding reference materials for clinical endoscopic images, a more professional evaluation was needed to verify the effectiveness of the endoscopic IE methods. Therefore, we invited 10 chief physicians from the Affiliated Hospital of Southwest Medical University with more than 5 years of experience in laparoscopic surgery to score the enhanced images. The subjective evaluation score standard is shown in Table 4. Subjective evaluation criteria included edge sharpening, sharpness, invariance, and acceptability. The subjective quality evaluation results of the clinicians for different algorithms are shown in Table 5; the quality score adopted the mean $\pm$ variance.

Table 4. Subjective evaluation score method.

Score	Enhanced Image Features
1	Some areas of the image are severely distorted
2	Mild image distortion
3	Harder to spot image distortion
4	The visual effect of the image is better
5	Image is very clear

Table 5. Diagnostic quality assessment by different algorithms in Hamlin's laparoscopic dataset (mean $\pm$ standard deviation).

Algorithm	Edge Sharpening	Clarity	Invariance	Acceptability
GIF	3.2 ± 0.16	3.5 ± 0.21	0.2 ± 0.25	1.4 ± 0.24
WGIF	3.8 ± 0.24	3.6 ± 0.21	0.5 ± 0.16	2.7 ± 0.41
GDGI	4.2 ± 0.16	3.8 ± 0.16	0.5 ± 0.25	3.8 ± 0.21
EGIF	4.0 ± 0.40	4.0 ± 0.29	0.6 ± 0.24	3.9 ± 0.29
Proposed	4.1 ± 0.29	4.1 ± 0.24	0.7 ± 0.24	4.2 ± 0.16

In Table 4, edge sharpening, image sharpness, and acceptability were rated on a scale of 1 (worst) to 5 (best). A score of 1 indicated a nondiagnostic image, and a score of 5 indicated excellent diagnostic image quality. Meanwhile, pathological invariance was scored with 0 (change) or 1 (no change).

The evaluations of 10 clinicians are shown in Table 5; the proposed quadratic WGF algorithm obtained the best subjective quality evaluation, which was attributable to the improved unsharp masking algorithm of WGF. Images enhanced using WGF had better texture details. Compared to other filtering methods, WGF had advantages in clarity, invariance, and acceptability on the Hamlin Center laparoscopy dataset.

Figure 9 shows that the proposed algorithm can better preserve the basic structure of endoscopic images, as well as enhance tissue contours and vessel details. The brightness and contrast were considerably improved, and the dehighlight effect was better, validating the feasibility of the proposed algorithm.

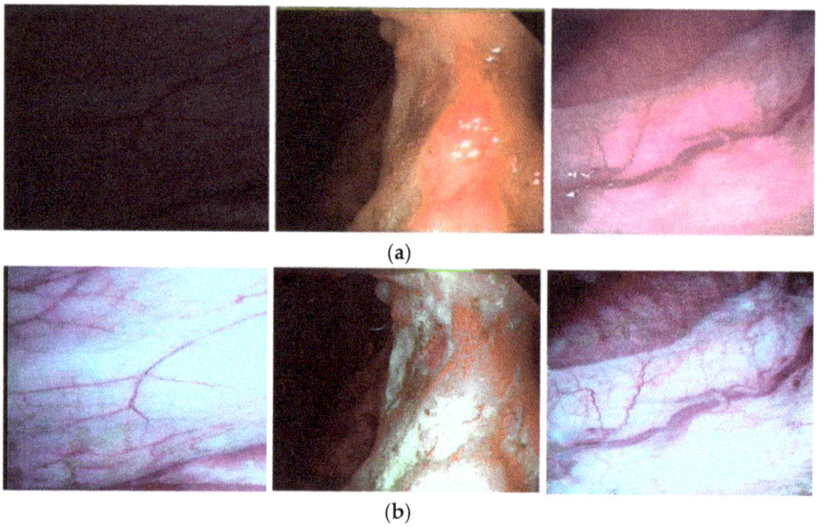

Figure 9. Endoscopic IE results: (**a**) original images and (**b**) enhanced images using our algorithm.

In the subjective evaluation, objective evaluation, and comparison results, the proposed improved quadratic WGF algorithm made the endoscope image clearer and the vascular contrast was significantly enhanced. The performance of the proposed algorithm was superior to GIF, WGIF, GDGIF, and EGIF. A contrast-enhancing algorithm was used to train the endoscopic images after the detail was enhanced. By enhancing the G and B components of an image and reducing the R component, the tissue background and the tones of the blood vessels had a distinct contrast effect. Guided filtering based on the original image made the luminance and detail layers of each channel separated. The detailed layer with vascular features was enhanced. The contrast of the image was further enhanced, and a set of optimal parameters $\alpha = 0.75$, $m = 0.525$, $E = 2.15$, and $L = 1.241$ were obtained. This ensured that the tissue background and blood vessels met the relevant requirements of the human visual angle.

5. Conclusions

An image enhancement algorithm based on secondary weighted guided filtering was proposed for endoscopy, which is a widely employed procedure in minimally invasive surgery. In the proposed algorithm, four modules—detail enhancement, contrast enhancement, brightness enhancement, and highlighted area removal—were simultaneously used to achieve contrast and sharpness enhancement of image vessels and contours. The modules can also be operated individually. The effectiveness of the proposed algorithm was verified using experiments. Both subjective evaluations and objective results showed that the proposed algorithm could preserve edges, reduce halo effects, and detect and remove highlights. Compared with other algorithms, the endoscopic image quality improved considerably. It was demonstrated that the proposed algorithm can be applied to endoscopic image processing. Therefore, the proposed algorithm has clinical application prospects in endoscopic image processing. Compared with other algorithms, the proposed algorithm had the least noise, but there was still some noise. In future work, we will continue to optimize the filtering algorithm. To meet the real-time and accuracy requirements of clinical operations, we will conduct research on smoke removal, super-resolution reconstruction, and 3D reconstruction of endoscopic images based on deep learning methods.

Author Contributions: Conceptualization, Y.P. and W.S.; methodology and guidance of the project, W.S. and G.Z.; validation, formal analysis, and data analysis, W.S. and G.Z.; writing—G.Z., J.L., E.C., Y.P. and W.S. All authors have read and agreed to the published version of the manuscript.

Funding: This work was supported by the National Natural Science Foundation of China (grant no. U21A20447 and 61971079), the Basic Research and Frontier Exploration Project of Chongqing (grant no. cstc2019jcyjmsxmX0666), Chongqing Technological Innovation and Application Development Project (cstc2021jscx-gksbx0051), the Innovative Group Project of the National Natural Science Foundation of Chongqing (grant no. cstc2020jcyj-cxttX0002), the Regional Creative Cooperation Program of Sichuan (2020YFQ0025), the Science and Technology Research Program of Chongqing Municipal Education Commission (KJZD-k202000604), the Doctoral Innovative Talents Project of Chongqing University of Posts and Telecommunications (BYJS202107), Chongqing Natural Science Foundation of China (cstc2021jcyj-bsh0218), and the Chongqing Science and Technology Bureau of China (D63012021013).

Institutional Review Board Statement: Not applicable.

Informed Consent Statement: Not applicable.

Data Availability Statement: Not applicable.

Acknowledgments: The authors thank everyone who contributed to this article.

Conflicts of Interest: The authors declare no conflict of interest.

References

1. Bray, F.; Ferlay, J.; Soerjomataram, I.; Siegel, R.L.; Jemal, A. Global cancer statistics 2018: Globocan estimates of incidence and mortality worldwide for 36 cancers in 185 countries. *CA Cancer J. Clin.* **2018**, *68*, 394–424. [CrossRef] [PubMed]
2. Togashi, K.; Osawa, H.; Koinuma, K.; Hayashi, Y.; Miyata, T.; Sunada, K.; Nokubi, M.; Horie, H.; Yamamoto, H. A comparison of conventional endoscopy, chromoendoscopy, and the optimal-band imaging system for the differentiation of neoplastic and non-neoplastic colonic polyps. *Gastrointest. Endos.* **2009**, *69*, 734–741. [CrossRef]
3. Li, T.; Ni, B.; Xu, M.; Wang, M.; Gao, Q.; Yan, S. Data-driven affective filtering for images and videos. *IEEE Trans. Cybern.* **2015**, *45*, 2336–2349. [CrossRef] [PubMed]
4. Li, T.; Yan, S.; Mei, T.; Hua, X.S.; Kweon, I.S. Image decomposition with multilabel context: Algorithms and applications. *IEEE Trans. Image Processing* **2010**, *20*, 2301–2314.
5. Schuellerweidekamm, C.; Schaeferprokop, C.M.; Weber, M.; Herold, C.J.; Prokop, M. CT angiography of pulmonary arteries to detect pulmonary embolism: Improvement of vascular enhancement with low kilovoltage settings. *Radiology* **2006**, *241*, 899–907. [CrossRef] [PubMed]
6. Zhang, K.; Wang, H.; Yuan, B.; Wang, L. An image enhancement technique using nonlinear transfer function and unsharp masking in multispectral endoscope. In *International Conference on Innovative Optical Health Science*; International Society for Optics and Photonics: Bellingham, WA, USA, 2017; Volume 10245, p. 1024504.
7. Yang, S.F.; Cheng, C.H. Fast computation of Hessian-based enhancement filters for medical images. *Comput. Meth. Prog. Biomedcine* **2014**, *116*, 215–225. [CrossRef]
8. Oh, J.; Hwang, H. Feature enhancement of medical images using morphology-based homomorphic filter and differential evolution algorithm. *Int. J. Control. Autom.* **2010**, *8*, 857–861. [CrossRef]
9. Yin, X.; Ng, B.W.; He, J.; Zhang, Y.; Abbott, D. Accurate image analysis of the retina using Hessian matrix and binarisation of thresholded en-tropy with application of texture mapping. *PLoS ONE* **2014**, *9*, e95943.
10. Ajam, A.; Aziz, A.A.; Asirvadam, V.S.; Izhar, L.I.; Muda, S. Cerebral vessel enhancement using bilateral and Hessian-based filter. In Proceedings of the 2016 6th International Conference on Intelligent and Advanced Systems (ICIAS), Kuala Lumpur, Malaysia, 15–17 August 2016.
11. Kim, J.Y.; Kim, L.S.; Hwang, S.H. An advanced contrast enhancement using partially overlapped sub-block histogram equalization. *IEEE Trans. Circ. Syst. Vid. Technol.* **2001**, *11*, 475–484.
12. Ma, J.; Fan, X.; Yang, S.X.; Zhang, X.; Zhu, X. Contrast limited adaptive histogram equalization-based fusion in YIQ and HSI color spaces for underwater image enhancement. *Int. J. Pattern Recognit. Artif. Intell.* **2017**, *32*, 1854018. [CrossRef]
13. Yang, Y.; Su, Z.; Sun, L. Medical image enhancement algorithm based on wavelet transform. *Electron. Lett.* **2010**, *46*, 120–121. [CrossRef]
14. Thirumala, K.; Pal, S.; Jain, T.; Umarikarb, A.C. A classification method for multiple power quality disturbances using EWT based adaptive filtering and multiclass SVM. *Neurocomputing* **2019**, *334*, 265–274. [CrossRef]
15. Tian, C.; Fei, L.; Zheng, W.; Xu, Y.; Zuo, W.; Ling, C.W. Deep learning on image denoising: An overview. *Neural Netw.* **2020**, *131*, 251–257. [CrossRef] [PubMed]
16. Tchaka, K.; Pawar, V.M.; Stoyanov, D. Chromaticity based smoke removal in endoscopic images. In *Medical Imaging 2017: Image Processing*; International Society for Optics and Photonics: Bellingham, WA, USA, 2017; Volume 10133, p. 101331M.

17. Okuhata, H.; Nakamura, H.; Hara, S.; Tsutsui, H.; Onoye, T. Application of the real-time Retinex image enhancement for endoscopic images. In Proceedings of the 2013 35th Annual International Conference of the IEEE Engineering in Medicine and Biology Society (EMBC), Osaka, Japan, 3–7 July 2013; pp. 3407–3410.
18. Gopi, V.P.; Palanisamy, P. Capsule endoscopic image denoising based on double density dual tree complex wavelet transform. *Int J. Imag. Robot.* **2013**, *9*, 48–60.
19. Imtiaz, M.S.; Mohammed, S.K.; Deeba, F.; Wahid, K.A. Tri-Scan: A three stage color enhancement tool for endoscopic images. *J Med. Syst.* **2017**, *41*, 102. [CrossRef] [PubMed]
20. Zhang, S.; Wang, T.; Dong, J.; Yu, H. Underwater image enhancement via extended multi-scale Retinex. *Neurocomputing* **2017**, *245* 1–9. [CrossRef]
21. Zheng, S.; Han, D.; Yuan, Y. 2-D image reconstruction of photoacoustic endoscopic imaging based on time-reversal. *Comput. Biol Med.* **2016**, *76*, 60–68. [CrossRef] [PubMed]
22. Ren, S.; He, K.; Girshick, R.; Sun, J. Faster R-CNN: Towards Real-Time Object Detection with Region Proposal Networks. *IEEE Trans. Pattern. Anal.* **2017**, *39*, 1137–1149. [CrossRef]
23. Li, Z.; Zheng, J.; Zhu, Z.; Yao, W.; Wu, S. Weighted Guided Image Filtering. *IEEE Trans. Image Process.* **2015**, *24*, 120–129.
24. Li, T.; Asari, V.K. Adaptive and integrated neighborhood-dependent approach for nonlinear enhancement of color images. *J Electronc. Imaging* **2005**, *14*, 043006.
25. Ghimire, D.; Lee, J. Nonlinear transfer function-based local approach for color image enhancement. *IEEE Trans. Consum. Electr* **2011**, *57*, 858–865. [CrossRef]
26. Hong, G.; Koo, M.; Saha, A.; Kim, B. Efficient local stereo matching technique using weighted guided image filtering (WGIF). In Proceedings of the 2016 IEEE International Conference on Consumer Electronics (ICCE), Las Vegas, NV, USA, 7–11 January 2016 pp. 484–485.
27. Zhao, D.; Xu, L.; Yan, Y.; Chen, J.; Duan, L.Y. Multi-scale Optimal Fusion model for single image dehazing. *Signal. Process-Image* **2019**, *74*, 253–265. [CrossRef]
28. Fragkou, P.; Galiotou, E.; Matsakas, M. Enriching the e-GIF Ontology for an Improved Application of Linking Data Technologies to Greek Open Government Data. *Procedia Soc. Behav. Sci.* **2014**, *147*, 167–174. [CrossRef]
29. Sato, T. TXI: Texture and color enhancement imaging for endoscopic image enhancement. *J. Healthc. Eng.* **2021**, *2021*, 5518948 [CrossRef] [PubMed]
30. Wang, Q.; Tao, P.; Yuan, B.; Wang, L. Vessel enhancement of endoscopic image based on multi-color space. *Opto-Electron. Eng.* **2020**, *47*, 190268.
31. Qayyum, A.; Sultani, W.; Shamshad, F.; Tufail, R.; Qadir, J. Single-Shot Retinal Image Enhancement Using Untrained and Pretrained Neural Networks Priors Integrated with Analytical Image Priors. *TechRxiv* **2021** *Preprint*. [CrossRef]
32. Fang, S.; Xu, C.; Feng, B.; Zhu, Y. Color Endoscopic Image Enhancement Technology Based on Nonlinear Unsharp Mask and CLAHE. In Proceedings of the 2021 IEEE 6th International Conference on Signal and Image Processing (ICSIP), Nanjing, China, 22–24 October 2021; pp. 234–239.
33. Gómez, P.; Semmler, M.; Schützenberger, A.; Bohr, C.; Döllinger, M. Low-light image enhancement of high-speed endoscopic videos using a convolutional neural network. *Med. Biol. Eng. Comput.* **2019**, *57*, 1451–1463. [CrossRef]

mathematics

MDPI

Article

A Novel Method of Chinese Herbal Medicine Classification Based on Mutual Learning

Meng Han [1,†], Jilin Zhang [1,*], Yan Zeng [1], Fei Hao [2] and Yongjian Ren [1]

[1] Computer & Software School, Hangzhou Dianzi University, Hangzhou 310018, China; hanm@hdu.edu.cn (M.H.); yz@hdu.edu.cn (Y.Z.); yongjian.ren@infocore.cn (Y.R.)
[2] School of Computer Science, Shaanxi Normal University, Xi'an 710119, China; fhao@snnu.edu.cn
* Correspondence: jilin.zhang@hdu.edu.cn; Tel.: +86-152-5880-1227
† Current address: Hangzhou Economic Development Zone, No. 1158, No. 2 Street, Baiyang Street, Hangzhou 310018, China.

Abstract: Chinese herbal medicine classification is an important research task in intelligent medicine, which has been applied widely in the fields of smart medicinal material sorting and medicinal material recommendation. However, most current mainstream methods are semi-automatic, with low efficiency and poor performance. To tackle this problem, a novel Chinese herbal medicine classification method based on mutual learning has been proposed. Specifically, two small student networks are designed for collaborative learning, and each of them collects knowledge learned from the other one respectively. Consequently, student networks obtain rich and reliable features, which will further improve the performance of Chinese herbal medicinal classification. In order to validate the performance of the proposed model, a dataset with 100 Chinese herbal classes (about 10,000 samples) was utilized and extensive experiments were performed. Experimental results verify that the proposed method is superior to those of the latest models with equivalent or even fewer parameters, specifically, obtaining 3∼5.4% higher accuracy rate and 13∼37% lower loss. Moreover, the mutual learning model achieves 80.8% Chinese herbal medicine classification accuracy.

Keywords: Chinese herbal medicine; classification; mutual learning; deep neural network

MSC: 68T07

1. Introduction

Chinese herbal medicine (CHM) classification plays a vital role in the field of intelligent medicine. Furthermore, it has been widely applied in the fields of smart medicinal material sorting and medicinal material recommendation. The classification of CHM still faces many challenges, such as small datasets and large scale of model parameters.

To achieve promising CHM classification performance, many researchers have carried out a lot of research work. Wang et al. proposed a new Local Linear Embedding Algorithm (LLE) and Linear Discriminant Analysis (LDA) processing techniques to handle high-dimensional nonlinear data in the classification of CHM [1]. However, the dataset employed in their method only contains six classes, which is very small and cannot meet the needs of real-world applications. Zhang et al. utilized a supervised local projection strategy to identify plant leaves and achieved excellent classification performance [2]. Unger et al. applied support vector machine (SVM) with a Fourier feature and a morphological measuring approach to classify the medicinal materials in the two test sets, which consisted of 26 and 17 categories, respectively, with around 10 samples in each category [3]. In the two test sets, their approaches had an accuracy of 73.21% and 84%, respectively. Principal Component Analysis (PCA) and SVM were adopted by Luo et al. to classify Chinese medicinal materials [4]. Experimental results demonstrated that the SVM approach produces superior experimental results than that of the PCA method. The Self-organizing Map (SOM) algorithm was introduced to classify CHM images in 2016 [5]. Although these methods have achieved promising CHM classification performance, the datasets utilized by them are limited, with only a few examples per category. On the other hand, these methods rely on less robust hand-crafted features and are not feasible for classification on large-scale datasets. In order to further enhance the classification performance, several deep convolutional neural networks, such as AlexNet [6], VGG [7], GoogleNet [8] and ResNet [9,10], have been employed and shown good performance in classification in recent years [11–13]. Liu et al. [14] utilized GoogleNet to improve the performance of CHM classification. Cai et al. [15] used the convolutional neural network with broad learning system method to identify Chinese herbal medicines, and their method achieved good performance. However, the dataset they used was still small, with just 17 categories and 1700 images. Unfortunately, due to the large scale of parameters, these models are not suitable for classification tasks in platforms or applications with small memory, such as mobile phones.

Mutual learning, a realistic method which can produce promising classification results via small yet powerful deep neural networks. Mutual learning starts with a group of students learning collaboratively [16]. Among them, each student is constrained by two loss terms, including the standard supervised learning loss and the mimicry loss respectively, which will encourage the class probabilities of each student to match those of other students, leading to more robust and richer discriminative features.

In fact, traditional Chinese herbal medicine classification methods have lower accuracy. On the other hand, although deep learning methods have higher accuracy, their training speed are usually slow. To address the aforementioned issues and improve the effectiveness and efficiency of CHM classification, this paper proposes to leverage the mutual learning to handle CHM classification approach, inspired by its superiority. Specifically, in the mutual learning framework, two student networks are employed to learn collaboratively, and each student network can receive information from the other one through the whole training process. Consequently, all student networks will learn more robust and richer features in this strategy, resulting in superior performance than that of the corresponding single network with the same or even much more layers.

In summary, our contributions can be concluded as follows:

1. A novel CHM classification approach based on mutual learning has been explored, which has achieved promising CHM classification performance in terms of both effectiveness and efficiency. Specifically, the mutual learning framework in this paper is based on two basic student networks. They perform collaborative learning during the whole training phase, aiming at extracting more robust and rich features without increasing the scale of parameters, and further enhance the performance of CHM classification.
2. Numerous experiments have been done to assess the effectiveness of our method, including the evaluation of the superiority of the mutual learning, the evaluation of the performance of mutual learning based on two identical student networks, the evaluation of the performance of mutual learning based on two different student networks, respectively. Experimental results illustrate that the mutual learning model can obtain significantly superior performance than those of the corresponding single networks without mutual learning with the same or even deep layers, in terms of both accuracy and speed.

The rest of this paper is organized as follows. Detailed information of the materials and methods are illustrated in Section 2. Section 3 depicts the experimental results and analyses. Section 4 concludes this paper.

2. Materials and Methods

2.1. Dataset

In order to validate the effectiveness of the mutual learning model, a CHM classification dataset CHMC with medium-scale [17] has been applied. Specifically, CHMC has 100 categories of Chinese herbal medicines, and each category contains about 100 images.

Therefore, the dataset owns a total of 10,000 images. Among them, 4/5 samples are utilized for training, and the rest are applied for testing. Some examples from the CHMC dataset are presented in Figure 1. Furthermore, most of the samples in the CHMC dataset have natural environment backgrounds, which will motivate their application in real-world scenarios.

Figure 1. Samples of CHMC dataset [17].

2.2. Problem Definition

Assume the dataset X contains $\mathcal{N}$ samples of class $\mathcal{C}$, $X = \{x_i\}_{i=1}^{\mathcal{N}}$, and the corresponding label can be denoted as $Y = \{y_i\}_{i=1}^{\mathcal{N}}$, where $y_i \in \{1, 2, \cdots, \mathcal{C}\}$.

Among them, $\mathcal{C}$ indicates the number of CHM categories, $\mathcal{N}$ denotes the number of Chinese herbal medicine samples. X/Y presents the CHM samples/label set, x_i and y_i indicate the i-th sample and its corresponding label.

The probability $q_1^c(x_i)$ that the ith sample x_i is predicted to be class c in the student network1 (*ConvNet*1) can be calculated by the following definition:

$$q_1^c(x_i) = \frac{\exp(s_1^c(x_i))}{\sum_{c=1}^{\mathcal{C}} \exp(s_1^c(x_i))} \tag{1}$$

where $s_1^c(x_i)$ indicates the logit value from the softmax layer of *ConvNet*1.

The probability $q_2^c(x_i)$ that the ith sample x_i is predicted to be class c in the student network2 (*ConvNet*2) can be obtained via the following equation:

$$q_2^c(x_i) = \frac{\exp(s_2^c(x_i))}{\sum_{c=1}^{\mathcal{C}} \exp(s_2^c(x_i))} \tag{2}$$

where $s_2^c(x_i)$ indicates the logit value from the softmax layer of *ConvNet*2.

The loss functions $\mathcal{L}_{ConvNet_1}$ and $\mathcal{L}_{ConvNet_2}$ of two student networks can be defined as follows:

$$\mathcal{L}_{ConvNet_1} = (1-\alpha) * \mathcal{L}_{C_1} + \alpha * D_{KL}(q_2 \| q_1) \tag{3}$$

$$\mathcal{L}_{ConvNet_2} = (1-\alpha) * \mathcal{L}_{C_2} + \alpha * D_{KL}(q_1 \| q_2) \tag{4}$$

where $\mathcal{L}_{ConvNet_1}/\mathcal{L}_{ConvNet_2}$ denotes the cross entropy loss of the $ConvNet1/ConvNet2$ network. q_1/q_2 indicates the predicted probability of the *Net1*/*Net2* network. $D_{KL}(q_2\|q_1)$ presents the Kullback Leibler (*KL*) divergence loss, indicates the KL distance from q_1 to q_2. $D_{KL}(q_1\|q_2)$ has the similar meaning with that of $D_{KL}(q_2\|q_1)$. Furthermore, α denotes a hyperparameter which is employed to balance the two loss items.

The cross entropy losses $\mathcal{L}_{C_1}$ and $\mathcal{L}_{C_2}$ can be defined as:

$$\mathcal{L}_{C_1} = -\sum_{i=1}^{\mathcal{N}}\sum_{c=1}^{\mathcal{C}} y_i^c * \log(q_1^c(x_i)) \tag{5}$$

$$\mathcal{L}_{C_2} = -\sum_{i=1}^{\mathcal{N}}\sum_{c=1}^{\mathcal{C}} y_i^c * \log(q_2^c(x_i)) \tag{6}$$

where y_i denotes the ground truth label of sample x_i, y_i^c is the indicator function, when $y_i = c, y_i^c = 1$, when $y_i \neq c, y_i^c = 0$.

$\mathcal{L}_{C_1}$ and $\mathcal{L}_{C_2}$ represent the cross entropy losses between the ground truth label of the sample and the corresponding network prediction value, which will force the model to predict results that close to the true label for the corresponding sample.

To enhance the generalization ability of $ConvNet1/ConvNet2$ on the test samples, the posterior probability q_2/q_1 of another student network $ConvNet1/ConvNet2$ is integrated into the model. Further, the matching degree of the posterior probability of the two networks can be obtained by the following equations:

$$D_{KL}(q_2\|q_1) = \sum_{i=1}^{\mathcal{N}}\sum_{c=1}^{\mathcal{C}} q_2^c(x_i) * \log(\frac{q_2^c(x_i)}{q_1^c(x_i)}) \tag{7}$$

$$D_{KL}(q_1\|q_2) = \sum_{i=1}^{\mathcal{N}}\sum_{c=1}^{\mathcal{C}} q_1^c(x_i) * \log(\frac{q_1^c(x_i)}{q_2^c(x_i)}) \tag{8}$$

where $q_1^c(x_i)$ denotes the probability that sample x_i is predicted to be class c in $ConvNet1$ and $q_2^c(x_i)$ indicates the probability that x_i is predicted to be class c in $ConvNet2$.

2.3. Network Structure

The mutual learning model for CHM classification proposed in this paper contains two student networks (shown in Figure 2). Specifically, student network mainly involves four networks: ResNet18, ResNet34, ResNet50, and ResNet101 [18], respectively. During the training process, the two student networks can learn from each other and obtain better features, which improves their accuracy in CHM classification. Concerning the testing phase, each student network can be utilized to perform the CHM classification task. Meanwhile, they can obtain uniformly better performance than that of the single network without mutual learning.

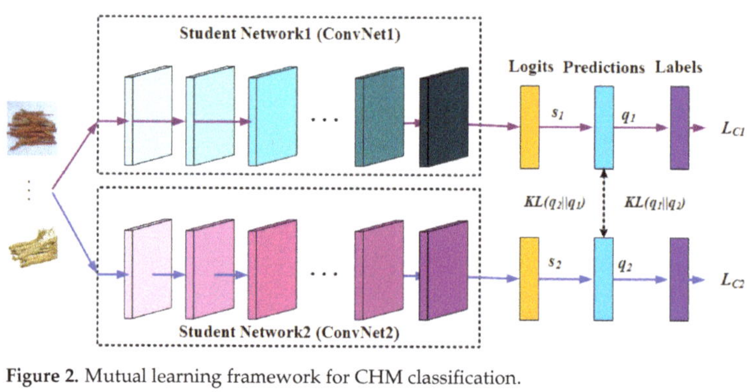

Figure 2. Mutual learning framework for CHM classification.

2.4. Model Training

For fair comparisons, all models mentioned in the experiments utilized stochastic gradient descent (SGD) [19,20] to learn the parameters, with a batch size of 32 (the number of samples input to the model at one time). The initial learning rate is 0.01, which decreased to 0.1 of its previous value after every 80 epochs, and the training phase stopped at 200 epochs. The momentum is set as 0.9, and the hyperparameter α is 0.8.

2.5. Evaluation Criteria

In order to evaluate the effectiveness of different models, several commonly utilized popular evaluation criteria, including Accuracy, Parameters, and Loss are considered. The accuracy represents the classification performance of the model, the higher the better. Parameters indicate the number of parameters of the model and can be utilized to measure the efficiency of the model, the smaller the better. The loss value demonstrates the difference between the model predicted value and the ground truth label of the sample, the smaller the better. Note that all experiments are performed on Nvidia's Titan X GPUs (12 GB), Intel's TMi7-7800X CPUs, 96 GB of RAM, and Ubuntu 18.04.

3. Experimental Results and Analysis

3.1. Evaluation of the Performance of the Mutual Learning Models

In order to verify the performance of the mutual learning model for CHM classification in this paper, we have compared it with several current popular deep learning models, including MobileNetV2 [21], MobileNetV3 [22], ResNet18 [18] and ResNet50 [18] respectively. The results are shown in Table 1. In Table 1, Mul18(50) and Mul50(18) indicate the mutual learning models based on two student networks (ResNet18 and ResNet50). Specifically, Mul18(50) refers to the model that shares the same structure with that of ResNet18 and learns knowledge from ResNet50. Furthermore, Mul50(18) has the similar meaning with that of Mul18(50), which denotes the model that has the same structure with that of ResNet50 and achieves knowledge from ResNet18.

Table 1 illustrates that the two variants of the residual networks, ResNet18 and ResNet50, have obtained superior accuracies than those of MobileNetV2 and MobileNetV3. Furthermore, our model Mul18(50) and Mul50(18) obtain the better CHM classification results than those of ResNet18 and ResNet50, which validate the effectiveness of the mutual learning models.

Table 1. Comparison results of different models.

Model	Accuracy (%)
MobileNetV2	70.75
MobileNetV3	73.05
ResNet18	74.05
ResNet50	76.90
Mul18(50) (Mutual learning model)	**77.95**
Mul50(18) (Mutual learning model)	**80.10**

Moreover, the superiority of our model can be illustrated from the following two aspects. On the one hand, the mutual learning model can achieve surpassing performance without increasing the number of parameters. Specifically, Mul18(50) has 5.3% higher accuracy than that of ResNet18, and the accuracy Mul50(18) is 4.2% better than that of ResNet50, respectively. On the other hand, the shallow mutual learning model can achieve comparable or even better performance than that of the deep single model. For example, Mul18(50) obtained 1.3% better classification accuracy than that of ResNet50 (the parameters of ResNet50 model is nearly twice times of Mul18(50)). The reason is that, during training, Mul18(50) not only learned the knowledge from the ResNet50 model, but also from its own. This learning strategy is comparable to ensemble learning, which integrates several low-performing weak classifiers (ResNet18 + ResNet50) into a high-performing strong classifier Mul18(50), resulting in a superior outcome.

3.2. Ablation Studies

In order to further assess the effectiveness of the mutual learning model in CHM classification, several ablation studies have been designed in the following. Specifically, one design is to verify the mutual learning model's performance under two identical student networks setting, and the other one is to evaluate the mutual learning model's performance under two distinct student networks setting, respectively.

3.2.1. Evaluation of the Performance of the Mutual Learning Model under Two Identical Student Networks

In order to verify the performance of the mutual learning model under two identical student networks setting, we compare two group models that with or without mutual learning, including Sig$i$ and Mul$i$(i) respectively. Among them, i indicates the model with ith layers, $i \in \{18, 34, 50, 101\}$. Sig$i$ indicates the single ResNet$i$ model without mutual learning and Mul$i$(i) denotes the mutual learning models with two identical student networks ResNet$i$. Mul$i$(i)-1 indicates the first student network and Mul$i$(i)-2 represents the second student network. Table 2 shows the compared results.

Table 2. Comparison results of the mutual learning models based on two identical student networks.

Model	Accuracy (%)	Parameters (M)	Loss Value
Sig18	74.05	11.69	0.0542
Mul(18)-1	**76.50**	11.69	**0.0440**
Mul(18)-2	**76.25**	11.69	**0.0440**
Sig34	75.00	21.80	0.0548
Mul(34)-1	**78.15**	21.80	**0.0432**
Mul(34)-2	**78.15**	21.80	**0.0432**
Sig50	76.90	25.56	0.0542
Mul(50)-1	**79.25**	25.56	**0.0382**
Mul(50)-2	**79.20**	25.56	**0.0382**
Sig101	77.45	44.64	0.0554
Mul(101)-1	**79.85**	44.64	**0.0373**
Mul(101)-2	**79.80**	44.64	**0.0373**

Table 2 shows that when the two student networks are identical, the mutual learning models can achieve significant better results than those of single network model in terms of accuracy and loss value, without increasing the parameters. Specifically, the accuracy of Mul18(18)-1/Mul18(18)-2 is 3.0% higher than that of Sig18, and the loss value of Mul18(18)-1/Mul18(18)-2 is 18.8% lower than that of Sig18; Mul34(34)-1/Mul34(34)-2 has a 4.2% higher accuracy than that of Sig34, and the loss value of Mul34(34)-1/Mul34(34)-2 is 30.3% lower than that of Sig34; Mul50(50)-1/Mul50(50)-2 achieves 3.1% higher than that of Sig50 in terms of accuracy, and Mul50(50)-1/Mul50(50)-2 is 29.5% lower than that of Sig50 in terms of loss value; Mul101(101)-1/Mul101(101)-2 obtains 3.1% higher than that of Sig101, and Mul101(101)-1/Mul101(101)-2 has 32.7 % lower loss value than that of Sig101, respectively.

Moreover, the shallow mutual learning models can obtain better results than those of deep single models at both accuracy and loss value, with much less parameters. Concretely, Mul18(18) obtains about 2% higher accuracy and 19.7% lower loss value than those of Sig34; Mul34(34) achieves about 1.62% higher accuracy and 20.3% lower loss value than those of Sig50; Mul34(34) acquires about 0.9% higher accuracy and 22% lower loss value than those of Sig101 and Mul50(50) obtains about 2.32% higher accuracy and 31.04% lower loss value than those of Sig101, separately.

Those results verify the effectiveness of the mutual learning model based on two identical student networks in terms of effectiveness and efficiency.

It should be noted that the two student networks of the mutual learning model (such as Mul18(18)-1/Mul18(18)-2) have the same parameter values as those of their corresponding single counterpart without mutual learning (such as Sig18). In this case, the mutual learning models can achieve higher accuracy and lower loss value, indicating that the mutual learning model can allow two identical student networks to learn additional knowledge about the other network during training, thereby obtaining better performance. Although the two student networks have the same structure, their initial parameter values are different, resulting in diverse knowledge throughout the training process, which may be employed to guide the learning of another student network. Furthermore, due to the similar structure, these two student networks are all converge to the same tiny range of values after training, resulting in approximately same accuracy and loss value.

To intuitively compare the performance of different models, Figures 3 and 4 present the accuracies and loss values of different models under different training epochs respectively. These two figures illustrate that during the whole training process, the accuracies/losses of the two student networks of the mutual learning model are higher/lower than those of the corresponding single counterpart models without mutual learning, which further verifies the effectiveness of mutual learning models under two identical student networks setting.

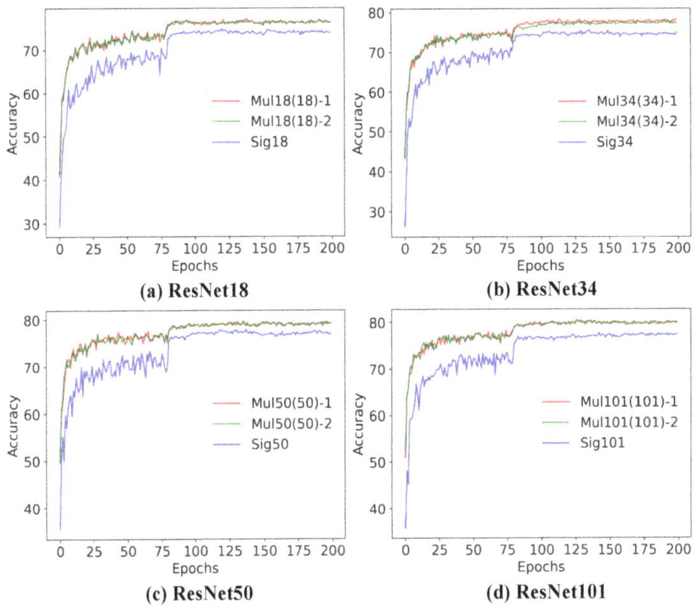

Figure 3. Comparison of the accuracy of two same student networks with or without mutual learning.

3.2.2. Evaluation of the Performance of Mutual Learning under Two Different Student Networks

Considering the performance of the mutual learning model under two different student networks setting, we also compare two set of models that with or without mutual learning, including [Sig$i$, Sig$j$] and [Mul$i$(j), Mul$j$(i)] respectively. Among them, i/j indicates the model with ith/jth layers, $i, j \in \{18, 34, 50, 101\}$, $i \neq j$. Sig$i$ indicates the single ResNet$i$ model without mutual learning, Sig$j$ has the similar meaning with that of Sig$i$. Mul$i$(j) and Mul$j$(i) represent the mutual learning models with two different student networks ResNet$i$ and ResNet$j$. Mul$i$(j) represents the one student network in mutual learning that has the same structure with Sig*i* and receives the knowledge from Sig*j*, Mul*j*(*i*) shares the similar meaning with that of Mul*i*(*j*). The comparison results are shown in Table 3.

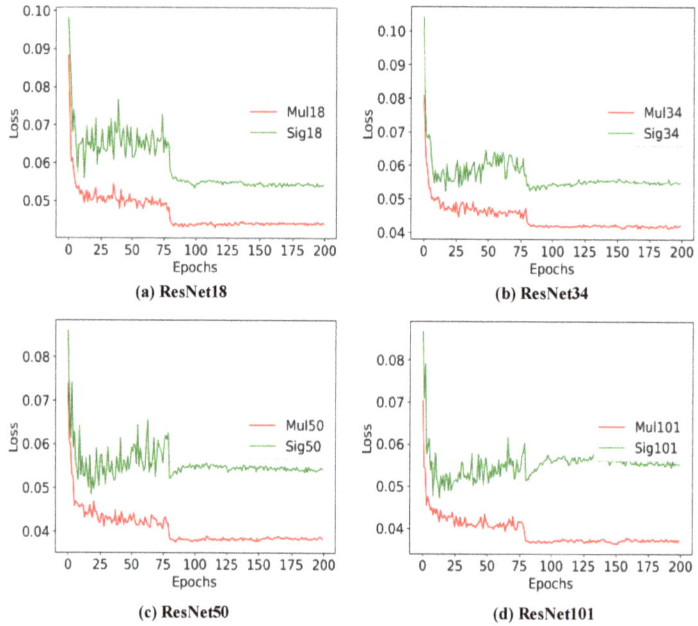

Figure 4. Comparison of the loss of two same student networks with or without mutual learning.

Table 3 demonstrates that when the two student networks are different, the mutual learning models have achieved better performance than those of their corresponding single networks with the same number of layers. Specifically, Mul18(34)/Mul34(18) receives 4.69%/4.37% higher accuracy and 30.1%/30.8% lower than Sig18/Sig34 in terms of accuracy and loss value; Mul18(50)/Mul50(18) obtains 5.27%/4.16% better accuracy and 32.1%/32.1% lower loss value than those of Sig18/Sig50; Mul18(101)/Mul101(18) achieves 4.86%/3.68% better accuracy and 34.1%/33.4% lower loss value than those of Sig18/Sig101; Mul34(50)/Mul50(34) receives 4.26%/5.07% better accuracy and 34.1%/33.4% lower loss value than those of Sig34/Sig50; Mul34(101)/Mul101(34) obtains 5.40%/3.29% better accuracy and 33.2%/33.9% lower loss value than those of Sig34/Sig101; Mul50(101)/Mul101(50) achieves 3.97%/4.20% higher accuracy and 36.0%/37.3% lower loss value than those of Sig50/Sig101, respectively.

Furthermore, Table 3 also illustrates that the small student networks (such as Mul18(34)) in mutual learning models also receive superior performance than a single network (such as Sig34) corresponding to the large student network in the mutual learning model. Concretely, Mul18(34) obtains 3.33% higher accuracy and 30.1% lower loss value than that of Sig34. Mul18(50) achieves 1.36% better accuracy and 1.36% lower loss value than that of Sig50. Mul18(101) receives a 2.60% better accuracy and 32.3% lower loss value than that of Sig101. Mul34(50) obtains 1.70% superior accuracy and 34.1% lower loss value than that of Sig50; Mul34(101) receives 2.06% superior accuracy and 33.2% lower loss value than that of Sig101; Mul50(101) receives 3.23% superior accuracy and 36.0% lower loss value than that of Sig101, respectively.

Table 3. Comparison results of the mutual learning models based on two different student networks.

Model	Accuracy (%)	Parameters (M)	Loss Value
Sig18	74.05	11.69	0.0542
Sig34	75.00	21.80	0.0548
Mul18(34)	77.50	11.69	0.0379
Mul34(18)	78.55	21.80	0.0379
Sig18	74.05	11.69	0.0542
Sig50	76.90	25.56	0.0542
Mul18(50)	77.95	11.69	0.0368
Mul50(18)	80.10	25.56	0.0368
Sig34	75.00	21.80	0.0548
Sig50	76.90	25.56	0.0542
Mul34(50)	78.20	21.80	0.0361
Mul50(34)	80.80	25.56	0.0361
Sig18	74.05	11.69	0.0542
Sig101	77.45	44.64	0.0554
Mul18(101)	77.65	11.69	0.0367
Mul101(18)	80.35	44.64	0.0367
Sig34	75.00	21.80	0.0548
Sig101	77.45	44.64	0.0554
Mul34(101)	79.50	21.80	0.0366
Mul101(34)	80.00	44.64	0.0366
Sig50	76.90	25.56	0.0542
Sig101	77.45	44.64	0.0554
Mul50(101)	79.95	25.56	0.0347
Mul101(50)	80.70	44.64	0.0347

Those results verify the effectiveness of the mutual learning models based on two different student networks in terms of effectiveness and efficiency.

It should be noted that although Mul18(34) is the small student network in the mutual learning model, it receives better performance not only than that of small single network Sig18 but also than that of big single network Sig34. Reasons are that, during the whole training process, Mul18(34) collaborative learns knowledge from ResNet18 and ResNet34, which results in richer and much more reliable features, leading to improved performance in CHM classification.

In order to intuitively compare the performance of different models, Figures 5 and 6 show the accuracies and loss values of different models under different training epochs respectively. These two figures demonstrate that during the whole training process, the accuracies/losses of the two student networks of the mutual learning model are significantly higher/lower than those of the corresponding single counterpart models without mutual learning, which further validates the effectiveness of mutual learning models under two different student networks setting. In the future, we will employ a deep no-reference image quality metric [23] to objectively assess the performance of the proposed method in the presence of image artefacts of varying degrees of severity.

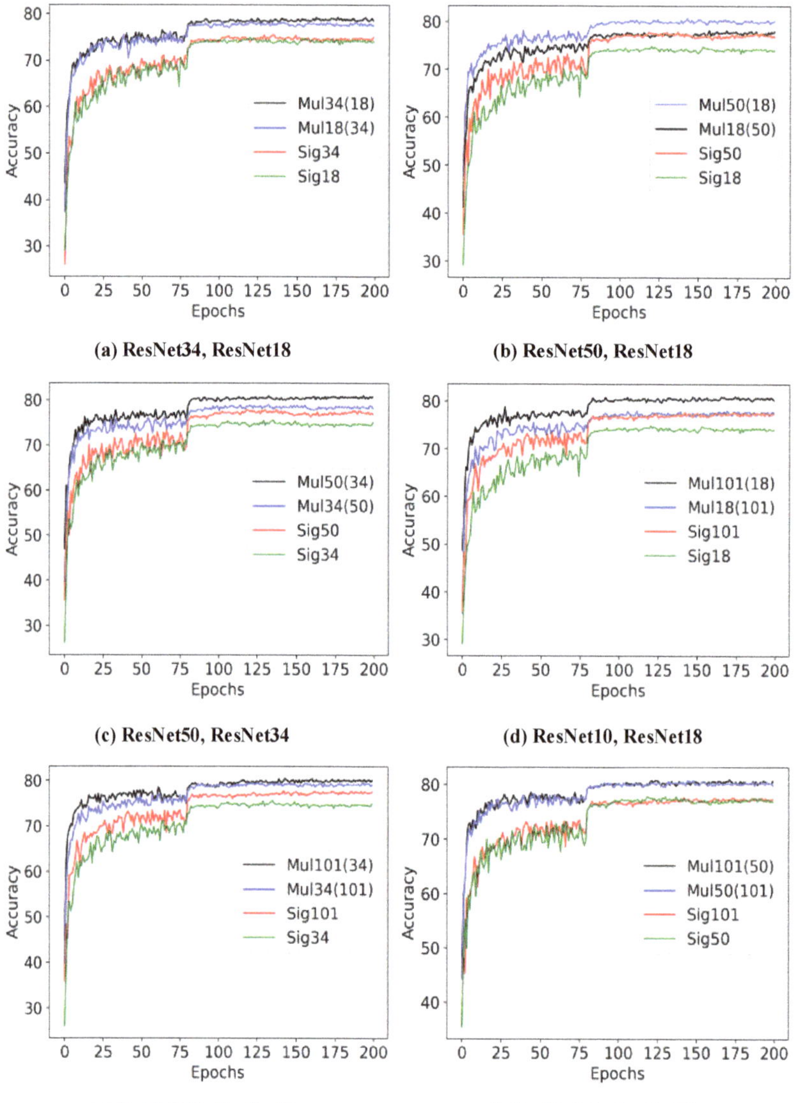

(a) ResNet34, ResNet18 **(b) ResNet50, ResNet18**

(c) ResNet50, ResNet34 **(d) ResNet10, ResNet18**

(e) ResNet101, ResNet34 **(f) ResNet101, ResNet50**

Figure 5. Comparison of the accuracy of two different student networks with or without mutual learning.

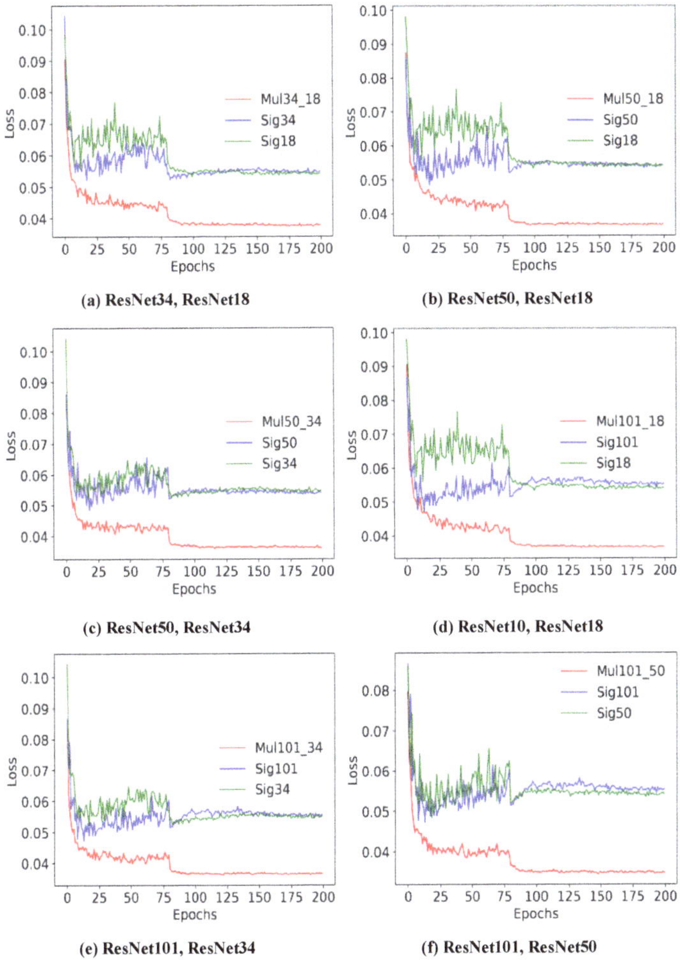

(a) ResNet34, ResNet18 (b) ResNet50, ResNet18 (c) ResNet50, ResNet34 (d) ResNet10, ResNet18 (e) ResNet101, ResNet34 (f) ResNet101, ResNet50

Figure 6. Comparison of the loss of two different student networks with or without mutual learning.

4. Conclusions

This paper has proposed to utilize a novel mutual learning model to perform CHM classification. This model can transfer the knowledge from one student network to another one. Furthermore, benefit from the mutual learning, a set of basic student neural networks can cooperatively update parameters and achieve information from each other throughout the training process, resulting in the learning of rich and robust features. Consequently, our model obtains promising CHM classification results with better efficiency and effectiveness. Specifically, experiments achieve 4.16~13.2% higher accuracy and 8.8~36.0% lower loss value than those of the non-mutual learning models, which verifies the effectiveness of the mutual learning model in CHM classification.

Author Contributions: Conceptualization, J.Z. and Y.R.; methodology, M.H.; validation, M.H.; formal analysis, F.H.; investigation, M.H.; resources, M.H.; data curation, M.H.; writing—original draft preparation, M.H.; writing—review and editing, M.H. and Y.Z.; supervision, J.Z.; project administration, J.Z. All authors have read and agreed to the published version of the manuscript.

Funding: This work was supported by the National Natural Science Foundation of China (NSFC) under Grant (No. 62072146, No. 61972358); the Key Research and Development Program of China (2019YFB2102101); the Key Research and Development Program of Zhejiang Province (2019C01059, 2019C03135) and Natural Science Basic Research Plan in Shaanxi Province of China (2022JM-371).

Institutional Review Board Statement: Not applicable.

Informed Consent Statement: Not applicable.

Data Availability Statement: The datasets generated during and/or analysed during the current study are available from the corresponding author on reasonable request.

Conflicts of Interest: We declare that this paper has no conflicts of interest. Furthermore, we do not have any commercial or associative interest that represents a conflict of interest in connection with the work submitted.

Abbreviations

The following abbreviations are used in this manuscript:

CHM	Chinese Herbal Medicine
LLE	Local Linear Embedding
LDA	Linear Discriminant Analysis
SVM	Support Vector Machine
PCA	Principal Component Analysis
SOM	Self-organizing Map
CHMC	Chinese Herbal Medicine Classification
KL	Kullback Leibler

References

1. Wang, J.; Wong, R.K.W.; Lee, T.C.M. Locally linear embedding with additive noise. *Pattern Recognit. Lett.* **2019**, *123*, 47–52. [CrossRef]
2. Zhang, S.; Lei, Y.; Dong, T.; Zhang, X.P. Label propagation based supervised locality projection analysis for plant leaf classification. *Pattern Recognit.* **2013**, *46*, 1891–1897. [CrossRef]
3. Unger, J.; Merhof, D.; Renner, S. Computer vision applied to herbarium specimens of German trees: Testing the future utility of the millions of herbarium specimen images for automated identification. *BMC Evol. Biol.* **2016**, *16*, 248. [CrossRef] [PubMed]
4. Luo, D.; Wang, J.; Chen, Y. Classification of Chinese Herbal medicines based on SVM. In Proceedings of the International Conference on Information Science, Electronics and Electrical Engineering (ISEEE), Sapporo, Japan, 26–28 April 2014; pp. 453–456.
5. Wang, M.; Li, L.; Yu, C.; Yan, A.; Zhao, Z.; Zhang, G.; Jiang, M.; Lu, A.; Gasteiger, J. Classification of Mixtures of Chinese Herbal Medicines Based on a Self-organizing Map (SOM). *Mol. Inform.* **2016**, *35*, 109–115. [CrossRef] [PubMed]
6. Mu, L.; Gao, Z.; Cui, Y.; Li, K.; Liu, H.; Fu, L. Kiwifruit Detection of Far-view and Occluded Fruit Based on Improved AlexNet. *Trans. Chin. Soc. Agric. Mach.* **2019**, *50*, 24–34.
7. Chen, Y.Y.; Gong, C.Y.; Liu, Y.Q. Fish Identification Method Based on FTVGG16 Convolutional Neural Network. *Trans. Chin. Soc. Agric. Mach.* **2019**, *50*, 223–231.
8. Xue, Y.; Wang, L.; Zhang, Y.; Shen, Q. Defect Detection Method of Apples Based on GoogLeNet Deep Transfer Learning. *Trans. Chin. Soc. Agric. Mach.* **2020**, *51*, 30–35.
9. Jiao, J.; Wang, W.; Hou, J. Freshness Identification of Iberico Pork Based on Improved Residual Network. *Trans. Chin. Soc. Agric. Mach.* **2019**, *50*, 364–371.
10. Chen, J.; Chen, L.Y.; Wang, S.S.; Zhao, H.Y.; Wen, C.J. Pest Image Recognition of Garden Based on Improved Residual Network. *Trans. Chin. Soc. Agric. Mach.* **2019**, *50*, 187–195.
11. Wang, C.; Zhao, Q.; Ma, Y. Crop Identification of Drone Remote Sensing Based on Convolutional Neural Network. *Trans. Chin. Soc. Agric. Mach.* **2019**, *50*, 161–168.
12. Liu, X.; Fan, C.; Li, J. Identification Method of Strawberry Based on Convolutional Neural Network. *Trans. Chin. Soc. Agric. Mach.* **2020**, *51*, 237–244.
13. Hou, J.; Yao, E.; Zhu, H. Classification of Castor Seed Damage Based on Convolutional Neural Network. *Trans. Chin. Soc. Agric. Mach.* **2020**, *51*, 440–449.
14. Liu, S.; Chen, W.; Dong, X. Automatic Classification of Chinese Herbal Based on Deep Learning Method. In Proceedings of the 2018 14th International Conference on Natural Computation, Fuzzy Systems and Knowledge Discovery (ICNC-FSKD), Huangshan, China, 28–30 July 2018.

15. Cai, C.; Liu, S.; Wang, L.; Yang, B.; Zhi, M.; Wang, R.; He, W. Classification of Chinese Herbal Medicine Using Combination of Broad Learning System and Convolutional Neural Network. In Proceedings of the 2019 IEEE International Conference on Systems, Man and Cybernetics (SMC), Bari, Italy, 6–9 October 2019.
16. Zhang, Y.; Xiang, T.; Hospedales, T.M.; Lu, H. Deep Mutual Learning. In Proceedings of the 2018 IEEE/CVF Conference on Computer Vision and Pattern Recognition (CVPR), Salt Lake City, UT, USA, 18–22 June 2018; pp. 4320–4328.
17. Hao, W.; Han, M.; Yang, H.; Hao, F.; Li, F. A novel Chinese herbal medicine classification approach based on EfficientNet. *Syst. Sci. Control Eng.* **2021**, *9*, 304–313. [CrossRef]
18. He, K.; Zhang, X.; Ren, S.; Sun, J. Deep Residual Learning for Image Recognition. In Proceedings of the IEEE Conference on Computer Vision and Pattern Recognition (CVPR), Las Vegas, NV, USA, 26–30 June 2016; pp. 770–778.
19. Bottou, L. Stochastic Gradient Descent Tricks. In *Neural Networks: Tricks of the Trade*; Springer: Berlin/Heidelberg, Germany, 2012; pp. 421–436.
20. Chen, W.; Mirdehghan, P.; Fidler, S.; Kutulakos, K.N. Auto-Tuning Structured Light by Optical Stochastic Gradient Descent. In Proceedings of the 2020 IEEE/CVF Conference on Computer Vision and Pattern Recognition (CVPR), Seattle, WA, USA, 13–19 June 2020.
21. Sandler, M.; Howard, A.; Zhu, M.; Zhmoginov, A.; Chen, L.C. MobileNetV2: Inverted Residuals and Linear Bottlenecks. In Proceedings of the 2018 IEEE/CVF Conference on Computer Vision and Pattern Recognition (CVPR), Salt Lake City, UT, USA, 18–22 June 2018.
22. Howard, A.; Sandler, M.; Chu, G.; Chen, L.C.; Chen, B.; Tan, M.; Wang, W.; Zhu, Y.; Pang, R.; Vasudevan, V.; et al. Searching for MobileNetV3. In Proceedings of the 2019 IEEE/CVF International Conference on Computer Vision(ICCV), Seoul, Korea, 27 October–3 November 2019.
23. Mukherjee, S.; Valenzise, G.; Cheng, I. Potential of deep features for opinion-unaware, distortion-unaware, no-reference image quality assessment. In Proceedings of the International Conference on Smart Multimedia, San Diego, CA, USA, 16–18 December 2019.

mathematics

Article

Multimedia Applications Processing and Computation Resource Allocation in MEC-Assisted SIoT Systems with DVS

Xianwei Li [1], Guolong Chen [1,2,*], Liang Zhao [3] and Bo Wei [4]

[1] School of Computer and Information Engineering, Bengbu University, Bengbu 233000, China; lixianwei163@163.com
[2] School of Information Engineering, Suzhou University, Suzhou 234000, China
[3] School of Computer Science, Shenyang Aerospace University, Shenyang 110000, China; lzhao@sau.edu.cn
[4] Graduate School of Fundamental Science and Engineering, Waseda University, Tokyo 169-0051, Japan; weibo0504@fuji.waseda.jp
* Correspondence: cglbox@sina.com

Abstract: Due to the advancements of information technologies and the Internet of Things (IoT), the number of distributed sensors and IoT devices in the social IoT (SIoT) systems is proliferating. This has led to various multimedia applications, face recognition and augmented reality (AR). These applications are computation-intensive and delay-sensitive and have become popular in our daily life. However, IoT devices are well-known for their constrained computational resources, which hinders the execution of these applications. Mobile edge computing (MEC) has appeared and been deemed a prospective paradigm to solve this issue. Migrating the applications of IoT devices to be executed in the edge cloud can not only provide computational resources to process these applications but also lower the transmission latency between the IoT devices and the edge cloud. In this paper, computation resource allocation and multimedia applications offloading in MEC-assisted SIoT systems are investigated. We aim to optimize the resource allocation and application offloading by jointly minimizing the execution latency of multimedia applications and the consumed energy of IoT devices. The studied problem is a formulation of the total computation overhead minimization problem by optimizing the computational resources in the edge servers. Besides, as the technology of dynamic voltage scaling (DVS) can offer more flexibility for the MEC system design, we incorporate it into the application offloading. Since the studied problem is a mixed-integer nonlinear programming (MINP) problem, an efficient method is proposed to address it. By comparing with the baseline schemes, the theoretic analysis and simulation results demonstrate that the proposed multimedia applications offloading method can improve the performances of MEC-assisted SIoT systems for the most part.

Keywords: multimedia applications; resource allocation; mobile edge computing

MSC: 90C26

1. Introduction

Due to the advancements of information technologies [1–3], as well as the expansion of the IoT [4–7], the number of sensors and other IoT devices distributed by IoT users in the SIoT systems is growing explosively [8,9]. It is reported by Cisco that the number of the IoT devices and connections in the globe will be 13.5 billion by the year 2022, as can be observed from Figure 1 [10]. Accordingly, various multimedia applications, such as face recognition and augmented reality (AR), are appearing and have become popular in our daily life [11]. These multimedia applications are typically computation-intensive and need real-time processing [12]. However, the computation resources of these IoT nodes are insufficient enough to meet the demands of these applications [13,14].

Mobile cloud computing (MCC) was once regarded as an important paradigm to conquer the limitations of IoT devices, where the computation-intensive IoT applications can be migrated and processed in the distant public cloud [15]. However, one of the obvious shortcomings of this method is the high latency for the long transmission delay, which is not a suitable choice for the processing of latency-sensitive multimedia applications. Therefore, a promising paradigm, which is MEC, has been introduced [16–18]. By distributing the cloud resources near the edge of the wireless networks, MEC can not only provide computing resources to the IoT devices but also lower the latency from the transmission of the IoT devices to the edge cloud.

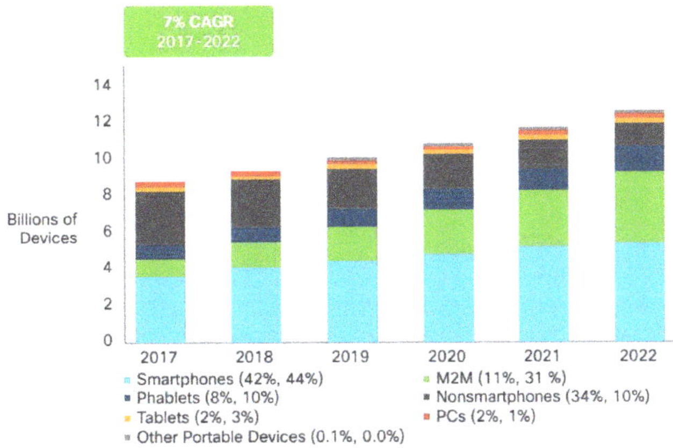

Figure 1. The growth of devices and connections worldwide [10].

Despite the advantages that the MEC has, how efficiently to allocate the computing resources of the MEC servers, such that both the application execution latency and consumed energy of IoT devices are minimized, is a challenging issue. From the viewpoint of the SIoT systems, designing efficient resources allocation algorithms can improve its safety, reliability and security, which ultimately contributes to the improvement of the reliability [19,20]. The DVS technology can vary the voltage and clock frequency of IoT devices according to the computation load such that the desired performance is provided [21]. By resorting to the DVS technique, the IoT devices cloud make adjustments to their computational speeds in order to reduce the application completion time and consumed energy. Therefore, combining the DVS technology with the application offloading can make the offloading strategy design more flexible. Although a significant amount of research attention has been paid to resource allocation and applications offloading in the MEC systems, joint consideration of the computational resources in the edge servers and adopting the DVS technology is not fully investigated.

In this paper, we make efforts to study computation resource allocation and multimedia applications offloading problems to optimize the performances in MEC-assisted SIoT systems. We formulate the studied problem as a latency and energy consumption minimization problem by optimizing the computational resources in the edge servers. Besides, as the DVS can offer more flexibility for the MEC system design, we incorporate it into the application offloading. Since the studied problem is an MINP problem, a method proven to be efficient is proposed to address it. Simulation results are presented to demonstrate the efficiency of the proposed multimedia applications offloading scheme by comparing it with the baseline schemes.

In summary, we demonstrate the main contributions in this paper as follows:

- The minimization problem of multimedia application execution latency and energy consumption of IoT devices is studied by the allocation of computing resources in the edge servers while adopting the DVS technology.

- The studied problem of latency and energy consumption is formulated. Due to the formulated problem being an MINP problem, an efficient multimedia applications offloading scheme is proposed, and the solution of it is obtained.
- Simulation results are performed to evaluate the efficacy of the proposed multimedia applications offloading scheme by comparing with the two baseline schemes. The theoretical analysis and simulation results indicate that the multimedia applications' offloading scheme proposed in this paper can perform better than the baseline methods, which can integrate the dependability aspects into the design of SIoT systems.

2. Related Work

Applications offloading, also known as data offloading, task offloading and computation offloading, and together with resource allocation, has been broadly studied in the current works. The allocated resources can be computing resources of MEC servers, radio resources, transmission power, and caching resources. The main objectives of them focus on the minimization of energy consumption, the application execution time, and both the application processing time and the consumed energy. We have referred to many of the relevant studies in the top renowned journals, which are included in the famous databases in the literature, such as IEEE Xplore and Elsevier. Based on the relevant studies, we discuss the related work from the following three perspectives.

(1) Energy consumption minimization.

In [22], Li et al. studied computation offloading problem for total energy consumption minimization by allocating transmission power in the dual connectivity (DC)-and nonorthogonal multiple access (NOMA)-assisted MEC systems. As the formulated problem is an MINLP problem, they proposed an iterative optimization method to obtain the solution. In [23], Wang et al. studied transmit power allocation and computing resources allocation for task offloading in order to obtain the minimization of the energy consumption of the mobile user equipment. In particular, they consider the imperfect channel state information (CSI). In [24], Liu et al. investigated the minimization of energy consumption of mobile devices in MCC systems under the constraints of transmission error rate and time delay. In [25], You et al. studied computing resource allocation of edge servers for mobile energy consumption minimization with computation latency constraint in MEC systems based on TDMA and OFDMA. In [26], Lyu et al. studied energy-efficient task admission for delay-sensitive applications in MEC systems. They formulated the total energy consumption minimization under the constraints of computational resources in the edge servers and latency. In [27], Zhao et al. studied the problem of energy consumption minimization by optimizing radio and computational resources of edge servers for smart mobile devices of the MEC system with multiple users. As the formulated problem is MINP, they proposed a method to obtain the optimal result. In [28], Zeng and Fodor investigated the problem of transmission energy consumption by allocating radio and computational resources jointly under a delay constraint. In [29], Meskar et al. studied commutation offloading in a MEC system to obtain the reduction of energy consumption. They used the competitive game to model the system, and a Gauss–Seidel method was introduced to determine the equilibrium. The optimization of resource allocation is not considered. In [14], Li et al. studied computation offloading for big data processing in the energy efficient large-scale IoT systems. For the research line of these previous studies, they either just paid attention to minimize the energy consumption or ignored the joint consideration of DVS technology and computation resource allocation.

(2) Application execution time minimization.

In [30], the problem of spectrum allocation and transmission power allocation for applications offloading is investigated to reduce the execution time, including computational time of MEC servers and transmission time of all mobile users. Because of the complexity of the optimized problem, they developed a reinforcement learning-based method to obtain the solution for the problem. In [31], Sun et al. studied the management of energy-aware mobility for MEC systems in the ultra-dense networks environment. They optimized the computation delay under the constraint of energy consumption by applying the Lyapunov optimization method. However, they did not consider resource allocations. In [32], Qian et al. studied the overall completing time reduction of the workload of smart terminal by formulating the optimization problem of computation resource allocation of edge servers. An efficient layered algorithm was proposed by them to obtain the optimal solution. In [33], Liu et al. studied a MEC system with two IoT devices offloading their tasks to an edge server so that the execution latency of IoT users can be minimized by considering the hybrid NOMA-OMA transmission. In [34], Chen et al. studied the minimization of compression execution time of multimedia applications in MEC systems. However, they only considered the optimization of radio and computation resources and ignored the adoption of DVS technology. As far as the research line of the aforementioned studies is concerned, their focus was concentrated on minimizing the application execution time, ignoring the joint consideration of DVS technology.

(3) Both the energy and application processing time minimization.

In [21], Wang et al. studied partial computation offloading by allocating the transmit power of mobile devices with DVS. They have two system design objectives, namely, the minimization of consumed energy and task execution time. In [35], Zhong et al. investigated the problem of task offloading by intelligently and efficiently manage resources in MEC for minimizing delay and energy consumption. They put forward a CL-ADMM framework that can reduce the delay and energy consumption effectively. In [36], Yang et al. studied task offloading for minimizing the energy and delay in the NOMA-enabled MEC systems with small cell networks. A hybrid genetic hill climbing (HGHC) algorithm is put forward to obtain the optimal solution to the formulated problem. In [37], Zhang et al. studied the tradeoff of energy and latency in the energy-aware MEC systems. A task offloading scheme was presented by the optimal allocation of the communication resource and using the DVS technology under the constraints of energy and delay. In our previous work [38], we studied bandwidth allocation for minimizing the system cost, which is measured by the task completion time and consumed energy of IoT devices, adopting the DVS technology. In [39], the authors studied transmission power and communication resources allocation for the balance of energy and latency task offloading in the full-duplex MEC systems. In [40], Zhu and Wen studied the allocation of transmission power, wireless resources, and computing resources in the edge servers to obtain the tradeoff of delay and energy. A computation task offloading policy was proposed by using the genetic algorithm. Although these previous studies considered the objectives of minimizing both energy and execution time, the DVS technology is overlooked.

From the above analysis, it is obvious that the allocation of computing resources in the edge cloud and the technology of DVS are not jointly considered in these previous works. Although the authors in [41] studied resource allocation for big data processing, their study is conducted in the geo-distributed federated public clouds. In addition, the joint objectives of the task completion time and energy consumed by IoT devices are not fully studied. We compare these previous works with the study of this paper, the results of which are listed in Table 1. From Table 1, it is clearly observed that the study in this paper can overcome the shortcomings that exist in the previous works and also provide a complement to them.

Table 1. Comparison.

Reference	DVS	Application Execution Time	Energy Consumption	Computation Resources
Chen et al. [16]	No	No	Yes	No
Wang et al. [21]	Yes	Yes	Yes	No
Wang et al. [30]	No	No	No	No
Zhong et al. [35]	No	Yes	Yes	No
Li et al. [22]	No	Yes	Yes	No
Wang et al. [23]	No	No	Yes	Yes
Liu et al. [33]	No	No	Yes	No

Table 1. *Cont.*

Reference	DVS	Application Execution Time	Energy Consumption	Computation Resources
Li et al. [14]	No	No	Yes	No
Li et al. [38]	Yes	Yes	Yes	No
Yang et al. [36]	No	Yes	Yes	No
Liu et al. [24]	No	Yes	Yes	Yes
Lyu et al. [26]	No	Yes	Yes	Yes
You et al. [25]	No	Yes	Yes	Yes
Zhao et al. [27]	No	Yes	Yes	Yes
Kabir et al. [39]	No	Yes	Yes	No
Zhang et al. [37]	Yes	Yes	Yes	No
Sun et al. [31]	No	Yes	Yes	No
Meskar et al. [29]	No	Yes	Yes	No
Zeng et al. [28]	No	Yes	Yes	No
Zhu et al. [40]	No	Yes	Yes	Yes
This Study	Yes	Yes	Yes	Yes

3. System Architecture

The system architecture is introduced in this section. Suppose that there is a MEC-assisted SIoT system with N IoT devices and one base station (BS), as Figure 2 shows. Each IoT device has a multimedia application that needs a lot of computation resources to be computed. Besides, an edge cloud is deployed near the BS to provide computation resources. As far as the IoT device i is concerned, $i \in \{1, 2, 3, ..., N\}$, its application can be represented by $I_i = (D_i, C_i)$, where D_i is the data size, and C_i is the needed number of CPU cycles for computing this application. The user of the IoT device i can use the methods in [42] to obtain the information of D_i and C_i. The IoT devices will make offloading decisions on whether to offload and process their applications in the edge servers or not. Let O_i denote the application offloading decision made by IoT device i. If the IoT device i offloads its application via BS to the edge cloud, $O_i = 1$, otherwise, $O_i = 0$. It should be noted that the system architecture of this paper can be utilized in numerous real-life cases. For example, the IoT devices may correspond to networked cameras of the surveillance monitoring systems, whose sensed video data require real-time execution, and the multimedia applications can face recognition applications.

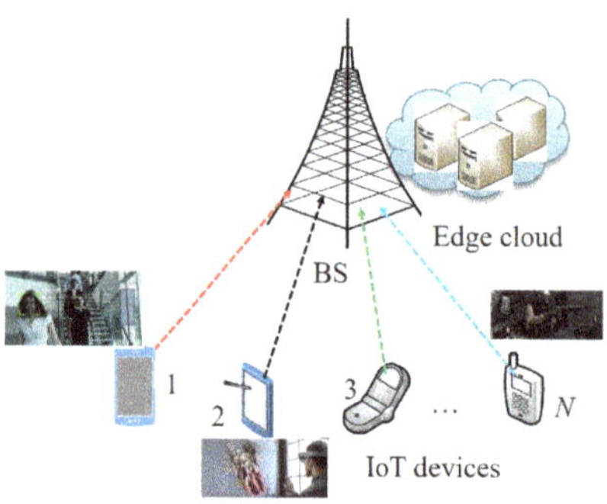

Figure 2. MEC-assisted social IoT system.

3.1. Local Computation Model

In this model, the application of the IoT device i is computed locally using its resources. We use f_i^l to denote the computing capacity in cycles per second. For IoT device i, the corresponding application execution time and consumed energy can be, respectively, denoted as [16]

$$t_{i,l} = \frac{C_i}{f_i^l} \tag{1}$$

$$e_{i,l} = P_{i,l} t_{i,l} \tag{2}$$

where $P_{i,l}$ is the consumed consumption for one CPU cycle.

The CPU power consumption per cycle is [16]

$$P_{i,l} = k_i (f_i^l)^3 \tag{3}$$

where k_i is a constant parameter, and its value relies on the chip architecture [37].

Therefore,

$$e_{i,l} = k_i C_i (f_i^l)^2 \tag{4}$$

Based on Equations (1) and (4), the local computation cost in the measure of the application execution time and the consumed energy is denoted as

$$\begin{aligned} G_i &= \lambda_{i,t} t_{i,l} + \lambda_{i,e} e_{i,l} \\ &= \lambda_{i,t} \frac{C_i}{f_i^l} + \lambda_{i,e} k_i C_i (f_i^l)^2 \end{aligned} \tag{5}$$

where $\lambda_{i,t}$ and $\lambda_{i,e} \in [0,1]$ represent the weight coefficient of the application processing time and consumed energy, respectively. If $\lambda_{i,t} > \lambda_{i,e}$, the IoT user puts more weight on processing time. Otherwise, if $\lambda_{i,t} < \lambda_{i,e}$, the IoT user puts more weight on the consumed energy such that its battery energy can be saved.

3.2. Edge Cloud Model

For the edge cloud model, IoT device i will offload and process its application in the edge cloud via wireless access, such as a macrocell BS or a WIFI access point.

For IoT device i, the uplink transmission data rate is

$$r_i = w_i \log_2(1 + \frac{q_i h_i}{\varpi_0}) \tag{6}$$

where q_i is the transmit power, w_i is the channel bandwidth, h_i is the channel gain, and ϖ_0 is the background noise power.

Then, the consumed time of IoT device i in the uplink is

$$t_{i,t} = \frac{D_i}{r_i} = \frac{D_i}{w_i \log_2(1 + \frac{q_i h_i}{\varpi_0})} \tag{7}$$

Accordingly, the consumed energy in the uplink is

$$e_{i,o} = q_i t_{i,t} = q_i \frac{D_i}{w_i \log_2(1 + \frac{q_i h_i}{\varpi_0})} \tag{8}$$

After the applications of IoT devices are migrated to the edge cloud, the computing resources will be allocated to process them. For the IoT device i, its application processing time is

$$t_{i,e} = \frac{C_i}{f_i^e} \tag{9}$$

Based on Equations (7) and (9), the application offloading time is

$$t_{i,o} = t_{i,t} + t_{i,e} = \frac{D_i}{w_i \log_2(1 + \frac{q_i h_i}{\varpi_0})} + \frac{C_i}{f_i^e} \tag{10}$$

Therefore, according to the Equations (8) and (10), the computation cost of application offloading for mobile device i is

$$\begin{aligned} H_i &= \lambda_{i,t} t_{i,o} + \lambda_{i,e} e_{i,o} \\ &= \lambda_{i,t} \left(\frac{D_i}{w_i \log_2(1 + \frac{q_i h_i}{\varpi_0})} + \frac{C_i}{f_i^e} \right) \\ &+ \lambda_{i,e} q_i \frac{D_i}{w_i \log_2(1 + \frac{q_i h_i}{\varpi_0})} \end{aligned} \tag{11}$$

3.3. Problem Formulation

The optimization problem is formulated by minimization of the computation cost for the local computation and edge cloud computation of IoT devices, which is

P:

$$\begin{aligned} &\min_{f_i^l, f_i^e, O_i} \sum_{i=1}^{N} Z_i \\ \text{s.t.} \quad & 0 < f_i^l \leq f_{i,m}^l \\ & \sum_{i=1}^{N} f_i^e \leq F \\ & O_i \in \{0, 1\} \end{aligned} \tag{12}$$

where Z_i is denoted as

$$\begin{aligned} Z_i &= (1 - O_i) G_i + O_i H_i \\ &= (1 - O_i)[\lambda_{i,t} t_{i,l} + \lambda_{i,e} e_{i,l}] \\ &+ O_i[\lambda_{i,t} t_{i,o} + \lambda_{i,e} e_{i,o}] \end{aligned} \tag{13}$$

where G_i and H_i are shown in the Equations (5) and (11), respectively.

In the above problem, constraint one is the processing capacity of the IoT device i, constraint two is the computation resources constraints of edge servers, and constraint three means the offloading decision that the IoT device i will make.

For convenient investigation, the notations are summarized in Table 2.

Remark 1. *Problem **P** is a typical MINP problem, the function of which is non-convex and notoriously hard to be solved [43]. This is due to the fact that the application offloading decision is binary, but the computation resource allocation is continuous. We can apply the Alternating Direction Method of Multipliers (ADMM), dandelion algorithm (DA) [44], Bat algorithm [45], and branch-and-bound methods to solve the MINP problem. However, the time-complexity is prohibitive [26]. The authors in [46] solved the MINP problem using the algorithms of benders' decomposition, admm, dinkelbach, and branch-and-bound, and compared the performances of these algorithms. In the following section, a method is proposed to obtain the optimal solution.*

Table 2. A summary of notations.

Notation	Description
f_i^l	The processing rate of the IoT device i
$t_{i,l}$	The local processing time of the IoT device i
$e_{i,l}$	The local energy consumption of the IoT device i
$t_{i,e}$	The transmission time of the IoT device i
$e_{i,o}$	The transmission energy consumption of the IoT device i
D_i	The application i's data size

Table 2. *Cont.*

Notation	Description
C_i	The needed CPU cycles to process application of IoT device i
$\lambda_{i,t}$	The weighting parameter of application processing time
$\lambda_{i,e}$	The weighting parameter of energy consumption
w_i	The channel bandwidth
q_i	The transmit power of the IoT device i
h_i	The channel gain
ϖ_0	The background noise power
r_i	The uplink transmission rate for the IoT device i
O_i	The application offloading decision that make by the IoT device i
f_i^e	The allocated computational resources in the edge cloud to device i
$f_{i,m}$	The maximum processing rate of the IoT device i
F	The total computational resources in the edge servers

4. Solution Method

In this section, the proposed solution method for the formulated application execution time and consumed energy minimization problem is introduced.

4.1. Solution Method

Before presenting the solution method, a lemma is firstly introduced, the proof of which is shown in [47]. Based on this lemma, the proposed solution method is introduced.

Lemma 1. *The following result is always true*

$$\sup_{x,y} f(x,y) = \sup_{x} \tilde{f}(x),$$

where $\tilde{f}(x) = \sup_y f(x,y)$.

Lemma 1 shows that when trying to minimize a function, some variables can firstly be chosen to be minimized, and then the left ones are to be minimized.

Based on **Lemma 1**, Problem **P** can be solved by maximizing over f_i^l, and f_i^e sequentially. Therefore, the problem **P** can be solved from the solution of the below three subproblems:

(1) Local computation problem;
(2) Edge cloud computation problem;
(3) The offloading decision problem.

4.2. Local Computation Problem

When $O_i = 0$, the users of IoT devices will accomplish their applications on their own mobile devices. In this case, problem **P** becomes the following problem:
P1:

$$\begin{aligned} \min_{f_i^l} \; & G_i(f_i^l) = \lambda_{i,t} \frac{C_i}{f_i^l} + \lambda_{i,e} k_i C_i (f_i^l)^2 \\ \text{s.t.} \quad & 0 < f_i^l \le f_{i,m} \end{aligned} \tag{14}$$

From $\frac{\partial^2 G_i}{\partial (f_i^l)^2} > 0$, we know that $G_i(f_i^l)$ is convex. Hence, from the first derivative of $G_i(f_i^l)$ with respect to f_i^l,

$$\frac{\partial G_i}{\partial f_i^l} = -\frac{\lambda_{i,t} C_i}{(f_i^l)^2} + 2\lambda_{i,e} k_i f_i^l C_i = 0 \tag{15}$$

From Equation (15), the following optimal solution is obtained.

$$f_i^{l*} = \sqrt[3]{\frac{\lambda_{i,t}}{2k_i\lambda_{i,e}}} \tag{16}$$

It is obviously observed that $G_i(f_i^l)$ monotonously increases when $f_i^l > f_i^{l*}$ and monotonously increases when $f_i^l < f_i^{l*}$.

Therefore, the optimal solution for problem P1 is

$$G_i(f_i^l) = \begin{cases} G_i(f_{i,m}), f_i^{l*} \geq f_{i,m} \\ G_i(f_i^{l*}), f_i^{l*} < f_{i,m} \end{cases} \tag{17}$$

4.3. Edge Cloud Computation Problem

If the users of IoT devices make decisions to offload and process their applications in the edge cloud, problem **P** becomes the following problem:
P2:

$$\begin{aligned} &\min_{f_i^e} \sum_{i=1}^{N} H_i \\ &\sum_{i=1}^{N} f_i^e \leq F \\ &f_i^e > 0 \end{aligned} \tag{18}$$

The objective function in the problem **P2** is easily checked as an obvious convex function. Hence, the Lagrangian function for problem **P2** is

$$\begin{aligned} L_i(f_i^e, \mu) = \lambda_{i,t}(&\frac{D_i}{w_i \log_2(1 + \frac{q_i h_i}{\varpi_0})} \\ &+ \frac{C_i}{f_i^e}) + \lambda_{i,e} q_i \frac{D_i}{w_i \log_2(1 + \frac{q_i h_i}{\varpi_0})} \\ &+ \mu(\sum_{i=1}^{N} f_i^e - F) \end{aligned} \tag{19}$$

where $\mu \geq 0$ denotes the Lagrangian multiplier.

Based on the KKT conditions [47], we have the following results.

$$\frac{\partial L_i}{\partial f_i^e} = -\frac{C_i \lambda_{i,t}}{r_i (f_i^e)^2} + \mu = 0 \tag{20}$$

$$\frac{\partial L_i}{\partial \mu} = \sum_{i=1}^{N} f_i^e - F = 0 \tag{21}$$

$$\mu \geq 0 \tag{22}$$

From Equation (20), it is evident that $\mu > 0$. Therefore, we obtain

$$f_i^e = \sqrt{\frac{C_i \lambda_{i,t}}{r_i \mu}} \tag{23}$$

Substituting Equation (23) back into Equation (21), we obtain

$$\mu = \left(\frac{\sum_{i=1}^{N}\sqrt{\frac{C_i\lambda_{i,t}}{r_i}}}{F}\right)^2 \tag{24}$$

Substituting Equation (24) back into Equation (23), we obtain the optimal computational resource allocation of edge servers, which is denoted as

$$f_i^e = F\frac{\sqrt{\frac{C_i\lambda_{i,t}}{r_i}}}{\sum_{i=1}^{N}\sqrt{\frac{C_i\lambda_{i,t}}{r_i}}} \tag{25}$$

By solving the above two subproblems, we can obtain the computation cost in the two computation models.

4.4. Application Offloading Decision

In this part, the proposed efficient application offloading algorithm will be introduced, which is motivated by the work of [37]. The users of IoT devices will make decisions to offload and process their applications in the edge cloud if the computation cost of the edge cloud model is not higher than that of the local model [16]. The user of the IoT device i will make an application offloading decision by comparing the computation cost of the local and edge cloud computation,

$$O_i = \begin{cases} 1, G_i \geq H_i \\ 0, G_i < H_i \end{cases} \tag{26}$$

After the minimum computation cost of each IoT device is obtained, the total minimum system computation cost is denoted as

$$Z^* = \sum_{i=1}^{N}((1 - O_i)G_i^* + O_i H_i^*) \tag{27}$$

Accordingly, the application offloading decisions of IoT devices in the MEC systems are made according to Algorithm 1.

Algorithm 1 Computational Resource Allocation and Applications Offloading Algorithm

Input:

N applications;

Output:

The application offloading decision made by each user of IoT device and the system computation overhead;

Obtain the optimal resource allocation of each IoT device by solving problem **P1**;

Based on Equation (16), IoT devices make adjustments to their voltage and clock frequency to obtain the adaptive CPU frequency according to the weight coefficient values by applying the DVS technology;

Obtain the optimized local computation cost of each IoT device based on Equation (17);

Calculate the allocated computational resource of each IoT device by solving problem **P2**;

Obtain the optimal computation cost of the edge cloud computation model from Equation (11);

if $G_i \geq H_i$ **then**

    $O_i = 1$;

else

    $O_i = 0$;

end if

5. Simulation Results

The proposed computational resource allocation and application offloading algorithm is evaluated in this section by simulation results. The proposed application offloading algorithm is compared with the following two benchmark algorithms:

Local Computing (LC) Algorithm: In this algorithm, all the IoT devices do not take the offloading strategy. They compute their applications by using the computing resources of their devices.

Edge Cloud (EC) Algorithm: In this algorithm, there is no local computation. All the IoT devices take the offloading strategy, offload and process their applications in the edge cloud.

5.1. Parameter Setting

Suppose that a MEC-assisted IoT system exists with $N = 5$ IoT devices, randomly distributed over a region, with a BS being placed at the center of this region. There are servers located near the BS, whose computation capacity F is set as 20 GHz, and the maximum computation capacity for the IoT device i is $f_{i,m} = 1$ GHz. Each IoT device has one multimedia application which needs computation resources to be executed. The data sizes of multimedia applications have a uniform distribution in [0.42, 4.2] Mb, which corresponds to the face recognition application. The requirement of the number of CPU cycles of these applications have a uniform distribution in [0.1, 1] $\times 10^9$ cycles. The transmission power of each IoT device is set as 1 W. The allocated bandwidth for each IoT device is 1.6 MHz. The channel gain is $h_i = 2.6 \times 10^{-7}$. The background noise power is set to be 10^{-7} W. The weight coefficient coefficient values $\lambda_{i,t}$ and $\lambda_{i,e}$ are randomly chosen from $\{0.2, 0.5, 0.8\}$ and $\lambda_{i,t} + \lambda_{i,e} = 1$. The main simulation parameter values are listed in Table 3. These parameter values are set according to [16,26].

Table 3. Simulation parameter values.

Parameters	Values
The number of IoT devices N	5
The bandwidth allocation w_i	1.6 MHz
The data sizes of multimedia applications D_i	[0.42, 4.2] Mb
The transmission power q_i	1 W
The needed computation resources C_i	[0, 1] $\times 10^9$ cycles
k_i	10^{-26}
The channel gain h_i	2.6×10^{-7}
The maximum processing rate $f_{i,m}$	1 GHz
The background noise power ϖ_0	10^{-7} W
The computation capacity of the edge cloud F	20 GHz

5.2. Effect of Weight Coefficient Values

In this section, the effect of the values of weight parameters on the offloading decisions, application completion time, and consumed energy of IoT devices are analyzed. The values of $\lambda_{i,e}$ are set to be 0.2, 0.5, and 0.8. Figure 3a shows the effect of weight parameter values on the application offloading decisions for IoT users. It can be observed from Figure 3a that as the data sizes of their applications are small, IoT users 1 and 2 compute their applications by their own devices under different values. However, for the IoT users 3, 4, and 5, as their applications have larger data sizes, they compute their applications by using the computation resources of the edge cloud under the values of 0.2 and 0.5. Furthermore, all the IoT users make the decisions on computing their applications on their own devices when the value is 0.8. This is due to the reason that offloading these applications to the edge cloud will consume more energy.

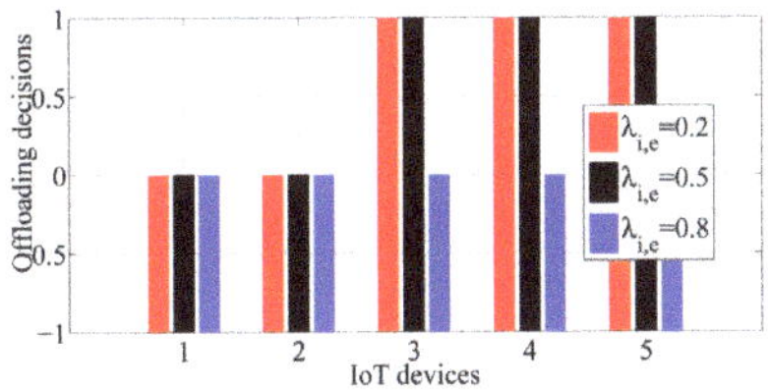

(a) Offloading decisions

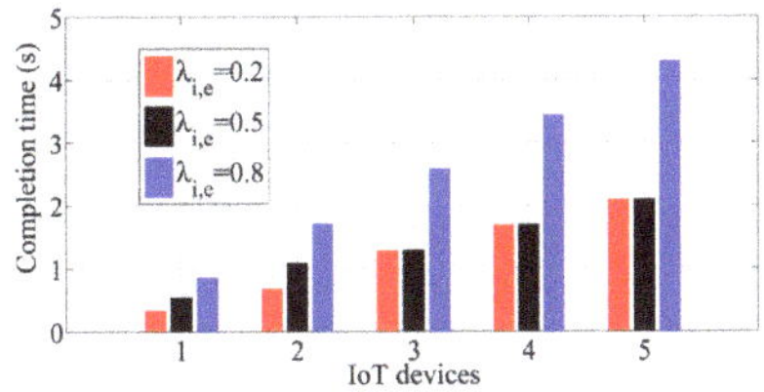

(b) Application completion time

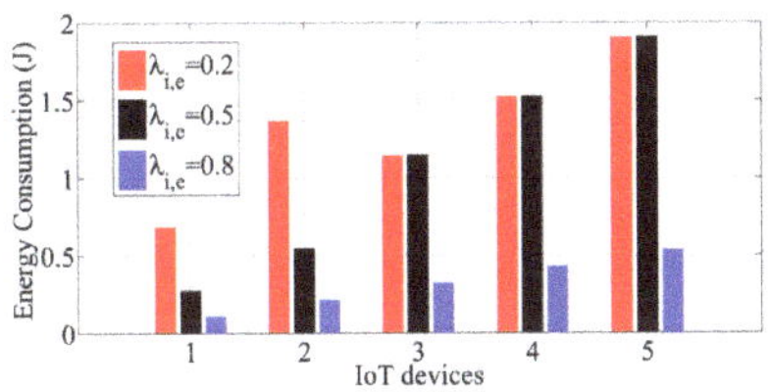

(c) Computation Cost

Figure 3. The effect of the weight coefficient values.

Figure 3b,c show the effect of weight coefficient values on the application completion time and the consumed energy, respectively. It can be obviously observed from Figure 3b that the completion time of the applications of IoT devices increases with the value of $\lambda_{i,e}$ increasing. The IoT devices, whose applications are of larger data sizes, will cost more time to complete their applications. Meanwhile, we have the observation from Figure 3c that the energy consumed by the IoT devices will decrease if the weight coefficient value $\lambda_{i,e}$ increases. This is because with the weight coefficient increasing value of $\lambda_{i,e}$, IoT users pay more attention to the factor of energy consumption in this scenario. Figure 3b,c also indicates that we could tune the values of the weight coefficient in different scenarios to meet the requirements of the MEC-assisted SIoT system.

5.3. Effect of the Edge Cloud Capacity

The effect of the edge cloud capacity on the offloading decisions of IoT users and the computation cost is analyzed in this section. The simulation results are shown in Figures 4–7. Figure 4a–c depict how the edge cloud capacity affects the offloading decisions that IoT users will make versus the weight coefficient values. From Figure 4a, we observe that when $\lambda_{i,e} = 0.2, \lambda_{i,t} = 0.8$, IoT devices 1 and 2 do not offload their applications even if the capacity of the edge cloud increases. This is because these IoT devices pay more attention to the completion time, and local processing will cost less execution time for them. IoT devices 3, 4, and 5 will offload applications with the capacity of the edge cloud increasing. Through Figure 4b, we find that the users of IoT devices would like to offload their applications if the edge cloud capacity increases. In particular, all the users of IoT devices offload their applications when $F = 30$ GHz. When $\lambda_{i,e} = 0.8, \lambda_{i,t} = 0.2$, we see from Figure 4c that all the IoT devices are to complete their applications locally. This is due to the reason that more attention is paid to the energy consumption in this scenario, and offloading applications to the edge cloud may cost more energy than the consumed energy in the local computing model. Therefore, IoT users would like to execute their applications locally. Figure 4a–c demonstrate that the offloading decisions that the IoT users make depend not only on the chosen weight coefficient values, but also the capacity of the edge cloud.

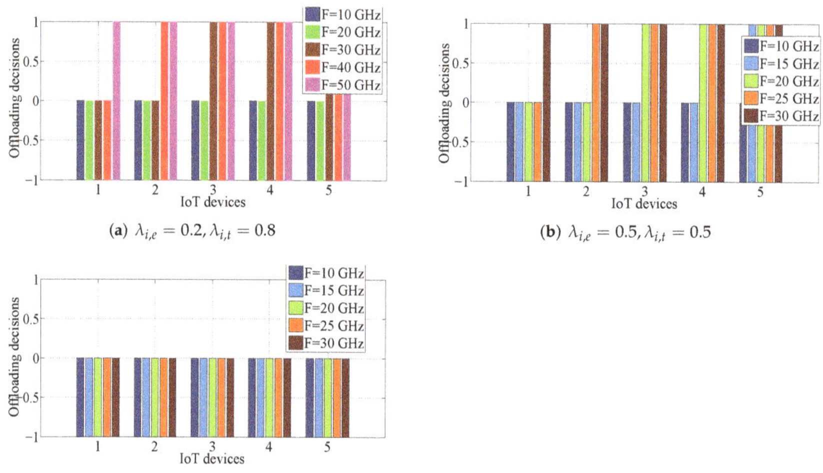

(a) $\lambda_{i,e} = 0.2, \lambda_{i,t} = 0.8$

(b) $\lambda_{i,e} = 0.5, \lambda_{i,t} = 0.5$

(c) $\lambda_{i,e} = 0.8, \lambda_{i,t} = 0.2$

Figure 4. The effect of the edge cloud capacity on the offloading decisions.

Figure 5a,b depict how the edge cloud capacity affects the application completion time under different values of weight coefficient. We see that the application completion time for each IoT device will decrease if the edge cloud capacity increases. By comparing Figure 5a,b, we find that the application completion time for each IoT device in Figure 5b is smaller than that in the Figure 5a under fixed edge cloud capacity. This is owing to the fact that the coefficient value of $\lambda_{i,t}$ is smaller in Figure 5a.

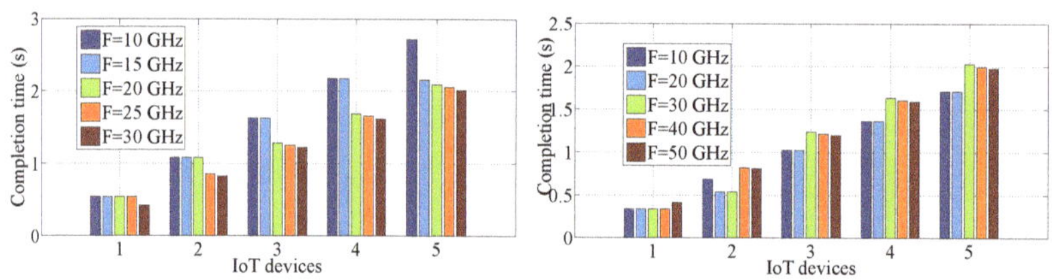

(a) $\lambda_{i,e} = 0.5, \lambda_{i,t} = 0.5$

(b) $\lambda_{i,e} = 0.2, \lambda_{i,t} = 0.8$

Figure 5. The effect of the edge cloud capacity on the application completion time.

Figure 6a,b depict how the edge cloud capacity affects the consumed energy under different values of weight coefficient. By comparing the two figures, we observe that the consumed energy for each IoT device in Figure 6a is lower than that in Figure 6b. This is owing to the fact that the coefficient value of $\lambda_{i,e}$ is bigger in Figure 6a.

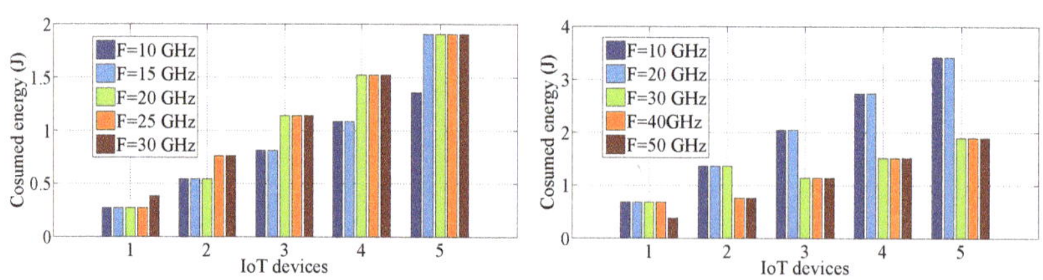

(a) $\lambda_{i,e} = 0.5, \lambda_{i,t} = 0.5$

(b) $\lambda_{i,e} = 0.2, \lambda_{i,t} = 0.8$

Figure 6. The effect of the edge cloud capacity on the consumed energy.

Figure 7a,b show how the edge cloud capacity impacts the computation cost with different values of weight parameters. The proposed algorithm is compared with two baseline algorithms. It is obviously shown in these figures that the computation costs under the **EC Algorithm** and the **Proposed Algorithm** decrease with the increase in the edge cloud capacity. As the edge cloud capacity does not affect the local computation cost, the computation cost in the **LC Algorithm** has the constant value. From Figure 7a,b, as anticipated, the **Proposed Algorithm** can achieve less computation cost compared with the **LC Algorithm** and the **EC Algorithm**. By comparing Figure 7a,b, it can also be obviously observed that the computation cost is lower when $\lambda_{i,e} = \lambda_{i,t} = 0.5$. Moreover, the two figures show that the computation cost in the **LC Algorithm** is lower than that in the **EC Algorithm** until the edge cloud capacity reaches a threshold value. When $\lambda_{i,e} = 0.5, \lambda_{i,t} = 0.5$, the threshold value is comparatively smaller.

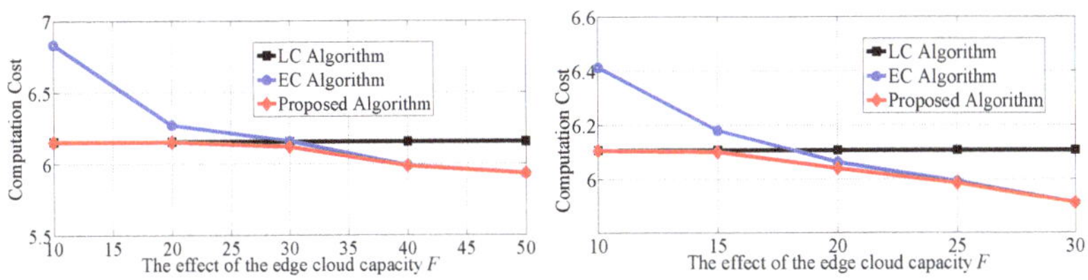

(**a**) $\lambda_{i,e} = 0.2, \lambda_{i,t} = 0.8$

(**b**) $\lambda_{i,e} = 0.5, \lambda_{i,t} = 0.5$

Figure 7. The effect of the edge cloud capacity on the computation cost.

There are several factors that could potentially affect the simulation results. For example, the weight coefficient values of $\lambda_{i,e}$ and $\lambda_{i,t}$ should be selected properly. In addition, the computing resources provided by the edge cloud provider should be adjusted according to data sizes of applications and the number of IoT users. Otherwise, there will be biases in the experimental results.

6. Conclusions

This paper has investigated resource allocation and multimedia applications offloading in a MEC-assisted SIoT system. Specifically, we analyzed the allocation of computation resources and the adoption of the DVS technology to minimize the computation cost in the measure of the application completion time and consumed energy for the processing of multimedia applications of IoT devices. We formulated the application completion time and consumed energy of IoT devices as an optimization problem. As the formulated problem is MINP, it is non-convex and NP-hard. The problem is decomposed into three sub-problems, and the solution for each one has been analyzed and solved. Theoretic analysis and simulation results have demonstrated the performance of the proposed algorithm by comparing the two baseline methods. The proposed method is beneficial for the efficient allocation of computation resource and application offloading in the MEC-assisted SIoT system. The experiment results highlight that the weight coefficient values and the edge cloud capacity impact the offloading decisions IoT users dramatically. In contrast to the two benchmark algorithms, the proposed algorithm reveals its advantages in terms of application completion time, consumed energy, and computation cost.

Several research issues should be studied in the future works. First, we will extend our study to consider the allocation of the caching resources [48] and apply the deep learning algorithms to solve the objective problem [49]. Second, as the backscatter communication (BackCom) can improve the transmission rate [50], we will combine the BackCom with computation offloading in MEC. Third, the Software Defined Network (SDN) technique will be integrated into the application offloading [51]. In addition, the security issue in the MEC-assisted SIoT system is also an interesting research topic [52].

Author Contributions: Conceptualization, X.L.; Funding acquisition, G.C. and B.W.; Investigation, X.L. and B.W.; Methodology, G.C.; Project administration, G.C.; Software, X.L.; Supervision, G.C. and L.Z.; Validation, L.Z. and B.W.; Writing–original draft, X.L.; Writing–review & editing, L.Z. and B.W. All authors have read and agreed to the published version of the manuscript.

Funding: This research was funded by Start up funds for the scientific research of high level talents of Bengbu University (BBXY2020KYQD02), Funding project for the cultivation of outstanding talents in Colleges and Universities (gxyqZD2021135), Key research and development projects in Anhui Province (202004a05020043), High level scientific research and Cultivation Project of Benbu University (2021pyxm05), Peak discipline construction of Bengbu University (2021GFXK03), JSPS KAKENHI Grant Number 20K14740 and JST, PRESTO Grant Number JPMJPR21PB, Japan, and Scientific Research and Development Fund of Suzhou University (2021fzjj29).

Acknowledgments: The authors would like to pay thanks to the anonymous reviewers for their valuable comments and suggestions, which greatly improve the quality of this paper.

Conflicts of Interest: The authors declare no conflict of interest.

Abbreviations

The following abbreviations are used in this manuscript:

MEC	Mobile Edge Computing
MCC	Mobile Cloud Computing
SIoT	Social Internet of Things
DVS	Dynamic voltage scaling
MINP	Mixed-integer nonlinear programming

References

1. Gong, Y.; Zhang, L.; Liu, R.P.; Yu, K.; Srivastava, G. Nonlinear mimo for industrial internet of things in cyberphysical systems *IEEE Trans. Ind. Inform.* **2021**, *8*, 5533–5541. [CrossRef]
2. Ding, F.; Zhu, G.; Alazab, M.; Li, X.; Yu, K. Deep-learning-empowered digital forensics for edge consumer electronics in 5g hetnets. *IEEE Consum. Electron. Mag.* **2022**, *11*, 42–50. [CrossRef]
3. Guo, Z.; Yu, K.; Li, Y.; Srivastava, G.; Lin, J.C.-W. Deep Learning-Embedded Social Internet of Things for Ambiguity-Aware Social Recommendations. *IEEE Trans. Netw. Sci. Eng.* **2021**, 1. [CrossRef]
4. Tan, L.; Yu, K.; Ming, F.; Chen, X.; Srivastava, G. Secure and resilient artificial intelligence of things: A honeynet approach for threat detection and situational awareness. *IEEE Consum. Electron. Mag.* **2021**, *11*, 69–78. [CrossRef]
5. Li, H.; Yu, K.; Liu, B.; Feng, C.; Qin, Z.; Srivastava, G. An efficient ciphertext-policy weighted attribute based encryption for the internet of health things. *IEEE J. Biomed. Health Inform.* **2021**, *26*, 1949–1960. [CrossRef]
6. Zhao, L.; Zheng, T.; Lin, M.; Hawbani, A.; Shang, J.; Fan, C. SPIDER: A Social Computing Inspired Predictive Routing Scheme for Softwarized Vehicular Networks. *IEEE Trans. Intell. Transp.* **2021**, 1–12. [CrossRef]
7. Zhen, L.; Zhang, Y.; Yu, K.; Kumar, N.; Barnawi, A.; Xie, Y. Early collision detection for massive random access in satellite-based internet of things. *IEEE Trans. Veh. Technol.* **2021**, *70*, 5184–5189. [CrossRef]
8. Zhao, L.; Wang, C.; Li, W.; Zhao, K.; Tarchi, D.; Wan, S.; Kumar, N. INTERLINK: A Digital Twin-Assisted Storage Strategy for Satellite-Terrestrial Networks. *IEEE Trans. Aerosp. Electron. Syst.* **2021**, 1. [CrossRef]
9. Feng, C.; Liu, B.; Guo, Z.; Yu, K.; Qin, Z.; Choo, K.-K.R. Blockchain-based cross-domain authentication for intelligent 5g-enabled internet of drones. *IEEE Internet Things* **2022**, *9*, 6224–6238. [CrossRef]
10. Cisco Visual Networking Index: Global Mobile Data Traffic Forecast Update 2017–2022 White Paper. Available online: http://media.mediapost.com/uploads/CiscoForecast.pdf (accessed on 6 April 2022).
11. Sun, Y.; Liu, J.; Yu, K.; Alazab, M.; Lin, K. Pmrss: Privacy-preserving medical record searching scheme for intelligent diagnosis in iot healthcare. *IEEE Trans. Veh. Technol.* **2022**, *18*, 1981–1990. [CrossRef]
12. Shang, W.-L.; Chen, J.; Bi, H.; Sui, Y.; Chen, Y.; Yu, H. Impacts of covid-19 pandemic on user behaviors and environmental benefits of bike sharing: A big-data analysis. *Appl. Energy* **2022**, *285*, 116429–116429. [CrossRef]
13. Sheng, Z.; Wang, H.; Yin, C.; Hu, X.; Yang, S.; Leung, V.C.M. Lightweight management of resource-constrained sensor devices in internet of things. *IEEE Internet Things* **2015**, *2*, 402–411. [CrossRef]
14. Li, G.; He, J.; Peng, S.; Jia, W.; Wang, C.; Niu, J.; Yu, S. Energy efficient data collection in large-scale internet of things via computation offloading. *IEEE Internet Things* **2019**, *35*, 4176–4187. [CrossRef]
15. Tan, L.; Yu, K.; Shi, N.; Yang, C.; Wei, W.; Lu, H. Towards secure and privacy-preserving data sharing for COVID-19 medical records: A blockchain-empowered approach. *IEEE Trans. Netw. Sci. Eng.* **2022**, *1*, 271–281. [CrossRef]
16. Chen, X.; Jiao, L.; Li, W.; Fu, X. Efficient multi-user computation offloading for mobile-edge cloud computing. *IEEE/ACM Trans. Netw.* **2016**, *24*, 2795–2808. [CrossRef]

17. Shi, W.; Cao, J.; Zhang, Q.; Li, Y.; Xu, L. Edge computing: Vision and challenges. *IEEE Internet Things* **2016**, *5*, 637–646. [CrossRef]
18. Liu, L.; Feng, J.; Pei, Q.; Chen, C.; Ming, Y.; Shang, B.; Dong, M. Blockchain-enabled secure data sharing scheme in mobile-edge computing: An asynchronous advantage actorcritic learning approach. *IEEE Internet Things* **2021**, *4*, 2342–2353. [CrossRef]
19. Mahmoud, R.; Yousuf, T.; Aloul, F.; Zualkernan, I. Internet of things (IoT) security: Current status, challenges and prospective measures. In Proceedings of the 10th International Conference for Internet Technology and Secured Transactions (ICITST 2015), London, UK, 14–16 December 2015; pp. 336–341.
20. Bures, M.; Klima, M.; Rechtberger, V.; Ahmed, B.S.; Hindy, H.; Bellekens, X. Review of Specific Features and Challenges in the Current Internet of Things Systems Impacting Their Security and Reliability. In Proceedings of the Trends and Applications in Information Systems and Technologies, Terceira Island, Azores, Portugal, 30 March–2 April 2021; pp. 546–556.
21. Wang, Y.; Sheng, M.; Wang, X.; Wang, L.; Li, J. Mobile-edge computing: Partial computation offloading using dynamic voltage scaling. *IEEE Trans. Commun.* **2016**, *10*, 4268–4282. [CrossRef]
22. Li, C.; Wang, H.; Song, R. Intelligent offloading for noma-assisted mec via dual connectivity. *IEEE Internet Things* **2021**, *4*, 2802–2813. [CrossRef]
23. Wang, J.; Feng, D.; Zhang, S.; Liu, A.; Xia, X.-G. Joint computation offloading and resource allocation for mec-enabled iot systems with imperfect csi. *IEEE Internet Things* **2021**, *5*, 3462–3475. [CrossRef]
24. Liu, K.; Peng, J.; Li, H.; Zhang, X.; Liu, W. Multi-device task offloading with time-constraints for energy efficiency in mobile cloud computing. *Perform. Eval. Rev.* **2016**, *64*, 1–14. [CrossRef]
25. You, C.; Huang, K.; Chae, H.; Kim, B.-H. Energy-Efficient Resource Allocation for Mobile-Edge Computation Offloading. *IEEE Wirel. Commun.* **2017**, *16*, 1397–1411. [CrossRef]
26. Lyu, X.; Tian, H.; Ni, W.; Zhang, Y.; Zhang, P.; Liu, R.P. Energy-efficient admission of delay-sensitive tasks for mobile edge computing. *IEEE Trans. Commun.* **2018**, *6*, 2603–2616. [CrossRef]
27. Zhao, P.; Tian, H.; Qin, C.; Nie, G. Energy-saving offloading by jointly allocating radio and computational resources for mobile edge computing. *IEEE Access* **2017**, 11255–11268. [CrossRef]
28. Zeng, M.; Fodor, V. Energy minimization for delay constrained mobile edge computing with orthogonal and non-orthogonal multiple access. *Ad Hoc Netw.* **2020**, *98*, 102060. [CrossRef]
29. Meskar, E.; Todd, T.D.; Zhao, D.; Karakostas, G. Energy aware offloading for competing users on a shared communication channel. *IEEE Trans. Mobile Comput.* **2017**, *1*, 87–96. [CrossRef]
30. Wang, S.; Chen, M.; Liu, X.; Yin, C.; Cui, S.; Poor, H.V. A machine learning approach for task and resource allocation in mobile-edge computing-based networks. *IEEE Internet Things* **2021**, *3*, 1358–1372. [CrossRef]
31. Sun, Y.; Zhou, S.; Xu, J. Emm: Energy-aware mobility management for mobile edge computing in ultra dense networks. *IEEE Trans. J. Sel. Areas Commun.* **2017**, *11*, 2637–2646. [CrossRef]
32. Qian, L.P.; Shi, B.; Wu, Y.; Sun, B.; Tsang, D.H.K. NOMA enabled mobile edge com puting for internet of things via joint communication and compu tation resource allocations. *IEEE Internet Things* **2020**, *7*, 718–733. [CrossRef]
33. Liu, L.; Sun, B.; Wu, Y.; Tsang, D.H.K. Latency optimization for computation offloading with hybrid noma-oma transmission. *IEEE Internet Things* **2021**, *8*, 6677–6691. [CrossRef]
34. Chen, G.; Zhao, L.; Li, X.; Zhao, F.; Zeng, X. Optimal Resource Allocation for Multimedia Applications Offloading in Mobile Edge Computing. *IEEE Open J. Comput. Soc.* **2021**, *2*, 360–369. [CrossRef]
35. Zhong, X.; Wang, X.; Li, L.; Yang, Y.; Qin, Y.; Yang, T.; Zhang, B.; Zhang, W. Cl-admm: A cooperative-learning-based optimization framework for resource management in MEC. *IEEE Internet Things* **2021**, *8*, 8191–8209. [CrossRef]
36. Yang, L.; Guo, S.; Yi, L.; Wang, Q.; Yang, Y. NOSCM: A Novel Offloading Strategy for NOMA-Enabled Hierarchical Small Cell Mobile-Edge Computing. *IEEE Internet Things* **2021**, *10*, 8107–8118. [CrossRef]
37. Zhang, J.; Hu, X.; Ning, Z.; Ngai, E.C.-H.; Zhou, L.; Wei, J.; Cheng, J.; Hu, B. Energy-latency tradeoff for energy-aware offloading in mobile edge computing networks. *IEEE Internet Things* **2018**, *4*, 2633–2645. [CrossRef]
38. Li, X.; Zhao, L.; Yu, K.; Aloqaily, M.; Jararweh, Y. A cooperative resource allocation model for IoT applications in mobile edge computing. *Comput. Commun.* **2021**, *173*, 183–191. [CrossRef]
39. Kabir, M.T.; Masouros C. A scalable energy vs. latency trade-off in fullduplex mobile edge computing systems. *IEEE Trans. Commun.* **2019**, *67*, 5848–5861. [CrossRef]
40. Zhu, A.; Wen, Y. Computing offloading strategy using improved genetic algorithm in mobile edge computing syste. *J. Grid Comput.* **2021**, *19*, 38. [CrossRef]
41. Ebadifard, F.; Babamir, S.M. Federated geo-distributed clouds: Optimizing resource allocation based on request type using autonomous and multi-objective resource sharing model. *Big Data Res.* **2021**, *24*, 100188. [CrossRef]
42. Yang, L.; Cao, J.; Tang, S.; Li, T.; Chan, A.T. A framework for partitioning and execution of data stream applications in mobile cloud computing. *Perform. Eval. Rev.* **2013**, *4*, 23–32. [CrossRef]
43. Pochet, Y.; Wolsey, L.A. *Production Planning by Mixed Integer Programming*; Springer: Berlin, Germany, 2006.
44. Li, X.-G.; Han, S.-F.; Zhao, L.; Gong, C.-Q.; Liu, X.-J. New dandelion algorithm optimizes extreme learning machine for biomedical classification problems. *Comput. Intell. Neurosci.* **2017**, *2017*, 4523754. [CrossRef]
45. Lin, N.; Tang, J.; Li, X.; Zhao, L. A novel improved bat algorithm in uav path planning, Computers. *Comput. Mater. Contin.* **2019**, *61*, 323–344. [CrossRef]

46. Yu, Y.; Bu, X.; Yang, K.; Wu, Z.; Han, Z. Green large-scale fog computing resource allocation using joint benders decomposition, dinkelbach algorithm, admm, and branch-and-bound. *Comput. IEEE Internet Things* **2019**, *6*, 4106–4117. [CrossRef]
47. Boyd, S.; Vandenberghe, L. *Convex Optimization*; Computational Cambridge University Press: Cambridge, UK, 2004.
48. Zhu, A.; Wen, Y. Efficient caching strategy in wireless networks with mobile edge computing. *Comput. Peer-to-Peer Netw. Appl.* **2020**, *13*, 1756–1766.
49. Yu, K.; Tan, L.; Lin, L.; Cheng, X.; Yi, Z.; Sato, T. Deep-learning-empowered breast cancer auxiliary diagnosis for 5gb remote e-health. *Comput. IEEE Wirel. Commun.* **2021**, *3*, 54–61. [CrossRef]
50. Xu, Y.; Gu, B.; Hu, R.Q.; Li, D.; Zhang, H. Joint computation offloading and radio resource allocation in MEC-based wireless-powered backscatter communication networks. *Comput. IEEE T. Veh. Technol.* **2021**, *6*, 6200–6205. [CrossRef]
51. Zhao, L.; Zhao, W.; Hawbani, A.; Al-Dubai, A.Y.; Min, G.; Zomaya, A.Y.; Gong, C. Novel online sequential learning-based adaptive routing for edge software-defined vehicular networks. *Comput. IEEE Trans. Wirel. Commun.* **2021**, *5*, 2991–3004. [CrossRef]
52. Yu, K.; Guo, Z.; Shen, Y.; Wang, W.; Lin, J.C.-W.; Sato, T. Secure artificial intelligence of things for implicit group recommendations. *Comput. IEEE Trans. Wirel. Commun.* **2022**, *4*, 2698–2707. [CrossRef]

mathematics

MDPI

Article

Boosting Unsupervised Dorsal Hand Vein Segmentation with U-Net Variants

Szidónia Lefkovits [1,*], Simina Emerich [2] and László Lefkovits [3]

1 Department of Electrical Engineering and Information Technology, Faculty of Engineering and Information Technology, George Emil Palade University of Medicine, Pharmacy, Science, and Technology of Targu Mures, Gheorghe Marinescu Street 38, 540139 Târgu Mureș, Romania

2 Communications Department, Faculty of Electronics, Telecommunications and Information Technology, Technical University of Cluj-Napoca, Memorandumului 28, 400114 Cluj-Napoca, Romania; simina.emerich@com.utcluj.ro

3 Computational Intelligence Research Group, Departament of Electrical Engineering, Sapientia Hungarian University of Transylvania, Sos. Sighișoarei 1/C, 540485 Corunca, Romania; lefkolaci@ms.sapientia.ro

* Correspondence: szidonia.lefkovits@umfst.ro

Abstract: The identification of vascular network structures is one of the key fields of research in medical imaging. The segmentation of dorsal hand vein patterns form NIR images is not only the basis for reliable biometric identification, but would also provide a significant tool in assisting medical intervention. Precise vein extraction would help medical workers to exactly determine the needle entry point to efficiently gain intravenous access for different clinical purposes, such as intravenous therapy, parenteral nutrition, blood analysis and so on. It would also eliminate repeated attempts at needle pricks and even facilitate an automatic injection procedure in the near future. In this paper, we present a combination of unsupervised and supervised dorsal hand vein segmentation from near-infrared images in the NCUT database. This method is convenient due to the lack of expert annotations of publicly available vein image databases. The novelty of our work is the automatic extraction of the veins in two phases. First, a geometrical approach identifies tubular structures corresponding to veins in the image. This step is considered gross segmentation and provides labels (Label I) for the second CNN-based segmentation phase. We visually observe that different CNNs obtain better segmentation on the test set. This is the reason for building an ensemble segmentor based on majority voting by nine different network architectures (U-Net, U-Net++ and U-Net3+, all trained with BCE, Dice and focal losses). The segmentation result of the ensemble is considered the second label (Label II). In our opinion, the new Label II is a better annotation of the NCUT database than the Label I obtained in the first step. The efficiency of computer vision algorithms based on artificial intelligence algorithms is determined by the quality and quantity of the labeled data used. Furthermore, we prove this statement by training ResNet–UNet in the same manner with the two different label sets. In our experiments, the Dice scores, sensitivity and specificity with ResNet–UNet trained on Label II are superior to the same classifier trained on Label I. The measured Dice scores of ResNet–UNet on the test set increase from 90.65% to 95.11%. It is worth mentioning that this article is one of very few in the domain of dorsal hand vein segmentation; moreover, it presents a general pipeline that may be applied for different medical image segmentation purposes.

Keywords: dorsal hand vein; segmentation; tubular structure extraction; ResNet–UNet; U-Net++; U-Net3+

MSC: 68T45

1. Introduction

Information security and identification have become a crucial part of everyday life. Traditionally secured systems are not reliable enough and are vulnerable to brute force attacks.

Instead of these conventional mechanisms, biometric physical or behavioral characteristics are used for personal identification or in security systems. Although biometrics-based identification is a complex task, its use is increasingly widespread. There are several well-known biometric parameters related to physiological characteristics, such as DNA, face recognition, iris, retina, hand geometry, palm print, fingerprint, palm vein, finger vein and dorsal hand vein, or behavioral characteristics such as voice style, typing rhythm, signature and its dynamics.

Blood vessel segmentation is a topic of great interest in medical image segmentation because it can help in establishing the correct diagnosis, identifying adequate treatment and planning the execution of surgery. In the literature, the most widespread vein segmentation systems are applied on retinal vessel segmentation [1], liver vessel segmentation [2], coronary vessel from angiogram images [3] or brain vessels [4]. The purpose of this paper is not human identification, but the accurate segmentation of dorsal hand veins. These veins are under the subcutaneous fat and are very difficult to detect, with only some parts of the veins being located under the skin at a distance of approximately 3–5 mm. Observation and, thereby, automatic detection of the vessels presents great difficulties, especially in the obese. The veins on the surface can be better visualized in infrared light at a wavelength of 700–1000 nm due to the differences in the absorption capacity of hemoglobin in vessels compared to other surrounding tissues.

The aim of this paper is to propose and implement a robust dorsal hand vein segmentation system that combines unsupervised traditional segmentation used as labels in subsequent steps that boost the labels obtained initially with different U-Net-based CNN methods. Currently, there are extremely few researchers [5,6] in the medical field concentrating on dorsal hand vein segmentation due to the lack of an expert-annotated database.

The role of the automatic segmentation of dorsal hand veins would assist nurses and doctors in determining the precise placement of a needle for injection, a butterfly needle for perfusion or a catheter. Automatic non-contact insertion of the needle would not only eliminate multiple misplaced needle pricks, but also possible infection with contagious diseases.

The main contribution of this article is an automatic segmentation of dorsal hand vein NIR images from the NCUT [7] database. In every computer vision application, the results obtained are greatly influenced by the quality and quantity of the images used. In our work, we propose a two-phase automatic segmentation system that does not require manual labeling. The creation of an overall accepted ground truth manually labeled by experts is a demanding and time-consuming task, and still not perfect. In our paper, we combine unsupervised traditional image processing techniques with supervised CNN segmentation. In the first phase, we implement automatic segmentation using different geometric image processing steps to detect the veins. This segmentation result is designated Label I. It is known that more annotators can improve the quality and accuracy of annotation. Thus, we wanted to improve the segmentation first obtained using supervised segmentation. In the second phase, we apply an ensemble of different CNN networks adapted for vein segmentation. The ensemble model obtained by supervised learning based on Label I substantially corrects the initial labels. This result constitutes Label II. The improvement between Label I and Label II is experimentally demonstrated by training the ResNet–UNet model in the same way on both labels. The performance obtained shows an improvement of approximately 5%, from a Dice score of 90.65% to 95.11%.

To the best of our knowledge, there are only two research papers in the field of dorsal hand vein segmentation that apply CNNs. The two articles report a mIoU of 78.12% [5] and a Dice score of 78.21% [6], both using other proprietary datasets instead of NCUT. All the other papers in the literature neglect the rigorous segmentation of the veins; rather, they concentrate on human biometric identification based on veins. Instead of segmentation performance (overlap: mIoU, Dice score), they measure human identification parameters: FAR (false acceptance rate), impostor acceptance of or FRR (false rejection rate) rejection of authentic matching. Our segmentation results are not comparable to authentication errors.

The rest of the paper is organized as follows: after a short review of the currently known dorsal hand vein authentication systems in the literature, the methods applied are presented. First, an unsupervised vein extraction method is proposed, which is further improved by two-phase supervised CNN segmentation. Finally, we describe our experiments and results on the networks studied and adapted for dorsal vein segmentation. Here, we are able to experimentally prove the effect of the two-phase boosting of labels used in training. The article ends with the discussion and conclusions.

2. Related Work

There are several state-of-the-art vein recognition methods that involve the steps of image acquisition, preprocessing, feature extraction and classification. In the domain of biometric identification, the most used methods are based on shape or texture.

Shape-based methods extract the topological structures of the vessels, extracting segments, bifurcation and endpoints. This kind of local shape can be described using LBP [8], PLBP [9], BGM [10] and the Width Skeleton Model [11]. In [8], the authors propose to combine global and local shape representations using several techniques, such as the cross-sectional profile of the veins, Gaussian matched filter, extraction of extreme points, skeletonization, binary coding (BC)-based local binary pattern (LBP) and factorized graph matching (FGM). Ref. [9] introduces partition local binary patterns (PLBP), where the image is divided into subregions and partial LBPs are computed to extract uniform pattern features. In [10], Biometric Graph Matching (BGM) is used to compare graph-like templates; this method includes registration to the template, graph matching and distance computation. The final identification is done using the k-Nearest Neighbors method. The Width Skeleton Model (WSM) [11] is also a graph model that takes both the topology of the vessels and their width into account.

The most important texture-based methods use various types of texture descriptors, such as Gabor features [12], SIFT [13] or local keypoint matching features, such as Oriented Gradient Maps (OGM) [14] or Centroid-Based Circular Keypoint Grid (CCKG) and fine-grained matching [15]. Ref. [13] uses Contrast-Limited Adaptive Histogram Equalization (CLAHE), Harris–Laplace corner detector and Scale Invariant Feature Transform (SIFT). In [16], the distinctiveness of vein patterns and the surrounding textures is measured using OGMs, and final matching is done through SIFT keypoint matching.

From the perspective of classification, the most widely used classifiers were unsupervised methods such as k-NN [10] or its weighted variants and SVM [17] until the most recent advances in the field of CNNs.

The convolutional neural network approach is not very widespread in this domain. The CNNs known in the literature are used especially for hand vein-based recognition and authentication, but not for segmentation. The reason is the lack of an annotated vein database required for segmentation. All of the following articles use CNNs for personal authentication with the NCUT [7] or other proprietary databases. Wang et al. [18] present a four-layered (one conv. layer) RCNN and test the identification accuracy on a self-made database. Li et al. [11] compare AlexNet, VGG-16 and GoogleNet for personal identification. Wan et al. [19] describe a VGG-based and an ensemble CNN made up of a combination of four SqueezeNet layers. Deep Hashing Networks (DHN) were first introduced in [20] and used for dorsal hand vein-based feature extraction and matching with a simplified CNN implementation [21]. In [22], the authors describe an identification system based on palm and dorsal hand vein features using DHN and BGM or finger vein + fingerprint + face.

In recent years, deep learning, i.e., convolutional neural networks, has been used with great success in medical image segmentation compared to traditional methods. The CNNs used for object detection or localization, such as AlexNet, VGG, Inception, ResNet, MobileNet and others, were not suitable for image segmentation. Fully convolutional (FCN) networks were adaptations containing two major parts, which are downconvolution (encoder) and upconvolution (decoder). These types of networks can aggregate context features, capturing, in each stage, a reduced resolution of the original image. In this way, a pixelwise segmentation of the whole test image can be obtained over a single pass through the trained network. The most important drawback in this case is the loss of information during each convolution and pooling. The loss of detail leads to incorrect margins and rough segmentations. The most widely used network in pixelwise segmentation is U-Net, introduced in [23]. U-Net introduced so-called skip connections, which refined the features in the upsampling part by concatenating the corresponding encoder feature map with its decoder pair. Different types of U-Nets have been used to segment different organs or tumors. U-Net is also applied in several engineering applications, such as manufacturing defects [24], fringe pattern denoising [25], concrete crack detection [26] and fluid dynamics [27]. V-Net [28] was initially proposed for prostate segmentation, while 3D U-Net [29] was aimed at kidney segmentation. The weighted Res-UNet [30] was proposed first for retinal vessel segmentation; Recurrent Residual U-Net [31] was applied in lung segmentation, skin cancer and retinal vessel segmentation; and H-DenseUNet [32] was used in liver and tumor segmentation.

Recently, participants in the Medical Segmentation Decathlon Challenge [33] have proposed general methods that test different types of architectures and different parametrization schemes that can generally be applied in several segmentation tasks. AutoML [34] and nnU-Net [35] have the great advantage of not needing manual fine-tuning of the CNN or its hyperparameters. They perform computations and set the parameter search space based on the data (resolution), and test some of the extant CNN architectures and produce a segmentation result based on the best ensemble obtained. This automated process is extremely long-lasting.

The segmentation of vessels via convolutional neural networks is a computationally complex problem. The above-mentioned CNN architectures can be applied only in supervised learning, where not only the original image but the expert gold-standard segmentation is also provided. For retinal vessel segmentation [36], the DRIVE [37] and CHASE DB1 [38] databases are the most widely used, containing 40 and 28 expert-segmented images, respectively. Several architectural variants have been evaluated; for instance, U-Net is used in [39]. The authors of [40] propose a pyramid self-attention-module, and Guo et al. [41] segment the retinal vessels with a Residual Spatial Attention Network.

The subcutaneous veins (finger [42,43], palm [44] or dorsal-hand [7]) are usually obtained from near-infrared images. The publicly available images used in the literature have low contrast and low resolution, and only the superficial parts of the vein can be seen and detected. They are not expert-annotated, and thus the segmentation with CNNs is only possible through a combination of manual segmentation and traditional geometrical feature extraction. In other cases, the original images and their annotations are self-acquired and not available publicly for further comparison [43]. In palm print and palm vein recognition, research is focused only on the distinction between impostor and genuine [45] or personal identification [44].

In the domain of dorsal hand vein identification, traditional methods are the most widespread, even nowadays. There are only a few systems that propose dorsal hand vein recognition based on deep learning solutions. This article proposes AlexNet and VGG combined with logistic regression for this purpose [19]. A fine-tuned VGG16 network was proposed for human identification in [46]. A deep biometric hash learning framework has been proposed for palm vein, palm print or dorsal hand vein recognition [47].

To the best of our knowledge, there are only two convolutional neural network approaches for the segmentation of dorsal hand veins, due to the lack of a corresponding vein annotation database.

In [6], the authors propose a GAN network for obtaining dorsal hand vein image segmentation. The generative part is a U-Net network, and no architecture for the two discriminators is specified, only their inputs. One has input pairs of the original image x and the segmentation y, requiring $D(x,y)$ to be minimized. The other discriminator has input pairs of the original image and the generated image $G(x)$, where the $D(x,G(X))$ has to be maximized. The article says nothing about the 50 images used in the training set and the 20 images in the test set. It similarly gives no information on how they obtained the labels used in the generator network. It is probably a proprietary database with manual labeling. The results of this article are compared with our experiments.

The authors of [5] propose a modified U-Net architecture for dorsal hand vein segmentation. They describe a self-labeled, publicly unavailable database of 116 subjects and 1439 images. They obtain the labeling by hand, marking the vein part pixel by pixel. The proposed architecture uses VGGNet as the backbone for feature extraction, an attention mechanism made up of matrix multiplication and three bottleneck $1 \times 1 \times 1$ layers, as well as a U-Netup layer that combines feature outputs 4 and 5 in VGGNet. The results obtained in this article are the best in the literature so far, and they are also compared with our results.

3. Materials and Methods

3.1. The Database

The pipeline proposed in this paper is trained and evaluated on the NCUT (North China University of Technology) Part A [7] dorsal hand vein dataset. This database contains 2040 near-infrared images of dorsal hands from 102 people, with 10 samples for both hands of the subjects, aged between 18 to 29 years, of which 50 are male and 52 were female. Every image has a resolution of 640×480 pixels on an 8-bit grayscale. The images have been acquired using a CCD camera with an IR filter. The IR light can illuminate the subcutaneous region to a depth of 3 mm. The blood absorbs more IR light than the skin, which is why it appears as a darker valley compared to the skin. The vein, where it is visible, is not very distinguishable from the surrounding bio-tissue. Furthermore, the number of local features (endpoint, crossing point) is extremely limited, between 5 and 10. Even though the equipment uses an IR filter, the images are of low quality because of the circular illumination source, which introduces the so-called inhomogeneity into the images. The veins near the margins are barely observable and not visible on the images. The central part is very luminous, with the veins hardly discernible, while the margins are shaded and barely detectable. However, the total intensity range is very restrictive. From the $[0, 255]$ grayscale intensity interval, the intensity domain of the dataset only extends to between $[101, 180]$.

3.2. Automated Unsupervised Labeling

The efficiency of computer vision algorithms based on supervised methods is determined by the quality and quantity of labeled data on which an iterative learning algorithm can be trained. One of the most important tasks in machine learning is to obtain high-quality annotations, often called the ground truth (GT). Generally, the ground truth is obtained by precise manual annotation involving experts in the domain. The algorithms are usually trained, validated and tested on different disjunct parts of the same labeled dataset. Semantic segmentation is an image annotation technique that provides the correct label to each pixel of an image from the perspective of a given task. This technique requires pixel-level classification, which is a laborious task and requires the right image processing tools corroborated by expertise in the domain. Our automated labeling pipeline is shown in Figure 1 and consists of the following three steps: preprocessing, vein structure enhancement and segmentation.

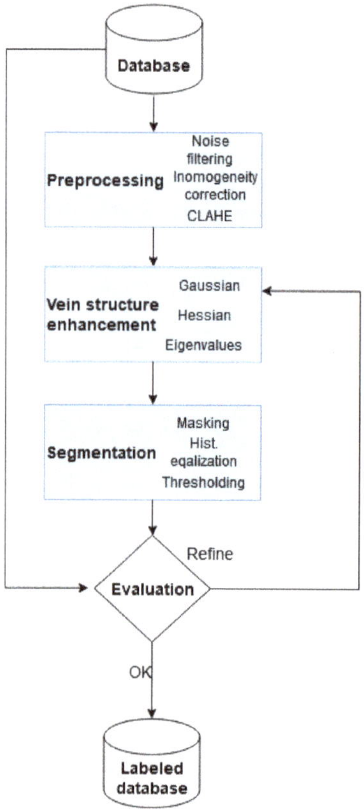

Figure 1. Automated labeling.

3.2.1. Preprocessing

An important preprocessing step in image segmentation is the correction of non-uniform illumination and the elimination of shading artifacts. The efficient removal of inhomogeneities can reveal information about veins that may be hidden due to artifacts and noise. Intensity inhomogeneity may be considered as a spatially varying function that alters image intensities expected to be constant through the image.

There are two main types of approaches applied to minimize intensity inhomogeneity, namely the prospective and retrospective methods [48]. Prospective correction adjusts the calibration and improves the image acquisition process. These types of deficiencies in the image acquisition system can be reduced by a careful and accurate hardware setup process. Retrospective methods are capable of correcting the intensity inhomogeneity that appears due to the interaction of objects and light. These correction methods mainly rely on information from the images acquired. In the image construction process, the corresponding shading effects are described by a simple linear model, assuming that intensity inhomogeneity is a smooth multiplicative or additive field that alters the real image intensities. The most widely used model is the multiplicative model with additive noise:

$$v(x) = u(x) \cdot b(x) + n(x), \tag{1}$$

where $v(x)$ is the real image, $u(x)$—homogeneous image, $b(x)$—bias image, $n(x)$—noise image.

The NCUT image database was acquired using simple hardware and without any inhomogeneity correction. The vein segmentation process requires similar images without any noise or artifacts. Illumination correction is compulsory in this case because, in this type of image, the center part is much brighter, and the illumination decreases towards the margins. We had to apply one efficient algorithm to unify the illumination.

In our work, we corrected the inhomogeneity of intensities by applying the N4 algorithm using standard settings. First, we transformed the intensity values into real numbers; next, we filtered the spike noise using a Gaussian blur with sigma 2 pixels. The correction works well when we define the region of interest (ROI). The ROI can be determined by eliminating the background pixels. The ROI is further eroded because the margin of the hand is very blurry and is in fact a transitional part. In this way, we obtained a binary mask determining the ROI, which is used during subsequent processing steps. The results of these operations are shown in Figure 2. The effect of the preprocessing steps on intensity variations are analyzed in 1D along the visualized black line shifted over the whole image. Inhomogeneity correction over the original image (Figure 2a) is shown in Figure 2b. We can assess that there is a smooth variation in intensity values, and the valleys correspond to detected veins. Unfortunately, minimum values differ from image to image, their values varying over a wide interval. The differences between peak and valley can be further amplified by applying the Contrast-Limited Adaptive Histogram Equalization algorithm (CLAHE), shown in Figure 2c.

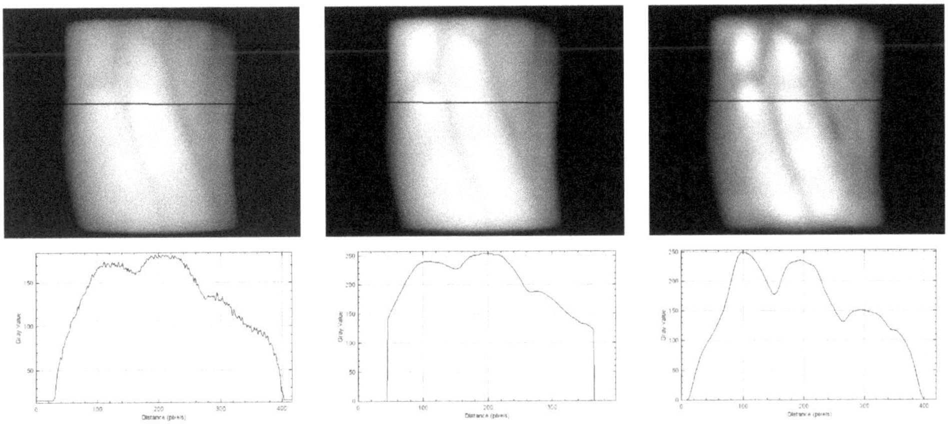

(a) (b) (c)

Figure 2. Preprocessing steps. (**a**) Original image and its profile; (**b**) inhomogeneity-corrected image and profile; (**c**) CLAHE image and corresponding profile.

3.2.2. Vein Structure Enhancement (Tubular Shape Detection)

The next step in our pipeline is to delineate the most important veins in the preprocessed images. A 2D grayscale image is considered as a surface in three-dimensional space, where the pixel intensity value is the z coordinate. The shape of veins in three dimensions is tubular and parallel to the hand plane. One of the best-known algorithms for extracting a tubular shape is the principal curvature method [49]. This method is a filtering process that detects tubular geometrical structures by evaluating the curvatures of surfaces. The local behavior of a surface can be described by the first- and second-order derivatives of intensity variations in each point of an image. The first-order derivative through the gradient vector can be interpreted as the direction of the surface. The Hessian matrix, given by the second-order derivative of the local intensity, shows the curvature structures in each point $I(\mathbf{x}) = I(x,y)$

$$\nabla^2 I(\mathbf{x}) = \begin{bmatrix} I_{xx}(\mathbf{x}) & I_{xy}(\mathbf{x}) \\ I_{yx}(\mathbf{x}) & I_{yy}(\mathbf{x}) \end{bmatrix} \quad (2)$$

where the second-order partial derivatives are $I_{xx}(\mathbf{x}) = \frac{\partial^2}{\partial x^2}I(\mathbf{x})$, $I_{xy}(\mathbf{x}) = \frac{\partial^2}{\partial x \partial y}I(\mathbf{x})$, $I_{yx}(\mathbf{x}) = \frac{\partial^2}{\partial y \partial x}I(\mathbf{x})$, $I_{yy}(\mathbf{x}) = \frac{\partial^2}{\partial y^2}I(\mathbf{x})$.

The Hessian matrix has two eigenvalues λ_1 and λ_2 and the corresponding eigenvectors v_1 and v_2. The eigenvalues λ_1 and λ_2 represent the principal curvatures along the principal directions, and v_1 and v_2 are the directions of the maximum and the minimum curvatures, respectively. Supposing $\lambda_1 > \lambda_2$, then v_1 is directed across the tubular direction, while vector v_2 is directed along the tubular direction [50].

Since vessels appear in different sizes, it is important to introduce a measurement scale that varies within a certain range. In linear scale space theory, the differentiation of a function is defined as a convolution with derivatives of Gaussians [51].

$$\frac{\partial}{\partial \mathbf{x}}L(\mathbf{x},\sigma) = \sigma^{\gamma}L(\mathbf{x}) * G(\mathbf{x},\sigma) \tag{3}$$

where γ is a normalization factor, σ is the scale of computation and $G((\mathbf{x}),\sigma)$ is the corresponding Gaussian function in D dimension and σ scale.

$$G(\mathbf{x},\sigma) = \frac{1}{\sqrt{2\pi\sigma^2}^D}e^{-\frac{\|x^2\|}{2\sigma^2}} \tag{4}$$

Namely, to obtain the partial derivatives of order n of a rescaled image $I(\mathbf{x}\sigma)$, one only has to convolve the original image $I(\mathbf{x})$ with the corresponding partial derivatives of the n-th order Gaussian $G(\mathbf{x},\sigma)$. Intuitively, the presence of a vein increases the difference between the inside and outside of the region considered. This operation is achieved by the second-order derivative of the Gaussian kernel. The σ parameter of the Gaussian is the operation scale.

In this paper, we followed this approach for vein detection. In order to segment the vein, we convolved dorsal hand images with the second-order derivative of the Gaussian kernel at various scales σ and determined the Hessian matrix of each image point. The eigenvalues λ_1 and λ_2 of the Hessian represent the principal curvatures along the principal directions, and v_1 and v_2 are the directions of maximum and minimum curvatures, respectively. Supposing $\lambda_1 > \lambda_2$, then v_1 is directed across the tubular direction and vector v_2 is directed along the tubular direction [50]. The image created using the larger eigenvalues λ_1 of the Hessian matrix shows the tubular structures of the image at σ scale. We proposed to segment only the significantly visible veins of a certain width. The σ scale used is determined experimentally by analyzing the images obtained at different scales in the range of $\sigma = 2$–12, shown in Figure 3.

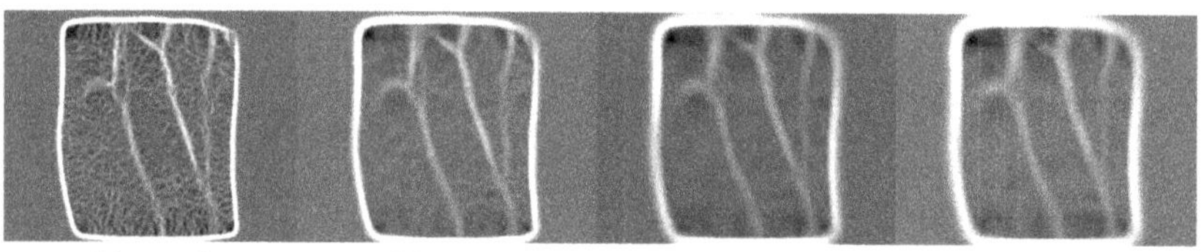

(a) $\sigma = 2$ **(b)** $\sigma = 6$ **(c)** $\sigma = 8$ **(d)** $\sigma = 12$

Figure 3. Hessian images of the veins at different scales.

In each image, the veins can be distinguished, but the most realistic image is obtained for a scale of $\sigma = 8$. The image contour is also a tubular structure, which must be removed for the next processing step. The contour is eliminated using the mask image obtained in the previous preprocessing step.

3.2.3. Image Segmentation

Analyzing the previously obtained image, it is obvious that a simple threshold is suitable for extracting the veins. A thresholding level for all the images in the database cannot be adequate because the veins have different intensities over all the images. We had to choose between several auto-thresholding methods. We determined that the threshold level based on maximum entropy can be one of the most efficient methods for vein segmentation in this particular image processing pipeline. The images resulting from previous steps are histogram-equalized, masked and automatically binarized with the maximum entropy threshold level. Figure 4 shows the 3 steps of image segmentation.

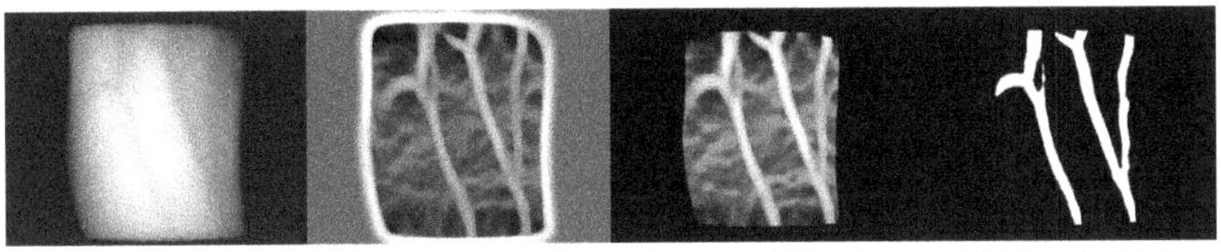

(**a**) Orig. (**b**) Hessian hist. eq. (**c**) Masked Hessian (**d**) Thresholded

Figure 4. Image segmentation steps.

The final binarized image is the label obtained during this automated image processing pipeline. All the parameters of the image processing procedure proposed are chosen after rigorous visual evaluation of the images obtained at each step. The annotation process presented is based on our expertise and knowledge in the domain of image processing. To improve segmentation, multiple annotators should be used and the results should be cross-checked, thereby eliminating mistakes and inaccuracies. In addition, more annotators may improve the quality and accuracy of image segmentation. Our idea is to replace the increased number of annotators with different probabilistic classifiers based on CNNs being tuned in different ways.

3.3. Adapted Convolutional Neural Networks for Vein Segmentation

Deep learning-based semantic segmentation has been gaining more and more importance in recent years, relegating traditional image processing methods and supervised machine learning algorithms to the background. The convolutional neural networks used for semantic segmentation were developed from the CNNs for image classification, object detection with bounding box delimitation and region proposal networks. Out of these applications and the networks, created especially for the ImageNet Challenge [52], several architectures have been developed for pixelwise image segmentation. Overall, we have studied the following best-known VGG [53] and ResNet [54] feature encoder networks originally used for object classification. In our experiments, we have made use of pretrained weights from these networks and initialized the fully convolutional encoder–decoder networks (FCN [55] and U-Nets [23]) with these weights. After applying transfer learning in the encoder with convolutions and downsampling, we applied the same symmetrical deconvolutions or upsampling in the decoder part. We studied and adapted the following CNNs for dorsal hand vein segmentation: adapted and tuned variants of U-Net, VGGU-Net, FCN32, FCN8, ResNet–UNet, U-Net++ and U-Net3+.

3.3.1. U-Net

This U-shaped network was first introduced in [23] and is most often used for medical image segmentation. The total number of convolutional layers is 23. Here, the input image is grayscale and not RGB. The original article considers 5 different layer sizes (each being half of the previous size) for the encoder, doubling from the current layer to the next in the decoder. For each size, there are two convolutional layers, each using convolutional filters of 3×3 and a ReLU activation function. The original input size is $572 \times 572 \times 1$ pixels ($W \times H \times D$). In the original U-Net [23], the input and output layer sizes are not fitted. The input image size is 572×572 pixels, but the output is only 388×388 pixels. This means an area reduction of over 54%. The feature-level output sizes on the 5 encoder stages are 572×572, 280×280, 136×136, 64×64 and 28×28. Each of these stages contains two conv. layers of the same size. However, their depth doubles from one stage to the next. The depths of the subsequent conv. layers are 64, 64; 128, 128; 256, 256; 512, 512, and the greatest depth of 1024, 1024 is attained on the smallest size of 28×28. The issue with the original U-Net is the unfitted encoder–decoder layers on each stage. The decoder layer sizes are 56×56, 104×104, 200×200 and 392×392. These differences come from the application of a 3×3 kernel size and a stride of 1. To be able to join the output of the corresponding stage of the encoder to the input of the same stage of the decoder, a crop and copy operation is needed. Thus, 64×64 is cropped and joined to a 56×56 layer, and in the same way, 136×136 to 104×104; 280×280 to 200×200 and finally 568×568 to 392×392. This cropping represents a 23%, 41%, 49% and 52% loss of information due to area cropping. To maintain the input–output sizes in each stage, a filter size of 3×3 is used in our case, with a stride of 1 and the zero-padding also set to 1. This setup will maintain the dimensions (before and after every convolution layer), leading to the concatenation of same-sized layers in the encoder to the corresponding layer in the decoder. Respecting these adjustments, for an input of $W \times H$, the same $W \times H$ output can be obtained by our implementation. The 6-stage layer setup in our implementation has an input of $W \times H = 640 \times 480$ pixels. Stage 1 consists of two conv. layers of $640 \times 480 \times 64$, followed by a 2×2 max-pooling for halving the dimension. Stage 2 has a size of $W/2 \times H/2$, with one conv. layer of depth 64. Stage 3 is $W/4 \times H/4$, and the four consecutive convolutions are of depth 64. Stage 4 has a dimension of $W/8 \times H/8$ and all 4 conv. layers are of depth 128. Stage 5 has 4 conv. layers of depth 256. The very last stage in our case is 20×15 pixels with 2 conv. layer depths of 512 and 512. The decoder part has the corresponding structure, but, instead of convolution layers, we use transpose convolutions to double the size of the previous stage. In this way, the cropping operation of the original U-Net becomes useless because the concatenation joins layers of the same size every time. Figure 5 presents the layers in our case.

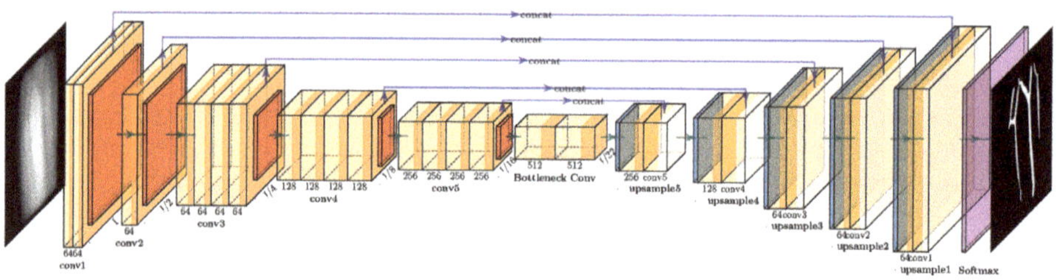

Figure 5. U-Net for vein segmentation. Orange layer is convolution layer, red is max-pooling, blue is upconvolution and purple is softmax.

3.3.2. VGG–UNet

The VGG was the best architecture at the ImageNet Challenge in 2014, invented by Oxford's Visual Geometry Group [53]. The most important idea in this simple linear network, containing the usual building blocks of CNNs, is the use of 3×3 convolutional filters in each layer. They use two or three stacked convolutional layers for every stage. The stages are considered layers of the same size. A transition from one stage to the next is a downsampling by a factor of 2, obtained by max-pooling. The first 13 layers are the encoder part. This is made up of two conv. layers with a depth of 64 on the original size. The next two conv. layers consider the input in half size both in height and width and double the depth to 128. The next three layers on $1/4$, $1/8$ and $1/16$ of the original dimension are made up of 3 stacked conv. layers, each having a depth of 256, 512 and 512, respectively. Each conv. layer is batch-normalized and their outputs are passed though ReLU activation functions. After the activation function, the spatial resolution is preserved, which means that the stride is 1 and the zero-padding is also 1. The decrease to half from one layer to the next is obtained by 4 max-pooling layers, each having a 2×2 kernel and a stride of 2. After the last conv. layer comes another (the 5th) max-pooling. Thus, the dimension of the last encoding layer is $1/16$. The decoder part is obtained with symmetrical transpose convolution layers of depth 512, 256, 128 and 64. In our approach, we used the encoder part of the VGG and created the decoder in the same manner as U-Net does. The proposed VGG-UNet used in our experiments is shown in Figure 6.

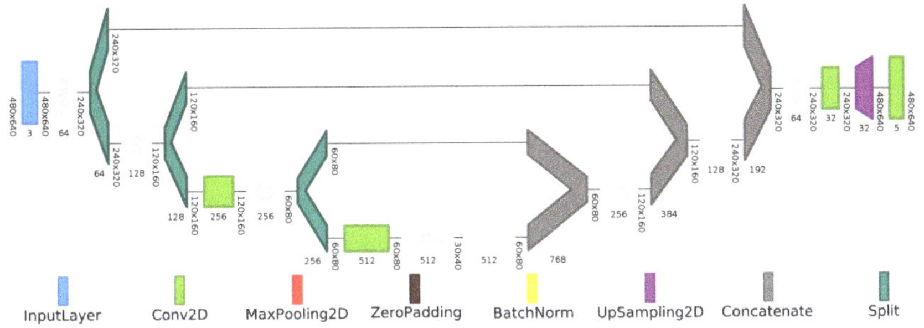

Figure 6. VGG–UNet for vein segmentation.

3.3.3. Fully Convolutional Network

FCN [55] is a fully convolutional network that uses the VGG-16 network in the encoder part. The first 13 layers remain the same in VGG-16. Instead of being fully connected (FC), they were converted to fully convolutional layers. The upsampling part is done using deconvolution layers. There are three different versions of upsampling according to the measure of upsampling (FCN32, FCN16 and FCN8). After 5 max-pooling layers of VGG-16, the last conv. layer size is $W/2^5 \times H/2^5$, where W and H are the input image width and height. Therefore, to increase this $1/2^5$ size back to the original size, the transposed convolution layer must have a stride of 32 (FCN32). This abrupt upsampling is not very successful. The edges of the segmentation result are blurred and rough. The second FCN16 version tries to correct this error in one step. This means that the output combines the partial outputs of the $1/16$ sized layer (after the 4th max-pooling) and the $1/32$ sized layer. This sum is only possible if the dimensions of these two layers are brought to the same size. Accordingly, the $1/32$ sized layer is first upsampled by 2, which results in a dimension of $1/16W \times 1/16H$, which is the same size as the output of the $1/16$ sized layer. The next step is the upsampling of this sum of two layers 16 times to obtain the original $W \times H$ image. However, the best result out of these three FCN versions is obtained using FCN8, which combines the partial output of the last layer ($1/32$), the penultimate ($1/16$) and the one before it ($1/8$). Thus, to bring all of them to the same size, the $1/32$ layer is upsampled 4 times, the $1/16$ twice and the $1/8$ is left unchanged. The sum of these three layers is then upsampled 8 times to obtain the original image. The upsampling is obtained each time using transpose convolution with a stride of f, where f is the upsample rate. Figure 7 shows the layers in our case.

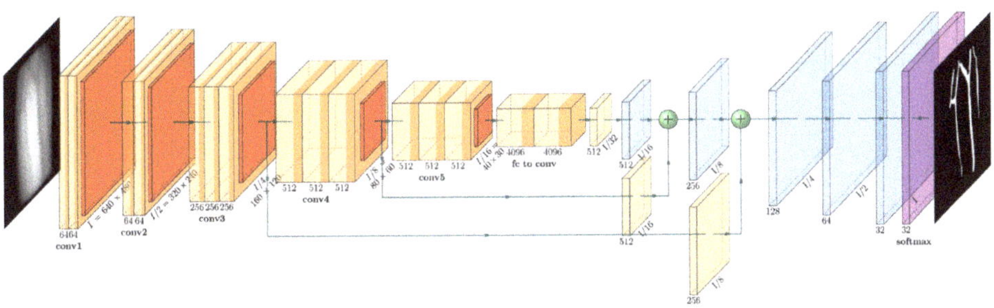

Figure 7. Fully convolutional network (FCN8) for vein segmentation. Orange layer is convolution layer, red is max-pooling, blue is upconvolution and purple is softmax.

3.3.4. ResNet–UNet

ResNet networks were introduced in [54]. The authors solved the problem of very deep networks, namely 16 and 30 convolutional layers. The more layers that were added in a deep neural network, the worse its performance and accuracy became. This happened owing to the vanishing or exploding gradient problem, which led to a non-convergent CNN network, and the increasing number of layers made the training process more difficult to optimize. They addressed this problem by introducing the deep residual building block. This block only learns the residual between the input and output using a so-called residual block $R(x) = Out(x) - x$, where x is the input of the residual block and $Out(x)$ is its output. In other words, $Out(x) = R(x) + x$. Thus, instead of optimizing the input–output mapping with convolutional layers, they use a bypass connection and the identity is mapped directly to the output, which means that only the difference (residual) between the input and output is optimized and estimated by 2 or 3 stacked convolutional layers. In this way, the limit of 16 layers is surpassed and they introduce very deep networks with 18, 34, 50, 101 and 152 conv. layers. Every conv. layer is batch-normalized and undergoes ReLU activation.

Our experiments for vein segmentation used the ResNet50 architecture, which considers 5 different sizes, each being half the size of the previous. Input size is $640 \times 480 \times 1$ pixels. The first conv. layer uses a kernel of 7×7 with depth 64, stride 2 and padding 3, resulting in an output size of 320×240. This is followed by a max-pooling layer of stride 2 and padding 1, meaning an output size of 160×120. For this size, there are two residual blocks, each containing $2 - 2$ conv. layers with 3×3 filters and a depth of 64. Here, the depth of all four layers is 64, while the output size is 160×120. These 4-layered residual blocks are repeated three more times (four times in total), obtaining an output of 80×60 and a depth of 128 for the second residual block (RB2), followed by the third RB3 with an output of 40×30 and a depth of 256, and the last RB4 with a 20×15 output and a depth of 512. In our ResNet–UNet, the encoder part was previously described as ResNet50. The decoder is symmetrical, containing transpose convolutions and concatenation in a U-Net-like manner. Figure 8 presents the layers in our case. We created Figures 6 and 8 using the Net2Viz [56] platform.

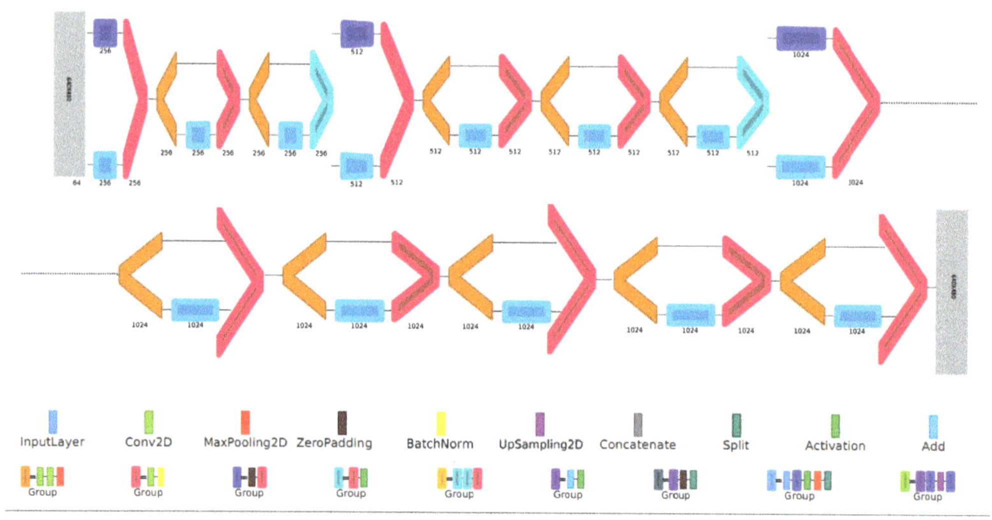

Figure 8. ResNet–UNet for vein segmentation.

3.3.5. U-Net++

U-Net++ [57] is a variant of the U-Net encoder–decoder architecture, but it uses full-scale skip connections. These have the advantage of combining low-level details of early layers with high-level features of deeper layers, aggregating feature maps at different scales. This type of skip connection corrects the disadvantage of U-Net—namely, obtaining only an approximate boundary segmentation because of the encoder–decoder down- and upsampling, respectively. In this case, the boundary of the segmented region becomes clearer. The details are obtained based on the interconnection between the encoder and decoder as in the simple U-Net, but there are also intra-connections between decoders. The architecture of U-Net++ can be seen as a right upper triangular architecture where the main diagonal elements are the encoder layers and the second, third, fourth and fifth diagonals are upconvolution layers, similar to those in U-Net.

In our case, the input layer is of size $(640, 480, 1)$ and the encoding layers are convolutional layers of filter size 3×3 with padding and stride 1. The layers of the encoder are: $Enc_{00}(640, 480, 64)$, $Enc_{10}(320, 240, 128)$, $Enc_{20}(160, 120, 256)$, $Enc_{30}(80, 60, 512)$ and $Enc_{40}(40, 30, 1024)$. The triplets represent the $width \times height \times depth$ of feature maps. Between each of these layers, there is a maxpool layer. The intermediate layers Int are transpose convolutions in our case, with kernel size = 4, padding and stride = 1. The second main diagonal is $Int_{01}(640, 480, Enc_{00} + upconv(Enc_{10}))$, $Int_{11}(320, 240, conv_{10} + upconv(Enc_{20}))$, $Int_{21}(160, 120, Enc_{20} + upconv(Enc_{30}))$, $Dec_{31}(80, 60, Enc_{30} + upconv(Enc_{40}))$. The third main diagonal is $Int_{02}(640, 480, Enc_{00} + Int_{01} + upconv(Int_{11}))$, $Int_{12}(320, 240, Enc_{10} + Int_{11} + upconv(Int_{21}))$, $Dec_{22}(160, 120, Enc_{20} + Int_{21} + upconv(Int_{31}))$, the fourth diagonal is $Int_{03}(640, 480, Enc_{00} + Int_{01} + Int_{02} + upconv(Int_{12}))$, $Dec_{13}(320, 240, Enc_{10} + Int_{11} + Int_{12} + upconv(Dec_{22}))$, and the last diagonal is $Dec_{04}(640, 480, Enc_{00} + Int_{01} + Int_{02} + Int_{03} + upconv(Dec_{12}))$. The final decision layer is the responses of Int_{01}, Int_{02}, Int_{03}, Dec_{04}, each sent through a separate convolutional layer of depth 64. The final decision map is divided by 4 in order to obtain a mean value as a response; see Figure 9.

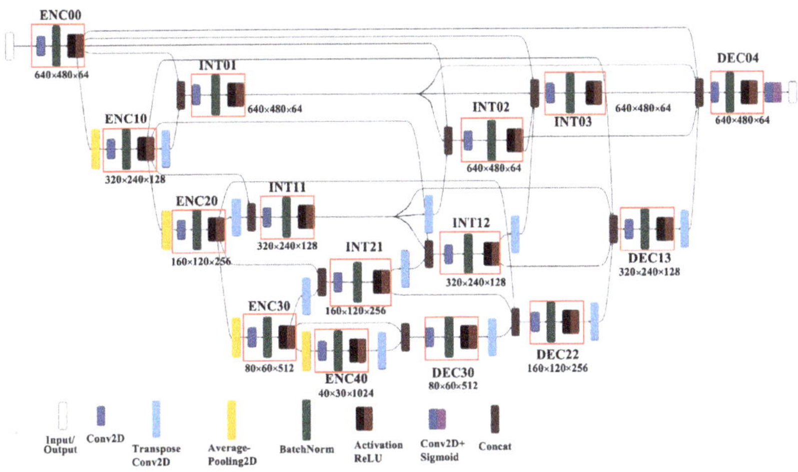

Figure 9. Our implementation of U-Net++.

3.3.6. U-Net3+

U-Net3+ [58] is a redesign of U-Net++ that combines all the smaller and same-sized feature maps of previous layers into the encoder, and all larger feature maps into the decoder. Here, the intermediate layers are eliminated, but there are more direct skip connections, meaning one from every encoder to every equal or smaller decoder. The $1\times$, $2\times$, $4\times$ or $8\times$ downsampling is solved using a corresponding maxpool layer and of course a convolution layer, batch-norm layers for regularization and ReLU as the activation function. The encoding layers are the same as in U-Net++, while the computation of the decoding layers is different, reducing the number of parameters drastically. Figure 10 shows the architecture of U-Net3+. The DEC_{31} is obtained from 4 feature maps $DEC_{31}(80, 60, upconv(DEC_{40} = ENC_{40}) + ENC_{30} + pool_{2\times 2}conv(ENC_{20}) +$

$pool_{4\times4} + conv(ENC_{10}) + pool_{8\times8}conv(ENC_{00}))$. The general formula for computing the decoder part is:

$$DEC_{ij}\left(W/2^i, H/2^i, \sum_{k=i+1}^{4}(upconv(DEC_{k0})) + ENC_{i0} + \sum_{p=0}^{i-1}(pool_{2^{i-p}\times2^{i-p}}conv(ENC_{p0}))\right) \tag{5}$$

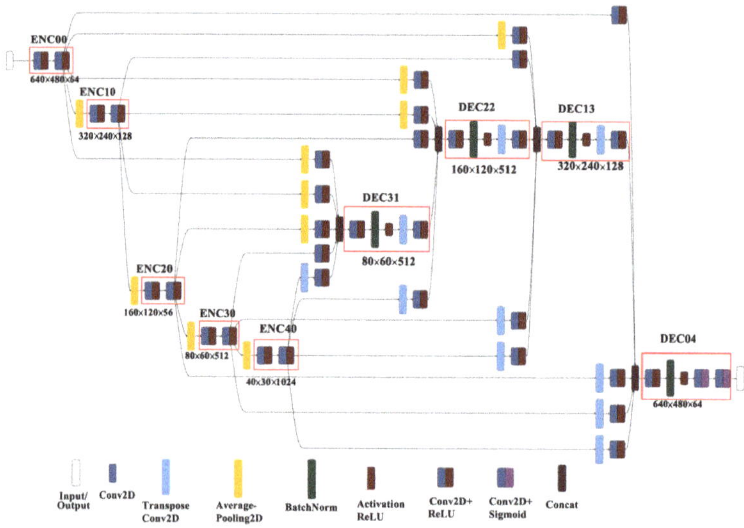

Figure 10. Our implementation of U-Net3+.

In this case, the only layer used for computing the loss is DEC_{04}, which is fed into a convolution layer obtaining an output feature map of $(640, 480, numclass)$. Finally, the softmax converts the feature map into a probability map. This probability map and the one-hot-encoded label image are compared using different types of loss functions and optimization algorithms during the training process. The weights of the CNNs presented are iteratively corrected using the training loss with different optimization algorithms, applying a backpropagation algorithm.

3.3.7. Loss Functions

In this section, we describe in detail the different types of loss functions used in our experiments. The cross-entropy or joint entropy of two discrete probability distributions p and q of a given random variable is:

$$H(p,q) = -\frac{1}{n}\sum_{i=1}^{n} p(x_i)log(q(x_i)) \tag{6}$$

This is in fact the number of additional bits to represent an event using q instead of p. For classification, $p(x_i)$ is the target value y_i and $q(x_i)$ is the predicted value $\hat{y}_i$. For binary cross-entropy, we have two classes and a random variable, which takes a value of 1 ($\hat{y}_i$) with probability y_i and the value of 0 ($1 - \hat{y}_i$) with probability $1 - y_i$. The binary cross-entropy weighted by the coefficient β is:

$$L_{BCE} = -\frac{1}{n}\sum_{i=1}^{n}(\beta y_i \log \hat{y}_i + (1-\beta)(1-y_i)\log(1-\hat{y}_i)), \tag{7}$$

where $\beta = 1 - \frac{y}{W \times H}$ If β is subunitary, false positives are reduced; if supraunitary, false negatives are reduced.

The Dice coefficient, or Dice–Sørensen coefficient, is a common metric for pixel segmentation that can also be modified to act as a loss function:

$$L_{Dice_c} = \sum\nolimits_{c \in Class} (1 - DSC_c) \tag{8}$$

The DSC_c denotes the Dice score from the perspective of a given class c. The Sørensen index equals twice the number of elements common to both sets divided by the sum of the number of elements in each set.

$$DSC = \frac{2|X \cap Y|}{|X| + |Y|}, \tag{9}$$

where $|\cdot|$ is the cardinality of the set (namely, the number of elements in each set); in binary case, it can be expressed as:

$$DSC = \frac{2y\hat{y}}{y + \hat{y} + \epsilon} \tag{10}$$

In practice, a smoothing score ϵ is introduced in the nominator to avoid division by 0. It measures the similarity of 2 overlapping areas and is similar to IoU or the Jaccard coefficient:

$$J = \frac{|X \cap Y|}{|X \cup Y|} = \frac{DSC}{2 - DSC} \tag{11}$$

The focal loss is a modification of the L_{BCE}, where a modulating factor is added to the power of γ; γ is a focusing factor and it means that well-classified examples are downweighted:

$$L_{Focal} = -\frac{1}{n}\sum_{i=1}^{n} \left(y_i(1 - \hat{y}_i)^{\gamma} \log \hat{y}_i + (1 - y_i)\hat{y}_i^{\gamma} \log(1 - \hat{y}_i)\right) \tag{12}$$

If an example is misclassified, the $(1 - \hat{y}_i)^{\gamma}$ factor is almost 1, and if an example is well classified, the factor tends towards 0. Thus, well-classified examples play a minor role in the total loss. In our experiment, the $\gamma = 2$. This type of loss yielded better convergence of the CNNs and reached the same accuracy values and Dice score on the vein in fewer epochs.

4. Experiments and Results

In this work, we propose to create a fully automated system for dorsal hand vein segmentation for NIR images. The main contribution of this paper is the boosting of the labels obtained using geometry-based image processing methods and correcting them via multiple U-Net networks. The boosted labels facilitate better segmentation via CNN training. The novelty of this paper is a two-stage CNN-based segmentation. First, multiple networks were trained on labels obtained without supervision. In this step, we have chosen the U-Net, U-Net++ and U-Net3+ networks with different loss types to reevaluate labels and decide on new labels. Secondly, the ResNet–UNet network was chosen to be trained on both labels. The more accurate Dice scores demonstrate the relevancy of boosting the labels. The method presented is useful, especially in the absence of precisely annotated ground truth labels made by experts. However, the pixelwise annotation of medical data, particularly vein images, is very tiresome and requires accurate pixelwise annotation from expert physicians.

The pipeline (Figure 11) of our boosted segmentation method is as follows.

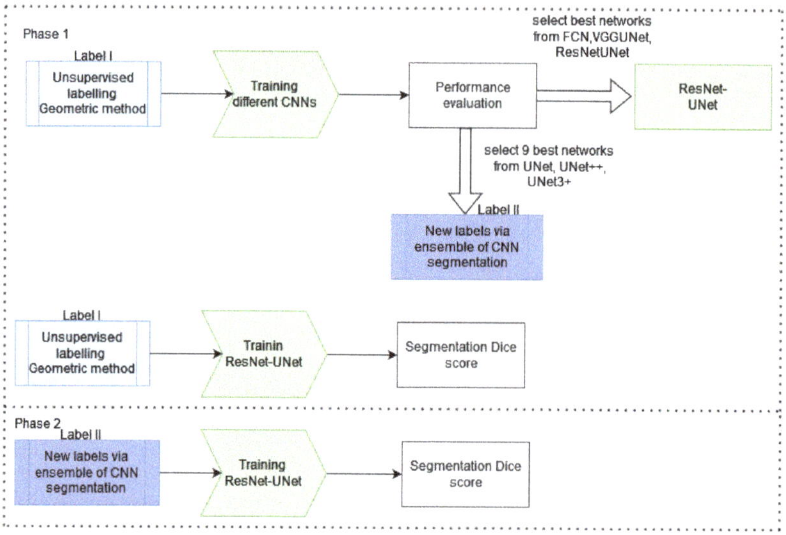

Figure 11. Pipeline for the system.

Phase 1 (upper part of our pipeline) represents the training and evaluation of different types of segmentation networks to determine which is best suited for vein segmentation. The segmentation performance of the networks studied is evaluated and measured, comparing them to the labeled images described in Section 3.2. These labels are denoted Label I.

In phase 2, the labels obtained before are boosted using an experimentally defined group of networks that proves to be sufficiently accurate and has a more complex architecture with better generalization properties. The segmentation thus obtained is named Label II. The best networks not included in the creation of Label II are trained for these more accurate labels, and their segmentation performance is measured and compared to the same networks, but trained on Label I instead.

In our experiments, the original training dataset from NCUT [7] was augmented using well-known augmentation steps. From every image, we generated 10 other augmented images, applying a random scale between 80 and 120%, a crop and padding to the original size, a translation of 5–10%, horizontal and vertical flipping with a probability of 50% and 20%, respectively, a rotation of $\pm 45^\circ$ and shearing of $\pm 10^\circ$. Each image was augmented using different and randomly selected methods. In this way, we obtained a total of $10 \times 2040 = 20{,}400$ vein images.

The datasets obtained in this manner were split into training, validation and test sets in a proportion of 60%, 20% and 20%. We tried both two-class segmentation considering vein and background and three-class segmentation, taking into account vein, hand and background separately, motivated by the different grayscale levels of hand and background. The hand is usually light gray and the background black or masked into black. For both two-class and three-class segmentation, we computed the masks for all the images and annotations. The masking process was described in detail in Section 3.2. Figure 12 shows a sequence of the augmented original images and their pairs of augmented segmentations.

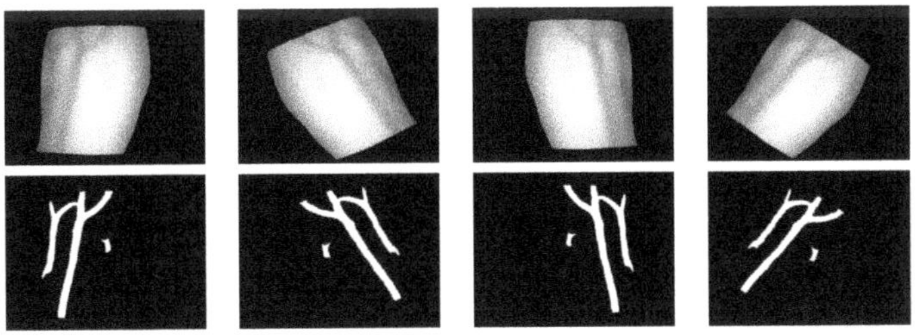

Figure 12. Different augmented images of the original image (**first column**), augmented images (**first row**) and corresponding labels (**second row**).

During our experiments, we compared different variants of segmentation networks fine-tuned and adapted for dorsal hand vein segmentation. The role of creating different types of segmentation architectures was to determine the architecture and hyperparameters of the networks that are suitable for vein segmentation. All these networks were trained on the labels annotated with no supervision (Label I) and proved to have a high capacity for generalization. The first set of networks that were trained were VGG–UNet, FCN32, FCN8 and the ResNet–UNet architectures. Out of these architectures, we determined the most suitable network for our purpose of vein segmentation. The second set of networks that were trained were U-Net, U-Net++ and U-Net3+. The role of these networks was to build an ensemble segmentor.

The components of a single CNN training process are shown in Figure 13.

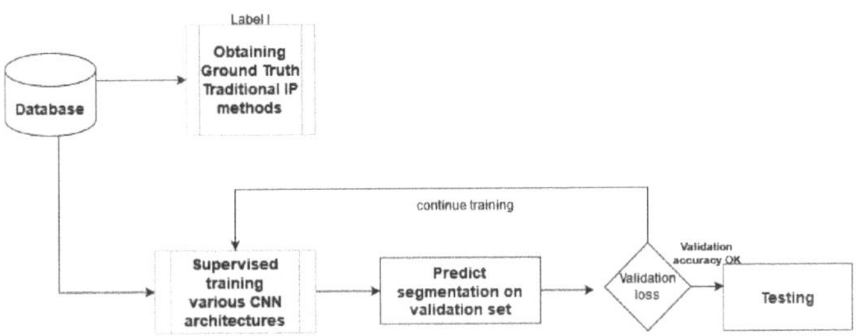

Figure 13. Training process of a single CNN.

Our first group of experiments compared four CNN networks adapted and trained for vein segmentation: FCN32, FCN8, VGG–UNet and ResNet–UNet. All four architectures were trained on the NCUT augmented dataset, with 12,240 images in the training set, 4080 images in the validation and 4080 images in the test set, respectively. The training process ran for 100 epochs, with a batch size of 16. The optimization algorithm was Adadelta, set to an initial learning rate of 0.1 and a decay rate of 0.95. Adadelta is an extended and more robust version of Adagrad. Instead of considering all past gradients, it considers the moving average of the previous gradients. In this way, it adapts its learning rate by considering a fixed-size moving window. With this type of optimization, Adadelta continues to learn, even after many update steps in iterations and epochs. The networks were optimized on the weighted DSC loss with a weight of 93/100 for the vein pixels 7/100 for the background pixels.

The Dice similarity score (DSC) measures the overlap similarity between the result and the target label. In our case, it measures the similarity between the segmentation obtained via CNN supervised learning and the unsupervised labels. The DSC is computed in every epoch and for each of the 765 iterations per epoch. It is computed for every image in the 16-sized batch:

$$DSC_I = \frac{2|CNNSeg_I \cap Label_I|}{|CNNSeg_I| + |Label_I|} \tag{13}$$

The Dice loss is computed from the mean Dice score (Equation (8)), and the mean Dice score is the mean over all images.

$$mDSC = \sum_{I \in Images} DSC_I \tag{14}$$

The Dice loss is $L_{DSC} = 1 - mDSC$. We have trained one of the networks studied both on weighted and unweighted Dice loss. The introduction of weights into the loss computation improves the training process considerably. The role of minimizing the CNN architecture on the weighted Dice loss is to balance the quite unbalanced NCUT dataset. On average, the total number of vein points was 6.8% of the image. This consideration led to us introducing a weight of 93/100 for vein pixels and 7/100 for the background (skin and black background pixels in total).

In the case of weighted Dice loss, the formula can be written as:

$$wmDSC = \sum\nolimits_{I \in Images} \frac{2\sum_{c \in Cl=\{0,1\}} weight_c|CNNSeg_I \cap Label_I|}{\sum_{c \in Cl=\{0,1\}} weight_c(|CNNSeg_I| + |Label_I|)} \tag{15}$$

Figure 14 and Table 1 show the accuracy of ResNet–UNet trained with unweighted and weighted Dice loss. It is clear that the unweighted loss performs 4–5% worse. The results only refer to the test set.

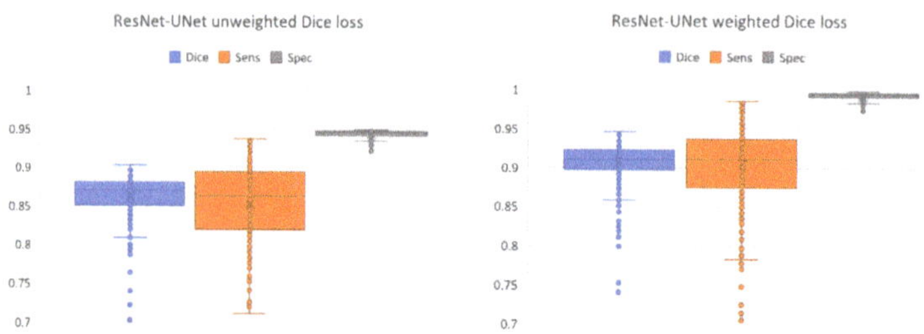

Figure 14. Comparison of ResNet–UNet network trained with unweighted Dice loss and weighted Dice loss.

Table 1. Results of the ResNet–UNet trained with unweighted and weighted Dice loss.

	ResNet–UNet Unweighted Loss			ResNet–UNet Weighted Loss		
	Dice	**Sens**	**Spec**	**Dice**	**Sens**	**Spec**
Max	0.9032	0.9382	0.9497	0.9472	0.9864	0.9994
Q3	0.8811	0.8946	0.9479	0.9233	0.9379	0.997
Mean	0.8631	0.8523	0.9449	0.9065	0.9046	0.9937
Q1	0.8512	0.8204	0.9429	0.8977	0.8753	0.9917
Min	0.7032	0.6076	0.9228	0.7413	0.7058	0.9749
Std	0.0274	0.0543	0.0043	0.0268	0.0487	0.0045

After setting the most suitable hyperparameters for all the networks, the four segmentor networks that were compared were the FCN32, FCN8, VGG–UNet and ResNet–UNet, all with weighted Dice loss. Figure 15 illustrates the training process. As can be seen, FCN8 and FCN32 are slightly worse in training than VGG–UNet and ResNet–UNet. The training and validation accuracies for all four networks are presented in Table 2 and Figures 15 and 16.

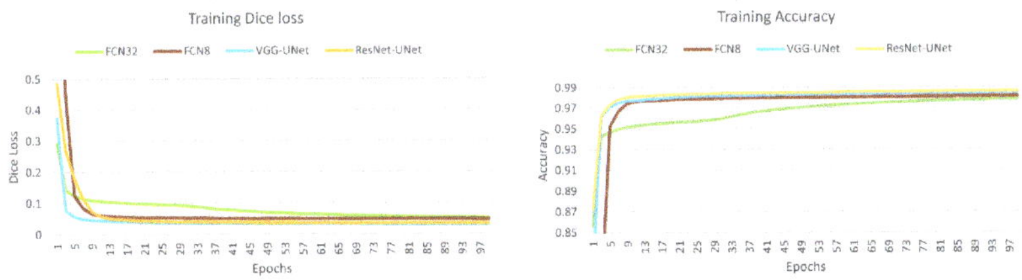

Figure 15. Loss and accuracy of FCN32, FCN8, VGG–UNet and ResNet–UNet networks in training.

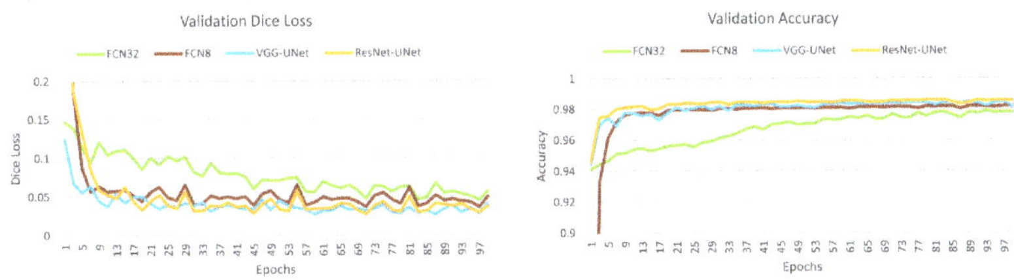

Figure 16. Loss and accuracy of FCN32, FCN8, VGG–UNet and ResNet–UNet networks in validation.

Table 2. Accuracy of networks FCN32, FCN8 and VGG–UNet in training and validation.

Epoch	acc. FCN32	val_acc. FCN32	acc. FCN8	val_acc. FCN8	acc. VGG–UNet	val_acc. VGG–UNet	acc. Res–UNet	val_acc. Res–UNet
1	0.8560	0.9413	0.5753	0.6723	0.8128	0.9450	0.8736	0.9461
10	0.9516	0.9516	0.9740	0.9762	0.9768	0.9779	0.9807	0.9810
20	0.9558	0.9561	0.9781	0.9790	0.9799	0.9774	0.9831	0.9832
30	0.9585	0.9592	0.9791	0.9793	0.9817	0.9797	0.9840	0.9842
40	0.9659	0.9685	0.9797	0.9804	0.9824	0.9818	0.9847	0.9844
50	0.9703	0.9699	0.9801	0.9807	0.9830	0.9821	0.9851	0.9850
60	0.9732	0.9731	0.9804	0.9809	0.9836	0.9840	0.9854	0.9851
70	0.9751	0.9738	0.9806	0.9809	0.9839	0.9837	0.9857	0.9847
80	0.9766	0.9753	0.9807	0.9814	0.9843	0.9843	0.9859	0.9856
90	0.9777	0.9778	0.9809	0.9817	0.9847	0.9845	0.9861	0.9841
100	0.9786	0.9778	0.9813	0.9819	0.9850	0.9814	0.9863	0.9852

We compared not only the losses during the training and validation processes, but the segmentation performance of these four networks as well, which we deemed the most important. We can draw the following conclusions based on the Dice scores, sensitivities and specificities measured on the test tests: FCN32 is the worst network in this case, with a Dice score of only 0.8024, followed by FCN8 (Dice = 0.8271) and VGG–UNet (0.8594). The best segmentor network out of the four shown is ResNet–UNet (Dice = 0.9065). We measured the Dice score, sensitivity (TPR = true positive rate) and specificity (TNR = true negative rate) for our segmentations for further comparison (Table 3 and Figure 17).

Table 3. Performance measures of FCN32, FCN8 and VGG–UNet.

	FCN32			FCN8			VGG–UNet		
	Dice	Sens	Spec	Dice	Sens	Spec	Dice	Sens	Spec
Max	0.8748	0.9728	0.9741	0.8698	0.9307	0.9593	0.9071	0.9598	0.9647
Q3	0.8379	0.8611	0.9719	0.8466	0.8725	0.9552	0.8850	0.9202	0.9622
Mean	0.8024	0.789	0.9523	0.8271	0.8373	0.9516	0.8594	0.8677	0.9569
Q1	0.7785	0.7257	0.9506	0.8150	0.8077	0.9486	0.8493	0.8328	0.9539
Min	0.5869	0.4611	0.7219	0.6674	0.6701	0.9256	0.6367	0.6078	0.9167
Std	0.0498	0.0989	0.0364	0.0300	0.0483	0.0052	0.039	0.0655	0.0074

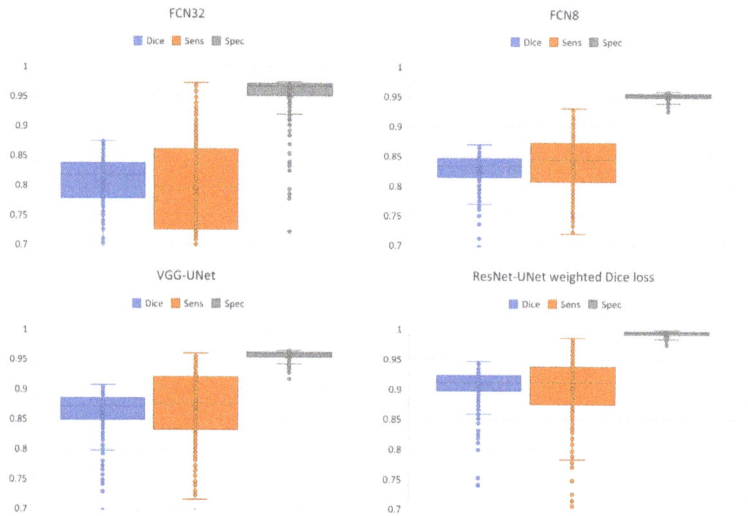

Figure 17. Boxplot comparison of FCN32, FCN8, VGG–UNet and ResNet–UNet.

Figure 18 shows a segmentation result from these four networks.

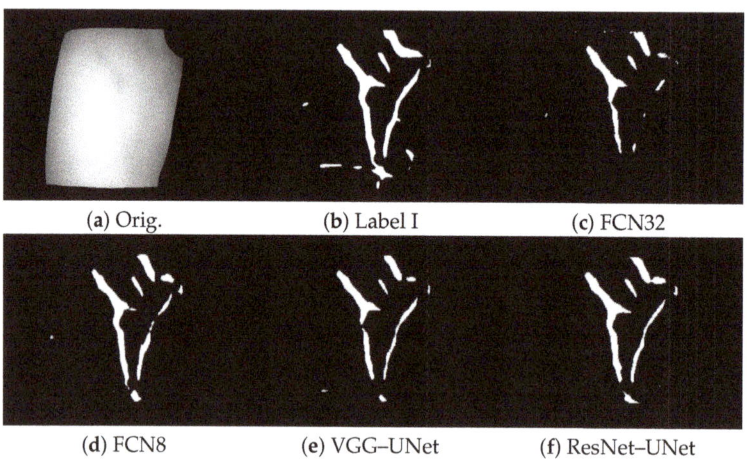

Figure 18. Segmentation results of the networks trained.

Based on the segmentation results and training time, we decided to continue our experiments with the best network obtained only, namely ResNet–UNet, having the best Dice score of 0.9065.

By analyzing the segmentation results visually, we observed that the best networks detected supplementary veins or connected discontinuous regions by joining them, or even eliminated incorrect patches considered noise in Label I. We drew the conclusion that Label I obtained without supervision should be over-evaluated via training some other good networks and computing their ensemble response. In this second group of experiments, we considered three different CNN architectures (U-Net, U-Net++, U-Net3+) not used in the first experiment, and for each one, three different loss functions (BCE loss, Dice loss and focal loss) were computed in the optimization phase.

Figure 19 shows an example of the segmentation obtained by the three network architectures with Dice loss.

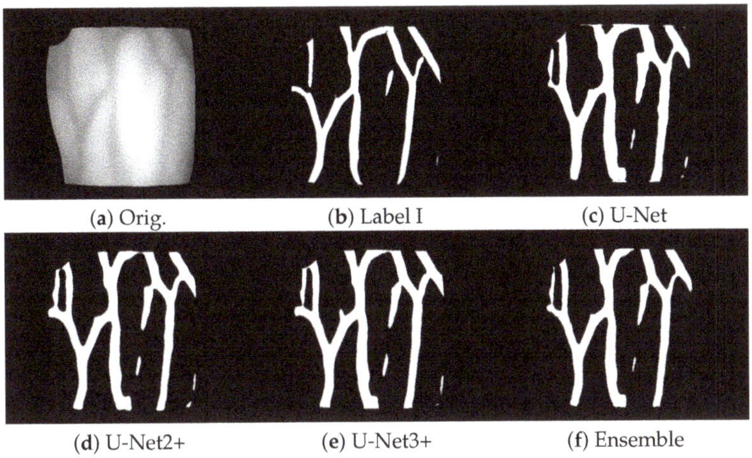

Figure 19. Visual comparison of U-Net, U-Net++ and U-Net3+ with Dice loss.

We have chosen these architectures for relabeling because they are even more complex than the FCN or VGG–UNet networks. U-Net++ and U-Net3+ have a greater capacity for generalization and similar performance on Label I compared to ResNet–UNet. The advantage of these architectures, selected to obtain the ensemble network, is the multiple interconnectivity between layers to consider more complex feature maps at each stage, leading to accurate segmentation.

In this way, we have created nine differently trained architectures. The segmentation responses from these networks were used to create the ensemble. The final response of the ensemble is considered as the new labeling of veins (Label II).

The hyperparameters of the U-Net, U-Net++ and U-Net3+ architectures are: a learning rate of 0.001, the Adadelta optimizer, 100 epochs and different losses—BCE, Dice or focal losses. For the focal loss, the learning rate had to be changed to 0.0002. The batch size is 8 for U-Net, 4 for U-Net++ and 2 for U-Net3+.

The comparison of the different loss functions can be seen in Figure 20, showing the Dice scores, sensitivity and specificity of every network from each of the nine architectures. The last box gives the performance of the ensemble network.

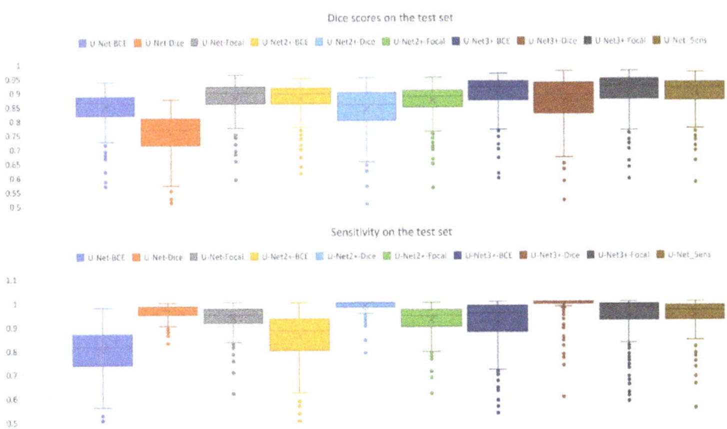

Figure 20. *Cont.*

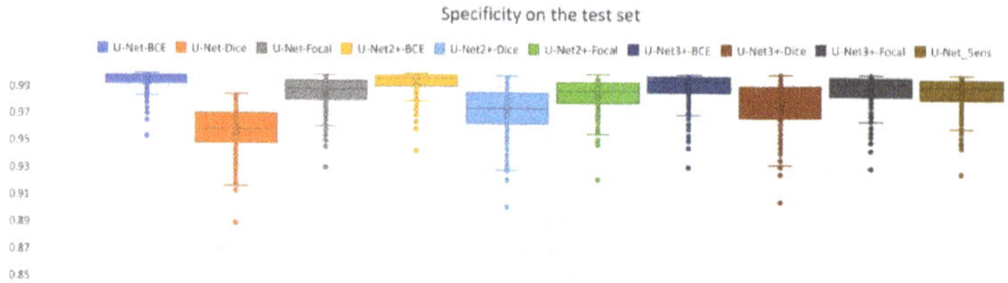

Figure 20. Boxplot comparison of the 9 networks and ensemble on images of the test set.

According to the Dice scores, sensitivities and specificities, focal loss is the best loss out of the three losses studied. The progress of focal loss on the three architectures during the validation process is shown in Figure 21. All three networks perform visibly well, but the best validation performance is given by U-Net3+.

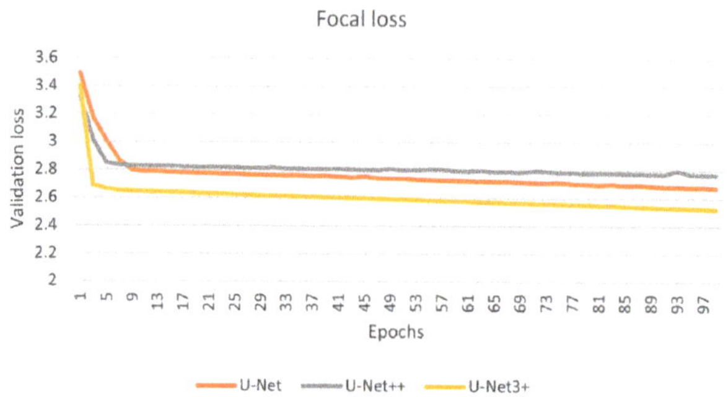

Figure 21. The progress of focal loss during training for the validation set.

The majority voting of the ensemble of nine networks was what defined the new label, namely Label II. Figure 22 shows an example of differences between the original label (Label I) and the new label (Label II). The Dice coefficient between the old labels and the new labels is 0.8872. Clearly, all three networks detect more vein regions, especially at the borders, and furthermore, U-Net2+ and U-Net3+ also detect continuous vein regions, linking perhaps discontinuous vein parts in Label I. The first row in Figure 22 shows the original image and the segmentation obtained by U-Net, U-Net2+ and U-Net3+. Row 2 shows Label I and the differences in row 1 segmentation to Label I. Row 3 shows the ensemble segmentation (Label II) and the differences in row 1 segmentation to Label II.

Our last group of experiments proves the assumption of this article—namely, that the slightly inaccurate segmentation obtained by unsupervised traditional image processing techniques can be improved by applying an ensemble of multiple CNN networks trained on the labels obtained in previous steps.

We trained our best ResNet–UNet network using the same training parameters and the most common loss function, the Dice loss and the best loss obtained in our previously described experiment, namely the focal loss. All the other hyperparameters were set to the same as previously. The results, as expected, show a 2–5% improvement in the Dice score on Label II compared to Label I. Table 4 and Figure 23 show the results on Label I for both Dice and focal losses. Table 5 and Figure 24 show the results on Label II for both Dice and focal losses.

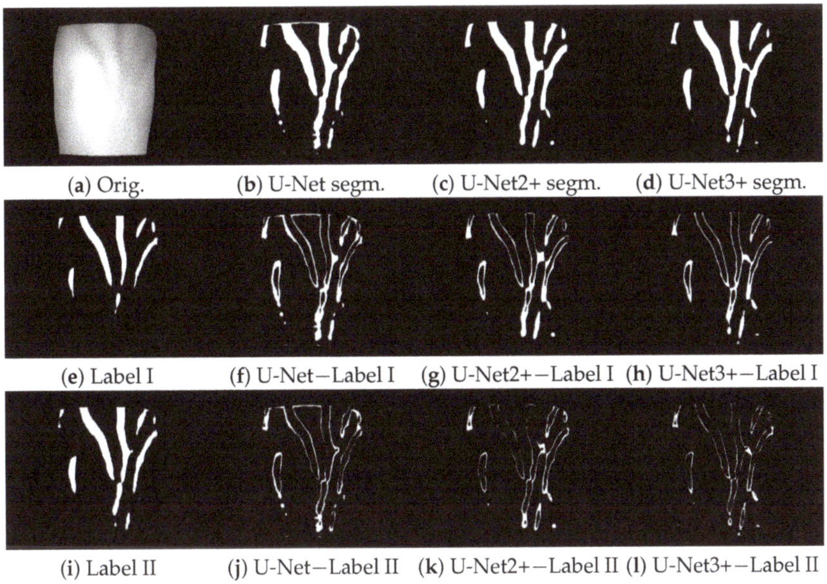

Figure 22. Visual comparison of U-Net, U-Net++ and U-Net3+ and their differences in Label I and Label II.

Table 4. Test set results of the ResNet–UNet network trained with Dice or focal loss in phase 1.

	ResNet-UNet Dice—Label I			**ResNet-UNet Focal Label I**		
	Dice	**Sens**	**Spec**	**Dice**	**Sens**	**Spec**
Max	0.9472	0.9864	0.9994	0.9604	0.9941	0.9992
Q3	0.9233	0.9379	0.9970	0.9333	0.9586	0.9966
Mean	0.9065	0.9046	0.9937	0.9145	0.9285	0.9928
Q1	0.8977	0.8753	0.9917	0.9044	0.9082	0.9906
Min	0.7413	0.7058	0.9749	0.7655	0.7452	0.9685
Std	0.0268	0.0487	0.0045	0.0290	0.0427	0.0051

Table 5. Test set results of the ResNet–UNet network trained with Dice or focal loss in phase 2.

	ResNet-UNet Dice—Label II			**ResNet-UNet Focal—Label II**		
	Dice	**Sens**	**Spec**	**Dice**	**Sens**	**Spec**
Max	0.9675	0.9742	0.9993	0.9596	0.9501	0.9992
Q3	0.9578	0.9605	0.9969	0.9439	0.9300	0.9975
Mean	0.9511	0.9504	0.9960	0.9357	0.9182	0.9962
Q1	0.9462	0.9424	0.9951	0.9294	0.9091	0.9954
Min	0.9162	0.8818	0.9920	0.8946	0.8294	0.9907
Std	0.0088	0.0135	0.0014	0.0106	0.0161	0.0015

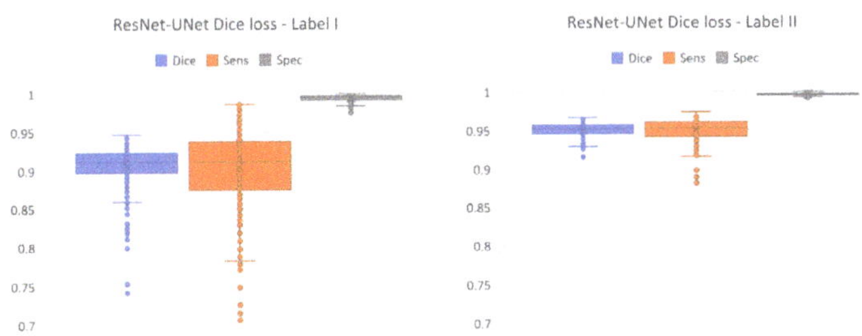

Figure 23. Improvement in labels in the two phases on the test set for Dice loss.

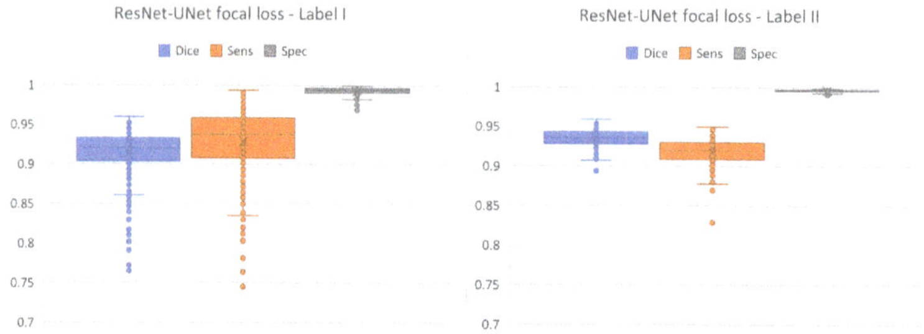

Figure 24. Improvement in labels in the two phases on the test set for focal loss.

Analyzing the boxplots of the corresponding experiments on the same test set, we can see that the segmentation after phase 2 is much better than after phase 1. The boxplots for both losses become flatter, which means that the interquartile range (IQR) is much smaller. For the Dice loss, the IQR is Q3 − Q1 = 0.9233 − 0.8977 = 0.0256, whereas in the second phase, it becomes equal to IQR = 0.9578 − 0.9462 = 0.011, which represents a 2.3-fold improvement. The difference is even better if we consider that the worst segmentation response is 0.7413 (minimum) in phase 1 and 0.9162 (minimum) in phase 2. The segmentation of the worst image improves by 17.49%. Better results are obtained for focal loss as well if we compare the two ResNet–UNet networks trained on the focal loss. The difference between Dice scores here is 2.12%, while the difference between minimums is 12.91%.

Figure 25 shows an image with significant differences between Label I and Label II and ResNet–UNet phase 1 and ResNet–UNet phase 2, both trained with Dice loss.

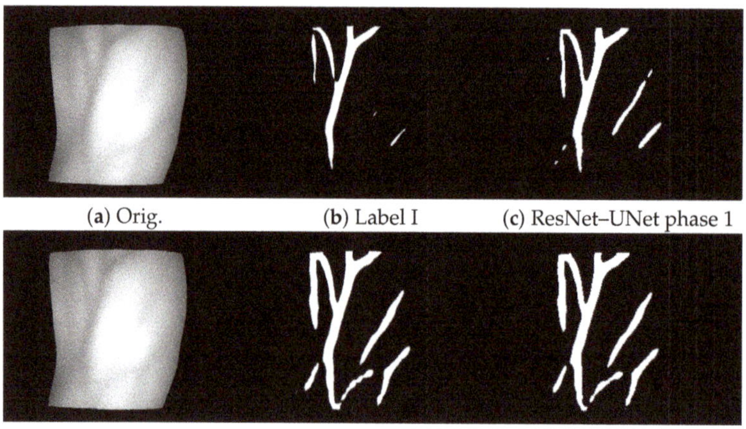

(**a**) Orig. (**b**) Label I (**c**) ResNet–UNet phase 1

(**d**) Orig. (**e**) Label II (**f**) ResNet–UNet phase 2

Figure 25. Visual comparison of the approach proposed: phase 1 and phase 2 segmentation.

All our experiments related to CNN training were done on a dual Nvidia Geforce RTX 2080 GPU system with 11 GB memory on each graphics card. Our experiments were run in Keras Tensorflow and Pytorch as well. Each of these deep learning frameworks relies on the Python programming language. The traditional image processing steps were implemented, and the correct workflow was experimentally set up via ImageJ and the ITK image processing software.

5. Discussion

There are very few articles in the literature that describe dorsal hand vein segmentation, due to the lack of expert annotation on dorsal hand or palm vein images. Most dorsal hand vein databases are made not for precise vein segmentation, but rather for personal identification. The papers discussing human identification rely on traditional image processing methods that extract geometrical features such as bifurcation, angel, segment length or certain local or global image features [15]. The two existing articles in the domain, also mentioned in the state-of-the-art section, are Gao et al. [5] from 31 December 2021 and Yakno et al. [6], which appeared in February 2022. Gao et al. present a system based on the U-Net network, introducing the so-called U-Netup that uses an attention module in the U-Net and joins the outputs of conv. layers 4 and 5, called feature 4 and feature 5, followed by two other convolutions to form the output of the CNN. They use a self-made dorsal hand vein database from 116 subjects, totaling 2024 images. The labels used for training are hand-marked, pixel by pixel. As we can see, these initial images are not standardized and the hand-marked labels are not quite accurate in the examples given in their article, with only 1–3 vein sections being marked with a maximum of 1–2 bifurcations. The results reported by the authors are defined as the mean intersection over reunion (mIoU) as a sum of (TP+TN)/2, considering the weights of both classes equal. In general, when computing mIOU, the correct class matches must be weighted by the number of elements in that class over the total number of elements. In this way, the background TN percentage does not have a weight of 1/2 in the final formula. The authors have not considered this, allowing for a straightforward comparison of the mIOU reported in [5] with our TP (sensitivity) and TN (specificity) values. Table 6 shows the results of paper [5] compared to our results.

Table 6. Comparison of the results.

Network	Database	TP	TN	mIoU = (TP + TN)/2 [5]
PSPNet [5]	Proprietary Unavailable	-	-	62.53
U-Net [5]	Proprietary Unavailable	-	-	68.07
U-Netup [5]	Proprietary Unavailable	-	-	78.12
Our ResNet–UNet Dice Level I	NCUT	90.46	99.37	94.91
Our ResNet–UNet focal Level I	NCUT	92.85	99.28	96.06
Our ResNet–UNet Dice Level II	NCUT	95.04	99.6	97.37
Our ResNet–UNet focal Level II	NCUT	91.82	99.62	95.72

The most recent article in dorsal hand vein segmentation is [6]. Yakno et al. present a system that achieves vein segmentation using Vein-Generative Adversarial Network (V-GAN). They use only 50 images for training and 20 for testing. The resolution of the images is 640 × 480 pixels. Based on the single visualization figure from the article and the resolution of the original images, it cannot be excluded that they used a small part of the same NCUT database that we used. The generative part of the GAN is U-Net, but the discriminative part is not specified; only the loss functions of the two discriminators are described, while their exact structure is not detailed at all. They trained the networks on ground truth labels, although their actual origin is not specified. They present two segmentation results, with and without preprocessing. As preprocessing, they applied ROI extraction of 192 × 192 pixels, CLAHE and gamma correction. Their sensitivity, specificity and Dice scores can be compared to ours (Table 7).

Table 7. Comparison of the results.

Network	Database	TP	TN	Dice
Without preprocessing [6]	Unknown	65.95	99.06	73.27
With preprocessing [6]	Unknown	80.33	98.36	78.21
Our ResNet–UNet Dice Level I	NCUT	90.46	99.37	90.65
Our ResNet–UNet focal Level I	NCUT	92.85	99.28	91.45
Our ResNet–UNet Dice Level II	NCUT	95.04	99.60	95.11
Our ResNet–UNet focal Level II	NCUT	91.82	99.62	93.57

In addition to comparing our results to the articles in the literature, we have studied the same procedure on databases other than only the NCUT. The Sakarya University of Applied Sciences (SUAS) database [59] consists of 919 vein images from 155 different subjects, measuring 640 × 480 pixels. We have also extracted the veins from these images with the traditional segmentation method proposed and applied the already trained ensemble network to segment these types of images as well.

The results were surprisingly good. The segmentations obtained are shown in Figure 26. Some post-processing steps of erosion and deleting small unconnected false veins would correct the segmentation. The purpose here was to examine the model obtained trained only on the NCUT with other types of dorsal hand images as well. The veins here are considered wider, influenced by the transition intensity from the vein to the skin that had a greater width in the original database, but that is not the case here.

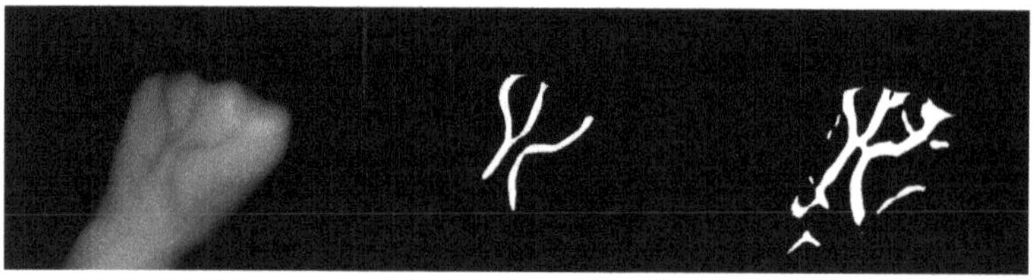

(**a**) SUAS Orig. (**b**) Label I segm. (**c**) Label II segm.

Figure 26. Segmentation of the ensemble on the SUAS database.

The same unsupervised vein extraction and CNN testing process was performed on the PUT database [60] as well. It consists of 1200 wrist images from 50 persons, containing three series of four images each for the left and right hands, meaning 24 images for each person. The resolution of the images is 1280 × 960 pixels. Here, the segmentation appears more precise than for the SUAS, but the horizontal line across the wrist introduces horizontal noise, especially in unsupervised segmentation, but in supervised testing as well. The results are shown in Figure 27.

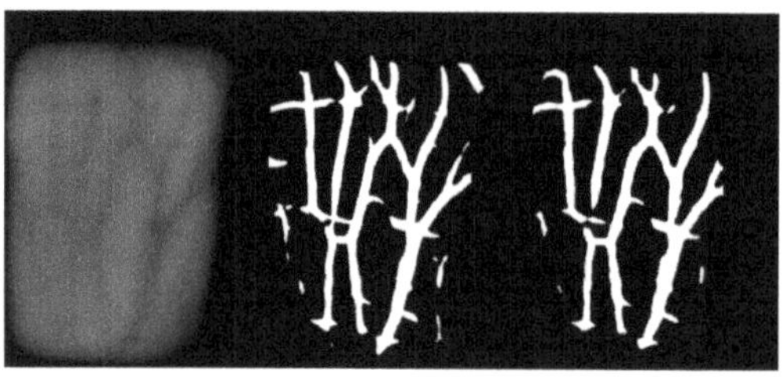

(**a**) PUT Orig. (**b**) Label I segm. (**c**) Label II segm.

Figure 27. Segmentation of the ensemble on the PUT database.

Considering these two different databases, which were not included in the training process of our model, we can conclude that the veins are being detected, but the segmentation results are noisy. This result can be explained by the different vein acquisition equipment and the lack of an identical acquisition protocol. Some images can be standardized over a series of preprocessing steps, but in certain situations, it is impossible to unify the images acquired by different equipment. To generalize the supervised segmentation, the model should be rebuilt, including these diverse images in the training process. The numerical results were not measured in this case because the entire automatic labeling and training procedure should have been redone from scratch, which was not the goal of this research effort.

6. Conclusions

The lack of ground truth labels of medical images means that the standard segmentation performance measure compares two results between each other and not the results with the gold standard. The ground truth is non-existent both in our case and in many other segmentation applications. In practice, it is essential to define the goal of segmentation and accepted error rates. In this paper, we proposed a novel pipeline for image segmentation, presenting a case study on dorsal hand vein NIR images. However, vein annotation can never be perfect because of the anatomical structure of the veins. The vascular system is arborescent, with many branches and bifurcations. Additionally, the veins become increasingly thinner in the extremities or in different organs. In the images used, vein width was between 4 and 25 pixels, corresponding to 0.6–4 mm, while 1 pixel was 0.15 mm. As a comparison, by applying a morphological operation of erosion or dilatation of only 1 pixel on the segmented images, the results changed by 4% in the Dice score. This is the reason for considering only the detectable, meaning the visible, subcutaneous veins in our labeling process.

The approach combines unsupervised segmentation with supervised learning. The first major step in our system is gross segmentation by applying traditional image processing techniques. The processing steps here include essential steps of image correction, such as inhomogeneity reduction and contrast-limited adaptive histogram equalization, to visualize and analyze the valleys on the horizontal profile image, which is followed by the extraction of tubular structures from the image. The final step in the unsupervised part is the local threshold, for obtaining the binary segmentation used further on as labels.

The second major step of the system proposed was the adaptation, training and fine-tuning of different CNN architectures initially used for object detection or medical image segmentation. These types of networks require supervised training; thus, they require not only the original image, but the ground truth segmentation as well. Lacking expert annotations on any of the publicly available dorsal hand vein images, we had to use the previously obtained segmentations as labels in our CNNs. Surprisingly, during visual verification, some of the CNNs performed even better than the labels given. This observation caused us to decide in favor of the second phase segmentation. An ensemble classifier based on majority voting by nine networks created more accurate image labels. These new labels were considerably better than the initial ones and led to better training and generalization of the initially studied convolutional networks that were not included in the ensemble. By using the second labeled dataset, the ResNet–UNet classifier presented improves the initial Dice score by approximately 4–5% and increases the sensitivity significantly. In this way, we obtained our best Dice score for the test set of 95.11%.

The ResNet–UNet classifier was also tested on two different databases not involved in the training process. The results are promising and are a compelling reason to include other types of images in the training process. It is possible to improve our results even more; we propose to study other CNN networks in the field of medical image segmentation.

The limitations of the paper presented are the restricted selection of geometric image processing segmentation steps used for obtaining Label I. The steps shown may work very well for some datasets and less so for others. This traditional segmentation pipeline needs further fine-tuning and adjustment to obtain the best possible labels for different kinds of vein images. On the other hand, in the second phase, the drawbacks include the general limitations of CNNs due to different stages of downconvolution and upconvolution. The more complex networks presented and applied in our case detect vein contours more precisely, with increasing computational complexity and training time. In addition, the accuracy of the resulting model is highly influenced by the quality, quantity and diversity of input data.

In the future, we intend to analyze networks that can handle the border pixels of the vein region. A more accurate detection of border pixels may lead to a Dice improvement of 1–2%. For this purpose, we will apply attention-guided networks and multi-pathway multi-resolution networks. We also propose to apply SegAN [61] to generate more images in our dataset and to investigate and train the nnU-Net [35] model, which is considered a benchmark in medical image segmentation.

At present, there are few research efforts studying dorsal hand vein segmentation in the clinical medical field because of a lack of ground truth images labeled by experts [5]. This article may be considered a starting point for non-contact injection in the dorsal hand veins to efficiently gain intravenous access, to administer different medications, apply intravenous therapy, perfusion, or to perform several types of blood tests, intravenous cannulation or catheter insertion. Nowadays, especially in hospitals for contagious and infectious diseases, where medical staff have to wear protective equipment such as gloves, goggles, surgery masks, aprons and gowns, the precise determination of the vein for an accurate needle prick is essential.

Furthermore, the pipeline proposed not only solves the problem of dorsal hand vein segmentation, but may also be applied in other vessel segmentation tasks, such as retinal vessel segmentation on fundus images to supplement computer-aided diagnosis and surgery planning for diabetic patients, lung vessel segmentation to detect pulmonary vascular diseases or identifying blocked or narrowed veins in the heart from a coronary angiogram. All these applications require well-acquired and standardized datasets of several thousand images collected thoroughly and according to a well-defined imaging protocol.

Author Contributions: Conceptualization, S.L. and L.L.; methodology, S.L. and L.L.; software, S.L.; validation, S.L. and L.L.; formal analysis, S.L. and L.L.; investigation, S.L. and L.L.; resources, S.E., S.L. and L.L.; data curation, L.L. and S.E.; validation: S.L. and L.L.; visualization, S.L., L.L. and S.E.; writing—original draft preparation, S.L.; writing—review and editing, S.L., L.L. and S.E.; supervision, L.L.; project administration, S.L.; funding acquisition, S.L. All authors have read and agreed to the published version of the manuscript.

Funding: The work was supported by George Emil Palade University of Medicine, Pharmacy, Science, and Technology of Târgu Mureș.

Institutional Review Board Statement: Not applicable.

Informed Consent Statement: Not applicable.

Data Availability Statement: Data was available upon request from authors of [7].

Conflicts of Interest: The authors declare no conflict of interest.

Abbreviations

The following abbreviations are used in this manuscript:

acc.	Accuracy
BC	Binary Coding
BCE	Binary Cross-Entropy
BGM	Biometric Graph Matching
CCKG	Centroid-Based Circular Keypoint Grid
CE	Cross-Entropy
CLAHE	Contrast-Limited Adaptive Histogram Equalization
CNN	Convolutional Neural Network
DHN	Deep Hashing Networks
DSC	Dice Similarity Score
FAR	False Acceptance Rate
FC	Fully Connected
FCN	Fully Convolutional Network
FGM	Factorized Graph Matching
FRR	False Rejection Rate
IQR	Inter-Quartile Range
GT	Ground Truth
IP	Image Processing
k-NN	k-Nearest Neighbor

LBP	Local Binary Pattern
mIoU	Mean Intersection over Union
OGM	Oriented Gradient Maps
PLBP	Partition Local Binary Patterns
PUT	Poznan University of Technology
RB	Residual Block
ResNet	Residual Network
ROI	Region of Interest
Sens	Sensitivity
SIFT	Scale-Invariant Feature Transform
Spec	Specificity
SUAS	Sakarya University of Applied Sciences
SVM	Support Vector Machines
TP	True Positive
TN	True Negative
VGG	Oxford's Visual Geometry Group
WSM	Width Skeleton Model

References

1. Galdran, A.; Anjos, A.; Dolz, J.; Chakor, H.; Lombaert, H.; Ayed, I.B. State-of-the-art retinal vessel segmentation with minimalistic models. *Sci. Rep.* **2022**, *12*, 6174. [CrossRef] [PubMed]
2. Su, J.; Liu, Z.; Zhang, J.; Sheng, V.S.; Song, Y.; Zhu, Y.; Liu, Y. DV-Net: Accurate liver vessel segmentation via dense connection model with D-BCE loss function. *Knowl.-Based Syst.* **2021**, *232*, 107471. [CrossRef]
3. Iyer, K.; Najarian, C.P.; Fattah, A.A.; Arthurs, C.J.; Soroushmehr, S.M.R.; Subban, V.; Sankardas, M.A.; Nadakuditi, R.R.; Nallamothu, B.K.; Figueroa, C.A. AngioNet: A convolutional neural network for vessel segmentation in X-ray angiography. *Sci. Rep.* **2022**, *11*, 18066. [CrossRef] [PubMed]
4. Tetteh, G.; Efremov, V.; Forkert, N.D.; Schneider, M.; Kirschke, J.; Weber, B.; Zimmer, C.; Piraud, M.; Menze, B.H. DeepVesselNet: Vessel Segmentation, Centerline Prediction, and Bifurcation Detection in 3-D Angiographic Volumes. *Front. Neurosci.* **2020**, *14*, 1285. [CrossRef]
5. Gao, X.; Zhang, G.; Wang, K. Segmentation Model of Dorsal Hand Vein Based on Improved U-Net. In Proceedings of the 2021 5th International Conference on Electronic Information Technology and Computer Engineering (EITCE 2021), Xiamen, China, 22–24 October 2021; Association for Computing Machinery: New York, NY, USA, 2021; pp. 1361–1365. [CrossRef]
6. Yakno, M.; Mohamad-Saleh, J.; Ibrahim, M.Z. Dorsal Hand Vein Segmentation Using Vein-Generative Adversarial Network (V-GAN) Model. In Proceedings of the 11th International Conference on Robotics, Vision, Signal Processing and Power Applications, Penang, Malaysia, 6 May 2021; Mahyuddin, N.M., Mat Noor, N.R., Mat Sakim, H.A., Eds.; Springer: Singapore, 2022; pp. 585–591.
7. Wang, Y.; Li, K.; Cui, J. Hand-dorsa vein recognition based on partition Local Binary Pattern. In Proceedings of the IEEE 10th International Conference on Signal Processing Proceedings, Beijing, China, 24–28 October 2010; pp. 1671–1674. [CrossRef]
8. Zhu, X.; Huang, D.; Wang, Y. Hand Dorsal Vein Recognition Based on Shape Representation of the Venous Network. In Proceedings of the Advances in Multimedia Information Processing—PCM 2013 (14th Pacific-Rim Conference on Multimedia), Nanjing, China, 13–16 December 2013; Huet, B., Ngo, C.W., Tang, J., Zhou, Z.H., Hauptmann, A.G., Yan, S., Eds.; Springer International Publishing: Cham, Switzerland, 2013; pp. 158–169.
9. Li, K.; Zhang, G.; Wang, Y.; Wang, P.; Ni, C. Hand-dorsa Vein Recognition Based on Improved Partition Local Binary Patterns. In *Biometric Recognition*; Yang, J., Yang, J., Sun, Z., Shan, S., Zheng, W., Feng, J., Eds.; Springer International Publishing: Cham, Switzerland, 2015; pp. 312–320.
10. Lajevardi, S.M.; Arakala, A.; Davis, S.; Horadam, K.J. Hand vein authentication using biometric graph matching. *IET Biom.* **2014**, *3*, 302–313. [CrossRef]
11. Li, X.; Huang, D.; Zhang, R.; Wang, Y.; Xie, X. Hand dorsal vein recognition by matching Width Skeleton Models. In Proceedings of the 2016 IEEE International Conference on Image Processing (ICIP), Phoenix, AZ, USA, 25–28 September 2016; pp. 3146–3150. [CrossRef]
12. Russakovsky, O.; Lin, Y.; Yu, K.; Fei-Fei, L. Object-Centric Spatial Pooling for Image Classification. In *Computer Vision—ECCV 2012, Proceedings of the 12th European Conference on Computer Vision, Florence, Italy, 7–13 October 2012*; Fitzgibbon, A., Lazebnik, S., Perona, P., Sato, Y., Schmid, C., Eds.; Springer: Berlin/Heidelberg, Germany, 2012; pp. 1–15.
13. Chanthamongkol, S.; Purahong, B.; Lasakul, A. Dorsal Hand Vein Image Enhancement for Improve Recognition Rate Based on SIFT Keypoint Matching. In Proceedings of the 2nd International Symposium on Computer, Communication, Control and Automation, Singapore, 1–2 December 2013; Atlantis Press: Dordrecht, The Netherlands, 2013; pp. 174–177. [CrossRef]
14. Huang, D.; Ben Soltana, W.; Ardabilian, M.; Wang, Y.; Chen, L. Textured 3D face recognition using biological vision-based facial representation and optimized weighted sum fusion. In Proceedings of the CVPR 2011 WORKSHOPS, Colorado Springs, CO, USA, 20–25 June 2011; pp. 1–8.

15. Huang, D.; Zhang, R.; Yin, Y.; Wang, Y.; Wang, Y. Local feature approach to dorsal hand vein recognition by Centroid-based Circular Key-point Grid and fine-grained matching. *Image Vis. Comput.* **2017**, *58*, 266–277. [CrossRef]
16. Huang, D.; Tang, Y.; Wang, Y.; Chen, L.; Wang, Y. Hand Vein Recognition Based on Oriented Gradient Maps and Local Feature Matching. In *Computer Vision—ACCV 2012, Proceedings of the 11th Asian Conference on Computer Vision, Daejeon, Korea, 5–9 November 2012*; Lee, K.M., Matsushita, Y., Rehg, J.M., Hu, Z., Eds.; Springer: Berlin/Heidelberg, Germany, 2013; pp. 430–444.
17. Li, X.; Liu, X.; Liu, Z. A dorsal hand vein pattern recognition algorithm. In Proceedings of the 2010 3rd International Congress on Image and Signal Processing, Yantai, China, 16–18 October 2010; Volume 4, pp. 1723–1726. [CrossRef]
18. Wang, J.; Wang, G. Hand-dorsa vein recognition with structure growing guided CNN. *Optik* **2017**, *149*, 469–477. [CrossRef]
19. Wan, H.; Chen, L.; Song, H.; Yang, J. Dorsal hand vein recognition based on convolutional neural networks. In Proceedings of the 2017 IEEE International Conference on Bioinformatics and Biomedicine (BIBM), Kansas City, MO, USA, 13–16 November 2017, pp. 1215–1221. [CrossRef]
20. Cao, Z.; Long, M.; Wang, J.; Yu, P.S. HashNet: Deep Learning to Hash by Continuation. *arXiv* **2017**, arXiv:1702.00758. [CrossRef]
21. Zhong, D.; Shao, H.; Liu, Y. Hand Dorsal Vein Recognition Based on Deep Hash Network. In *Pattern Recognition and Computer Vision*; Lai, J.H., Liu, C.L., Chen, X., Zhou, J., Tan, T., Zheng, N., Zha, H., Eds.; Springer International Publishing: Cham, Switzerland, 2018; pp. 26–37.
22. Cherrat, E.M.; Alaoui, R.; Bouzahir, H. Convolutional Neural Networks Approach for Multimodal Biometric Identification System Using the Fusion of Fingerprint, Finger-vein and Face images. *PeerJ Comput. Sci.* **2020**, *6*, e248. [CrossRef]
23. Ronneberger, O.; Fischer, P.; Brox, T. U-Net: Convolutional Networks for Biomedical Image Segmentation. *arXiv* **2015**, arXiv:1505.04597.
24. Segmentation of Additive Manufacturing Defects Using U-Net. Volume 2: 41st Computers and Information in Engineering Conference (CIE). International Design Engineering Technical Conferences and Computers and Information in Engineering Conference. V002T02A029. 2021. Available online: http://xxx.lanl.gov/abs/https://asmedigitalcollection.asme.org/IDETC-CIE/proceedings-pdf/IDETC-CIE2021/85376/V002T02A029/6801303/v002t02a029-detc2021-68885.pdf (accessed on 1 May 2022). [CrossRef]
25. Gurrola-Ramos, J.; Dalmau, O.; Alarcón, T. U-Net based neural network for fringe pattern denoising. *Opt. Lasers Eng.* **2022**, *149*, 106829. [CrossRef]
26. Tang, Y.; Chen, Z.; Huang, Z.; Nong, Y.; Li, L. Visual measurement of dam concrete cracks based on U-net and improved thinning algorithm. *J. Exp. Mech.* **2022**, *37*, 209–220. [CrossRef]
27. Le, Q.T.; Ooi, C. Surrogate modeling of fluid dynamics with a multigrid inspired neural network architecture. *Mach. Learn. Appl.* **2021**, *6*, 100176. [CrossRef]
28. Milletari, F.; Navab, N.; Ahmadi, S.A. V-Net: Fully Convolutional Neural Networks for Volumetric Medical Image Segmentation. *arXiv* **2016**, arXiv:1606.04797.
29. Çiçek, O.; Abdulkadir, A.; Lienkamp, S.S.; Brox, T.; Ronneberger, O. 3D U-Net: Learning Dense Volumetric Segmentation from Sparse Annotation. *arXiv* **2016**, arXiv:1606.06650.
30. Xiao, X.; Lian, S.; Luo, Z.; Li, S. Weighted Res-UNet for High-Quality Retina Vessel Segmentation. In Proceedings of the 2018 9th International Conference on Information Technology in Medicine and Education (ITME), Hangzhou, China, 19–21 October 2018; pp. 327–331. [CrossRef]
31. Alom, M.Z.; Hasan, M.; Yakopcic, C.; Taha, T.M.; Asari, V.K. Recurrent Residual Convolutional Neural Network based on U-Net (R2U-Net) for Medical Image Segmentation. *arXiv* **2018**, arXiv:1802.06955.
32. Li, X.; Chen, H.; Qi, X.; Dou, Q.; Fu, C.W.; Heng, P.A. H-denseunet: Hybrid densely connected unet for liver and tumor segmentation from ct volumes. *IEEE Trans. Med. Imaging* **2018**, *37*, 2663–2674. [CrossRef]
33. Medical Decathlon. 2022. Available online: http://medicaldecathlon.com/ (accessed on 1 May 2022).
34. Rippel, O.; Weninger, L.; Merhof, D. AutoML Segmentation for 3D Medical Image Data: Contribution to the MSD Challenge 2018. *arXiv* **2020**, arXiv:2005.09978.
35. Isensee, F.; Jaeger, P.F.; Kohl, S.A.; Petersen, J.; Maier-Hein, K.H. nnU-Net: A self-configuring method for deep learning-based biomedical image segmentation. *Nat. Methods* **2021**, *18*, 203–211. [CrossRef]
36. Hemelings, R.; Elen, B.; Stalmans, I.; Van Keer, K.; De Boever, P.; Blaschko, M.B. Artery–vein segmentation in fundus images using a fully convolutional network. *Comput. Med. Imaging Graph.* **2019**, *76*, 101636. [CrossRef]
37. DRIVE: Digital Retinal Images for Vessel Extraction. 2022. Available online: https://drive.grand-challenge.org/ (accessed on 1 May 2022).
38. Chase BD1 Retinal Image Database. 2022. Available online: https://blogs.kingston.ac.uk/retinal/chasedb1/ (accessed on 1 May 2022).
39. Zhang, L.; Cheng, Z.; Shen, Y.; Wang, D. Palmprint and Palmvein Recognition Based on DCNN and A New Large-Scale Contactless Palmvein Dataset. *Symmetry* **2018**, *10*, 78. [CrossRef]
40. Wu, C.Z.; Sun, J.; Wang, J.; Xu, L.F.; Zhan, S. Encoding-decoding Network With Pyramid Self-attention Module for Retinal Vessel Segmentation. *Int. J. Autom. Comput.* **2021**, *18*, 973. [CrossRef]
41. Guo, C.; Szemenyei, M.; Yi, Y.; Zhou, W.; Bian, H. Residual Spatial Attention Network for Retinal Vessel Segmentation. *arXiv* **2020**, arXiv:2009.08829.

42. Jalilian, E.; Uhl, A. Improved CNN-Segmentation-Based Finger Vein Recognition Using Automatically Generated and Fused Training Labels. In *Handbook of Vascular Biometrics*; Springer International Publishing: Cham, Switzerland, 2020; pp. 201–223. [CrossRef]
43. Qin, H.; El-Yacoubi, M.A. Finger-Vein Quality Assessment by Representation Learning from Binary Images. In *Neural Information Processing*; Arik, S., Huang, T., Lai, W.K., Liu, Q., Eds.; Springer International Publishing: Cham, Switzerland, 2015; pp. 421–431.
44. Cho, S.; Oh, B.S.; Toh, K.A.; Lin, Z. Extraction and Cross-Matching of Palm-Vein and Palmprint From the RGB and the NIR Spectrums for Identity Verification. *IEEE Access* **2020**, *8*, 4005–4021. [CrossRef]
45. Zhang, Y.; Chung, A.C.S. Deep Supervision with Additional Labels for Retinal Vessel Segmentation Task. In *Medical Image Computing and Computer Assisted Intervention—MICCAI 2018, Granada, Spain, 16–20 September 2018*; Springer International Publishing: Berlin/Heidelberg, Germany, 2018; pp. 83–91. [CrossRef]
46. Kumar, R.; Singh, R.C.; Kant, S. Dorsal Hand Vein-Biometric Recognition Using Convolution Neural Network. In *International Conference on Innovative Computing and Communications*; Gupta, D., Khanna, A., Bhattacharyya, S., Hassanien, A.E., Anand, S., Jaiswal, A., Eds.; Springer: Singapore, 2021; pp. 1087–1107.
47. Shao, H.; Zhong, D.; Du, X. A deep biometric hash learning framework for three advanced hand-based biometrics. *IET Biom.* **2021**, *10*, 246–259. [CrossRef]
48. Vovk, U.; Pernuš, F.; Likar, B. Intensity inhomogeneity correction of multispectral MR images. *NeuroImage* **2006**, *32*, 54–61. [CrossRef]
49. Frangi, A.F.; Niessen, W.J.; Vincken, K.L.; Viergever, M.A. Multiscale vessel enhancement filtering. In *Medical Image Computing and Computer-Assisted Intervention—Proceedings of the MICCAI'98, Cambridge, MA, USA, 11–13 October 1998*; Wells, W.M., Colchester, A., Delp, S., Eds.; Springer: Berlin/Heidelberg, Germany, 1998; pp. 130–137.
50. Sato, Y.; Nakajima, S.; Shiraga, N.; Atsumi, H.; Yoshida, S.; Koller, T.; Gerig, G.; Kikinis, R. Three-dimensional multi-scale line filter for segmentation and visualization of curvilinear structures in medical images. *Med. Image Anal.* **1998**, *2*, 143–168. [CrossRef]
51. Florack, L.M.; ter Haar Romeny, B.M.; Koenderink, J.J.; Viergever, M.A. Scale and the differential structure of images. *Image Vis. Comput.* **1992**, *10*, 376–388. [CrossRef]
52. Russakovsky, O.; Deng, J.; Su, H.; Krause, J.; Satheesh, S.; Ma, S.; Huang, Z.; Karpathy, A.; Khosla, A.; Bernstein, M.; et al. ImageNet Large Scale Visual Recognition Challenge. *Int. J. Comput. Vis. (IJCV)* **2015**, *115*, 211–252. [CrossRef]
53. Simonyan, K.; Zisserman, A. Very Deep Convolutional Networks for Large-Scale Image Recognition. *arXiv* **2014**, arXiv:1409.1556.
54. He, K.; Zhang, X.; Ren, S.; Sun, J. Deep Residual Learning for Image Recognition. *arXiv* **2015**, arXiv:1512.03385.
55. Long, J.; Shelhamer, E.; Darrell, T. Fully Convolutional Networks for Semantic Segmentation. *arXiv* **2015**, arXiv:1411.4038.
56. Bäuerle, A.; van Onzenoodt, C.; Ropinski, T. Net2Vis—A Visual Grammar for Automatically Generating Publication-Tailored CNN Architecture Visualizations. *IEEE Trans. Vis. Comput. Graph.* **2021**, *27*, 2980–2991. [CrossRef] [PubMed]
57. Zhou, Z.; Rahman Siddiquee, M.M.; Tajbakhsh, N.; Liang, J. UNet++: A Nested U-Net Architecture for Medical Image Segmentation. In *Deep Learning in Medical Image Analysis and Multimodal Learning for Clinical Decision Support*; Stoyanov, D., Taylor, Z., Carneiro, G., Syeda-Mahmood, T., Martel, A., Maier-Hein, L., Tavares, J.M.R., Bradley, A., Papa, J.P., Belagiannis, V., et al., Eds.; Springer International Publishing: Cham, Switzerland, 2018; pp. 3–11.
58. Huang, H.; Lin, L.; Tong, R.; Hu, H.; Zhang, Q.; Iwamoto, Y.; Han, X.; Chen, Y.W.; Wu, J. UNet 3+: A Full-Scale Connected UNet for Medical Image Segmentation. In Proceedings of the ICASSP 2020—2020 IEEE International Conference on Acoustics, Speech and Signal Processing (ICASSP), Barcelona, Spain, 4–8 May 2020; pp. 1055–1059. [CrossRef]
59. Yildiz, M.Z.; Boyraz, O.F.; Guleryuz, E.; Akgul, A.; Hussain, I. A Novel Encryption Method for Dorsal Hand Vein Images on a Microcomputer. *IEEE Access* **2019**, *7*, 60850–60867. [CrossRef]
60. Kabacinski, R.; Kowalski, M. Vein pattern database and benchmark results. *Electron. Lett.* **2011**, *47*, 1. [CrossRef]
61. Xue, Y.; Xu, T.; Zhang, H.; Long, L.R.; Huang, X. SegAN: Adversarial Network with Multi-scale L1 Loss for Medical Image Segmentation. *Neuroinformatics* **2018**, *16*, 383–392. [CrossRef]

mathematics

MDPI

Article

Multi-Level Cross-Modal Semantic Alignment Network for Video–Text Retrieval

Fudong Nian [1,2,*], Ling Ding [1], Yuxia Hu [2] and Yanhong Gu [1]

1 School of Advanced Manufacturing Engineering, Hefei University, Hefei 230601, China
2 Anhui International Joint Research Center for Ancient Architecture Intellisencing and Multi-Dimensional Modeling, Anhui Jianzhu University, Hefei 230601, China
* Correspondence: nianfd@hfuu.edu.cn

Abstract: This paper strives to improve the performance of video–text retrieval. To date, many algorithms have been proposed to facilitate the similarity measure of video–text retrieval from the single global semantic to multi-level semantics. However, these methods may suffer from the following limitations: (1) largely ignore the relationship semantic which results in semantic levels are insufficient; (2) it is incomplete to constrain the real-valued features of different modalities to be in the same space only through the feature distance measurement; (3) fail to handle the problem that the distributions of attribute labels in different semantic levels are heavily imbalanced. To overcome the above limitations, this paper proposes a novel multi-level cross-modal semantic alignment network (MCSAN) for video–text retrieval by jointly modeling video–text similarity on global, entity, action and relationship semantic levels in a unified deep model. Specifically, both video and text are first decomposed into global, entity, action and relationship semantic levels by carefully designing spatial–temporal semantic learning structures. Then, we utilize KLDivLoss and a cross-modal parameter-share attribute projection layer as statistical constraints to ensure that representations from different modalities in different semantic levels are projected into a common semantic space. In addition, a novel focal binary cross-entropy (FBCE) loss function is presented, which is the first effort to model the unbalanced attribute distribution problem for video–text retrieval. MCSAN is practically effective to take the advantage of the complementary information among four semantic levels. Extensive experiments on two challenging video–text retrieval datasets, namely, MSR-VTT and VATEX, show the viability of our method.

Keywords: video–text retrieval; multi-level space learning; cross-modal similarity calculation

MSC: 68T09

1. Introduction

With the popularity of online short video sharing platforms (e.g., TikTok), video–text retrieval (using a video clip as query to find similar sentences and vice versa) becomes a fundamental and crucial information retrieval problem for both users and platforms. As a specific cross-modal retrieval [1] task, many research papers about video–text retrieval have been presented and achieved remarkable progress from 2018 to the present [2–6].

Measuring the semantic similarity between any pair of video–text is very important for video–text retrieval. Basically, existing studies on video–text retrieval can be summarized into two categories according to the roughness of video and text semantic representations: (1) The first one is single-level encoding methods [2,6–8], which leverage convolutional neural networks (CNN), recurrent neural networks (RNN) or Transformer to learn global representation (i.e., single level) of video/text. However, compacting video/text into a single global level representation is insufficient due to neglecting the local and fine-grained static/dynamic information that widely existed in video/text. (2) The second one is multi-level encoding methods [3,4,9–11], which convert video/text into hybrid attribute spaces (e.g., global, entity and action). The total similarity of the video–text pair is the fusion of the cross-modal similarities in different semantic levels.

Recently, large-scale visual-and-language pretraining (VLP) models (e.g., DALL-E [12], CLIP [13] and MVP [14]), which can learn representations grounded in both visual textual contexts via a self-supervised learning manner, have been successfully applied in various downstream multi-modal tasks such as visual question answering [15], video captioning [16] and visual reasoning [17]. Some video–text retrieval methods utilize VLP models to obtain more representative video and text features [18–21]. Although these approaches show promising performance on video–text retrieval tasks, training VLP means leveraging lots of extra multi-modal training data and a video–text retrieval framework with the VLP model also means adding a number of parameters.

Despite the significance and value of the methods in the above algorithms, they still suffer from three critical shortcomings: (1) *Semantic levels are insufficient*. Though action and entity semantic levels are considered in [3,9,11] and get better performance, the semantic similarity in relationship level is ignored. However, several works [22–24] demonstrate that modeling relationships can improve the performance of many multi-modal understanding tasks significantly. Similarly, as shown in Figure 1, relationships are also common clues in video–text retrieval scenarios. (2) *Incomplete joint space representation*. To compare the cross-modal representations in different semantic levels, most existing works [25,26] utilize ranking or classification losses. Although it has achieved certain results, there is no statistical guarantee that real-valued vectors encoded from different modalities are in a common space. (3) *Unbalanced data distribution problem is neglected*. Figure 2 shows the number of five entities in MSR-VTT [27] dataset, from it we can see that attributes distribution has a serious long tail effect. Unfortunately, to the best of our knowledge, no video–text retrieval frameworks are handling this problem explicitly.

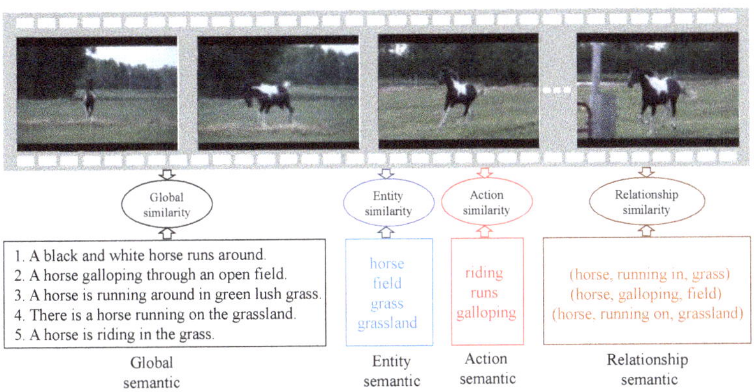

Figure 1. An illustration of both video and text are decomposed into global, entity, action and relationship semantic levels.

To tackle these limitations, in this paper, we present a novel **M**ulti-Level **C**ross-Modal **S**emantic **A**lignment **N**etwork (MCSAN) for video–text retrieval by jointly modeling the video/text context information and unbalanced attributes distribution challenges in a unified deep model. To achieve a robust video–text retrieval, as shown in Figure 1, besides the global representation, we first construct multi-level semantic dictionaries (entity, action and relationship) from the corpus. Then, we design several practical semantic encoding modules including CNN, RNN, GNN [28] and Multi-head self-attention [29], which are utilized to encode both video and text into multi-level semantic spaces (i.e., global, entity, action and relationship). Meanwhile, not only using feature distance, we also utilize KLDivLoss and a cross-modal parameter-share attribute projection layer as statistical constraints to ensure that representations from different modalities in different semantic levels are projected into a common semantic space. In addition, we design a novel multi-label regression loss to handle the unbalanced attributes distribution problem. Extensive experimental results on two widely-used video–text retrieval benchmark datasets, i.e., MSR-VTT [27] and VATEX [30], to validate the effectiveness and superiority of our MCSAN.

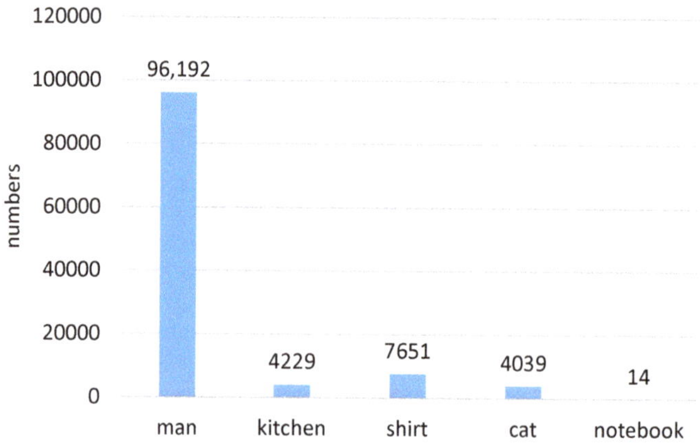

Figure 2. The number of 5 entities in MSR-VTT corpus, we can see that attributes distribution is very uneven.

In summary, this paper makes the following contributions.

- A novel Multi-Level Cross-Modal Semantic Alignment Network (MCSAN) is developed for video–text retrieval tasks. The semantic similarity between video and text is fully considered at four semantic levels (global, action, entity and relationship) by carefully designing spatial–temporal semantic learning structures and cross-modal representation distribution constraints in an end-to-end framework, which offers an alternative orientation for video-text retrieval.
- Compared with existing works, we are the first to measure the similarity of video–text pairs using relationship semantic level. We demonstrate that relationship, which is also a complementary and crucial clue for video–text retrieval.
- We introduce a novel focal binary cross-entropy (FBCE) loss function for multi-label attributes regression. Though several papers adopt attributes to improve the performance of video–text retrieval, to the best of our knowledge, this is the first effort to consider and handle the unbalanced attributes distribution problem in video–text retrieval scenarios.
- By carefully incorporating spatial–temporal semantic learning structures, cross-modal representation distribution constraints, novel multi-label classification loss function, adaptive graph learning, and cross-modal contextual attention module, our proposed method can jointly enjoy the merits of alleviate semantic gap and long-tailed multi-level multi-modal attributes learning for video–text retrieval. Moreover, we conduct extensive experiments on two popular benchmarks, i.e., MSR-VTT [27] and VATEX [30], demonstrating the rationality and effectiveness of the proposed multi-level cross-modal semantic alignment network.

The remainder of this paper is organized as follows: Section 2 reviews the related work. We present the detailed architecture of the multi-level cross-modal semantic alignment network in Section 3, while Section 4 describes the datasets, settings, implementation details, experimental results, and limitations. Finally, we conclude the paper with future work in Section 5.

2. Related Work

The general process of the current video–text retrieval framework can be roughly divided into two blocks, namely, modality encoding (embedding video and text into vectors), and similarity calculation (predicting the similarity score of two modalities). Therefore, in this section, we briefly review typical video–text retrieval algorithms in the above two views.

2.1. Modality Encoding

Existing video and text encoding methods can be roughly divided into two categories. The first one is single-level encoding methods [2,6–8,31,32], which leverage convolutional neural networks (CNN), recurrent neural networks (RNN) or Transformer to learn global representation (i.e., single level) of video/text. However, compacting video/text into a single global level representation is insufficient due to neglecting the local and fine-grained static/dynamic information that widely existed in video/text. The second one is multi-level encoding methods [3,4,9–11], which convert video/text into hybrid attribute spaces (e.g., global, entity and action). The total similarity of the video–text pair is the fusion of the cross-modal similarities in different semantic levels. The popular pipeline for video/text encoding is that: (1) For video encoding, using the pre-trained image classification or video clip classification model to extract the frame-wise feature. For text encoding, using Word2Vec, Glove, or Bert to extract the word-wise feature. (2) Utilizing CNN, RNN, or Transformer to handle temporal information of both video and text.

To enhance the representation ability, Yang et al. [33] constructed a tree structure to model text. Dong et al. [34] proposed a reading-strategy-inspired visual representation learning framework to represent videos. Some works [35–38] made full use of multi-modal cues, e.g., appearance, audio, motion, OCR and face, for video encoding. Although these methods have made some progress, the training pipeline of these methods are very complex, and even a large amount of additional annotation information is required.

Recently, thanks to the rapid development of VLP models [12–14], there are some works [18–21] tend to utilize the VLP model encoding the video and text directly. Although these approaches show promising performance on video–text retrieval tasks since they have better feature representation ability, training VLP means leveraging lots of extra multi-modal training data and the video–text retrieval framework with the VLP model also means adding a mount of parameters. Moreover, due to the training codes of these VLP based video–text retrieval algorithms are not publicly available, we have not compared these methods in this paper.

2.2. Similarity Calculation

The most common method of calculating cross-modal similarity in video–text retrieval task is that first project video and text into a common semantic space and then compute the feature distance in the common space [34,39–42]. Additionally, Lei et al. [39] concatenated video and text features, and fed them into a transformer for multi-modal fusion. Directly predicting the cross-modal similarity by fusing multi-modal representations without learning the common semantic space explicitly in other cross-modal understanding tasks [43,44] is not uncommon. Yu et al. [43] proposed a guided attention module to fuse text and image representations for visual question answering. Yu et al. [44] presented a multi-modal Transformer to cascade the image and text features in depth. for image captioning. Though the recent image-text retrieval literature [45] has demonstrated that multi-modal fusion can make the model more stable, extending it for video retrieval is unwise because it is at the expense of efficiency. It should be noted that all existing methods (whether it is common space base framework) calculate the similarity score either in global or entity and action semantic levels, which neglect the relationship information widely existing in multimedia data. Instead, we are the first to measure the similarity of video–text pairs using relationship semantic level, which is also a complementary and crucial clue for video–text retrieval.

3. Methodology

3.1. Problem Statement

Video–text retrieval includes two aspects: (1) Providing a sentence as a query and return the corresponding videos. (2) Providing a video as a query and return the corresponding sentences. The major challenge to achieve these goals is modeling the similarity between any video–text pairs. Formally, given a video V and a sentence T, the video–text retrieval model will output $S(V,T) = (0,1)$ to indicate the similarity of this video–text pair, where the larger the value of $S(V,T)$, the more similar the semantics of video V and text T.

3.2. Overall Framework

We introduce a novel multi-level cross-modal semantic alignment network (MCSAN) to improve the performance of video–text retrieval tasks. In order to precisely handle both the semantics of video and sentence, we employ several carefully designed spatial–temporal representation structures to encode both video and sentence into four semantic levels (global, action, entity and relationship). To calculate the similarity of video and sentence, we utilize metric learning, statistical distribution constraints and cross-modal parameter-share attribute projection layers to ensure multi-level representations extracted from different modalities are in multi-level common spaces. As the semantic distribution is seriously uneven, we propose a novel multi-label regression loss that can automatical focus on samples that are hard to be identified. The overall architecture of MCSAN is illustrated in Figure 3; in that which follows, we depict it in detail.

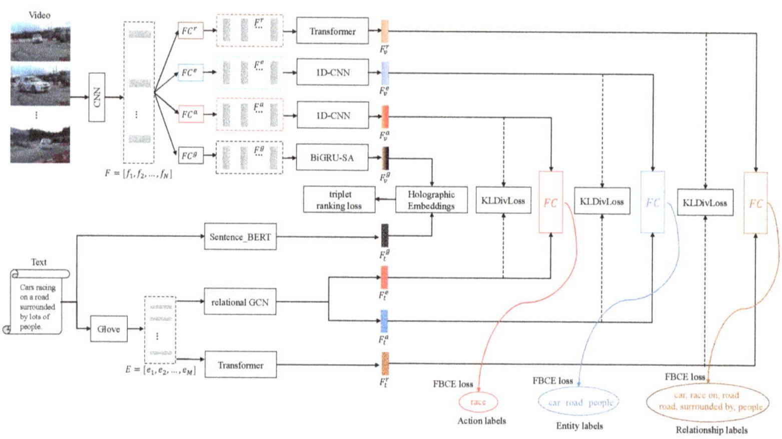

Figure 3. Framework of the proposed multi-level cross-modal semantic alignment network (MCSAN).

The proposed MCSAN is reasonable: (1) Obviously, as shown in Figure 3, a query sentence (e.g., *"Cars racing on a road surrounded by lots of people."*) corresponding to a specific video clip has multiple semantic levels including global-level (the whole sentence), verb-level (actions), and noun-level (entities). The multiple semantic levels involves complicated interactions between them, which are actually organized as a relationship structure, indicating that a textual query can be effectively grounded onto the video by properly aligning different semantic levels with the corresponding video parts. Although some previous methods attempt to utilize the multi-level semantic structure, they fail to capture the fine-grained and explicit relationship information. (2) Intuitively, in video retrieval or video captioning tasks, humans usually takes the relation-aware context of the visual structure into consideration and select the correct temporal moment.

3.3. Multi-Level Attributes Vocabulary Construction

As mentioned above, besides global representation, we also represent both video and text into three attribute spaces, i.e., action, entity and relationship. To achieve this goal, attribute vocabulary is necessary for training the encoding modules. In this work, we employ the Stanford CoreNLP Natural Language Processing Toolkit [46] to build action, entity and relationship vocabularies. Specifically, for a video–text retrieval dataset, we collect all sentences as original corpus, and extract nouns, verbs and subject–verb–object (SVO) triplets, which are deemed as entity, action and relationship, respectively. Then, we lemmatize all words to eliminate duplication of attributes. Finally, based on the frequency statistics, we select the top K_e nouns, K_a verbs and K_r SVO triplets as the final entity, action and relationship vocabularies, respectively.

3.4. Multi-Level Text and Video Semantics Encoding

In this section, we detail how to encode both video/text into global, entity, action and relationship semantic spaces.

3.4.1. Multi-Level Text Semantics Encoding

(1) Text parsing and initial embedding.

For a given sentence T, we first utilize the pre-trained word embedding model as the textual encoder to extract word initial embeddings $E = [e_1, e_2, ..., e_M]$, where M denotes the number of words in sentence T.

(2) Text global semantic encoding.

The text global semantic encoding F_t^g is calculated by pre-trained *Sentence_BERT* [47] since it sets a new state-of-the-art performance on semantic textual similarity task:

$$F_t^g = Sentence\_BERT(T), \tag{1}$$

(3) Text entity, action semantic encoding.

Since prior works [10,11] demonstrate that relational GCN [48] performs well on local-level text representations, we adopt relational GCN to encode the semantics of text entity and action, which are denoted as F_t^e and F_t^a, respectively. The structure of relational GCN is the same as [11] except not handle global feature, please refer to [11] for details.

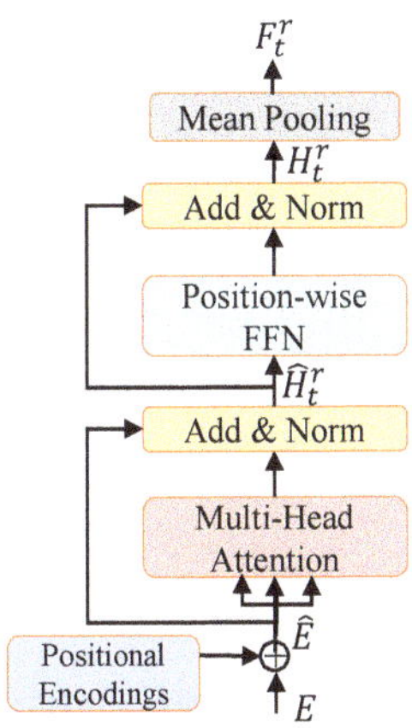

Figure 4. Text relationship semantic encoding architecture.

(4) Text relationship semantic encoding.

Compared with entity or action, the relationship in a sentence is complex, e.g., "*A dog is chasing a frisbee on the grass*" includes two relationships ("*dog chasing frisbee*" and "*dog on grass*") and words in these relationships are nonadjacent. Addressing it, we utilize a Transformer with multi-head self-attention block (as shown in Figure 4) to encode the text relationship semantic.

Specifically, the self-attention layer produces the attention output as follows:

$$S_t^r = softmax(\frac{Q_t K_t^\top}{\sqrt{d}})V_t, \tag{2}$$

where d indicates the feature dimension. Q_t, K_t and V_t are Query, Key and Value matrixes of the self-attention layer, which are based on the original word initial embedding with positing encoding $\widehat{E}$:

$$Q_t = W_t^q \widehat{E}, K = W_t^k \widehat{E}, V = W_t^v \widehat{E}, \tag{3}$$

where W_t^q, W_t^k, and W_t^v are the embedding weights of the self-attention layer.

Based on several affinity matrixes, then compute the context representation H_t^r:

$$\widehat{H}_t^r = LayerNorm(S_t^r + \widehat{E}), \tag{4}$$

$$H_t^r = LayerNorm(\widehat{H}_t^r + Linear(ReLU(Linear(\widehat{H}_t^r)))), \tag{5}$$

where *LayerNorm* is the layer normalization operation and *Linear(ReLU())* is a fully connected position-wise FFN layer.

Finally, the text relationship semantic encoding F_t^r is obtained by applying mean pooling on H_t^r, that is:

$$F_t^r = \frac{1}{N}\sum_{i=1}^{N} H_{t_i}^r, \tag{6}$$

where $H_{t_i}^r$ is the context representation of i-th word.

3.4.2. Multi-Level Video Semantics Encoding

Parallel to multi-level text semantics encoding, we also encode video into global, action, entity and relationship spaces.

(1) Video parsing and initial embedding.

Given a video V, we first uniformly sample N frames, then use the pre-trained feature extraction model to extract general frame-wise features, i.e., $F = [f_1, f_2, ..., f_N]$, here, f_i represents the i-th frame general feature of video V. We then leverage four residual sub-networks to convert the general frame-level features to level-specific frame initial embeddings as follows:

$$F^g = ReLU(F + FC^g(F)), \tag{7}$$

$$F^e = ReLU(F + FC^e(F)), \tag{8}$$

$$F^a = ReLU(F + FC^a(F)), \tag{9}$$

$$F^r = ReLU(F + FC^r(F)), \tag{10}$$

where $F^g = [f_1^g, f_2^g, ..., f_N^g] \in R^{N \times D_v}$, $F^e = [f_1^e, f_2^e, ..., f_N^e] \in R^{N \times D_v}$, $F^a = [f_1^a, f_2^a, ..., f_N^a] \in R^{N \times D_v}$ and $F^r = [f_1^r, f_2^r, ..., f_N^r] \in R^{N \times D_v}$ are frame-wise global, entity, action and relationship initial embeddings, respectively. Here, D_v is the dimension of the extracted visual feature. FC^g, FC^e, FC^a and FC^r are four different fully connected layers.

(2) Video global semantic encoding.

Bi-directional recurrent neural network [49] is an effective structure to handle both past and future contextual information of a given video sequence. We adopt a bidirectional GRU with soft attention (BiGRU-SA) structure to learn video global semantic encoding from frame-wise global initial embedding F^g.

As shown in Figure 5, to extract more salient global semantic and suppress unimportant frames automatically, we first utilize the attention mechanism to refine the F^g, i.e.,

$$\widehat{F^g} = \alpha F^g, \tag{11}$$

where $\widehat{F^g}$ is frame-wise global initial embedding after soft attention, and α is the attention score which is computed as follows:

$$\alpha = softmax(F^g W), \tag{12}$$

where W is the learnable weight matrix.

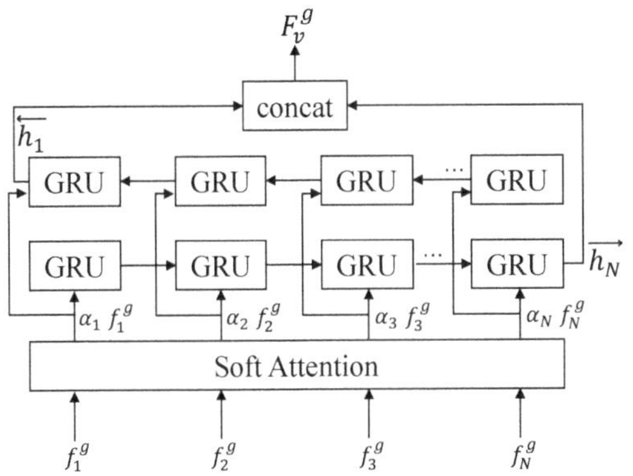

Figure 5. Video global semantic encoding architecture.

Let $\overrightarrow{GRU}$ and $\overleftarrow{GRU}$ indicate the forward and backward GRUs, $\overrightarrow{h}$ and $\overleftarrow{h}$ are corresponding hidden states generated as follows:

$$\overrightarrow{h} = \overrightarrow{GRU}(\widehat{F^g}), \tag{13}$$

$$\overleftarrow{h} = \overleftarrow{GRU}(\widehat{F^g}), \tag{14}$$

Finally, we concatenate the last hidden states of $\overrightarrow{h}$ and $\overleftarrow{h}$ to obtain the final video global semantic encoding:

$$F_v^g = concat(\overrightarrow{h_N}, \overleftarrow{h_1}), \tag{15}$$

where *concat* denotes the concatenate operation, $\overrightarrow{h_N}$ represents the hidden vector at the N-th time step of the forward GRU layer, and $\overleftarrow{h_1}$ represents the hidden vector at the 1-th time step of the backward GRU layer.

(3) Video entity semantic encoding.

Intuitively, the video entity depends on each frame. To be specific, on the one hand, if any frame contains a certain entity means that the entire video also has this entity concept. On the other hand, if the video does not contain a certain entity concept means that all frames do not contain this entity concept. We adapt 1D CNN with kernel size 1 to model this characteristic, as illustrated in Figure 6a, the final video entity semantic encoding F_v^e can be represented as follows:

$$F_v^e = ReLU(Conv1d_{k=1}(F^e)), \tag{16}$$

(4) Video action semantic encoding.

We also adapt 1D CNN to encode video action semantic. However, different from entity, action is motion information, which depends on several continuous video frames. Therefore, we integrate three 1D CNN with different kernel sizes to handle this challenge, the final video action semantic encoding F_v^a can be represented as follows:

$$F_v^a = \beta_1 ReLU(Conv1d_{k=2}(F^e)) + \beta_2 ReLU(Conv1d_{k=3}(F^e)) + \beta_3 ReLU(Conv1d_{k=5}(F^e)), \tag{17}$$

where β_1, β_2, and β_3 serve as the balance factor.

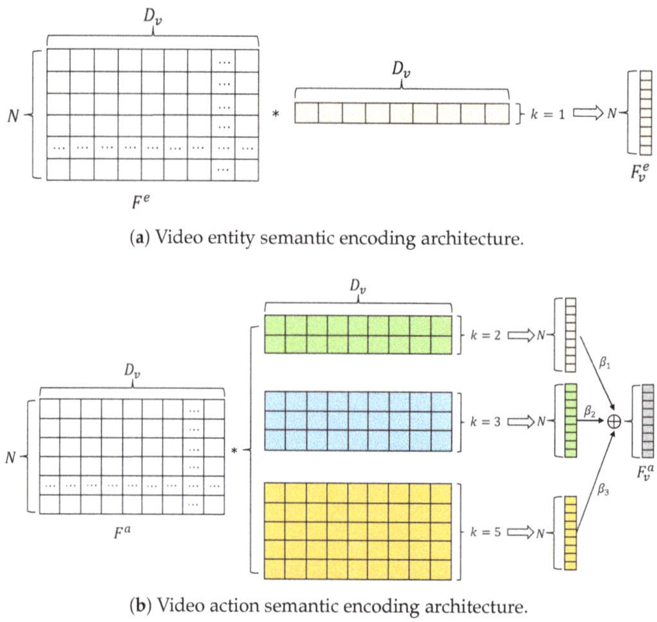

Figure 6. The structures of video entity and action semantic encoding using different 1D CNN.

(5) Video relationship semantic encoding.

Different from entity and action, the relationship semantics associated two objects may appear in discontinuous frames. To address this challenge, consistent with text relation semantic extraction, we also present a self-attention based transformer encoder (as shown in Figure 7) to compute the final video relationship semantic encoding F_v^r from the frame-wise relationship initial embedding F^r.

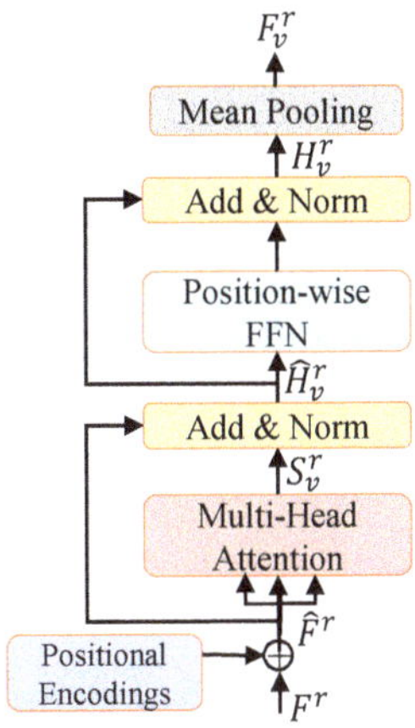

Figure 7. Video relationship semantic encoding architecture.

Specifically, the self-attention layer produces the attention output S_v^r as follows:

$$S_v^r = softmax(\frac{Q_v K_v^\top}{\sqrt{d}})V_v, \tag{18}$$

where d indicates the feature dimension. Q_v, K_v and V_v are query, key and value matrixes of the self-attention layer, which are based on the original frame-wise relationship initial embedding with positing encoding $\widehat{F}^r$:

$$Q_v = W_v^q \widehat{F}^r, K = W_v^k \widehat{F}^r, V = W_v^v \widehat{F}^r, \tag{19}$$

where W_v^q, W_v^k, and W_v^v are the embedding weights of the self-attention layer.

Based on several affinity matrixes, then compute the context representation H_v^r:

$$\widehat{H}_v^r = LayerNorm(S_v^r + \widehat{F}^r), \tag{20}$$

$$H_v^r = LayerNorm(\widehat{H}_v^r + Linear(ReLU(Linear(\widehat{H}_v^r)))), \tag{21}$$

where *LayerNorm* is the layer normalization operation and *Linear(ReLU())* is a fully connected position-wise FFN layer.

Finally, the video relationship semantic encoding F_v^r is obtained by applying mean pooling on H_v^r, that is:

$$F_v^r = \frac{1}{N}\sum_{i=1}^{N} H_{v_i}^r, \tag{22}$$

where $H_{v_i}^r$ is the context representation of ith frame.

3.5. Multi-Level Text and Video Semantics Alignment

In this section, we detail how to project the real-valued semantic vectors extracted from different modalities into a common space and calculate their similarity at different semantic levels.

3.5.1. Global Alignment

In order to make different dimensions in F_v^g and F_t^g fully interactive, we first use Holographic Embeddings [50] to fusion F_v^g and F_t^g, then leverage a fully connected layer (FC) to calculate the similarity of F_v^g and F_t^g, formally:

$$sim(F_v^g, F_t^g) = \sigma(FC(F_v^g \star F_t^g)), \tag{23}$$

where $sim(F_v^g, F_t^g)$ denotes the global semantic similarity, σ is Sigmoid non-linear function which projects the similarity score into $(0, 1)$, $\star$ represents circular correlation operation, i.e., $[a \star b]_k = \sum_{i=0}^{d_f-1} a_i b_{k+i\%d_f}$, here d_f is feature dimension.

3.5.2. Entity, Action and Relationship Alignment

(1) Statistical distribution constraints.

In order to ensure entity, action and relationship features extracted from different modalities that are projected into a common space, we leverage cross-modal parameter-share attribute projection layer (i.e., FC_*^{share}) in different semantic levels. That is,

$$p_v^e = ReLU(FC_e^{share}(F_v^e)), p_t^e = ReLU(FC_e^{share}(F_t^e)), \tag{24}$$

$$p_v^a = ReLU(FC_a^{share}(F_v^a)), p_t^a = ReLU(FC_a^{share}(F_t^a)), \tag{25}$$

$$p_v^r = ReLU(FC_r^{share}(F_v^r)), p_t^r = ReLU(FC_r^{share}(F_t^r)), \tag{26}$$

where p_v^e, p_v^a and p_v^r are the predicted entity, action and relationship of the video. p_t^e, p_t^a and p_t^r are the predicted entity, action and relationship of the text.

In addition, we also consider minimizing the cross-modal feature distribution in different semantic levels as follows:

$$min(distribution(\mathbf{F}_v^e), distribution(\mathbf{F}_t^e)), \tag{27}$$

$$min(distribution(\mathbf{F}_v^a), distribution(\mathbf{F}_t^a)), \tag{28}$$

$$min(distribution(\mathbf{F}_v^r), distribution(\mathbf{F}_t^r)), \tag{29}$$

where $\mathbf{F}$ denotes semantic representation matrix of a mini-batch.

(2) Similarity calculation.

We use the cosine similarity to measure cross-modal similarity in entity, action and relationship levels, that is:

$$sim(F_v^e, F_t^e) = cos(F_v^e, F_t^e), \tag{30}$$

$$sim(F_v^a, F_t^a) = cos(F_v^a, F_t^a), \tag{31}$$

$$sim(F_v^r, F_t^r) = cos(F_v^r, F_t^r), \tag{32}$$

where $sim(F_v^e, F_t^e)$, $sim(F_v^a, F_t^a)$ and $sim(F_v^r, F_t^r)$ denote the entity, action and relationship semantic similarities of the video V and the sentence T, respectively.

3.6. Training and Inference

3.6.1. Training

Once all similarity scores in four semantic levels are computed, the similarity between the video V and the sentence T is calculated by:

$$sim(V, T) = (sim(F_v^g, F_t^g) + sim(F_v^e, F_t^e) + sim(F_v^a, F_t^a) + sim(F_v^r, F_t^r))/4, \tag{33}$$

where $sim(V, T)$ denotes the overall similarity of the the video V and the sentence T.

We use the triplet ranking loss with hard negative sampling strategy (i.e., L_{rank}) to optimize MCSAN, that is:

$$L_{rank} = max(0, m + sim(V, T^-) - sim(V, T)) + max(0, m + sim(V^-, T) - sim(V, T)), \quad (34)$$

where (V, T) are the positive pair, T^- and V^- are the hardest negatives of text and video in a mini-batch, and m is a positive constant, which we term the margin.

In addition, we also use a novel multi-label regression loss for entity, action and relationship semantic learning. The original video–text retrieval dataset has no attribute annotations. Therefore, annotating entity, action and relationship for each video/text is crucial for learning multi-level representations. To ensure video and text share a common attribute space, we annotate video/text with the same vocabulary (Section 3.3). To be specific, for each sentence, we also use Standford NLP ToolKit to parse its entity, action and relationship as annotations. For each video, we parse all corresponding sentences and take their union as the annotations. Finally, all annotations are labeled in one-hot format based on the vocabulary (that is, entity, action and relationship can be predicted by a multi-label regression manner).

As illustrated in Section 1, the distribution of attributes (i.e., entity, action and relationship) is very imbalanced. Thus, the widely-used binary cross-entropy (BCE) loss may affect the generalization performance of the video–text retrieval model. To address it, inspired by the Focal loss [51], which performed successfully on unbalanced object detection tasks, we propose a novel focal binary cross-entropy (FBCE) loss for entity, action and relationship learning as:

$$\begin{aligned} L_e = &-\frac{1}{K}\sum_{i=1}^{K}(y^e_{v,i}\alpha_e(1-p^e_{v,i})^{\gamma_e}log(p^e_{v,i}) + (1-y^e_{v,i})\alpha_e(1-p^e_{v,i})^{\gamma_e}log(1-p^e_{v,i})) \\ &-\frac{1}{K}\sum_{i=1}^{K}(y^e_{t,i}\alpha_e(1-p^e_{t,i})^{\gamma_e}log(p^e_{t,i}) + (1-y^e_{t,i})\alpha_e(1-p^e_{t,i})^{\gamma_e}log(1-p^e_{t,i})), \end{aligned} \quad (35)$$

$$\begin{aligned} L_a = &-\frac{1}{K}\sum_{i=1}^{K}(y^a_{v,i}\alpha_a(1-p^a_{v,i})^{\gamma_a}log(p^a_{v,i}) + (1-y^a_{v,i})\alpha_a(1-p^a_{v,i})^{\gamma_a}log(1-p^a_{v,i})) \\ &-\frac{1}{K}\sum_{i=1}^{K}(y^a_{t,i}\alpha_a(1-p^a_{t,i})^{\gamma_a}log(p^a_{t,i}) + (1-y^a_{t,i})\alpha_a(1-p^a_{t,i})^{\gamma_a}log(1-p^a_{t,i})), \end{aligned} \quad (36)$$

$$\begin{aligned} L_r = &-\frac{1}{K}\sum_{i=1}^{K}(y^r_{v,i}\alpha_r(1-p^r_{v,i})^{\gamma_r}log(p^r_{v,i}) + (1-y^r_{v,i})\alpha_r(1-p^r_{v,i})^{\gamma_r}log(1-p^r_{v,i})) \\ &-\frac{1}{K}\sum_{i=1}^{K}(y^r_{t,i}\alpha_r(1-p^r_{t,i})^{\gamma_r}log(p^r_{t,i}) + (1-y^r_{t,i})\alpha_r(1-p^r_{t,i})^{\gamma_r}log(1-p^r_{t,i})), \end{aligned} \quad (37)$$

where K is the batch size. $y^e_{v,i}$, $y^a_{v,i}$and $y^r_{v,i}$ are the ground-truth entity, action and relationship of the i-th video. $y^e_{t,i}$, $y^a_{t,i}$and $y^r_{t,i}$ are the ground-truth entity, action and relationship of the i-th text. Please refer to [51] for the details of factors α and γ.

In addition, we leverage Kullback–Leibler divergence loss (KLDivLoss) to constrain that features from different modalities have the same distribution. That is:

$$L_{e\_kl} = KLDivLoss(\mathbf{F}^e_v, \mathbf{F}^e_t), \quad (38)$$

$$L_{a\_kl} = KLDivLoss(\mathbf{F}^a_v, \mathbf{F}^a_t), \quad (39)$$

$$L_{r\_kl} = KLDivLoss(\mathbf{F}^r_v, \mathbf{F}^r_t), \quad (40)$$

Finally, we combine the above losses to obtain the total objective function L_{total} as follows:

$$L_{total} = L_{rank} + \lambda_1(L_e + L_a + L_r) + \lambda_2(L_{e\_kl} + L_{a\_kl} + L_{r\_kl}), \quad (41)$$

where λ_1, λ_2 are trade-off hyper-parameters.

3.6.2. Inference

We simply sort the similarity scores of all video–text pairs for video–text retrieval.

4. Experiments and Results

To justify the effectiveness of our MCSAN model, we carried out extensive experiments under the bidirectional retrieval scenario including (1) text-to-video retrieval, i.e., retrieving videos that are semantically consistent with a given sentence query; and (2) video-to-text retrieval, i.e., retrieving sentences that are semantically consistent with a given video query. In this section, we first give the details about experimental settings, including datasets, evaluation metrics and implementation details. Then, we compare our MCSAN with several state-of-the-art baselines. Next, we explore the effectiveness of each component in our model via ablation studies. Finally, several qualitative and visualization experimental results are reported.

4.1. Experimental Settings

4.1.1. Datasets

We conduct extensive experiments on two most widely-used video–text retrieval datasets, namely, MSR-VTT [27] and VATEX [30], to evaluate our proposed method and several state-of-the-art baselines.

MSR-VTT consists of 10,000 video clips, where each video is described by 20 different sentences. Following the official setting, this dataset is split into 6573 training videos, 497 validation videos, and 2990 testing videos.

VATEX is a large-scale dataset including more than 30,000 video clips, where each video is associated with 10 English and 10 Chinese sentences. Here, only English sentences are used in our experiments. Following the settings in previous work [3,9,11], where 25,991, 1500, 1500 video clips are utilized for training, validation and testing, respectively.

4.1.2. Evaluation Metrics

Following prior cross-modal retrieval works [11,52], rank-based metric, i.e., Recall at K (R@K for short), Sum of all Recalls (SumR for short), are adopted to measure the overall video–text retrieval performance. The higher R@K and SumR indicate that the model has better retrieval performance.

4.1.3. Implementation Details

For a fair comparison with all the compared methods, we apply the same feature as HANet [11]. To be specific, for visual embedding, we use the pre-trained ResNet152 [53] and I3D [54] to extract frame features of MSR-VTT and VATEX, respectively. For text embedding, we use the pre-trained Glove [55] to extract word features of both MSR-VTT and VATEX. Here, the dimension of text embedding is 300 (extracted from Glove), and the dimension of visual embedding are 2048 (extracted from ResNet152) and 1024 (extracted from I3D) for MSR-VTT and VATEX, respectively. We optimized our MCSAN using PyTorch on 1 GeForce RTX 2080Ti GPU. Following HANet [11], the Adam [56] optimizer is employed with learning rate of 1×10^{-4} and the model is trained for 50 epochs with the batch size of 64. The trade-off hyper-parameters λ_1 and λ_2 are empirically set to 0.1 and 0.001, respectively. We estimate the hyperparameter margin m by running a grid search on the corresponding dataset, and the optimal value of m is empirically set to 0.25. In our FBCE loss, following the original Focal loss [51], α_e, α_a and α_r are empirically set to 0.25, γ_e, γ_a and γ_r are empirically set to 2. Note that, the model with the highest SumR value on validation set is deemed as the best model to report the performance on the test set.

4.2. Comparison with State-of-the-Art Methods

We compare our model with two types of baselines: compute the similarity between video and text only using the global features, i.e., VSE [57], VSE++ [58], Mithum et al. [2], W2VV [41], W2VV++ [8], Dual Encoding [3], CE [36], TCE [33], Zhao et al. [59], and compute the similarity between video and text using several level features, i.e., HGR [9], HANet [11], HSL [60]. The experimental results of our proposed MCSAN and all baseline approaches are reported in Tables 1 and 2. Note that all models are trained using the same initial video/text features on the same dataset. From Tables 1 and 2, we can have the following observations:

(1) In the two datasets, methods utilizing multi-level features perform better than these algorithms only use the global feature significantly, indicating that representations extracted from different semantic levels are complementary for video–text retrieval task.

(2) For all video–text retrieval methods, video-to-text has better performance than text-to-video. We think the reason is that on existing video–text retrieval dataset, one video corresponds to multiple sentences; however, one text can only correspond to one video. The results indicate that collecting a new video–text retrieval dataset with proportional numbers of video and text may be a feasible research direction.

(3) The proposed MCSAN outperforms all the baselines on MSR-VTT and VATEX datasets. The results demonstrate that the proposed model can jointly model multi-modal context information and multi-level semantics of both video and text in a unified deep model, which can better capture the underlying complementary representation of video/text, so as to improve the performance of video–text retrieval.

Table 1. Comparisons with the state-of-the-art video–text retrieval methods on the MSR-VTT dataset. The best performance are marked in bold. Our proposed model performs the best.

Method	Text-to-Video			Video-to-Text			SumR
	R@1	R@5	R@10	R@1	R@5	R@10	
VSE [57]	5.0	16.4	24.6	7.7	20.3	31.2	105.2
VSE++ [58]	5.7	17.1	24.8	10.2	25.4	35.1	118.3
Mithum et al. [2]	5.8	17.6	25.2	10.5	26.7	35.9	121.7
W2VV [41]	6.1	18.7	27.5	11.8	28.9	39.1	132.1
Dual Encoding [3]	7.7	22.0	31.8	13.0	30.8	43.3	148.6
TCE [33]	7.7	22.5	32.1	-	-	-	-
Zhao et al. [59]	8.8	25.5	36.5	14.0	33.1	44.9	162.8
HGR [9]	9.2	26.2	36.5	15.0	36.7	48.8	172.4
HANet [11]	9.3	27.0	38.1	16.1	39.2	52.1	181.8
HSL [60]	10.8	29.2	38.5	20.3	45.1	55.9	201.7
MCSAN	**10.9**	**29.6**	**40.1**	**21.1**	**46.8**	**57.4**	**205.3**

Table 2. Comparisons with the state-of-the-art video–text retrieval methods on the VATEX dataset. The best performance are marked in bold. The overall performance are indicated by Sum of Recalls (SumR). MCSAN is the best.

Method	Text-to-Video			Video-to-Text			SumR
	R@1	R@5	R@10	R@1	R@5	R@10	
W2VV [41]	14.6	36.3	46.1	39.6	69.5	79.4	285.5
VSE++ [58]	31.3	65.8	76.4	42.9	73.9	83.6	373.9
CE [36]	31.1	68.7	80.2	41.3	71.0	82.3	374.6
W2VV++ [8]	32.0	68.2	78.8	41.8	75.1	84.3	380.2
Dual Encoding [3]	31.1	67.4	78.9	-	-	-	-
HGR [9]	35.1	73.5	83.5	-	-	-	-
HSL [60]	**36.8**	73.6	83.7	46.8	75.7	85.1	401.7
HANet [11]	36.4	74.1	84.1	49.1	79.5	86.2	409.4
MCSAN	36.6	**74.2**	**84.1**	**51.4**	**81.3**	**86.8**	**411.8**

4.3. Ablation Studies

Because the proposed MCSAN contains multiple key components, we additional compare variants of MCSAN with respect to the following perspectives to verify the effectiveness of each component in MCSAN: (1) the effect of the relationship information, (2) the impact of the statistical distribution constraints, and (3) the effect of the proposed FBCE loss for handling unbalanced attributes. The following MCSAN variants are designed for comparison. The following MCSAN variants are designed for comparison.

(1) MCSAN¬R: A variant of MCSAN with the relationship encoding level being removed.

(2) MCSAN¬S: A variant of MCSAN with the statistical distribution constraints being removed.

(3) MCSAN¬L: A variant of MCSAN with the FBCE loss being removed, and only using the conventional BCE loss for entity, action and relationship learning.

The ablation study results are shown in Table 3. We can observe that the combination of all three components has the best performance and the performance will degrade if remove any components. The results demonstrate that all components in our MCSAN are effective. Moreover, we can also observe that if the relationship encoding is removed, the performance will degrade the most, which indicates that explicitly relationship understanding is crucial for video–text retrieval.

Table 3. Results of comparison among different variants in MCSAN on MSR-VTT dataset. The best performance are marked in bold. MCSAN exploiting all the four semantic levels (global, entity, action and realtionship) is the best.

Method	Text-to-Video			Video-to-Text			SumR
	R@1	R@5	R@10	R@1	R@5	R@10	
MCSAN¬R	9.4	27.1	37.9	17.2	42.3	54.7	195.8
MCSAN¬S	10.1	27.8	39.8	19.9	45.9	57.0	202.6
MCSAN¬L	10.6	28.8	39.2	20.8	46.4	56.6	203.7
MCSAN	**10.9**	**29.6**	**40.1**	**21.1**	**46.8**	**57.4**	**205.3**

4.4. Qualitative Analyses

We visualize three text-to-video retrieval examples on the MSR-VTT test set in Figure 8. For each query sentence, Figure 8 shows the top-3 scored videos evaluated by our MCSAN. We find that the proposed model is able to recognize the relationship *"man at top speed"* since comprehensive relationship between concepts is explicitly modeled in our framework. The results demonstrate that the proposed method can handle different types of video/text semantics well.

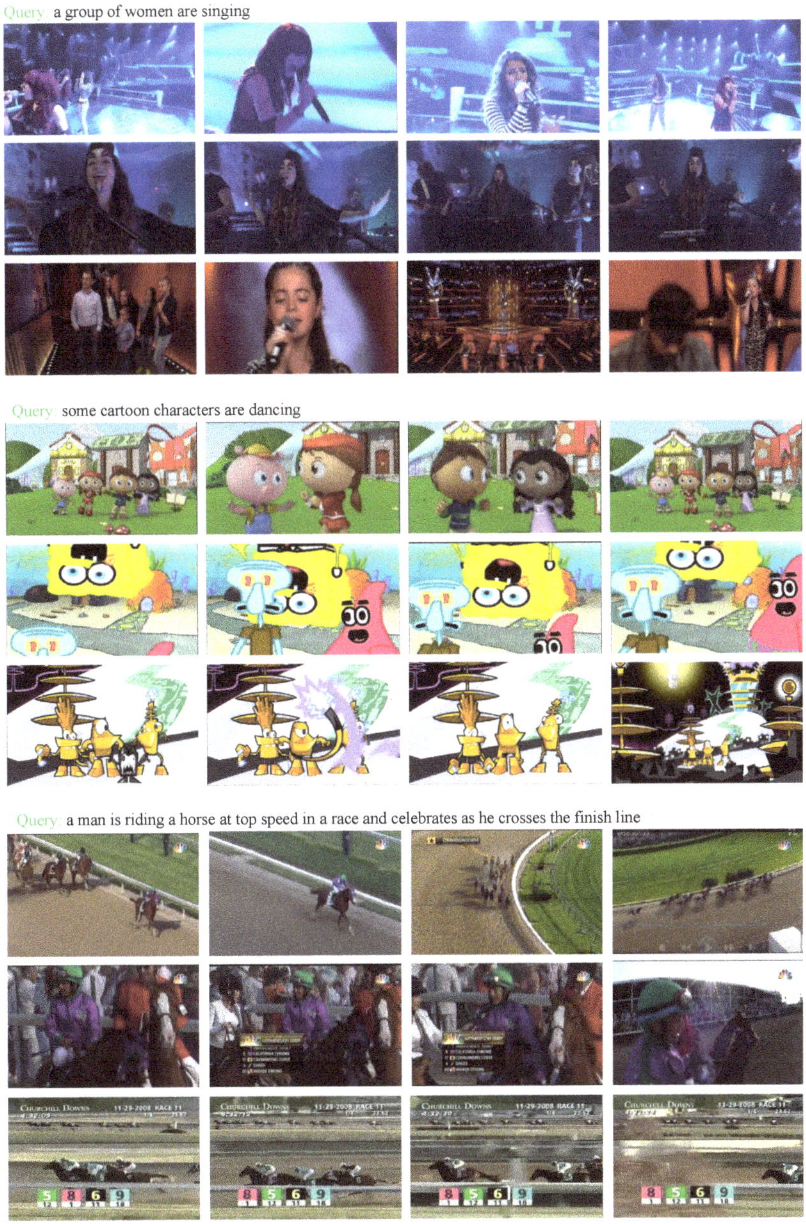

Figure 8. Top 3 text-to-video retrieval examples on the MSR-VTT test set.

4.5. Limitations

Although we achieve good results in the previous experiments, there are still some inevitable problems. Note that Rao et al. [45] demonstrated that modality embedding is crucial for the cross modal retrieval performance improvement. However, only simple CNN/Transformer structures are adopted in this paper. Thus, we will explore a more effective way to extract text/video semantic features in the future. Moreover, we will try to leverage additional knowledge information (e.g., knowledge embedding learnt from the external sentence corpus) since it can provide useful complementary information for video–text retrieval.

5. Conclusions

In this paper, we propose a novel Multi-Level Cross-Modal Semantic Alignment Network (MCSAN) for video–text retrieval tasks. The semantic similarity between video and text is fully considered at four semantic levels (global, action, entity and relationship) by carefully designed spatial–temporal semantic learning structures and cross-modal representation distribution constraints in an end-to-end framework. We make the first attempt to handle the cross-modal relationship semantic consistency without relying on any extern corpus in video–text retrieval task. Moreover, we introduce a novel focal binary cross-entropy (FBCE) loss function, which also is the first effort to model the unbalanced attribute distribution problem for video–text retrieval. We conduct extensive experiments on two video–text retrieval benchmarks, i.e., MSR-VTT and VATEX. The quantitative and qualitative experimental results demonstrate the effectiveness of the proposed framework. We achieve state-of-the-art performance against existing non-VLP-based video–text retrieval frameworks. Due to that most recent VLP based video–text retrieval algorithms are not publicly available, we hope that future work in the field of video–text retrieval should pay more attention to the reproducibilities and capabilities of the model, rather than use all the tricks to report a hard-to-reproduce better performance.

Author Contributions: Conceptualization, methodology, and writing—original draft preparation, F.N.; writing—review and editing, Y.G.; visualization, L.D.; funding acquisition, Y.H. All authors have read and agreed to the published version of the manuscript.

Funding: This work was supported by the National Natural Science Foundation (NSF) of China (No. 61902104), the Anhui Provincial Key Research and Development Program (No. 2022a05020042, No. 2022a05020043), the Anhui Provincial Natural Science Foundation (No. 2008085QF295, No. 2008085QF316), the University Natural Sciences Research Project of Anhui Province (No. KJ2020A0651), New Energy Vehicle and Intelligent Networked Vehicle Innovation Project (No. wfgcyh2020477), and Anhui International Joint Research Center for Ancient Architecture Intellisencing and Multi-Dimensional Modeling (No. GJZZX2021KF01).

Institutional Review Board Statement: Not applicable.

Informed Consent Statement: Not applicable.

Data Availability Statement: Data available in a publicly accessible repository. The data presented in this study are openly available at https://github.com/Roc-Ng/HANet, accessed on 26 July 2021.

Conflicts of Interest: The authors declare no conflict of interest.

References

1. Kaur, P.; Pannu, H.S.; Malhi, A.K. Comparative analysis on cross-modal information retrieval: A review. *Comput. Sci. Rev.* **2021**, *39*, 100336. [CrossRef]
2. Mithun, N.C.; Li, J.; Metze, F.; Roy-Chowdhury, A.K. Learning joint embedding with multimodal cues for cross-modal video–text retrieval. In Proceedings of the 2018 ACM on International Conference on Multimedia Retrieval, Yokohama, Japan, 11–14 June 2018; pp. 19–27.
3. Dong, J.; Li, X.; Xu, C.; Ji, S.; He, Y.; Yang, G.; Wang, X. Dual encoding for zero-example video retrieval. In Proceedings of the IEEE/CVF Conference On Computer Vision and Pattern Recognition, Long Beach, CA, USA, 16–20 June 2019; pp. 9346–9355.
4. Wang, W.; Gao, J.; Yang, X.; Xu, C. Learning coarse-to-fine graph neural networks for video–text retrieval. *IEEE Trans. Multimed.* **2020**, *23*, 2386–2397. [CrossRef]
5. Jin, W.; Zhao, Z.; Zhang, P.; Zhu, J.; He, X.; Zhuang, Y. Hierarchical cross-modal graph consistency learning for video–text retrieval. In Proceedings of the 44th International ACM SIGIR Conference on Research and Development in Information Retrieval, Virtual Event, 11–15 July 2021; pp. 1114–1124.
6. Gorti, S.K.; Vouitsis, N.; Ma, J.; Golestan, K.; Volkovs, M.; Garg, A.; Yu, G. X-Pool: Cross-Modal Language-Video Attention for Text-Video Retrieval. In Proceedings of the IEEE/CVF Conference on Computer Vision and Pattern Recognition, New Orleans, LA, USA, 21–24 June 2022; pp. 5006–5015.
7. Feng, Z.; Zeng, Z.; Guo, C.; Li, Z. Exploiting visual semantic reasoning for video–text retrieval. *arXiv* **2020**, arXiv:2006.08889.

8. Li, X.; Xu, C.; Yang, G.; Chen, Z.; Dong, J. W2vv++ fully deep learning for ad-hoc video search. In Proceedings of the 27th ACM International Conference on Multimedia, Nice, France, 21–25 October 2019; pp. 1786–1794.
9. Chen, S.; Zhao, Y.; Jin, Q.; Wu, Q. Fine-grained video–text retrieval with hierarchical graph reasoning. In Proceedings of the IEEE/CVF Conference on Computer Vision and Pattern Recognition, Seattle, WA, USA, 14–19 June 2020; pp. 10638–10647.
10. Wray, M.; Larlus, D.; Csurka, G.; Damen, D. Fine-grained action retrieval through multiple parts-of-speech embeddings. In Proceedings of the IEEE/CVF International Conference on Computer Vision, Seoul, Korea, 27 October–3 November 2019; pp. 450–459.
11. Wu, P.; He, X.; Tang, M.; Lv, Y.; Liu, J. HANet: Hierarchical Alignment Networks for Video–text Retrieval. In Proceedings of the 29th ACM international conference on Multimedia, Virtual Event, 20–24 October 2021; pp. 3518–3527.
12. Reddy, M.D.M.; Basha, M.S.M.; Hari, M.M.C.; Penchalaiah, M.N. Dall-e: Creating images from text. *UGC Care Group I J.* **2021**, *8*, 71–75.
13. Radford, A.; Kim, J.W.; Hallacy, C.; Ramesh, A.; Goh, G.; Agarwal, S.; Sastry, G.; Askell, A.; Mishkin, P.; Clark, J.; et al. Learning transferable visual models from natural language supervision. In Proceedings of the International Conference on Machine Learning (PMLR), Virtual Event, 18–24 July 2021; pp. 8748–8763.
14. Wei, L.; Xie, L.; Zhou, W.; Li, H.; Tian, Q. MVP: Multimodality-guided Visual Pre-training. *arXiv* **2022**, arXiv:2203.05175.
15. Yang, Z.; Garcia, N.; Chu, C.; Otani, M.; Nakashima, Y.; Takemura, H. Bert representations for video question answering. In Proceedings of the IEEE/CVF Winter Conference on Applications of Computer Vision, Snowmass Village, CO, USA, 1–5 March 2020; pp. 1556–1565.
16. Tang, M.; Wang, Z.; Liu, Z.; Rao, F.; Li, D.; Li, X. Clip4caption: Clip for video caption. In Proceedings of the 29th ACM International Conference on Multimedia, Virtual Event, 20–24 October 2021; pp. 4858–4862.
17. Wang, Z.; Codella, N.; Chen, Y.C.; Zhou, L.; Yang, J.; Dai, X.; Xiao, B.; You, H.; Chang, S.F.; Yuan, L. CLIP-TD: CLIP Targeted Distillation for Vision-Language Tasks. *arXiv* **2022**, arXiv:2201.05729.
18. Luo, J.; Li, Y.; Pan, Y.; Yao, T.; Chao, H.; Mei, T. CoCo-BERT: Improving video-language pre-training with contrastive cross-modal matching and denoising. In Proceedings of the 29th ACM International Conference on Multimedia, Virtual Event, 20–24 October 2021; pp. 5600–5608.
19. Fang, H.; Xiong, P.; Xu, L.; Chen, Y. Clip2video: Mastering video–text retrieval via image clip. *arXiv* **2021**, arXiv:2106.11097.
20. Luo, H.; Ji, L.; Zhong, M.; Chen, Y.; Lei, W.; Duan, N.; Li, T. Clip4clip: An empirical study of clip for end to end video clip retrieval. *arXiv* **2021**, arXiv:2104.08860.
21. Gao, Z.; Liu, J.; Chen, S.; Chang, D.; Zhang, H.; Yuan, J. Clip2tv: An empirical study on transformer-based methods for video–text retrieval. *arXiv* **2021**, arXiv:2111.05610.
22. Nian, F.; Bao, B.K.; Li, T.; Xu, C. Multi-modal knowledge representation learning via webly-supervised relationships mining. In Proceedings of the 25th ACM International Conference on Multimedia, Mountain View, CA, USA, 23–27 October 2017; pp. 411–419.
23. Yao, T.; Pan, Y.; Li, Y.; Mei, T. Exploring visual relationship for image captioning. In Proceedings of the European conference on computer vision (ECCV), Munich, Germany, 8–14 September 2018; pp. 684–699.
24. Wang, S.; Wang, R.; Yao, Z.; Shan, S.; Chen, X. Cross-modal scene graph matching for relationship-aware image-text retrieval. In Proceedings of the IEEE/CVF Winter Conference on Applications of Computer Vision, Snowmass Village, CO, USA, 1–5 March 2020; pp. 1508–1517.
25. Shvetsova, N.; Chen, B.; Rouditchenko, A.; Thomas, S.; Kingsbury, B.; Feris, R.S.; Harwath, D.; Glass, J.; Kuehne, H. Everything at Once-Multi-Modal Fusion Transformer for Video Retrieval. In Proceedings of the IEEE/CVF Conference on Computer Vision and Pattern Recognition, New Orleans, LA, USA, 21–24 June 2022; pp. 20020–20029.
26. Wray, M.; Doughty, H.; Damen, D. On semantic similarity in video retrieval. In Proceedings of the IEEE/CVF Conference on Computer Vision and Pattern Recognition, Virtual, 19–25 June 2021; pp. 3650–3660.
27. Xu, J.; Mei, T.; Yao, T.; Rui, Y. Msr-vtt: A large video description dataset for bridging video and language. In Proceedings of the IEEE Conference on Computer Vision and Pattern Recognition, Las Vegas, NV, USA, 27–30 June 2016; pp. 5288–5296.
28. Wu, Z.; Pan, S.; Chen, F.; Long, G.; Zhang, C.; Philip, S.Y. A comprehensive survey on graph neural networks. *IEEE Trans. Neural Netw. Learn. Syst.* **2020**, *32*, 4–24. [CrossRef]
29. Vaswani, A.; Shazeer, N.; Parmar, N.; Uszkoreit, J.; Jones, L.; Gomez, A.N.; Kaiser, Ł.; Polosukhin, I. Attention is all you need. In Proceedings of the Advances in Neural Information Processing Systems, Long Beach, CA, USA, 4–9 December2017; pp. 6000–6010.
30. Wang, X.; Wu, J.; Chen, J.; Li, L.; Wang, Y.F.; Wang, W.Y. Vatex: A large-scale, high-quality multilingual dataset for video-and-language research. In Proceedings of the IEEE/CVF International Conference on Computer Vision, Seoul, Korea, 27 October–3 November 2019; pp. 4581–4591.
31. Li, T.; Ni, B.; Xu, M.; Wang, M.; Gao, Q.; Yan, S. Data-driven affective filtering for images and videos. *IEEE Trans. Cybern.* **2015**, *45*, 2336–2349. [CrossRef]
32. Nian, F.; Li, T.; Wu, X.; Gao, Q.; Li, F. Efficient near-duplicate image detection with a local-based binary representation. *Multimed. Tools Appl.* **2016**, *75*, 2435–2452. [CrossRef]
33. Yang, X.; Dong, J.; Cao, Y.; Wang, X.; Wang, M.; Chua, T.S. Tree-augmented cross-modal encoding for complex-query video retrieval. In Proceedings of the 43rd International ACM SIGIR Conference on Research and Development in Information Retrieval, Xi'an, China, 25–30 July 2020; pp. 1339–1348.

34. Dong, J.; Wang, Y.; Chen, X.; Qu, X.; Li, X.; He, Y.; Wang, X. Reading-strategy inspired visual representation learning fo text-to-video retrieval. *IEEE Trans. Circuits Syst. Video Technol.* **2022**, *32*, 5680–5694. [CrossRef]
35. Gabeur, V.; Sun, C.; Alahari, K.; Schmid, C. Multi-modal transformer for video retrieval. In Proceedings of the Europear Conference on Computer Vision, Glasgow, UK, 23–28 August 2020; pp. 214–229.
36. Liu, Y.; Albanie, S.; Nagrani, A.; Zisserman, A. Use what you have: Video retrieval using representations from collaborative experts. *arXiv* **2019**, arXiv:1907.13487.
37. Miech, A.; Laptev, I.; Sivic, J. Learning a text-video embedding from incomplete and heterogeneous data. *arXiv* **2018** arXiv:1804.02516.
38. Gabeur, V.; Nagrani, A.; Sun, C.; Alahari, K.; Schmid, C. Masking modalities for cross-modal video retrieval. In Proceedings o the IEEE/CVF Winter Conference on Applications of Computer Vision, Waikoloa, HI, USA, 3–8 January2022; pp. 1766–1775.
39. Song, X.; Chen, J.; Wu, Z.; Jiang, Y.G. Spatial–temporal graphs for cross-modal text2video retrieval. *IEEE Trans. Multimed.* **2021** *14*, 2914–2923. [CrossRef]
40. Miech, A.; Zhukov, D.; Alayrac, J.B.; Tapaswi, M.; Laptev, I.; Sivic, J. Howto100m: Learning a text-video embedding by watching hundred million narrated video clips. In Proceedings of the IEEE/CVF International Conference on Computer Vision, Seoul Korea, 27 October–3 November 2019; pp. 2630–2640.
41. Dong, J.; Li, X.; Snoek, C.G. Predicting visual features from text for image and video caption retrieval. *IEEE Trans. Multimed* **2018**, *20*, 3377–3388. [CrossRef]
42. Dong, J.; Long, Z.; Mao, X.; Lin, C.; He, Y.; Ji, S. Multi-level alignment network for domain adaptive cross-modal retrieval *Neurocomputing* **2021**, *440*, 207–219. [CrossRef]
43. Yu, Z.; Yu, J.; Cui, Y.; Tao, D.; Tian, Q. Deep modular co-attention networks for visual question answering. In Proceedings of the IEEE/CVF Conference on Computer Vision and Pattern Recognition, Long Beach, CA, USA, 16–20 June 2019; pp. 6281–6290.
44. Yu, J.; Li, J.; Yu, Z.; Huang, Q. Multimodal transformer with multi-view visual representation for image captioning. *IEEE Trans Circuits Syst. Video Technol.* **2019**, *30*, 4467–4480. [CrossRef]
45. Rao, J.; Wang, F.; Ding, L.; Qi, S.; Zhan, Y.; Liu, W.; Tao, D. Where Does the Performance Improvement Come From?—A Reproducibility Concern about Image-Text Retrieval. *arXiv* **2022**, arXiv:2203.03853.
46. Manning, C.D.; Surdeanu, M.; Bauer, J.; Finkel, J.R.; Bethard, S.; McClosky, D. The Stanford CoreNLP natural language processing toolkit. In Proceedings of the 52nd Annual Meeting of the Association for Computational Linguistics: System Demonstrations Baltimore, MD, USA, 23–24 June 2014; pp. 55–60.
47. Reimers, N.; Gurevych, I. Sentence-bert: Sentence embeddings using siamese bert-networks. *arXiv* **2019**, arXiv:1908.10084.
48. Schlichtkrull, M.; Kipf, T.N.; Bloem, P.; Berg, R.v.d.; Titov, I.; Welling, M. Modeling relational data with graph convolutional networks. In Proceedings of the European Semantic Web Conference, Heraklion, Greece, 3–7 June 2018; pp. 593–607.
49. Schuster, M.; Paliwal, K.K. Bidirectional recurrent neural networks. *IEEE Trans. Signal Process.* **1997**, *45*, 2673–2681. [CrossRef]
50. Nickel, M.; Rosasco, L.; Poggio, T. Holographic embeddings of knowledge graphs. In Proceedings of the AAAI Conference on Artificial Intelligence, Phoenix, AZ, USA, 12–17 February 2016; pp. 1955–1961.
51. Lin, T.Y.; Goyal, P.; Girshick, R.; He, K.; Dollár, P. Focal loss for dense object detection. In Proceedings of the IEEE International Conference on Computer Vision, Venice, Italy, 22–29 October 2017; pp. 2980–2988.
52. Qu, L.; Liu, M.; Wu, J.; Gao, Z.; Nie, L. Dynamic modality interaction modeling for image-text retrieval. In Proceedings of the 44th International ACM SIGIR Conference on Research and Development in Information Retrieval, Virtual, 11–15 July 2021, pp. 1104–1113.
53. He, K.; Zhang, X.; Ren, S.; Sun, J. Deep residual learning for image recognition. In Proceedings of the IEEE Conference on Computer Vision and Pattern Recognition, Las Vegas, NV, USA, 27–30 June 2016; pp. 770–778.
54. Carreira, J.; Zisserman, A. Quo vadis, action recognition? a new model and the kinetics dataset. In Proceedings of the IEEE Conference on Computer Vision and Pattern Recognition, Honolulu, HI, USA, 21–26 July 2017; pp. 6299–6308.
55. Pennington, J.; Socher, R.; Manning, C.D. Glove: Global vectors for word representation. In Proceedings of the 2014 Conference on Empirical Methods in Natural Language Processing (EMNLP), Doha, Qatar, 25–29 October 2014; pp. 1532–1543.
56. Kingma, D.P.; Ba, J. Adam: A method for stochastic optimization. *arXiv* **2014**, arXiv:1412.6980.
57. Kiros, R.; Salakhutdinov, R.; Zemel, R.S. Unifying visual-semantic embeddings with multimodal neural language models. *arXiv* **2014**, arXiv:1411.2539.
58. Faghri, F.; Fleet, D.J.; Kiros, J.R.; Fidler, S. Vse++: Improving visual-semantic embeddings with hard negatives. *arXiv* **2017**, arXiv:1707.05612.
59. Zhao, R.; Zheng, K.; Zha, Z.J. Stacked convolutional deep encoding network for video–text retrieval. In Proceedings of the 2020 IEEE International Conference on Multimedia and Expo (ICME), Virtual, 6–10 July 2020; pp. 1–6.
60. Dong, J.; Li, X.; Xu, C.; Yang, X.; Yang, G.; Wang, X.; Wang, M. Dual encoding for video retrieval by text. *IEEE Trans. Pattern Anal. Mach. Intell.* **2021**, *44*, 4065–4080. [CrossRef]

Σ mathematics

MDPI

Article

Deep Spatial-Temporal Neural Network for Dense Non-Rigid Structure from Motion

Yaming Wang [1,2], Minjie Wang [1], Wenqing Huang [1,*], Xiaoping Ye [2] and Mingfeng Jiang [1]

[1] Pattern Recognition and Computer Vision Lab, Zhejiang Sci-Tech University, Hangzhou 310000, China
[2] Key Laboratory of Digital Design and Intelligent Manufacture in Culture & Creativity Product of Zhejiang Province, Lishui University, Lishui 323000, China
* Correspondence: wenqinghuang@zstu.edu.cn

Abstract: Dense non-rigid structure from motion (NRSfM) has long been a challenge in computer vision because of the vast number of feature points. As neural networks develop rapidly, a novel solution is emerging. However, existing methods ignore the significance of spatial–temporal data and the strong capacity of neural networks for learning. This study proposes a deep spatial–temporal NRSfM framework (DST-NRSfM) and introduces a weighted spatial constraint to further optimize the 3D reconstruction results. Layer normalization layers are applied in dense NRSfM tasks to stop gradient disappearance and hasten neural network convergence. Our DST-NRSfM framework outperforms both classical approaches and recent advancements. It achieves state-of-the-art performance across commonly used synthetic and real benchmark datasets.

Keywords: dense non-rigid structure from motion; weighted spatial constraint; layer normalization layers; deep spatial–temporal neural

MSC: 68T07; 68T45

1. Introduction

Non-rigid structure from motion (NRSfM) recovers the non-rigid 3D structure and camera pose from given monocular 2D point trajectories. It is ill-posed by its inherent ambiguities, and requires motion and deformation cues as well as prior assumptions to achieve 3D reconstruction. Moreover, it can be further subdivided into sparse NRSfM and dense NRSfM. Dense NRSfM is more complex and advances more slowly because it must reconstruct thousands of times more feature points compared with the sparse NRSFM. Most algorithms that address the dense NRSfM issue [1–5] extend the sparse reconstruction approach, and generally achieve unsatisfactory results. Recent developments have been made in dense NRSfM-specific algorithms [6–9]. Additionally, gradually introducing the neural network into the NRSfM area has provided new insights for resolving the dense NRSfM issue, despite the current primary focus on tackling sparse NRSfM.

The first 3D reconstruction of dense non-rigid objects from motion using an unsupervised neural network was completed by V. Sidhu [9] in 2020, and he gave the NRSfM network framework its moniker, neural non-rigid structure from motion (N-NRSfM). He developed a neural network framework for fitting deformations, employed latent space constraints for dense NRSfM, and obtained excellent reconstruction results. However, the final results heavily rely on conventional algorithms that first derive shape priors because of the reconstruction requirement for a rigid three-dimensional prior. This severely restricts the neural network's ability to learn, thereby rendering these approaches less robust.

This study presents a deep spatiotemporal NRSfM framework (DST-NRSfM) network structure to address the dense NRSfM problem. The proposed DST-NRSfM is trained by an entirely unsupervised drawing on the auto-encoder [10,11] principle, which uses layer normalization layers to both prevent gradient disappearance and accelerate neural network convergence; additionally, it uses temporal–spatial constraints to enhance the 3D reconstruction output accuracy. The complete network model is divided into two modules: shape estimation and rotation estimation. These two modules, respectively, derive the 3D structure and camera posture of the reconstructed object from an input 2D point trajectory matrix. The shape-estimation module abandons the shape prior and builds the most appropriate end-to-end network model for dense objects based on the properties of distinct datasets. In the rotation estimation module, considering the uniqueness of the NRSfM problem, we implemented a rotation matrix corrector after the rotation estimation network. This corrector will further orthogonally limit the resulting rotation matrix and eliminate its potential reflection ambiguity. Experiments demonstrated that our proposed method outperformed rival methods and achieved cutting-edge outcomes on the most popular dense datasets. What follows is a summary of the primary contributions of this study.

- We propose a novel deep neural network framework called DST-NRSfM to address the dense NRSfM challenge, which is superior for reconstructing objects with significant deformations because it does not require shape priors.
- We introduce the weighted spatial constraint to minimize the reconstruction error, improve mesh quality, and ensure that the reconstructed item is closer to the original shape. The second set of comparison experiments in Section 4.2 demonstrates the success of the weighted spatial constraint.
- The proposed technique achieves state-of-the-art performance on the most popular dense benchmark datasets. Section 4.3 provides evidence to support this hypothesis.

The remainder of this study is organized as follows. First, Section 2 discusses related work. Section 3 introduces problem settings, reviews the NRSfM problem and subsequently provides a detailed description of our network architecture. Section 4 details the experiments, presents the results, and analyzes the model's overall performance. Section 5 summarizes the proposed approach.

2. Related Works

NRSfM. Utilizing prior knowledge of shape and camera motion is a popular method for solving the inherently ambiguous NRSfM problem. Note that each frame's 3D shape is assumed to be composed of a few shape bases [12] or trajectory bases [13,14], and methods, such as probabilistic principal component analysis (PPCA) [15], metric constraints [16], complementary space models [17], block sparse dictionary learning [18], or force-based models [19], are employed to enhance the outcomes of the non-rigid 3D reconstruction produced via factoring. However, because the ideal number of bases is typically unpredictable (different bases occur in various sequences), this strategy is not robust. Recently, NRSfM has advanced significantly as the BMM algorithm [20], isometric priors [21], elastic priors [22], local-rigidity prior [23,24], space–time smooth constraints [25], variational methods [7], and tensor-based models [26] have been successively proposed.

Dense NRSfM. Reconstruction is more challenging for dense NRSfM, which is an extension of the NRSfM problem, owing to the significantly greater number of key points that must be restored. To address this issue, Collins et al. [27] suggested a segmentation approach that first uses a straightforward local model to reconstruct local patches and then stitches all local reconstruction results to create a smooth surface. However, sewing local reconstruction results together presents a hurdle. A template-based approach for reconstructing dense surfaces was proposed by Russell et al. [28] in 2012; however, in this approach, an appropriate 3D template must first be selected. The initial method for sparse reconstruction [1–5] was expanded to address the dense NRSfM problem because of the proliferation of NRSfM problem-solving techniques; however, the outcome remains subpar. Currently, an increasing number of studies are focused on solving the dense NRSfM problem; these include the following: (1) Agudo et al. [6] proposed modeling time-varying shapes using a probabilistic linear subspace of modal shapes obtained from continuum mechanics. (2) Garg et al. [7] treated the dense NRSfM problem as a global variational energy minimization problem by estimating the per-frame and camera motion matrices.

(3) Kumar et al. [8,29,30] assumed that non-rigid deformations are collections of local linear subspaces and time, and used Grassmann manifolds to represent shapes as a set of smooth low-dimensional surfaces embedded in higher-dimensional Euclidean space, thus providing a practical solution and new theoretical insights for dense NRSfM. (4) Sidhu et al. [9] completed 3D reconstruction of dense non-rigid motion with an unsupervised neural network; excellent reconstruction results were obtained with the auto-decoder deformation model and latent-space constraints, but their method is not robust because it strongly depends on the mean shape.

NRSfM based on neural networks. Although the application of neural networks in solving dense NRSfM problems is still new, they are crucial in solving numerous NRSfM problems. In 2018, Cha et al. [31] developed a 3D unsupervised reconstruction network that could accurately predict the 3D results of omitted instances from the same category, and successfully reconstructed the 3D results of instances in a certain object category from 2D features using an orthographic camera model. In 2019, Facebook presented the C3DPO algorithm [32], which introduced a fresh regularization technique and substituted neural networks for traditional matrix decomposition. The deep NRSfM and deep NRSfM++ algorithms were proposed by Lucy et al. [33,34] to interpret NRSfM as multilayer sparse coding. By switching out the traditional low-rank assumption [18,35] for hierarchical block sparsity, which is more durable and comprehensible than single-level block sparsity. In 2020, Park et al. [36,37], inspired by the Procrustean alignment scheme [38], created a Procrustean regression network with a loss function that can automatically identify the correct rotation matrix. In 2021, Zeng et al. [39] first introduced a residual recurrent network (RRN) and two new loss compositions: pairwise contrast and pairwise consistency losses. RRN alone can accurately reconstruct non-rigid shapes and further improve the reconstruction results with two new losses. Wang et al. [5] used the 3D depth auto-encoder framework as the NRSfM prior and successfully recovered the 3D shape from a 2D image group with no time sequence and large deformation. Recently, Deng et al. [40] introduced a new technique for applying subspace joint structures, thereby enabling end-to-end batch training, and proposed a sequence-to-sequence translation perspective for deep NRSfM.

Although neural-network-based NRSfM has advanced significantly in recent years, it has focused primarily on the 3D reconstruction of sparse objects. There is still room for the development of dense NRSfM based on neural networks.

3. Methods

This section points out the problem setting of this study, reviews the classical architectures for the NRSfM problem to better explain the design rationale and subsequently describes our method in detail.

3.1. Preliminary

Problem setup. A network framework capable of dense NRSfM with deep neural networks without shape priors is needed. Specifically, given a dense non-rigid 2D trajectory matrix $W \in \mathbb{R}^{2F \times P}$, which contains the 2D coordinates of P keypoints in F frame, we want to recover the dense non-rigid 3D structure $S \in \mathbb{R}^{3F \times P}$.

Revisiting NRSfM. NRSfM aims to recover the 3D structure of an non-rigid object and the camera pose from a collection of 2D films acquired by a monocular camera. It can be represented by the following linear equation for orthogonal cameras:

$$W = R_{xy}S + t_{xy}, \tag{1}$$

where $W \in \mathbb{R}^{2F \times P}$ represents a 2D image sequence with P key-points in F frames and stacks F following $2 \times P$ matrix: $W_i = \begin{bmatrix} x_{i1} & \cdots & x_{ip} \\ y_{i1} & \cdots & y_{ip} \end{bmatrix}$, where $(x_{ij}, y_{ij})^T$ denotes the 2D coordinates of j-th key-point captured in the i-th frame; $S \in \mathbb{R}^{3F \times P}$ is the stack of 3D shapes S_i of reconstructed objects for each frame, where S_i contains the 3D coordinates of every key-point in the i-th frame and $S_i = \begin{bmatrix} x_{i1} & \cdots & x_{ip} \\ y_{i1} & \cdots & y_{ip} \\ z_{i1} & \cdots & z_{ip} \end{bmatrix}$; $R_{xy} \in \mathbb{R}^{2F\times 3F}$ and $t_{xy} \in \mathbb{R}^{2F}$ both are the $x - y$ component of a rigid transformation. $R_{xy} = \begin{bmatrix} R_1 & \cdots & 0 \\ \vdots & \ddots & \vdots \\ 0 & \cdots & R_F \end{bmatrix}$, where R_i is the first two rows of the rotation matrix $R_i^{'} \in \mathbb{R}^{3\times 3}$ for the i-th frame; and the translation parameter t_{xy} of the camera can be eliminated by centralization when all the feature points are visible. Experiments in this study were implemented assuming that the camera translation component was eliminated.

When the reconstruction object of the NRSfM problem is a dense non-rigid object, both global and local features must be considered, and the computations required increase dramatically, thereby complicating the dense NRSfM. Kumar et al. [8,29,30] introduced the Grassmann manifold to address this problem, whereas Sidhu et al. [9] used the average face plus neural network method. This study developed an unsupervised deep neural network based on the basic theory of NRSfM. This network can deeply mine the relationship between dense video stream frames and frames, points, and points and leverage the learning capabilities of the neural network to achieve better reconstruction effects.

3.2. Deep Spatial-Temporal NRSfM

The architecture of the DST-NRSfM model, which operates end-to-end without requiring any real data for supervision, is shown in Figure 1. It takes the 2D feature point trajectory matrix W acquired by video optical flow processing as input and outputs the 3D structure S and the camera's rotation matrix $R \in \mathbb{R}^{3F\times 3F}$ (shown in Figure 2). First, the reconstructor provides us with the initial reconstruction result; subsequently, we further optimize the reconstruction results in time and space according to the traits of high coupling between adjacent feature points of dense reconstruction objects and modest changes in neighboring frames. The outcomes of the second experiment in Section 4.2 indicate the effectiveness of the proposed spatial and temporal constraints.

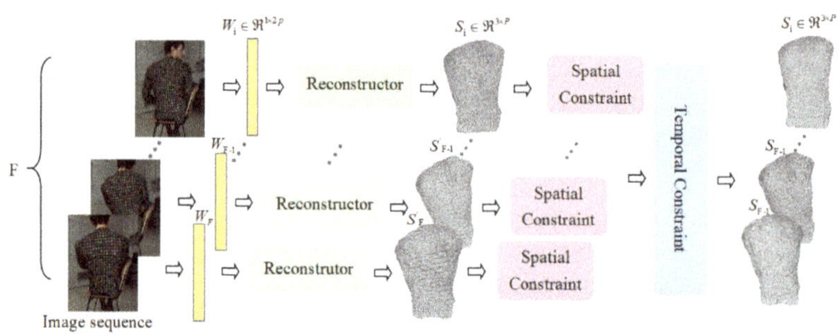

Figure 1. Overall framework of the deep spatial–temporal non-rigid structure from motion (DST-NRSfM) model.

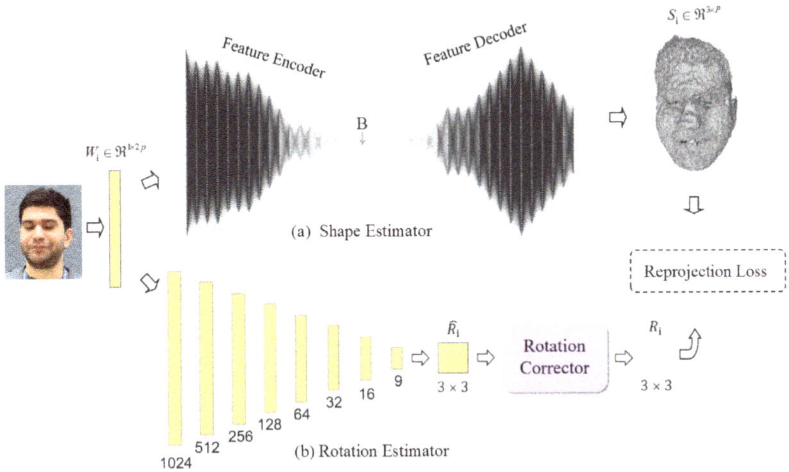

Figure 2. Schematic of the reconstructor: (**a**) Shape estimator for predicting the 3D structure of the reconstructed object. (**b**) Rotation estimator for estimating camera poses in each frame.

3.2.1. Shape Estimator in Reconstructor

An illustration of the proposed shape estimator is shown in Figure 2a, which is inspired by the typical autoencoder neural network architecture and N-NRSfM [9]. However, our network structure fully utilizes the neural network's inherent learning capacity, unlike N-NRSfM. With the addition of a feature encoder f_e and the removal of the shape priors that lead to over-dependence issues, the complete network can learn how to reconstruct the 3D structure of an non-rigid object from its 2D trajectory matrix W. The number B of neurons in the middlemost hidden layer of the whole network framework (i.e., the output layer of f_e) is set significantly lower than that of the input and output layers to ensure that the shape estimator first obtains the low-dimensional expression of the input data through f_e and then uses the feature decoder f_d to reconstruct the 3D structure from the low-dimensional expression. This successfully reduces the difficulty of the solution caused by the dense input data and allows the entire shape-estimation network to have a certain level of noise resistance. The entire shape-estimation technique is summarized as follows:

$$S_i' = f_d \circ f_e(W_i), \tag{2}$$

where W_i is reshaped into a $1 \times 2P$ feature tensor to be fed into the fully connected layers.

Network structure of the feature decoder f_d. To improve the ability of the neural network to fit complex functions and better reconstruct the 3D structure of dense objects, we expanded the number of network layers based on the deformation auto-decoder [9], which is a series of nine fully connected layers with small hidden dimensions (2, 8, 8, 8, 16, 32, 32, 32, $|S_i|$), set the maximum number of layer nodes except for the output layer to 1024, used exponential linear units (ELU) as the activation units (except for the last layer), and added a layer normalization (LN) layer between each activation function and the neural network's output. To alleviate the problem of network degradation induced by network deepening, we set the network to its residual form. When the number of neurons in the middle layer B is one, the entire network can be divided into four residual blocks. When $B = 64$, the entire network has a large residual block. The main architecture of f_d in Figure 3.

Network structure of the feature encoder f_e. Feature encoder f_e is comparable to feature decoder f_d in that it uses a fully connected residual network with a LN layer added before the output of each layer of the neural network enters the activation function ELU.

The cone-shaped wiring runs throughout the decoder network. The input layer nodes can reach 1024, whereas the output layer nodes can only go down to B, which is the number of neurons in the middlemost layer determined by the features of various datasets. f_e substitutes for the original shape prior and enhances the neural network's ability to recover highly deformed objects, as demonstrated by the experimental results on the pants dataset in Section 4.3. The architecture of f_e is shown in Figure 3.

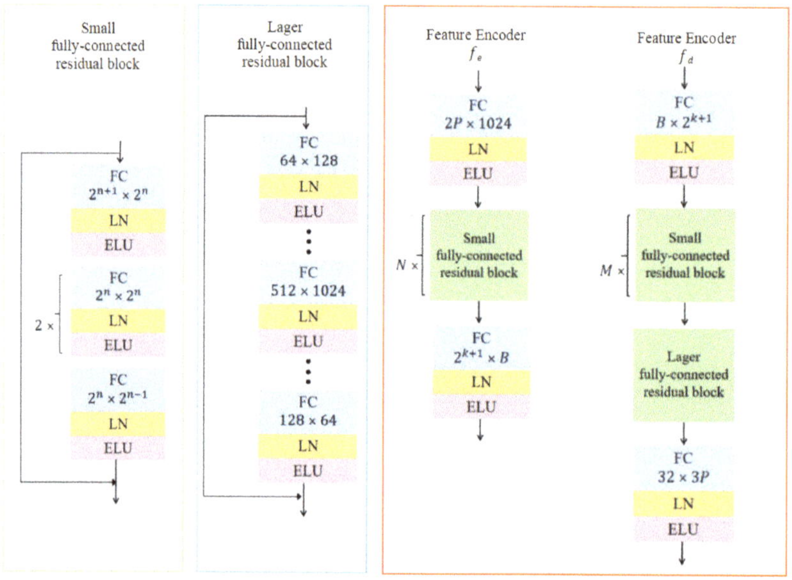

Figure 3. The architecture of the feature encoder f_e and feature decoder f_d. All neural networks framework increase or decrease exponentially. B is determined by the characteristics of the reconstructed object, $k = \log_2 B$, and $n \in (10, k)$. N and M mainly depend on the size of B, and $N \in [2, 4]$ and $M \in [0, 3]$.

Configuration for the middlemost hidden layer. The size of the number B of neurons in the middlemost hidden layer represents the low-dimensional expression of the reconstructed object, and modifying B influences the function fitting ability of the neural network as the number of neural network parameters changes. A reasonable selection of B allows us to better reconstruct the target object. When B is extremely low, the original information is lost , whereas if B is set extremely high, the reconstruction result is easily disrupted by noise in the input data and severely deformed objects cannot be recovered.

However, the number of neurons in the middlemost hidden layer is not a fixed value. It changes with the characteristics of different datasets, and can only be based on experience or trials to obtain a better value. In this study, B is defined as corresponding to different types of datasets based on the features of various datasets and trials. The settings for B for each dataset are presented in Section 4.

Layer normalization layers. The 2D trajectory matrix of the entire sequence serves as the input to our network to maintain the temporal information of the input sequence, which makes neural network training more challenging. Additionally, although choosing the ELU activation function eliminates the issue of network mean shift, soft saturation in the negative range also contributes to gradient disappearance and sluggish convergence during model training. To address the aforementioned issues, we introduced an LN layer [41] according to the network topology and properties of the incoming data. After every layer of the shape-estimation network (except the last layer), we added LN layers for data normalization. The output of each layer of the shape-estimation network, following the addition of the LN layer, can be stated as follows, assuming that the activation function is f.

$$y = f(\frac{x - E(x)}{\sqrt{var(x) - \varepsilon}} \times g + b), \tag{3}$$

where ε is a small decimal value, which prevents the denominator from being 0. Herein, gain (g) and bias (b) ensure that the normalization process does not eliminate the preceding data. Both are altered by the model training and are selected by the neural network itself.

3.2.2. Rotation Estimation Network in Reconstructor

Figure 2b shows the rotation estimator module in the DST-NRSfM model, which can be divided into two sections: a rotation estimation network and rotation matrix corrector. The two sections collaborate to deduce the rotation matrix R. The rotation estimation network, which has only eight fully connected layers, and each layer is followed by an ELU (except the last layer), can be represented by the following formula.

$$\hat{R}_i = g_\omega(W_i). \tag{4}$$

Simultaneously, because the input data are captured by an orthogonal camera and reflection ambiguity, that is, if the rotation matrix at the i-th frame is assumed to be R_i, then both R_i and $-R_i$ are valid rotation matrices, but the choice of different rotation symbols will result in different recovery shapes, that is, $S_f = [S_{fx}; S_{fy}; S_{fz}]$ and $S_f = [-S_{fx}; -S_{fy}; -S_{fz}]$ may appear when reconstructing the rotation matrix. Therefore, we solved these problems by adding a rotation matrix corrector after the rotation estimation module. The entire correction process is as follows.

In Figure 4, ① represents the singular value decomposition (SVD) of $\hat{R}_i$:

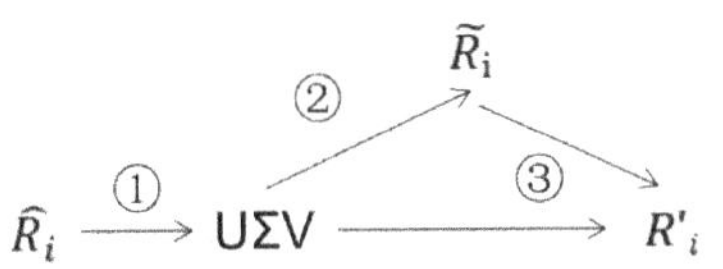

Figure 4. Rotation matrix corrector workflow.

$$\hat{R}_i = U\Sigma V; \tag{5}$$

② imposes an orthogonal constraint, that is, $\tilde{R}_i\tilde{R}_i^T = 1$, on the rotation matrix:

$$\tilde{R}_i \longleftarrow UV^T; \tag{6}$$

③ resolves the reflection ambiguity by placing the estimated rotation matrix into a special orthogonal group with $\left|R_i'\right| = 1$:

$$R_i' \longrightarrow U \begin{bmatrix} 1 & 0 & 0 \\ 0 & 1 & 0 \\ 0 & 0 & |\tilde{R}_i| \end{bmatrix} V^T. \tag{7}$$

Finally, the 3D structure S_i' estimated by the shape estimator network is reprojected to a 2D shape using the rotation matrix R_i' to measure the degree of agreement between the projection of the 3D reconstruction result and the given 2D feature point. The reprojection loss was calculated as follows.

$$L_{reproj} = \sum_{i=1}^{F} \left\| W_i - PR_i'S_i' \right\|_\varepsilon, \tag{8}$$

where $\|\cdot\|_\varepsilon$ denotes the Huber loss:

$$L_\delta(e) = \begin{cases} \frac{1}{2}e^2, & if|e| \le \delta, \\ \delta \cdot (|e| - \frac{1}{2}\delta), & otherwise, \end{cases} \tag{9}$$

where $\delta = 1$, and e usually stands for residuals. Because we performed the experiments using the orthogonal camera model, the projection matrix P can be expressed as:

$$P = \begin{bmatrix} 1 & 0 & 0 \\ 0 & 1 & 0 \end{bmatrix}. \tag{10}$$

3.3. Temporal Constraint and Spatial Constraint

According to any dense NRSfM's object that consists of dense feature points, we can assume that points in adjacent fields move in the same direction and most points between adjacent frames do not change significantly. Hence, we introduced temporal and spatial constraints to further improve the reconstruction outcomes.

Temporal constraint. The temporal constraint, also known as time-smoothing loss, limits the 3D trajectory smoothness of dense non-rigid reconstructions from the temporal dimension, as follows.

$$L_{temp} = \sum_{f=1}^{F-1} \left\| S_{f+1} - S_f \right\|_\varepsilon. \tag{11}$$

Weighted spatial constraint. The spatial constraint aims to constrain the smoothness of 3D structures in each frame from the spatial dimension. Although the spatial smoothing described by Sidhu et al. [9] can achieve this effect, their algorithm causes undesirable deformations. Herein, we presented the weighted spatial constraint to improve the reconstruction performance. This guaranteed that the points in the local field of any vertex had the same motion trend and the local details of the reconstructed object can be preserved. These are all crucial for dense NRSfM, which brings the reconstruction result closer to the real value without deformation while ensuring smoothness. L_{w_spat} is given as:

$$L_{w\_spat} = \sum_{f=1}^{F} \sum_{i \in S_f} \left\| i - \frac{\sum_{j \in N(i)} \omega_{ij} * j}{\sum_{j \in N(i)} \omega_{ij}} \right\|_\varepsilon, \tag{12}$$

$$\omega_{ij} = \frac{1}{2}(\cot \alpha_{ij} + \cot \beta_{ij}), \tag{13}$$

where $N(i)$ represents the set of all vertices in 1-ring field of vertex i, $i \in S_f$; and α_{ij} and β_{ij} are the opposite corners of the two adjoining triangular patches of edge ij.

3.4. Alternative Training

The final training loss function L of DST-NRSfM is:

$$L = \lambda_1 L_{reproj} + \lambda_2 L_{temp} + \lambda_3 L_{w\_spat}, \tag{14}$$

where λ_1, λ_2, and λ_3 are the weight coefficients that balance the influence of each loss function on the final structure. We discovered that training the networks with L_{temp} and L_{w_spat} yields superior results.

Finally, the priors that solve the dense NRSfM problem are significantly reduced, and the complexity of the rotation estimation network is reduced because of a suitable shape-estimation network.

4. Experiments

4.1. Implementation Details

Datasets. The following three types of datasets were used. (1) Widely used dense benchmarks with 3D ground truth S_{gt}: actor mocap (100 frames with 36,349 points) [42], synthetic faces syn3 and syn4 with different camera trajectories (99 frames with 28,000 points) [7], Kinect paper sequences (193 frames with 58,000 points) and t-shirt sequences (313 frames with 77,000 points) [43]. (2) Relatively sparse datasets with 3D ground truth geometry : expressions (384 frames with 997 points) [44] and pants (291 frames with 2859 points) [45], which are significantly deformed. (3) Real video sequence: back (150 frames with 20,474 points) [46], heart surgery sequence (201 frames with 55,115 points) [47], and real face (120 frames with 28,332 points) [7].

Evaluation indicator. We utilized the normalized error (NE) to assess the algorithm's performance for datasets with three-dimensional true values, defined as

$$e_{3D} = \frac{1}{F}\sum_{f=1}^{F}\frac{\left\|S_{est}^{f} - S_{gt}^{f}\right\|_{F}}{\left\|S_{gt}^{f}\right\|_{F}}, \tag{15}$$

where S_{gt}^{f} denotes the actual 3D structure of the f-th frame of the reconstructed object and S_{est}^{f} is the f-th frame of our anticipated 3D structure, which is aligned to the ground truth after using the Procrustes algorithm.

Training Details. We employed RProp [48] as the optimizer with a learning rate of 0.0001 because we input the entire dataset during training to effectively retain the spatiotemporal information. All proposed network frameworks were initialized with He [49]. The experiment set the weights to $\lambda_1 = 1000$, $\lambda_2 = 1$, and $\lambda_3 = 1 \times 10^{-5}$ and trained for 60,000 epochs. The number B of neurons in the middlemost layer of the shape-estimation network, which is affected by the essential characteristics of the given dataset, extent of deformation, amount of noise, and degree of density, was selected empirically by the determined ranges $[1, 64]$ throughout Sections 4.2 and 4.3. In general, the larger the noise and deformation variables of the dataset, the closer B is to 1, and the sparser the dataset, and the smaller the value of B.

Experimental environment. DST-NRSfM was programmed using the PyTorch and trained on a server with 12 GB RAM, RTX2080Ti graphics card, and Ubuntu operating system.

4.2. Network Structure Analysis

The necessity for layer normalization layers. To demonstrate the importance of LN layers in the shape-estimation network, we designed a series of controlled trials for shape-estimation networks with and without LN layers using the same loss function on the synthetic faces syn3, the real dataset actor mocap, expressions (sparser), and the Kinect dataset paper. The convergence curves of each dataset are shown in Figure 5.

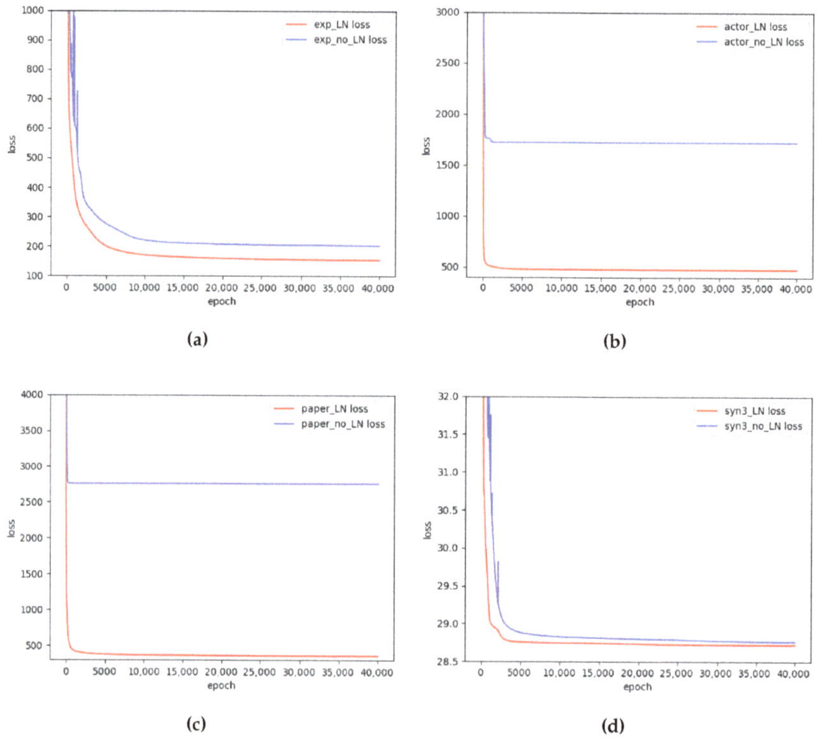

Figure 5. Decline curve corresponding to whether to add layer normalization layers (LN) in the proposed network architecture with reprojection loss and temporal constraint in expressions, actor mocap, paper, and syn3. (**a**) expressions; (**b**) actor mocap; (**c**) paper; (**d**) syn3.

Figure 5 demonstrates how the LN layers cause the actor mocap and paper datasets to converge at a lower loss while improving the stability and speed of the expressions and syn3 dataset models. We effectively incorporated the LN layers into the proposed shape-estimation network. It improved the model's problem-solving abilities, increased model stability, and hastened convergence.

Effectiveness of temporal constraint and weighted spatial constraint. We conducted ablation experiments on the loss function of the DST-NRSfM network to confirm the efficiency of the temporal constraint and the newly implemented weighted spatial constraint. Table 1 reports the experimental results. The results show that despite the reconstruction results being considerably improved by the temporal constraints, the extension of the weighted spatial constraint further enhanced the reconstruction accuracy. Figure 6a–d visualize the reconstruction results of actor mocap, expressions, syn3, and syn4 with and without spatial constraints in the presence L_{reproj} and L_{temp} loss conditions. The results following the spatial constraints are more accurate and smoother, as can be seen in Figure 6a,c,d. In contrast, Figure 6b does not exhibit a notable qualitative difference because the expressions are sparser; however, careful inspection of the reconstructed point cloud (reconstructed points are yellow, and the reconstructed points after flipping are black) revealed that there were fewer flipped reconstruction points in the reconstruction results after the weighted spatial constraint. This suggests that the weighted spatial constraint aids in mesh quality improvement.

Table 1. Results of ablation experiments.

	syn3	syn4	Expressions	Actor Mocap	Paper
L_{reproj}	0.1196	0.1201	0.2205	0.2624	0.0376
$L_{reproj} + L_{temp}$	0.0149	0.0255	0.0273	0.0174	0.0342
$L_{reproj} + L_{temp} + L_{w\_spat}$	0.0134	0.0241	0.0226	0.0163	0.0296

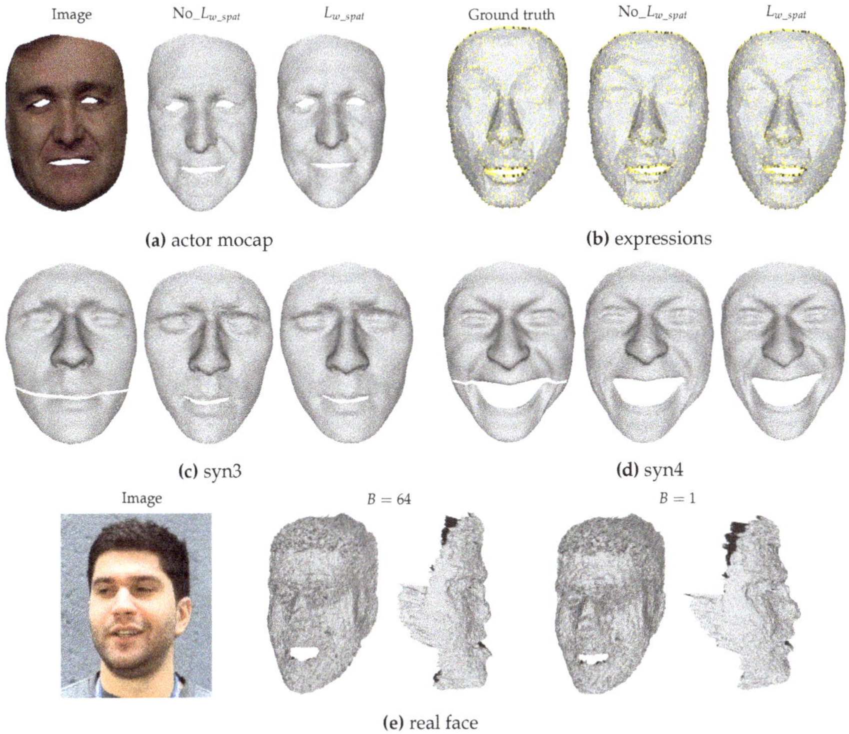

Figure 6. Visualized ablation and contrast experiment results. From left to right, genuine pictures, and 3D reconstruction without and with the weighted spatial constraint are displayed in (**a**–**d**). (**a**–**d**) depict the ablation experiment results of actor mocap, expressions, syn3, and syn4, respectively; the yellow points in (**b**) are the reconstructed point clouds, whereas the black points are the inverted 3D points. From left to right, (**e**) displays the true images of the real face dataset and the front and side views of the reconstruction results when the number of neurons in the middlemost layer of the shape-estimation network is $B = 1$ and $B = 64$.

Analysis of model computational complexity. For smoother deployments in empirical applications, we analyzed the computational complexity of the DST-NRSfM model. As the complexity of the neural network model is mainly determined by two parameters: parameters (Params) and floating-point operations per second (FLOPS), we separately count the two parameters of the shape estimator and the rotation estimator, as shown in Table 2. It is clearly visible that the computational complexity of the model differs depending on the number of neurons in the middle layer and the input dimensions. We found that model complexity is strongly influenced by dataset density, and model complexity increases as dataset density increases. Therefore, the model we designed still has a lot of room for improvement in the frame structure.

Table 2. Computational complexity analysis of DST-NRSfM model.

	Dataset	Actor Mocap ($B = 64$)	syn3 ($B = 64$)	Paper ($B = 2$)	Expressions ($B = 2$)	Heart Surgery ($B = 2$)	Back ($B = 2$)	Real Face ($B = 1$)
Shape Estimator	FLOPS	8.06×10^{10}	6.40×10^{9}	2.51×10^{10}	1.88×10^{9}	2.43×10^{10}	7.00×10^{9}	7.62×10^{9}
	Params	8.07×10^{7}	6.47×10^{7}	1.31×10^{8}	4.90×10^{7}	1.21×10^{8}	4.67×10^{7}	6.35×10^{7}
Rotation Estimator	FLOPS	7.51×10^{9}	5.93×10^{9}	2.36×10^{10}	1.05×10^{9}	2.28×10^{10}	6.39×10^{9}	7.05×10^{9}
	Params	7.51×10^{7}	5.99×10^{7}	1.22×10^{8}	2.74×10^{6}	1.14×10^{8}	4.26×10^{7}	5.87×10^{7}

4.3. Results and Analysis

Actor mocap. The actor mocap sequence, as real face data with S_{gt}, allows us to analyze the reconstruction results of our method qualitatively and quantitatively. The visible results are shown in the third image of Figure 6a. Comparing to actual images, our method successfully reconstructed the 3D structure of the actor mocap. Furthermore, we qualitatively compared our approach to face model learning (FML) [50], scalable monocular surface reconstruction (SMSR) [51], consolidating monocular dynamic reconstruction (CMDR) [52,53], optimization neural network (RONN) [54], and N-NRSfM [9]. Moreover, e_{3D} for the actor mocap is listed in Table 3, which revealed that our method is significantly superior to other methods.

Table 3. e_{3D} on the the actor mocap.

Dataset	FML [50]	SMSR [51]	CMDR [52]	RONN [54]	N-NRSfM [9]	Ours ($B = 64$)
actor mocap	0.092	0.054	0.0257	0.0226	0.0181	**0.0163**

Synthetic Faces. The widely usage of synthetic faces allows us to compare DST-NRSfM to more methods. To more intuitively understand the efficacy of our approach, we compared the experimental outcomes of DST-NRSfM with classical sparse NRSfM methods, such as metric projections (MP) [55], complementary rank-3 spaces (CSF2) [17], block-matrix-method (BMM) [20], and organic priors based approach (OP) [3], traditional dense NRSfM methods, such as variational approach (VA) [7], dense spatio-temporal approach (DSTA) [25], CMDR [52,53], Grassmannian manifold (GM) [8], jumping manifolds (JM) [29], SMSR [51], and probabilistic point trajectory approach (PPTA) [14], and the latest neural-based dense NRSfM approaches, such as N-NRSfM [9], and RONN [54]. Table 4 presents the final comparative experimental results, where OP is the newest method that solves the dense NRSfM problem by extending the sparse approach to the dense domain; however, the accuracy of our proposed framework remained nearly twice as accuracy. Although DSTA also employs space-time limitations to enhance reconstruction accuracy, the reconstruction accuracy of the proposed framework was substantially higher than that of DSTA because our spatial constraint theory fundamentally differs from that proposed by DSTA; moreover, our solution is more flexible. Additionally, our approach performed better than state-of-the-art learning-based dense NRSfM approaches, despite syn4 being more challenging to reconstruct than syn3. The visual reconstruction outcomes for syn3 and syn4 are shown in Figure 6c,d, respectively.

Table 4. e_{3D} on the synthetic face sequences (syn3 and syn4).

	Classical Sparse NRSfM Methods				Neural Dense NRSFM Methods		
Dataset	MP [55]	CSF2 [17]	BMM [20]	OP [3]	N-NRSfM [9]	RONN [54]	Ours ($B = 64$)
syn3	0.0611	0.5474	0.0784	0.0279	0.0320	0.0309	**0.0134**
syn4	0.0762	0.5292	0.0918	0.0419	0.0389	0.0359	**0.0263**

	Conventional Dense NRSfM Methods						
Dataset	VA [7]	DSTA [25]	GM [8]	JM [29]	PPTA [14]	CMDR [52]	SMSR [51]	Ours ($B = 64$)
syn3	0.0346	0.0374	0.0294	0.0280	0.0390	0.0324	0.0304	**0.0134**
syn4	0.0379	0.0428	0.0309	0.0327	0.052	0.0369	0.0319	**0.0263**

Kinect Sequences. In contrast to the face sequences, the Kinect sequences exhibited larger deformations, more key points, and a simpler camera trajectory. To ensure a fair evaluation, we preprocessed the Kinect sequences as described by Kumar et al. [8] and ran a multi-frame optical flow [56] with default parameters to obtain dense correspondences. e_{3D} for the Kinect sequences are presented in Table 5. Visualizations are shown in the second row of Figure 7. Our approach outperformed all competing methods in the Kinect paper sequence. In the t-shirt sequence, owing to insufficient device memory, the weighted spatial constraint cannot be applied, causing a suboptimal reconstruction effect, but the result remains resistant.

Table 5. e_{3D} on the Kinect paper and t-shirt sequences.

Dataset	MP [55]	DSTA [25]	GM [8]	JM [29]	N-NRSfM [9]	Ours
paper	0.0827	0.0612	0.0394	0.0338	0.0332	**0.0296** ($B = 2$)
t-shirt	0.0741	0.0636	0.0362	0.0386	**0.0309**	0.0396 ($B = 2$)

Expressions. As the expressions dataset is horizontally shifted and relatively sparse, we set $B = 2$. Using this dataset, we can compare our method with two new algorithms: Kernel Shape Trajectory Approach (KSTA) [57] and Global Model with Local Interpretation (GMLI) [44]. Herein, e_{3D} for the expressions are presented in Table 6. The reconstruction results are shown in Figure 6b. We achieved $e_{3D} = 0.023$, which is better than the best result of 0.026, for this sequence. Experiments demonstrated that DST-NRSfM can also be applied to sparser datasets with significant horizontal shifts.

Table 6. e_{3D} on the expressions dataset.

Dataset	CSF2 [17]	KSTA [57]	GMLI [44]	N-NRSfM [9]	RONN [54]	Ours ($B = 2$)
expressions	0.030	0.035	0.026	0.026	0.026	**0.023**

Pants. The pants dataset collects sequences that document how pants appear when people jump and rotate. Extremely violent deformation makes the reconstruction extremely challenging. To highlight the benefits of DST-NRSfM in reconstructing severely distorted objects, we used it to reconstruct the pants dataset. Table 7 presents the reconstruction results quantitatively, and the visualization is shown in the last row of Figure 7. Experiments demonstrated that the proposed framework had the best reconstruction effect on this dataset, and accuracy was enhanced by nearly 20% over the second-place finisher. Note that these are merely experimental results produced without spatial constraints because the dataset lacks a mesh template.

Table 7. e_{3D} on the pants dataset.

Dataset	KSTA [57]	BMM [20]	PPTA [14]	Ours ($B = 1$)
pants	0.220	0.183	0.203	**0.148**

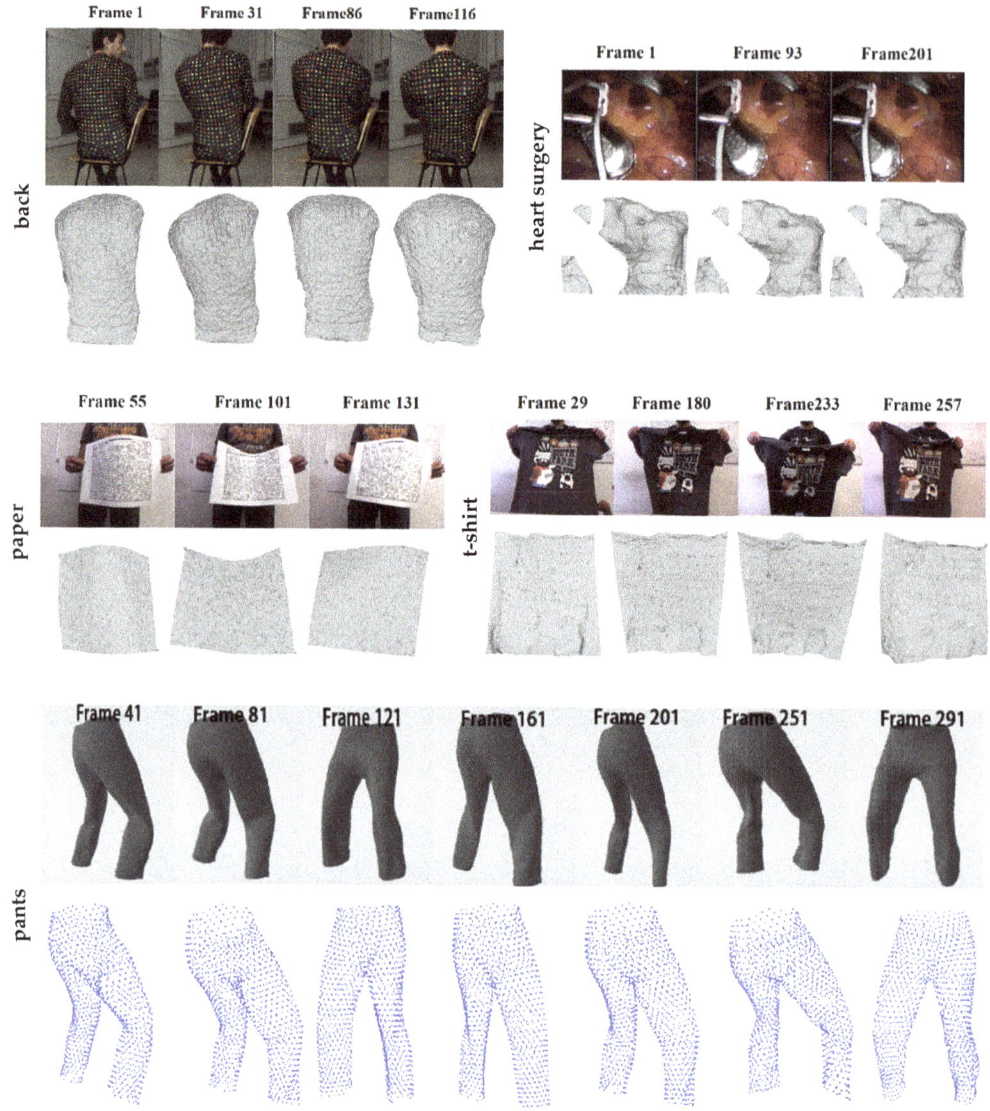

Figure 7. Visualizations of real sequence reconstruction results. The first row shows the reconstructed results of back and heart surgery sequences. The second row is the visualization of Kinect sequences' reconstruction results. The third row shows the reconstruction effect of the heavily deformed sparse pants sequence, where DST-NRSfM achieves the lowest e_{3D} among all examined approaches. The reconstruction result of the real face sequence is shown in Figure 6e.

Real video sequence. We constructed several real video sequences, such as the back, heart surgery sequence, and real face. We adjusted the size of B according to the features of each dataset and expertise. The real face sequence contains a significant amount of noise; therefore, we set $B = 1$. Figure 6e shows the effect of the size of B on the reconstruction results. For the back and heart surgery sequences, we assumed that their essential characteristics were 2; hence, $B = 2$. The back and heart surgery sequences are shown in the first row of Figure 7. Evidently, the DST-NRSfM generated highly realistic outcomes.

5. Conclusions

This study provided a novel end-to-end unsupervised DST-NRSfM for solving tough dense NRSfM. We discarded shape prior and designed a network architecture that leverages the neural network's capacity for learning according to the properties of various datasets. Therefore, even for objects with significant deformations, the best reconstruction results may be achieved with only reprojection loss and temporal constraints. To further enhance the reconstruction results, we introduced a new spatial constraint called a weighted spatial constraint. This constraint enhances the reconstruction accuracy and the mesh quality and smooths out the reconstruction. Aiming at the problem of gradient disappearance and model instability found in the experiment, we implemented layer normalization layers in dense NRSfM. Quantitative and qualitative results demonstrated that our method achieves competitive performance with state-of-the-art dense NRSfM methods.

In DST-NRSfM the number of neurons in the middlemost layer of the shape-estimation network can only be hypothesized based on the features of different datasets, which is similar to the bases in the conventional NRSfM technique. The model framework consists of fully connected networks, resulting in redundancy of parameters and high computational complexity. Moreover, because it involves matrices of size $P \times P$, where P is the number of feature points and requires a mesh template for computation, the weighted spatial constraint approach cannot be utilized for arbitrary datasets.

DST-NRSfM substantially enhances the reconstruction accuracy of dense NRSfM and provides a broader perspective of using neural networks to address such issues. Future research will focus on enabling a neural network with low computational complexity to automatically select the most appropriate structure based on the dataset features.

Author Contributions: Conceptualization, Y.W., W.H. and M.J.; methodology, Y.W., W.H. and M.W.; software, M.W.; validation, Y.W., W.H. and M.J.; formal analysis, Y.W. and M.W.; investigation, M.W. and X.Y.; data curation, M.W. and X.Y.; writing—original draft preparation, M.W. and W.H.; writing—review and editing, Y.W., W.H. and M.W.; visualization, Y.W. and M.W.; supervision,Y.W. and W.H. All authors have read and agreed to the published version of the manuscript.

Funding: This research is supported by the Natural Science Foundation of Zhejiang Province (LZ20F020003, LZ21F020003, LSZ19F010001, LY17F020003), and the National Natural Science Foundation of China (61272311, 61672466).

Institutional Review Board Statement: Not applicable.

Informed Consent Statement: Not applicable.

Data Availability Statement: The data presented in this study are available on request from the corresponding author. The data are not publicly available due to privacy.

Conflicts of Interest: The authors declare no conflict of interest.

References

1. Russell, C.; Fayad, J.; Agapito, L. Dense non-rigid structure from motion. In Proceedings of the 2012 Second International Conference on 3D Imaging, Modeling, Processing, Visualization & Transmission, Zurich, Switzerland, 13–15 October 2012; pp. 509–516.
2. Golyanik, V.; Stricker, D. Dense batch non-rigid structure from motion in a second. In Proceedings of the 2017 IEEE Winter Conference on Applications of Computer Vision (WACV), Santa Rosa, CA, USA, 24–31 March 2017; pp. 254–263.
3. Kumar, S.; Van Gool, L. Organic Priors in Non-Rigid Structure from Motion. *arXiv* **2022**, arXiv:2207.06262.
4. Song, J.; Patel, M.; Jasour, A.; Ghaffari, M. A Closed-Form Uncertainty Propagation in Non-Rigid Structure From Motion.*IEEE Robot. Autom. Lett.* **2022**, *7*, 6479–6486. [CrossRef]
5. Wang, C.; Lucey, S. PAUL: Procrustean Autoencoder for Unsupervised Lifting. In Proceedings of the IEEE/CVF Conference on Computer Vision and Pattern Recognition, Nashville, TN, USA, 20–25 June 2021; pp. 434–443.
6. Agudo, A.; Montiel, J.; Agapito, L.; Calvo, B. Online Dense Non-Rigid 3D Shape and Camera Motion Recovery. In Proceedings of the BMVC, Nottingham, UK, 1–5 September 2014.
7. Garg, R.; Roussos, A.; Agapito, L. Dense variational reconstruction of non-rigid surfaces from monocular video. In Proceedings of the IEEE Conference on Computer Vision and Pattern Recognition, Portland, OR, USA, 23–28 June 2013; pp. 1272–1279.

8. Kumar, S.; Cherian, A.; Dai, Y.; Li, H. Scalable dense non-rigid structure-from-motion: A grassmannian perspective. In Proceedings of the IEEE Conference on Computer Vision and Pattern Recognition, Salt Lake City, UT, USA, 18–23 June 2018; pp. 254–263.
9. Sidhu, V.; Tretschk, E.; Golyanik, V.; Agudo, A.; Theobalt, C. Neural dense non-rigid structure from motion with latent space constraints. In *Proceedings of the European Conference on Computer Vision*; Springer: Berlin/Heidelberg, Germany, 2020; pp. 204–222
10. Rumelhart, D.E.; Hinton, G.E.; Williams, R.J. Learning representations by back-propagating errors. *Nature* **1986**, *323*, 533–536 [CrossRef]
11. Hinton, G.E.; Osindero, S.; Teh, Y.W. A fast learning algorithm for deep belief nets. *Neural Comput.* **2006**, *18*, 1527–1554. [CrossRef] [PubMed]
12. Zhou, Z.; Shi, F.; Xiao, J.; Wu, W. Non-rigid structure-from-motion on degenerate deformations with low-rank shape deformation model. *IEEE Trans. Multimed.* **2014**, *17*, 171–185. [CrossRef]
13. Wang, Y.M.; Zheng, J.B.; Jiang, M.F.; Xiong, Y.L.; Huang, W.Q. A Trajectory Basis Selection Method for Non-Rigid Structure from Motion. In *Applied Mechanics and Materials*; Trans Tech Publications Ltd.: Bach, Switzerland, 2014; Volume 644, pp. 1396–1399.
14. Agudo, A.; Moreno-Noguer, F. A scalable, efficient, and accurate solution to non-rigid structure from motion. *Comput. Vis. Image Underst.* **2018**, *167*, 121–133. [CrossRef]
15. Torresani, L.; Hertzmann, A.; Bregler, C. Nonrigid structure-from-motion: Estimating shape and motion with hierarchical priors *IEEE Trans. Pattern Anal. Mach. Intell.* **2008**, *30*, 878–892. [CrossRef]
16. Paladini, M.; Del Bue, A.; Stosic, M.; Dodig, M.; Xavier, J.; Agapito, L. Factorization for non-rigid and articulated structure using metric projections. In Proceedings of the 2009 IEEE Conference on Computer Vision and Pattern Recognition, Miami, FL, USA, 20–25 June 2009; pp. 2898–2905.
17. Gotardo, P.F.; Martinez, A.M. Non-rigid structure from motion with complementary rank-3 spaces. In Proceedings of the CVPR 2011, Colorado Springs, CO, USA, 20–25 June 2011; pp. 3065–3072.
18. Kong, C.; Lucey, S. Prior-less compressible structure from motion. In Proceedings of the IEEE Conference on Computer Vision and Pattern Recognition, Las Vegas, NV, USA, 27–30 June 2016; pp. 4123–4131.
19. Agudo, A.; Moreno-Noguer, F. Force-based representation for non-rigid shape and elastic model estimation. *IEEE Trans. Pattern Anal. Mach. Intell.* **2017**, *40*, 2137–2150. [CrossRef]
20. Dai, Y.; Li, H.; He, M. A simple prior-free method for non-rigid structure-from-motion factorization. *Int. J. Comput. Vis.* **2014**, *107*, 101–122. [CrossRef]
21. Parashar, S.; Pizarro, D.; Bartoli, A. Isometric non-rigid shape-from-motion in linear time. In Proceedings of the IEEE Conference on Computer Vision and Pattern Recognition, Las Vegas, NV, USA, 27–30 June 2016; pp. 4679–4687.
22. Agudo, A.; Moreno-Noguer, F.; Calvo, B.; Montiel, J.M.M. Sequential non-rigid structure from motion using physical priors. *IEEE Trans. Pattern Anal. Mach. Intell.* **2015**, *38*, 979–994. [CrossRef]
23. Cha, G.; Lee, M.; Cho, J.; Oh, S. Non-rigid surface recovery with a robust local-rigidity prior. *Pattern Recognit. Lett.* **2018**, *110*, 51–57. [CrossRef]
24. Li, X.; Li, H.; Joo, H.; Liu, Y.; Sheikh, Y. Structure from recurrent motion: From rigidity to recurrency. In Proceedings of the IEEE Conference on Computer Vision and Pattern Recognition, Salt Lake City, UT, USA, 18–23 June 2018; pp. 3032–3040.
25. Dai, Y.; Deng, H.; He, M. Dense non-rigid structure-from-motion made easy—A spatial-temporal smoothness based solution. In Proceedings of the 2017 IEEE International Conference on Image Processing (ICIP), Beijing, China, 17–20 September 2017; pp. 4532–4536.
26. Graßhof, S.; Brandt, S.S. Tensor-Based Non-Rigid Structure From Motion. In Proceedings of the IEEE/CVF Winter Conference on Applications of Computer Vision, Waikoloa, HI, USA, 3–8 January 2022; pp. 3011–3020.
27. Collins, T.; Bartoli, A. Locally affine and planar deformable surface reconstruction from video. In Proceedings of the International Workshop on Vision, Modeling and Visualization, Siegen, Germany, 15–17 November 2010; pp. 339–346.
28. Bartoli, A.; Gérard, Y.; Chadebecq, F.; Collins, T. On template-based reconstruction from a single view: Analytical solutions and proofs of well-posedness for developable, isometric and conformal surfaces. In Proceedings of the 2012 IEEE Conference on Computer Vision and Pattern Recognition, Providence, RI, USA, 16–21 June 2012; pp. 2026–2033.
29. Kumar, S. Jumping manifolds: Geometry aware dense non-rigid structure from motion. In Proceedings of the IEEE/CVF Conference on Computer Vision and Pattern Recognition, Long Beach, CA, USA, 15–20 June 2019; pp. 5346–5355.
30. Kumar, S.; Van Gool, L.; de Oliveira, C.E.; Cherian, A.; Dai, Y.; Li, H. Dense Non-Rigid Structure from Motion: A Manifold Viewpoint. *arXiv* **2020**, arXiv:2006.09197.
31. Cha, G.; Lee, M.; Oh, S. Unsupervised 3d reconstruction networks. In Proceedings of the IEEE/CVF International Conference on Computer Vision, Seoul, Korea, 27 October–2 November 2019; pp. 3849–3858.
32. Novotny, D.; Ravi, N.; Graham, B.; Neverova, N.; Vedaldi, A. C3dpo: Canonical 3d pose networks for non-rigid structure from motion. In Proceedings of the IEEE/CVF International Conference on Computer Vision, Seoul, Korea, 27 October–2 November 2019; pp. 7688–7697.
33. Kong, C.; Lucey, S. Deep non-rigid structure from motion. In Proceedings of the IEEE/CVF International Conference on Computer Vision, Seoul, Korea, 27 October–2 November 2019; pp. 1558–1567.
34. Wang, C.; Lin, C.H.; Lucey, S. Deep NRSfM++: Towards Unsupervised 2D-3D Lifting in the Wild. In Proceedings of the 2020 International Conference on 3D Vision (3DV), Fukuoka, Japan, 25–28 November 2020.

35. Kumar, S. Non-rigid structure from motion: Prior-free factorization method revisited. In Proceedings of the IEEE/CVF Winter Conference on Applications of Computer Vision, Waikoloa, HI, USA, 4–8 January 2020; pp. 51–60.
36. Park, S.; Lee, M.; Kwak, N. Procrustean regression: A flexible alignment-based framework for nonrigid structure estimation. *IEEE Trans. Image Process.* **2017**, *27*, 249–264. [CrossRef] [PubMed]
37. Park, S.; Lee, M.; Kwak, N. Procrustean regression networks: Learning 3d structure of non-rigid objects from 2d annotations. In *Proceedings of the European Conference on Computer Vision*; Springer: Berlin/Heidelberg, Germany, 2020; pp. 1–18.
38. Lee, M.; Cho, J.; Choi, C.H.; Oh, S. Procrustean normal distribution for non-rigid structure from motion. In Proceedings of the IEEE Conference on Computer Vision and Pattern Recognition, Portland, OR, USA, 23–28 June 2013; pp. 1280–1287.
39. Zeng, H.; Dai, Y.; Yu, X.; Wang, X.; Yang, Y. PR-RRN: Pairwise-Regularized Residual-Recursive Networks for Non-rigid Structure-from-Motion. In Proceedings of the IEEE/CVF International Conference on Computer Vision, Montreal, BC, Canada, 11–17 October 2021; pp. 5600–5609.
40. Deng, H.; Zhang, T.; Dai, Y.; Shi, J.; Zhong, Y.; Li, H. Deep Non-rigid Structure-from-Motion: A Sequence-to-Sequence Translation Perspective. *arXiv* **2022**, arXiv:2204.04730.
41. Ba, J.L.; Kiros, J.R.; Hinton, G.E. Layer normalization. *arXiv* **2016**, arXiv:1607.06450.
42. Valgaerts, L.; Wu, C.; Bruhn, A.; Seidel, H.P.; Theobalt, C. Lightweight binocular facial performance capture under uncontrolled lighting. *ACM Trans. Graph.* **2012**, *31*, 1–11. [CrossRef]
43. Varol, A.; Salzmann, M.; Fua, P.; Urtasun, R. A constrained latent variable model. In Proceedings of the 2012 IEEE Conference on Computer Vision and Pattern Recognition, Providence, RI, USA, 16–21 June 2012; pp. 2248–2255.
44. Agudo, A.; Moreno-Noguer, F. Global model with local interpretation for dynamic shape reconstruction. In Proceedings of the 2017 IEEE Winter Conference on Applications of Computer Vision (WACV), Santa Rosa, CA, USA, 24–31 March 2017; pp. 264–272.
45. White, R.; Crane, K.; Forsyth, D.A. Capturing and animating occluded cloth. *ACM Trans. Graph.* **2007**, *26*, 34–es. [CrossRef]
46. Russell, C.; Fayad, J.; Agapito, L. Energy based multiple model fitting for non-rigid structure from motion. In Proceedings of the CVPR 2011, Providence, RI, USA, 20–25 June 2011; pp. 3009–3016.
47. Stoyanov, D. Stereoscopic scene flow for robotic assisted minimally invasive surgery. In *Proceedings of the International Conference on Medical Image Computing and Computer-Assisted Intervention*; Springer: Berlin/Heidelberg, Germany, 2012; pp. 479–486.
48. Riedmiller, M.; Braun, H. A direct adaptive method for faster backpropagation learning: The RPROP algorithm. In Proceedings of the IEEE International Conference on Neural Networks, San Francisco, CA, USA, 28 Maarch–1 April 1993; pp. 586–591.
49. He, K.; Zhang, X.; Ren, S.; Sun, J. Delving deep into rectifiers: Surpassing human-level performance on imagenet classification. In Proceedings of the IEEE International Conference on Computer Vision, Santiago, Chile, 1–13 December 2015; pp. 1026–1034.
50. Tewari, A.; Bernard, F.; Garrido, P.; Bharaj, G.; Elgharib, M.; Seidel, H.P.; Pérez, P.; Zollhofer, M.; Theobalt, C. Fml: Face model learning from videos. In Proceedings of the IEEE/CVF Conference on Computer Vision and Pattern Recognition, Long Beach, CA, USA, 15–20 June 2019; pp. 10812–10822.
51. Ansari, M.D.; Golyanik, V.; Stricker, D. Scalable dense monocular surface reconstruction. In Proceedings of the 2017 International Conference on 3D Vision (3DV), Qingdao, China, 10–12 October 2017; pp. 78–87.
52. Golyanik, V.; Jonas, A.; Stricker, D. Consolidating segmentwise non-rigid structure from motion. In Proceedings of the 2019 16th International Conference on Machine Vision Applications (MVA), Tokyo, Japan, 27–31 May 2019; pp. 1–6.
53. Golyanik, V.; Jonas, A.; Stricker, D.; Theobalt, C. Intrinsic dynamic shape prior for fast, sequential and dense non-rigid structure from motion with detection of temporally-disjoint rigidity. *arXiv* **2019**, arXiv:1909.02468.
54. Wang, Y.; Peng, X.; Huang, W.; Wang, M. A Convolutional Neural Network for Nonrigid Structure from Motion. *Int. J. Digit. Multimed. Broadcast.* **2022**, *2022*, 3582037. [CrossRef]
55. Paladini, M.; Del Bue, A.; Xavier, J.; Agapito, L.; Stošić, M.; Dodig, M. Optimal metric projections for deformable and articulated structure-from-motion. *Int. J. Comput. Vis.* **2012**, *96*, 252–276. [CrossRef]
56. Garg, R.; Roussos, A.; Agapito, L. A variational approach to video registration with subspace constraints. *Int. J. Comput. Vis.* **2013**, *104*, 286–314. [CrossRef] [PubMed]
57. Gotardo, P.F.; Martinez, A.M. Kernel non-rigid structure from motion. In Proceedings of the 2011 International Conference on Computer Vision, Barcelona, Spain, 6–13 November 2011; pp. 802–809.

mathematics

MDPI

Article

Ocular Biometrics with Low-Resolution Images Based on Ocular Super-Resolution CycleGAN

Young Won Lee, Jung Soo Kim and Kang Ryoung Park *

Division of Electronics and Electrical Engineering, Dongguk University, 30 Pildong-ro 1-gil, Jung-gu, Seoul 04620, Korea
* Correspondence: parkgr@dongguk.edu; Tel.: +82-2-2260-3329; Fax: +82-2-2277-8735

Abstract: Iris recognition, which is known to have outstanding performance among conventional biometrics techniques, requires a high-resolution camera and a sufficient amount of lighting to capture images containing various iris patterns. To address these issues, research is actively conducted on ocular recognition to include a periocular region in addition to the iris region, which also requires a high-resolution camera to capture images, indicating limited applications due to costs and size limitation. Accordingly, this study proposes an ocular super-resolution cycle-consistent generative adversarial network (OSRCycleGAN) for ocular super-resolution reconstruction, and additionally proposes a method to improve recognition performance in case that ocular images are acquired at a low-resolution. The results of the experiment conducted using open databases, namely, CASIA-iris-Distance and Lamp v4, and IIT Delhi iris database, showed that the equal error rate of recognition of the proposed method was 3.02%, 4.06% and 2.13% for each database, respectively, which outperformed state-of-the-art methods.

Keywords: biometrics; ocular recognition; super-resolution reconstruction; OSRCycleGAN

MSC: 68T07; 68U10

1. Introduction

Background of Biometrics

Among various biometrics technologies [1,2], iris recognition is commonly applied in the fields that require personal identification or security above a certain level due to unique characteristics of an iris region (unaffected by aging, no changes in characteristics due to external factors), thus guaranteeing a high level of security [3–8]. Iris images are captured from a certain long distance [9], unlike the close-distance iris recognition system environment in which image quality may be reduced. To overcome these drawbacks, replacing the environment or equipment is generally considered first, but entails a high cost. Therefore, ocular or periocular recognition has been researched using an ocular region containing the iris region or periocular region not containing the iris region [10,11]. However, ocular or periocular recognition method also has a problem of low-resolution or poor-quality images when they are captured from a quite far distance or when a low-performance camera is used, which degrades the recognition performance. Super-resolution reconstruction (SRR) may be applied as an alternative to solve the issue [12,13]. However, conventional SRR techniques have been embodied for the purpose of enhancing visibility in images using traditional image processing techniques [14,15]. Thus, ocular recognition performance improvement in low-resolution images cannot be achieved.

In recent years, deep learning technology was advanced, which enables a convolutional neural network (CNN)-based SRR to be extensively conducted [16,17]. Moreover, other studies on SRR have been conducted for applying a generative adversarial network (GAN) [18] to further enhance the performance of SRR [19]. The purpose SRR in general scenes is to improve visibility and increase resolution for the entire image rather than for details of a specific region. However, improvement in recognition performance is considered as a major purpose in biometric images for iris and ocular recognition than improving visibility through SRR as the details of biometrics of each individual are important.

From this perspective, this study proposes an ocular super-resolution cycle-consistent generative adversarial network (OSRCycleGAN)-based SRR method. Our research has contributions in the following three ways compared to previous works:

- Different from a conventional CycleGAN, our proposed OSRCycleGAN reduces the number of weight filters by half in generator and discriminator. Consequently, it can decrease system complexity and memory usage while increasing the processing speed.
- The proposed OSRCycleGAN does not use identity loss compared to conventional CycleGAN loss while using cycle consistent and perceptual losses. When calculating the perceptual loss in particular, it calculates authentic and imposter matching dissimilarities between mini-batch unit images in order to reflect them in cycle consistent and discriminator losses.
- For a fair performance evaluation by other researchers, the trained OSRCycleGAN model and algorithms are publicly available on request.

The rest of the paper is arranged as follows. Previous studies are analyzed in Section 2, while the explanations of OSRCycleGAN-based SRR and the ocular recognition method introduced in this study are provided in Section 3. Experimental results with analyses are presented in Section 4. Finally, conclusions and future works are offered in Section 5.

2. Related Work

Prior studies on iris and ocular recognition can be roughly categorized into those that considered SRR and those that did not consider SRR. The details are provided in the following sections.

2.1. Iris and Ocular Recognition without SRR

Iris recognition in initial phases targeted images taken from a close distance; iris recognition from a long distance has been researched to improve user convenience and to be applicable in a surveillance environment [20,21]. However, long-distance iris recognition requires a sufficiently strong near-infrared (NIR) lighting in addition to a camera with telescopic lens that can maintain high image quality even from a far distance. The iris region in images captured from a long distance has poorer quality than in images captured from a close distance and, therefore, high performance cannot be guaranteed. Accordingly, studies have been conducted using an ocular region including the iris, which is larger than the iris region.

An ocular region can be captured from a farther distance than the convention iris recognition method. Therefore, it can be obtained relatively easily although rich and unique features of iris cannot be used, and the rough iris region has been used as a substitute in the conventional iris recognition [22,23] and integrated in iris recognition methods [10,24,25]. Oishi et al. [24] proposed a method involving fusion of two scores of iris recognition and periocular recognition. Tan et al. [25] also obtained iris recognition result and periocular region recognition result through fusion.

The above methods are handcrafted feature-based methods, and deep feature-based methods have been recently researched to improve recognition performance. In a study by Gangwar et al. [26], after extracting a circular iris region from the input image as in conventional iris recognition methods, the region was then converted to a rectangular iris region in a polar coordinate for an input in the CNN for recognition. In a study by Lee et al. [27], when an iris image quality is poor in a noisy environment, a total of three images are captured by expanding the iris region with respect to the center of pupil and then the images are input in three CNN models for recognition. Liu et al. [28] applied the Hough transform as a preprocessing step of an input to detect the iris boundary to improve the iris recognition performance; then, an input image was configured by making the region excluding the iris region fuzzy using the Gaussian low-pass filter, and a CNN model was trained using the image to perform recognition. Vizomi et al. [29] attempted ocular recognition by applying a CNN. Lee et al. [30] obtained the ocular region using a rough pupil detection method from the face image captured by an NIR sensor and trained a deep CNN using this region.

However, all these studies focused on iris and ocular recognition without considering SRR, which implies degradation in recognition performance when low-resolution images are input.

2.2. Iris and Ocular Recognition with SRR

2.2.1. Conventional Image Processing-Based Method

There are studies that have applied SRR for restoring low-resolution images in a recognition system using iris and ocular regions. Nguyen et al. [21] detected the iris region in each image of a video sequence captured from a long distance and then determined whether each detected iris region has high resolution and high quality. Subsequently, Nguyen et al. [31] modeled the relationship between the original high-resolution iris image and the low-resolution iris image, which was then converted to feature-domain based on a maximum a posteriori probability (MAP) for SRR. Deshpande et al. [32] used Papoulis–Gerchberg (PG) and projection onto convex set (POCS) methods as SRR for improving the quality of a low-resolution iris image. In a study by Nguyen et al. [33], focus score weighted SRR was applied to restore low-resolution and low-quality images for performing iris recognition in images captured from a long distance and in a moving uncooperative environment.

2.2.2. Learning-Based Method

Traditional image processing-based SRR methods have limitations in performance improvement as the degradation function, which is the cause of degradation in quality of captured images, needs to be presumed by humans and the image restoration process is fairly difficult to perform. Thus, learning-based SRR methods have been researched. In a study by Fahmy et al. [34], a cross-correlation model was used to register and align the divided image into nine frame sets to apply SRR. Shirke et al. [35] applied the SRR method developed by Fahmy et al. [34] to restore iris images acquired from a distance for improving resolution and performance. In a study by Cui et al. [36], iris images were synthesized without a large iris image dataset due to the difficulty in constructing an iris image dataset during which PCA-based SRR was applied to improve the resolution and quality of images. Shin et al. [37,38] proposed a recognition method in which a low-resolution iris image is restored using multi-layered perceptron (MLP). Moreover, Shin et al. [39] proposed a method for generating and recognizing a high-resolution iris image using MLP and constraint least square (CLS) filter. Alonso-Fernandez et al. [40] proposed a PCA hallucination method in which low-resolution (LR) patches are obtained using PCA eigen-transformation from a low-resolution input image and then high-resolution (HR) patches for the training dataset are obtained to restore a high-resolution iris image.

2.2.3. Deep Feature-Based Method

Traditional learning-based methods have the disadvantage of limited improvement in SRR performance for images captured in various environments; therefore, deep learning-based methods have been researched. In a previous study [41], an iris super-resolution method involving a CNN model consisting of three general layers that restore LR patch to HR patch, and a stacked auto-encoder containing several auto-encoders was proposed. In a study by Reddy et al. [42], an ocular sequence image was captured, and subpixel registration was first performed using a discrete cosine transform interpolation filter (DCTIF) for images in each frame. Ocular recognition was then performed by applying deblurring using an additional CNN for the ocular sequence image. In another study [43], texture or natural image was pre-trained with a CNN model and the weight was trained as well; then, transfer learning for learning iris images was applied to an SRCNN model and very deep convolutional networks (VDCNN) model.

In advanced deep learning-based methods, they conducted various experiments such as image steganography using GAN and attention modules [44–46]. In [44], they performed image steganography by using called CHAT-GAN implemented by GANs combined with a channel attention module. Based on this method, they achieved high-performance for image steganography without losing hiding information and image qualities. In a study by Liao [45,46], they proposed a new method that decreases or distributes the payload in color image steganography. Image steganography is quite difficult to implement because its goal is to hide additional key information in an image without any noticeable differences. In other words, the method may have high system complexities if implemented. Therefore, they attempted to decrease or distribute the payload by proposing a method based on image texture complexity and distortion distribution. As a result, they got a satisfactory performance by implementing the proposed method called embedding strategy based on image texture complexity (ES-ITC), embedding strategy based on distortion distribution (ES-DD), and amplifying channel modification probabilities strategy (ACMP).

In the wild, various degradation factors can reduce image quality, and these factors may appear at any time, which cannot be noticed. This can decrease system performance, so these factors should be removed. Based on this background, Yin et al. [47] proposed a method that eliminates the degradation factor and obtains the super-resolution image by single conditional hyper-network architecture.

The deep learning-based methods explained above all use general CNNs or encoders, thus having limitations in SRR and performance improvements for iris and ocular images in various environments, which is caused by not using the scheme of competitive training of generator and discriminator. This study, therefore, proposes an OSRCycleGAN based SRR method for improving the SRR performance through competitive learning of generator and discriminator, and a method for improving recognition performance of ocular images captured at a low resolution.

Table 1 below compares the strengths and weaknesses between previous studies and the proposed method.

Table 1. Comparisons of previous studies and the proposed method.

<table>
<tr><th colspan="3">Category</th><th>Method(s)</th><th>Strength</th><th>Weakness</th></tr>
<tr><td rowspan="4">Without SRR</td><td rowspan="4">Handcrafted feature-based</td><td rowspan="3">Iris</td><td>Daugman's method [5,8]</td><td rowspan="3">Does not require an additional graphics processing unit</td><td rowspan="3">Does not consider the performance degradation for low-resolution iris images</td></tr>
<tr><td>Stabilized iris encoding and Zernike moments phase features [20]</td></tr>
<tr><td>Noisy image captured at a distance [39]</td></tr>
<tr><td>Iris + ocular</td><td>Used ocular region including iris and periocular [10,22–25]</td><td>High recognition performance in various environments as both iris and periocular region information are used</td><td>Poorer recognition performance than the deep-feature-based method</td></tr>
</table>

Table 1. *Cont.*

Category			Method(s)	Strength	Weakness
	Deep feature-based	Iris	DeepIrisNet [26]	Improved recognition performance for noisy iris images as multiple CNNs are used	Training time for each model is increased as multiple CNNs are used
		Ocular	Multiple CNN-based noisy ocular recognition [27]	Solves existing iris segmentation accuracy problem and low-quality image issue by using both iris and ocular regions	- Training time increases because of multiple CNNs - Does not consider the performance degradation for low-resolution images
With SRR	Image processing-based	Iris	SRR for captured image at a distance [21,33], MAP [31], PG + POCS [32], FCM [35]	SRR was applied to prevent performance degradation due to low-resolution image captured from a long distance	Limitations in resolution restoration because of existing image processing technique
	Learning-based		PCA + ICA [34], PCA [36,40], MLP [37–39]	Better restoration results than traditional image processing methods	Limited improvement of SRR performance in various environments
	Deep feature-based	Iris	Stacked auto-encoder [41], SRCNN + VDCNN [43]	Higher SRR performance than image processing-based or learning-based methods	Limited recognition and SRR accuracies in various environments as a general CNN or encoder are used
		Ocular	Multi-frame SRR + CNN-based deblurring [42]	Improved performance by separating SRR and deblurring processes	
			OSRCycleGAN (proposed method)	Generator and discriminator improve SRR performance through competitive learning	Requires intensive training procedure

3. Proposed Method

3.1. Overview of Proposed Method

Figure 1 shows the overview of the proposed method. A low-resolution ocular image is used as an input (Step 1 of Figure 1). This is converted to a high-resolution ocular image by OSRCycleGAN proposed in this study (Step 2 of Figure 1). Then, the restored image is used as an input of a residual neural network (ResNet) pretrained with ocular images; ocular features are extracted from a pooling layer before the last fully connected layer (FCL) (Step 3 of Figure 1). Matching distance is calculated based on the Euclidean distance between the features extracted from the input image and the features extracted from the registered image. It is accepted as genuine matching if the calculated distance is less than the threshold and rejected as imposter matching otherwise (Step 4 of Figure 1).

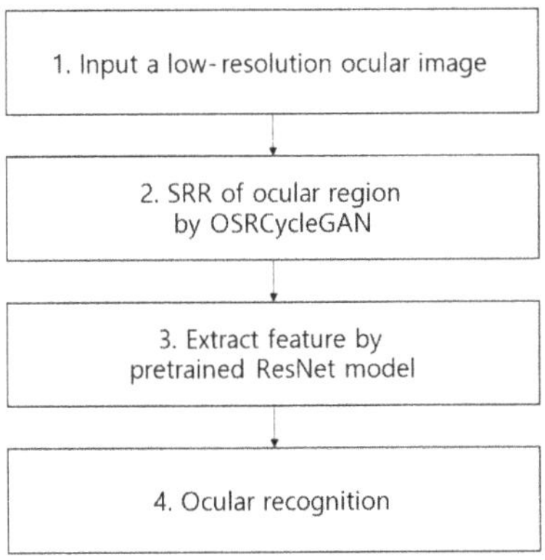

Figure 1. Overview of the proposed method.

3.2. *SRR by OSRCycleGAN*

In general, the process of capturing a low-resolution image can be represented in the equation [48,49].

$$y = H(x) + n \tag{1}$$

Here, y, x, $H(\cdot)$, and n refer to low-resolution image, original high-resolution image, degradation function, and additional noise, respectively. In this equation, $H(\cdot)$ is the two-dimensional point spread function (PSF) that degrades the quality of the original image x. Accordingly, accurately modeling PSF and n improves SRR performance, but it is still difficult to accurately model low-resolution images captured in various environments. Accordingly, this study proposes an OSRCycleGAN-based SRR method.

3.2.1. Architecture of CycleGAN

OSRCycleGAN proposed in this study is based on a cycle-consistent generative adversarial network (CycleGAN) model. In the SRR method involving only a general CNN or an encoder, the original form of the image being restored is not maintained well or the image information is not considered during restoration. The model is trained in one direction for the region viewed by the filter based on the calculation of the weight of simple convolution filtering. Conversely, CycleGAN [50] has been mostly applied in image translation and style transfer. Style is learned by learning the difference between each domain through cycle loss and image generating capability of a GAN based on which loss is reflected in the GAN so that an image of another domain can be generated in one desired domain. In this study, CycleGAN is used for high-resolution image reconstruction rather than for style transfer or image translation. If each domain is, respectively, designated as low resolution and high resolution, the result of our image SRR can be attained when an image is transformed from the low-resolution to the high-resolution fields to be produced via GAN and cycle loss.

CycleGAN generally consists of two generators and two discriminators in which a generator generates images having the difference between domains and a discriminator discerns the difference between the image generated by converting the domain and the ground-truth image of the respective domain. Equation (2) below shows how generators $G(\cdot)$ and $F(\cdot)$ that had received x, y as input and ground truth are processed in CycleGAN. Here, x is the low-resolution image, while y is the respective high-resolution image input.

$$x' = F(G(x)), \;\; y' = G(F(y)) \tag{2}$$

$$G(\cdot) : X \rightarrow Y, \qquad F(\cdot) : Y \rightarrow X \tag{3}$$

Here, $G(\cdot)$ and $F(\cdot)$ each represent generators which generate images for the domain characteristics of $X- > Y$ and $Y- > X$, respectively. Using two generators is the unique characteristic of CycleGAN where the generator that converts $X- > Y$ gives the input x to $G(\cdot)$ to obtain $\widetilde{y}$ and then goes through $F(\cdot)$ to obtain x'. Similarly, the same process is followed for the opposite case of $Y- > X$. The difference is calculated when the model is back to $X- > Y- > X$ or $Y- > X- > Y$ through conversion between domains and generation using two generators, and this difference can be reduced to perform conversion between the targeted domains more accurately. The equation for calculating this process is called cycle loss, as expressed in Equation (4) below.

$$\mathcal{L}_{cyc}(G, F) = \mathbb{E}_{x\sim P_{data}(x)}[\| F(G(x)) - x \|_1] + \mathbb{E}_{y\sim P_{data}(y)}[\| G(F(y)) - y \|_1] \tag{4}$$

Here, x is the low-resolution image, while y is the respective high-resolution image input. Because $G(\cdot)$ and $F(\cdot)$ each represent generators which generate images for the domain characteristics of $X- > Y$ and $Y- > X$, respectively, $F(G(x))$ shows x' image (as shown in Equation (2)) obtained by $X- > Y- > X$ while $G(F(y))$ represents y' image (as shown in Equation (2)) obtained by $Y- > X- > Y$. $x \sim P_{data}(x)$ and $y \sim P_{data}(y)$ are data distributions. $\| \cdot \|_1$ shows L1 distance, and $\mathbb{E}$ represents expectation value.

The discriminator is trained so that it cannot distinguish between the image generated by the generator and the ground-truth image, and this process can be referred to as adversarial loss. Equations below show the adversarial loss of $X- > Y$ and $Y- > X$.

$$\mathcal{L}_{\text{adv}}(G, D_Y, X, Y) = \mathbb{E}_{\text{y}\sim \text{P}_{\text{data}}(\text{y})}[\log D_y(y)] + \mathbb{E}_{\text{x}\sim \text{P}_{\text{data}}(\text{x})}[\log(1 - D_y(G(x))] \tag{5}$$

$$\mathcal{L}_{\text{adv}}(F, D_X, Y, X) = \mathbb{E}_{\text{x}\sim \text{P}_{\text{data}}(\text{x})}[\log D_x(x)] + \mathbb{E}_{\text{y}\sim \text{P}_{\text{data}}(\text{y})}[\log(1 - D_x(G(y))] \tag{6}$$

Here, $D_y(y)$ represents the discriminator using y (real high-resolution image) as input, and $D_y(G(x))$ shows the discriminator using $G(x)$ (generated (fake) high-resolution image by the generator $G(\cdot)$ using x (low-resolution image) as input). In addition, $D_x(x)$ represents the discriminator using x (real low-resolution image) as input, and $D_x(G(y))$ shows the discriminator using $G(y)$ (generated (fake) low-resolution image by the generator $G(\cdot)$ using y (high-resolution image) as input). The $log(\cdot)$ is a logarithmic function.

Based on Equations (4)–(6), the final CycleGAN loss is as follows.

$$\mathcal{L}(G, F, D_X, D_Y) = \mathcal{L}_{adv}(F, D_X, Y, X) + \mathcal{L}_{adv}(G, D_Y, X, Y) + \mathcal{L}_{cyc}(G, F) \tag{7}$$

3.2.2. Architecture of OSRCycleGAN

The process of converting low-resolution ocular image to a high-resolution image based on OSRCycleGAN is shown in Figure 2, where the image y', which corresponds to the conversion result of generator $G_x(\cdot)$, is the final restored high-resolution image. OSRCycleGAN reduces the number of weighted filters by half to reduce the number of parameters in a conventional CycleGAN model; consequently, system complexity and memory usage are reduced, and processing speed is increased by reducing the channel dimension of a feature map. Parallel computation through graphics processing unit (GPU) is essential for applying deep learning in which an increase in the number of weighted filters requires high-performance GPU for training and testing, thus being difficult to be applied in diverse environments.

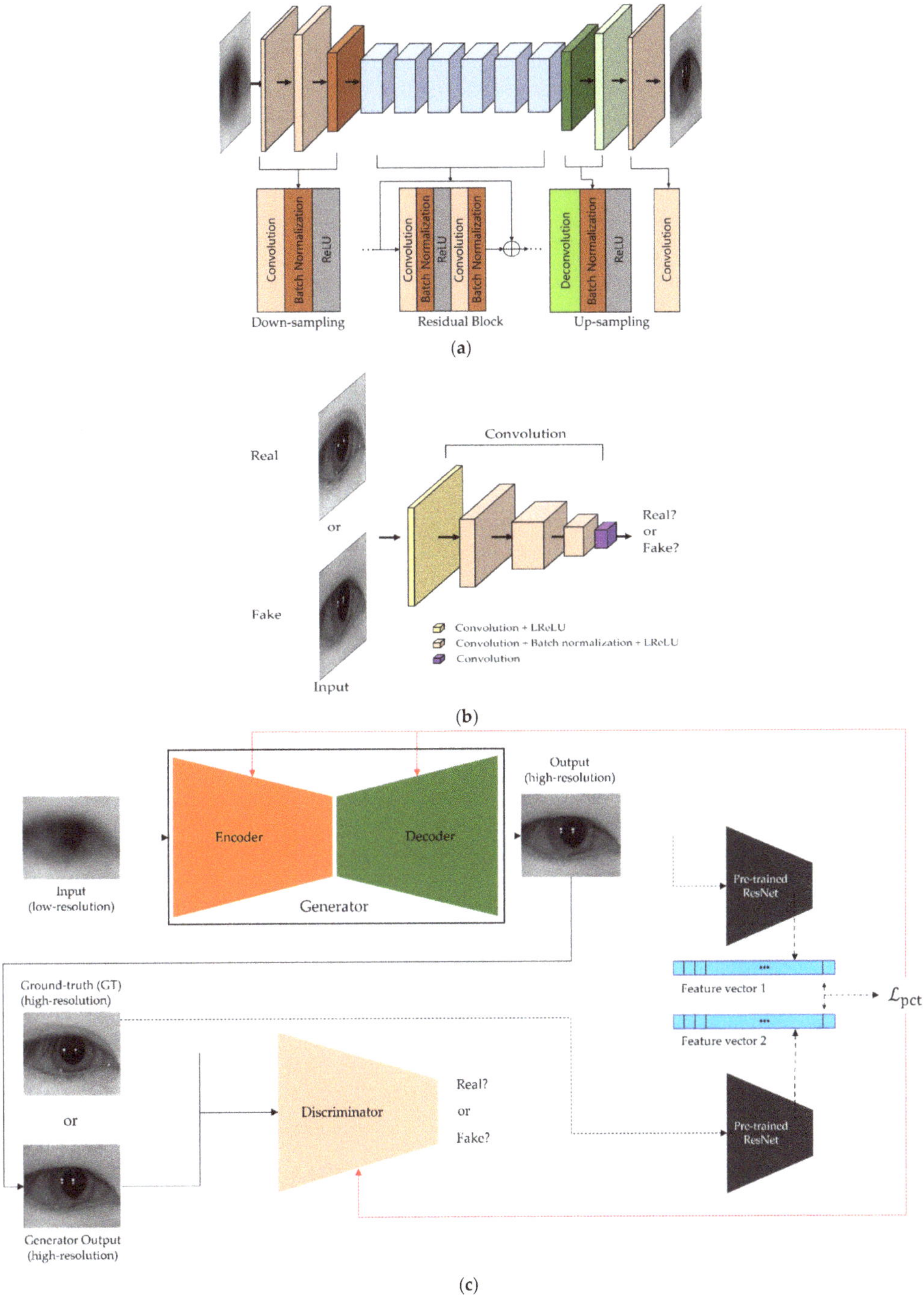

Figure 2. OSRCycleGAN. (**a**) Generator, (**b**) discriminator, and (**c**) whole flow of proposed method with proposed the perceptual loss calculations.

The generator model of OSRCycleGAN was modified to reduce the channel dimension based on a six-layer model consisting of residual connection with batch normalization (BN). The discriminator model was also modified in the same manner. Tables 2 and 3 present the details of generator and discriminator of OSRCycleGAN used in this study. The ocular image used in this study includes the information of the eyelid, eyelash, pupil, iris, and sclera. The general shape of the eye is longer width-wise than length-wise. Therefore, a rectangular shape, as shown in Tables 2 and 3, was used, instead of a square shape, as an input in a conventional CycleGAN to prevent the information from being lost. Because the basic architecture of proposed OSRCycleGAN is referred to the original CycleGAN, we followed the positions of BN batch normalization based on the structure of original CycleGAN.

Table 2. Generator of OSRCycleGAN (* and ** means that the BN + ReLU and Conv + BN + ReLU + Conv + BN combinations are applied after the Conv or in each residual block, respectively. BN, ReLU, and Conv mean batch normalization, rectified linear unit, and convolution layer, respectively).

Layers	Feature Map Size (Width × Height × Channels)	Filter Size	Number of Filters	Stride
Input layer	380 × 280 × 3			
Conv-1 *	380 × 280 × 32	7 × 7 × 3	32	1
Conv-2 *	190 × 140 × 64	3 × 3 × 32	64	2
Conv-3 *	95 × 70 × 128	3 × 3 × 64	128	2
Residual 1–6 **	95 × 70 × 128	3 × 3 × 128	128	1
Deconv1 *	190 × 140 × 64	4 × 4 × 128	64	2
Deconv2 *	380 × 280 × 32	4 × 4 × 64	32	2
Output *	380 × 280 × 3	7 × 7 × 32	3	1

Table 3. Discriminator of OSRCycleGAN (#filter and S mean the number of filters and strides, respectively) (* and ** means that the Leaky ReLU (LReLU) and BN + LReLU combination are applied after the Conv, respectively. ReLU, BN, and Conv mean rectified linear unit, batch normalization, and convolution layer, respectively).

Layers	Feature Map Size (Width×Height×Channels)	Filter Size	Number of Filters	Stride
Input layer	380 × 280 × 3			
Conv-1 *	190 × 140 × 32	4 × 4 × 3	32	2
Conv-2 **	95 × 70 × 64	4 × 4 × 32	64	2
Conv-3 **	48 × 35 × 128	4 × 4 × 64	128	2
Conv-4 **	24 × 18 × 256	4 × 4 × 128	256	1
Conv-5 (Output)	24 × 18 × 1	4 × 4 × 256	1	1

3.2.3. Loss of OSRCycleGAN

In OSRCycleGAN, identity loss used in CycleGAN loss was eliminated, and the perceptual loss shown in Equation (8) was applied to improve the SRR performance as shown in Figure 2c.

$$\mathcal{L}_{\text{pct}} = \sqrt{\sum_{1}^{T}\left(\frac{C(y_i)}{\sum_{1}^{T} C(y_i)} - \frac{C(x_i')}{\sum_{1}^{T} C(x_i')}\right)^2} \quad \text{for } i = 1 \ldots T \tag{8}$$

Equation (8) expresses a perceptual loss used for our proposed method. First, each ground truth image and restored image by proposed OSRCycleGAN are passed in ResNet-101 model. Here, ResNet-101 model is denoted by $C(\cdot)$. Ground truth image and restored image are denoted by y and x', respectively. In addition, the ith extracted features from average pooling layer of the model $C(\cdot)$ are represented as $C(y_i)$ and $C(x'_i)$, respectively, and T is 2048. Using Equation (8), the difference of mean is calculated for each 2048 feature, and they are summated. From that, the dissimilarity between restored and original (ground truth) image is calculated as shown in Equation (8).

Rather than simply calculating the loss by comparing the restored image with the ground-truth image, features were extracted by having the images restored at a mini-batch unit input in the previously trained CNN model, and the distance between the extracted feature and the feature of ground-truth image was calculated based on authentic and imposter matching to be reflected in the GAN loss. When this loss is used, a significant effect can be observed on the final GAN loss depending on the distance value. The loss value increases as the distance increases so that inadequate restoration can be reflected in the model through which better restoration results can be expected. For extracting features to calculate the perceptual loss, a ResNet model pretrained with ocular images was used. Ultimately, cycle consistent loss of Equation (7) and perceptual loss of Equation (8) were used together in OSRCycleGAN, as expressed in Equation (9).

$$\mathcal{L}_{\text{loss}} = \mathcal{L}(G,\ F,\ D_x,\ D_y) + \mathcal{L}_{\text{pct}} \quad (9)$$

3.2.4. Difference between OSRCycleGAN and Original CycleGAN

In this section, the differences between the proposed OSRCycleGAN and the original CycleGAN are presented:

- Different from a conventional CycleGAN, our proposed OSRCycleGAN reduces the number of weight filters by half in generator and discriminator. Consequently, it can decrease system complexity and memory usage while increasing the processing speed.
- The proposed OSRCycleGAN does not use identity loss compared to conventional CycleGAN loss while using cycle consistent and perceptual losses. When calculating the perceptual loss in particular, it calculates authentic and imposter matching dissimilarities between mini-batch unit images in order to reflect them in cycle consistent and discriminator losses.

3.3. *Ocular Recognition*

In this study, ResNet-101 was used for ocular recognition based on the results of a previous study [30]. Generally, when only the layer depth is extended without any supplementation, training accuracy is reduced, and global minimum cannot be reached because repeatedly processing convolutions causes features of the original image to be reduced through computation and, thus, loses characteristics. This problem was solved by using the concept of identify mapping and short-cut-(skip-connection)-based residual block. For training with the datasets used in this study, fine-tuning was proceeded based on a pre-trained ResNet model [51]. Several hundreds of thousands of datasets are required to train the weights of many layers in ResNet, and the experimental dataset used in this study is insufficient. This model was pre-trained with ImageNet database, which consists of several hundreds of thousands of images [52] and was used in ImageNet large-scale visual recognition competition (ILSVRC). Therefore, the image size is resized into the input size of the ImageNet data in this study. Here, it is determined in which layer fine-tuning is performed for retraining. In this study, only Conv5 and the fully connected layer were fine-tuned. Several hyper-parameters and optimizers need to be selected for training a CNN. Most processes of model training can be separated into forward and backward ones. The forward process arbitrarily initializes the weight, and the computation is proceeded sequentially according to how the model is designed. Then, in the backward process, the desired ground-truth value and the value computed in the forward process are compared to calculate the loss, which is then used to adjust the weight in backward. An activation function is considered important in the forward process. A sigmoid function was used commonly in the past, but due to an extensive period of time and computation amount, a rectified linear unit (ReLU) [53] is more commonly used an activation function recently. A ReLU function is easy to compute and does not output negative values, thus exhibiting a better performance when training is converged and not requiring extensive computation for finding a slope value.

A basic multinomial logistic loss is used in ResNet for which the jth output ($\sigma(z)_j$ of Equation (10)) predicted using the softmax function in Equation (10) was used for calculation. Accordingly, numerical stability can be maintained when calculating the slope.

$$\sigma(z)_j = \frac{e^{zj}}{\sum_{k=1}^{K} e^{zk}} \quad for\ j = 1 \ldots, K \tag{10}$$

Here, K is the number of outputs (classes) of ResNet. In case that the array of output neurons is set to z, the probability of the neurons belonging to the jth class is obtained by dividing the value of the jth class by the sum of the values of all classes. Using the calculated results as input, a multinomial logistic loss (MLL) of Equation (11) [54] is calculated, as expressed in Equation (11).

$$\text{MLL} = -\frac{1}{K}\sum_{n=1}^{K} \log(\hat{p}_n, l_n), \tag{11}$$

Here, $\hat{p}_n$ represents predicted probability, and l_n is a ground-truth label ($l_n \in [0, 1, 2, \ldots, K-1]$ among the K classes).

In most studies related to biometrics, measuring a recognition performance is in a closed world and open world settings. Closed world setting is when the classes of data for training and testing are the same, while open world setting is when the classes of data for training and testing are different. Typically, it is difficult to presume that the classes of data for training and testing biometrics are the same. Thus, open world setting is deemed more appropriate for real-world applications and, thus, was adopted in this study as well. In the biometrics classification, the output of an FCL of the CNN is used or the feature vector extracted from the layer before the last FCL is used to calculate the matching distance from the feature vector of the registered image. In closed world setting, the classes of data for training and testing are the same. Therefore, the output of an FCL of CNN can be directly used; in open world setting, as the classes of data for training and testing are different, the feature vector extracted from the layer before the last FCL is used to calculate the matching distance from the feature vector of the registered image to perform recognition.

In this study, ocular images processed by SRR using OSRCycleGAN are inputted to ResNet which extracts the 2048 features from the average pooling layer. A total of 2048 features are used to calculate the Euclidean distance from the 2048 features extracted from the enrolled ocular image. It is accepted as genuine matching if the calculated distance is smaller than the threshold, and rejected as imposter matching otherwise. With the training data, the optimal distance threshold was set at the point where false acceptance error (FAR) is identical to false rejection error (FRR). FAR denotes the error of incorrectly determining imposter data as genuine, whereas FRR incorrectly denies genuine data as an imposter. FAR and FRR generally have a tradeoff relationship, and the error when FAR is identical to FRR is named as the equal error rate (EER).

4. Experimental Results

4.1. Dataset and Experimental Environments

To evaluate the performance of the proposed method, the experiment was conducted using three open databases obtained with an NIR camera: CASIA-Iris-Distance and CASIA-Iris-Lamp [55], and Indian Institute of Technology Delhi (IIT Delhi) databases [56]. Each database was divided into two sub-sets to conduct twofold cross-validation. For example, 282 classes including two eyes of 141 individuals in the CASIA-Iris-Distance database were divided into sub-database 1 (DB 1) of 142 classes (71 individuals) and sub-database 2 (DB 2) of 140 classes (70 individuals) to perform data augmentation before conducting training. For data augmentation, translation and cropping were applied for six pixels in all four directions to augment the data by 169 times [30]. Data augmentation based on translation and cropping has been commonly used to other previous studies [57]. Hence, misalignment between registered and recognition images was covered by training the CNN, and the problem of inadequate training from having insufficient dataset was solved. Furthermore, the augmented data were only used for training, while the original data were used for testing. By separately conducting training and testing through twofold cross-validation, the problem of overfitting, which leads to degradation in performance for testing data, caused by the training data being excessively trained by CNN, was prevented. The average accuracy attained from two testing by twofold cross-validation was utilized as the final accuracy of the proposed method. Table 4 depicts the detailed descriptions of the experimental databases used in the study.

Table 4. Detailed descriptions of the experimental databases.

Category	Number of Classes		Number of Images			
			Before Augmentation		After Augmentation	
	DB1	DB2	DB1	DB2	DB1	DB2
CASIA-Iris-Distance	142	140	2080	2056	351,520	347,464
CASIA-Iris-Lamp	408	408	8054	8036	1,361,126	1,358,084
IIT Delhi iris database	210	223	1120	1120	189,280	189,280

Bilinear interpolation was used with respect to the original ground-truth image in Table 4 to compose low-resolution images having 1/16 resolution of the original images. In actual environments, Gaussian blur was additionally applied to compose a dataset considering how a blur or other types of noises may occur due to movements.

Training and testing of the proposed method were conducted in a desktop computer installed with central processing unit (CPU) Intel i7-6700 3.40 GHz, random access memory (RAM) of 32 GB, and NVIDIA GeForce GTX1070 graphic processing unit (GPU) [58]. Compute unified device architecture (CUDA) of version 8.0 and CUDA deep neural network library (cuDNN) of version 5.0 were employed; our algorithms were made using open computer vision (OpenCV) of version 3.3.0 and Visual Studio 2015. TensorFlow of version 2.1.0 [59] and Windows Caffe of version 1.0.0 [60] were used for the implementation of OSRCycleGAN and ocular recognition model, respectively.

4.2. Training of the Proposed Model

Training of OSRCycleGAN

For the hyper-parameters for training OSRCycleGAN that restores high-resolution images, 200 epochs of repeated training, mini batch size of 10, and Adaptive moment estimation (Adam) as optimizer [61] were applied. Beta_1, which is a parameter for Adam, was 0.5 for which the initial learning rate was 2×10^{-4} for the exponential decay rate of Adam optimizer. For the estimate of first and second moment, 0.9 and 0.999 were applied, respectively. We did not employ learning rate strategies, i.e., linear decay. These values were maintained in all the experiments. When training SRR models using the dataset used in previous studies on SRR and in this experiment, the hyper-parameters of the proposed model were applied under the same condition for a fair evaluation. To solve the inherent problem of a GAN where a generator is difficult to train, the generator was repeatedly trained for five times, while the discriminator was trained once for one mini batch. Due to this training strategy, the optimization of generator of OSRCycleGAN model was possible along with discriminator. Figure 3 depicts the loss graphs of generator and discriminator of OSRCycleGAN. As depicted in Figure 3, OSRCycleGAN was trained enough with the training data.

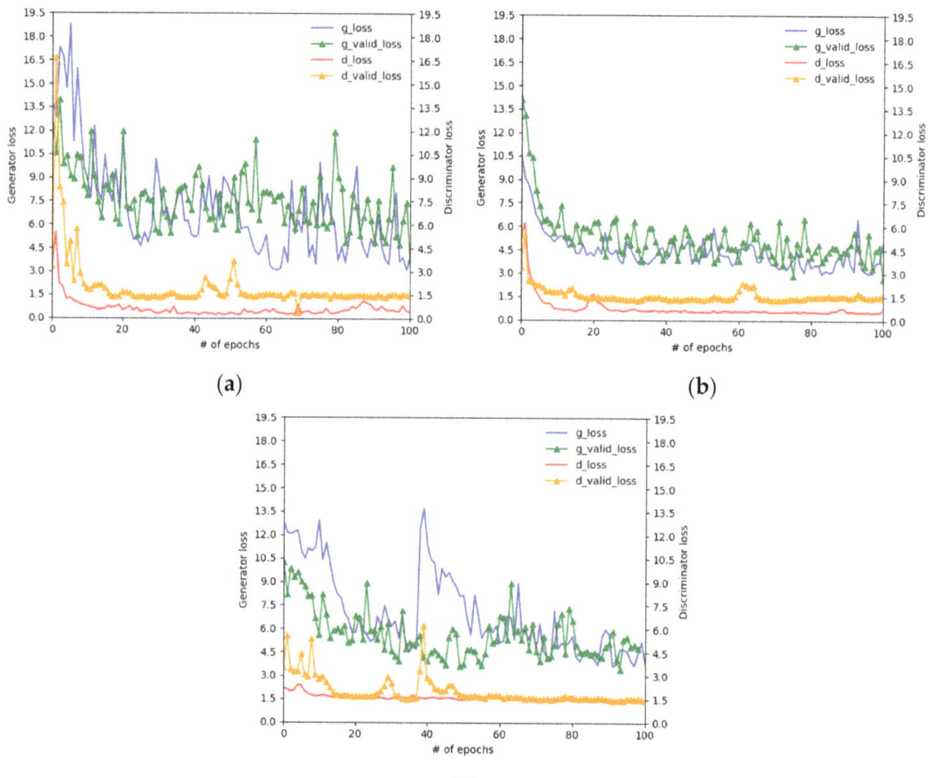

Figure 3. Graphs of training losses of generator (g_loss) and discriminator (d_loss) by OSRCycleGAN with (**a**) CASIA-Iris-Distance, (**b**) CASIA-Iris-Lamp, and (**c**) IIT Delhi iris databases.

We adopted twofold cross-validation because the previous deep learning-based ocular recognition study [30] has chosen the same twofold cross-validation. In our research, we do not focus on ocular recognition method but ocular super-resolution reconstruction by OSRCycleGAN. Therefore, we adopted the ocular recognition method of [30] in our research, and we used the same twofold cross-validation in order to follow the experimental protocol of [30]. Additionally, we added the valid loss plots in Figure 3, which were obtained with validation data. We set 10% of training data as validation data, and these validation data were not used for training. As shown in Figure 3, validation loss graphs are also decreased and stabilized according to the increment of epochs, which confirms that our OSRCycleGAN was not overfitted with training data.

Stochastic gradient descent (SGD) optimizer [62] was used for training the ResNet-101, during which a step policy was used as a learning rate policy for optimization where a gamma value is multiplied at a certain iteration. As one of the characteristics of SGD, training was conducted at the mini-batch size unit. Each model in the study was trained for 3–10 epochs. The learning rate was set to 0.0001, which is fairly small as fine-tuning was proceeded using the pre-trained weight. Momentum and weight decay values were set to 0.9 and 0.0001, respectively, while the gamma value was set to 0.1. Each dataset consisted of a different number of images, accordingly, the number of steps was varied in order to achieve the optimal performance. Figure 4 shows the graphs of training accuracy and training loss obtained during training of the ResNet-101 model. As shown in Figure 4, training loss almost went to 0, while training accuracy converged to 100% as the training epoch increased, which indicates that the ResNet-101 model used in this study was successfully trained.

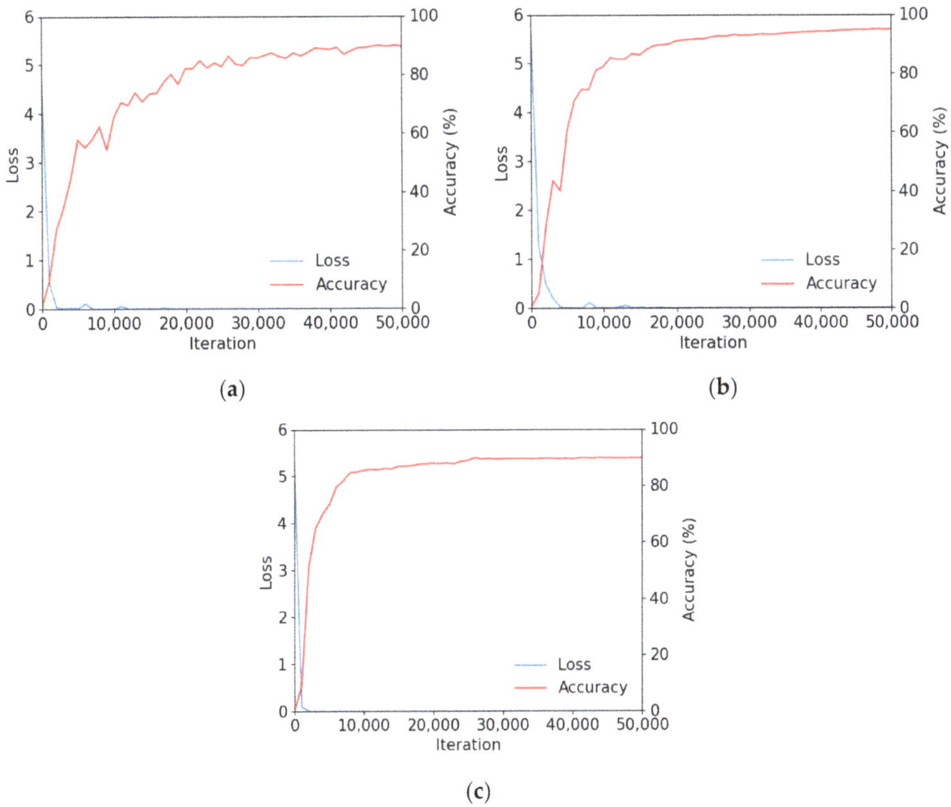

Figure 4. Graphs of training loss and accuracy by ResNet-101 with (**a**) CASIA-Iris-Distance, (**b**) CASIA-Iris-Lamp, and (**c**) IIT Delhi iris databases.

4.3. Testing of the Proposed Method

4.3.1. Ablation Studies

To evaluate the performance of SRR by OSRCycleGAN, the similarity between the original high-resolution image and the image restored by SRR was measured using signal-to-noise ratio (SNR) [63], peak signal-to-noise ratio (PSNR) [64], and structural similarity (SSIM) [65], as expressed in Equations (12)–(15). The SRR performance is higher as all the values of SNR, PSNR, and SSIM are high.

$$\mathrm{MSE} = \frac{1}{mn}\sum_{i=0}^{m-1}\sum_{j=0}^{n-1}[I_o(i, j) - I_e(i, j)]^2 \tag{12}$$

$$\text{SNR} = 10\log_{10}\left(\frac{\frac{\sum_{i=0}^{m-1}\sum_{j=0}^{n-1}[I_o(i,j)]^2}{mn}}{\text{MSE}}\right) \tag{13}$$

$$\text{PSNR} = 10\log_{10}\left(\frac{255^2}{\text{MSE}}\right) \tag{14}$$

Here, I_o is the original high-resolution image, while I_e is the image obtained with SRR. m and n indicate width and height of the image, respectively. Equation (15) below shows the mathematical equation of SSIM.

$$\text{SSIM} = \frac{(2\mu_e\mu_o + C1)(2\sigma_{eo} + C2)}{({\mu_e}^2 + {\mu_o}^2 + C1)({\sigma_e}^2 + {\sigma_o}^2 + C2)} \tag{15}$$

Here, μ_o and σ_o indicate mean and standard deviation of pixel values of an original high-resolution image, while μ_e and σ_e indicate mean and standard deviation of pixel values of the image generated with SRR. σ_{eo} is the covariance of two images. C1 and C2 are positive constants preventing the denominator from becoming 0. As shown in Table 5, the OSRCycleGAN had better SRR performance than most of the state-of-the-art methods except the Pix2Pix method. Although Pix2Pix shows the higher PSNR, SNR, and SSIM, the recognition accuracies with the restored images by Pix2Pix are lower than those by proposed method.

Table 5. Comparisons on SRR by the proposed method and state-of-the-art methods.

Methods	PSNR	SNR	SSIM
SRGAN [19]	15.64	1.15	0.68
Pix2Pix [66]	27.2	5.91	0.78
CycleGAN [50]	18.4	1.74	0.71
OSRCycleGAN	22.66	2.03	0.74

Figure 5 shows the comparisons on SRR by the proposed method and state-of-the-art methods. As shown in Figure 5, the images restored by OSRCycleGAN are closer to the original high-resolution images than the images restored by state-of-the-art methods except for Pix2Pix.

We prepared a real low resolution dataset from the original benchmark datasets of CASIA-Iris-Distance, CASIA-Iris-Lamp, and IIT Delhi iris database. That is, all our experiments were conducted on real low-resolution images that were downsampled from original high-resolution images by using bilinear interpolation techniques [67]. For example, the actual size of low-resolution images of Figure 5b is $1/16$ compared to that of the original high-resolution images of Figure 5a. However, in order to make the better visibility for readers, we increased the size of images in Figure 5b same to that of Figure 5a. In addition, we did not used Gaussian noise to obtain the low-resolution image. Instead, we applied Gaussian blurring as point spread function (PSF) of image degradation as shown in Equation (1). In details, we did not use any noise term (n of Equation (1)), but used both downsampling and Gaussian blurring as the PSF of image degradation ($H(\cdot)$ of Equation (1)) based on [48,49]. The kernel size and sigma value of Gaussian blurring function are 3×3 and 3, respectively.

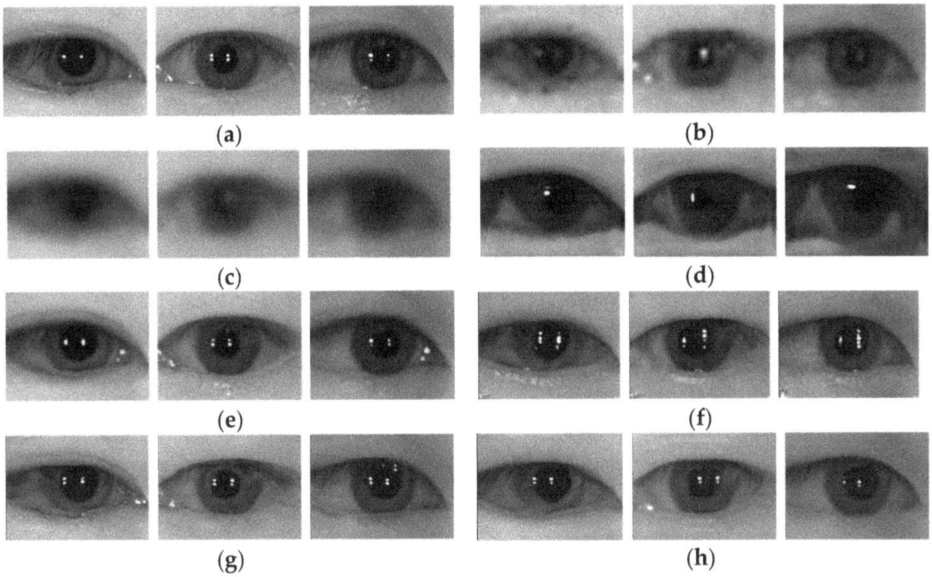

Figure 5. Comparisons on SRR by the proposed method and the state-of-the-art methods. (**a**) Original high-resolution images. (**b**) Low-resolution images by bilinear interpolation. (**c**) Low-resolution images by bilinear interpolation + Gaussian blurring. (**d**) Output images by SRGAN with (**c**). (**e**) Output images by Pix2Pix with (**c**). (**f**) Output images by CycleGAN with (**c**). (**g**) Output images by OSRCycleGAN with (**b**). (**h**) Output images by OSRCycleGAN with (**c**).

For the second experiment, ocular recognition accuracy using the images obtained with SRR was compared. For performance comparison, the ResNet-101 model for ocular recognition was experimented by testing without training, testing after fine-tuning, and testing after training from scratch. Recognition performance was compared by dividing the input cases of the ResNet-101 model into bilinear interpolation image (3 channels), reconstructed image (3 channels), and bilinear interpolation image (2 channels) + reconstructed image (1 channel). Furthermore, the cases for adding a perceptual loss and not adding a perceptual loss to the existing loss equation were compared. As presented in Tables 6 and 7, the recognition accuracy was the highest when bilinear interpolation image (2 channels) + reconstructed image by OSRCycleGAN (1 channel) was used as an input in addition to cycle consistent loss + perceptual loss as proposed in this study.

As shown in the caption of Table 6, fine-tuning* means the fine-tuning using the model pretrained with original high-resolution ocular images, and fine-tuning** represents the fine-tuning using the model pretrained with ImageNet [52]. In case of fine-tuning, training were performed with our experimental data (reconstructed high-resolution images) for only the weights of remained layers while the weights of some layers were frozen. In case of train from scratch, the weights of all the layers were trained with our experimental data. The number of original high-resolution ocular images is much smaller than that of ImageNet. Therefore, some weights were not sufficiently trained by fine-tuning* (where our model was fine-tuned with original high-resolution ocular images). That is why the accuracy of fine-tuning* is lower than that by train from scratch.

Table 6. Ocular recognition accuracy comparison in the case of using only bilinear interpolation when generating a low-resolution image (* means fine-tuning using the model pretrained with original high-resolution ocular images, and ** means fine-tuning using the model pretrained with ImageNet).

High-Resolution Image Obtained by	Recognizer Input	Recognizer Training Method	Loss for OSRCycleGAN	EER (%)
Bilinear interpolation	Interpolated image (three channels)	Without training (only testing)	Loss is not used	11.41
		Fine-tuning *		4.58
OSRCycleGAN	Reconstruction image (three channels)	Without training (only testing)	Cycle consistent loss	8.55
			Cycle consistent loss + Perceptual loss	11.68
		Fine-tuning *	Cycle consistent loss	13.98
			Cycle consistent loss + Perceptual loss	4.28
Bilinear interpolation + OSRCycleGAN (proposed)	Interpolated image (two channels) + reconstruction image(one channel)	Fine-tuning *	Cycle consistent loss	9.26
			Cycle consistent loss + Perceptual loss	7.01
		Fine-tuning **	Cycle consistent loss	13.25
			Cycle consistent loss + Perceptual loss	3.28
		Train from scratch	Cycle consistent loss	4.23
			Cycle consistent loss + Perceptual loss	3.93

In addition, we performed the additional experiments using less or more loss functions in OSRCycleGAN as shown in Table 7. The EER of using cycle consistent loss and perceptual loss (with adversarial loss) is 3.02% which is lower than those of using cycle consistent loss (with adversarial loss) (6.95%), using cycle consistent loss, perceptual loss, and identity loss (with adversarial loss) (6.26%), and using cycle consistent loss, perceptual loss, identity loss, and focal loss (with adversarial loss) (5.88%). These results confirm that proposed OSRCycleGAN using cycle consistent loss, perceptual loss, and adversarial loss shows the best accuracies of ocular recognition.

Table 7 presents the results in the case of using bilinear interpolation + Gaussian blurring when generating a low-resolution image whereas Table 6 shows the results in the case of using only bilinear interpolation when generating a low-resolution image. Applying additional noises of Gaussian blurring makes the changes in the overall feature distribution of ocular images. Thus, it becomes more challenging to fine-tune the model by fine-tuning* and fine-tuning**. Therefore, train from scratch where the weights of all the layers were trained with our experimental data (reconstructed high-resolution images) shows the better accuracy than those by the fine-tuning* and fine-tuning** where only the weights of some layers were trained as shown in Table 7.

Table 7. Ocular recognition accuracy comparison in the case of using bilinear interpolation + Gaussian blurring when generating a low-resolution image (* means fine-tuning using the model pretrained with original high-resolution ocular images, and ** means fine-tuning using the model pretrained with ImageNet).

High-Resolution Image Obtained by	Recognizer Input	Recognizer Training Method	Loss for OSRCycleGAN	EER (%)
Bilinear interpolation + Gaussian Blurring	Interpolated image (three channels)	Without training (only testing)	Loss is not used	13.99
		Fine-tuning *		4.82
OSRCycleGAN	Reconstruction image (three channels)	Without training (only testing)	Cycle consistent loss	10.84
			Cycle consistent loss + Perceptual loss	6.15
		Fine-tuning *	Cycle consistent loss	13.26
			Cycle consistent loss + Perceptual loss	5.41
Bilinear interpolation + OSRCycleGAN (proposed)	Interpolated image (two channels) + reconstruction image(one channel)	Fine-tuning *	Cycle consistent loss	4.42
			Cycle consistent loss + Perceptual loss	3.80
		Fine-tuning **	Cycle consistent loss	5.56
			Cycle consistent loss + Perceptual loss	10.69
		Train from scratch	Cycle consistent loss	6.95
			Cycle consistent loss + Perceptual loss	3.02
			Cycle consistent loss + Perceptual loss + Identity loss	6.26
			Cycle consistent loss + Perceptual loss + Identity loss + Focal loss	5.88

4.3.2. Comparisons with the State-of-the-Art Methods

For the next experiment, ocular recognition accuracy was compared between the proposed method and state-of-the-art methods. Comparative experiment was conducted for low-resolution images as bilinear interpolation + Gaussian blurring is more frequently used [67] than only bilinear interpolation when generating a low-resolution image. Three types of open databases, CASIA-Iris-Distance, CASIA-Iris-Lamp, and IIT Delhi iris databases were experimented; as shown in Tables 8–10, the proposed method exhibited the highest ocular recognition accuracies in all cases.

The reason why Fast-SRGAN [68] shows much higher EER compared to our method is that Fast-SRGAN was used for SR of visible-light iris images which have different image characteristics (i.e., more noises, reflections, and shadow, etc.) from those of near-infrared light images used in our experiments. The reason why Iris-GAN [69] shows much higher EER compared to our method is that Iris-GAN was based on DCGAN which generates images from random noises instead of images, and the goal of Iris-GAN is not SR but image generation for the increment of training data. The reason why DeblurGAN [70] shows much higher EER compared to our method is that DeblurGAN was used for image deblurring instead of SR. As shown in Table 8, proposed OSRCycleGAN outperforms all the traditional, learning-based, and depth-based methods.

Table 8. Comparisons with the state-of-the-art methods with CASIA-Iris-Distance database (using bilinear interpolation + Gaussian blurring when generating a low-resolution image). For the training of recognizer, train from scratch was used.

High-Resolution Image Obtained by		Recognizer Input	Loss for GAN	EER (%)
Traditional image processing-based	PCT [71]	Reconstruction image (three channels)	Null	13.23
Learning-based	SRCNN [16]		Mean Squared Error loss	7.54
Deep learning-based	MobileNetV2 [72]		Mean Squared Error loss	6.78
	SRGAN [19]		Original SRGAN loss	11.18
	Pix2Pix [66]		Original Pix2pix loss	4.21
	CycleGAN [50]		Original CycleGAN loss	4.19
	Bilinear interpolation + CycleGAN [50]	Interpolated image (two channels) + reconstruction image (one channel)	Original CycleGAN loss	4.41
	Fast-SRGAN [68]	Reconstruction image (three channel)	Original Fast-SRGAN loss + VGG content loss	20.86
	Iris-GAN [69]		Original Iris-GAN loss	14.43
	DeblurGAN [70]		Original DeblurGAN loss	34.86
	Bilinear interpolation +OSRCycleGAN (proposed)	Interpolated image (two channels) + reconstruction image (one channel)	Cycle consistent loss + Perceptual loss	3.02

Table 9. Comparisons with state-of-the-art methods with the CASIA-Iris-Lamp database (using bilinear interpolation + Gaussian blurring when generating a low-resolution image). For the training of recognizer, train from scratch was used.

High-Resolution Image Obtained by	Recognizer Input	Loss for GAN	EER (%)
SRGAN [19]	Reconstruction image (three channels)	Original SRGAN loss	6.39
Pix2Pix [66]	Reconstruction image (three channels)	Original Pix2pix loss	6.24
CycleGAN [50]	Reconstruction image (three channels)	Original CycleGAN loss	6.65
Bilinear interpolation + CycleGAN [50]	Interpolated image (two channels) + reconstruction image (one channel)	Original CycleGAN loss	6.11
Bilinear interpolation + OSRCycleGAN (proposed)	Interpolated image (two channels) + reconstruction image (one channel)	Cycle consistent loss + Perceptual loss	4.06

Table 10. Comparisons with state-of-the-art methods with the IIT Delhi iris database (using bilinear interpolation + Gaussian blurring when generating a low-resolution image). For the training of recognizer, train from scratch was used.

High-Resolution Image Obtained by	Recognizer Input	Loss for GAN	EER (%)
SRGAN [19]	Reconstruction image (three channels)	Original SRGAN loss	5.57
Pix2Pix [66]	Reconstruction image (three channels)	Original Pix2pix loss	3.09
CycleGAN [50]	Reconstruction image (three channels)	Original CycleGAN loss	4.46
Bilinear interpolation + CycleGAN [50]	Interpolated image (two channels) + reconstruction image (one channel)	Original CycleGAN loss	3.35
Bilinear interpolation + OSRCycleGAN (proposed)	Interpolated image (two channels) + reconstruction image (one channel)	Cycle consistent loss + Perceptual loss	2.13

For hypothesis tests, we conducted an additional experiments of the *t*-test [73] and test of Cohen's d-value [74] about the accuracies by proposed method and second best method in Tables 8–10. If the *p*-value by *t*-test is less than 0.01, it means that the null hypothesis (that two observations (the accuracies by proposed method and second best method in our case) does not show the difference) is rejected and there is a significant difference between the two observations based on 99% significant level. If the *p*-value is larger than 0.01 and less than 0.05, it means that there is a significant difference between the two observations based on 95% significant level [73]. Cohen's d-value larger than 0.8 means the large effect size of the significant difference between the two observations (the accuracies proposed method and second best method in our case) [74]. Firstly, we calculated the *p*-value and Cohen's d-value in Table 8. The results were 0.01274 and 6.279, respectively. For Table 9, the *p*-value and Cohen's d-value were 0.01317 and 6.126, respectively. For Table 10, we got 0.02957 and 4.196, respectively. From these results, we confirm that our method shows the higher accuracies than the second best method in Tables 8–10 based on 95% significant level and large effect size.

Figure 6a–c show the receiver operating characteristic (ROC) curve of the measured recognition accuracy presented in Tables 8–10. The genuine acceptance rate is calculated as 1-FRR. Each graph is the average of the two graphs found through twofold cross-validations. As shown in Figure 6, the proposed method had the highest ocular recognition accuracies in all cases.

Figure 7 shows the examples of correct recognition cases by the proposed method. As shown in Figure 7, recognition was correctly executed even if there are differences between registered image and recognition image. That is because recognition is attempted using features extracted through a deep learning model rather than just using pixel information of the image.

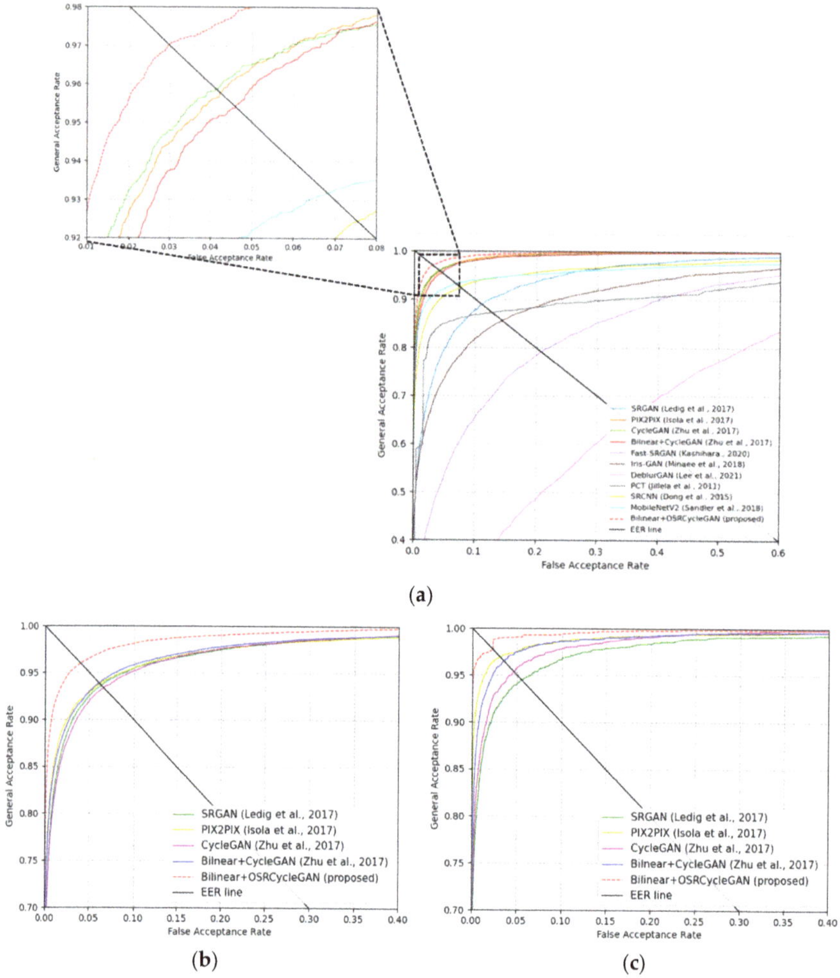

Figure 6. ROC curves of ocular recognition by the proposed method and state-of-the-art methods with (**a**) CASIA-Iris-Distance, (**b**) CASIA-Iris-Lamp, and (**c**) IIT Delhi iris database.

Figure 8 shows the examples of false rejection and false acceptance cases by the proposed method. As shown in Figure 8, in case that recognition and enrolled images are quite similar, a false acceptance case may occur like (a) and (b), or an image belonging to the same class may not be recognized because it is restored incorrectly during restoration like (c)–(f).

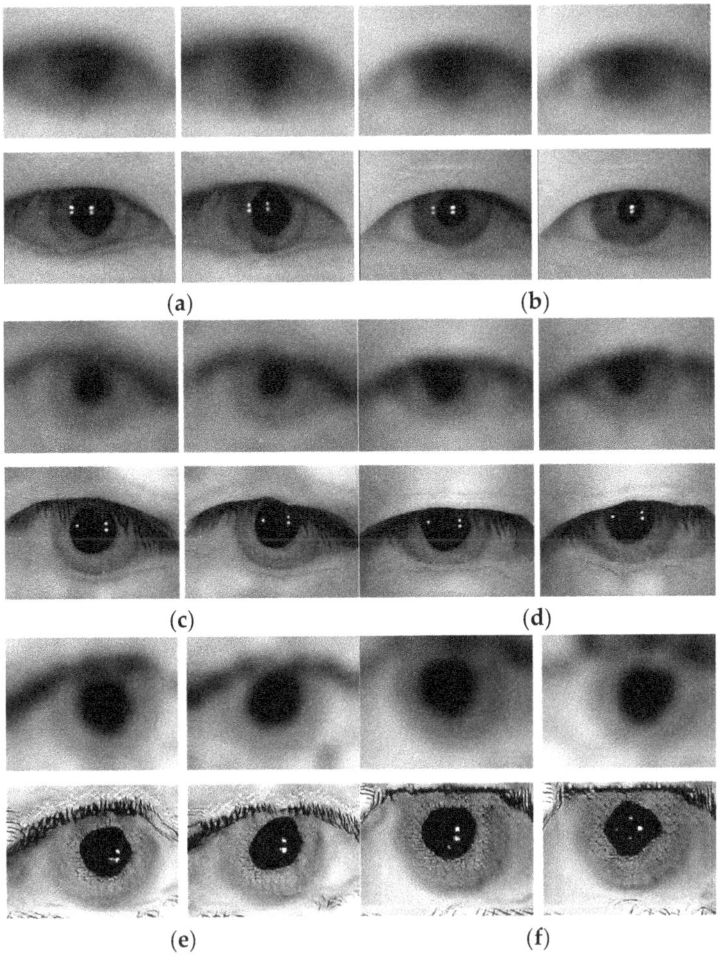

Figure 7. Example of correct recognition cases by the proposed method. (**a**,**b**) CASIA-Iris-Distance database. (**c**,**d**) CASIA-Iris-Lamp database. (**e**,**f**) IIT Delhi iris database. The left-hand and right-hand side images in (**a**–**f**) show registered images and recognition images, respectively. 1st and 2nd row images in (**a**–**f**) show low-resolution and high-resolution images restored by OSRCycleGAN, respectively.

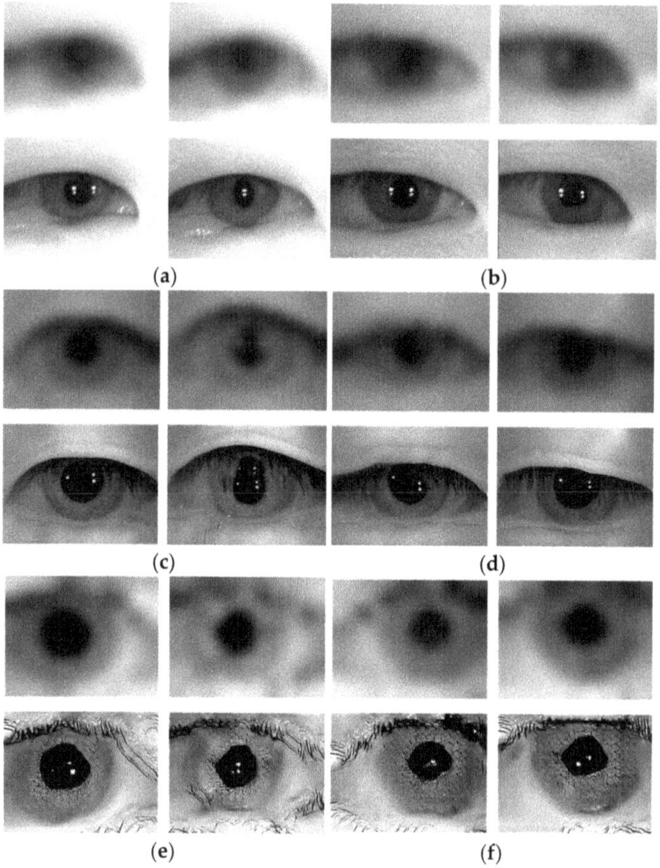

Figure 8. Example of recognition error cases by the proposed method. (a,b) CASIA-Iris-Distance database. (c,d) CASIA-Iris-Lamp database. (e,f) IIT Delhi iris database. (a,c,e) show false rejection cases. (b,d,f) show false acceptance cases. The left-hand and right-hand side images in (a–f) show registered images and recognition images, respectively. 1st and 2nd row images in (a–f) show low-resolution images and high-resolution images restored by OSRCycleGAN, respectively.

4.3.3. Evaluation Based on Cross-Database Matching Performance

As next experiment, we evaluated cross-database matching performance to validate the generalization capability of the proposed method. As the 1st experiment, we performed the training of our OSRCycleGAN for SR and ResNet-101 for ocular recognition with CASIA-Iris-Lamp database, and testing with CASIA-Iris-Distance database (case 1). As the 2nd experiment, we performed the training of OSRCycleGAN and ResNet-101 with CASIA-Iris-Distance database, and testing with CASIA-Iris-Lamp database (case 2). As shown in Table 11 and Figure 9, we confirm that the recognition accuracies by cross-database matching are not much reduced compared to those by same database matching of Tables 8 and 9, and Figure 6a,b, which validates the generalization capability of the proposed method.

Table 11. Evaluation based on cross-database matching performance. Case 1 means the training of OSRCycleGAN for SR and ResNet-101 for ocular recognition with CASIA-Iris-Lamp database, and testing with CASIA-Iris-Distance database. Case 2 means the training of OSRCycleGAN and ResNet-101 with CASIA-Iris-Distance database, and testing with CASIA-Iris-Lamp database.

Cases	EER (%)
Case 1	3.68
Case 2	6.46

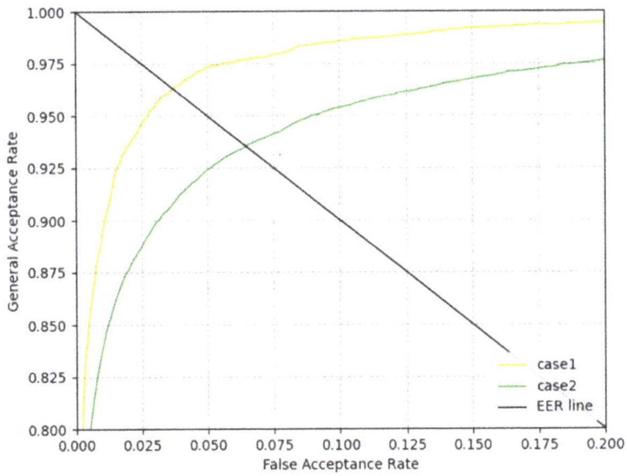

Figure 9. ROC curves of ocular recognition based on cross-database matching.

4.3.4. Processing Time and System Complexity

For the last experiment, as shown in Table 12, the processing speed of the proposed method was compared in a desktop computer, as explained in Section 4.1 and in the Jetson TX2-embedded system, shown in Figure 10. The Jetson TX2-embedded system is widely used for on-board deep learning processing. Jetson TX2 has NVIDIA Pascal^{TM}-family GPU (256 CUDA cores), having 8 GB of memory shared between the central processing unit (CPU) and GPU and 59.7 GB/s of memory bandwidth; it uses less than 7.5 W of power [75]. As presented in Table 13, the proposed OSRCycleGAN had a faster processing speed than the original CycleGAN and Pix2Pix in which the proposed method had a processing speed of 145 frames/sec (1000/6.89) on a desktop computer and 9.1 frames/sec (1000/110) on the Jetson TX2-embedded system. The Jetson TX2-embedded system has limited processing power such as a number of GPU cores, thus having a slower processing speed than the desktop computer, but the proposed method was still executable.

Table 12. Average processing time of one image by the proposed method (unit: ms).

Environments	OSRCycleGAN	ResNet-101	Total
Desktop computer	6.89	47	53.89
Jetson TX2 embedded system	110	313	423

Figure 10. Jetson TX2 embedded system.

Table 13. Average processing time of one image by Pix2Pix, original CycleGAN, and proposed OSRCycleGAN (unit: ms).

Environments	Pix2Pix [66]	CycleGAN [50]	OSRCycleGAN
Desktop computer	25.53	22.22	6.89
Jetson TX2 embedded system	273	177	110

In addition, we compared the number of floating point operations per second (#FLOPS) of Pix2Pix and CycleGAN with proposed OSRCycleGAN. As shown in Table 14, proposed OSRCycleGAN shows the better performance in #FLOPS compared to Pix2Pix. In addition, as shown in Tables 13–15, we confirm that the system complexity (#FLOPS), memory usage, and processing time by OSRCycleGAN are much less than those by CycleGAN.

Table 14. Comparisons on #FLOPS of one image by Pix2Pix, original CycleGAN, and proposed OSRCycleGAN (unit: #FLOPS).

Pix2Pix [66]	CycleGAN [50]	OSRCycleGAN
111.6×10^6	24.07×10^6	3.69×10^6

Table 15. Comparisons on memory usage by CycleGAN and proposed OSRCycleGAN (unit: Giga Bytes).

CycleGAN [50]	4.11
OSRCycleGAN	2.04

4.4. Analysis with Class Activation Maps

In this section, to determine whether the features useful for ocular recognition are extracted adequately in ResNet-101 layers for which the images restored by OSRCycleGAN are used as input, a gradient class activation map (Grad-CAM) [76] was extracted, as shown in Figure 11.

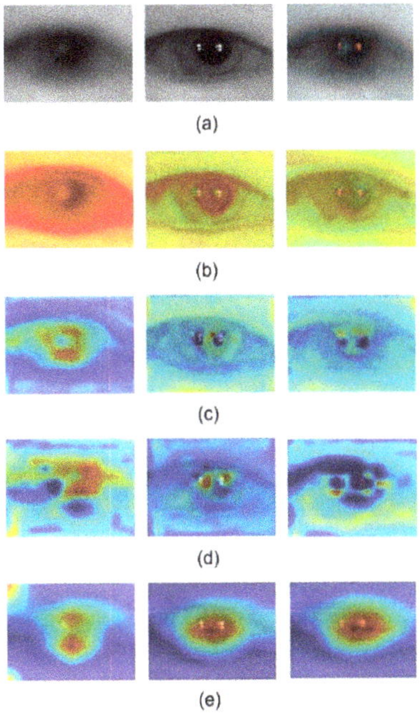

Figure 11. Grad-CAM extraction results. Each row in the figure is a low-resolution image before restoration, bilinear interpolated high-resolution image, high-resolution image after being restored by OSRCycleGAN, and when mixed images of bilinear interpolation (two channels) + OSRCycleGAN (one channel) in Tables 8–10 are used as input in the ResNet-101. (**a**) of each column is the input image. (**b**) Grad-CAM image extracted from second residual block layer, (**c**–**e**) are Grad-CAM image extracted from third, fourth and fifth residual block, respectively.

As shown in Figure 11b,c, weight is reflected in the pupil, iris region, and periocular region in the layer before the ResNet-101. Furthermore, a higher weight was reflected in the ocular region toward the subsequent layers, as shown in Figure 11d,e. Compared to low-resolution images, a higher weight was trained in the iris region in images restored to higher resolution, resulting in better recognition performance.

5. Conclusions

Existing iris or ocular recognition systems have a problem of capturing low-quality images due to low resolution; low-quality images with a blur are generated due to the movement of users when images are acquired from a far distance or low-resolution images are captured when low-priced camera equipment is used. To address these drawbacks, the study proposed an OSRCycleGAN-based SRR method. It also proposed a method for enhancing the recognition accuracy of low-resolution ocular image. When the experiments were conducted using three types of open databases, the proposed method exhibited more outstanding SRR and ocular recognition performance than state-of-the-art methods. Moreover, OSRCycleGAN had a faster processing speed than the conventional CycleGAN in a desktop computer and the Jetson TX2-embedded system, but it was still executable in an embedded system with limited processing power. The results of analyzing class activation maps showed that effective features were extracted more adequately from the images restored to high resolution using the proposed method than from low-resolution images.

Although the two loss functions (cycle consistent loss and perceptual loss) used in this method are not proposed by us, we propose a new method for calculating the perceptual loss based on both authentic and imposter matching distances between mini-batch unit images. As shown in Tables 8–10, our OSRCycleGAN using cycle consistent loss, perceptual loss, and adversarial (discriminator) loss shows the higher accuracies of ocular recognition than the original CycleGAN using cycle consistent loss, identity loss, and adversarial (discriminator) loss, which confirms the superiority of using perceptual loss instead of identity loss. Because authentic matching (matching from same class) and imposter matching (matching from different classes) should be considered as important factor in biometric system including ocular recognition, the perceptual loss based on these two matching could enhance the accuracy by our OSRCycleGAN compared to CycleGAN which does not consider the two matching even with less number of filters, system complexity, memory usage, and processing time. In addition, the identity loss of CycleGAN cannot avoid performance degradation from various effects such as pixel shifting because it just calculates the pixel differences between two images. Therefore, the identity loss was not used in our OSRCycleGAN, and we compensate the gap that comes from removing the identity loss by adding perceptual loss. These are also our innovative points compared to CycleGAN.

As shown in Table 13, proposed OSRCycleGAN shows the processing speed faster than the second best one (CycleGAN) by about 322% and 161% in desktop computer and Jetson TX2 embedded system, respectively. In addition, proposed OSRCycleGAN shows much lower number (15.3%) of #FLOPS than that by the second best one (CycleGAN) as shown in Table 14. Although the EER by our OSRCycleGAN is not much reduced compared to the second best method as shown in Tables 8–10 and Figure 6, the proportions of EER reduction by our OSRCycleGAN are 27.9% ((4.19 − 3.02)/4.19), 33.6% ((6.11 − 4.06)/6.11), and 31.1% ((3.09 − 2.13)/3.09) compared to the second best method in Tables 8–10, respectively. Because OSRCycleGAN is the enhanced model of original CycleGAN, if we compare OSRCycleGAN with the original CycleGAN having same input, the proportions of EER reduction by OSRCycleGAN are 31.5% ((4.41 − 3.02)/4.41), 33.6% ((6.11 − 4.06)/6.11), and 36.4% ((3.35 − 2.13)/3.35) compared to the original CycleGAN having same input in Tables 8–10, respectively.

In future work, the applicability of OSRCycleGAN in face recognition or vein recognition, which are other biometrics modality and person re-identification, will be analyzed. Furthermore, a lighter OSRCycleGAN model will be researched for improving the processing speed in embedded systems.

Author Contributions: Methodology, Y.W.L.; conceptualization, J.S.K.; supervision, K.R.P.; writing—original draft, Y.W.L.; writing—editing and review, K.R.P. All authors have read and agreed to the published version of the manuscript.

Funding: This research was supported in part by the National Research Foundation of Korea (NRF) funded by the Ministry of Science and ICT (MSIT) through the Basic Science Research Program (NRF-2021R1F1A1045587), in part by the NRF funded by the MSIT through the Basic Science Research Program (NRF-2022R1F1A1064291), and in part by the NRF funded by the MSIT through the Basic Science Research Program (NRF-2020R1A2C1006179).

Institutional Review Board Statement: Not applicable.

Informed Consent Statement: Not applicable.

Data Availability Statement: Not applicable.

Conflicts of Interest: The authors declare no conflict of interest.

References

1. Proenca, H.; Neves, J.C. Deep-PRWIS: Periocular recognition without the iris and sclera using deep learning frameworks. *IEEE Trans. Inf. Forensics Secur.* **2017**, *13*, 888–896. [CrossRef]
2. Noh, K.J.; Choi, J.; Hong, J.S.; Park, K.R. Finger-vein recognition based on densely connected convolutional network using score-level fusion with shape and texture images. *IEEE Access* **2020**, *8*, 96748–96766. [CrossRef]
3. Daugman, J.G. High confidence visual recognition of persons by a test of statistical independence. *IEEE Trans. Pattern Anal. Mach. Intell.* **1993**, *15*, 1148–1161. [CrossRef]

4. Daugman, J.G. Biometric Personal Identification System Based on Iris Analysis. U.S. Patent 5291560, 1 March 1994.
5. Daugman, J.G. Statistical richness of visual phase information: Update on recognizing persons by iris patterns. *Int. J. Comput. Vis.* **2001**, *45*, 25–38. [CrossRef]
6. Daugman, J.G. The importance of being random: Statistical principles of iris recognition. *Pattern Recognit.* **2003**, *36*, 279–291. [CrossRef]
7. Daugman, J.G. How iris recognition works. *IEEE Trans. Circuits Syst. Video Technol.* **2004**, *14*, 21–30. [CrossRef]
8. Daugman, J.G. New methods in iris recognition. *IEEE Trans. Syst. Man, Cybern. Part B (Cybern.)* **2007**, *37*, 1167–1175. [CrossRef]
9. Nguyen, K.; Fookes, C.; Jillela, R.; Sridharan, S.; Ross, A. Long range iris recognition: A survey. *Pattern Recognit.* **2017**, *72*, 123–143. [CrossRef]
10. Verma, S.; Mittal, P.; Vatsa, M.; Singh, R. At-a-distance person recognition via combining ocular features. In Proceedings of the IEEE International Conference on Image Processing, Phoenix, AZ, USA, 25–28 September 2016; pp. 3131–3135.
11. Bharadwaj, S.; Bhatt, H.S.; Vasta, M.; Singh, R. Periocular biometrics: When iris recognition fails. In Proceedings of the 4th IEEE International Conference on Biometrics: Theory, Application, and Systems, Washington, DC, USA, 27–29 September 2010; pp. 1–6.
12. Su, H.; Tang, L.; Wu, Y.; Tretter, D.; Zhou, J. Spatially adaptive block-based super-resolution. *IEEE Trans. Image Process.* **2011**, *21*, 1031–1045. [CrossRef]
13. Babacan, S.D.; Molina, R.; Katsaggelos, A.K. Variational Bayesian super resolution. *IEEE Trans. Image Process.* **2011**, *20*, 984–999. [CrossRef]
14. Hu, J.; Wu, X.; Zhou, J. Noise robust single image super-resolution using a multiscale image pyramid. *Signal Process.* **2018**, *148*, 157–171. [CrossRef]
15. Taniguchi, K.; Ohashi, M.; Han, X.-H.; Iwamoto, Y.; Sasatani, S.; Chen, Y.-W. Example-based super-resolution using locally linear embedding. In Proceedings of the 6th International Conference on Computer Sciences and Convergence Information Technology, Jeju Island, Korea, 29 November 2011–1 December 2011; pp. 861–865.
16. Dong, C.; Loy, C.C.; He, K.; Tang, X. Image super-resolution using deep convolutional networks. *IEEE Trans. Pattern Anal. Mach. Intell.* **2016**, *38*, 295–307. [CrossRef] [PubMed]
17. Kim, J.; Lee, J.K.; Lee, K.M. Accurate image super-resolution using very deep convolutional networks. In Proceedings of the IEEE Conference on Computer Vision and Pattern Recognition, Las Vegas, NV, USA, 27-30 June 2016; pp. 1646–1654.
18. Goodfellow, I.J.; Pouget-Abadie, J.; Mirza, M.; Xu, B.; Warde-Farley, D.; Ozair, S.; Courville, A.; Bengio, Y. Generative adversarial nets. In Proceedings of the 28th Conference on Neural Information Processing Systems, Montreal, QC, Canada, 8–13 December 2014; pp. 2672–2680.
19. Ledig, C.; Theis, L.; Huszár, F.; Caballero, J.; Cunningham, A.; Acosta, A.; Aitken, A.P.; Tejani, A.; Totz, J.; Wang, Z.; et al. Photo-Realistic Single Image Super-Resolution Using a Generative Adversarial Network. In Proceedings of the 2017 IEEE Conference on Computer Vision and Pattern Recognition (CVPR), Honolulu, HI, USA, 21–26 July 2017.
20. Tan, C.-W.; Kumar, A. Accurate iris recognition at a distance using stabilized iris encoding and Zernike moments phase features. *IEEE Trans. Image Process.* **2014**, *23*, 3962–3974. [CrossRef]
21. Nguyen, K.; Fookes, C.; Sridharan, S.; Denman, S. Quality-driven super-resolution for less constrained iris recognition at a distance and on the move. *IEEE Trans. Inf. Forensics Secur.* **2011**, *6*, 1248–1258. [CrossRef]
22. Rodriguez, A.; Panza, J.; Kumar, B.V.K.V. Segmentation-free ocular detection and recognition. In Proceedings of the SPIE Defense, Security, and Sensing, Orlando, FL, USA, 25–29 April 2011; p. 8029. [CrossRef]
23. Cho, S.R.; Nam, G.P.; Shin, K.Y.; Nguyen, D.T.; Pham, T.D.; Lee, E.C.; Park, K.R. Periocular-based biometrics robust to eye rotation based on polar coordinates. *Multimedia Tools Appl.* **2015**, *76*, 11177–11197. [CrossRef]
24. Oishi, S.; Ichino, M.; Yoshiura, H. Fusion of iris and periocular user authentication by AdaBoost for mobile devices. In Proceedings of the IEEE International Conference on Consumer Electronics, Las Vegas, NV, USA, 9–12 January 2015; pp. 428–429. [CrossRef]
25. Tan, C.-W.; Kumar, A. Towards online iris and periocular recognition under relaxed imaging constraints. *IEEE Trans. Image Process.* **2013**, *22*, 3751–3765. [CrossRef]
26. Gangwar, A.; Joshi, A. DeepIrisNet: Deep iris representation with applications in iris recognition and cross-sensor iris recognition. In Proceedings of the IEEE International Conference on Image Processing, Phoenix, AZ, USA, 25–28 September 2016; pp. 2301–2305. [CrossRef]
27. Lee, M.B.; Gil Hong, H.; Park, K.R. Noisy ocular recognition based on three convolutional neural networks. *Sensors* **2017**, *17*, 2933. [CrossRef]
28. Liu, M.; Zhou, Z.; Shang, P.; Xu, D. Fuzzified image enhancement for deep learning in iris recognition. *IEEE Trans. Fuzzy Syst.* **2019**, *28*, 92–99. [CrossRef]
29. Vizoni, M.V.; Marana, A.N. Ocular recognition using deep features for identity authentication. In Proceedings of the International Conference on System, Signals and Image Processing, Niteroi, Brazil, 1–3 July 2020; pp. 155–160.
30. Lee, Y.W.; Kim, K.W.; Hoang, T.M.; Arsalan, M.; Park, K.R. Deep residual CNN-based ocular recognition based on rough pupil detection in the images by NIR camera sensor. *Sensors* **2019**, *19*, 842. [CrossRef]
31. Nguyen, K.; Fookes, C.; Sridharan, S.; Denman, S. Feature-domain super-resolution for iris recognition. *Comput. Vis. Image Underst.* **2013**, *117*, 1526–1535. [CrossRef]

32. Deshpande, A.; Patavardhan, P.P.; Rao, D.H. Super-resolution for iris feature extraction. In Proceedings of the IEEE Inter-national Conference on Computational Intelligence and Computing Research, Coimbatore, India, 18–20 December 2014; pp. 1–4.
33. Nguyen, K.; Fookes, C.; Sridharan, S.; Denman, S. Focus-score weighted super-resolution for uncooperative iris recognition at a distance and on the move. In Proceedings of the 25th International Conference of Image and Vision Computing New Zealand, Queenstown, New Zealand, 8–9 November 2010; pp. 1–8. [CrossRef]
34. Fahmy, G. Super-resolution construction of iris images from a visual low resolution face video. In Proceedings of the 9th International Symposium on Signal Processing and Its Applications, Sharjah, United Arab Emirates, 12–15 February 2007; pp. 1–4.
35. Shirke, S.D.; Rajabhushnam, C. Biometric personal iris recognition from an image at long distance. In Proceedings of the 3rd International Conference on Trends in Electronics and Informatics, Tirunelveli, India, 23–25 April 2019; pp. 560–565.
36. Cui, J.; Wang, Y.; Huang, J.Z.; Tan, T.; Sun, Z. An iris image synthesis method based on PCA and super-resolution. In Proceedings of the 17th International Conference on Pattern Recognition, Cambridge, UK, 26 August 2004; pp. 471–474.
37. Shin, K.Y.; Park, K.R.; Kang, B.J.; Park, S.J. Super-resolution method based on multiple multi-layer perceptrons for iris recognition. In Proceedings of the 4th International Conference on Ubiquitous Information Technologies & Applications, Fukuoka, Japan, 20–22 December 2009; pp. 1–5.
38. Shin, K.Y.; Kang, B.J.; Park, K.R.; Shin, J.-h. A Study on the restoration of a low-resolution iris image into a high-resolution one based on multiple multi-layered perceptrons. *J. Korea Multimed. Soc.* **2010**, *13*, 1581–1592.
39. Shin, K.Y.; Kang, B.J.; Park, K.R. Super-resolution iris image restoration based on multiple MLPs and CLS filter. *J. Internet Technol.* **2012**, *13*, 233–244.
40. Alonso-Fernandez, F.; Farrugia, R.A.; Bigun, J. Eigen-patch iris super-resolution for iris recognition improvement. In Proceedings of the 23rd European Signal Processing Conference (EUSIPCO), Nice, France, 31 August–4 September 2015; pp. 76–80. [CrossRef]
41. Ribeiro, E.; Uhl, A.; Alonso-Fernandez, F.; Farrugia, R.A. Exploring deep learning image super-resolution for iris recognition. In Proceedings of the 25th European Signal Processing Conference (EUSIPCO), Kos, Greece, 28 August 2017–2 September 2017. [CrossRef]
42. Reddy, N.; Noor, D.F.; Li, Z.; Derakhshani, R. Multi-frame super resolution for ocular biometrics. In Proceedings of the IEEE/CVF Conference on Computer Vision and Pattern Recognition Workshops, Salt Lake City, UT, USA, 18–22 June 2018; pp. 566–574.
43. Ribeiro, E.; Uhl, A. Exploring Texture Transfer Learning via Convolutional Neural Networks for Iris Super Resolution. In Proceedings of the International Conference of the Biometrics Special Interest Group (BIOSIG), Darmstadt, Germany, 20–22 September 2017. [CrossRef]
44. Tan, J.; Liao, X.; Liu, J.; Cao, Y.; Jiang, H. Channel attention image steganography with generative adversarial networks. *IEEE Trans. Netw. Sci. Eng.* **2021**, *9*, 888–903. [CrossRef]
45. Liao, X.; Yu, Y.; Li, B.; Li, Z.; Qin, Z. A new payload partition strategy in color image steganography. *IEEE Trans. Circuits Syst. Video Technol.* **2019**, *30*, 685–696. [CrossRef]
46. Liao, X.; Yin, J.; Chen, M.; Qin, Z. Adaptive payload distribution in multiple images steganography based on image texture features. *IEEE Trans. Dependable Secur. Comput.* **2022**, *19*, 897–911. [CrossRef]
47. Yin, G.; Wang, W.; Yuand, Z.; Ji, W.; Yue, D.; Sun, S.; Chua, T.-S.; Wang, C. Conditional hyper-network for blind super-resolution with multiple degradations. *IEEE Trans. Image Process.* **2022**, *31*, 3949–3960. [CrossRef]
48. Martins, A.L.D.; Homem, M.R.P.; Mascarenhas, N.D.A. Super-resolution Image reconstruction using the ICM Algorithm. In Proceedings of the IEEE International Conference on Image Processing, San Antonio, TX, USA, 16–19 September 2007; pp. 1–4.
49. Han, Y.; Shu, F.; Zhang, Q. Image super-resolution reconstruction based on adaptive interpolation norm regularization. In Proceedings of the International Symposium on Intelligent Signal Processing and Communication Systems, Xiamen, China, 28 November–1 December 2007; pp. 1–4.
50. Zhu, J.-Y.; Park, T.; Isola, P.; Efros, A.A. Unpaired image-to-image translation using cycle-consistent adversarial networks. In Proceedings of the IEEE International Conference on Computer Vision, Venice, Italy, 22–29 October 2017; pp. 2242–2251.
51. He, K.; Zhang, X.; Ren, S.; Sun, J. Deep residual learning for image recognition. In Proceedings of the IEEE Conference on Computer Vision and Pattern Recognition, Las Vegas, NV, USA, 26 June 2016; pp. 770–778.
52. Deng, J.; Dong, W.; Socher, R.; Li, L.-J.; Li, K.; Fei-Fei, L. ImageNet: A large-scale hierarchical image database. In Proceedings of the IEEE Conference on Computer Vision and Pattern Recognition, Miami, FL, USA, 20–25 June 2009; pp. 248–255.
53. Nair, V.; Hinton, G.E. Rectified linear units improve restricted Boltzmann machines. In Proceedings of the 27th International Conference on Machine Learning, Haifa, Israel, 21–24 June 2010; pp. 807–814.
54. Multinomial Logistic Loss. Available online: http://caffe.berkeleyvision.org/doxygen/classcaffe_1_1MultinomialLogisticLossLayer.html (accessed on 1 July 2022).
55. CASIA-iris Version 4. Available online: http://biometrics.idealtest.org/dbDetailForUser.do?id=4#/datasetDetail/4 (accessed on 3 July 2022).
56. Kumar, A.; Passi, A. Comparison and combination of iris matchers for reliable personal authentication. *Pattern Recognit.* **2010**, *43*, 1016–1026. [CrossRef]
57. Krizhevsky, A.; Sutskever, I.; Hinton, G.E. Imagenet classification with deep convolutional neural networks. In Proceedings of the 25th International Conference on Neural Information Processing Systems, Lake Tahoe, NV, USA, 3–8 December 2012; pp. 1097–1105.

58. NVIDIA GeForce GTX 1070. Available online: https://www.nvidia.com/en-us/geforce/products/10series/geforce-gtx-1070/ (accessed on 3 July 2022).
59. Abadi, M.; Agarwal, A.; Barham, P.; Brevdo, E.; Chen, Z.; Citro, C.; Corrado, G.S.; Davis, A.; Dean, J.; Devin, M.; et al. TensorFlow: Large-Scale Machine Learning on Heterogeneous Systems. 2015. Available online: https://www.tensorflow.org (accessed on 10 July 2022).
60. Jia, Y.; Shelhamer, E.; Donahue, J.; Karayev, S.; Long, J.; Girshick, R.; Guadarrama, S.; Darrell, T. Caffe: Convolutional architecture for fast feature embedding. In Proceedings of the 22nd ACM International Conference on Multimedia, Orlando, FL, USA, 3–7 November 2014; pp. 675–678.
61. Kingma, D.P.; Ba, J. Adam: A method for stochastic optimization. In Proceedings of the International Conference on Learning Representation, San Diego, CA, USA, 7–9 May 2015; pp. 1–15.
62. Bottou, L. Stochastic Gradient Descent Tricks. In *Neural Networks: Tricks of the Trade*; Montavon, G., Orr, G.B., Müller, K.R., Eds.; Lecture Notes in Computer Science; Springer: Berlin, Heidelberg, 2012; p. 7700.
63. Stathaki, T. *Image Fusion: Algorithms and Applications*; Academic Press: Cambridge, MA, USA, 2008.
64. Salomon, D. *Data Compression: The Complete Reference*, 4th ed.; Springer: New York, NY, USA, 2006.
65. Wang, Z.; Bovik, A.; Sheikh, H.; Simoncelli, E. Image quality assessment: From error visibility to structural similarity. *IEEE Trans. Image Process.* **2004**, *13*, 600–612. [CrossRef]
66. Isola, P.; Zhu, J.-Y.; Zhou, T.; Efros, A.A. Image-to-image translation with conditional adversarial networks. In Proceedings of the IEEE Conference on Computer Vision and Pattern Recognition, Honolulu, HI, USA, 21–26 July 2017; pp. 1125–1134.
67. Gonzalez, R.C.; Woods, R.E. *Digital Image Processing*; Prentice Hall: Upper Saddle River, NJ, USA, 2010.
68. Kashihara, K. Iris recognition for biometrics based on CNN with super-resolution GAN. In Proceedings of the IEEE Conference on Evolving and Adaptive Intelligent Systems, Bari, Italy, 27–29 May 2020; pp. 1–6.
69. Minaee, S.; Abdolrashidi, A. Iris-GAN: Learning to Generate Realistic Iris Images Using Convolutional GAN. *arXiv* **2018**, arXiv:1812.04822. Available online: https://arxiv.org/abs/1812.04822 (accessed on 10 July 2022).
70. Lee, M.B.; Kang, J.K.; Yoon, H.S.; Park, K.R. Enhanced Iris Recognition Method by Generative Adversarial Network-Based Image Reconstruction. *IEEE Access* **2021**, *9*, 10120–10135. [CrossRef]
71. Jillela, R.; Ross, A.; Flynn, P.J. Information fusion in low-resolution iris videos using Principal Components Transform. In Proceedings of the IEEE Workshop on Applications of Computer Vision (WACV), Kona, HI, USA, 5–7 January 2011; pp. 262–269. [CrossRef]
72. Sandler, M.; Howard, A.; Zhu, M.; Zhmoginov, A.; Chen, L.C. Mobilenetv2: Inverted residuals and linear bottlenecks. In Proceedings of the IEEE Conference on Computer Vision and Pattern Recognition, Salt Lake City, UT, USA, 18–22 June 2018; pp. 4510–4520.
73. Student's T-Test. Available online: https://en.wikipedia.org/wiki/Student%27s_t-test (accessed on 3 October 2022).
74. Cohen, J. A power primer. *Psychol. Bull.* **1992**, *112*, 155. [CrossRef]
75. Jetson TX2 Module. Available online: https://www.nvidia.com/en-us/autonomous-machines/embedded-systems/ (accessed on 15 July 2022).
76. Selvaraju, R.R.; Cogswell, M.; Das, A.; Vedantam, R.; Parikh, D.; Batra, D. Grad-CAM: Visual Explanations from Deep Networks via Gradient-Based Localization. In Proceedings of the 2017 IEEE International Conference on Computer Vision (ICCV), Venice, Italy, 22–29 October 2017; pp. 618–626. [CrossRef]

mathematics

MDPI

Article

Deep-Learning-Based Complex Scene Text Detection Algorithm for Architectural Images

Weiwei Sun [1], Huiqian Wang [1], Yi Lu [1], Jiasai Luo [1], Ting Liu [1], Jinzhao Lin [1], Yu Pang [1,*] and Guo Zhang [1,2,*]

[1] Chongqing Key Laboratory of Photoelectronic Information Sensing and Transmitting Technology, Chongqing University of Posts and Telecommunications, Chongqing 400065, China
[2] School of Medical Information and Engineering, Southwest Medical University, Luzhou 646000, China
* Correspondence: pangyu@cqupt.edu.cn (Y.P.); zhangguo@swmu.edu.cn (G.Z.); Tel.: +86-13372653576 (Y.P.); +86-13438598188 (G.Z.)

Abstract: With the advent of smart cities, the text information in an image can be accurately located and recognized, and then applied to the fields of instant translation, image retrieval, card surface information recognition, and license plate recognition. Thus, people's lives and work will become more convenient and comfortable. Owing to the varied orientations, angles, and shapes of text, identifying textual features from images is challenging. Therefore, we propose an improved EAST detector algorithm for detecting and recognizing slanted text in images. The proposed algorithm uses reinforcement learning to train a recurrent neural network controller. The optimal fully convolutional neural network structure is selected, and multi-scale features of text are extracted. After importing this information into the output module, the Generalized Intersection over Union algorithm is used to enhance the regression effect of the text bounding box. Next, the loss function is adjusted to ensure a balance between positive and negative sample classes before outputting the improved text detection results. Experimental results indicate that the proposed algorithm can address the problem of category homogenization and improve the low recall rate in target detection. When compared with other image detection algorithms, the proposed algorithm can better identify slanted text in natural scene images. Finally, its ability to recognize text in complex environments is also excellent.

Keywords: building detection; geographic position; EAST; smart cities

MSC: 68T07; 68U15

1. Introduction

In recent years, more and more devices (smartphones, smart watches, high-definition surveillance cameras, etc.) for acquiring images and videos have been widely used in various industries. People have access to massive amounts of image data. Some important text information is often included in these image data, such as license plate numbers, product introduction text in billboards, road information and direction indication text in street signs, etc. [1,2]. Therefore, the text in the image is detected and recognized by the computer, and the obtained text information plays an important role in promoting the development of human–computer interaction [3], geographic location positioning [4], real-time translation [5], robot navigation [6], and industrial automation [7]. However, the texts in the images have different sizes, different font shapes and orientations, and even overlap and contamination, which make text detection very difficult. Therefore, text extraction in natural scenes has gradually become a research hotspot in the field of image processing.

The traditional text-detection algorithms are cumbersome and less robust. For example, Neumann et al. [8] searched for candidate character features through the Maximally Stable Extremal Region algorithm, and combined the extracted features into word or text regions according to custom rules or classifiers. This method is relatively efficient, but the performance is poor in the case of uneven lighting. Louloudis et al. [9] used the parallel or symmetrical properties of upper and lower edges between text lines to achieve the effective detection of text candidates. However, this method lags behind the deep learning methods that have appeared in recent years in terms of accuracy and adaptability. In particular, dealing with scene features such as low resolution and geometric distortion, the text in the picture is disturbed by the complex background, which increases the difficulty of text detection.

With the continuous progress of deep learning [10–18] technology and the popularization of high-computing-power hardware in recent years, the application fields of deep learning are becoming more and more extensive, such as computer vision (biometric recognition, image processing, video analysis), natural language processing (speech recognition, text data mining, text translation), data mining (consumption habit, weather data, recommendation systems), and composite applications (unmanned driving, unmanned aerial vehicles, robots), etc. Text detection algorithms based on deep learning have become the mainstream direction of current text detection technology research. The basic objective of a text detection algorithm is to use a neural network structure to automatically extract text features from natural scene images. The weight parameters are updated based on feedback via a loss function to achieve text localization [19]. Natural scene text detection methods based on deep learning can be divided into three types: bounding box (BBOX) regression [20–24], semantic segmentation [25–28], and a combination of these two [29–33]. Of these, the text detection method based on BBOX regression is the most widely used one. A combination of semantic segmentation and BBOX regression can achieve better text detection results. However, such a method uses more steps, which increases the processing time. The operation of the combined method is similar to that of the Mask-RCNN algorithm [34]. Huang et al. [35] used the MSER algorithm to find candidate characters, and then used a deep neural network algorithm as a classifier to screen out the final text lines. Jaderberg et al. [36] scanned images with the help of sliding windows and used a convolutional neural network model to generate multi-scale feature images. Shi et al. [37] proposed a Connectionist Text proposal network model to extract features by combining a CNN and RNN deep network. This method enhances the connection of text lines and improves the detection accuracy. However, this method can only detect horizontal text. In addition, the receptive field range of common convolutional neural networks is limited, and it is more challenging to directly detect long text lines. Therefore, Zhi et al. [38] proposed the SegLink text detection algorithm. The method detects the local areas of words or text lines, and then connects these local areas to form complete words or text lines. However, the subsequent processing method is complex and slow, and the detection of text with long feeling fields is not very good. In addition, Zhou et al. [39] proposed an efficient and accurate scene text detector (EAST) algorithm in 2017. The algorithm can predict multi-angle quad text areas in natural scene images. The previous text detection algorithm often contained intermediate steps such as candidate text box proposal, text box formation, word segmentation, and related post-processing, which made the algorithm structure more complicated. As an end-to-end text detection algorithm, EAST simplifies the entire work process into two phases. First, the full convolutional network is used to obtain multi-scale characteristic images, and then the feature fusion is carried out to obtain a feature map; the position information of the text box is predicted on this feature image. Then, non-maximum suppression and fusion of text boxes are performed; finally, the predicted text box is output. The EAST algorithm has a simple structure and good performance. The output text box is also suitable for the detection of the text area in the street sign scene. However, the EAST algorithm has a poor effect on complex scenes and in multi-scale text detection (Figure 1).

Figure 1. Textual information in multi-scale and complex scene natural imagery.

In this study, we proposed a Neural Architecture Search—Feature Pyramid Network EAST (NEAST) text detection algorithm to solve the problem whereby images are difficult to detect in complex scenes and multi-scale text. The algorithm consists of a feature extraction layer and an output layer. The feature extraction layer adopts an automatic architecture search network. It can extract features at various levels with diverse scales. The output layer first addresses the class imbalance problem in the scene image, and then improves the Intersection over Union (IoU) [40] algorithm to obtain the Generalized Intersection over Union (GIoU) [41] algorithm. A text suggestion box is selected to obtain the final text detection result. The algorithm not only better solves the classification homogeneity problem, but also improves the problem of low recall in target detection. Compared with other image detection algorithms, our proposed NEAST algorithm can better recognize skewed text in natural scene images. The algorithm shows excellent text recognition capability in complex environments.

2. Materials and Methods

2.1. EAST Algorithm

Scene text detection methods have achieved encouraging results on various benchmarks. However, these methods, even those using deep neural network models, have shortcomings when dealing with challenging scenarios. Because the overall performance of a text detection model depends on the interactions among the modules in the algorithmic model, a simple model can optimize the loss function and neural network structure in a targeted manner and improve text detection. Therefore, text regions in natural scene images can be detected quickly and accurately using a simple and efficient EAST algorithm. The model structure is depicted in Figure 2. The simple structure and fast operation are the advantages of the EAST algorithm. However, its accuracy of text detection in complex scenes is not satisfactory.

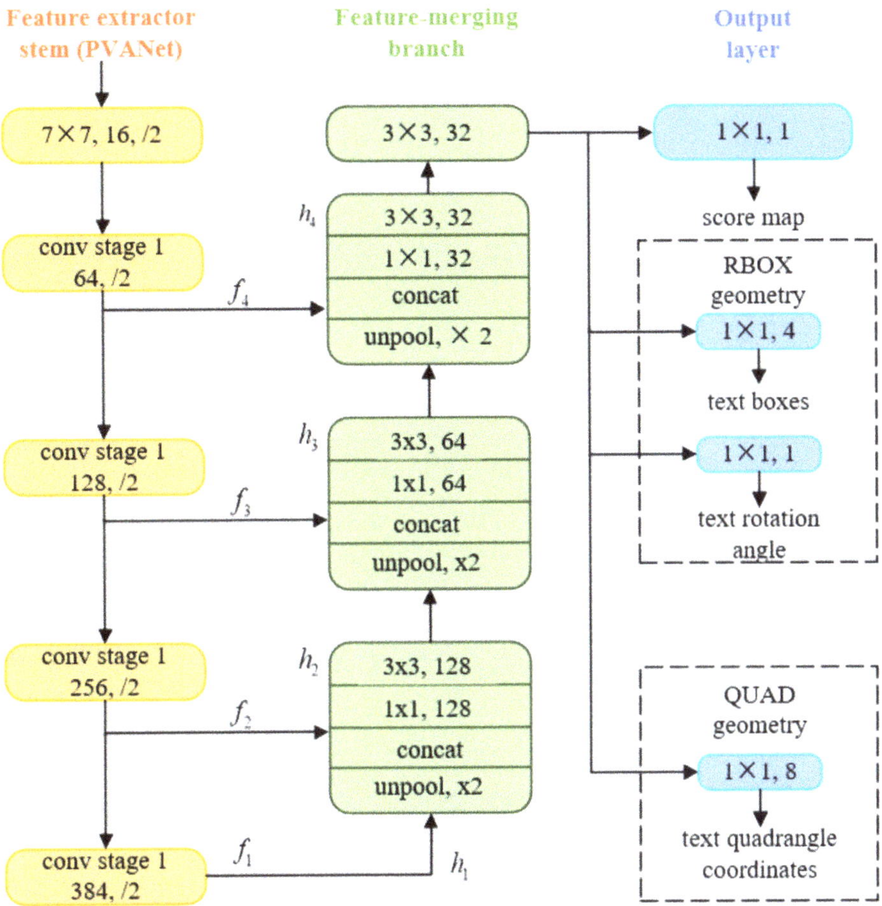

Figure 2. EAST algorithm model.

The network structure of EAST is shown in Figure 2. We use the Performance vs. Accuracy Network (PVANet) to extract features, and merge the features of different layers after upsampling. Then, the final score and box are predicted. The box is represented by RBOX and QUAD. If box data are annotated in the form of RBOX, the model finally predicts the 1-channel score_map and the 4-channel box_map. If the box data are annotated in the form of QUAD, the model finally predicts the 1-channel score_map and the 8-channel BOX_map.

2.1.1. Feature Extraction Network

After an image is input, feature extraction is performed using a feature pyramid network (FPN). Pre-training is performed using a CNN with interleaved convolutional and pooling layers. Four levels of feature maps, f_i, are obtained, whose sizes are $1/32$, $1/16$, $1/8$, and $1/4$ of the original image. The objective of this step is to address the problem of scale diversity of text lines. Low- and high-level features are used to predict smaller- and larger-sized text lines, respectively.

2.1.2. Feature Fusion

In the feature fusion step, the feature map extracted in the preceding stage is first de-pooled. The size of the feature map is increased, and it is connected in series with the current feature map. Next, a 1×1 convolution kernel is used to perform the convolution operation to reduce the calculation load of the model. Subsequently, the convolution operation is performed through a 3×3 convolution kernel to fuse the feature information. Finally, the result of the text detection feature fusion stage is output. When the feature fusion process is completed, a 3×3 convolution kernel is used to perform the convolution operation. The resulting final feature map is input to the output layer. The feature fusion operates as follows:

$$
\begin{array}{l}
g_i = \begin{cases} \text{unpool}(h_i) & \text{if } i \leq 3 \\ \text{conv}_{3\times3}(h_i) \text{ if } i = 4 & \text{if } i = 1 \end{cases} \\
h_i = \begin{cases} f_i & \text{otherwise} \\ \text{conv}_{3\times3}(\text{conv}_{1\times1}([g_{i-1}; f_i])) & \text{othere} \end{cases}
\end{array}
\quad (1)
$$

2.1.3. Output Layer

The output layer is obtained using the convolution operation with many 1×1 convolution kernels. Then, 32-channel feature maps are projected to generate 1-channel fractional and multi-channel geometry feature maps. The geometry output can be rectangular or quadrilateral (see Table 1).

Table 1. EAST algorithm output.

Geometry	Channels	Description
AABB	4	$G = R = \{d_i \mid i \in \{1,2,3,4\}\}$
RBOX	5	$G = \{R, \theta\}$
QUAD	8	$G = Q = \{(\Delta x_i, \Delta y_i) \mid i \in \{1,2,3,4\}\}$

In Table 1, AABB is a horizontal rectangular frame. The four channels represent the four distances from the pixel positions to the top, right, bottom, and left borders of the rectangle, respectively. RBOX is a rotating rectangular box, and the geometric shape is represented by the horizontal BBOX of four channels and the rotation angle θ of one channel. QUAD is an arbitrary quadrilateral, and numeral 8 represents the coordinate offsets from the four vertices of the rectangle to the pixel position. Because each coordinate offset includes two values of the abscissa and ordinate $(\Delta x_i, \Delta y_i)$, the output of its geometry needs to contain eight channels.

This method mainly includes a fully convolutional network and non-maximum suppression. The algorithm model can flexibly generate word-level or text-line-level text prediction boxes, and the predicted geometric shapes can be rotated or horizontal boxes. However, the picture detection in complex scenes is not satisfactory.

2.2. *NEAST Oblique Text Detection Method*

The objective of the proposed algorithm is to obtain a network structure in the search space and set it as a sub-network through a recurrent neural network (RNN) [42] controller. Subsequently, this network structure is trained on a dataset. After its accuracy R is obtained by testing on the validation set, the accuracy values are returned to the controller. The controller continues to optimize to obtain another network structure. This is repeated until an optimal feature extraction network structure is obtained. Thereafter, the output layer is improved to enhance the accuracy, and the final detection result is obtained.

The proposed detection model is shown in Figure 3. We used the Learning Scalable Feature Pyramid Architecture for Object Detection (NAS-FPN) to combine the features of multiple layers. NAS-FPN reorganizes the feature images on five scales. FPN uses five layers of resolution features (C3, C4, C5, C6, C7), and C5 is subsampled to obtain C6 and C7. The resolution downsampling of the features in the five layers is (8, 16, 32, 64, 128), and (P3, P4, P5, P6, P7) can be obtained through FPN. The output layer convolves the extracted feature map through several 1×1 convolution kernels to generate the score plot and the rectangle detection block diagram in any direction. The text box regression is guided by the GIoU algorithm. Positive and negative samples are selected from the prior box. Then, the positive samples are encoded according to the proposed encoding. The problem that IoU cannot be optimized without overlap is solved, and it can also be used as a measure in the target detection task. The regression effect of the text box will be improved. We use the focus loss (FL) function (including position loss and classification loss) to solve the problem of positive and negative sample imbalance and hard classification sample learning.

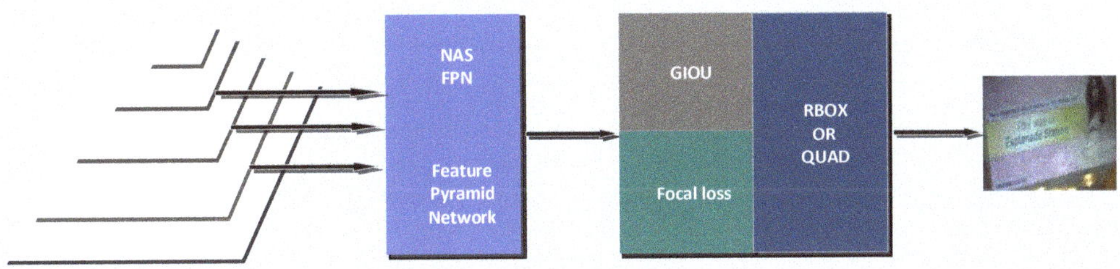

Figure 3. Text detection model based on NEAST.

2.2.1. Feature Extraction Module

Text regions in natural scene images are multi-scale and multi-object. Two types of features (low resolution, strong semantics; high resolution, low semantics) are combined to form the FPN structure through top-down paths and lateral connections. This structure is an inevitable choice for feature extraction. The text region occupies a small proportion of the image area. The shape of the region is mostly narrow and long. The target size and structure are significantly different from other target detections. Therefore, an artificially designed FPN is not necessarily the optimal structure. The combination number of feature fusion at various scales also increases with an increase in the number of network layers. Therefore, an FPN is constructed using the neural network architecture search. A search space that covers all cross-scale connections and captures multi-scale features is designed. Next, an RNN controller is obtained through reinforcement learning training to select the optimal FPN structure. The objective of the search is to find particle architectures that have the same input and output feature levels and can be applied repeatedly. The pyramid architecture can also be made manageable by modularizing the search space.

The NAS-FPN network architecture is designed based on RetinaNet and includes two parts: the Backbone Network (Basic Classification Network, MobileNet, ResNet) and Feature Pyramid Network (FPN). In NAS-FPN, a duplicate FPN module can be searched. We obtain a tradeoff between speed and accuracy by controlling the number of repetitions of this module. Then, we output the prediction results at different stages according to the different computing resources. In RetinaNet, the feature fusion strategy of FPN is adopted. NAS-FPN replaces the FPN portion of RetinaNet with the searched fusion architecture. This can find a better FPN architecture of the retinal network framework and improve the accuracy of text detection. The RetinaNet framework with NAS-FPN is depicted in Figure 4.

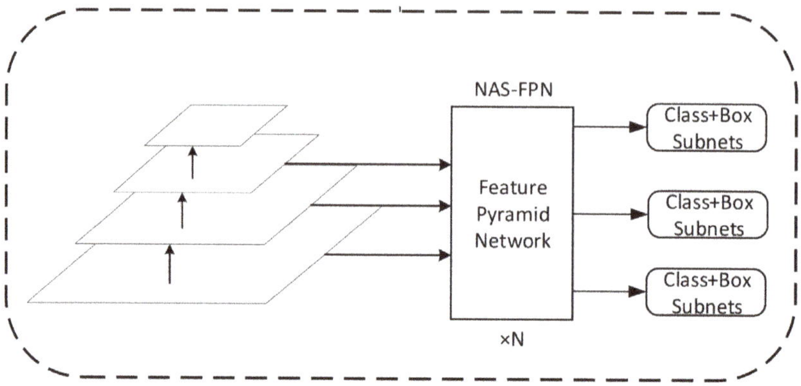

Figure 4. The NAS-FPN RetinaNet. N is the number of module repetitions.

A neural architecture search algorithm is used to search the FPN. The backbone network models for class and BBOX predictions follow the original design of RetinaNet. The FPN, input feature layers generated with multiple sizes, and output feature layers generated with the same size are depicted in Figure 4. The design of the RetinaNet network is adopted, using the output of the last layer in each group of networks as the input of the pyramid network. The output of the previous pyramid network is used as the input for the next pyramid network. Next, five scales are used as input features (C1, C2, C3, C4, C5), and their feature steps are (8, 16, 32, 64, 128), respectively. Feature C3 is obtained by the maximum pooling of C4 or C5 with strides 2 and 4. The input features are passed onto a pyramid network, which consists of a series of fused units connected across scales. The pyramid network finally outputs an enhanced multi-scale feature representation. Because both the input and output of the pyramid network are feature layers of the same size, the architecture of the FPN can be stacked N times to improve the accuracy.

Multiple cross-scale connections of FPN networks can constitute a huge search space. In the search space, the FPN network is composed of many merging cells (MC), which are merged with feature representations. The fusion unit connects and fuses the feature maps from two different levels of feature layers as a feature output. The unit structure constitutes the meta-structure of the FPN network. The component feature combination of the fusion unit constitutes the search space of the algorithm. The structure of the fusion unit is depicted in Figure 5.

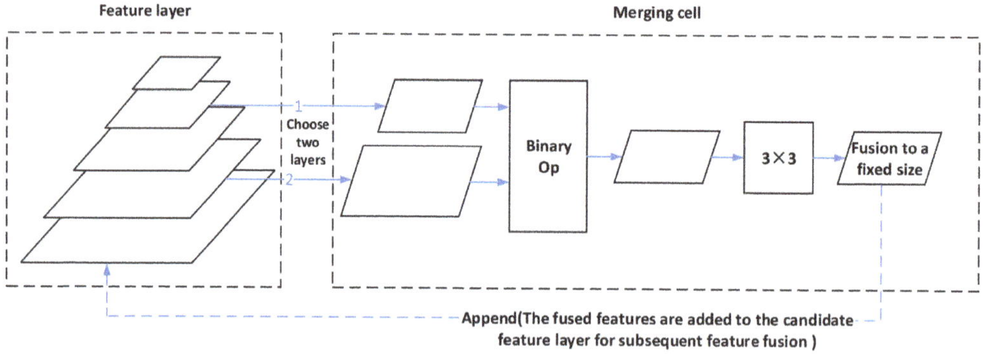

Figure 5. Structure of fusion unit.

The fusion unit comprises three processes: first, two feature layers are selected from the candidates; second, the dimension of the output feature is selected; and, finally, the two previously selected feature layers are combined and output to a specific scale based on the fusion method. The feature fusion methods are mainly divided into two types: sum and global pooling. Their structures are depicted in Figure 6.

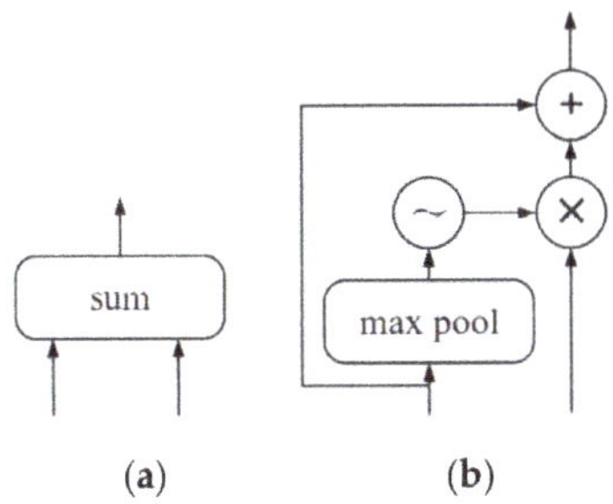

Figure 6. Feature fusion methods: (**a**) sum and (**b**) global pooling.

The two feature fusion methods are characterized by simplicity and effectiveness. No further trainable parameters are required. Before applying binary operations, the size of the input feature layer must be adjusted to the desired output size by upsampling the adjacent layers or by max pooling, if necessary. The merged feature layer includes a ReLu activation function, convolution operation with kernel size 3×3, and batch normalization. The NAS-FPN network selects the optimal model architecture in a given search space by training the RNN controller through reinforcement learning. The RNN controller updates the parameters using the accuracy of the submodel in the search space as a reward signal. After repeated training, the controller gradually learns how to obtain the optimal architectural model. A schematic of the learning process is depicted in Figure 7.

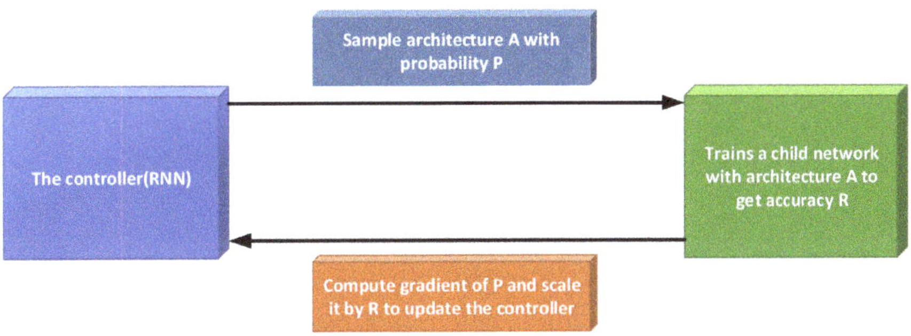

Figure 7. Controller reinforcement learning.

The structure and internal connections of the neural network are specified using a variable-length string. Therefore, the RNN can be used to generate variable-length network structures. The predicted network contains only convolutional layers, whose hyperparameters are generated using the RNN. These hyperparameters include the following: the height, width, and number of convolution kernels, and the height and width of the sliding stride of the convolution kernel. As depicted in Figure 8, the output predicted by each SoftMax function in the RNN is used as the next input.

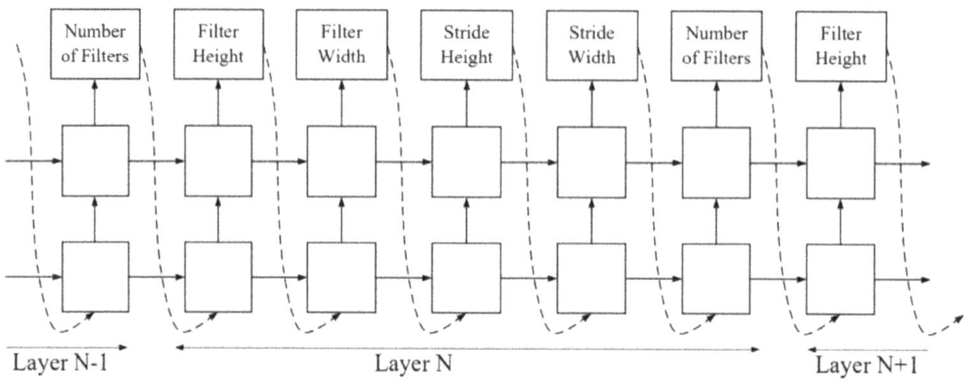

Figure 8. Predictive structure flowchart for RNN controller.

The controller generates a set of hyperparameters, and the accuracy of the generated model on the validation set is used as a feedback signal to optimize its expected value. The algorithm regards the actions of the controller as a function. Parameter updates are carried out via feedback signals. Then, the optimization of the feedback signal is realized. The termination condition in generating the network structure is to stop when the number of network layers reaches an optimal value.

After a parameter θ_c in the controller RNN is optimized, the resulting network structure can achieve good accuracy on the validation set.

After generating the network structure, the controller uses the training data to train until convergence. Next, the accuracy of the controller is confirmed after testing it on the validation set. The termination condition for the generated network structure is the number of network layers reaching a specified value. Parameter θ_c in the RNN controller is optimized. The generated network structure achieves improved accuracy on the verification set. The RNN controller predicts a series of outcomes, corresponding to a series of operations $a_{1:T}$ to design sub-networks. The generated network is tested on the validation set and the accuracy R is obtained. The R value is used as a feedback signal, and reinforcement learning is used to train the controller. To optimize the network structure, the controller is required to maximize its expected value. The formula is as follows:

$$J(\theta_c) = E_{P(a_{1:T};\theta_c)}[R] \tag{2}$$

Feedback signal R is not differentiable. The policy gradient algorithm is used to iteratively update θ_c as follows:

$$\nabla\theta_c J(\theta_c) = \sum_{t=1}^{T} E_{P(a_{1t};\theta_c)}\left[\nabla\theta_c \log P\left(a_t \middle| a_{(t-1):1};\theta_c\right) R\right] \tag{3}$$

The approximate calculation formula is as follows:

$$\nabla\theta_c J(\theta_c) = \frac{1}{m}\sum_{k=1}^{m}\sum_{t-1}^{T} \nabla\theta_c \log P\left(a_t \middle| a_{(t-1):1};\theta_c\right) R_k \tag{4}$$

where m is the number of various neural network architectures in a batch of samples during controller training, T is the number of predicted hyperparameters in the controller design network structure, and R_k is the tested accuracy on the validation set after the kth neural network is trained.

The advantage of the feature extraction network is that it designs a search space covering all possible cross-scale connections, which can be used to generate multi-scale feature representations. Particle architectures that have the same input and output feature levels and can be applied repeatedly are found during the search process. The modular search space also makes the search pyramid architecture manageable. Furthermore, feature extraction network models employing automatic architecture search algorithms can obtain feature pyramid representations at the output of any given pyramid network. The network model does not need to complete the forward pass of all pyramid networks, providing a solution that can dynamically allocate computational resources to generate detections. Therefore, an optimal FPN structure can be obtained to extract the feature of the text region.

2.2.2. Generalized Intersection over Union Algorithm

Currently, the optimization of a BBOX in the text detection method is performed mostly by reducing the regression loss of the BBOX. In this study, we trained on regression tasks with IoU as a direct metric. In the anchor-node-based target detection method, the IoU can be used not only to determine the positive and negative samples but also to judge the accuracy of the prediction frame. In addition, the IoU is insensitive to scale. Assuming that A and B denote the predicted box and labeled text area, respectively, the IoU and loss function are given as follows:

$$\mathrm{IOU} = \frac{|\mathrm{A} \cap \mathrm{B}|}{|\mathrm{A} \cup \mathrm{B}|} \tag{5}$$

$$\mathrm{Loss}_{\mathrm{giou}} = 1 - \mathrm{IOU} \tag{6}$$

There are two problems with using the IoU directly as the loss function. First, when the two boxes do not intersect, $\mathrm{IOU} = 0$ can be obtained by definition. In this case, the contact ratio of the two boxes cannot be reflected. Second, when $\mathrm{Loss} = 0$, model training cannot be performed because there is no gradient backhaul. As depicted in Figure 9, when the IoU is the same, the detection results of the prediction boxes may also be different. The text detection result on the far right is the worst.

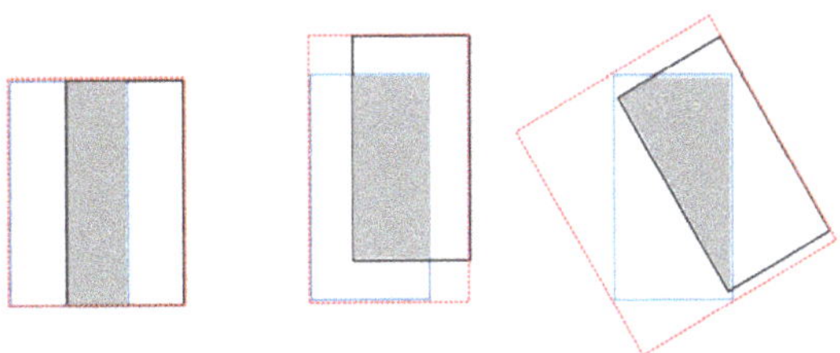

Figure 9. Text detection results with the same IoU value.

Because the use of IoU has many drawbacks, we propose to use another metric, GIoU, which is given as follows:

$$\mathrm{GIoU}(\mathrm{A}, \mathrm{B}) = \mathrm{IoU}(\mathrm{A}, \mathrm{B}) - \frac{|\mathrm{C}| - |\mathrm{AUB}|}{|\mathrm{C}|} \tag{7}$$

As shown in Figure 10, A is the prediction box, B is the real box, and S is the set of all boxes. Whether A and B intersect or not, C is the smallest box containing A and B (the smallest convex closed box containing A and B), and C also belongs to the S set.

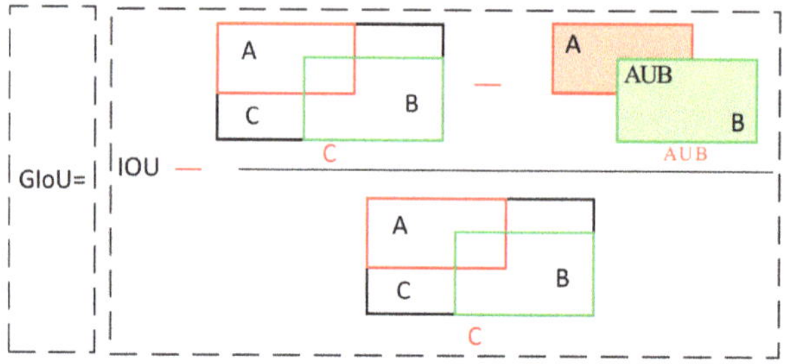

Figure 10. Structure diagram of GIoU.

We calculate IoU (the ratio of the intersection of A and B), and then calculate the area ratio of the C (no A and B) to C. Finally, the GIoU is obtained by subtracting the specific gravity value from the IoU.

The coordinates of prediction box B^p and marker box B^G are as follows:

$$B^P = \left(x_1^P,\ y_1^P, x_2^P, y_2^P\right), B^G = \left(x_1^G, y_1^G, x_2^G, y_2^G\right) \tag{8}$$

For prediction box B^p, ensure that $x_2^P > x_1^P$ and $y_2^P > y_1^P$:

$$\begin{aligned} \hat{x}_1^p &= \min\left(x_1^P, x_2^P\right) \\ \hat{x}_2^p &= \max\left(x_1^P, x_2^P\right) \\ \hat{y}_1^p &= \min\left(y_1^P, y_2^P\right) \\ \hat{y}_2^p &= \max\left(y_1^P, y_2^P\right) \end{aligned} \tag{9}$$

The areas of predicted box B^p and labeled box B^G are calculated as follows:

$$\begin{aligned} A^P &= \left(\hat{x}_2^p - \hat{x}_1^p\right) \times \left(\hat{y}_2^p - \hat{y}_1^p\right) \\ A^G &= \left(x_2^p - x_1^p\right) \times \left(y_2^p - y_1^p\right) \end{aligned} \tag{10}$$

The coordinates and area of area I where B^p and B^G intersect are calculated as follows:

$$\begin{aligned} x_1^I &= \min\left(x_1^I, x_2^I\right) \\ x_2^I &= \max\left(x_1^I, x_2^I\right) \\ y_1^I &= \min\left(y_1^I, y_2^I\right) \\ y_2^I &= \max\left(y_1^I, y_2^I\right) \end{aligned} \tag{11}$$

$$I = \begin{cases} \left(x_2^I - x_1^I\right) \times \left(y_2^I - y_1^I\right) & \text{if} \quad x_2^I > x_1^I, y_2^I > y_1^I \\ 0 & \text{otherwise} \end{cases} \tag{12}$$

The same method is used to obtain the coordinates and area A^C of the smallest BBOX C. The area of the text area is defined as U, and the value of U is calculated as follows:

$$U = A^p + A^G - I \tag{13}$$

GIoU is calculated as follows:

$$\text{GIOU} = \frac{I}{U} - \frac{A^C - U}{A^C} \tag{14}$$

When GIoU is used as the loss function, $L_{\text{GIOU}} = 1 - \text{GIOU}$, which can meet the basic requirements of the loss function. In addition, GIoU is also independent of size. It is the lower bound of IoU. When the two boxes overlap infinitely, IOU = GIOU and the value is between (0, 1). However, the value range of GIoU is (−1, 1). When the positions of the two boxes overlap completely, the maximum value is 1; when the two boxes do not overlap fully, the minimum value is −1. Therefore, GIoU is a very good distance metric. However, unlike IoU, GIoU calculates not only the overlapping part but also the non-overlapping area. In addition, GIoU calculates the overlapping area in the same manner as does the IoU in text detection. To calculate the minimum closure area, only the maximum and minimum coordinates are required.

2.3. Class Imbalance

Class imbalance refers to the significant difference in the numbers of training examples of various classes in the target classification [43]. Owing to the limited number of samples with BBOX as the target category in an image, the results of the statistical analysis of the ICDAR2013 [44] dataset are as depicted in Figure 11. The text areas in most images occupy only 30% of the entire image. Most of the widths are also concentrated between 0 and 0.3. The height ratio is concentrated between 0 and 0.15. Therefore, the proportion of text areas in natural scene images is generally small. Furthermore, the shape of the area is narrow and long.

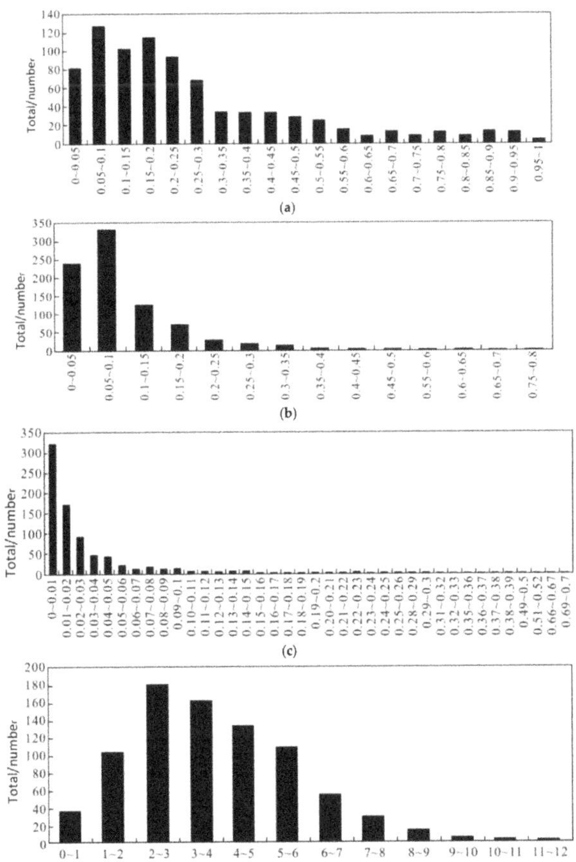

Figure 11. Characteristic analysis of text area in ICDAR2013 database. (**a**) Width of text area/width of full image, (**b**) height of text area/width of full image, (**c**) text regional area/full image area, and (**d**) width of text area/height of text area.

As depicted in Figure 12, the BBOX required to calculate the loss value is divided into two types: positive and negative. When the GIoU between the BBOX and ground truth (GT) is greater than a threshold value, the BBOX is a positive BBOX. When GIoU is less than the threshold value, the BBOX is a negative BBOX.

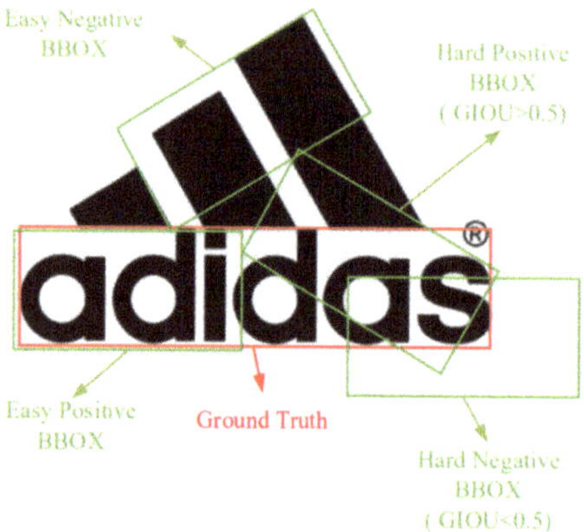

Figure 12. Schematic of four samples.

When an original image is input, the proportion of the target is only a small part of the whole image. Therefore, the two types of BBOXs are mainly negative, and most of the negative BBOXs are not in the transition area between the foreground and background. This clearly classified negative BBOX is called easy negative and is common. This leads to two problems:

1. An extremely negative BBOX will cause its loss value to be significantly large. The loss value of a positive BBOX is overwhelmed, which is not conducive to the convergence of the target.
2. When the parameter changes in the training process are not evident, the model cannot be effectively trained, and the problem of gradient disappearance may occur. However, when the easy negative sample is trained, the corresponding target score is small. That is, the loss value of a single BBOX sample is small. The parameter changes during model training backpropagation are also significantly small. Small parameter changes are not conducive to model training. Therefore, for text detection, it is extremely necessary to find BBOX samples with larger loss values and a greater impact on parameter convergence—namely, a hard BBOX.

The detection and analysis of the EAST algorithm indicate that class imbalance is another reason for its poor performance. Therefore, it is necessary to reduce the proportion of simple sample loss values. Furthermore, the sample loss values with confidence greater than 0.5 must be suppressed.

The cross-entropy (CE) loss for binary classification is calculated as follows:

$$CE(p,y) = \begin{cases} -\log(p) \; y = 1 \\ -\log(1-p) \;\; \text{otherwise} \end{cases} \tag{15}$$

where $y = 1$ represents a positive sample and the p value is the model's estimated probability for the class with the $y = 1$ label. Parameter p_t is defined as follows:

$$p_t = \begin{cases} p & y = 1 \\ 1-p & \text{otherwise} \end{cases} \tag{16}$$

$$CE(p, \mathrm{y}) = CE(p_t) = -\log(p_t) \tag{17}$$

A parameter is added to control and balance the proportion of positive and negative sample loss values:

$$CE(p_t) = -\alpha_t \log(p_t) \tag{18}$$

Although the proportion of positive and negative samples is balanced, easy and difficult examples are not distinguished. A modulation factor $(1 - p_t)^\gamma$ is added to the CE loss function, where $\gamma \geq 0$. The FL loss function is defined as

$$FL(P_t) = -(1 - P_t)^\gamma \log(p_t) \tag{19}$$

Figure 13 is the FL diagram at the $\gamma = 0,\ 1,\ 2,\ 5$ value, whereas the CE loss is represented by curve 1.

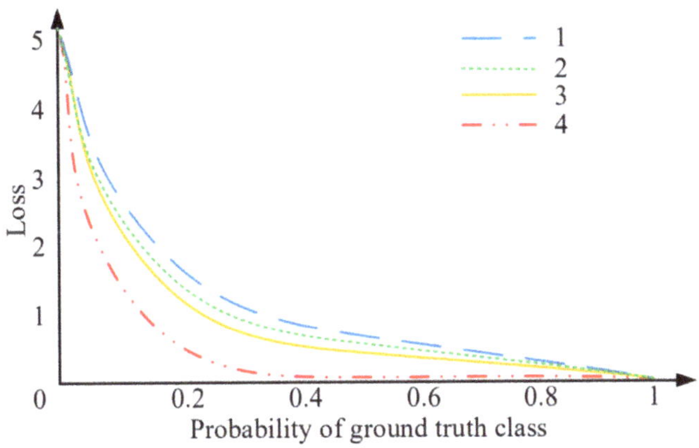

Figure 13. Loss function change curve.

As depicted in Figure 13, when the example is misclassified and p_t is small, modulation factor $(1 - p_t)^\gamma$ is close to 1 and the loss is not affected. When $p_t \to 1$, the factor becomes 0 and the loss on well-classified examples is weighted. Furthermore, the focus parameter z smoothly adjusts the weights of simple examples. When $\gamma = 0$, FL is equal to CE. As the parameter increases, the effect of the modulation factor also increases. For the third curve $\gamma = 2$, FL works the best. The modulation factor reduces the loss contribution in the simple example. Furthermore, the range of the sample reception low loss is extended. Finally, the b-balanced variant of FL is used.

The α of FL is used to balance the variant:

$$FL(p_t) = -\alpha_t(1 - p_t)^\gamma \log(p_t) \tag{20}$$

This approach improves the accuracy when compared with the non-α-balanced form. AP is the average precision. The formula is as follows:

$$\sum_{k=1}^{N} P(k)\Delta r(k) \tag{21}$$

where N represents the number of all pictures in the test set; $P(k)$ represents the precision value when k images can be recognized. Delta $r(k)$ represents the change in the recall value when the number of recognized images changes from $k - 1$ to k.

2.4. Experimental Dataset

The datasets that we used are ICDAR 2013 and ICDAR 2015 [45]. Resolutions range from 720 × 480 to 1280 × 960. They include real-world images (road signs, billboards, posters, etc.). ICDAR 2013 contains 229 training images and 233 test images of focused scene text. Text is in English and aligned horizontally. Annotations are axis-aligned bounding boxes that divide a total of 1015 cropped word images. ICDAR 2015 contains 1000 training images and 500 test images. Annotations are word-level quadrilateral tilted text. The details of the datasets are listed in Table 2.

Table 2. Experimental datasets.

Dataset	Size	Number of Images (Train/Test)	Amount of Text
ICDAR 2013	250 M	462 (229/233)	1943
ICDAR 2015	131.8 M	1500 (1000/500)	17,548

3. Results

3.1. Impact of Pyramid Network on Text Detection

The text detection model can be controlled by adjusting the dimensions of the backbone model and pyramid network. The model was trained and evaluated on the ICDAR2015 dataset. The training parameters were set as listed in Table 3.

Table 3. Training parameter settings.

Type	Setting
Batch size	16
learning rate	10^{-3}
Focal loss	$\alpha = 0.25$, $\gamma = 2$
Learning decay rate	0.9/10,000
Iterations	100,000

Pyramid networks offer the advantage that they can be extended to larger architectures by stacking multiple repeated architectures. We first changed the number of FPNs to test their impact on text detection. The experimental results are depicted in Figure 14a, where the numbers on the lines indicate the number of pyramid networks. Stacking FPN architectures does not always improve the performance of the model; however, stacking NAS-FPN can significantly improve the accuracy. This result indicates that the proposed search algorithm can find a scalable pyramid network architecture suitable for text detection.

The backbone architecture has a significant impact on the pyramid network. We performed comparative experiments with the ResNet-50, ResNet-101, and MobilenetV2 backbone networks. The results of these experiments are depicted in Figure 14b. When the number of pyramid networks increases, the performance of NAS-FPN on all these backbone architectures increases. The results indicate that the text detection model can work well with various architectures. However, the text detection is better on the ResNet network.

3.2. Impact of Modules on Text Detection

The NEAST text detection model used in this study is an improved text detection algorithm based on the EAST algorithm. It has an improved FPN, addresses the problem of class imbalance, and corrects the IoU of the output module. To evaluate the impact of each module on the entire algorithm model, the modules of the model were disabled in turn on the ICDAR 2015 dataset to compare the recall, precision, and F-Measure values. The comparative data are listed in Table 4, where Tt represents the time spent in training the model and Dt is the time spent in detecting text.

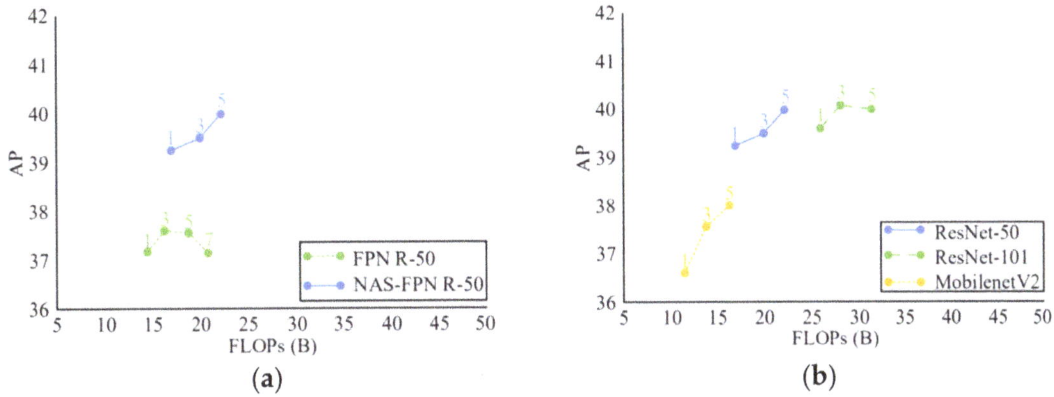

Figure 14. Impact of NAS-FPN on text detection. Impact of (**a**) search algorithm and (**b**) backbone network on model performance.

Table 4. Experimental results for various modules.

Method	Tt/h	Dt/ms	R	P	F
EAST	19.7	150.9	0.73	0.84	0.78
FL+GIOU	33.4	198.0	0.79	0.85	0.82
NAS+GIOU	139.3	307.8	0.76	0.87	0.81
NAS+FL	144.9	323.5	0.82	0.85	0.83
Proposed	145.6	337.4	0.84	0.89	0.87

The proposed method takes the longest times for model training and text detection because the temporal neural network architecture search algorithm and class equalization process both generate many parameters and increase the complexity of the model. However, the proposed method is the best in terms of the recall, precision, and comprehensiveness metrics. The FL function addresses the problem of class imbalance and mitigates the problem of low recall rate during object detection. The GIoU algorithm can further improve the accuracy of text detection. Although the GIoU algorithm generates fewer additional parameters, the accuracy of the text detection model is significantly improved. Experimental results confirmed that the proposed neural network architecture search algorithm achieved significantly improved detection results.

4. Discussion

A comparison of the text detection performance between the proposed model and some commonly used text detection algorithms on the ICDAR 2013 and ICDAR 2015 datasets was conducted in this work. By implementing the model on different datasets, the applicability and generalization parameters of the model were evaluated.

We discuss fine-scale detection strategies for FASText [46] and Faster R-CNN [47]. As shown in Table 5, it is difficult for a single RPN to perform accurate text localization due to the large amount of error detection (low accuracy). Improvements were made to the RPN algorithm by using the Fast R-CNN detection model, which significantly improves the positioning accuracy, with an F-measure of 0.73. Faster R-CNN also improves the recall of the original RPN. This may benefit from the joint bounding box regression mechanism of Fast R-CNN, which improves the accuracy of bounding box prediction. Although FASText can roughly locate the text line or the main part of a word, it cannot capture the most precise location compared to the ICDAR 2013 standard. Obviously, the proposed NEAST significantly improves Faster R-CNN and FASText in terms of accuracy and recall, which indicates that NEAST predicts a fine-scale text proposal of a sequence rather than a whole line of text. Nonetheless, our detection algorithm is more accurate and reliable. As can be seen from the data in Table 5, our proposed detection algorithm achieves the optimal recall, accuracy, and F-measure values on the ICDAR2013 and IDDAR2015 datasets.

Table 5. Comparison of text detection results of various methods on the ICDAR 2013 dataset.

Method	R	P	F
Ren [46]	0.67	0.81	0.73
Faster RCNN [47]	0.68	0.72	0.73
SSD [48]	0.60	0.80	0.68
Diaz-Escobar [49]	0.74	0.83	0.78
Proposed	0.81	0.86	0.83

The complexity and quantity of natural scenes and images in different datasets are different. The results based on different datasets show that the NEAST text detection algorithm can achieve better detection results and is more robust in complex backgrounds. We discussed the impact of repeated connections on NEAST. Compared with the data listed in Table 6, it is clear that the proposed text detection method performs better on the ICDAR 2015 dataset. Therefore, the conclusion is that the larger the training dataset, the better the text detection model. Contextual information helps to reduce error detection, such as text outliers, which is important for recovering highly ambiguous text—for example, very small text. It is one of the main strengths of our NEAST, which can dramatically increase the F-measure of EAST from 0.78 to 0.87 through our repeated connections.

Table 6. Comparison of text detection results of various methods on the ICDAR 2015 dataset.

Method	R	P	F
Xue [50]	0.78	0.86	0.82
EAST [39]	0.73	0.84	0.78
SSTD [51]	0.74	0.80	0.77
Jiang [52]	0.83	0.87	0.85
R2CNN [27]	0.80	0.85	0.83
PixelLink [53]	0.82	0.85	0.84
Proposed	0.84	0.89	0.87

From the ICDAR2015 dataset, we selected three natural scene images with high background complexity, oblique text, and multiple scales. Experiments were performed on the models with and without the improvement of the EAST algorithm to compare their text detection performance. Figures 15 and 16 depict the text detection performance obtained using the EAST algorithm without and with improvement, respectively. It is evident that the proposed improved text detection model can accurately detect the text regions in horizontal and oblique directions, and the detection effect on long texts is also satisfactory. Through targeted training, the proposed detection method can more accurately exclude non-text regions, thereby improving the accuracy of the final detection results. It is also evident that the performance of the proposed algorithm for oblique text detection in any direction is significantly improved when compared with that of the EAST algorithm.

(**a**) (**b**) (**c**)

Figure 15. Text detection results of EAST algorithm: (**a**) test image 1, (**b**) test image 2, and (**c**) test image 3.

(**a**) (**b**) (**c**)

Figure 16. Text detection results of proposed improved EAST algorithm: (**a**) test image 1, (**b**) test image 2, and (**c**) test image 3.

The performance of the proposed NEAST text detection algorithm was evaluated on complex natural scenes with oblique multi-scale text. The results are depicted in Figure 17a–c. The algorithm accurately identified multi-scale text at various shooting angles. As depicted in Figure 17d–f, the algorithm can also detect text in scenes with dynamic light conditions. These results confirm the high detection strength and accuracy of the proposed algorithm against complex scenes.

Figure 17. Oblique text detection results in natural scenes.

5. Conclusions

In this paper, an improved NEAST algorithm is proposed for skewed text detection in complex scenes and images with multi-scale text. We propose the following innovations. Firstly, we use the Learning Scalable Feature Pyramid Architecture for Object Detection (NAS-FPN) to integrate features of multiple layers and construct an FPN by means of a neural architecture search. By designing a search space that can cover all cross-scale connections and acquire multi-scale features, an RNN controller is acquired through reinforcement learning training to select the optimal FPN structure. Secondly, the GIoU algorithm is used to replace the IoU algorithm, so as to improve the regression of text BBOX. Finally, the focal loss function is used to resolve the class imbalance problem. The core idea of our proposed algorithm is to obtain a network structure in the FPN search space by an RNN controller, set it as a subnetwork, and then use this network structure to train on the dataset. The final accuracy is obtained by testing on the validation set. This accuracy rate is applied on the controller, and the controller continues to optimize to obtain another network structure. This practice is repeated until the best feature extraction network structure is obtained, and, finally, the detection result of skewed text is realized. In future research, we will continue to improve the NEAST text recognition algorithm by targeting the diversity of languages, including Chinese and numbers. The unsupervised ultra-lightweight backbone network will be used to mine the deep semantic information of complex natural scenes and images.

Author Contributions: Conceptualization, Y.P. and G.Z.; methodology and guidance of the project, W.S., Y.P. and G.Z.; validation, formal analysis, and data analysis, W.S. and G.Z.; writing, W.S., H.W., Y.L., J.L. (Jiasai Luo), T.L., J.L. (Jinzhao Lin), Y.P. and G.Z. All authors have read and agreed to the published version of the manuscript.

Funding: This work was supported by the Doctoral Innovative Talents Project of Chongqing University of Posts and Telecommunications (BYJS202107), the Natural Science Foundation of Chongqing (grant number cstc2021jcyj-bsh0218); the Science and Technology Bureau of Chongqing (D63012021013); the National Natural Science Foundation of China (Grant No. U21A20447 and 61971079); the Basic Research and Frontier Exploration Project of Chongqing (Grant No. cstc2019 jcyjmsxmX0666); the Chongqing Technological Innovation and Application Development Project (cstc2021jscx-gksbx0051); the Innovative Group Project of the National Natural Science Foundation of Chongqing (Grant No. cstc2020jcyj-cxttX0002); the Regional Creative Cooperation Program of Sichuan (2020YFQ0025); and the Science and Technology Research Program of Chongqing Municipal Education Commission (KJZD-k202000604).

Data Availability Statement: Not applicable.

Conflicts of Interest: The authors declare no conflict of interest.

References

1. Fang, S.; Xie, H.; Wang, Y.; Mao, Z.; Zhang, Y. Read like humans: Autonomous, bidirectional and iterative language modeling for scene text recognition. In Proceedings of the 2021 IEEE/CVF Conference on Computer Vision and Pattern Recognition (CVPR), Nashville, TN, USA, 20–25 June 2021; pp. 7098–7107.
2. Wu, F.; Zhu, C.; Xu, J.; Bhatt, M.W.; Sharma, A. Research on image text recognition based on canny edge detection algorithm and k-means algorithm. *Int. J. Syst. Assur. Eng.* **2022**, *13*, 72–80. [CrossRef]
3. Kisacanin, B.; Pavlovic, V.; Huang, T.S. *Real-Time Vision for Human-Computer Interaction*; Springer Science & Business Media: Berlin/Heidelberg, Germany, 2015.
4. Barber, D.B.; Redding, J.D.; McLain, T.W.; Beard, R.W.; Taylor, C.N. Vision-based target geo-location using a fixed-wing miniature air vehicle. *J. Intell. Robot. Syst.* **2006**, *47*, 361–382. [CrossRef]
5. Haritaoglu, I. Scene text extraction and translation for handheld devices. In Proceedings of the 2001 IEEE Computer Society Conference on Computer Vision and Pattern Recognition (CVPR), Kauai, HI, USA, 8–14 December 2001; p. II.
6. DeSouza, G.N.; Kak, A.C. Vision for mobile robot navigation: A survey. *IEEE Tran. Pattern Anal.* **2002**, *24*, 237–267. [CrossRef]
7. Ham, Y.K.; Kang, M.S.; Chung, H.K.; Park, R.H.; Park, G.T. Recognition of raised characters for automatic classification of rubber tires. *Opt. Eng.* **1995**, *34*, 102–109. [CrossRef]
8. Neumann, L.; Matas, J. Real-time lexicon-free scene text localization and recognition. *IEEE Tran. Pattern Anal.* **2015**, *38*, 1872–1885. [CrossRef]
9. Louloudis, G.; Gatos, B.; Pratikakis, I.; Halatsis, C. Text line detection in handwritten documents. *Pattern Recogn.* **2008**, *41*, 3758–3772. [CrossRef]
10. Hinton, G.E.; Salakhutdinov, R.R. Reducing the dimensionality of data with neural networks. *Science* **2006**, *313*, 504–507. [CrossRef]
11. Jinqiang, W.; Basnet, P.; Mahtab, S. Review of machine learning and deep learning application in mine microseismic event classification. *Min. Miner. Deposits* **2021**, *15*, 19–26. [CrossRef]
12. Peng, P.; He, Z.; Wang, L.; Jiang, Y. Automatic classification of microseismic records in underground mining: A deep learning approach. *IEEE Access* **2020**, *8*, 17863–17876. [CrossRef]
13. Kamilaris, A.; Prenafeta-Boldú, F.X. Deep learning in agriculture: A survey. *Comput. Electron. Agr.* **2018**, *147*, 70–90. [CrossRef]
14. Jospin, L.V.; Laga, H.; Boussaid, F.; Buntine, W.; Bennamoun, M. Hands-on Bayesian neural networks—A tutorial for deep learning users. *IEEE Comput. Intell. Mag.* **2022**, *17*, 29–48. [CrossRef]
15. Su, X.; Xue, S.; Liu, F.; Wu, J.; Yang, J.; Zhou, C.; Hu, W.; Paris, C.; Nepal, S.; Jin, D.; et al. A Comprehensive Survey on Community Detection with Deep Learning. *IEEE Trans. Neural Netw. Learn. Syst.* **2022**. *Early Access*. [CrossRef]
16. Li, T.; Wang, Y.; Hong, R.; Wang, M.; Wu, X. pDisVPL: Probabilistic discriminative visual Part Learning for image classification. *IEEE MultiMedia* **2018**, *25*, 34–45. [CrossRef]
17. Li, T.; Cheng, B.; Ni, B.; Liu, G.; Yan, S. Multitask low-rank affinity graph for image segmentation and image annotation. *ACM T. Intel. Syst. Tec.* **2016**, *7*, 1–18. [CrossRef]
18. Li, T.; Ni, B.; Xu, M.; Wang, M.; Gao, Q.; Yan, S. Data-driven affective filtering for images and videos. *IEEE T. Cybernetics* **2015**, *45*, 2336–2349. [CrossRef]

19. Wang, W.; Xie, E.; Li, X.; Hou, W.; Lu, T.; Yu, G.; Shao, S. Shape Robust Text Detection with Progressive Scale Expansion Network In Proceedings of the 2019 IEEE/CVF Conference on Computer Vision and Pattern Recognition (CVPR), Long Beach, CA, USA, 15–20 June 2019; pp. 9328–9337.
20. Wang, T.; Wu, D.J.; Coates, A.; Ng, A.Y. End-to-end text recognition with convolutional neural networks. In Proceedings of the 21st International Conference on Pattern Recognition (ICPR2012), Tsukuba, Japan, 11–15 November 2012; pp. 3304–3308.
21. Zang, D.; Zhang, J.; Zhang, D.; Bao, M.; Cheng, J.; Tang, K. Traffic sign detection based on cascaded convolutional neural networks. In Proceedings of the 2016 17th IEEE/ACIS International Conference on Software Engineering, Artificial Intelligence, Networking and Parallel/Distributed Computing (SNPD), Shanghai, China, 30 May–1 June 2016; pp. 201–206.
22. Zhang, Z.; Zhang, C.; Shen, W.; Yao, C.; Liu, W.; Bai, X. Multi-oriented Text Detection with Fully Convolutional Networks. In Proceedings of the 2016 IEEE Conference on Computer Vision and Pattern Recognition (CVPR), Las Vegas, NV, USA, 27–30 June 2016; pp. 4159–4167.
23. Liu, X.; Liang, D.; Yan, S.; Chen, D.; Qiao, Y.; Yan, J. FOTS: Fast Oriented Text Spotting with a Unified Network. In Proceedings of the 2018 IEEE/CVF Conference on Computer Vision and Pattern Recognition, Salt Lake City, UT, USA, 18–23 June 2018; pp. 5676–5685.
24. He, W.; Zhang, X.; Yin, F.; Liu, C. Deep Direct Regression for Multi-oriented Scene Text Detection. In Proceedings of the 2017 IEEE International Conference on Computer Vision (ICCV), Venice, Italy, 22–29 October 2017; pp. 745–753.
25. Qin, S.; Ren, P.; Kim, S.; Manduchi, R. Robust and Accurate Text Stroke Segmentation. In Proceedings of the 2018 IEEE Winter Conference on Applications of Computer Vision (WACV), Lake Tahoe, NV, USA, 12–15 March 2018; pp. 242–250.
26. Feng, W.; He, W.H.; Yin, F.; Liu, C.L. Scene Text Detection with Recurrent Instance Segmentation. In Proceedings of the 2018 24th International Conference on Pattern Recognition (ICPR), Beijing, China, 20–24 August 2018; pp. 2227–2232.
27. Jiang, Y.; Zhu, X.; Wang, X.; Yang, S.; Li, W.; Wang, H.; Fu, P.; Luo, Z. R^2 CNN: Rotational Region CNN for Arbitrarily-Oriented Scene Text Detection. In Proceedings of the 2018 24th International Conference on Pattern Recognition (ICPR), Beijing, China, 20–24 August 2018; pp. 3610–3615.
28. Liao, M.; Zhu, Z.; Shi, B.; Xia, G.; Bai, X. Rotation-Sensitive Regression for Oriented Scene Text Detection. In Proceedings of the 2018 IEEE/CVF Conference on Computer Vision and Pattern Recognition, Salt Lake City, UT, USA, 18–23 June 2018; pp. 5909–5918.
29. Liu, X.; Zhou, G.; Zhang, R.; Wei, X. An Accurate Segmentation-Based Scene Text Detector with Context Attention and Repulsive Text Border. In Proceedings of the 2020 IEEE/CVF Conference on Computer Vision and Pattern Recognition Workshops (CVPRW), Seattle, WA, USA, 14–19 June 2020; pp. 2344–2352.
30. Long, S.; Ruan, J.; Zhang, W.; He, X.; Wu, W.; Yao, C. TextSnake: A Flexible Representation for Detecting Text of Arbitrary Shapes. In Proceedings of the Computer Vision (ECCV), Munich, Germany, 8–14 September 2018; pp. 19–35.
31. Lyu, P.; Yao, C.; Wu, W.; Yan, S.; Bai, X. Multi-oriented Scene Text Detection via Corner Localization and Region Segmentation. In Proceedings of the 2018 IEEE/CVF Conference on Computer Vision and Pattern Recognition, Salt Lake City, UT, USA, 18–23 June 2018; pp. 7553–7563.
32. Nayef, N.; Yin, F.; Bizid, I.; Choi, H.; Feng, Y.; Karatzas, D.; Luo, Z.; Pal, U.; Rigaud, C.; Chazalon, J.; et al. ICDAR2017 Robust Reading Challenge on Multi-Lingual Scene Text Detection and Script Identification-RRC-MLT. In Proceedings of the 2017 14th IAPR International Conference on Document Analysis and Recognition (ICDAR), Kyoto, Japan, 9–15 November 2017; pp. 1454–1459.
33. Li, J.; Lin, Y.; Liu, R.; Ho, C.M.; Shi, H. RSCA: Real-time Segmentation-based Context-Aware Scene Text Detection. In Proceedings of the 2021 IEEE/CVF Conference on Computer Vision and Pattern Recognition Workshops (CVPRW), Nashville, TN, USA, 19–25 June 2021; pp. 2349–2358.
34. He, K.; Gkioxari, G.; Dollár, P.; Girshick, R. Mask R-CNN. In Proceedings of the 2017 IEEE International Conference on Computer Vision (ICCV), Venice, Italy, 22–29 October 2017; pp. 2980–2988.
35. Huang, W.; Qiao, Y.; Tang, X. Robust scene text detection with convolution neural network induced mser trees. In Proceedings of the European Conference on Computer Vision (ECCV), Zürich, Switzerland, 6–7 and 12 September 2014; pp. 497–511.
36. Jaderberg, M.; Vedaldi, A.; Zisserman, A. Deep features for text spotting. In Proceedings of the European Conference on Computer Vision (ECCV), Zürich, Switzerland, 6–7 and 12 September 2014; pp. 512–528.
37. Shi, B.; Bai, X.; Belongie, S. Detecting Oriented Text in Natural Images by Linking Segments. In Proceedings of the 2017 IEEE Conference on Computer Vision and Pattern Recognition (CVPR), Honolulu, HI, USA, 21–26 July 2017; pp. 3482–3490.
38. Tian, Z.; Huang, W.; He, T.; He, P.; Qiao, Y. Detecting text in natural image with connectionist text proposal network. In Proceedings of the European Conference on Computer Vision (ECCV), Amsterdam, The Netherlands, 8–16 October 2016; pp. 56–72.
39. Zhou, X.; Yao, C.; Wen, H.; Wang, Y.; Zhou, S.; He, W.; Liang, J. East: An efficient and accurate scene text detector. In Proceedings of the IEEE Conference on Computer Vision and Pattern Recognition (CVPR), Honolulu, HI, USA, 21–26 July 2017; pp. 5551–5560.
40. Rezatofighi, H.; Tsoi, N.; Gwak, J.; Sadeghian, A.; Reid, I.; Savarese, S. Generalized Intersection Over Union: A Metric and a Loss for Bounding Box Regression. In Proceedings of the 2019 IEEE/CVF Conference on Computer Vision and Pattern Recognition (CVPR), Long Beach, CA, USA, 15–20 June 2019; pp. 658–666.
41. Hou, F.; Lei, W.; Li, S.; Xi, J.; Xu, M.; Luo, J. Improved Mask R-CNN with distance guided intersection over union for GPR signature detection and segmentation. *Automat. Constr.* **2021**, *121*, 103414. [CrossRef]

42. Cho, K.; Van Merriënboer, B.; Gulcehre, C.; Bahdanau, D.; Bougares, F.; Schwenk, H.; Bengio, Y. Learning phrase representations using RNN encoder-decoder for statistical machine translation. *arXiv* **2014**, arXiv:1406.1078.
43. Ma, J.; Shao, W.; Ye, H.; Wang, L.; Wang, H.; Zheng, Y.; Xue, X. Arbitrary-Oriented Scene Text Detection via Rotation Proposals. *IEEE T. Multimed.* **2018**, *20*, 3111–3122. [CrossRef]
44. Stamatopoulos, N.; Gatos, B.; Louloudis, G.; Pal, U.; Alaei, A. ICDAR 2013 Handwriting Segmentation Contest. In Proceedings of the 2013 12th International Conference on Document Analysis and Recognition, Washington, DC, USA, 25–28 August 2013; pp. 1402–1406.
45. Karatzas, D.; Gomez-Bigorda, L.; Nicolaou, A.; Ghosh, S.; Bagdanov, A.; Iwamura, M.; Matas, J.; Neumann, L.; Chandrasekhar, V.R.; Lu, S.; et al. ICDAR 2015 competition on Robust Reading. In Proceedings of the 2015 13th International Conference on Document Analysis and Recognition (ICDAR), Tunis, Tunisia, 23–26 August 2015; pp. 1156–1160.
46. Buta, M.; Neumann, L.; Matas, J. FASText: Efficient Unconstrained Scene Text Detector. In Proceedings of the 2015 IEEE International Conference on Computer Vision (ICCV), Santiago, Chile, 7–13 December 2015; pp. 1206–1214.
47. Kumar, A.; Zhang, Z.J.; Lyu, H. Object detection in real time based on improved single shot multi-box detector algorithm. *EURASIP J. Wirel. Comm.* **2020**, *2020*, 204. [CrossRef]
48. Ren, S.; He, K.; Girshick, R.; Sun, J. Faster R-CNN: Towards Real-Time Object Detection with Region Proposal Networks. *ITPAM* **2017**, *39*, 1137–1149. [CrossRef]
49. Diaz-Escobar, J.; Kober, V. Natural Scene Text Detection and Segmentation Using Phase-Based Regions and Character Retrieval. *Math. Probl. Eng.* **2020**, *2020*, 7067251. [CrossRef]
50. Xue, C.; Lu, S.; Zhang, W. MSR: Multi-scale shape regression for scene text detection. *arXiv* **2019**, arXiv:1901.02596.
51. He, P.; Huang, W.; He, T.; Zhu, Q.; Qiao, Y.; Li, X. Single Shot Text Detector with Regional Attention. In Proceedings of the 2017 IEEE International Conference on Computer Vision (ICCV), Venice, Italy, 22–29 October 2017; pp. 3066–3074.
52. Jiang, X.; Xu, S.; Zhang, S.; Cao, S. Arbitrary-Shaped Text Detection with Adaptive Text Region Representation. *IEEE Access* **2020**, *8*, 102106–102118. [CrossRef]
53. Deng, D.; Liu, H.; Li, X.; Cai, D. Pixellink: Detecting scene text via instance segmentation. In Proceedings of the Thirty-Second AAAI Conference on Artificial Intelligence, New Orleans, LA, USA, 7–8 February 2018; Volume 32.

mathematics

MDPI

Article

Interactive Learning of a Dual Convolution Neural Network for Multi-Modal Action Recognition

Qingxia Li [1], Dali Gao [2,3], Qieshi Zhang [4], Wenhong Wei [5] and Ziliang Ren [5,*]

1 School of Computer and Information, Dongguan City College, Dongguan 523419, China
2 School of Mathematics and Computer Science, Quanzhou Normal University, Quanzhou 362000, China
3 Fujian Provincial Key Laboratory of Data-Intensive Computing, Quanzhou 362000, China
4 Shenzhen Institute of Advanced Technology, Chinese Academy of Sciences, Shenzhen 518055, China
5 School of Computer Science and Technology, Dongguan University of Technology, Dongguan 523808, China
* Correspondence: renzl@dgut.edu.cn

Abstract: RGB and depth modalities contain more abundant and interactive information, and convolutional neural networks (ConvNets) based on multi-modal data have achieved successful progress in action recognition. Due to the limitation of a single stream, it is difficult to improve recognition performance by learning multi-modal interactive features. Inspired by the multi-stream learning mechanism and spatial-temporal information representation methods, we construct dynamic images by using the rank pooling method and design an interactive learning dual-ConvNet (ILD-ConvNet) with a multiplexer module to improve action recognition performance. Built on the rank pooling method, the constructed visual dynamic images can capture the spatial-temporal information from entire RGB videos. We extend this method to depth sequences to obtain more abundant multi-modal spatial-temporal information as the inputs of the ConvNets. In addition, we design a dual ILD-ConvNet with multiplexer modules to jointly learn the interactive features of two-stream from RGB and depth modalities. The proposed recognition framework has been tested on two benchmark multi-modal datasets—NTU RGB + D 120 and PKU-MMD. The proposed ILD-ConvNet with a temporal segmentation mechanism achieves an accuracy of 86.9% and 89.4% for Cross-Subject (C-Sub) and Cross-Setup (C-Set) on NTU RGB + D 120, 92.0% and 93.1% for Cross-Subject (C-Sub) and Cross-View (C-View) on PKU-MMD, which are comparable with the state of the art. The experimental results shown that our proposed ILD-ConvNet with a multiplexer module can extract interactive features from different modalities to enhance action recognition performance.

Keywords: convolutional neural network; rank pooling; feature interactive learning; action recognition

MSC: 65Z05

1. Introduction

As an important means of information and intelligent human–computer cooperation, action recognition has a broad application prospect in video monitoring, video retrieval, virtual reality, human–computer interaction, etc. [1–5]. Recently, deep convolutional neural networks (ConvNets) have strong feature learning and model generalization ability by automatically learning feature information from the bottom to the top, which have been applied to many fields, such as video understanding [6–10]. However, it is difficult to further improve the performance of models because of the limited ability of information representation and discrimination feature learning.

In recent years, most approaches mainly focus on designing deep ConvNets to learn spatial-temporal features, which improved action recognition performance through extracting the discriminative features from different modalities [11–15]. Most of those approaches are designed to work on a single frame or a single stack of frames in a short clip for extracting spatial-temporal features, while some methods obtain rich information by compressing action videos [16–20]. Although these ConvNets based methods have achieved amazing performance in action recognition, the performance improvement of the models is limited due to the inherent limitations, e.g., some video frame sparse sampling methods are easy to cause the loss of temporal information and most single-stream ConvNets cannot jointly learn interactive features of different modalities.

Inspired by the video compression representation method proposed in [17,21,22], in this paper, we use the compression method to generate visual dynamic images (VDIs) and depth dynamic images (DDIs) to obtain rich information from those two modalities, and a multi-modal feature interactive learning model (ILD-ConvNet) is provided to extract the interactive features of RGB and depth modalities in order to improve recognition performance.

The main contributions of this paper are as follows:

1. An effective 2D-ConvNet framework is proposed to extract interactive features from different modalities to recognize human action, which jointly learn features from different modalities for human action recognition.
2. We experimentally demonstrate that the constructed VDIs and DDIs can effectively represent spatial-temporal information from the whole RGB-D sequences.
3. The proposed ILD-ConvNet recognition framework has been evaluated on large-scale human action datasets. The results show that our proposed ILD-ConvNet achieved better recognition performance and generalization performance, which demonstrated the effectiveness of our ILD-ConvNet.

2. Related Work

The extraction of underlying features is mainly divided into spatial and temporal features as for RGB and depth sequences, which can well describe the details of human actions. Early low-level feature information extraction mainly includes feature extraction algorithms with prior knowledge, geometric features, motion information, and Histogram of Oriented Gradient (HOG). [23,24]. In addition, some recognition methods used to represent time information mainly focus on spatial configuration modeling, dynamic time axis (DTW), Hidden Markov model (HMM), and the recognition methods based on hand-draft are summarized in [25,26].

In the past two decades, with the development of deep learning networks, action recognition methods based on RGB and depth modalities have made great progress. Simonyan et al. proposed a two-stream ConvNet recognition framework to fuse RGB and optical flow features, which achieved the effect of combining spatial-temporal information [27]. Wang et al. [28] present a series of good training practices for deep action recognition, Temporal Segment Networks (TSN), which included a sparse temporal sampling strategy and video-level supervision. However, it is difficult to ensure that the interactive information between different streams can be differentiated and explored. Zhang et al. [29] designed a cross-stream ConvNet to investigate syndicated information from multiple modalities. Wang et al. [30] provided a Temporal Difference Network (TDN) to learn multi-scale temporal information. In addition, 3D ConvNets can obtain more comprehensive spatiotemporal feature information, such as C3D, I3D, and X3D [31–33]. However, the amount of computation is too large and requires a lot of computing resources. In addition, transformer-based methods achieved remarkable results due to globally connected patterns across spatial and temporal dimensions [34–36].

Recently, some researchers have designed a series of ConvNets to realize human action recognition based on depth sequences, because it can reflect the comprehensive three-dimensional geometric information. Wang et al. [37,38] expressed the depth sequences to dynamic images through rank pooling and applied 3D point cloud mapping transformation to improve recognition performance, which achieved relatively good recognition results on multi-modal datasets. In addition, Recurrent Neural Networks (RNNs) can capture the feature information of temporal well, which have developed rapidly in action recognition [39–41].

The above feature learning methods have achieved success in improving the human action recognition performance. However, the single-modality data cannot provide the comprehensive information required for action recognition. Based on the multi-stream recognition framework, some strategies are proposed to capture distinguishing features, such as sparse temporal sampling [14], motion image [33] and dynamic image representation [17,21,22]. In [42], a cooperative ConvNets is designed to jointly learn the middle-level feature information of RGB and depth sequences, which obtained good recognition performance on the existing RGB-D datasets such as NTU RGB + D 60 [43]. In addition, the joint learning mechanisms are designed to learn single-modal and cross-modal information for action recognition tasks, such as c-ConvNet [42], SC-ConvNets [44] and J-ResNet-CMCB [45]. In addition, some approaches improved recognition performance through fusing RGB, depth and skeleton in multi-stream feature learning, such as Modality Compensation Network [46] and multi-modal action recognition model [47].

To overcome the lack of the above multi-stream ConvNets, with the advent of an increasing amount of multi-modal data, we are motivated to design more efficient recognition frameworks to represent spatial-temporal information from entire action sequences and extract complimentary features from different modalities.

3. The Proposed Method

The proposed ILD-ConvNet architecture as shown in Figure 1, which has three parts: the ILD-ConvNet, network input representation and joint optimization.

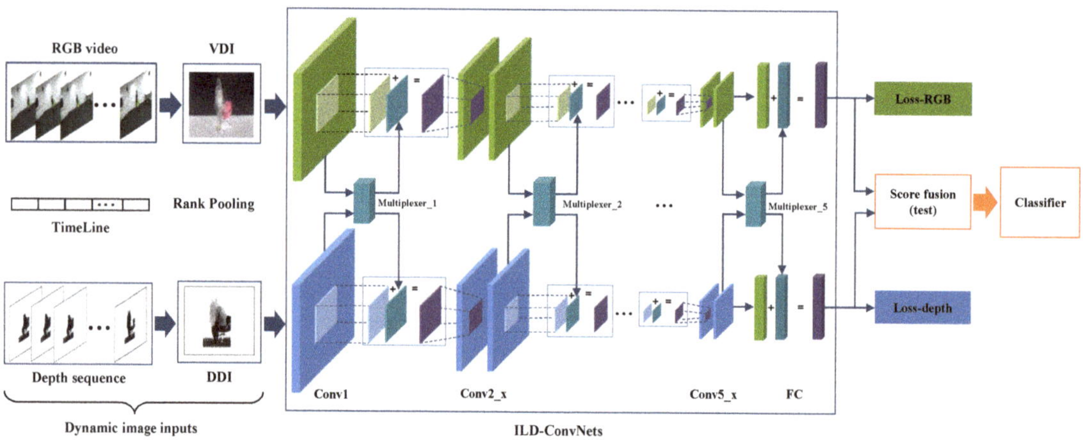

Figure 1. Overview of the proposed recognition framework.

3.1. ILD-ConvNet Framework

By considering 2D ConvNets, 3D ConvNets and RNNs, a dual ConvNets framework is designed based on the multi-modal feature interactive learning and fusion strategy. The designed multi-modal interactive learning dual flow network ILD-ConvNet consists of two separate paths, multiplexer modules and two losses. Given an RGB and depth sequences, the rank pooling method converted them into a pair of dynamic images $\langle VDI, DDI \rangle$. Then, a designed single ResNet with multiplexer modules is used to extract the discriminative features from $\langle VDI, DDI \rangle$. Then, the two losses and effective fusion strategy are used to jointly optimize and fuse multi-modal features.

Due to the high modularity, ResNet is selected as the basic module for RGB and depth information flow learning [48]. The ILD-ConvNet recognition framework includes two independent information flow learning networks. Each network includes 7×7 convolution layer, four bottleneck blocks, a full connection layer and softmax mapping layer. The network adopts the same strategies as ResNet. The network framework based on the

ResNet$_{50}$ model is summarized in Table 1. In the ResNet$_{50}$ model, the input maps of the 4 bottleneck blocks are 64, 256, 512 and 1024. To reduce the number of parameters of the multiplexer module, the network is placed before each bottleneck block to learn the interaction characteristics of different modalities.

Table 1. The network architecture of ILD-ConvNet-based ResNet$_{50}$. Down sampling is performed by conv3_x, conv4_x and conv5_x with a stride of 2.

Layer Name	Output Size	ILD-ConvNet$_{50}$	
		RGB Stream	Depth Stream
Conv1	112 × 112	14 × 14, 64, stride 2	7 × 7, 64, stride 2
Multiplexer_1	112 × 112	$\begin{bmatrix} 1\times1,\ 64\times2 \\ 1\times1,\ 64 \end{bmatrix}\times1$	
Conv2_x	56 × 56	$\begin{bmatrix} 1\times1,\ 64 \\ 3\times3,\ 64 \\ 1\times1,\ 256 \end{bmatrix}\times3$	$\begin{bmatrix} 1\times1,\ 64 \\ 3\times3,\ 64 \\ 1\times1,\ 256 \end{bmatrix}\times3$
Multiplexer_2	56 × 56	$\begin{bmatrix} 1\times1,\ 256\times2 \\ 1\times1,\ 256 \end{bmatrix}\times1$	
Conv3_x	28 × 28	$\begin{bmatrix} 1\times1,\ 128 \\ 3\times3,\ 128 \\ 1\times1,\ 512 \end{bmatrix}\times4$	$\begin{bmatrix} 1\times1,\ 128 \\ 3\times3,\ 128 \\ 1\times1,\ 512 \end{bmatrix}\times4$
Multiplexer_3	28 × 28	$\begin{bmatrix} 1\times1,\ 512\times2 \\ 1\times1,\ 512 \end{bmatrix}\times1$	
Conv4_x	14 × 14	$\begin{bmatrix} 1\times1,\ 256 \\ 3\times3,\ 256 \\ 1\times1,\ 1024 \end{bmatrix}\times23$	$\begin{bmatrix} 1\times1,\ 256 \\ 3\times3,\ 256 \\ 1\times1,\ 1024 \end{bmatrix}\times23$
Multiplexer_4	14 × 14	$\begin{bmatrix} 1\times1, 1024\times2 \\ 1\times1, 1024 \end{bmatrix}\times1$	
Conv5_x	7 × 7	$\begin{bmatrix} 1\times1,\ 512 \\ 3\times3,\ 512 \\ 1\times1,\ 2048 \end{bmatrix}\times3$	$\begin{bmatrix} 1\times1,\ 512 \\ 3\times3,\ 512 \\ 1\times1,\ 2048 \end{bmatrix}\times3$
Multiplexer_5	7 × 7	$\begin{bmatrix} 1\times1,\ 2048\times2 \\ 1\times1,\ 2048 \end{bmatrix}\times1$	
FC	1 × 1	FC-RGB	FC-depth

3.2. Network Inputs

Represent RGB or depth sequences as $\langle I_1, I_2, I_3, \ldots, I_T\rangle$. $\varnothing(I_t) \in R^d$ is the feature vector extracted therefrom of I_t, and the average feature vector at the time t is defined as

$$V_t = \frac{1}{t}\sum\nolimits_{\tau=1}^{t} \varnothing(I_\tau), \tag{1}$$

where the sorting score function of V_t at the time t is as follows.

$$S(t|d) = \langle \mathrm{d}, V_t\rangle, \mathrm{d} \in R^d, \tag{2}$$

where d is the learned parameter vector. The score $S(t|d)$ reflects the ordering of each image frame in the sequence, which satisfies $q > t \rightarrow S(q|d) > S(t|d)$.

$$E(d) = \frac{\lambda}{2}||d||^2 + \frac{2}{T(T-1)}\sum\nolimits_{q>t} \max\{0, 1 - S(q|d) + S(t|d)\}, \tag{3}$$

where the first and second terms are the quadratic term of SVM optimization and the error accumulation of score ranking, respectively. The interval between q and t is set as 1 to distinguish the score ranking. The mapping function from video to parameter feature d^* vector is further defined as [49]:

$$d^* = \rho(I_1, \ldots, I_T; \varnothing) = argmin_d E(d), \tag{4}$$

where d^* is the optimal estimate of d. d^* contains all the ordering information of the video sequence, which is equal to the number of pixels of a single frame of the sequence. Therefore, it can be seen as a descriptor of the videos and interpreted as a standard image frame. For depth sequence, we first normalize them into single-channel images, and then use the introduced rank pooling method (d^*) to compress them into one dynamic image (DDI).

3.3. Multiplexer Modules

In terms of network architecture design, ResNet is selected as the basic network based on the highly modular residual unit. The proposed ILD-ConvNet is divided into two paths to process the input RGB and depth information flow characteristics, respectively. High-level interactive learning is conducted through the multiplexer module, as shown in Figure 2.

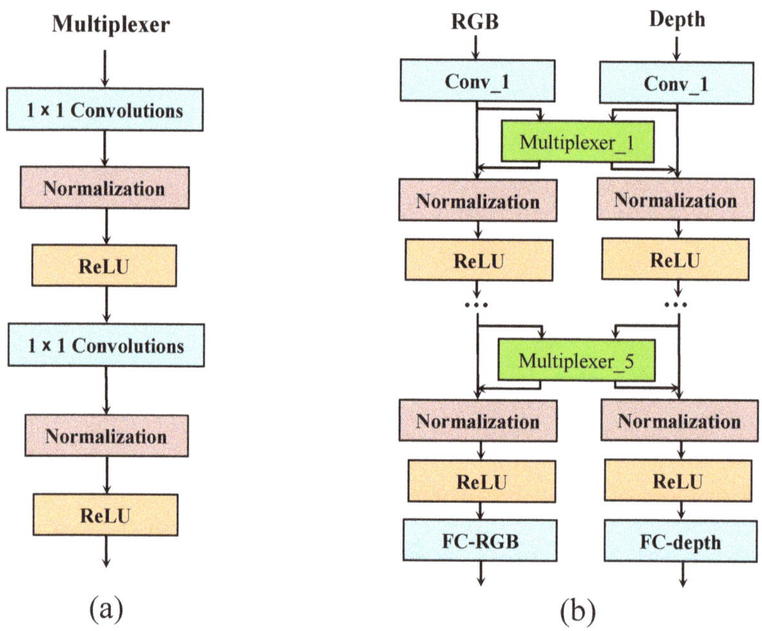

Figure 2. Multiplexer module and information stream. (**a**) Multiplexer module. (**b**) Two-stream information.

The multiplexer module combines the characteristics of two-path information flow. After weighted redirection interactive learning, it is input back to RGB and depth information flow, respectively. The characteristic output function of the multiplexer module can be defined as

$$F_{multiplexer}(x) = ReLU(BN(f_{1\times1}(ReLU(BN(f_{1\times1}(w * x)))))), \tag{5}$$

where $BN(\cdot)$ and $ReLU(\cdot)$ denote the batch normalization and rectified linear units activation function, respectively, and $f_{1\times 1}$ is a learnable 1×1 convolution kernel. The information flow input is defined as:

$$X_{RGB} = \lambda X_{RGB} + (1-\lambda)F_{multiplexer}\Big(X_{RGB} + X_{depth}\Big), \tag{6}$$

$$X_{depth} = \lambda X_{depth} + (1-\lambda)F_{multiplexer}\Big(X_{RGB} + X_{depth}\Big), \tag{7}$$

where X_{RGB} and X_{depth} represent the output of the information flow, respectively. $\lambda \in (0,1)$ is the adjustment coefficient.

3.4. Optimization Learning

Different from the ConvNets, which is trained on a single frame, the designed ILD-ConvNet has paired sample objects $\langle VDI, DDI\rangle$ for training. In order to eliminate the deviation between two different modalities, a dual loss function is used to jointly optimize RGB and depth information flows. In the meantime, standard cross-entropy loss functions are used in the training process.

The information flow of the training sample $\langle VDI, DDI\rangle$ is expressed as $X_{\langle VDI,DDI\rangle}$. The scores of VDI and DDI are obtained by using the softmax function. The classification probability score can be estimated as follows:

$$prob_c = \frac{\exp(W_c X + b_c)}{\sum_{c_i}\exp(w_{c_i} X + b_{c_i})}, \tag{8}$$

where W_c and b_c are the weights and offsets of the softmax layer. The loss function of the two streams can be described as:

$$L_{RGB}(y,C) = -\sum_{c=1}^{C} y_c(\log(prob_{c-RGB})), \tag{9}$$

$$L_{depth}(y,C) = -\sum_{c=1}^{C} y_c(\log(prob_{c-depth})), \tag{10}$$

where C is the classification number of actions, y_c is the ground truth label, $prob_{c-RGB}$ and $prob_{c-depth}$ are the classification probabilities, respectively.

Different from training on a single RGB or depth frame, ILD-ConvNet operates on $\langle VDI, DDI\rangle$ and obtains two-stream features. To make the proposed ConvNets more discriminative and eliminate the multi-modal variance between the RGB-D information streams, a dual loss function is adopted to jointly optimized ILD-ConvNet. In the training process, the standard cross-entropy loss is used to jointly optimize ILD-ConvNet. The overall loss function can be expressed as:

$$L(y,C) = L_{RGB} + L_{depth}, \tag{11}$$

The feature vectors v_{RGB} and v_{depth} of the dual stream network can be obtained in the testing process. The final score feature vectors of RGB and depth sequences can be obtained through feature fusion:

$$v_{fusion} = v_{RGB} \circ v_{\text{depth}}, \tag{12}$$

where "$\circ$" represents the maximum, minimum or inner product operation. Then, the maximum value of v_{fusion} is used as the classification result of RGB and depth sequences.

3.5. Datasets Implementation Details

3.5.1. Datasets

NTU RGB + D 120 [50] is the largest multi-modal human action dataset currently released. NTU RGB + D 120 includes RGB, depth, infrared IR and 3D skeleton modalities, and two evaluation protocols are defined. For the Cross-Subject (C-Sub) evaluation protocol, samples collected by subjects with camera numbers of 1, 2, 4, 5, 8, 9, 13, 14, 15, 16, 17, 18, 19, 25, 27, 28, 31, 34, 35, 38, 45, 46, 47, 49, 50, 52, 53, 54, 55, 56, 57, 58, 59, 70, 74, 78, 80, 81, 82, 83, 84, 85, 86, 89, 91, 92, 93, 94, 95, 97, 98, 100, and 103 were used for training (63,360 samples). The rest were selected for testing (51,120 samples). For the Cross-Setup (C-Set), the samples collected by the even ID cameras are divided into training (54,720 samples) and the rest for testing (59,760 samples).

The PKU-MMD dataset [51] includes multi-modal data such as RGB, depth, infrared radiation and skeleton modalities, and each modality includes 1074 long video sequences, and two action recognition evaluation protocols are designed for the dataset. For the Cross-Subject (C-Sub) evaluation protocol, it is divided into 18,134 training and 2600 testing samples. For the Cross-View (C-View) evaluation protocol, the training set have 13,815 samples and the testing have 6919 samples.

3.5.2. Implementation Details

Network input. The RGB and depth sequences are compressed to obtain the input of the ILD-ConvNet by adopting the rank pooling method proposed above. In order to adapt to the dual flow network training model, $\langle VDI, DDI \rangle$ is scaled to 224 $\times$ 224. The DDI sorted by depth sequence is scaled to $[0, 255]$. In addition, the training samples are incrementally processed by random clipping and dithering.

Model training and testing. The parameters of ILD-ConvNet can be initialized through the pre-trained weights of ResNet. In the training and testing process, we follow the good practice proposed in [16], the methods of mini batch, momentum, random gradient descent and data augmentation methods are used for feature learning, where the batch and momentum are set as 64 and 0.8, respectively. The initial learning rate is set as 0.01, which decreases to 0.1 times every 30 generations. In order to overcome the overfitting phenomenon, dropout technology was further adopted. The dropout rate was set to 0.5. Inspired by the good practices proposed in [16], we further verified the impact of segmentation strategy on recognition performance in our experiments.

4. Experimental Results and Analysis

4.1. Effectiveness of the Proposed ILD-ConvNet

4.1.1. Effectiveness

In order to evaluate the effectiveness of the proposed recognition framework, comparative experiments of different modalities are conducted on the NTU RGB + D 120 dataset, including RGB, depth and RGB + depth dual modalities. The parameter λ was set to 0.1 and the average fusion method is used in the experiments, Table 2 shows the experimental results. The recognition rate of VDI in ResNet_{50} model is 16.1% and 13.0% higher than that of RGB, and the DDI is 28.6% and 30.1% higher than that of depth on the basis of the evaluation protocols of the NTU RGB + D 120 dataset C-Sub and C-Set. The improvement of the recognition rate shows that the proposed video frame ranking method can improve the behavior recognition performance of the training mode. The results proves that this method can effectively represent the spatial-temporal information of samples.

Table 2 shows that the recognition rates of ResNet-50 model achieve 51.4% and 51.3%, respectively, by fusing RGB and depth modalities. The recognition rates of ILD-ConvNet_{50} achieve 55.4% and 55.0%, respectively. The recognition rates of ILD-ConvNet50 are 4.0% and 3.7% higher than those of ResNet_{50}. The recognition rates of ResNet_{50} model achieve 73.8% and 74.0% by fusing VDI and DDI modalities. ILD-ConvNet_{50} can obtain 75.3% and 75.2% recognition rates. The proposed ILD-ConvNet_{50} are 1.5% and 1.2% higher than those of ResNet_{50}. Furthermore, we can see that the recognition rate is greatly improved by fusing RGB and depth modalities, which indicates the interactive characteristics between RGB and depth sequences. Furthermore, the experimental results of our ILD-ConvNet show that learning the interactive characteristics between two different modalities can better improve recognition performance. The reason of the improvement of recognition rate is that the designed multiplexer module has learned the interaction characteristics of RGB and depth.

Table 2. The results of $ResNet_{50}$ and ILD-ConvNet.

Methods	Modality	C-Sub	C-Set
$ResNet_{50}$	*RGB*	40.6%	39.5%
$ResNet_{50}$	*depth*	43.6%	42.2%
$ResNet_{50}$	*RGB + depth*	51.4%	51.3%
$ResNet_{50}$	VDI	56.7%	52.5%
$ResNet_{50}$	DDI	72.2%	72.3%
$ResNet_{50}$	$\langle VDI, DDI \rangle$	73.8%	74.0%
ILD-$ConvNet_{50}$	$\langle RGB, depth \rangle$	55.4%	55.0%
ILD-$ConvNet_{50}$	$\langle VDI, DDI \rangle$	75.3%	75.2%

4.1.2. Comparison of Different Fusion Methods

The average fusion method was adopted to achieve the classification results in Table 2. To obtain better recognition performance, the weighted average, maximum and product score fusion methods are evaluated on the NTU RGB + D dataset, and the results are shown in Table 3. It can be seen from the experimental results that the recognition rates of the three feature fusion methods are similar, and the average method is relatively good. Therefore, the average fusion method is selected as the feature fusion method for the following experiments.

Table 3. Comparative accuracies of the proposed ILD-$ConvNet_{50}$ with $\langle VDI, DDI \rangle$ on the NTU RGB + D 120 dataset.

Methods	C-Sub	C-Set
Average	75.3%	75.2%
Product	75.2%	75.0%
Max	74.9%	74.9%

4.1.3. Effectiveness of Parameter λ

The parameter λ is varied from 0 to 0.5 to evaluate recognition performance. The comparison results are summarized in Figure 3, and we can see that increasing λ will lead to worse performance. The results implies that increasing λ does not help obtain richer information from the other modality. Thus, $\lambda = 0.1$ is set in the following experiments.

4.2. *Comparison to the State of the Art*

4.2.1. Experimental on the NTU RGB + D Dataset

To further demonstrate the effectiveness of RGB and depth modalities, BNInception, $ResNet_{50}$, $ResNet_{101}$, ILD-$ConvNet_{50}$ and ILD-$ConvNet_{101}$ were selected for further experiments, and the comparison results are shown in Table 4. RGB and depth modalities are used as inputs in this group of experiments. In addition, BNInception, $ResNet_{50}$ and $ResNet_{101}$ are used to train RGB, depth, VDI and DDI, respectively. Meanwhile, image pairs $\langle RGB, depth \rangle$ and $\langle VDI, DDI \rangle$ are used as the inputs of ILD-$ConvNet_{50}$ and ILD-$ConvNet_{101}$.

The experimental results indicate that ILD-$ConvNet_{101}$ achieved 82.8% and 83.6% recognition rates, respectively, on the C-Sub and C-Set protocols of the NTU RGB + D 120 dataset. ILD-$ConvNet_{101}$ is 0.7% and 2.1% higher than $ResNet_{101}$, respectively, for the same input and base network, and our ILD-$ConvNet_{101}$ is 5.6% and 6.2% higher than

ResNet$_{101}$, respectively. Furthermore, inspired by the segmentation training mechanism proposed in [16], we conduct experiments in 3 segments on the NTU RGB + D 120 dataset, which obtain 86.9% and 89.4% on two protocols. In specially, the proposed ILD-ConvNet degenerates to the plain SC-ConvNet as in [44]. Although the proposed recognition framework is only 1.7% higher than SC-ConVnet in C-Set protocol, it also shows the effectiveness of our designed multiplexer module. Moreover, some subtle actions are easier to recognize, such as "jump table tennis ball". The experimental results demonstrated that the interactive features of RGB and depth modalities learned by the designed multiplexer module can improve recognition performance.

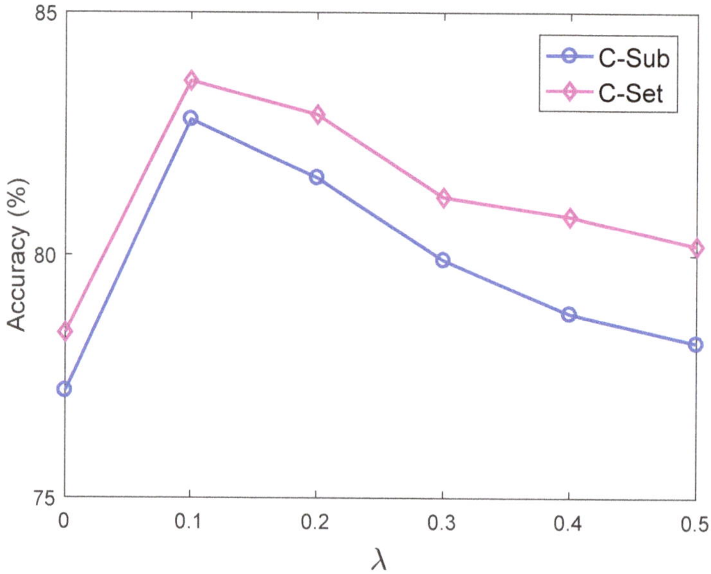

Figure 3. Comparison of weight λ for two protocols using the ILD-ConvNet101 with the inputs $\langle VDI, DDI\rangle$.

Table 4. Comparative accuracies of different networks, and the segment is set 3 in TSN [16].

Methods	Modality	C-Sub	C-Set
BNInception	$\langle RGB, depth\rangle$	52.5%	53.1%
ResNet$_{50}$	$\langle RGB, depth\rangle$	51.4%	51.3%
ResNet$_{101}$	$\langle RGB, depth\rangle$	56.5%	54.1%
BNInception	$\langle VDI, DDI\rangle$	75.4%	76.2%
ResNet$_{50}$	$\langle VDI, DDI\rangle$	73.8%	74.0%
ResNet$_{101}$	$\langle VDI, DDI\rangle$	77.2%	78.4%
ILD-ConvNet$_{50}$	$\langle RGB, depth\rangle$	55.4%	55.0%
ILD-ConvNet$_{101}$	$\langle RGB, depth\rangle$	57.2%	56.2%
ILD-ConvNet$_{50}$	$\langle VDI, DDI\rangle$	75.3%	75.2%
ILD-ConvNet$_{101}$	$\langle VDI, DDI\rangle$	82.4%	83.1%
J-ResNet-CMCB [45]	$\langle VDI, DDI\rangle$	82.8%	83.6%
TSN [16] + SC-ConvNet [44]	$\langle VDI, DDI\rangle$	86.9%	87.7%
TSN [16] + ILD-ConvNet$_{101}$	$\langle VDI, DDI\rangle$	86.9%	89.4%

4.2.2. Experimental on the PKU-MMD Dataset

To evaluate the effectiveness and generalization ability of the proposed ILD-ConvNet, we further conducted experiments on the multi-modal human action dataset PKU-MMD with different scales and application backgrounds. The basic network is ResNet$_{101}$, and λ is set to 0.1. Table 5 shows the experimental comparison results.

Table 5. Comparative accuracies of different networks on the PKU-MMD dataset; the segment is set 3 in TSN [16].

Methods	Modality	C-Sub	C-View
SA-LSTM [52]	*skeleton*	86.3%	91.4%
TA-LSTM [52]	*skeleton*	86.6%	92.3%
STA-LSTM [52]	*skeleton*	86.9%	92.6%
ResNet_{101}	VDI	77.3%	74.8%
ResNet_{101}	DDI	81.7%	79.0%
ResNet_{101}	$\langle VDI, DDI \rangle$	83.6%	82.7%
ILD-ConvNet_{101}	$RGB + depth$	80.7%	79.8%
J-ResNet-CMCB [45]	$\langle VDI, DDI \rangle$	90.4%	91.4%
TSN [16] + SC-ConvNet [44]	$\langle VDI, DDI \rangle$	92.1%	93.2%
TSN [16] + ILD-ConvNet_{101}	$\langle VDI, DDI \rangle$	92.0%	93.1%

Table 5 shows that the proposed ILD-ConvNet based on ResNet_{101} obtained 92.0% and 93.1% recognition rates, respectively, on the two protocols. The results show that the proposed ILD-ConvNet obtained generalization ability on different types and scales of datasets.

4.3. Analysis

Compared with other ConvNet-based methods, the experimental results on the NTU RGB + D and PKU-MMD datasets have shown the effectiveness of our ILD-ConvNet. It can be seen that the proposed dual-stream framework can achieve better recognition performance. The experimental results also implied that the introduced rank pooling mechanism can represent spatial-temporal information from entire RGB and depth sequences, and the designed multiplexer module can enhance recognition performance by extracting the interactive features from different modalities.

Figures 4 and 5 shows the confusion matrix under the two evaluation protocols. It can be seen that the designed ILD-ConvNet can effectively identify most of the actions, but some refined actions, such as "make an OK sign" and "snap fingers". On the C-Sub test protocol, highly similar actions of human–object interaction are easy to be confused, such as "put on glasses" and "take off glasses", "reading" and "writing". In addition, it is difficult to effectively distinguish actions with similar behavior trajectories, such as "rub two hands" and "clasping".

Figures 6 and 7 are the confusion matrix under the two test protocols in the PKU-MMD dataset. The PKU-MMD is a long video sequence multi-modal dataset. Each video sequence contains a series of actions, which needs to be preceded by segmentation. We can see from Figures 6 and 7 that the proposed ILD-ConvNet can distinguish most human actions after segmentation. However, some actions cannot be effectively identified, such as "eat meal/snack", "drink water", "tear up paper" and "put on glasses".

The hyper parameter λ controls the weights of the previous convolution layers in ILD-ConvNet. Adjusting λ should improve the recognition performance of the proposed ILD-ConvNet. We first roughly get the range of λ through analyzing the contribution of different item in Equations (6) and (7). The higher λ forces the RGB and depth streams to obtain more interactive features from different modalities. However, more noise will be introduced at the same time, which will affect the recognition performance of the proposed network model. Therefore, we should select the optimal λ through verifying the results in practice.

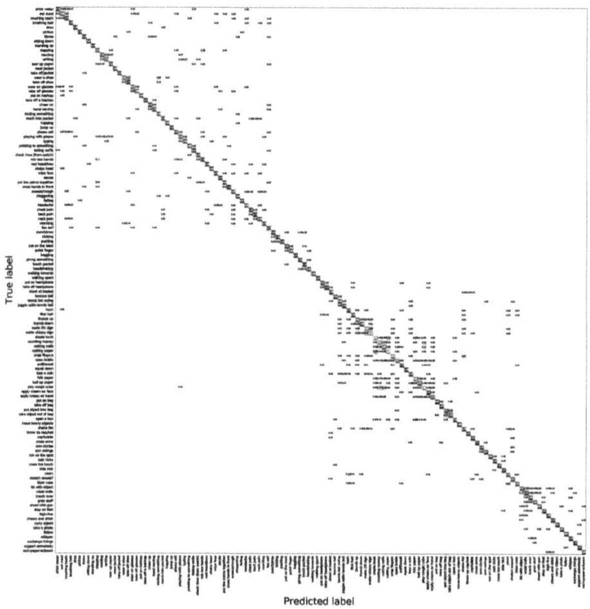

Figure 4. Confusion matrix of the ILD-ConvNet$_{101}$ using C-Sub protocol on NTU RGB + D 120.

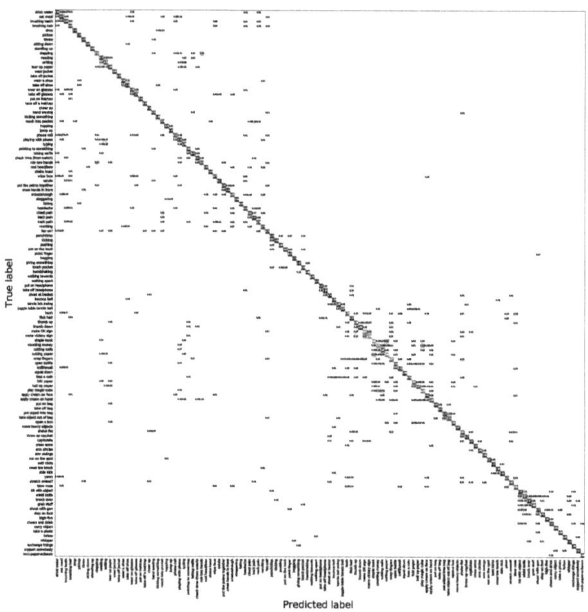

Figure 5. Confusion matrix of the ILD-ConvNet$_{101}$ using C-Set protocol on NTU RGB + D 120.

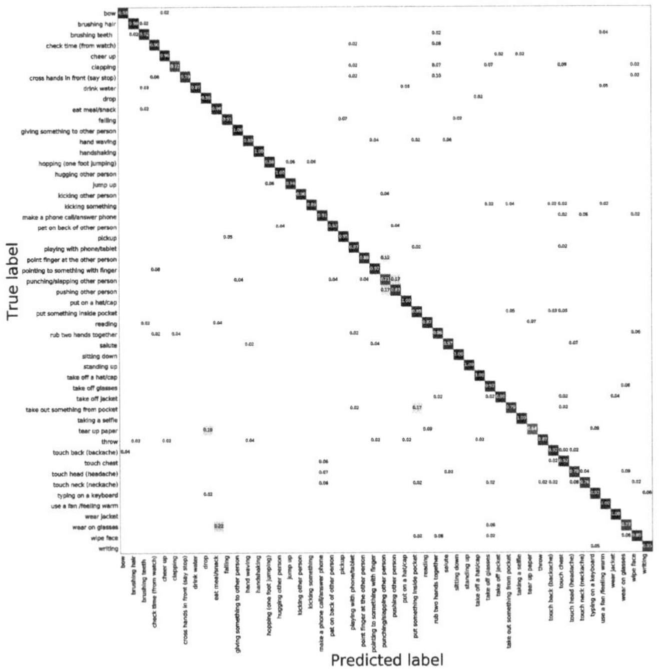

Figure 6. Confusion matrix using the C-Sub protocol on the PKU-MMD dataset.

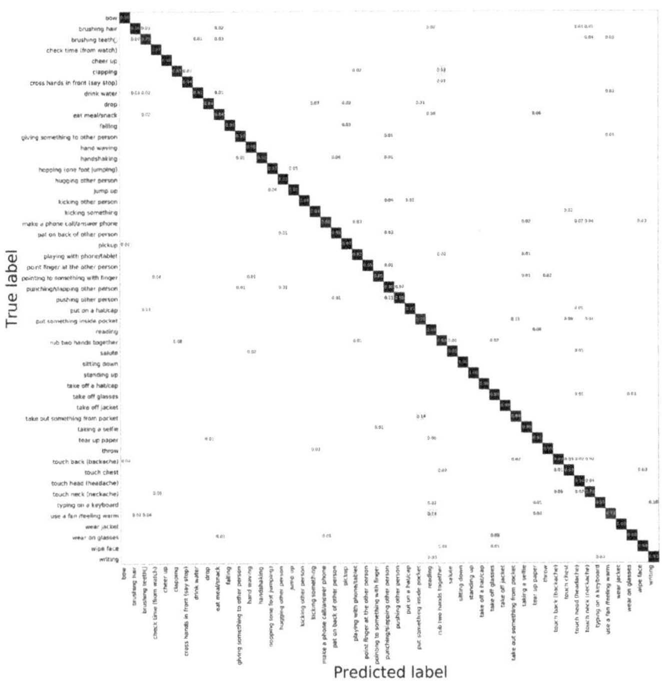

Figure 7. Confusion matrix using the C-View protocol on the PKU-MMD dataset.

5. Conclusions

A human action recognition method based on interactive learning of multi-modal features is proposed in this paper. The rank pooling method is used to construct $\langle VDI, DDI \rangle$ to obtain spatial-temporal information, and a dual-stream framework, ILD-ConvNet, with multiplexer modules is then employed to learn the interactive features from the RGB-D modalities for improving recognition performance. The experimental results illustrate the effectiveness of the rank pooling method and a multiplexer module. Compared with the state-of-the-art methods, our proposed recognition framework achieves comparable results on two multi-modal RGB-D datasets. The future research of this work is to extend the 2D ConvNet framework to 3D, and explore more effective feature fusion methods and reduce the number of model parameters.

Author Contributions: Conceptualization, Z.R. and Q.Z.; methodology, Q.L.; software, Z.R.; validation, Q.L., D.G. and W.W.; formal analysis, W.W.; investigation, Q.Z.; resources, D.G.; data curation, Q.Z.; writing—original draft preparation, Q.L.; writing—review and editing, Q.L. and D.G.; visualization, Q.Z. and W.W.; supervision, Z.R.; funding acquisition, W.W. All authors have read and agreed to the published version of the manuscript.

Funding: This work was supported by the Key Project of Science and Technology Innovation 2030 supported by the Ministry of Science and Technology of China (No. 2018AAA0101301), the National Natural Science Foundation of China (No. 61972090), the Key Projects of Artificial Intelligence of High School in Guangdong Province (No. 2019KZDZX1011), Innovation Project of High School in Guangdong Province (No. 2018KTSCX314), Dongguan Science and Technology Special Commissioner Project (No. 20221800500362), and Dongguan Social Development Science and Technology Project (No. 20211800904722).

Data Availability Statement: Not applicable.

Acknowledgments: The authors thank everyone who contributed to this article.

Conflicts of Interest: The authors declare no conflict of interest.

References

1. Liu, Y.; Lu, Z.; Li, J.; Yang, T.; Yao, C. Deep image-to-video adaptation and fusion networks for action recognition. *IEEE Trans. Image Process. TIP* **2020**, *29*, 3168–3182. [CrossRef] [PubMed]
2. Zhang, J.; Shen, F.; Xu, X.; Shen, H.T. Temporal reasoning graph for activity recognition. *IEEE Trans. Image Process. TIP* **2020**, *29*, 5491–5506. [CrossRef] [PubMed]
3. Rao, H.; Wang, S.; Hu, X.; Tan, M.; Guo, Y.; Cheng, J.; Liu, X.; Hu, B. A self-supervised gait encoding approach with locality-awareness for 3D skeleton based person re-identification. *IEEE Trans. Pattern Anal. Mach. Intell. TPAMI* **2021**, *44*, 6649–6666. [CrossRef] [PubMed]
4. Zhang, L.; Zhang, S.; Jiang, F.; Qi, Y.; Zhang, J.; Guo, Y.; Zhou, H. BoMW: Bag of manifold words for one-shot learning gesture recognition from Kinect. *IEEE Trans. Circuits Syst. Vid. Technol. TCSVT* **2017**, *28*, 2562–2573. [CrossRef]
5. Ji, X.; Zhao, Q.; Cheng, J.; Ma, C. Exploiting spatio-temporal representation for 3D human action recognition from depth map sequences. *Knowl.-Based Syst.* **2021**, *227*, 107040.
6. Ji, Y.; Yang, Y.; Shen, F.; Shen, H.T.; Zheng, W.-S. Arbitrary-View Human Action Recognition: A Varying-view RGB-D Action Dataset. *IEEE Trans. Circuits Syst. Video Technol. TCSVT* **2021**, *31*, 289–300. [CrossRef]
7. Lin, J.; Gan, C.; Han, S. TSM: Temporal shift module for efficient video understanding. In Proceedings of the IEEE International Conference on Computer Vision (ICCV), Seoul, Korea, 27 October–2 November 2019; pp. 7083–7093.
8. Li, Y.; Ji, B.; Shi, X.; Zhang, J.; Kang, B.; Wang, L. TEA: Temporal excitation and aggregation for action recognition. In Proceedings of the IEEE Conference on Computer Vision and Pattern Recognition (CVPR), Seattle, WA, USA, 14–19 June 2020; pp. 909–918.
9. Song, X.; Lan, C.; Zeng, W.; Xing, J.; Sun, X.; Yang, J. Temporal–Spatial Mapping for Action Recognition. *IEEE Trans. Circuits Syst. Video Technol. TCSVT* **2020**, *30*, 748–759. [CrossRef]
10. Feichtenhofer, C.; Fan, H.; Malik, J.; He, K. Slow-fast networks for video recognition. In Proceedings of the IEEE International Conference on Computer Vision (ICCV), Seoul, Korea, 27 October–2 November 2019; pp. 6202–6211.
11. Song, Y.-F.; Zhang, Z.; Shan, C.; Wang, L. Richly activated graph convolutional network for robust skeleton-based action recognition. *IEEE Trans. Circuits Syst. Vid. Technol. TCSVT* **2021**, *31*, 1915–1925.
12. Ijjina, E.P.; Chalavadi, K.M. Human Action Recognition in RGB-D Videos using Motion Sequence Information and Deep Learning. *Pattern Recognit.* **2017**, *72*, 504–516.

13. Li, C.; Hou, Y.; Wang, P.; Li, W. Multiview-Based 3D Action Recognition using Deep Networks. *IEEE Trans. Hum.-Mach. Syst. THMS* **2019**, *49*, 95–104. [CrossRef]
14. Joze, H.R.V.; Shaban, A.; Iuzzolino, M.L.; Koishida, K. MMTM: Multimodal transfer module for CNN fusion. In Proceedings of the 2020 IEEE/CVF Conference on Computer Vision and Pattern Recognition (CVPR), Seattle, WA, USA, 13–19 June 2020; pp. 13286–13296.
15. Abavisani, M.; Joze, H.R.V.; Pate, V.M. Improving the performance of unimodal dynamic hand-gesture recognition with multimodal training. In Proceedings of the 2019 IEEE/CVF Conference on Computer Vision and Pattern Recognition (CVPR), Long Beach, CA, USA, 15–20 June 2019; pp. 1165–1174.
16. Wang, L.; Xiong, Y.; Wang, Z.; Qiao, Y.; Lin, D.; Tang, X.; Gool, L.V. Temporal segment networks for action recognition in videos. *IEEE Trans. Pattern Anal. Mach. Intell. TPAMI* **2019**, *41*, 2740–2755. [CrossRef] [PubMed]
17. Fernando, B.; Gavves, E.; Oramas, J.; Ghodrati, A.; Tuytelaars, T. Rank pooling for action recognition. *IEEE Trans. Pattern Anal. Mach. Intell. TPAMI* **2016**, *39*, 773–787. [CrossRef] [PubMed]
18. Tran, D.; Wang, H.; Feiszli, M.; Torresani, L. Video classification with channel-separated convolutional networks. In Proceedings of the IEEE International Conference on Computer Vision (ICCV), Seoul, Korea, 27 October–2 November 2019; pp. 5551–5560.
19. Wang, H.; Song, Z.; Li, W.; Wang, P. A Hybrid Network for Large-Scale Action Recognition from RGB and Depth Modalities. *Sensors* **2020**, *20*, 3305. [CrossRef] [PubMed]
20. Wu, H.; Ma, X.; Li, Y. Spatio-temporal multimodal learning with CNNs for video action recognition. *IEEE Trans. Circuits Syst. Video Technol. TCSVT* **2022**, *32*, 1250–1261. [CrossRef]
21. Fernando, B.; Anderson, P.; Hutter, M.; Gould, S. Discriminative Hierarchical Rank Pooling for Activity Recognition. In Proceedings of the IEEE Conference on Computer Vision and Pattern Recognition (CVPR), Vegas, NV, USA, 27–30 June 2016; pp. 1924–1932.
22. Bilen, H.; Fernando, B.; Gavves, E.; Vedaldi, A.; Gould, S. Dynamic image networks for action recognition. In Proceedings of the IEEE Conference on Computer Vision and Pattern Recognition (CVPR), Vegas, NV, USA, 27–30 June 2016; pp. 3034–3042.
23. Li, N.; Cheng, X.; Zhang, S.; Wu, Z. Realistic human action recognition by fast HOG3D and self-organization feature map. *Mach. Vis. Appl.* **2014**, *25*, 1793–1812. [CrossRef]
24. Ioffe, S.; Szegedy, C. Batch normalization: Accelerating deep network training by reducing internal covariate SHIFT. In Proceedings of the 32nd International Conference on Machine Learning (ICML), Lile, France, 6–11 July 2015; Volume 1, pp. 448–456.
25. Moghaddam, Z.; Piccardi, M. Training initialization of hidden Markov models in human action recognition. *IEEE Trans. Autom. Sci. Eng. TASE* **2014**, *11*, 394–408. [CrossRef]
26. Sempena, S.; Maulidevi, N.; Aryan, P. Human action recognition using dynamic time warping. In Proceedings of the International Conference on Electrical Engineering and Informatics (ICEEI), Bandung, Indonesia, 17–19 July 2011; pp. 1–5.
27. Simonyan, K.; Zisserman, A. Two-stream convolutional networks for action recognition in videos. *Proc. Adv. Neural Inf. Process. Syst. NIPS* **2014**, *1*, 568–576.
28. Wang, L.; Xiong, Y.; Wang, Z.; Qiao, Y.; Lin, D.; Tang, X.; Van Gool, L. Temporal Segment Networks: Towards Good Practices for Deep Action Recognition. In Proceedings of the European Conference on Computer Vision (ECCV), Amsterdam, The Netherlands, 11–14 October 2016; pp. 20–36.
29. Zhang, J.; Shen, F.; Xu, X.; Shen, H.T. Cooperative cross-stream network for discriminative action representation. *arXiv* **2019**, arXiv:1908.10136.
30. Wang, L.; Tong, Z.; Ji, B.; Wu, G. TDN: Temporal difference networks for efficient action recognition. In Proceedings of the IEEE/CVF Conference on Computer Vision and Pattern Recognition (CVPR), Nashville, TN, USA, 19–25 June 2021; pp. 1895–1904.
31. Tran, D.; Bourdev, L.; Fergus, R.; Torresani, L.; Paluri, M. Learning spatio-temporal features with 3D convolutional networks. In Proceedings of the IEEE International Conference on Computer Vision (ICCV), Santiago, Chile, 7–13 December 2015; pp. 4489–4497.
32. Jiang, S.; Qi, Y.; Zhang, H.; Bai, Z.; Lu, X.; Wang, P. D3D: Dual 3-D Convolutional Network for Real-Time Action Recognition. *IEEE Trans. Ind. Inform. TII* **2021**, *17*, 584–4593. [CrossRef]
33. Tao, L.; Wang, X.; Yamasaki, T. Rethinking Motion Representation: Residual Frames With 3D ConvNets. *IEEE Trans. Image Process. TIP* **2021**, *30*, 9231–9244. [CrossRef]
34. Dosovitskiy, A.; Beyer, L.; Kolesnikov, A.; Weissenborn, D.; Zhai, X.; Unterthiner, T.; Dehghani, M.; Minderer, M.; Heigold, G.; Gelly, S.; et al. An image is worth 16x16 words: Transformers for image recognition at scale. In Proceedings of the International Conference on Learning Representations (ICLR), Virtual Event, Austria, 3–7 May 2021.
35. Carion, N.; Massa, F.; Synnaeve, G.; Usunier, N.; Kirillov, A.; Zagoruyko, S. End to end object detection with transformers. In Proceedings of the European Conference on Computer Vision (ECCV), Glasgow, UK, 23–28 August 2020; pp. 213–229.
36. Girdhar, R.; Carreira, J.; Doersch, C.; Zisserman, A. Video action transformer network. In Proceedings of the IEEE Conference on Computer Vision and Pattern Recognition (CVPR), Long Beach, CA, USA, 16–20 June 2019; pp. 244–253.
37. Wang, P.; Li, W.; Gao, Z.; Tang, C.; Ogunbona, P.O. Depth pooling based large-scale 3-D action recognition with convolutional neural networks. *IEEE Trans. Multimed. TMM* **2018**, *20*, 1051–1061. [CrossRef]
38. Wang, P.; Li, W.; Gao, Z.; Zhang, J.; Tang, C.; Ogunbona, P.O. Action recognition from depth maps using deep convolutional neural networks. *IEEE Trans. Hum.-Mach. Syst.* **2016**, *46*, 498–509. [CrossRef]

39. Qi, M.; Wang, Y.; Qin, J.; Li, A.; Luo, J.; Van Gool, L. StagNet: An attentive semantic RNN for group activity and individual action recognition. *IEEE Trans. Circuits Syst. Video Technol. TCSVT* **2020**, *30*, 549–565. [CrossRef]
40. Si, C.; Chen, W.; Wang, W.; Wang, L.; Tan, T. An attention enhanced graph convolutional LSTM network for skeleton-based action recognition. In Proceedings of the 2019 IEEE/CVF Conference on Computer Vision and Pattern Recognition (CVPR), Long Beach CA, USA, 16–17 June 2019; pp. 1227–1236.
41. Liu, J.; Wang, G.; Duan, L.-Y.; Abdiyeva, K.; Kot, A.C. Skeleton based human action recognition with global context-aware attention LSTM networks. *IEEE Trans. Image Process. TIP* **2018**, *27*, 1586–1599. [CrossRef]
42. Wang, P.; Li, W.; Wan, J.; Ogunbona, P.; Liu, X. Cooperative Training of Deep Aggregation Networks for RGB-D Action Recognition. In Proceedings of the 32nd AAAI Conference on Artificial Intelligence (AAAI), New Orleans, LA, USA, 2–7 February 2018; pp. 7404–7411.
43. Shahroudy, A.; Liu, J.; Ng, T.; Wang, G. NTU RGB+D: A large scale dataset for 3D human activity analysis. In Proceedings of the IEEE Conference on Computer Vision and Pattern Recognition (CVPR), Vegas, NV, USA, 27–30 June 2016; pp. 1010–1019.
44. Ren, Z.; Zhang, Q.; Cheng, J.; Hao, F.; Gao, X. Segment spatial-temporal representation and cooperative learning of Convolution Neural Networks for multimodal-based action recognition. *Neurocomputing* **2021**, *433*, 142–153. [CrossRef]
45. Cheng, J.; Ren, Z.; Zhang, Q.; Gao, X.; Hao, F. Cross-Modality Compensation Convolutional Neural Networks for RGB-D Action Recognition. *IEEE Trans. Circuits Syst. Video Technol. TCSVT* **2022**, *32*, 1498–1509. [CrossRef]
46. Song, S.; Liu, J.; Li, Y.; Guo, Z. Modality compensation network: Cross-modal adaptation for action recognition. *IEEE Trans. Image Process. TIP* **2020**, *29*, 3957–3969. [CrossRef]
47. Xu, W.; Wu, M.; Zhao, M.; Xia, T. Fusion of skeleton and RGB features for RGB-D human action recognition. *IEEE Sens. J.* **2021**, *21*, 19157–19164.
48. He, K.; Zhang, X.; Ren, S.; Sun, J. Deep Residual Learning for Image Recognition. In Proceedings of the IEEE Conference on Computer Vision and Pattern Recognition (CVPR), Vegas, NV, USA, 27–30 June 2016; pp. 770–778.
49. Smola, A.J.; Schölkopf, B. A tutorial on support vector regression. *Statist. Comput.* **2004**, *14*, 199–222. [CrossRef]
50. Liu, J.; Shahroudy, A.; Perez, M.L.; Wang, G.; Duan, L.; Chichung, A.K. NTU RGB+D 120: A large-scale benchmark for 3D human activity understanding. *IEEE Trans. Pattern Anal. Mach. Intell. TPAMI* **2019**, *42*, 2684–2701. [CrossRef]
51. Liu, C.; Hu, Y.; Li, Y.; Song, S.; Liu, J. PKU-MMD: A large scale benchmark for continuous multi-modal human action understanding. *arXiv* **2017**, arXiv:1703.07475.
52. Song, S.; Lan, C.; Xing, J.; Zeng, W.; Liu, J. Spatio-temporal attention-based LSTM networks for 3D action recognition and detection. *IEEE Trans. Image Process. TIP* **2018**, *27*, 3459–3471. [CrossRef] [PubMed]

mathematics

MDPI

Article

Deep Learning-Based Plant Classification Using Nonaligned Thermal and Visible Light Images

Ganbayar Batchuluun, Se Hyun Nam and Kang Ryoung Park *

Division of Electronics and Electrical Engineering, Dongguk University, 30 Pildong-ro, 1-gil, Jung-gu, Seoul 04620, Korea
* Correspondence: parkgr@dongguk.edu

Abstract: There have been various studies conducted on plant images. Machine learning algorithms are usually used in visible light image-based studies, whereas, in thermal image-based studies, acquired thermal images tend to be analyzed with a naked eye visual examination. However, visible light cameras are sensitive to light, and cannot be used in environments with low illumination. Although thermal cameras are not susceptible to these drawbacks, they are sensitive to atmospheric temperature and humidity. Moreover, in previous thermal camera-based studies, time-consuming manual analyses were performed. Therefore, in this study, we conducted a novel study by simultaneously using thermal images and corresponding visible light images of plants to solve these problems. The proposed network extracted features from each thermal image and corresponding visible light image of plants through residual block-based branch networks, and combined the features to increase the accuracy of the multiclass classification. Additionally, a new database was built in this study by acquiring thermal images and corresponding visible light images of various plants.

Keywords: plant image; image classification; thermal image; visible light image; deep learning

MSC: 68T07; 68U10

1. Introduction

Many studies have investigated plant image classification methods and databases [1–21]. However, all these studies utilized visible light cameras, which are sensitive to light and have the drawback of obtaining low-quality images owing to shadows, illumination changes, and ambient light and its reflections. In addition, visible light cameras cannot be used in the absence of light.

To avoid such problems, a thermal camera was used in previous research [22]. However, there are still very few studies on plant image classification using thermal cameras, and the acquired thermal images of plants have mostly been analyzed with a naked eye examination [23,24]. In addition, thermal cameras are sensitive to atmospheric temperature and humidity; therefore, they have the disadvantage of capturing low-quality images owing to rainwater and ambient heat from surrounding objects. To solve these problems, Raza et al. [25] used thermal and visible light cameras simultaneously. However, they conducted experiments based on manual feature extraction. The extraction of the most suitable features from a database is difficult while using the manual feature extraction-based method. Furthermore, binary classification, which only classifies plant images into two classes, diseased and healthy, was performed in this previous study. Therefore, we conducted novel multiclass classification research based on automatic feature extraction using a deep learning method in this study. In the proposed method, we developed a plant classification residual (PlantCR) network by using VGG-Net [26] and ResNet [27]. Furthermore, we used this structure to extract features from thermal and visible light images of plants and to combine them. Then, the plants were classified into 28 classes. A detailed description of our method is described in Section 3. Moreover, we obtained and constructed a novel nonaligned thermal and visible light plant image database (TherVisDb) [28]. In addition, we used this constructed database to perform various experiments in the ablation study. The novelties of our study can be explained in the following four ways:

- Previous studies only dealt with the binary classification of plants based on thermal and corresponding visible light images. Therefore, this is the first research for the multiclass classification of plants using thermal and corresponding visible light images. In addition, previous studies used manual feature extraction, whereas automatic feature extraction was used in this study to obtain more suitable features.
- We proposed a novel PlantCR network in this study. To design the structure of PlantCR, we used the same grouped submodules for visible and thermal images, and the fusion of two feature sets extracted from these two images. By using the same grouped submodule, we could simplify the system architecture. Each grouped submodule included a residual block, and the accuracy of the multiclass classification increased through the fusion of two feature sets.
- We built a new TherVisDb database containing 9440 images of various flowers and flower leaves for the experiment. This self-constructed database contained both thermal images and the corresponding visible light images of plants. However, there was a significant difference between the field of view (FOV) and view of angle (VOA) of each camera, and, thus, the images were not aligned with each other. Therefore, it was challenging to conduct the plant image classification. In addition, this database had a larger number of classes and images than existing thermal plant image databases.
- Our model and database constructed in this study were disclosed via the site GitHub [28] so that they can be used by other researchers.

Existing related works are explained in Section 2, in which previous plant image-based studies were divided into visible light image-based, thermal image-based, and thermal and visible light image-based methods. Sections 2.1–2.3 provide the detailed descriptions of these methods. A detailed explanation of the proposed method is provided in Section 3, which is followed by the experimental results and analysis in Section 4. Lastly, the discussion and conclusion are presented in Sections 5 and 6, respectively.

2. Related Works

2.1. Visible Light Image-Based Methods

In the crop disease classification [1] method, experiments were previously performed using the PlantDoc database and proposed AAR network. In the fruit recognition method [2], classification experiments were conducted using AlexNet and CNN. This previous study compared the performance of the methods based on the Fruit-360 database. In the fruit variety classification [3] method, a CNN and the Fruit-360 database were used. In addition, regions of interest were created from apple images by using the YOLO network [29]. In the crop disease classification [4] method, experiments were conducted using the PlantDoc database and proposed DenseNet-121 model. In the fruit image classification [5] method, classification experiments were conducted using Inception V3 [30] and VGG16 [26]. This previous study compared the performance of methods based on the Fruit-360 database. In the grape variety recognition [6] method, the ExtResnet model was proposed, but the experiment was performed using the wine grape instance segmentation database [31]. In the fruit classification [7] method, DCNN and the Fruit-360 database were used. In the fruits recognition method [8], various experiments were conducted using the Fruits-360 image database. In addition, various feature extractions and machine-learning-based methods were used to perform experiments, after which the results were compared. The fruit classification [9] method used a CNN and the Fruit-360 database. In another fruit classification method, [10] proposed a multiclass CNN model. In this previous study, the experiment was performed on the FIDS30 database [32] and on the Fruits-360 database. In the fruit and vegetable classification [11] method, FruitVegCNN and MPSoC were proposed, but the Fruit-360 database was used for the experiment. The fruit classification [12] method proposed multiple deep learning models. In this previous study, the experiment was performed on the following databases: a supermarket produce and self-collected databases. Siddiqi [13] proposed FruitNet as a fruit image classification method and compared fourteen deep learning methods and compared the performance on the Fruit-360 database. In the fruit recognition method [14], experiments were conducted using EfficientNet-B0 and Fruit-360. In the crop disease classification [15] method, experiments were performed using the PlantDoc database and proposed OMNCNN. In the fruit classification [16] method, classification experiments were conducted using a histogram of oriented gradients. In the fruit image classification [17] method, the Fruit-360 database and ShuffleNet were used. Another fruit image-based classification method [18] proposed a deep learning method and used a model trained on ImageNet. In the crop and crop disease classification [19] method, experiments were performed using the PlantDoc database and five deep learning methods (MobileNetV1, MobileNetV2, NASNetMobile, DenseNet121, and Xception). Another crop and crop disease classification [20] method proposed a trilinear convolutional neural network model. Various experiments were conducted using the PlantVillage [33] and PlantDoc [34] databases and a pretrained model with ImageNet. In the apple classification [21] method, a CNN and the Fruit-360 database were used.

However, all these studies used visible light cameras. As explained in Section 1, visible light cameras are sensitive to light. Hence, they have the drawback of capturing low-quality images owing to shadows, illumination changes, and ambient light and its reflections. Moreover, visible light cameras cannot be used in the absence of light. To solve these problems, studies were conducted using thermal plant image-based methods, which were explained in Section 2.2.

2.2. Thermal Image-Based Method

Zhu et al. [23] studied plant image diagnosis and conducted experiments using a self-collected database. They proposed a method for diagnosing diseased plants. Lydia et al. [24] studied plant image identification and conducted experiments using a self-collected database. They proposed a data-gathering approach for the identification of diseased plants. In the plant image-based detection [22] method, experiments were conducted using thermal images for the detection of diseased areas in plant images based on the if–then rule. However, the previous thermal image-based studies typically analyzed thermal images with a naked eye examination, which is a time-consuming task. Moreover, very few studies on plant thermal images have been executed, and methods based on computer devices and algorithms have not been sufficiently developed. In addition, thermal cameras are sensitive to atmospheric temperature and humidity; therefore, they have the drawback of capturing low-quality images owing to rainwater and heat from surrounding objects. However, the studies described in Section 2.3 considered the drawbacks of thermal and visible light cameras and used them simultaneously.

2.3. Thermal and Visible Light Image-Based Method

A previous plant image classification [25] study considered the problems of thermal and visible light cameras and proposed a method based on computer devices and algorithms. Their method used thermal images and corresponding visible light images to perform the binary classification. Furthermore, in the study, thermal images and the corresponding multiple visible light images were obtained through three camera sensors, a thermal camera and two visible light cameras (left and right). By combining these three types of images, an improvement in the accuracy of the classification for dividing images into healthy and diseased plant images was possible. Moreover, the binary classification (healthy or diseased) was performed by using the analysis of variance [35] and support vector machine [36], and the features extracted through manual feature extraction methods.

However, this method increased the computation time and complexity of the system because of the simultaneous use of the three cameras. In addition, this method used manual feature extraction methods, which cannot extract suitable features. Moreover, since this method only performed a binary classification, it could not recognize various plant images.

Therefore, to solve these problems, a multiclass classification was performed in this study using plant images acquired using two camera sensors, thermal and visible light cameras. In addition, a deep learning-based automatic feature extraction method was used to extract more suitable features from the images.

In addition, Table 1 summarizes the existing methods explained in the Section 2 for ease of understanding. In Table 1, previous methods and the proposed method are also compared based on images, feature extractions, and methods. Moreover, the methods are compared by advantages and disadvantages of using such images and methods. As shown in Table 1, the proposed method was the first study on plant multiclass classification using thermal and visible light images.

Table 1. Summary and comparison of our and previous methods.

Categories		Methods	Advantages	Disadvantages
Visible light image-based	Based on automatic feature extraction	Binary and multiclass classification [1–21]	- Provides high-resolution and high-quality images in day or high illumination environments - Provides color information - Extracts features automatically based on big database	- Provides dark images in night or low illumination environments - Provides low-quality images in day or high illumination environments owing to shadows, illumination changes, and ambient light and its reflections
Thermal image-based	Based on manual feature extraction	Diagnosis [23], identification [24]	- Provides thermal information	- Sensitive to atmospheric temperature and humidity, and captures low-quality images owing to rainwater and heat from surrounding objects - Very difficult to extract suitable features
	Based on automatic feature extraction	Detection method [22]	- Provides thermal information - Automatically extracts features based on big database	- Sensitive to atmospheric temperature and humidity, and captures low-quality images owing to rainwater and heat from surrounding objects
Thermal and visible light image-based	Based on manual feature extraction	Binary classification [25]	- Provides high-resolution and high-quality images in day or high illumination environments - Provides color and thermal information	- Very difficult to extract suitable features - Does not consider multiclass problems - Computationally expensive owing to three camera sensors
	Based on automatic feature extraction	Multiclass classification (proposed method)	- Provides high-resolution and high-quality image in day or high illumination environments - Provides color and thermal information - Extracts features automatically based on big database - Considers multiclass problems	- Computationally expensive owing to two camera sensors

3. Proposed Method

3.1. Overall Explanation of the Proposed Method

This section thoroughly describes PlantCR. A simplified flowchart of PlantCR constructed in this study is presented in Figure 1. The proposed PlantCR network was constructed using the concepts of VGG-Net and ResNet. As presented in Figure 1, the proposed method used thermal images and corresponding visible light images of plants as its input and combined the extracted features to classify the images into 28 classes. The tables and figures in Section 3.2 describe the details of the structure. In addition, Section 3.2 extensively explains the input images, size of the outputs, and parameters used in the structure.

Figure 1. Overview of the PlantCR network for plant image classification.

3.2. Detailed Structure of the PlantCR Network

As presented in Figure 1, a visible light plant image (200 × 200 × 3 pixels) and a thermal plant image (200 × 200 × 1 pixels) were inputted into the PlantCR network proposed in this study. The details of the PlantCR structure are listed in Tables 2–4 and presented in Figure 2. The main structure of the PlantCR network is presented in Table 2, and it consisted of input layers (input layers one and two), group layers (group_1–3), the concatenate layer (concat), fully connected layer (FC), and global average pooling layer (GAP); the output (class#) of the FC layer was 28. The "Times" columns in Tables 2 and 3 represent the number of repetitions of each layer. Each layer in the column of parameters shows a sum of the parameters of only that layer. Table 3 summarizes a group of layers and residual blocks, consisting of an input layer, convolution layers (conv2d), a max pooling layer (max_pool), and residual blocks (res_block). Table 4 summarizes the residual block, consisting of an input layer, convolution layers, a parametric rectified linear unit (prelu), and an additional operation layer (add). In Tables 2–4, the filter size and stride were (3 × 3) and (1 × 1), respectively; the padding of the conv2d layers of the residual block was (1 × 1), and that of the remaining conv2d layers was (0 × 0). "#" indicates "number of" in all contents.

Table 2. Structure of the PlantCR network.

Layer#	Times	Layer Type	Filter#	Parameter#	Layer Connection
1	1	input layer_1 and 2	0	0	input
2	2	group_1	64/128	1,735,872	input layer_1
3	2	group_2	64/128	1,735,872	input layer_2
4	1	concat	0	0	group_1 and group_2
5	2	group_3	128	3,100,160	concat
6	1	GAP	28	0	group_3
7	1	FC (softmax)	class#	3612	GAP
Total number of parameters: 6,575,516					

Table 3. Structure of a group layer.

Times	Layer Type	Layer Connection
1	input layer	input
2	conv2d	input layer
1	max_pool	conv2d
4	res_block	max_pool

Table 4. Structure of a residual block.

Layer Type	Layer Connection
input layer	input
conv2d_1	input layer
prelu	conv2d_1
conv2d_2	prelu
add	conv2d_2 and input layer

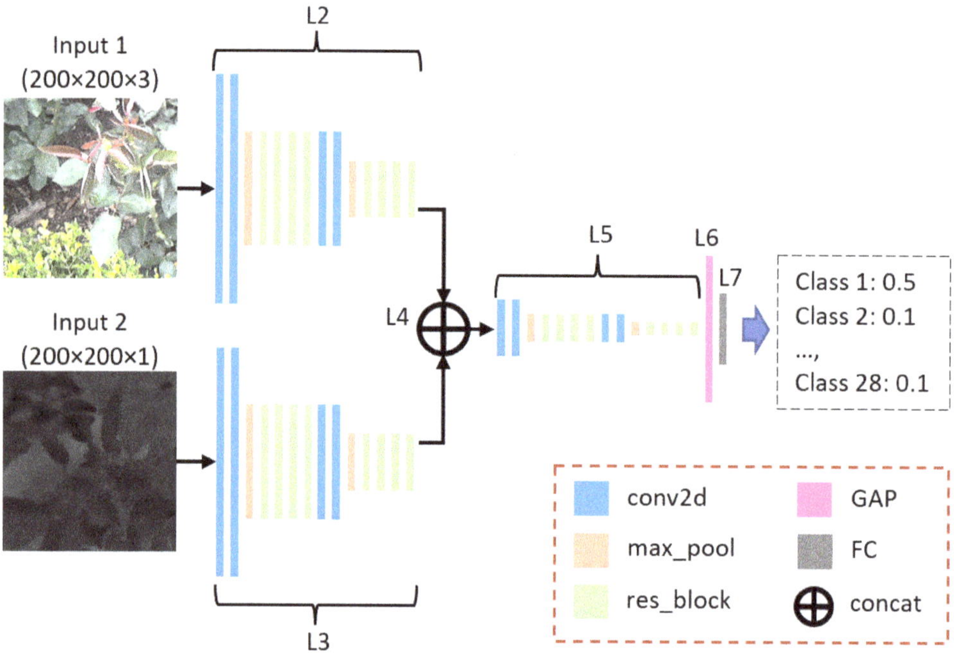

Figure 2. The detailed structure of PlantCR.

3.3. Details of Database and Experimental Setup

Experiments were conducted using TherVisDb [28], consisting of various rose and rose leaf images. The Tau® 2 FLIR thermal camera (Tau® 2) and Logitech C270 HD camera [37] were used to capture thermal images and corresponding visible light images. During the capturing of the images, the atmospheric humidity, temperature, wind speed, fine dust, ultrafine dust, and UV index were 91%, 30 °C, 3 m/s, 24 $\mu g/m^3$, 22 $\mu g/m^3$, and 8, respectively. Here, one UV index unit is equal to 25 milliWatts/m^2. The database was constructed in July 2022. The size and depth of the images captured using the thermal and visible light cameras were 640 × 512 × 1 pixels and 14 bits, respectively. Moreover, the depth and size of the images acquired using the visible light camera were 24 and 640 × 512 × 3, respectively. In this study, the size of the images in the database, prepared using the cropping operation, was 8 bits and 300 × 300 × 1 pixels for the thermal images and 24 bits and 300 × 300 × 3 pixels for the visible light images. The size of the depth of the images was 24 bits. The images used in this study had 24 bits. In detail, a single pixel in an image represented up to 256 numbers (or intensity), which could be represented by 8 bits in the binary number. Because we had RGB (three-channel) color images, the size of the depth of the images could be 24 bits (8 bits × 3 channels). Moreover, all the images had '.png' as the image file extension. In addition, all images of 300 × 300 pixels were downsized to 200 × 200 pixels when being inputted into the proposed model in this study. The total number of thermal and visible light plant images was 4720 and 4720, respectively. In addition, the training, test, and validation sets had 3314, 954, and 452 images, respectively. The training set images were augmented from 3314 images to 26,512 images through the use of augmentation methods (rotating three times by 90 degrees and flipping horizontally). The total number of classes in this database was 28, and Figure 3 shows example images. Table 5 lists the number of all images and names of plants for each class in the TherVisDb database. As presented in Figure 3, the thermal images and corresponding visible light images were not aligned, owing to the FOV and VOA of the cameras.

Table 5. Description of TherVisDb.

Class Index	Class Names	Thermal Image #	Visible Light Image #	Train Set	Test Set	Validation Set
1	Alexandra	120	120	168	48	24
2	Belvedere	48	48	68	20	8
3	Blue river	136	136	192	56	24
4	Charm of Paris	136	136	192	56	24
5	Cleopatra	152	152	214	62	28
6	Cocktail	112	112	158	46	20
7	Duftrausch	176	176	248	72	32
8	Echinacea sunset	64	64	90	26	12
9	Eleanor	144	144	202	58	28
10	Elvis	224	224	314	90	44
11	Fellowship	208	208	292	84	40
12	Goldeise	144	144	202	58	28
13	Goldfassade	184	184	258	74	36
14	Grand classe	264	264	370	106	52
15	Just Joey	72	72	102	30	12
16	Kerria japonica	104	104	146	42	20
17	Margaret	112	112	158	46	20
18	Oklahoma	312	312	438	126	60
19	Pink perfume	120	120	168	48	24
20	Queen Elizabeth	120	120	168	48	24
21	Rose gaujard	312	312	438	126	60
22	Rosenau	304	304	426	122	60
23	Roseraie du chatelet	352	352	494	142	68
24	Spiraea salicifolia l	64	64	90	26	12
25	Stella de oro	48	48	68	20	8
26	Twist	288	288	404	116	56
27	Ulrich brunner fils	120	120	168	48	24
28	White symphonie	280	280	392	112	56
	Total	4720	4720	6628	1908	904

The image classification algorithm was processed using a computer device with an NVIDIA GeForce GTX TITAN X GPU [38], a Core i7-6700 CPU@3.40 GHz CPU, and a 32 GB RAM. The model and source code were built by using libraries of OpenCV (version 4.3.0) [39], Python (version 3.5.4) [40], and the Keras API (version 2.1.6-tf) [41].

Figure 3. Example images of TherVisDb. From left to right: images of Alexandra, Belvedere, Elvis, and Fellowship. (**a**) Visible light images and (**b**) thermal images.

4. Experimental Results

4.1. Training Setup and Hyperparameters

The training setup of the proposed PlantCR was as follows: An adaptive moment estimation (Adam [42]) and a categorical cross-entropy loss [43] were used as the optimizer and the loss, respectively. The training loss curves and validation accuracy curves of the PlantCR are presented in Figure 4. Figure 4a,b present the loss curves and accuracy curves of the PlantCR according to the epoch number, respectively. As shown in Figure 4, the network constructed in this study was sufficiently trained without being overfitted by the training data. In detail, in machine learning, overfitting can be checked by validating the trained model using a validation dataset at each epoch in the training phase. For example, overfitting does not occur if validation accuracy increases with stabilization when the training loss decreases with stabilization. Therefore, as shown in Figure 4, the validation accuracy increased with stabilization (Figure 4b) when the training loss decreased with stabilization (Figure 4a). Therefore, we could confirm that the model was sufficiently trained without being overfitted. In addition, Table 6 lists the hyperparameters, and presents the selected values from the search spaces for the network.

Table 6. Selected values from search spaces of hyperparameters.

Parameters	Epochs	Learning Rate Decay (for SGD)	Batch Size	Learning Rate	Momentum (for SGD)	Optimizer
Search Space	(1~300)	(0.000001, 0.00001, 0.0001)	(1,4,8,16)	(0.0001, 0.001, 0.01, 0.1)	(0.9, 0.8, 0.7)	("SGD," "Adam")
Selected Value	260	0.00001	8	0.00001	0.9	"Adam"

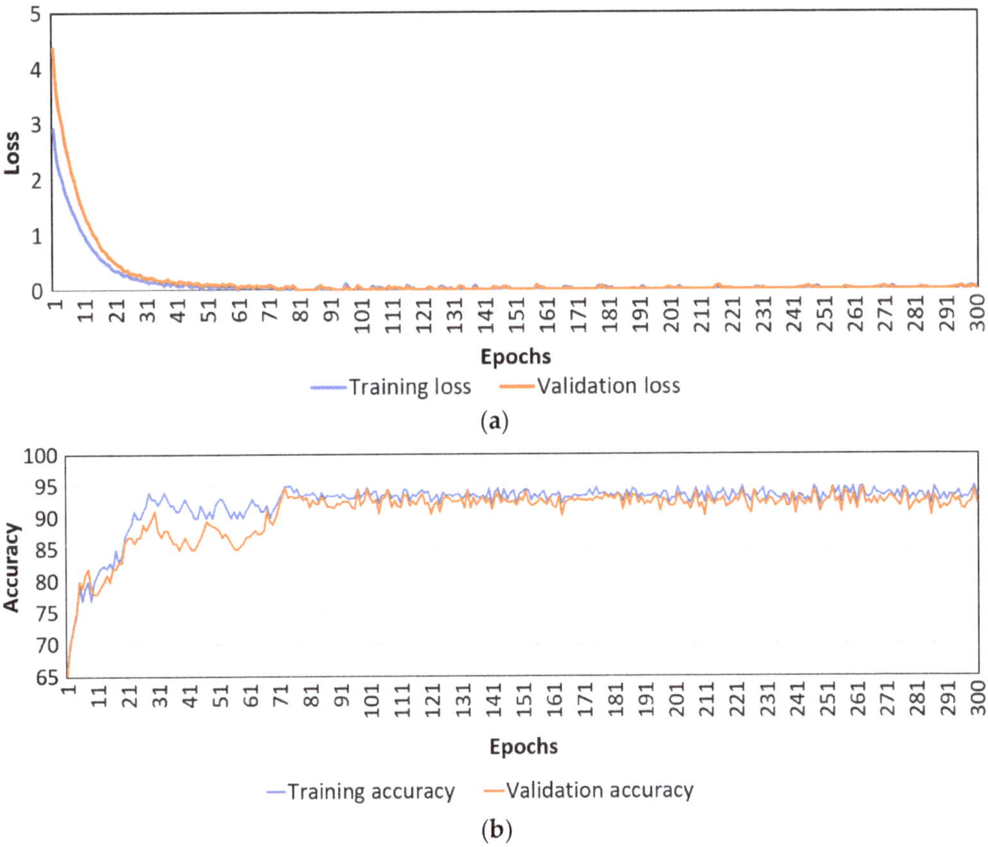

Figure 4. Loss curves and accuracy curves of PlantCR. (**a**) Training loss curves and validation loss curves; (**b**) training accuracy curves and validation accuracy curves.

4.2. Ablation Study

This section explains and compares the testing accuracies. The performance of the plant classification methods was calculated by using metrics given by Equations (1)–(4), positive predictive values (PPVs, also named precisions), the presenting true positive rate (TPR, also named the sensitivity and recall), F1-score (the harmonic mean of the precision and recall) [44], and accuracy (ACC) [45], respectively. In the equations, the numbers of true positive (#TP), false positive (#FP), false negative (#FN), and true negative (#TN) were given to calculate the accuracies.

$$\mathrm{PPV} = (\#\mathrm{TP})/(\#\mathrm{TP} + \#\mathrm{FP}) \tag{1}$$

$$\mathrm{TPR} = (\#\mathrm{TP})/(\#\mathrm{TP} + \#\mathrm{FN}) \tag{2}$$

$$\text{F1-score} = 2(\mathrm{PPV} \cdot \mathrm{TPR})/(\mathrm{PPV} + \mathrm{TPR}) \tag{3}$$

$$\mathrm{ACC} = (\#\mathrm{TP} + \#\mathrm{TN})/(\#\mathrm{TP} + \#\mathrm{TN} + \#\mathrm{FP} + \#\mathrm{FN}) \tag{4}$$

As shown in Table 7 and Figure 5, the experiment was conducted using seven methods. Methods (Figure 5) using only the thermal images, only the visible light images, and a combination of the two types of images in various ways were compared.

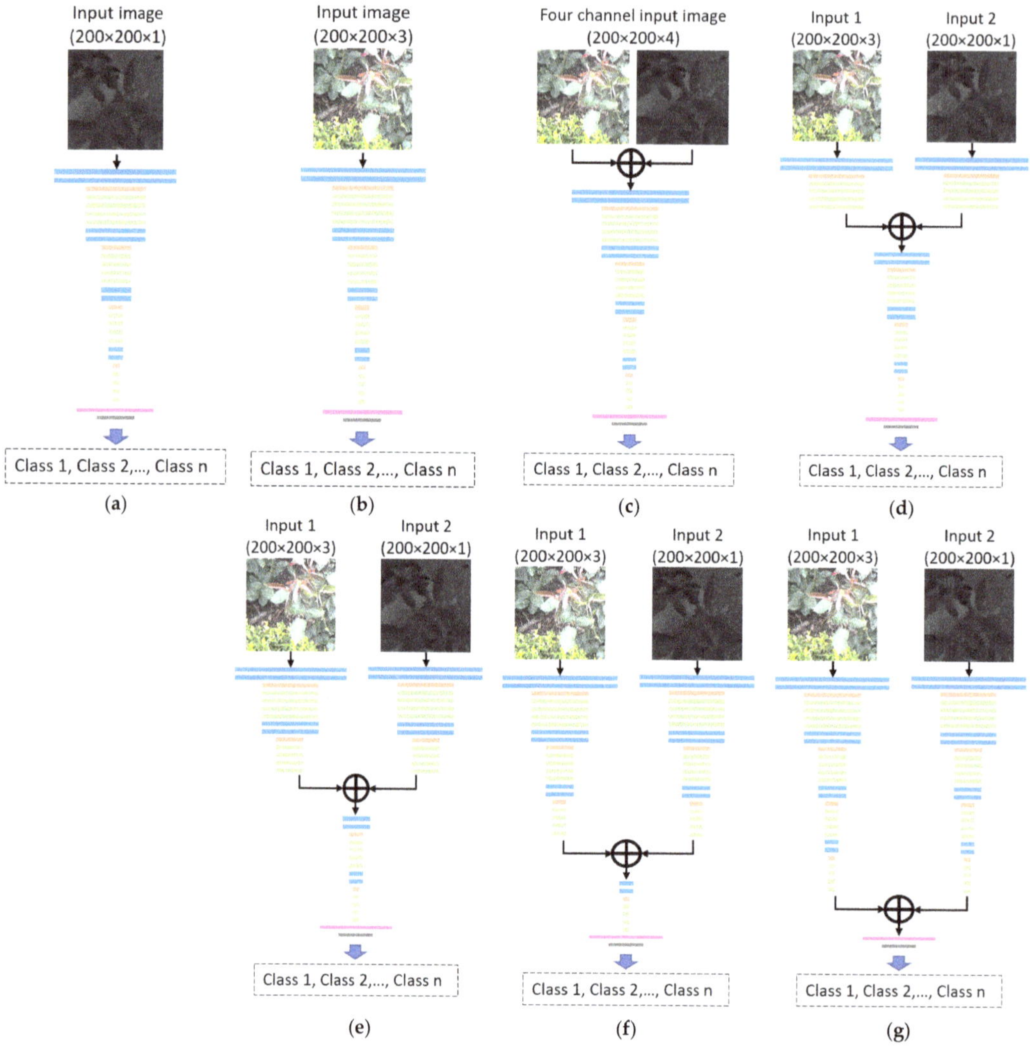

Figure 5. Variants of the classification network conducted in the ablation study. (**a**–**g**) Methods 1–7. The meaning of each color bar is explained in Figure 2.

Table 7. Accuracies obtained by using the proposed PlantCR network and variants of PlantCR.

Methods	TPR	PPV	F1-Score	ACC
Method 1 (thermal image)	80.4	81.69	80.28	98.58
Method 2 (visible light image)	81.65	78.79	79.32	98.52
Method 3 (combined)	84.5	83.47	83.17	98.69
Method 4 (combined)	86.97	86.11	86.32	99.04
Method 5 (combined) (proposed PlantCR)	90.26	90.42	90.05	99.28
Method 6 (combined)	87.58	86.63	86.68	99.08
Method 7 (combined)	86.67	83.99	84.7	98.87

As shown in Figure 5a–g, variants of the classification network were presented. Method 1 (Figure 5a) used a single thermal image as the input, whereas Method 2 (Figure 5b) used a single visible light image. Method 3 (Figure 5c) combined the thermal and visible light images by using a concatenate layer (Layer# 4 in Table 2) and obtained a single image with four channels, which was used as the input image. Methods 4–7 (Figure 5d–g) extracted features from each image using the branch networks and combined the features to classify the plant images. As shown in Figure 5d–g, features were extracted by using different numbers of groups (as in Layer# 2 and 3 in Tables 2 and 3) and combined at different points. The accuracies obtained using these methods were compared in Table 7. As shown in Table 7, Method 5 exhibited the highest accuracy. Therefore, we proposed Method 5 in this study.

Figures 6–8 and Table 8 show the accuracies obtained for each class using Methods 1, 2, and 5 (proposed PlantCR). In Figures 6–8, the darker colors represent the higher values.

In this study, training and validation accuracies in Figure 4b were different metrics from the ACC in Table 7. For the training and validation in the training phase, we used "accuracy" as the metric. Here, "accuracy" calculated how often predictions equaled labels. This metric created two local variables, such as the total number of training or validation images N and the count of correct predictions TP. Shortly, it was an operation that simply divided the TP by N (accuracy = TP/N). In another words, the training and validation accuracies were a ratio of the number of correct predictions and the number of the total data of the training or validation set. However, in the case of the ACC in Table 7, we used Equation (4), in which a sum of TP and TN was divided by the total number of testing images (#TP + #TN + #FP + #FN). The ACC results mostly had a higher accuracy compared to the other metrics, such as the TPR and PPV. This was because the number of TNs was much greater than others (TP, FP, and FN), and the number of TNs increased more if the class number increased. In the case of Method 5 in Table 7, the total number of TNs was 25,662 when the total number of the FP, FN, and TP was 96, 96, and 858, respectively. Because we had 28 classes, we had a much greater number of TNs than others (TP, FP, and FN).

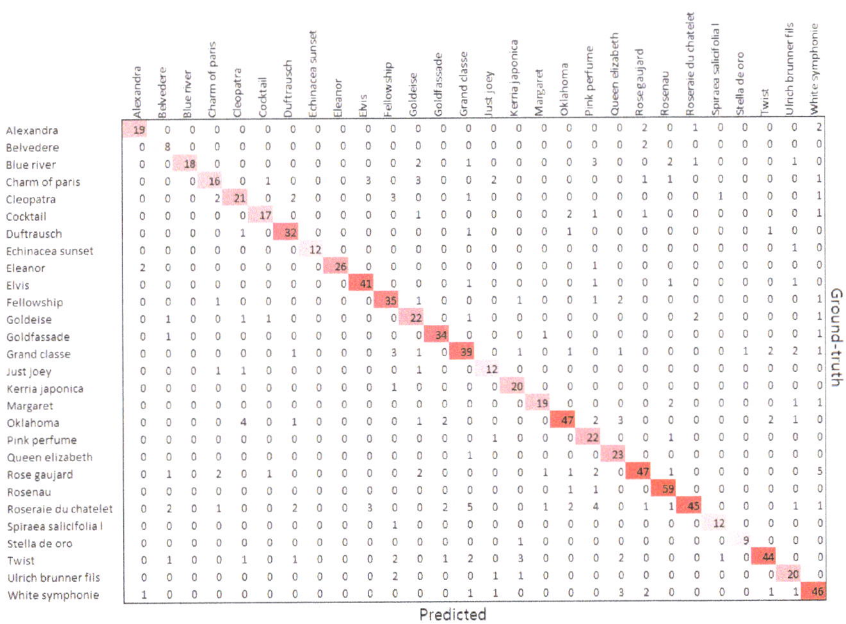

Figure 6. Confusion matrix obtained using Method 1 (Ther).

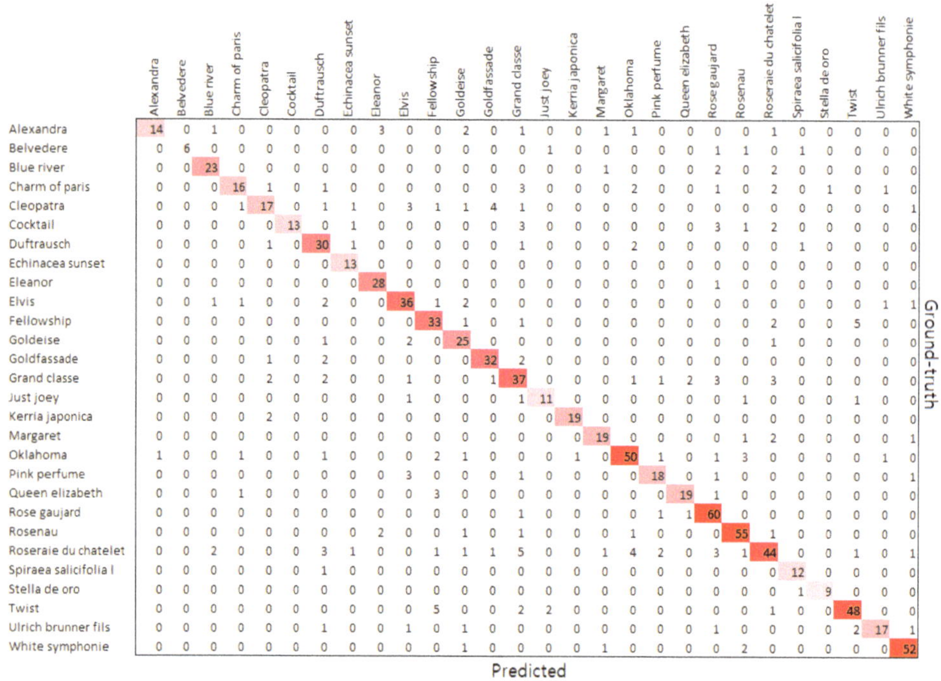

Figure 7. Confusion matrix obtained using Method 2 (Vis).

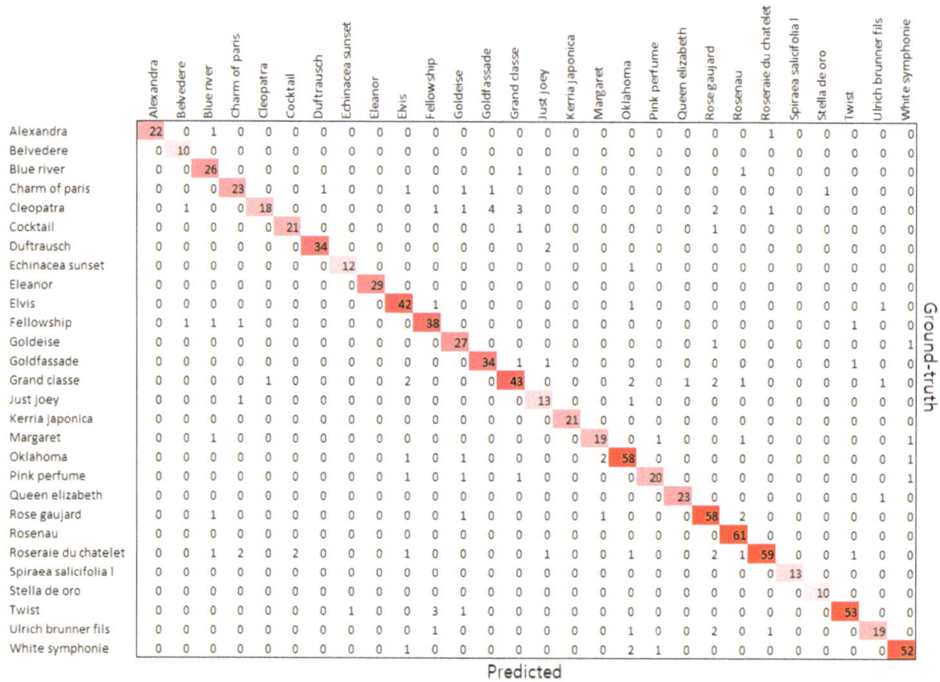

Figure 8. Confusion matrix obtained using proposed PlantCR (Th&V).

Table 8. Detailed accuracy of each class using Methods 1, 2, and PlantCR (using thermal image (Ther), visible light image (Vis), and both images (Th&V), respectively).

#	Class Names	TPR			PPV			F1-Score			ACC		
		Ther	Vis	Th&V	Ther	Vis	Th&V	Ther	Vis	Th&V	Ther	Vis	Th&V
1	Alexandra	86.36	93.33	100	79.17	58.33	91.67	82.61	71.79	95.65	99.16	98.85	99.79
2	Belvedere	57.14	100	83.33	80	60	100	66.67	75	90.91	99.16	99.58	99.79
3	Blue river	100	85.19	83.87	64.29	82.14	92.86	78.26	83.64	88.14	98.95	99.06	99.27
4	Charm of Paris	69.57	80	85.19	57.14	57.14	82.14	62.75	66.67	83.64	98.01	98.32	99.06
5	Cleopatra	72.41	70.83	94.74	67.74	54.84	58.06	70	61.82	72	98.11	97.8	98.53
6	Cocktail	85	100	91.3	73.91	56.52	91.30	79.07	72.22	91.3	99.06	98.95	99.58
7	Duftrausch	82.05	66.67	97.14	88.89	83.33	94.44	85.33	74.07	95.77	98.85	97.8	99.69
8	Echinacea sunset	100	76.47	92.31	92.31	100	92.31	96	86.67	92.31	99.9	99.58	99.79
9	Eleanor	100	84.85	100	89.66	96.55	100	94.55	90.32	100	99.69	99.37	100
10	Elvis	87.23	76.6	85.71	91.11	80	93.33	89.13	78.26	89.36	98.95	97.9	98.95
11	Fellowship	74.47	71.74	86.36	83.33	78.57	90.48	78.65	75	88.37	98.01	97.69	98.95
12	Goldeise	64.71	69.44	81.82	75.86	86.21	93.10	69.84	76.92	87.1	98.01	98.43	99.16
13	Goldfassade	87.18	84.21	87.18	91.89	86.49	91.89	89.47	85.33	89.47	99.16	98.85	99.16
14	Grand classe	73.58	61.67	86	73.58	69.81	81.13	73.58	65.49	83.5	97.06	95.91	98.22
15	Just Joey	70.59	78.57	76.47	80	73.33	86.67	75	75.86	81.25	99.16	99.27	99.37
16	Kerria japonica	74.07	95	100	95.24	90.48	100	83.33	92.68	100	99.16	99.69	100
17	Margaret	86.36	82.61	86.36	82.61	82.61	82.61	84.44	82.61	84.44	99.27	99.16	99.27
18	Oklahoma	85.45	81.97	86.57	74.60	79.37	92.06	79.66	80.65	89.23	97.48	97.48	98.53
19	Pink perfume	57.89	78.26	90.91	91.67	75	83.33	70.97	76.6	86.96	98.11	98.85	99.37
20	Queen Elizabeth	67.65	86.36	95.83	95.83	79.17	95.83	79.31	82.61	95.83	98.74	99.16	99.79
21	Rose gaujard	83.93	76.92	85.29	74.60	95.24	92.06	78.99	85.11	88.55	97.38	97.8	98.43
22	Rosenau	86.76	84.62	91.04	96.72	90.16	100	91.47	87.3	95.31	98.85	98.32	99.37
23	Roseraie du chatelet	91.84	72.13	95.16	63.38	61.97	83.1	75.00	66.67	88.72	96.86	95.39	98.43
24	Spiraea salicifolia L.	85.71	80	100	92.31	92.31	100	88.89	85.71	100	99.69	99.58	100
25	Stella de oro	90	90	90.91	90	90	100	90	90	95.24	99.79	99.79	99.9
26	Twist	88	84.21	94.64	75.86	82.76	91.38	81.48	83.48	92.98	97.9	98.01	99.16
27	Ulrich brunner fils	68.97	85.00	86.36	83.33	70.83	79.17	75.47	77.27	82.61	98.64	98.95	99.16
28	White symphonie	74.19	89.66	92.86	82.14	92.86	92.86	77.97	91.23	92.86	97.27	98.95	99.16
	Average	80.40	81.65	90.26	81.69	78.79	90.42	80.28	79.32	90.05	98.58	98.52	99.28

4.3. Comparisons with Existing Methods

This section describes the comparative experiments conducted using the latest existing methods. Tables 9–11 compare the previously proposed methods [6,7,21] and proposed PlantCR method. Tables 9–11 list the experimental results using a thermal, visible light, and thermal and visible light image databases, respectively. As could be observed, the proposed method obtained the highest accuracies in all cases.

Table 9. Comparison between previous methods and Method 1 (Ther).

Methods	TPR	PPV	F1	ACC
Rhamadiyanti et al., 2021 [21]	79.65	80.22	79.93	96.73
Hussain et al., 2020 [7]	80.16	81.57	80.26	97.08
Franczyk et al., 2020 [6]	79.12	80.44	79.77	97.16
Method 1	80.40	81.69	80.28	98.58

Table 10. Comparison between previous methods and Method 2 (Vis).

Methods	TPR	PPV	F1	ACC
Rhamadiyanti et al., 2021 [21]	81.50	78.42	79.23	98.09
Hussain et al., 2020 [7]	81.46	78.37	79.28	97.97
Franczyk et al., 2020 [6]	80.80	78.30	79.24	97.66
Method 2	81.65	78.79	79.32	98.52

Table 11. Comparison between previous methods and proposed PlantCR (Th&V).

Methods	TPR	PPV	F1	ACC
Rhamadiyanti et al., 2021 [21]	88.67	90.30	89.47	98.26
Hussain et al., 2020 [7]	89.52	89.67	89.59	98.42
Franczyk et al., 2020 [6]	88.33	90.28	89.29	98.29
PlantCR	90.26	90.42	90.05	99.28

4.4. Processing Time

The processing time of Methods 1 and 2 and PlantCR on variants of the database in the testing phase was compared in Table 12, and it was measured based on the computer specifications described in Section 3.3 (the last paragraph). As presented in Table 12, the frame rate of the method using the thermal images was 19.28 frames per second (fps) (1000/(51.85)), and that of the method using visible light images was 19.24 fps (1000/(51.97)). Moreover, the frame rate of the method using both thermal and visible light images (PlantCR) was 18.09 fps (1000/(55.25)).

Table 12. Processing time per image.

Methods	Processing Time
Method 1 (Ther)	51.85 ms
Method 2 (Vis)	51.97 ms
PlantCR (Th&V)	55.25 ms

5. Discussion

In this study, we investigated various classifications using thermal images and corresponding visible light images of plants. By combining the thermal image and corresponding visible light image, the proposed method (PlantCR) performed better than the methods using either thermal or visible light images on their own, as summarized in Tables 7 and 8. In addition, the proposed method was verified to perform better than the methods proposed in previous studies, as per the data listed in Tables 9–11.

In addition, there have been very few existing open databases of plant thermal images. Moreover, open databases of plant thermal and visible light images have never been available to the public. Therefore, in this study, we constructed a thermal and visible light plant image open database. This database had more images and a greater number of classes than existing thermal plant image open databases. The constructed database was called TherVisDb, and is publicly available for other researchers to use [28].

Figure 9 shows the error cases of PlantCR. Classification errors occurred due to the plant labels in the images as presented in Figure 9.

As shown in Table 5, each class had a different number of images. Moreover, some classes had low-quality images as shown in Figure 10. Therefore, the number of images of each class and the low-quality images comprised the differences of the model performances in the different classes. In detail, as shown in Figure 10, the image of duftrausch became dark due to rainwater on the plant and on the ground. Moreover, the image of the rose gaujard became blurry due to high humidity. Moreover, the image of rosenau became bright due to the hot temperature of the environment.

In addition, in the field of agriculture, machine-learning-based solutions are very helpful to human work. For example, such techniques increase the speed of human work in the analysis, disease detection, and crop classification in automated conveyor systems.

Similarly, machine-learning-based plant classification systems are very helpful for classifying plants (medicinal plants, medicinal herbs, and foods) in gardens and factories. For example, there are many medicinal plant factories, where processing is performed by humans by hand [46], whereas some factories use automated systems [47] based on machine learning algorithms such as the proposed method. Moreover, there are many wild plants that can be used as a food source [48]. The proposed method could also be used as a smartphone application; therefore, a person can check if a wild plant in front of them can be used as a food source or if it is a medicinal plant [49].

Figure 9. Example of error cases on TherVisDb. From left to right, the images of alexandra, charm of paris, cleopatra, and grand classes. (**a**) Thermal images; (**b**) corresponding visible light images.

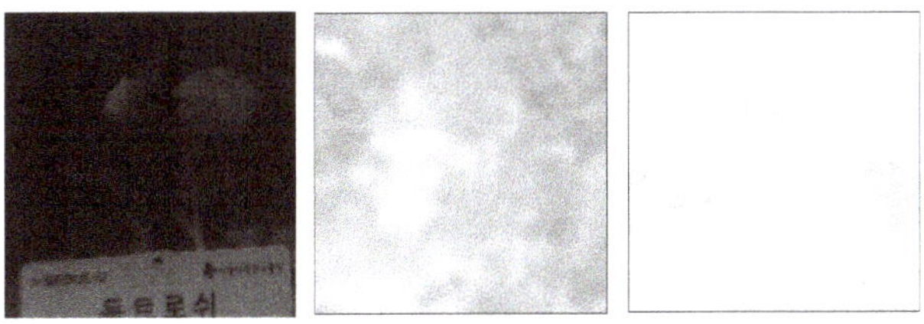

Figure 10. Example of error cases on TherVisDb. Images of (**a**) duftrausch, (**b**) rose gaujard, and (**c**) rosenau.

In our research, the thermal images were not aligned with the corresponding visible light images. For the alignment, an additional calibration process of the thermal and visible light cameras was required. Even with the calibration, the thermal and visible light images could not be aligned due to the different distances between the cameras and the objects. Therefore, we proposed the plant classification method, which could be operated without the alignment method.

6. Conclusions

We developed a plant classification method in this study, based on thermal and visible light images and conducted various experiments using the TherVisDb database, containing various rose and rose leaf images. The experimental results obtained using the TherVisDb database showed a higher accuracy of the proposed method (F1-score = 90.05%, ACC = 99.28%) than the latest methods.

Through this study, we confirmed that the classification accuracy could be increased by simultaneously using thermal images and corresponding visible light images of plants. Moreover, although the thermal images and corresponding visible light plant images used in this study exhibited large differences in the FOV and VOA, the increase in the accuracy was verified when two types of images were simultaneously used, compared to using only one image type. In addition, as shown in Figure 5 and Table 7, we confirmed that extracting features using different numbers of groups (Tables 2 and 3) resulted in different accuracies, and using two groups for each image showed a higher accuracy than using more or less groups.

There have been many machine-learning-based studies conducted in the field of agriculture. However, as explained in related works, mostly crop disease datasets and fruit datasets were used in various studies, namely, detection, classification, segmentation, etc. Furthermore, there have been very few plant image dataset-based studies. Therefore, we referenced previous agriculture and machine-learning-based studies in the Section 2.

To reduce the occurrence of classification errors in future work, as mentioned in Figure 9, we plan to conduct a classification study to increase the accuracy of PlantCR by considering various deep learning methods. Additionally, we plan to perform a plant segmentation by using the self-constructed thermal and visible light images database and increasing the corresponding classification performance. Moreover, we plan to count plants by using drones and machine learning algorithms [50] in our future works.

Author Contributions: Methodology, G.B.; validation, S.H.N.; supervision, K.R.P.; writing—original draft, G.B.; writing—review and editing, K.R.P. All authors have read and agreed to the published version of the manuscript.

Funding: This research was supported in part by the National Research Foundation of Korea (NRF) funded by the Ministry of Science and ICT (MSIT) through the Basic Science Research Program (NRF-2022R1F1A1064291), in part by the NRF funded by the MSIT through the Basic Science Research Program (NRF-2021R1F1A1045587), and in part by the NRF funded by the MSIT through the Basic Science Research Program (NRF-2020R1A2C1006179).

Institutional Review Board Statement: Not applicable.

Informed Consent Statement: Not applicable.

Data Availability Statement: Not applicable.

Conflicts of Interest: The authors declare no conflict of interest.

References

1. Abawatew, G.Y.; Belay, S.; Gedamu, K.; Assefa, M.; Ayalew, M.; Oluwasanmi, A.; Qin, Z. Attention augmented residual network for tomato disease detection and classification. *Turk. J. Electr. Eng. Comput. Sci.* **2021**, *29*, 2869–2885.
2. Hamid, N.N.A.A.; Razali, R.A.; Ibrahim, Z. Comparing bags of features, conventional convolutional neural network and AlexNet for fruit recognition. *Indones. J. Electr. Eng. Comput. Sci.* **2019**, *14*, 333–339. [CrossRef]
3. Katarzyna, R.; Paweł, M.A. Vision-based method utilizing deep convolutional neural networks for fruit variety classification in uncertainty conditions of retail sales. *Appl. Sci.* **2019**, *9*, 3971. [CrossRef]
4. Chakraborty, A.; Kumer, D.; Deeba, K. Plant leaf disease recognition using fastai image classification. In Proceedings of the 5th International Conference on Computing Methodologies and Communication (ICCMC), Erode, India, 8–10 April 2021; pp. 1624–1630. [CrossRef]
5. Siddiqi, R. Effectiveness of transfer learning and fine tuning in automated fruit image classification. In Proceedings of the 3rd International Conference on Deep Learning Technologies, Xiamen, China, 5–7 July 2019; pp. 91–100. [CrossRef]
6. Franczyk, B.; Hernes, M.; Kozierkiewicz, A.; Kozina, A.; Pietranik, M.; Roemer, I.; Schieck, M. Deep learning for grape variety recognition. *Procedia Comput. Sci.* **2020**, *176*, 1211–1220. [CrossRef]
7. Hussain, I.; Tan, S.; Hussain, W.; Ali, A. CNN Transfer learning for automatic fruit recognition for future class of fruit. *IJC.* **2020**, *39*, 88–96.
8. Kader, A.; Sharif, S.; Bhowmick, P.; Mim, F.H.; Srizon, A.Y. Effective workflow for high-performance recognition of fruits using machine learning approaches. *Int. Res. J. Eng. Technol.* **2020**, *7*, 1–5.
9. Dandekar, M.; Punn, N.S.; Sonbhadra, S.K.; Agarwal, S.; Kiran, R.U. Fruit classification using deep feature maps in the presence of deceptive similar classes. In Proceedings of the International Joint Conference on Neural Networks (IJCNN), Shenzhen, China, 18–22 July 2021; pp. 1–6.
10. Biswas, B.; Ghosh, S.K.; Ghosh, A. A robust multi-label fruit classification based on deep convolution neural network. In *Computational Intelligence in Pattern Recognition. Advances in Intelligent Systems and Computing*; Das, A., Nayak, J., Naik, B., Pati, S., Pelusi, D., Eds.; Springer: Singapore, 2020; Volume 999. [CrossRef]
11. Dey, S.; Saha, S.; Singh, A.; McDonald-Maier, K. FruitVegCNN: Power- and memory-efficient classification of fruits & vegetables using cnn in mobile MPSoC. In Proceedings of the IEEE 17th India Council International Conference (INDICON), New Delhi, India, 11–13 December 2020; pp. 1–7. [CrossRef]

12. Hossain, M.S.; Al-Hammadi, M.; Muhammad, G. Automatic fruit classification using deep learning for industrial applications. *IEEE Trans. Ind. Inform.* **2019**, *15*, 1027–1034. [CrossRef]
13. Siddiqi, R. Comparative performance of various deep learning-based models in fruit image classification. In Proceedings of the 11th International Conference on Advances in Information Technology, Bangkok, Thailand, 1–3 July 2020; Volume 14, pp. 1–9. [CrossRef]
14. Srivastava, S.; Singh, T.; Sharma, S.; Verma, A. A fruit recognition system based on modern deep learning technique. *Int. J. Eng. Res. Technol.* **2020**, *9*, 896–898. [CrossRef]
15. Ashwinkumar, S.; Rajagopal, S.; Manimaran, V.; Jegajothi, B. Automated plant leaf disease detection and classification using optimal MobileNet based convolutional neural networks. *Mater. Today Proc.* **2022**, *51*, 480–487. [CrossRef]
16. Muhathir, M.; Santoso, M.H.; Muliono, R. Analysis naïve bayes in classifying fruit by utilizing HOG feature extraction. *J. Inform. Telecommun. Eng.* **2020**, *4*, 1–10. [CrossRef]
17. Ghosh, S.; Mondal, M.J.; Sen, S.; Chatterjee, S.; Kar Roy, N.; Patnaik, S. A novel approach to detect and classify fruits using ShuffleNet V2. In Proceedings of the IEEE Applied Signal Processing Conference, Kolkata, India, 7–9 October 2020; pp. 163–167. [CrossRef]
18. Shahi, T.B.; Sitaula, C.; Neupane, A.; Guo, W. Fruit classification using attention-based MobileNetV2 for industrial applications. *PLoS ONE* **2022**, *17*, 1–21. [CrossRef] [PubMed]
19. Chompookham, T.; Surinta, O. Ensemble methods with deep convolutional neural networks for plant leaf recognition. *ICIC Express Lett.* **2021**, *15*, 553–565.
20. Wang, D.; Wang, J.; Li, W.; Guan, P. T-CNN: Trilinear convolutional neural networks model for visual detection of plant diseases. *Comput. Electron. Agric.* **2021**, *190*, 106468. [CrossRef]
21. Rhamadiyanti, D.T.; Suyanto, S. Robustness of convolutional neural network in classifying apple images. In Proceedings of the International Seminar on Intelligent Technology and Its Applications (ISITIA), Virtual Conference, 21–22 July 2021; pp. 226–231. [CrossRef]
22. Anasta, N.; Setyawan, F.X.A.; Fitriawan, H. Disease detection in banana trees using an image processing-based thermal camera. *IOP Conf. Ser. Earth Environ. Sci.* **2021**, *739*, 012088. [CrossRef]
23. Zhu, W.; Chen, H.; Ciechanowska, I.; Spaner, D. Application of infrared thermal imaging for the rapid diagnosis of crop disease. *IFAC-PapersOnLine* **2018**, *51*, 424–430. [CrossRef]
24. Lydia, M.S.; Aulia, I.; Jaya, I.; Hanafiah, D.S.; Lubis, R.H. Preliminary study for identifying rice plant disease based on thermal images. Journal of Physics: Conference Series, Volume 1566. In Proceedings of the 4th International Conference on Computing and Applied Informatics 2019 (ICCAI 2019), Medan, Indonesia, 26–27 November 2019.
25. Raza, S.-E.-A.; Prince, G.; Clarkson, J.P.; Rajpoot, N.M. Automatic Detection of Diseased Tomato Plants Using Thermal and Stereo Visible Light Images. *PLoS ONE* **2015**, *10*, e0123262. [CrossRef]
26. Simonyan, K.; Zisserman, A. Very deep convolutional networks for large-scale image recognition. *arXiv* **2015**, arXiv:1409.1556v6.
27. He, K.; Zhang, X.; Ren, S.; Sun, J. Deep residual learning for image recognition. In Proceedings of the IEEE Conference on Computer Vision and Pattern Recognition, Las Vegas, NV, USA, 27–30 June 2016; pp. 770–778. [CrossRef]
28. PlantCR & TherVisDb. Available online: https://github.com/ganav/PlantCR-TherVisDb/tree/main (accessed on 28 September 2022).
29. Redmon, J.; Farhadi, A. Yolo V3: An incremental improvement. *arXiv* **2018**, arXiv:1804.02767.
30. Szegedy, C.; Vanhoucke, V.; Ioffe, S.; Shlens, J.; Wojna, Z. Rethinking the inception architecture for computer vision. *arXiv* **2015**, arXiv:1512.00567.
31. Santos, T.; Leonardo, D.S.; Andreza, D.S.; Sandra, A. Embrapa wine grape instance segmentation dataset—Embrapa WGISD (1.0.0) [Data set]. *Zenodo* **2019**. Available online: https://zenodo.org/record/3361736#.YwgsOnZByUk (accessed on 16 September 2022). [CrossRef]
32. FIDS30 Database. Available online: https://www.kaggle.com/datasets/arnavmehta710a/fids30 (accessed on 16 September 2022).
33. PlantVillage Dataset. Available online: https://www.kaggle.com/datasets/emmarex/plantdisease (accessed on 16 September 2022).
34. Singh, D.; Jain, N.; Jain, P.; Kayal, P.; Kumawat, S.; Batra, N. PlantDoc: A dataset for visual plant disease detection. In Proceedings of the 7th ACM IKDD CoDS and 25th COMAD, Hyderabad, India, 5–7 January 2020; pp. 249–253. [CrossRef]
35. Analysis of Variance. Available online: https://en.wikipedia.org/wiki/Analysis_of_variance (accessed on 16 September 2022).
36. Tong, S.; Koller, D. Support vector machine active learning with applications to text classification. *J. Mach. Learn. Res.* **2002**, *2*, 45–66. [CrossRef]
37. Logitech C270 HD Web-Camera. Available online: https://www.logitech.com/en-us/products/webcams/c270-hd-webcam.960-000694.html (accessed on 6 September 2022).
38. NVIDIA GeForce GTX TITAN X. Available online: https://www.nvidia.com/en-us/geforce/products/10series/titan-x-pascal/ (accessed on 16 September 2022).
39. OpenCV, Intel, California, U.S. Available online: http://opencv.org/ (accessed on 16 September 2022).
40. Python, Python Software Foundation, Delaware, U.S. Available online: https://www.python.org/ (accessed on 16 September 2022).
41. Keras, Chollet, F., California, U.S. Available online: https://keras.io/ (accessed on 16 September 2022).
42. Kingma, D.P.; Ba, J.B. ADAM: A method for stochastic optimization. In Proceedings of the 3rd International Conference on Learning Representations, San Diego, CA, USA, 7–9 May 2015; pp. 1–15.

43. Categorical Cross-Entropy Loss. Available online: https://peltarion.com/knowledge-center/documentation/modeling-view/build-an-ai-model/loss-functions/categorical-crossentropy (accessed on 16 September 2022).
44. Derczynski, L. Complementarity, F-score, and NLP evaluation. In Proceedings of the Tenth International Conference on Language Resources and Evaluation 2016, Portorož, Slovenia, 23–28 May 2016; pp. 261–266. Available online: https://aclanthology.org/L16-1040 (accessed on 28 September 2022).
45. Powers, D.M.W. Evaluation: From precision, recall and f-measure to roc, informedness, markedness & correlation. *Mach. Learn. Technol.* **2011**, *2*, 37–63.
46. BOLIVIA Plant for Processing Medicinal and Aromatic Herbs, Chizchipani, Caranavi. Available online: https://www.alamy.com/stock-photo-bolivia-plant-for-processing-medicinal-and-aromatic-herbs-chizchipani-31914323.html (accessed on 25 October 2022).
47. Processing Lines for Medicinal Herbs and Plants. Available online: https://www.godioliebellanti.com/medical-herbs-and-plants/?lang=en (accessed on 25 October 2022).
48. Wild Plants for a Free Meal. Available online: https://morningchores.com/edible-wild-plants/ (accessed on 25 October 2022).
49. Medicinal Plants. Available online: https://www.plantscience4u.com/2018/08/10-medicinal-plants-and-their-uses-with.html (accessed on 25 October 2022).
50. Castellano, G.; Castiello, C.; Cianciotta, M.; Mencar, C.; Vessio, G. Multi-View Convolutional Network for Crowd Counting in Drone-Captured Images. In *Computer Vision—ECCV 2020 Workshops. ECCV 2020*; Lecture Notes in Computer Science; Bartoli, A., Fusiello, A., Eds.; Springer: Cham, Switzerland, 2020; Volume 12538. [CrossRef]

mathematics MDPI

Article

Learning Adaptive Spatial Regularization and Temporal-Aware Correlation Filters for Visual Object Tracking

Liqiang Liu [1,*,†], Tiantian Feng [2,†], Yanfang Fu [1,*], Chao Shen [1], Zhijuan Hu [1], Maoyuan Qin [1], Xiaojun Bai [1] and Shifeng Zhao [1]

1 School of Computer Science and Engineering, Xi'an Technological University, Xi'an 710021, China
2 School of Physics and Optoelectronic Engineering, Xidian University, Xi'an 710071, China
* Correspondence: liuliqiang@xatu.edu.cn (L.L.); fuyanfang@xatu.edu.cn (Y.F.)
† These authors contributed equally to this work.

Abstract: Recently, discriminative correlation filters (DCF) based trackers have gained much attention and obtained remarkable achievements for their high efficiency and outstanding performance. However, undesirable boundary effects occur when the DCF-based trackers suffer from challenging situations, such as occlusion, background clutters, fast motion, and so on. To address these problems, this work proposes a novel adaptive spatial regularization and temporal-aware correlation filters (ASTCF) model to deal with the boundary effects which occur in the correlation filters tracking. Firstly, our ASTCF model learns a more robust correlation filter template by introducing spatial regularization and temporal-aware components into the objective function. The adaptive spatial regularization provides a more robust appearance model to handle the large appearance changes at different times; meanwhile, the temporal-aware constraint can enhance the time continuity and consistency of this model. They make correlation filters model more discriminating, and also reduce the influence of the boundary effects during the tracking process. Secondly, the objective function can be transformed into three sub-problems with closed-form solutions and effectively solved via the alternating direction method of multipliers (ADMM). Finally, we compare our tracker with some representative methods and evaluate using three different benchmarks, including OTB2015, VOT2018 and LaSOT datasets, where the experimental results demonstrate the superiority of our tracker on most of the performance criteria compared with the existing trackers.

Keywords: spatial regularization; temporal-aware; correlation filter tracking; alternating direction method of multipliers; boundary effect

MSC: 68U10

1. Introduction

Visual tracking [1–5] plays a very important role in machine vision field and has been applied in many realistic scenes, including robots, traffic surveillance, self-driving cars, criminal investigation, and so on. It aims to predict the position and size of a tracked object with a bounding box in each frame, by employing a tracking method, where the position and size information is given in the first frame of each sequence. Although many advanced tracking methods [6–8] have been proposed in recent years due to the rapid development of computer sciences, many methods still have their weakness, including accuracy and robustness, speed and practicability in some specific scenes. Therefore, there are also lots of challenges urgently needing to be address.

Due to a high speed and a good performance, the DCF-based tracking method [9–12] has gained lots of attention, and various algorithms have been proposed in recent years. Traditional correlation filters (CF) based methods perform well both on accuracy and speed because of the usage of a circular shift operation. Thus, the training samples can be obtained using a circulant matrix and correlation filters can be optimized and solved in frequency domain by the fast Fourier transform (FFT). The CF-based tracking methods can be efficiently divided into background and object regions by learning a strong and discriminative classifier, and as a result a better performance can be achieved. The MOSSE algorithm [9] first proposed the correlation filters-based tacking method by introducing the correlation filter theory in the tracking field. It performed well, while the speed nearly reached 600 frames per second (fps). Then the kernel correlation filter (KCF) tracker [11] introduced a novel CF framework with kernel function, and also used multi-channel features including Histogram of Oriented Gradient (HOG) and gray features to build a robustness CF model. The KCF tracker can handle many challenging tracking problems, such as occlusion, color change, motion blur and so on

Standard DCF-based tracking methods have a high efficiency and a good performance [11,12]. Although the circular shifting operation can obtain the kernel CF-based training samples, it also generates many unreal samples, which leads to undesirable boundary effects [13]. The limitation of the introduced boundary effects on the standard DCF model is mainly reflected in two aspects. On the one hand, the discriminative ability of the learned model is weakened by the unreal training samples. On the other hand, the calculation of detection scores ignores the non-center of the region, which is heavily influenced by periodic repetitions of the detection sample [14]. In order to address the above mentioned boundary effect, which occurs in CF-based trackers, many excellent trackers have been proposed in recent years. Although these trackers have made good achievements both with tracking performances and tracking speed [15–21], there are still lots of challenges for the CF-based tracking field.

In this work, we propose a novel CF-based tracking method with adaptive spatial regularization and temporal-aware (ASTCF) terms. On the one hand, the introduced adaptive spatial regularization term is integrated with the formulation of multiple training samples for the purpose of coupling of DCF learning and model updating. This operation benefits the tracking accuracy and robustness, and also can be adapted to the appearance changes for different objects at different times. Meanwhile, in order to enhance the time continuity and consistency of this model, the temporal-aware component is introduced in the objective function to penalize a large variation in the correlation filters between two successive frames. The temporal-aware regularization can effectively prevent large changes in the correlation filters and keep the interframe variation smoother, thus making the learned appearance model more robust. On the other hand, unlike the high complexity produced by SRDCF because of the formulation of multiple training images, our ASTCF model can be effectively optimized with the ADMM algorithm. The related objective function can be transformed into three subproblems with analytical closed-form solutions. Figure 1 illustrates the tracking results of the ASTCF and the BACF on two video sequences with motion blur and deformation. Compared with the BACF [16], we can see that our ASTCF performs better to adapt the large appearance changes by introducing the spatial regularization and temporal-aware terms in the objective function. Finally, we have evaluated our method using two classical tracking benchmarks and a recent long-term tracking dataset, which are OTB2015 [22], VOT2018 [23] and LaSOT [24], respectively. These experimental results show the superior accuracy and real-time performance of our model compared with the advanced trackers. Moreover, the further ablation study also indicates the importance of the introduced adaptive spatial regularization and temporal-aware terms in the objective function.

The summary of our contribution in this work is as follows:

- We have proposed the ASTCF model by introducing adaptive spatial regularization and temporal-aware terms into the DCF framework. The adaptive spatial regularization can provide a more robust appearance model to handle large appearance changes at different times, while the temporal-aware constraint can enhance the time continuity and consistency of this model.

- In order to solve ASTCF efficiently, we have optimized it with the ADMM algorithm, where the related objective function can be transformed into three subproblems with analytical closed-form solutions. Moreover, our method can converge within a few iterations.
- Our ASTCF tracker has performed comparative experiments on both short-term tracking and long-term tracking datasets, including OTB2015, VOT2018 and LaSOT test dataset. These experiments indicate that our tracker achieves a very impressive performance and a real-time tracking speed in comparison with the state-of-the-art trackers.

Figure 1. The tracking results of ASTCF and BACF on two video sequences with motion blur and deformation.

2. Related Works

Many competing DCF-based tracking algorithms have been proposed in recent years. The traditional DCF-based trackers have been a great achievement and have addressed many tracking problems. Following the MOSSE [9] and the KCF [11] trackers, Danelljan et al. proposed the DSST tracker [15], which mainly deals with size change by employing a translation filter and multiscale filters to accurately predict position and size information, respectively. Bertinetto et al. proposed the Staple tracker [25] by using HOG and a color histogram to establish a robust appearance model to adapt to changes in target appearance. Subsequently, inspired by the Staple tracker, the CACF [26] tracker further proposed a framework structure based on context information, which makes full use of background information to establish samples and improve the discrimination of samples; this framework is universal. Furthermore, some long-term trackers have been proposed to address the tracking problems of long-term sequences [27–29]. For example, the LCT method [27] proposes a classifier based on an online random fern which is connected to the correlation filter tracker as a re-detector, and the response score is used to judge whether the target is lost or not. Moreover, Liu et al. [12] proposed a long-term tracker by learning multi-featured CF for tracking and a saliency detector to reposition the target.

To deal with the boundary effect of the CF-based tracker, many excellent methods have been proposed. For example, the SRDCF tracker [14] addresses the boundary effect problem by introducing a spatially regularized term in the objective function based on the standard DCF model that enables the correlation filters to be learned on larger image regions, leading to a more discriminative appearance model. However, the main drawback of the SRDCF tracker is that it involves a lot of computation. Because the spatial regularization term cannot make good use of the circular matrix of the traditional CF, a large number of linear equations and the Gauss-Seidel method are used, which are very time-consuming to solve. Therefore, its large computation cannot meet the real-time requirements. The BACF tracker [16] uses real background patches and target patches to learn the tracker, and uses an online adaptation strategy to update the tracker model according to the new appearance of the target and background. It perfectly solves the problem, which is that the CF tracker lacks real negative training samples and boundary effects, and the speed meets the real-time requirement. Recently, the ASRCF tracker [17] has introduced adaptive spatial regularization into the objective function, and has optimized the objective function through the ADMM algorithm [30], and it has finally obtained the reliable filtering coefficient. By introducing temporal regularization into the single-sample SRDCF method, a spatio-temporal regularized correlation filter (STRCF) [20] method is proposed, which can obtain multiple training samples and also help to establish a more robust target tracking appearance model. The AutoTrack tracking method [21] involves an automatic spatiotemporal regularization framework for high-performance Unmanned Aerial Vehicle (UAV) tracking, where local responses and global variations are used to constrain and control the learning of relevant filters, reaching a speed of 60fps on the CPU. With the advancement of convolutional neural networks (CNN) [31,32], many trackers use deep features from the deep network which have a strong discriminative ability to recognize objects. These methods increase the computational cost and decrease the tracking speed at the same time. Some deep trackers have also combined the correlation filter and the deep network to obtain a good balance between speed and performance, like the DeepSRDCF [33], the CFNet [34], the RPCF [35] and the DeepSTRCF [20].

3. The Proposed Method

In this section, we will introduce the proposed ASTCF method. The aim of ASTCF is to improve the robustness of the appearance model for visual tracking. We will first introduce the overall framework, then show how to construct and solve the adaptive spatial regularization and temporal-aware model.

3.1. Overall Framework

The framework of our ASTCF tracking method is shown in Figure 2, where the Coke sequence is taken as an example. Firstly, due to the position and scale of the tracked object shown in the first frame, we extract the features of the region of interest (ROI) to obtain the initial correlation filter template. The extracted features include shallow HOG features and deep CNN features, whose combination can effectively build a more robust appearance model. Secondly, we transform the objective function based on the adaptive regularization and temporal-aware terms into the frequency domain and solve the relevant sub-problems efficiently by using the ADMM algorithm. Therefore, we can obtain a more robust correlation filter. Thirdly, when the next frame comes, we extract the features of ROI in different scales and perform the correlation operation between the previous correlation filter template and the search region. Then we obtain the correlation response in the temporal domain via the inverse Fourier transform. So, the maximum value of the correlation response is defined as the object's position in the frame. Moreover, the object scale of the current frame can be estimated through a scale estimation model. Lastly, the filter template of the current frame is updated by employing the filter template of the previous frame and the object's position in the current frame.

For ASTCF, the model learns a spatial regularization whose value always varies adaptively for different objects at different times. As shown in Frame n of the Coke sequence in Figure 2, the spatial regularization can suppress the interference of occlusions and provide a greater penalty at related pixels during the tracking process. Moreover, the correlation responses reflected in our model still maintain their peaks of responses despite the target suffering from various interferences.

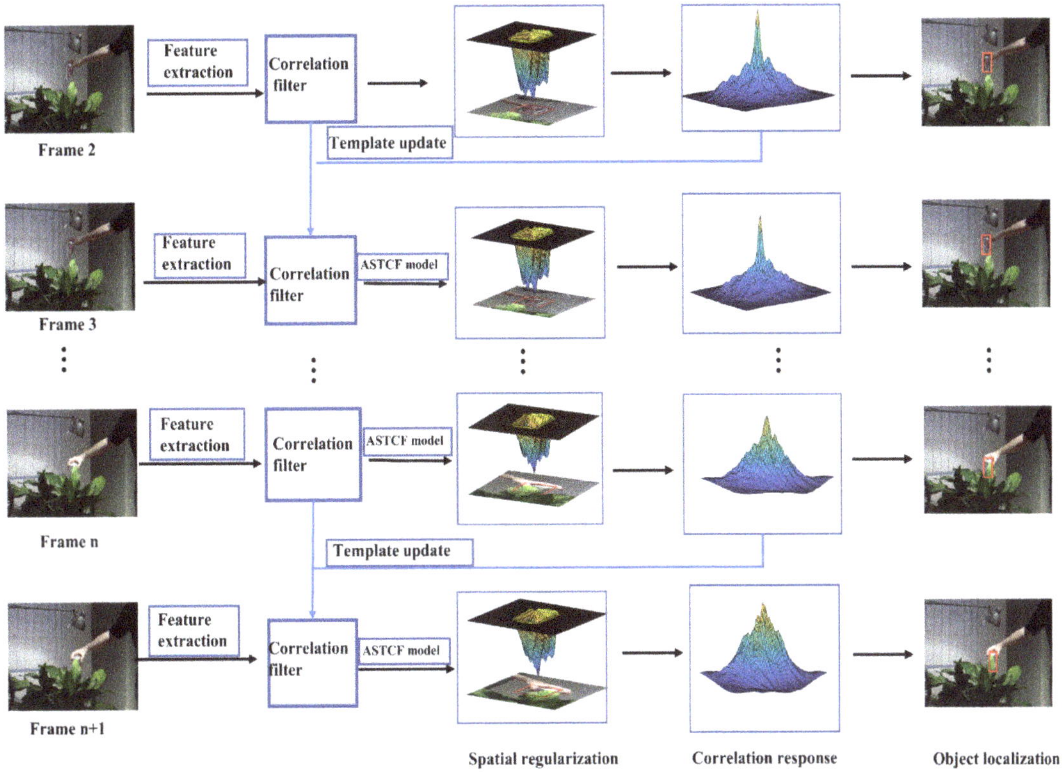

Figure 2. The framework of adaptive spatial regularization and temporal-aware. Red bounding-boxes donate the final results.

3.2. Adaptive Spatial Regularization and Temporal-Aware Model

3.2.1. Revisit the Objective Function of BACF Method

The BACF method [16] proposed a background-aware and multi-channels correlation filters based on standard DCF. The related objective function of BACF is as follows:

$$E(\boldsymbol{h}) = \frac{1}{2}\sum_{j=1}^{T}\left\| \sum_{k=1}^{K} \boldsymbol{h}_k{}^{\mathrm{T}} \boldsymbol{P} x_k[\Delta\tau_j] - y(\mathrm{j}) \right\|_2^2 + \frac{\lambda}{2}\sum_{k=1}^{K} \|\boldsymbol{h}_k\|_2^2 \tag{1}$$

where $[\Delta\tau_j]$ is the operation of cyclic shift, $x_k[\Delta\tau_j]$ donates the discrete cyclic shift of step j is operated on the features x_k of channel k. $\boldsymbol{P}$ is a binary mask matrix donates clips a $T \times D$ matrix from the object feature x_k, and $T >> D$, where T is the length of x. $x_k \in \mathbb{R}^T$ denotes the k-th channel of the vectorized image. $y \in \mathbb{R}^T$ is the desired response, which generally uses a Gaussian-shaped ground truth generally, and $\boldsymbol{h} \in \mathbb{R}^D$ denotes the k-th channel of the vectorized filter. The symbol ^{T} is the conjugate transpose.

The BACF method obtains positive and negative samples by using a binary mask matrix to search samples and by utilizing dense sampling, resulting in the reduction of the influence of boundary effect which is caused by cyclic shift.

3.2.2. Adaptive Spatial Regularization and Temporal-Aware Objective Function

To address the impact of tracking performance on unnecessary boundary effects, we have introduced spatial regularization and temporal-aware terms into the objective function. Firstly, inspired by the ASRCF [17] and BACF [16] methods, the adaptive spatial regularization term is introduced into the objective function for simulation to realize the learning and model update of DCF. The adaptive spatial regularization term is helpful to construct a more robust appearance description and a reliable correlation filter coefficient. Secondly, in order to enhance the temporal continuity and consistency of the model, we also introduce a temporal-aware term in the objective function to compensate for the large variation of the correlation filter between two consecutive frames. In this work, we take $\left\|\mathbf{P}^{\mathrm{T}}\mathbf{h}_k - \mathbf{P}^{\mathrm{T}}\mathbf{h}_k^{v-1}\right\|_2^2$ as the temporal-aware term, where $\mathbf{h}_k^{v-1}$ denotes the learned filter of the previous frame. Thus, our objective function can be formulated as follows:

$$E(\mathbf{h},\mathbf{w}) = \frac{1}{2}\sum_{j=1}^{T}\left\|\sum_{k=1}^{K}(\mathbf{P}^{\mathrm{T}}\mathbf{h}_k)*\mathbf{x}_k[\Delta\tau_j] - \mathbf{y}(\mathrm{j})\right\|_2^2 + \frac{\lambda_1}{2}\sum_{k=1}^{K}\|\mathbf{w}\odot\mathbf{h}_k\|_2^2 + \frac{\lambda_2}{2}\|\mathbf{w}-\mathbf{w}^r\|_2^2 + \frac{\beta}{2}\left\|\mathbf{P}^{\mathrm{T}}\mathbf{h}_k - \mathbf{P}^{\mathrm{T}}\mathbf{h}_k^{v-1}\right\|_2^2 \quad (2)$$

where $\mathbf{x}_k \in \mathbb{R}^T$ denotes the k-th channel of the vectorized image, $\mathbf{h} \in \mathbb{R}^D$ denotes the k-th channel of the vectorized filter, and $\mathbf{P} \in \mathbb{R}^{T\times T}$ donates a diagonal binary matrix. K is the total number of channels, $[\Delta\tau_j]$ is the operation of the cyclic shift, $\mathbf{x}_k[\Delta\tau_j]$ donates the discrete cyclic shift of step j is operated on the features $\mathbf{x}_k$ of channel k. The vector $\mathbf{y} \in \mathbb{R}^{D\times 1}$ is the desired response, which generally uses a Gaussian-shaped ground truth. The symbol $*$ denotes the spatial correlation operator. Unlike the $\mathbf{P}$ matrix making the correlation operator to apply on the true foreground and background samples in the BACF method, in this paper it is applied directly to the filter template, and then the correlation operators are evaluated on the object features. λ_1 and λ_2 are the spatial regularization parameters of the second and third terms, respectively. The $\|\mathbf{w}-\mathbf{w}^r\|_2^2$ term attempts to make the adaptive spatial weight $\mathbf{w}$ similar to a reference weight $\mathbf{w}^r$. It introduces a priori information in spatial weight $\mathbf{w}$ and effectively avoids the model degradation. β is the temporal-aware regularization parameter, and symbol ^{T} is the operation of conjugate transpose.

3.2.3. Optimization of Objective Function

The objective function in Equation (4) is convex, and it can be minimized to obtain the optimal solution. Inspired by the existing correlation filters tracking methods, the correlation filters can be learned efficiently in the frequency domain. Thus, we have converted the objective function into the frequency domain by using the Parseval's theorem, and also introduce an auxiliary variable $\hat{\mathbf{g}}$ for solutions. The formulation of the constrained optimization in the frequency domain can be expressed as follows:

$$\begin{aligned} &E(\mathbf{h},\hat{\mathbf{g}},\mathbf{w}) = \tfrac{1}{2T}\|\hat{\mathbf{X}}\hat{\mathbf{g}} - \hat{\mathbf{y}}\|_2^2 + \tfrac{\lambda_1}{2}\|\mathbf{w}\odot\mathbf{h}\|_2^2 + \tfrac{\lambda_2}{2}\|\mathbf{w}-\mathbf{w}^r\|_2^2 + \tfrac{\beta}{2}\|\hat{\mathbf{g}} - \hat{\mathbf{g}}_{v-1}\|_2^2 \\ &s.t.\ \hat{\mathbf{g}} = \sqrt{T}\mathbf{F}\mathbf{P}^{\mathrm{T}}\mathbf{h} \end{aligned} \quad (3)$$

where $\hat{\mathbf{X}} = \left[diag(\hat{x_1})^{\mathrm{T}},\ldots,diag(\hat{x_K})^{\mathrm{T}}\right] \in \mathbb{R}^{T\times KT}$, $\mathbf{h} = \left[\mathbf{h}_1^{\mathrm{T}},\ldots,\mathbf{h}_K^{\mathrm{T}}\right]^{\mathrm{T}} \in \mathbb{R}^{KT\times 1}$ donates a cascade of correlation filters vectorization with K channels, and $\hat{\mathbf{g}} = \left[\hat{\mathbf{g}}_1^{\mathrm{T}},\ldots,\hat{\mathbf{g}}_K^{\mathrm{T}}\right]^{\mathrm{T}} \in \mathbb{R}^{KT\times 1}$. The symbol ^ indicates the discrete Fourier transform of signal, $\mathbf{F}$ is the orthonormal $T\times T$ matrix of complex basis vectors to map any T dimensional vectorized signal into the Fourier domain, for example, $\hat{\mathbf{a}} = \sqrt{T}\mathbf{F}\mathbf{a}$. $\hat{\mathbf{g}}_{v-1} = \sqrt{T}\mathbf{F}\mathbf{P}^{\mathrm{T}}\mathbf{h}_{v-1}$ is an auxiliary variable, where $\mathbf{h}_{v-1}$ similar to $\mathbf{h}$.

It can be observed that the model in Equation (5) is convex, thus it could be solved iteratively to obtain the optimal solution via the ADMM algorithm. Therefore, we first use the Augmented Lagrangian Method (ALM) to optimize Equation (5), for which the Lagrangian function can be formulated as follows:

$$\begin{aligned} L(\mathbf{h},\hat{\mathbf{g}},\hat{\xi},\mathbf{w}) &= \tfrac{1}{2T}\|\hat{\mathbf{X}}\hat{\mathbf{g}} - \hat{\mathbf{y}}\|_2^2 + \tfrac{\lambda_1}{2}\|\mathbf{w}\odot\mathbf{h}\|_2^2 + \tfrac{\lambda_2}{2}\|\mathbf{w}-\mathbf{w}^r\|_2^2 + \tfrac{\beta}{2}\|\hat{\mathbf{g}} - \hat{\mathbf{g}}_{v-1}\|_2^2 \\ &+ \hat{\xi}^{\mathrm{T}}(\hat{\mathbf{g}} - \sqrt{T}\mathbf{F}\mathbf{P}^{\mathrm{T}}\mathbf{h}) + \tfrac{\mu}{2}\left\|\hat{\mathbf{g}} - \sqrt{T}\mathbf{F}\mathbf{P}^{\mathrm{T}}\mathbf{h}\right\|_2^2 \end{aligned} \quad (4)$$

where $\hat{\xi} = \left[\hat{\xi}_1^{\mathrm{T}}, \ldots, \hat{\xi}_K^{\mathrm{T}}\right]^{\mathrm{T}}$ is set of the Lagrange multipliers, and μ is a penalty factor. Then, the ADMM algorithm can be used for solving the subproblems $\hat{g}$, h, w and update $\hat{\xi}$.

- Subproblem h

If variables $\hat{g}$, w and $\hat{\xi}$ are fixed in Equation (5), we can get the closed-form solution for variable h. Thus, h can be computed as:

$$h = \underset{h}{\operatorname{argmin}}\left\{\frac{\lambda_1}{2}\|w \odot h\|_2^2 + \hat{\xi}^{\mathrm{T}}(\hat{g} - \sqrt{T}FP^{\mathrm{T}}h) + \frac{\mu}{2}\left\|\hat{g} - \sqrt{T}FP^{\mathrm{T}}h\right\|_2^2\right\} \tag{5}$$

Equation (5) also can be reformulated as follows:

$$C(h) = \frac{\lambda_1}{2}\|w \odot h\|_2^2 + \hat{\xi}^{\mathrm{T}}(\hat{g} - \sqrt{T}FP^{\mathrm{T}}h) + \frac{\mu}{2}\left\|\hat{g} - \sqrt{T}FP^{\mathrm{T}}h\right\|_2^2 \tag{6}$$

where $W = diag(w) \in \mathbb{R}^{T \times T}$ and $w \odot h = Wh$. Next, take the partial derivation of $C(h)$ and we can get the solution of h as:

$$\begin{aligned} h &= (\lambda_1 W^{\mathrm{T}}W + \mu\, T\, PP^{\mathrm{T}})^{-1}TP(\xi + \mu g) \\ &= \tfrac{Tp \odot (\xi + \mu g)}{\lambda_1 (w \odot w) + \mu T\ \ p} \end{aligned} \tag{7}$$

where $p = [P_{11}, P_{22}, \ldots, P_{TT}]$ denotes the row vectors with the binary matrix P, and $PP^{\mathrm{T}} = P$. By using an inverse transform, we can estimate the related spatial values of each element in variables $\hat{g}$ and $\hat{\xi}$, and then connected them to obtain variables g and ξ.

- Subproblem $\hat{g}$

Following the solution of subproblem h, fixing variables h, w and $\hat{\xi}$, we can get the closed-form solution for variable $\hat{g}$. The minimization of $\hat{g}$ can be formulated as follows:

$$\hat{g} = \underset{\hat{g}}{\operatorname{argmin}}\left\{\frac{1}{2T}\|\hat{X}\hat{g} - \hat{y}\|_2^2 + \frac{\beta}{2}\|\hat{g} - \hat{g}_{v-1}\|_2^2, + \hat{\xi}^{\mathrm{T}}(\hat{g} - \sqrt{T}FP^{\mathrm{T}}h) + \frac{\mu}{2}\left\|\hat{g} - \sqrt{T}FP^{\mathrm{T}}h\right\|_2^2\right\} \tag{8}$$

We can find that each element of $\hat{y}$ depends only on the K values of $\hat{x}$ and $\hat{g}$. Let $\hat{y}$ written as $\hat{y}(t)$, and $\hat{x}(t) = [\hat{x}_1(t), \ldots, \hat{x}_K(t)]^{\mathrm{T}}$, and $\hat{g}(t) = [\hat{g}_1(t), \ldots, \hat{g}_K(t)]^{\mathrm{T}}$. Thus, the solution of Equation (13) can be decomposed into T linear subsystems of size $K \times K$. Each independent objective function can be formulated as:

$$\hat{g}(t) = \underset{\hat{g}(t)}{\operatorname{argmin}}\left\{\frac{1}{2T}\left\|\hat{x}(t)^{\mathrm{T}}\hat{g}(t) - \hat{y}(t)\right\|_2^2 + \frac{\beta}{2}\|\hat{g}(t) - \hat{g}_{v-1}(t)\|_2^2 + \hat{\xi}^{\mathrm{T}}(t)(\hat{g}(t) - \hat{h}(t)) + \frac{\mu}{2}\|\hat{g}(t) - \hat{h}(t)\|_2^2\right\} \tag{9}$$

where $\hat{h}(t) = [\hat{h}_1(t), \ldots, \hat{h}_K(t)]^{\mathrm{T}}$, and $\hat{g}_{v-1}(t) = [\hat{g}_{v-1}^1(t), \ldots, \hat{g}_{v-1}^K(t)]^{\mathrm{T}}$.

Next,

$$C(\hat{g}(t)) = \frac{1}{2T}\left\|\hat{x}(t)^{\mathrm{T}}\hat{g}(t) - \hat{y}(t)\right\|_2^2 + \frac{\beta}{2}\|\hat{g}(t) - \hat{g}_{v-1}(t)\|_2^2 + \hat{\xi}^{\mathrm{T}}(t)(\hat{g}(t) - \hat{h}(t)) + \frac{\mu}{2}\|\hat{g}(t) - \hat{h}(t)\|_2^2 \tag{10}$$

Take the partial derivation of $C(\hat{g}(t))$ and let $\frac{\partial C(\hat{g}(t))}{\partial \hat{g}(t)} = 0$, then:

$$\hat{g}(t) = \left(\hat{x}(t)\hat{x}(t)^{\mathrm{T}} + T(\beta + \mu)I_K\right)^{-1}(\hat{x}(t)\hat{y}(t) - T\hat{\xi}(t) + T\mu\hat{h}(t) + T\beta\hat{g}_{v-1}(t)) \tag{11}$$

Following the theory of Sherman-Morrison, $(uv^{\mathrm{T}} + A) = A^{-1} - \frac{A^{-1}uv^{\mathrm{T}}A^{-1}}{1 + v^{\mathrm{T}}A^{-1}u}$. Putting $A = T(\beta + \mu)I_K$ and $u = v = \hat{x}(t)$ in Equation (17), the inverse matrix in Equation (17) can be formulated as:

$$\left(\hat{x}(t)\hat{x}(t)^{\mathrm{T}} + T(\beta + \mu)I_K\right)^{-1} = \frac{1}{T(\beta + \mu)}\left(I_K - \frac{\hat{x}(t)\hat{x}(t)^{\mathrm{T}}}{\mathrm{T}(\beta + \mu) + \hat{x}(t)^{\mathrm{T}}\hat{x}(t)}\right) \tag{12}$$

Next, combining Equations (18) and (17), we can get the solution as:

$$\hat{g}(t) = \frac{1}{(\beta+\mu)}\left(\frac{1}{T}\hat{x}(t)\hat{y}(t) - \hat{\xi}(t) + \mu\hat{h}(t) + \beta\hat{g}_{v-1}(t)\right) - \frac{\hat{x}(t)}{(\beta+\mu)b}\left(\frac{1}{T}\hat{S_x}(t)\hat{y}(t) - \hat{S_\xi}(t) + \mu\hat{S_h}(t) + \beta\hat{S}_{g_{v-1}}(t)\right) \quad (13)$$

where $\hat{S_x}(t) = \hat{x}(t)^{\mathrm{T}}\hat{x}(t)$, $\hat{S_\xi}(t) = \hat{x}(t)^{\mathrm{T}}\hat{\xi}(t)$, $\hat{S_h}(t) = \hat{x}(t)^{\mathrm{T}}\hat{h}(t)$, $\hat{S}_{g_{v-1}}(t) = \hat{x}(t)^{\mathrm{T}}\hat{g}_{v-1}(t)$ and invariant $b = \hat{S_x}(t) + T(\beta+\mu)$.

- Subproblem w

If h, $\hat{g}$ and $\hat{\xi}$ are given, we can get the closed-form solution of w, which can be formulated as:

$$w = \underset{w}{\operatorname{argmin}}\left\{\frac{\lambda_1}{2}\|w \odot h\|_2^2 + \frac{\lambda_2}{2}\|w - w^r\|_2^2\right\} \quad (14)$$

Take the partial derivation of Equation (14) as follows:

$$\frac{\partial}{\partial w}\left(\frac{\lambda_1}{2}\|wH\|_2^2 + \frac{\lambda_2}{2}\|w - w^r\|_2^2\right) = \lambda_1 wH + \lambda_2(w - w^r) \quad (15)$$

where $H = diag(h) \in \mathbb{R}^{T\times T}$. Let the partial derivation to be zero. Thus:

$$\begin{aligned} w &= (\lambda_1 H^{\mathrm{T}}H + \lambda_2 I)^{-1}\lambda_2 w^r \\ &= \frac{\lambda_2 w^r}{\lambda_1 h\odot h + \lambda_2 I} \end{aligned} \quad (16)$$

- Lagrange multiplier $\hat{\xi}$

After solving these subproblems, the Lagrange multiplier $\hat{\xi}$ can be updated. The updating formula is as follows:

$$\hat{\xi}^{(i+1)} = \hat{\xi}^{(i)} + \mu(\hat{g}^{(i+1)} - \hat{h}^{(i+1)}) \quad (17)$$

where $\hat{\xi}^{(i+1)}$ and $\hat{h}^{(i+1)}$ denote, respectively, the $(i+1)$th solution of $\hat{g}$ and $\hat{h}$ in the Fourier domain. And the $(i+1)$th regularization constant μ is set as $\mu^{(i+1)} = \min(\mu_{\max}, \delta\mu^{(i)})$, where δ is a size factor, and parameters μ and δ can be referred to the ADMM algorithm.

The ASTCF model is convex and each of its subproblems has a closed-form solution by using the ADMM algorithm. Therefore, this model satisfies the conditions of Eckstein-Bertsekas [36] and can converge to the global optimum. By using the ADMM algorithm, the evaluation of most sequences can be converged within three iterations.

3.2.4. Locate Object Position and Model Update

The object position can be obtained via the correlation response between $\hat{g}$ of the last frame and the feature map of the search region. Thus, the computation of the response map can be expressed as follows:

$$R(x_k) = \mathcal{F}^{-1}\left(\sum_{k=1}^{K}\hat{x}_k \odot \hat{g}_k^{v-1}\right) \quad (18)$$

where K is the number of channels in the feature map, and $\hat{g}_k^{v-1}$ denotes the learned correlation filter from the last frame via the ADMM algorithm in the frequency domain. The maximum response is defined as the position of the tracked object.

Following the ASRCF method [17], we can learn another scale CF to reduce the computation. The scale CF is trained with efficient shallow HOG features. Then, four scales search regions are selected and their related response maps are obtained. While the location-related CF is trained with fusion features with deep CNN features and shallow HOG features. In this work, we have chosen Conv4-3 of the pretrained VGG-16 [37] model on ImageNet [38] as CNN features. The scale CF is learned with 31 dimensions

HOG features, and the location-related CF is learned with 111 dimensions HOG and CNN fusion features.

For the update of the appearance model, we have employed the following formula:

$$\hat{X}_v^{model} = (1-\eta)\hat{X}_{v-1}^{model} + \eta\hat{X}_v \tag{19}$$

where v and $v-1$ denote the vth and $(v-1)$th frames respectively. η donates the learning rate of the appearance model. The specific steps of our ASTCF are shown as Algorithm 1.

Algorithm 1. The proposed ASTCF model

Input: The initial position p_0 and scale size s_0 of the object in the first frame, initialize parameter w.
Output: Estimate object position p_v and scale size s_v in the vth frame, tracking model, and CF template.
repeat:

1. Learn scale correlation filter by using HOG features and learn the location- related correlation filter by using features combined with HOG and CNN.
2. Use Equation (18) to compute response R of object localization CF. Define the maximum response value as the position of the object, and the maximum of the responses in four scale estimation CF is the scale of the object.
3. Update the appearance model by using Equation (19);
4. Compute subproblems $\boldsymbol{h}$ and $\hat{\boldsymbol{g}}$ by using Equations (13) and (7), and update subproblems $\hat{\boldsymbol{g}}$ and w in three iterations.

Until last frame of sequence

4. Experimental Results

We implemented our ASTCF method based on the MATLAB2017a platform with the MatConvNet toolbox, and ran it on a PC machine equipped with an Intel 3.7 GHz, 16 G RAM and a single NVIDIA GTX 1080ti GPU. For parameter setting, the regularization parameters λ_1 and λ_2 are chosen as 0.2 and 0.001, respectively. The initial value of w^r is set as 7. The learning rate of ASTCF is chosen as η = 0.0175, and the temporal-aware constraint parameter is set as β = 15. We use three iterations of the ADMM optimization process, and the penalty factor is set as μ = 1. The penalty factor at iteration $i+1$ is updated as $\mu^{(i+1)} = \min(\mu_{\max}, \delta\mu^{(i)})$, where $\delta = 10$ and $\mu_{\max} = 1000$.

We evaluate our tracker and other advanced trackers on three benchmarks. Our ASTCF method is first evaluated on the classical OTB2015 [22] with 100 sequences and VOT2018 [23] short-term datasets with 60 video sequences, respectively. Then, we evaluated our tracker on the LaSOT [24] long-term dataset with 280 sequences.

4.1. OTB2015 Dataset

As a popular dataset in the tracking field, the OTB2015 [22] dataset has 100 video sequences, which is twice as many as OTB2013 [39]. All sequences use uniform input and output formats, and each image of each sequence comes with an annotated data file to facilitate training and evaluation of the algorithm. For better analyzing the advantages and disadvantages of the tracking algorithm, the OTB dataset was based on Illumination Variation (IV), in-plane Rotation (IPR), scale change, out-of-plane rotation (OPR), Background Clutters (BC), Low Resolution (LR), and out-of-view (OV) attributes to classify sequences. The OTB dataset follows the one-pass evaluation (OPE), which consists of the accuracy plot of the central location error measurement and the success rate plot of the intersection measurement of the union of the predicted target box and the manually annotated data [39]. In addition, we have employed distance precision and overlap success metrics for evaluation among the compared trackers. For this experiment, we compare our tracker with 11 existing advanced trackers, including trackers using hand-crafted features and CNN features, such as SiamRPN++ [40], ECO [41], SRDCF [14], DeepSRDCF [33], MCPF [42], TADT [43], BACF [16], STRCF [20], MDNet [44], SiamFC [45] and VITAL [46].

Figure 3 shows the precision plots and success plots of the 11 compared trackers which are evaluated using the OTB2015 dataset [22], where the legend in the precision plots denote the distance precision (DP) score with the threshold at 20 pixels, and the legend in the success plots donates an area-under-the-curve (AUC) score [12] for each tracker, respectively. It can be seen that the proposed ASTCF tracker achieves the best results both on the DP score and the AUC score, reaching 0.699 and 0.927, respectively. The overall precision shows DP scores improving by 10.3% and 7% compared with those of the baseline BACF [16] and DeepSRDCF [33], respectively. In addition, the gained AUC scores are 7.8% and 6.2%, respectively.

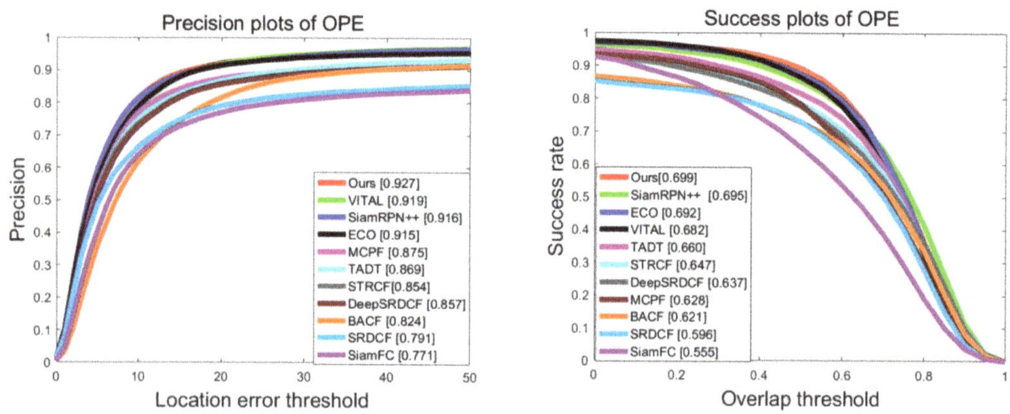

Figure 3. Overall precision plots and success plots of OPE evaluated on OTB2015.

Figure 4 shows the precision plots of the compared trackers with 11 different attributes. It can be seen that the performance of our tracker is pretty good, and ranks high on most attributions. Similarly, Figure 5 shows the overlap success plots of the compared trackers with 11 attributions. It can be seen that our ASTCF tracker has achieved good results on all the attributions, especially the occlusion, out-of-plane rotation and out of view. For example, in the background attribution, our tracker achieves remarkable improvements over the compared trackers, i.e., improves the AUC score by 0.7% and 7.5% compared with VITAL [46] and BACF [16], respectively.

Table 1 reports the overall DP scores, AUC scores, and speed between the five methods and our proposed tracker. It illustrates that the speed of our tracker is approximately 23.5 fps, which satisfies the real-time requirement. Compared with ECO [41] and MDNet [44], which cannot meet the real-time requirement, our proposed ASTCF tracker has an obvious advantage on speed.

Table 1. The comparisons of precision, success rate and speed.

	SRDCF	BACF	STRCF	ECO	MDNet	Ours
DP	0.791	0.824	0.854	0.915	0.910	0.927
AUC	0.596	0.621	0.647	0.692	0.677	0.699
FPS	5.8	26.5	24.8	9.9	1.4	23.5

4.2. VOT2018 Dataset

The VOT datasets publish a visual tracking challenge and hold an ECCV and ICCV workshop every year. They also build a tracking community which provides a precisely defined and repeatable way to compare trackers and they host a common platform to discuss evaluation and progress in the visual tracking field. Now the VOT Challenge has been held since 2013 and has gained more and more attention. Each year, the VOT Challenge is updated with a new dataset based on the previous year. We compare our ASTCF model with eight trackers, including DSTRCF [20], ECO [41], SiamDW [47], UpdateNet [48], DeepSRDCF [33], SRDCF [14], DSST [15] and Staple [25]. We have used some tracking algorithm evaluation indicators given by the official VOT competition, such as accuracy, robustness and Expected Average Overlap (EAO) [49].

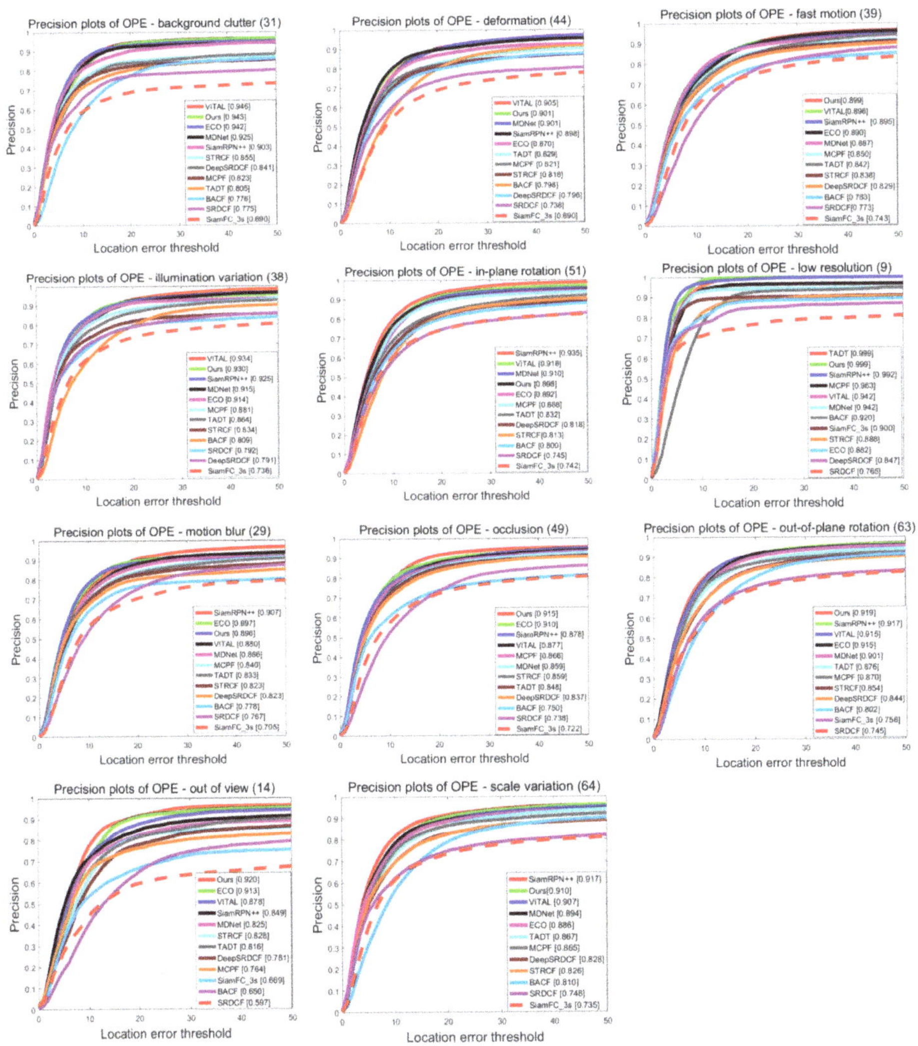

Figure 4. Precision plots of OPE on eleven video sequence attributions of OTB2015 dataset.

Table 2 shows the accuracy results of trackers with VOT dataset showing nine different attributes they are: empty, camera motion, motion change, illumination change, occlusion, size change, weighted mean, mean and pooled. The accuracy is used to evaluate the accuracy of the target tracking algorithm. The higher the value, the higher the accuracy. Table 2 reports that our ASTCF achieves the best result on the accuracy metric compared with other methods, and its attribution score on pooled reaches 0.6098. In addition, Table 3 presents the robustness results which represents the stability of the tracking algorithm when tracking the target in the sequence set, which represents the number of tracking failures. Table 3 shows that the robustness of the ASTCF is better than those of others, except on the attribution of camera motion and pooled. Table 4 shows the metrics of Expected Average Overlap results. The EAO evaluation metric is the average overlapping expected value of each tracker on a short-term image sequence. It can be seen that our ASTCF tracker ranks the first among all the trackers, and its EAO score is 0.3943.

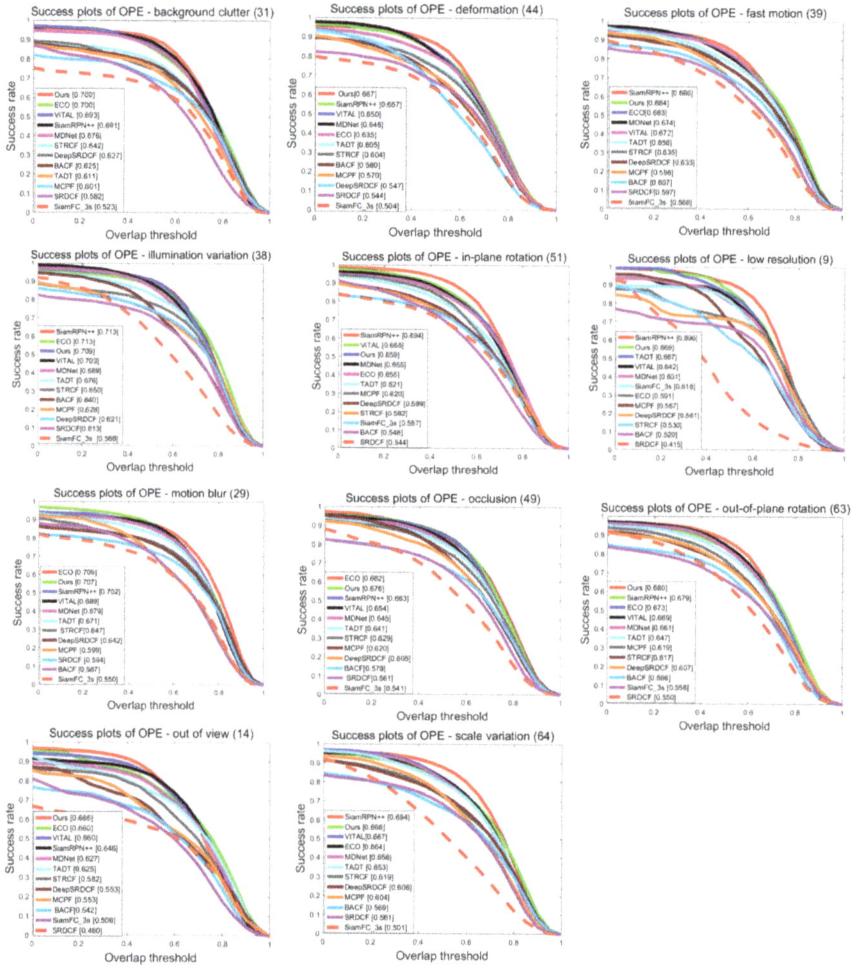

Figure 5. Success plots of OPE on eleven video sequence attributions of OTB2015.

4.3. LaSOT Dataset

The LaSOT dataset [24] is a new and huge dataset which was released in 2018. It has 1400 sequences in 70 categories, totaling 3.52 million frames. Each category contains exactly 20 sequences, keeping the dataset balanced across classes. It also provides longer time sequences containing more than 1000 frames (average 2512 frames) to meet the long-term trends currently tracked. For comparison, the LaSOT dataset also follows the one-pass evaluation (OPE) criteria of OTB. In this experiment, we used the test sets with 280 sequences, whose average frame length is more than 2500 frames. In this experiment, we compared our method with 12 advanced trackers, including ASRCF [17], SiamFC [45], ECO [41], STRCF [20], BACF [16], TRACA [50], Staple [25], LCT [27], SRDCF [14], MDNet [44], DSST [15] and KCF [11].

Table 2. Accuracy results among all compared trackers evaluate on VOT2018.

Methods	Camera Motion	Empty	Illum Change	Motion Change	Occlusion	Size Change	Mean	Weighted Mean	Pooled
Ours	0.5974	0.6322	0.6012	0.6131	0.4899	0.6201	0.6163	0.6094	0.6098
DSTRCF	0.5706	0.5898	0.5294	0.5286	0.4661	0.4660	0.5251	0.5399	0.5564
SiamDW	0.5707	0.6225	0.4819	0.5111	0.4981	0.4267	0.5185	0.5393	0.5594
ECO	0.5221	0.5598	0.5253	0.4775	0.3714	0.4436	0.4833	0.4978	0.5130
UpdateNet	0.5226	0.5713	0.5179	0.4936	0.4805	0.4842	0.5117	0.5194	0.5324
DSRDCF	0.4982	0.5716	0.5252	0.4842	0.4239	0.4569	0.4933	0.5016	0.5156
SRDCF	0.4855	0.5499	0.5912	0.4493	0.4322	0.4398	0.4913	0.4866	0.5009
Staple	0.5580	0.5958	0.5634	0.5187	0.4764	0.4799	0.5320	0.5405	0.5518
DSST	0.4219	0.4517	0.5110	0.3751	0.3482	0.3195	0.4046	0.4005	0.4090

Table 3. Robustness results among all compared trackers evaluate on VOT2018.

Methods	Camera Motion	Empty	Illum Change	Motion Change	Occlusion	Size Change	Mean	Weighted Mean	Pooled
Ours	19.000	6.000	1.000	15.000	10.000	6.000	9.000	9.083	38.000
DSTRCF	11.000	11.000	2.000	13.000	10.000	7.000	9.000	10.255	36.000
SiamDW	26.000	9.000	3.000	20.000	26.000	15.000	16.500	18.041	62.000
ECO	19.000	7.000	4.000	18.000	18.000	9.000	12.500	13.511	44.000
UpdateNet	29.000	11.000	3.000	33.000	21.000	13.000	18.333	20.876	75.000
DSRDCF	33.000	13.000	5.000	31.000	27.000	20.000	21.500	23.964	80.000
SRDCF	52.000	20.000	8.000	47.000	27.000	28.000	30.333	35.426	116.000
Staple	8.000	11.000	5.000	26.000	22.000	15.000	17.833	19.883	68.0000
DSST	103.000	45.000	6.000	76.000	32.000	36.000	49.667	63.072	206.000

Table 4. The EAO rank among all compared trackers.

Method	All
Ours	0.3943
DeepSTRCF	0.3723
ECO	0.3077
SiamDW	0.2925
Staple	0.2733
UpdateNet	0.2499
DeepSRDCF	0.2282
SRDCF	0.1621
DSST	0.0976

Figure 6 shows that our ASTCF method has achieved good results on both precision and success rate; most especially, it has an obvious advantage compared with the CF-based trackers. Figure 7 shows the overlap success plots of the compared trackers with 14 different attributes, such as illumination variation, deformation, full occlusion, and so on. It can be seen that our ASTCF method achieves outstanding results on most of the attributions, especially the partial occlusion, full occlusion and deformation attributions. Therefore, the results depict the effectiveness of our ASTCF method.

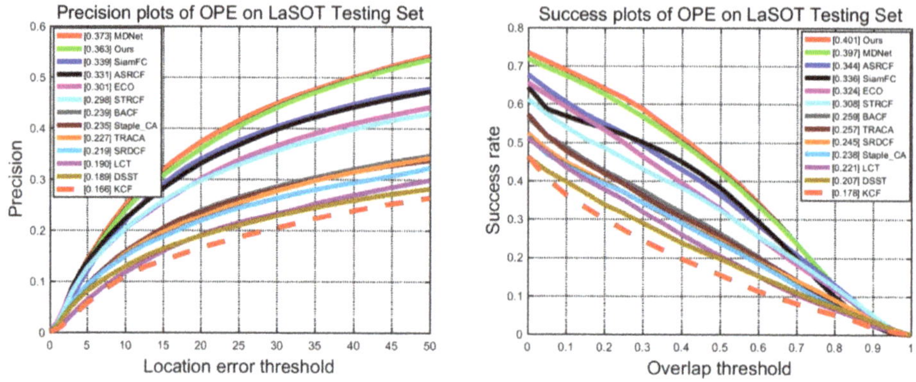

Figure 6. Precision plots and success plots of OPE on LaSOT test dataset.

4.4. Qualitative Evaluation

To further verify the effectiveness of our tracking algorithm, we have taken the qualitative evaluations of eight trackers with the representative sequences, including Bird1, Skiing, Soccer, Coke, Freeman4, Singer2, and Ironman. There are seven compared trackers, including DeepSRDCF [33], ECO [42], MCPF [43], TADT [43], SimaFC [45], BACF [16], SRDCF [14]. Figure 8 shows the results of the qualitative evaluation. It can be seen that the proposed ASTCF method has achieved better tracking performance on qualitative evaluation, especially the tracking results after 100 frames. Take the Birds sequence for example, we can see that our ASTCF method can still track the object accurately after it disappears and reappears, but other trackers lose their tracked objects.

4.5. Temporal-Aware Constraint Parameter

The choice of temporal constraint parameter β will influence the tracking performance, which is introduced in Equation (1) as the temporal-aware term. Table 5 shows the tracking performance when we choose different temporal regularization parameters. In this experiment, we present the value only from 10 to 20 at an interval of 1. It can be seen that the precision and success rates reached their highest values when we choose $\beta = 16$.

4.6. Ablation Studies

This ablation study is to verify the effectiveness of the adaptive spatial regularization and temporal-aware terms of our ASTCF tracker; the results of different versions of ASTCF tracker on OTB2015 can be seen in Table 6. ASTCF-s donates ASTCF without adaptive spatial regularization term, ASTCF-t donates ASTCF without temporal term and ASTCF-st donates ASTCF without adaptive spatial regularization and temporal-aware terms (equal baseline tracker). From the results of Table 6, we can see that the adaptive regularization and temporal-aware terms can effectively improve the performances of trackers, and they become better when fused together. Compared with ASTCF-s, ASTCF improves 6.0% in DP score and 4.7% in AUC score. Moreover, ASTCF also improves 1.2% in DP score and 1.0% in AUC score compared with ASTCF-t.

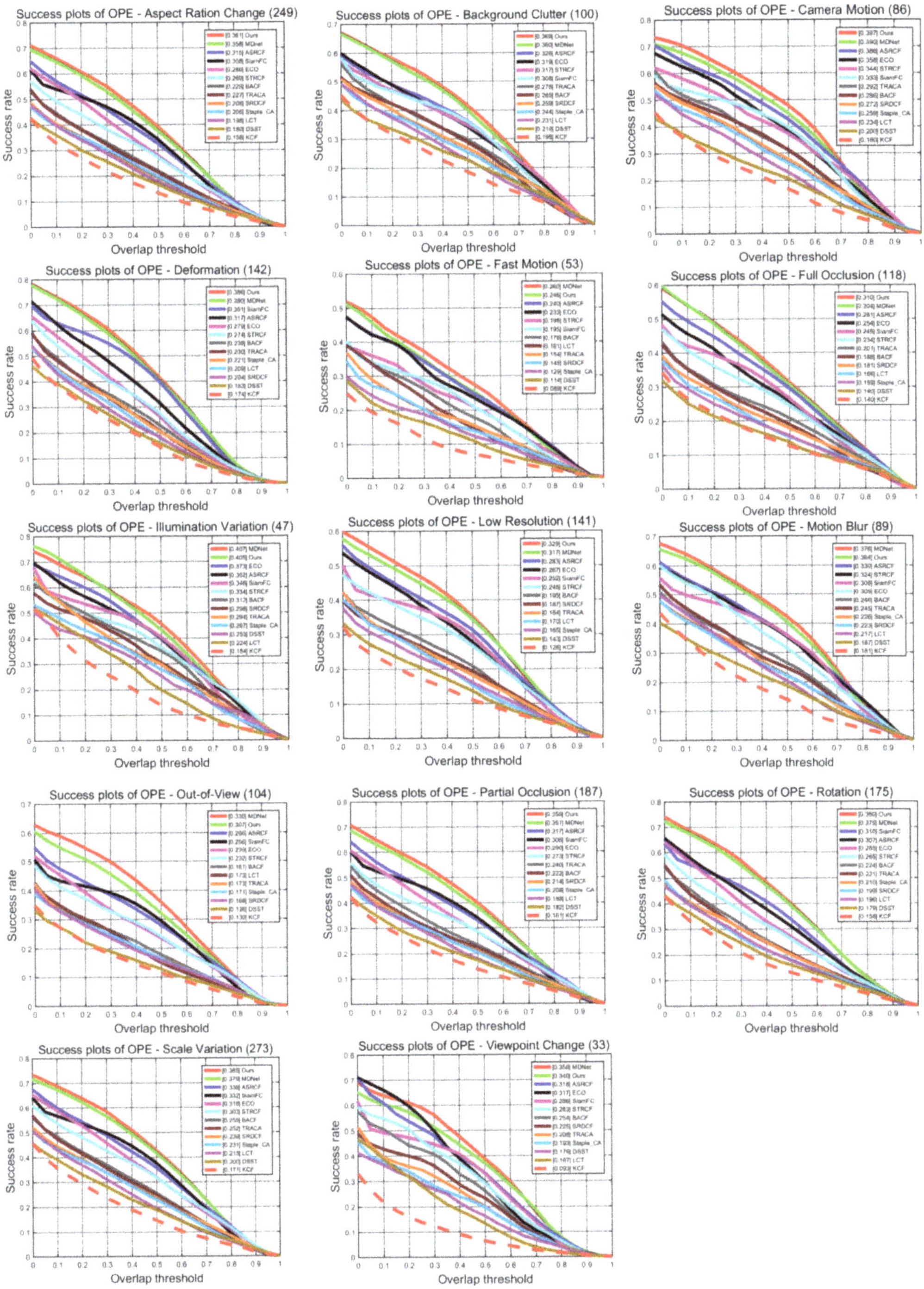

Figure 7. Success plots of OPE evaluate on fourteen sequence attributions.

Figure 8. Representative tracking results of qualitative evaluation. The selective sequences are Bird1, Skiing, Soccer, Coke, Freeman4, Singer2, and Ironman.

Table 5. Precision and success rates on OTB2015 dataset with different temporal-aware regularization parameters β.

β	Precision	Success
10	0.871	0.662
11	0.879	0.669
12	0.887	0.672
13	0.895	0.681
14	0.919	0.689
15	0.918	0.692
16	0.927	0.699
17	0.920	0.689
18	0.912	0.680
19	0.901	0.682
20	0.896	0.677

Table 6. DP scores and AUC scores of different versions of ASTCF on OTB2015 dataset.

Tracker	ASTCF	ASTCF-s	ASTCF-t	ASTCF-st
Precision (DP)	0.927	0.867	0.915	0.802
Success (AUC)	0.699	0.652	0.689	0.601

5. Conclusions

This paper proposes a novel adaptive spatial regularization and temporal-aware correlation filters (ASTCF) model for solving the unwanted boundary effects which occur in the correlation filters tracking. The proposed ASTCF method can help to build a robust appearance model and improve the tracking accuracy by introducing adaptive spatial regularization and temporal-aware terms into the objective function. Further, the objective function can be effectively optimized via the ADMM algorithm. The three related subproblems have analytical closed-form solutions, and greatly reduce the computational cost. Compared with other trackers on several benchmarks, the ASTCF method depicts obvious advantages on most of the evaluation metrics. For the OTB2015 dataset, our ASTCF tracker achieved the best results both on DP score and AUC score, which reached 0.699 and 0.927, respectively. Moreover, the speed of the ASTCF method is approximately 23.5 fps, which satisfies the requirements of real-time. In the future, we will further explore the application of this model for small object tracking on UAV and dark scenes.

Author Contributions: Conceptualization, L.L., T.F., C.S. and Y.F.; methodology, L.L., Y.F. and T.F.; software, L.L. and T.F.; validation, L.L., C.S., Z.H., X.B. and Y.F.; formal analysis, L.L. and T.F.; investigation, L.L., M.Q., Z.H., S.Z. and C.S.; resources, L.L. and Y.F.; data curation, L.L.; writing—original draft preparation, L.L., T.F.; writing—review and editing, L.L., C.S., Y.F. and T.F.; visualization, L.L., Z.H., S.Z., M.Q., X.B. and C.S.; project administration, L.L., C.S. and Y.F. All authors have read and agreed to the published version of the manuscript.

Funding: This research was supported by Shaanxi S&T Grants 2021KW-07 and Shaanxi Province Technology Innovation Guidance Special Fund 2022QFY01-14.

Institutional Review Board Statement: Not applicable.

Informed Consent Statement: Not applicable.

Data Availability Statement: All datasets evaluated in the paper can be found on official websites, OTB-100: http://cvlab.hanyang.ac.kr/tracker_benchmark/datasets.html, accessed on 30 September 2022, VOT-2018: https://www.votchallenge.net/vot2018/, accessed on 30 September 2022. LaSOT: https://cis.temple.edu/lasot/, accessed on 30 September 2022.

Acknowledgments: The authors appreciate all the people who build the benchmarks for tracking.

Conflicts of Interest: The authors declare no conflict of interest.

References

1. Li, P.X.; Wang, D.; Wang, L.J.; Lu, H.C. Deep visual tracking: Review and experimental comparison. *Pattern Recognit.* **2018**, *76*, 323–338. [CrossRef]
2. Smeulders, A.W.; Chu, D.M.; Cucchiara, R.; Calderara, S.; Dehghan, A. Visual tracking: An experimental survey. *IEEE Trans. Pattern Anal. Mach. Intell.* **2014**, *36*, 1442–1468. [PubMed]
3. Wang, N.Y.; Shi, J.; Yeung, D.Y.; Jia, J. understanding and diagnosing visual tracking systems. In Proceedings of the IEEE International Conference on Computer Vision (ICCV), Santiago, Chile, 7–13 December 2015; pp. 3101–3109.
4. Yilmaz, A.; Javed, O.; Shah, M. Object tracking: A survey. *ACM Comput. Surv.* **2006**, *38*, 1–45. [CrossRef]
5. Sundararaman, R.; De Almeida Braga, C.; Marchand, E.; Pettré, J. Tracking Pedestrian Heads in Dense Crowd. In Proceedings of the 2021 IEEE/CVF Conference on Computer Vision and Pattern Recognition (CVPR), Virtual, 19–25 June 2021; pp. 3864–3874. [CrossRef]
6. Jang, J.; Jiang, H. MeanShift++: Extremely Fast Mode-Seeking with Applications to Segmentation and Object Tracking. In Proceedings of the 2021 IEEE/CVF Conference on Computer Vision and Pattern Recognition (CVPR), Virtual, 19–25 June 2021; pp. 4100–4111. [CrossRef]
7. Yu: Yu, Y.; Chen, L.; He, H.; Liu, J.; Zhang, W.; Xu, G. Second-Order Spatial-Temporal Correlation Filters for Visual Tracking. *Mathematics* **2022**, *10*, 684. [CrossRef]

8. Liu, L.; Cao, J. End-to-end learning interpolation for object tracking in low frame-rate video. *IET Image Process.* **2020**, *14*, 997–1216. [CrossRef]
9. Bolme, D.S.; Beveridge, J.R.; Draper, B.A.; Lui, Y.M. Visual object tracking using adaptive correlation filters. In Proceedings of the Twenty-Third IEEE Conference on Computer Vision and Pattern Recognition, CVPR 2010, San Francisco, CA, USA, 13–18 June 2010; pp. 2544–2550. [CrossRef]
10. Henriques, J.F.; Caseiro, R.; Martins, P.; Batista, J. Exploiting the Circulant Structure of Tracking-by-Detection with Kernels. In *Computer Vision—ECCV*; Springer: Berlin/Heidelberg, Germany, 2012; pp. 702–715.
11. Henriques, J.F.; Caseiro, R.; Martins, P.; Batista, J. High-Speed Tracking with Kernelized Correlation Filters. *IEEE Trans. Pattern Anal. Mach. Intell.* **2015**, *37*, 583–596. [CrossRef] [PubMed]
12. Liu, L.; Feng, T.; Fu, Y. Learning Multifeature Correlation Filter and Saliency Redetection for Long-Term Object Tracking. *Symmetry* **2022**, *14*, 911. [CrossRef]
13. Galoogahi, H.K.; Sim, T.; Lucey, S. Correlation Filters with Limited Boundaries. In Proceedings of the 2015 IEEE Conference on Computer Vision and Pattern Recognition (CVPR), Boston, MA, USA, 7–12 June 2015; pp. 4630–4638.
14. Danelljan, M.; Hager, G.; Khan, F.S.; Felsberg, M. Learning Spatially Regularized Correlation Filters for Visual Tracking. In Proceedings of the 2015 IEEE International Conference on Computer Vision (ICCV), Santiago, Chile, 7–13 December 2015; pp. 4310–4318. [CrossRef]
15. Danelljan, M.; Hager, G.; Khan, F.S.; Felsberg, M. Discriminative Scale Space Tracking. *IEEE Trans. Pattern Anal. Mach. Intell.* **2017**, *39*, 1561–1575. [CrossRef] [PubMed]
16. Galoogahi, H.K.; Fagg, A.; Lucey, S. Learning Background-Aware Correlation Filters for Visual Tracking. In Proceedings of the 2017 IEEE International Conference on Computer Vision (ICCV), Venice, Italy, 22–29 October 2017; pp. 1144–1152. [CrossRef]
17. Dai, K.; Wang, D.; Lu, H.; Sun, C.; Li, J. Visual Tracking via Adaptive Spatially-Regularized Correlation Filters. In Proceedings of the 2019 IEEE/CVF Conference on Computer Vision and Pattern Recognition (CVPR) 2019, Long Beach, CA, USA, 16–20 June 2019; pp. 4665–4674. [CrossRef]
18. Han, R.; Feng, W.; Wang, S. Fast Learning of Spatially Regularized and Content Aware Correlation Filter for Visual Tracking. *IEEE Trans. Image Process.* **2020**, *29*, 7128–7140. [CrossRef]
19. Danelljan, M.; Hager, G.; Khan, F.S.; Felsberg, M. Adaptive Decontamination of the Training Set: A Unified Formulation for Discriminative Visual Tracking. In Proceedings of the 2016 IEEE Conference on Computer Vision and Pattern Recognition (CVPR), Las Vegas, NV, USA, 27–30 June 2016; pp. 1430–1438. [CrossRef]
20. Li, F.; Tian, C.; Zuo, W.; Zhang, L.; Yang, M. Learning Spatial-Temporal Regularized Correlation Filters for Visual Tracking. In Proceedings of the 2018 IEEE/CVF Conference on Computer Vision and Pattern Recognition, Salt Lake City, UT, USA, 18–22 June 2018; pp. 4904–4913. [CrossRef]
21. Li, Y.; Fu, C.H.; Ding, F.Q.; Huang, Z.Y.; Lu, G. AutoTrack: Towards High-Performance Visual Tracking for UAV with Automatic Spatio-Temporal Regularization. In Proceedings of the 2020 IEEE/CVF Conference on Computer Vision and Pattern Recognition (CVPR), Virtual, 13–19 June 2020; pp. 11920–11929. [CrossRef]
22. Wu, Y.; Lim, J.; Yang, M. Object Tracking Benchmark. *IEEE Trans. Pattern Anal. Mach. Intell.* **2015**, *37*, 1834–1848. [CrossRef] [PubMed]
23. Matej, K.; Ales, L.; Jiri, M.; Michael, F.; Roman, P.; Luka, C.; Tomas, V.; Goutam, B.; Alan, L.; Abdelrahman, E.; et al. The Sixth Visual Object Tracking VOT2018 Challenge Results. In *Computer Vision–ECCV 2018 Workshops. ECCV 2018. Lecture Notes in Computer Science*; Leal-Taixé, L., Roth, S., Eds.; Springer: Cham, Switzerland, 2018; Volume 11129. [CrossRef]
24. Fan, H.; Lin, L.; Yang, F.; Chu, P.; Deng, G.; Yu, S.; Bai, H.; Xu, Y.; Liao, C.; Ling, H. LaSOT: A High-Quality Benchmark for Large-Scale Single Object Tracking. In Proceedings of the 2019 IEEE/CVF Conference on Computer Vision and Pattern RECOgnition (CVPR), Long Beach, CA, USA, 16–20 June 2019; pp. 5369–5378. [CrossRef]
25. Bertinetto, L.; Valmadre, J.; Golodetz, S.; Miksik, O.; Torr, P.H.S. Staple: Complementary Learners for Real-Time Tracking. In Proceedings of the 2016 IEEE Conference on Computer Vision and Pattern Recognition (CVPR), Las Vegas, NV, USA, 27–30 June 2016; pp. 1401–1409. [CrossRef]
26. Mueller, M.; Smith, N.; Ghanem, B. Context-aware correlation filter tracking. In Proceedings of the IEEE Conference on Computer Vision and Pattern Recognition (CVPR), Honolulu, HI, USA, 21–26 July 2017; pp. 1396–1404.
27. Ma, C.; Yang, X.; Zhang, C.Y.; Yang, M. Long-term correlation tracking. In Proceedings of the IEEE Conference on Computer Vision and Pattern Recognition (CVPR), Boston, MA, USA, 7–12 June 2015; pp. 5388–5396.
28. Tang, F.; Ling, Q. Contour-Aware Long-Term Tracking with Reliable Re-Detection. *IEEE Trans. Circuits Syst. Video Technol.* **2020**, *30*, 4739–4754. [CrossRef]
29. Wang, N.; Zhou, W.; Li, H. Reliable Re-Detection for Long-Term Tracking. *IEEE Trans. Circuits Syst. Video Technol.* **2019**, *29*, 730–743. [CrossRef]
30. Boyd, S. Distributed Optimization and Statistical Learning via the Alternating Direction Method of Multipliers. *Found. Trends Mach. Learn.* **2010**, *3*, 1–122. [CrossRef]
31. Wu, X.; Sahoo, D.; Hoi, S.C. Recent advances in deep learning for object detection. *Neurocomputing* **2020**, *396*, 39–64. [CrossRef]
32. Chen, J.; Zhou, M.; Huang, H.; Zhang, D.; Peng, Z. Automated extraction and evaluation of fracture trace maps from rock tunnel face images via deep learning. *Int. J. Rock Mech. Min. Sci.* **2021**, *142*, 104745. [CrossRef]

33. Danelljan, M.; Hager, G.; Khan, F.S.; Felsberg, M. Convolutional Features for Correlation Filter Based Visual Tracking. In Proceedings of the 2015 IEEE International Conference on Computer Vision Workshop (ICCVW), Santiago, Chile, 7–13 December 2015; pp. 621–629. [CrossRef]
34. Valmadre, J.; Bertinetto, L.; Henriques, J.; Vedaldi, A.; Torr, P.H.S. End-to-End Representation Learning for Correlation Filter Based Tracking. In Proceedings of the 2017 IEEE Conference on Computer Vision and Pattern Recognition (CVPR), Honolulu, HI, USA, 21–26 July 2017; pp. 5000–5008. [CrossRef]
35. Sun, Y.; Sun, C.; Wang, D.; He, Y.; Lu, H. ROI Pooled Correlation Filters for Visual Tracking. In Proceedings of the 2019 IEEE/CVF Conference on Computer Vision and Pattern Recognition (CVPR), Long Beach, CA, USA, 16–20 June 2019; pp. 5776–5784. [CrossRef]
36. Eckstein, J.; Bertsekas, D.P. On the Douglas—Rachford splitting method and the proximal point algorithm for maximal monotone operators. *Math. Program.* **1992**, *55*, 293–318. [CrossRef]
37. Karen, S.; Andrew, Z. Very deep convolutional networks for large-scale image recognition. *arXiv* **2014**, arXiv:1409.1556.
38. Russakovsky, O.; Deng, J.; Su, H.; Krause, J.; Satheesh, S.; Ma, S.; Huang, Z.; Karpathy, A.; Khosla, A.; Bernstein, M.; et al. Imagenet large scale visual recognition challenge. *Int. J. Comput. Vis.* **2015**, *115*, 211–252. [CrossRef]
39. Wu, Y.; Lim, J.; Yang, M. Online Object Tracking: A Benchmark. In Proceedings of the 2013 IEEE Conference on Computer Vision and Pattern Recognition 2013, Portland, OR, USA, 23–28 June 2013; pp. 2411–2418. [CrossRef]
40. Li, B.; Wu, W.; Wang, Q.; Zhang, F.; Xing, J.; Yan, J. SiamRPN++: Evolution of Siamese Visual Tracking with Very Deep Networks. In Proceedings of the 2019 IEEE/CVF Conference on Computer Vision and Pattern Recognition (CVPR), Long Beach, CA, USA, 16–20 June 2019; pp. 4277–4286. [CrossRef]
41. Danelljan, M.; Robinson, A.; Shahbaz, K.F.; Felsberg, M. ECO: Efficient Convolution Operators for Tracking. In Proceedings of the 2017 IEEE Conference on Computer Vision and Pattern Recognition (CVPR), Honolulu, HI, USA, 21–26 July 2017; pp. 6931–6939. [CrossRef]
42. Zhang, T.; Xu, C.; Yang, M. Learning Multi-Task Correlation Particle Filters for Visual Tracking. *IEEE Trans. Pattern Anal. Mach. Intell.* **2019**, *41*, 365–378. [CrossRef] [PubMed]
43. Li, X.; Ma, C.; Wu, B.; He, Z.; Yang, M. Target-Aware Deep Tracking. In Proceedings of the 2019 IEEE/CVF Conference on Computer Vision and Pattern Recognition (CVPR), Long Beach, CA, USA, 16–20 June 2019; pp. 1369–1378. [CrossRef]
44. Nam, H.; Han, B. Learning Multi-domain Convolutional Neural Networks for Visual Tracking. In Proceedings of the 2016 IEEE Conference on Computer Vision and Pattern Recognition (CVPR), Las Vegas, NV, USA, 27–30 June 2016; pp. 4293–4302. [CrossRef]
45. Bertinetto, L.; Valmadre, J.; Henriques, J.F.; Vedaldi, A.; Torr, P.H.S. Fully-Convolutional Siamese Networks for Object Tracking. In *Computer Vision–ECCV 2016 Workshops. ECCV 2016. Lecture Notes in Computer Science*; Hua, G., Jégou, H., Eds.; Springer: Cham, Switzerland, 2016; Volume 9914. [CrossRef]
46. Song, Y.; Chao, M.; Wu, X.; Gong, L.; Yang, M. VITAL: Visual Tracking via Adversarial Learning. In Proceedings of the 2018 IEEE/CVF Conference on Computer Vision and Pattern Recognition, Salt Lake City, UT, USA, 18–22 June 2018; pp. 8990–8999. [CrossRef]
47. Zhang, Z.; Peng, H. Deeper and Wider Siamese Networks for Real-Time Visual Tracking. In Proceedings of the 2019 IEEE/CVF Conference on Computer Vision and Pattern Recognition (CVPR) Long Beach, CA, USA, 16–20 June 2019; pp. 4586–4595. [CrossRef]
48. Zhang, L.; Gonzalez-Garcia, A.; Weijer, J.V.D.; Danelljan, M.; Khan, F.S. Learning the Model Update for Siamese Trackers. In Proceedings of the 2019 IEEE/CVF International Conference on Computer Vision (ICCV), Seoul, Korea; 2019; pp. 4009–4018. [CrossRef]
49. Matej, K.; Jiri, M.; Alexs, L.; Tomas, V.; Roman, P.; Gustavo, F.; Georg, N.; Fatih, P.; Luka, C. A Novel Performance Evaluation Methodology for Single-Target Trackers. *IEEE Trans. Pattern Anal. Mach. Intell.* **2016**, *38*, 2137–2155. [CrossRef]
50. Choi, J.; Chang, H.J.; Fischer, T.; Yun, S.; Lee, K.; Jeong, J.; Demiris, Y.; Choi, J.Y. Context-Aware Deep Feature Compression for High-Speed Visual Tracking . In Proceedings of the 2018 IEEE/CVF Conference on Computer Vision and Pattern Recognition, Salt Lake City, UT, USA, 18–22 June 2018; pp. 479–488. [CrossRef]

mathematics

MDPI

Article

TransMF: Transformer-Based Multi-Scale Fusion Model for Crack Detection

Xiaochen Ju [1], Xinxin Zhao [1] and Shengsheng Qian [2,*]

[1] Railway Engineering Research Institute, China Academy of Railway Sciences Corporation Limited, Beijing 100081, China; juxc2008@163.com (X.J.); xyzxx000@163.com (X.Z.)

[2] Institute of Automation, Chinese Academy of Sciences, Beijing 100090, China

* Correspondence: shengsheng.qian@nlpr.ia.ac.cn

Abstract: Cracks are widespread in infrastructure that are closely related to human activity. It is very popular to use artificial intelligence to detect cracks intelligently, which is known as crack detection. The noise in the background of crack images, discontinuity of cracks and other problems make the crack detection task a huge challenge. Although many approaches have been proposed, there are still two challenges: (1) cracks are long and complex in shape, making it difficult to capture long-range continuity; (2) most of the images in the crack dataset have noise, and it is difficult to detect only the cracks and ignore the noise. In this paper, we propose a novel method called *Transformer-based Multi-scale Fusion Model* (TransMF) for crack detection, including an Encoder Module (EM), Decoder Module (DM) and Fusion Module (FM). The Encoder Module uses a hybrid of convolution blocks and Swin Transformer block to model the long-range dependencies of different parts in a crack image from a local and global perspective. The Decoder Module is designed with symmetrical structure to the Encoder Module. In the Fusion Module, the output in each layer with unique scales of Encoder Module and Decoder Module are fused in the form of convolution, which can release the effect of background noise and strengthen the correlations between relevant context in order to enhance the crack detection. Finally, the output of each layer of the Fusion Module is concatenated to achieve the purpose of crack detection. Extensive experiments on three benchmark datasets (CrackLS315, CRKWH100 and DeepCrack) demonstrate that the proposed TransMF in this paper exceeds the best performance of present baselines.

Keywords: crack detection; convolutional neural network; transformer; multi-scale fusion

MSC: 68T45

1. Introduction

With the development of Deep Learning (DL), Artificial Intelligence (AI) has ushered in great prosperity. It has become a popular trend to find ways to solve tasks automatically instead of manually, permeating all aspects of our lives, such as Facial Recognition (FR) [1], Vehicle License Plate Recognition (VLPR) [2], Image Classification [3–5] and so on. More importantly, AI has been able to provide support for the safety of life and property, in which a relatively popular task is crack detection. A crack is a line structure and crack detection is a kind of segmentation task, or object detection task, which detects cracks on the object surface in an automatic way, and has practical significance for human survival and life. Public service infrastructures, such as bridges [6–8], and pavements [9–12], are directly related to the safety of human life, and cracks on the surface of which, to some extent, represent the degree of damage of these public facilities. Therefore, it is critical and important to detect cracks more quickly and efficiently.

The encoder–decoder framework is a popular method to solve crack detection, which has been widely used in an image segmentation domain. The encoder takes an input image and generates a high-dimensional feature vector and the decoder takes a high-dimensional feature vector and generates a semantic segmentation mask. High-dimensional features can be aggregated with at multiple levels. U-Net [13] is a pioneering work in the field of crack detection, using a symmetric encoder–decoder framework with skip connection firstly, where both the decoder and encoder are implemented with Convolutional Neural Networks (CNNs). Based on U-Net [13], many excellent methods have been proposed [12,14,15]. However, the network framework of the above methods is relatively simple, and requires a large amount of data augmentation to improve the segmentation effect [16]. In addition, the Convolutional Neural Networks (CNN) have the limitation of the receptive field. During the convolution process, the weight calculation is performed in the receptive field of a certain size. Generally speaking, the receptive field is not very large, and combined with the slender feature of cracks, the convolution cannot capture the long-range dependencies of cracks, which may result in performance degradation. Recently, Transformer [17] was proposed to model long-range dependencies for contextual encoding of natural language, which has developed rapidly in the field of computer vision in the last 2 years, and a number of variants have been proposed, such as Vision Transformers [18], Swin Transformer [19], Star-Transformer [20], etc. CrackFormer [21] is a Crack Transformer network (CrackFormer) with a transformer encoder–decoder structure, which proposes a self-attention block and scaling-attention block for fine-grained crack detection. Today, there has been some research using a transformer-based multi-scale method on many applications. Kong et al. [22] proposed a multi-scale temporal transformer for skeleton-based action recognition.Xiao et al. [23] proposed a multi-scale spatiotemporal transformer to efficiently aggregate contextual information in long-time sequences of video frames. Yuan et al. [24] proposed a multi-scale adaptive segmentation network based on Swin Transformer for remote sensing image segmentation.

In addition, Deep Learning can obtain the deep contour features of an image, but the shallow features are rich in texture information of the image that contains unwanted noise. Noise is a thorny problem in crack detection [25], and how to design robust network architecture is very important for crack detection. A very common method is to simply fuse shallow features and deep features using a skip connection. For example, YOLOv3-Lite [26] adopts depthwise separable convolution, feature pyramid, and YOLOv3 to detect cracks in aircraft structures. CrackSeg [27] introduces a novel multi-scale dilated convolutional module to learn rich deep convolutional features under complex background. Although the above methods have achieved good results in solving the problem of background noise, they still cannot pay more attention to the detection object while removing the background noise.

Overall, there are two challenges that need to be addressed in order to effectively model crack detection:

- Challenge 1: Cracks on the surface of objects are thin and long with complex shapes, which makes it difficult to detect cracks. At present, many methods use Convolutional Neural Networks (CNNs) to extract deep features of cracks, but the convolutional features can only model local features, and ignore the global feature relationship that can capture long-range dependencies. The long-range dependencies can coordinate the overall characteristics of the cracks. Therefore, we conclude the first challenge is: how can we model the long-range dependencies of different parts in a crack image from a local and global perspective for a better crack image understanding?
- Challenge 2: Images of cracks are taken from various facilities, such as bridges, buildings, railways, roads and other public building facilities, or household items such as cups and tables. Therefore, the actual scene of cracks is complex and diverse, and the crack detection task cannot ignore these background noises, which leads to incorrect detection of cracks and reduces the detection efficiency. The crack features extracted by convolution are divided into shallow low-level features and deep high-level features. Shallow low-level features contain the texture information of cracks, and deep high-level features contain the general contour information of cracks. However,

shallow low-level features are highly affected by the background noise, while deep high-level features are less affected by background noise. So, we concluded that the second challenge is: how can we remove the effect of background noise from the low-level features of crack images, which is an important prerequisite to enhance the crack detection?

Motivated by the above discussions, we propose a novel method called *Transformer-based Multi-scale Fusion Model* (TransMF) for crack detection, which consists of three modules: Encoder Module (EM), Decoder Module (DM) and Fusion Module (FM). For *Challenge 1*, we use a hybrid of convolution and transformer approaches, combining global and local perspectives, to explore the long-range dependencies of various parts in the crack. Specifically, we design an Encoder Module (EM) and Decoder Module (DM), which are symmetrical and contain multiple layers of Conv-Block and Swin Transformer block, respectively, as shown in Figure 1. For *Challenge 2*, we design a Fusion Module (FM) to fuse the multi-scale features from different layers in the encoder and decoder to mitigate the effect of background noise through fusing low-level and high-level features in the form of convolution, which can assist in strengthening the correlations between the relevant context for enhancing the crack detection. In general, the contributions in this paper are summarized as follows:

- We propose a novel *Transformer-based Multi-scale Fusion Model* (TransMF) for crack detection, including an Encoder Module (EM), Decoder Module (DM) and Fusion Module (FM), which performs encoding and decoding symmetrically, and fuses at different levels to preserve the information of the underlying features and deep features.
- Both the Encoder Module (EM) and Decoder Module (DM) utilize a hybrid architecture of Convolutional Neural Networks (CNN) and Swin Transformers, which can capture both detailed spatial information from local features and the global context encoded by Transformers.
- In this paper, a multi-scale Fusion Module (FM) is designed, rather than a simple skip connection, to effectively fuse the encoder and decoder features of each layer with different scales to form a comprehensive representation, preventing wrong detection of noise.
- We evaluate TransMF on three benchmark datasets (CrackLS315 [28], CRKWH100 [28] and DeepCrack [14]). Experimental results demonstrate that the proposed TransMF exceeds the best performance of present baselines.

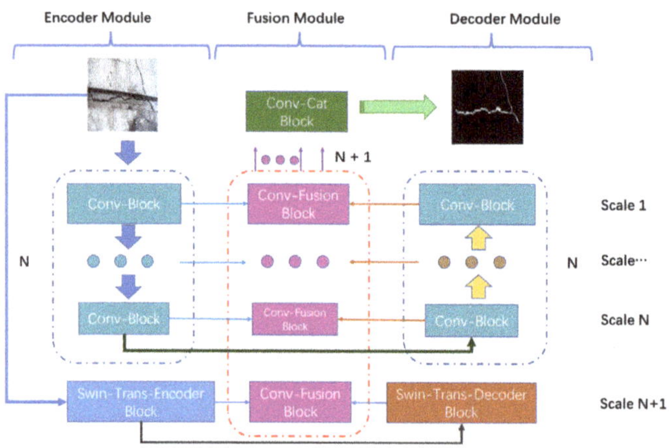

Figure 1. The overall framework of the proposed TransMF, which consists of three modules: an Encoder Module (EM), Decoder Module (DM) and Fusion Module (FM). Both the Encoder Module (EM) and Decoder Module (DM) utilize a hybrid of Convolutional Neural Networks (CNNs) and Swin Transformers, which are symmetrical. The Fusion Module (FM) fuses multi-scale features to form a comprehensive representation.

2. Related Work

2.1. Crack Detection

Surface cracks are everywhere around us, being on things such as daily necessities, public building facilities, transportation tools and so on. The existence of cracks brings us great inconvenience and will endanger our lives and health to a certain extent. Crack detection has thus become a popular research field. The traditional crack detection method is that the inspector goes to the scene to detect cracks using the detection instrument, which is time-consuming, laborious and costly, also bringing great danger to the inspector. As Machine Learning [29] evolved, people designed manual features to train models for initial automatic detection. As Deep Learning [30] then came to a boom, models were learned in a black-box manner, facilitating the further development of crack detection, during which Convolutional Neural Networks (CNNs) [31] were widely used. In recent years, much excellent crack detection work has been proposed, such as [13,14,28,32].

Currently, crack detection based on deep learning can be divided into two kinds of methods [33] as shown in the left part in Figure 2: (1) image processing-based method for crack detection; (2) machine learning method for crack detection. In the first method, which utilizes handcrafted features, high-resolution images are preprocessed to remove noise and shadows using filters, segmentation and other approaches. Edge detection, segmentation, or pixel analysis are used to highlight or segment the cracked part in the image. In the second method, the dataset is preprocessed and a machine learning model is used to classify the cracked regions.

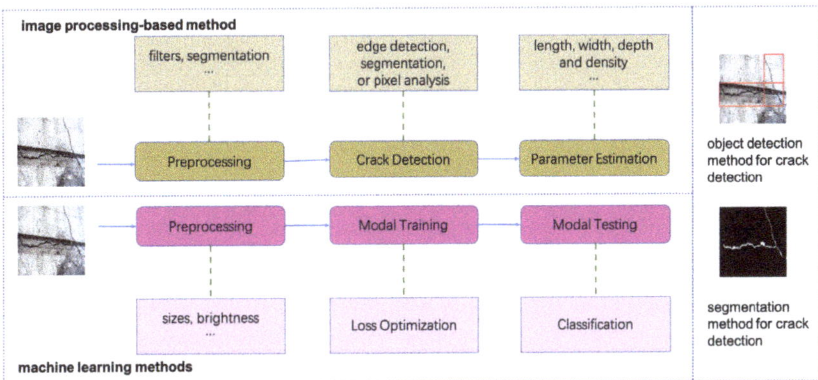

Figure 2. On the left are two methods of crack detection, including: (1) image processing-based method for crack detection, which utilizes handcrafted features; (2) machine learning method for crack detection, which utilizes learned features by the model. The right side shows that the methods based on machine learning include two categories, object detection method for crack detection and segmentation method for crack detection.

Among them, the methods based on machine learning include two categories, object detection method for crack detection and segmentation method for crack detection. The former detects regions containing cracks, and the latter segments crack contours, including semantic segmentation and instance segmentation, as shown as the right part in Figure 2. YOLOv3-Lite [26] uses the deep separable convolution to extract features, and utilizes the feature pyramid to preserve semantic information at different levels. A crack detection method based on the YOLOv4 algorithm is proposed in [34], which achieves good crack detection results with a lower trained model weight. To overcome the complicated and uneconomical disadvantages of traditional crack detection methods, a pavement crack detection network [35] is proposed to combine YOLOv5 and Transformer. Zhou et al. [36] propose a novel network architecture with richer feature fusion and attention mechanism and mixed pooling module for crack detection. Qu et al. [37] propose a deeply supervised convolutional neural network for crack detection via a novel multiscale convolutional feature fusion module. A more fine-grained method is utilized in [38], where raw images are cropped into smaller images, and cracks are detected with a trained CNN classifier and an exhaustive search with a sliding window. U-Net [13] utilizes Convolutional Neural Networks (CNNs) to design encoder and decoder forming a 'U'-shaped net and detect a crack in form of segmentation. Based on U-Net [13], many excellent methods have been proposed [12,14,15]. For example, Liu et al. [14] utilize an encoder–decoder architecture to learn hierarchical features of cracks in multiple scenes and scales effectively for crack detection. CrackU-net [12] uses a 'U'-shaped model architecture to achieve crack detection, including convolution, pooling, transpose convolution, and concatenation operations in it. Liu et al. [15] propose a two-step pavement crack detection and segmentation method based on modified U-Net, in which a residual neural network (ResNet-34) pre-trained by ImageNet [39] is used as the encoder and convolution layers as the decoder. Dense Attention U-Net [40] proposes a encoder with multi-stage dense blocks to improve its capability for extracting informative contextual features. In this paper, we mainly focus on the segmentation method for crack detection.

2.2. Semantic Segmentation for Crack Detection

Semantic segmentation is a computer vision task, which performs binary classification for each pixel according to its semantics: '0' for the background and '1' for the foreground [5]. Generally speaking, the segmentation network designs a feature extraction network to obtain a feature map which is the same size as the original image, and performs a class prediction operation on each pixel. To enrich the channel information, down-sampling and up-sampling are chosen to form a feature extraction network. With the development of Convolutional Neural Networks (CNN), the down-sampling and up-sampling parts are replaced by various convolutional networks, called encoder and decoder. In recent years, transformers [17], originally used for Natural Language Processing (NLP), have set off a boom in the field of Computer Vision (CV), and more and more methods use a transformer [17] to complete segmentation tasks.

The object detection method for crack detection can only achieve the classification and rough location of cracks. More intuitive and accurate detection results are obtained by pixel-level crack detection [41]. There are three major types of approaches in the field of Semantic segmentation for Crack Detection, namely thresholding-based, edge-based, and data driven-based methods [42]. The first two are rule-driven segmentation methods. In this paper, we mainly focus on data-driven segmentation methods using neural networks. The fully connected segmentation method is popular with many researchers [41,43]. Dung et al. [43] propose a crack detection method based on deep Fully Convolutional Network (FCN). To solve time-consuming and labor-consuming problems, Yang et al. [41] propose a Fully Convolutional Network (FCN) with multiple steps to realize automatic pixel-level Crack Detection and Measurement. A modified FCN architecture is proposed in [44] to provide pixel-level detection of multiple damages. The U-Net [13] network expresses the encoding and decoding with a 'U'-shape and becomes the basis of many works [45–48], in which Convolutional Neural Networks (CNNs) make a good effect. As transformer [17] is widely used in the field of Computer Vision (CV), many works [21] also use transformer for crack segmentation, in which self-attention block and scaling-attention block are utilized for fine-grained crack detection.

Unlike the above methods, Convolutional Neural Network (CNN) and Transformer are both used in TransMF to jointly coordinate feature learning from both global and local perspectives, and to predict cracks by integrating features of different scales, in which long-range dependencies can be grasped and the impact of noise is minimized as much as possible.

3. Methodology

3.1. Problem Definition

Generally speaking, crack detection is a kind of image segmentation task, which applies image segmentation to the scene of detecting cracks on objects. Therefore, the dataset and evaluation metrics of crack detection are basically the same as the requirements of image segmentation. Given an image $\mathbf{I} \in \mathbb{R}^{W \times H \times C}$, its label image is $\mathbf{L} \in \mathbb{R}^{W \times H}$, which is a binary image, and each pixel of the image belongs to a category, where W is image width, H is image height and C is the channel of the image. In this paper, the total number of categories is m. The trained model is used to predict the class of each pixel of the image and statistically evaluated using an evaluation metric.

3.2. Overall Framework

In this paper, we propose a novel Transformer-based Multi-scale Fusion Model (TransMF) to detect cracks on objects by designing an Encoder Module (EM), Decoder Module (DM) and Fusion Module (FM).

- **Encoder Module (EM)** : The Encoder Module (EM) proposed in this paper is stacked by N Conv-Block and one Swin-Trans-Encoder Block. Each layer of Conv-Block has different image scales. By extracting deep features of images with convolution, and extracting feature relations with Swin-Trans-Encoder Block, the features with deep semantic relations are obtained. In this way, we can model the long-range dependencies of different regions in the crack image from a local and global perspective.
- **Decoder Module (DM)**: The Encoder Module (EM) and Decoder Module (DM) in TransMF proposed in this paper are symmetric, that is to say, the Decoder Module (DM) is also composed of Swin-Trans-Encoder Block and Conv-Block, and is consistent with the parameter Settings of the Encoder Module (EM). It is worth noting that the feature dimension of the Encoder Module (EM) decreases layer-by-layer, while the dimension of the Decoder Module (DM) increases layer-by-layer. The output of each layer of the Encoder Module (EM) and Decoder Module (DM) are jointly input to the Fusion Module (FM).
- **Fusion Module (FM)**: In order to achieve the representation fusing both low-level features and deep features, in this paper, we design a Fusion Module (FM), which fuses the outputs of encoder and decoder where images are different scales. To fuse those multiple scales feature maps, we concatenate the fusion features of different levels together to form the comprehensive representation, which can mitigate the effects of background noise for crack detection.

In this section, we will introduce our Transformer-based Multi-scale Fusion Model (TransMF) in detail.

3.3. Encoder Module (EM)

To model the long-range dependencies relation of different parts in the crack image from a local and global perspective, we propose a method which is a hybrid of convolution and Transformer, to explore those relationships of various parts in the crack, in which Conv-Block and Swin-Trans-Encoder Block are proposed.

As mentioned as Section 3.1, the input of our model are image label pair: $\{\mathbf{I}, \mathbf{L}\}, \mathbf{I} \in \mathbb{R}^{W \times H \times C}, \mathbf{L} \in \mathbb{R}^{W \times H}$. Encoder Module (EM) is consists of Conv-Block and Swin-Trans-Encoder Block, the output feature is f_{en}.

Conv-Block: In order to alleviate the influence of noise and obtain the local feature from a local perspective, in this paper, we design Conv-Block to obtain multi-scale feature maps. In Encoder Module (EM), Nx Conv-Block is used to extract the features of crack image **I** forming different scale feature maps. The structure of Conv-Block is shown in Figure 3a: each convolution operation is followed by a RELU activation function called Conv-RELU Block, in which the size of the convolution kernel is 3×3. After Mx convolutions, the max-pooling feature is sent into the next Conv-Block. The i-th output feature of Conv-Block is $I^i_{en_{conv}}, i \in [1, N]$ as Equation (1)

$$I^{i+1}_{en_{conv}} = \text{MaxPooling}(\underbrace{RELU(Conv(I^i_{en_{conv}}))}_{M\times}) \tag{1}$$

where $I_{en^i_{conv}} \in \mathbb{R}^{W^i \times H^i \times C^i}$ and $I^1_{en_{conv}} = \mathbf{I}$.

Swin-Trans-Encoder Block: In order to model the long-range dependencies relation of different crack regions from a global perspective, in this paper, we divide the output feature map of the last Conv-Block and design a Swin-Trans-Encoder Block to explore this relationship. The structure is shown in Figure 3c, in which ST block [19] is shown as (e).

The Swin-Trans-Encoder Block is composed of a Patch-Embedding layer and two ST blocks (Swin Transformer Block). Through the Patch Embedding operation, we split the feature map into 4×4 patches following Swin Transformer [19] and embed the feature getting $I_{em} \in \mathbb{R}^{\frac{W^N}{4} \times \frac{H^N}{4} \times C^N}$. However, we only use two ST blocks to encode these patch features. The ST block is calculated as Equation (2)

$$\begin{cases} \hat{z}^l = \text{W-MSA}(\text{LN}(z^{l-1})) + z^{l-1} \\ z^l = \text{MLP}(\text{LN}(\hat{z}^l)) + \hat{z}^l \\ \hat{z}^{l+1} = \text{SW-MSA}(\text{LN}(z^l)) + z^l \\ z^{l+1} = \text{MLP}(\text{LN}(\hat{z}^{l+1})) + \hat{z}^{l+1} \end{cases} \tag{2}$$

where $\hat{z}^l$ is the output for (S)W-MSA and z^l for MLP.

In summary, the Swin-Trans-Encoder Block is described by Equation (4).

$$f_{en_{st}} = \underbrace{ST\_Block}_{4\times}(PosEmbed(I^N_{en_{conv}})) \tag{3}$$

where $I^N_{en_{conv}}$ is the output feature of the N-th Conv-Block.

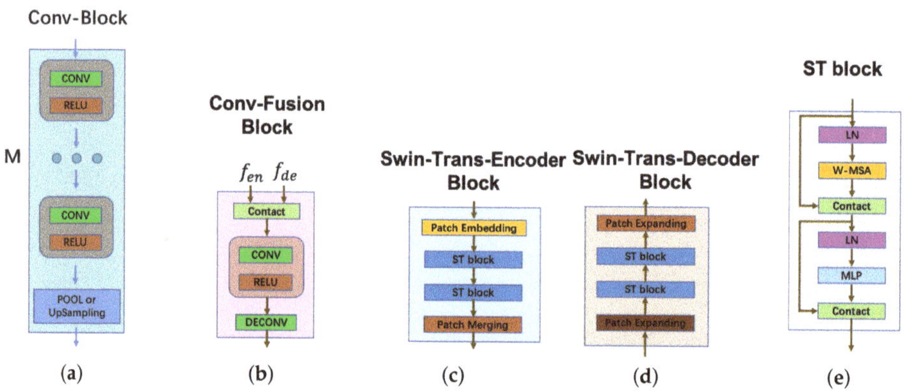

Figure 3. Subfigure (**a**) is Conv-Block, which consists of M convolution-activation blocks. The output in Encoder Module (EM) is the pooled feature, but the output in Decoder Module (DM) is the upsampling feature. Subfigure (**b**) is Conv-Fusion Block, which fuses the encoding feature and the decoding feature by concatenating, and then uses convolution fusing deeply. Subfigure (**c**) is Swin-Trans-Encoder Block, which uses Patch Embedding for image slicing and positional encoding, and uses two swin transformer blocks to extract features containing relationships, and uses Patch merging to merge image slices. Subfigure (**d**) is the Swin-Trans-Decoder Block, which uses the same number of swin transformer blocks as the Swin-Trans-Encoder Block. Subfigure (**e**) is the architecture of the swin transformer block.

3.4. Decoder Module (DM)

To decode the features from Encoder Module (EM), we design the Decoder Module (DM) symmetrically, including Swin-Trans-Decoder Block and Conv-Block, where the layer configuration of Conv-Block is symmetric to that in the Encoder Module (EM). Then we obtain the feature f_{de}.

Conv-Block: For details, refer to the explanation of Conv-Block in Encoder Module (EM). It should be noted that the pooling operation is performed when encoding, and the up-sampling operation is performed when decoding.

Swin-Trans-Decoder Block: The Swin-Trans-Decoder Block consists of two ST blocks and Patch Expanding, where the ST block is calculated as Equation (2). It is worth noting that the dimensions of the ST block in the Swin-Trans-Decoder Block and Swin-Trans-Encoder Block are the same.

For up-sampling, we design Patch Expanding through which we obtain the Swin-Trans-Decoder feature. The specific implementation is to use linear layers and normalization. After the Patch Expanding operation, the feature dimension is $W' \times H' \times C'$.

$$f_{de_{st}} = \text{PatchExpanding}(\underbrace{ST\_Block}_{4\times}(f_{en_{st}})) \tag{4}$$

Then, the output feature $I^i_{de}, i \in [0, N]$ of Swin-Trans-Decoder Block is sent to the stacked Conv-Block layers and the i-th layer is calculated as Equation (5).

$$I^i_{de_{conv}} = \text{UpSampling}(\underbrace{RELU(Conv(I^{i-1}_{de_{conv}}))}_{M\times}) \tag{5}$$

where $I^1_{de_{conv}} = f_{de_{st}}$

3.5. Fusion Module (FM)

In order to better fuse the encoding features and decoding features of different scales, in this paper, we design a Fusion Module (FM), as shown as Figure 3b. First, the concatenated features of encoding and decoding of each scale from different layers are fused in the form of 1×1 convolution, and deconv is as up-sampling to obtain the same scale feature map. Finally, the convolutional fusion features at different scales are concatenated to obtain the final feature as described in Figure 1.

Given the encoding feature f^i_{en} and decoding feature f^i_{de} of the i-th layer, the fusion feature I^i_{fusion} is calculated as Equation (6).

$$I^i_{fusion} = \text{Deconv}(\text{RELU}(\text{Conv}(\text{Concat}(f^i_{en}, f^i_{de})))) \tag{6}$$

where $i \in [1, N+1]$. Note that when $i \in [1, N]$, $f_{en} = I^i_{en_{conv}}, f_{de} = I^i_{de_{conv}}$, and when $i = N+1$, $f_{en} = f_{en_{st}}, f_{de} = f_{de_{st}}$. As shown as Equation (7).

$$f^i_{en} = \begin{cases} I^i_{en_{conv}}, & i \in [1, N] \\ f_{en_{st}}, & i = N+1 \end{cases} \quad f^i_{de} = \begin{cases} I^i_{de_{conv}}, & i \in [1, N] \\ f_{de_{st}}, & i = N+1 \end{cases} \tag{7}$$

Finally, the predicted feature is calculated according to the following Equation (8) referring to Figure 1.

$$I_{fusion} = Concat(I^i_{fusion}), i \in [1, N+1] \tag{8}$$

3.6. Loss Function

Given predicted feature I_{fusion}, we chose Binary Cross Entropy to calculate the loss as Equation (9). Given the number of pixels in an input image, denoted as $M = W \times H \times C$, the value of the j-th pixel on the feature map is F_j, and its label is L_j, the loss is calculated as Equation (9).

$$l(F_j; W) = \begin{cases} log(1 - Sigmoid(F_j; W)), & if \quad L_j = 0 \\ log(Sigmoid(F_j; W)), & if \quad L_j = 1 \end{cases} \tag{9}$$

Then, the final loss is calculated as Equation (10).

$$Loss = \sum_{j=1}^{M}(\sum_{i=1}^{N} l(F_j^i; W) + l(F_j^{fusion}; W)) \tag{10}$$

4. Experiments

Extensive experiments are performed on three public datasets, and the results are compared with the current state-of-the-art baselines. In this section, the experimental results and result analysis will be presented in detail.

4.1. Dataset

To demonstrate the effectiveness and robustness of the method TransMF proposed in this paper, we compare it with the state-of-the-art baselines on three benchmark datasets (CrackLS315 [28], CRKWH100 [28] and DeepCrack [14]). Data augmentation is used in these three datasets all in form of random blur and random color jitter. The details are shown in Table 1.

Table 1. The statistics of two benchmark Datasets .

Split	CrackLS315	CRKWH100
# train	252	80
# test	63	20
# total	315	100

4.1.1. CrackLS315 Dataset

In CrackLS315 [28], 315 asphalt road pavement images are captured under laser illumination with a line-array camera at the same ground sampling distance. The size of each image is 512 by 512 pixels. This dataset is divided into 265 images for train, 10 images for validation and 40 images for test in [28]. In this paper, for simplicity, we randomly shuffle the dataset and divide it into a train set and test set in a ratio of 4:1.

4.1.2. CRKWH100 Dataset

CRKWH100 [28] consists of 100 road pavement images of size 512 $\times$ 512 pixels, all of which are captured by a line-array camera at a ground sampling distance of 1 millimetre under visible-light illumination. In [28], this dataset is used as a validation set, and in this paper, this dataset is divided into a train set and test set according to the same rules as CrackLS315 [28].

4.1.3. DeepCrack Dataset

In DeepCrack [14], a public benchmark dataset with cracks in multi-scale and multi-scene is established, which consists of 537 RGB color images with manually annotated segmentations. The images in this dataset are of a fixed size of 544 $\times$ 384 pixels. In our experiments, we divide it into a train set and test set in a ratio of 4:1 following [28].

4.2. Evaluation Metrics

In order to compare with the current baseline methods quantitatively, in this paper, several evaluation metrics are selected and calculated referring to [14], including Global accuracy, Class average accuracy, Mean intersection over Union, Precision, Recall and F-score.

Given an image I, the label image of which is L. The number of pixel categories is m, and in the background of Crack Detection in this paper, $m = 2$. For the i-th class pixels which are predicted to class j, the number of pixels is denoted as n_{ij} and $i, j \in [0, m-1]$.

4.2.1. Global Accuracy (G)

The percentage of the pixels correctly predicted is measured by Global accuracy (G), which is calculated as following Equation (11)

$$G = \frac{\sum_{i=0}^{m} n_{ii}}{\sum_{i=0}^{m} \sum_{j=0}^{m} n_{ij}} \tag{11}$$

4.2.2. Class Average Accuracy (C)

The predictive accuracy over all classes is called Class average accuracy (C), which is calculated as Equation (12).

$$C = \frac{1}{m} \times \frac{\sum_{i=0}^{m} n_{ii}}{\sum_{j=0}^{m} n_{ij}} \tag{12}$$

4.2.3. Mean Intersection over Union (I/U)

Mean intersection over union (I/U) over all classes is calculated as Equation (13).

$$I/U = \frac{1}{m} \times \frac{\sum_{i=0}^{m} n_{ii}}{\sum_{j=0}^{m} n_{ij} + \sum_{j=0}^{m} n_{ji} - n_{ii}} \tag{13}$$

Intersection-Over-Union is a common evaluation metric for semantic image segmentation. For an individual class, the IOU metric is defined as Equation (14):

$$\text{IOU} = \frac{TP}{TP + FP + FN} \tag{14}$$

Mean intersection over union first computes IOUs for all individual classes, then returns the mean of these values, which is the standard metric of segmentation and widely used in crack detection

4.2.4. Precision (P)

According to the definition of the confusion matrix of machine learning, the Precision (P) is calculated as Equation (15).

$$P = \frac{n_{TP}}{n_{TP} + n_{FP}} \tag{15}$$

where n_{TP} is the number of True Positives, n_{FP} is the number of False Positives.

4.2.5. Recall (R)

According to the definition of the confusion matrix of machine learning, the Recall (R) is calculated as Equation (16).

$$R = \frac{n_{TP}}{n_{TP} + n_{FN}} \tag{16}$$

where n_{TP} is the number of True Positives, n_{FN} is the number of False Negatives.

4.2.6. F-Score (F)

Given Precision (P) and Recall (R), F-score (F) is calculated as Equation (17).

$$F = \frac{2PR}{P + R} \tag{17}$$

4.3. Baselines

In order to prove the effectiveness of TransMF proposed in this paper, with the above datasets and evaluation metrics, we select several strong baseline methods for comparison, including: HED [49], U-Net [13], SegNet [50], DeepCrack [14]. The details of the baseline methods are as follows:

- HED [49]: HED is an edge-detection algorithm consisting of fully convolutional neural networks and deeply-supervised nets, which can detect edges at a speed of practical relevance.
- U-Net [13]: U-Net consists of a contracting path to capture context and a symmetric expanding path that enables precise localization, which achieves very good performance due to data augmentation.
- SegNet [50]: SegNet detects cracks using semantic pixel-wise segmentation, which consists of an encoder network, a corresponding decoder network followed by a pixel-wise classification layer, eliminating the need for learning to upsample.
- DeepCrack [14]: DeepCrack predicts pixel-wise crack segmentation in an end-to-end method, which proposes a CNN-based learning method for semantic segmentation using the 'U'-shaped model architecture.
- DAUnet [40]: DAUnet is proposed to use the dense attention with U-Net, and utilizes a encoder with multi-stage dense blocks to improve its capability of extracting informative contextual features.
- MPRA [36]: MPRA uses a novel network architecture with richer feature fusion and attention mechanism and mixed pooling module for crack detection.

To demonstrate the effectiveness of all components in TransMF, several variants are designed, which are introduced in detail in Section 5.2.

4.4. Experimental Setting

We use three datasets, CrackLS315 [28], CRKWH100 [28] and DeepCrack [14], which are often used as test sets. Six evaluation strategies are used to evaluate the prediction effect, including Global accuracy (G), Class average accuracy (C), Mean intersection over Union (*I/U*), Precision (*P*), Recall (*R*) and F-score (*F*). The first three are widely used to evaluate semantic segmentation, and the latter three are commonly used for crack detection. A better I/U can highlight the superiority of our method in the field of image segmentation, and a better F1 score can be a convenient comparison in the field of crack detection, because crack detection is not only implemented by the method of image segmentation, but also the method of image detection, which is introduced in related work section.

We implement the network using the PyTorch deep learning framework. The initial value of the learning rate is 1×10^{-3}, which decays every 1000 iterations with a decay rate of 0.1. The momentum is set to 0.9 and withou weight decay. We use Adam as the optimizer and a NVIDIA GeForce GPU for training.

5. Discussion

5.1. Quantitative Results

Detailed results on three datasets are shown in Table 2. In addition, we also draw PR curves to qualitatively compare the performance of different methods, as shown in Figure 4. From which we can obtain the subsequent observations:

(1) As can be seen from Table 2, our proposed TransMF achieves the best results on all metrics except Precision (P) on both CrackLS315 [28] and CRKWH100 [28] datasets. However, the F1 score indicates that our method is the best, and the low Precision indicates that many hard cases in the dataset are still problems to be studied in crack detection. SegNet [50] is better than Unet showing that a simple skip connection cannot fuse feature information of different scales. HED [49] is implemented by a full connection network and contains rich information, but there is still redundant information. Our TransMF is better

than DeepCrack [14], indicating that the proposed Transformer-based Multi-scale Fusion Model could grasp long-range relation information from a local and global perspective.

Table 2. The results of comparison among baselines of TransMF on three datasets. The bold means that the best result for each baseline method.

Dataset	Methods	Metrics					
		G	C	I/U	P	R	F1
CrackLS315 [28]	HED	**99.81**	74.08	69.34	69.34	48.22	55.99
	Unet	99.75	72.32	65.42	50.45	44.75	47.43
	SegNet	**99.81**	69.15	66.79	**73.93**	38.34	50.5
	DeepCrack	99.60	73.99	61.51	31.28	48.25	37.95
	DAUnet	99.77	73.91	67.13	55.17	47.91	51.29
	MPRA	99.80	79.72	71.27	60.32	59.53	59.88
	TransMF	**99.81**	**80.78**	**72.24**	61.84	**61.67**	**61.75**
CRKWH100 [28]	HED	99.83	75.13	71.91	77.82	50.30	61.10
	Unet	99.78	72.84	67.54	60.72	45.75	52.18
	SegNet	99.84	73.97	72.40	**87.79**	47.96	62.03
	DeepCrack	99.59	73.97	61.83	32.48	48.22	38.81
	DAUnet	99.77	71.73	66.53	58.56	43.54	49.94
	MPRA	99.83	83.20	75.37	68.5	66.49	67.48
	TransMF	**99.85**	**84.08**	**77.37**	73.76	**68.22**	**70.88**
DeepCrack [14]	HED	98.55	90.54	81.76	75.86	81.97	78.80
	Unet	98.46	88.71	82.12	80.68	78.16	79.40
	SegNet	98.59	88.59	83.15	84.01	77.77	80.77
	DeepCrack	99.17	**94.57**	88.74	86.14	**89.64**	87.85
	TransMF	**99.27**	94.44	**89.78**	**88.89**	89.27	**89.08**

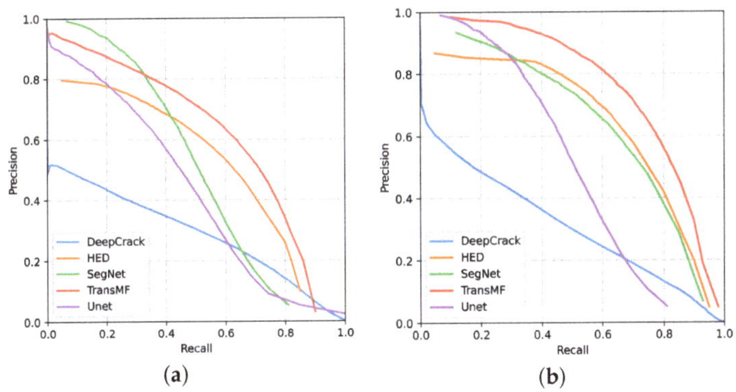

Figure 4. The Precision–Recall (PR) curve for crack detection. (**a**) on CrackLS315 dataset, (**b**) CRKWH100 dataset.

Compared to MPRA, which uses spatial attention and a channel-wise attention for low-level features and high-level features separately, our proposed TransMF utilizes an encoder–decoder structure to extract multi-scale visual features and construct the multi-scale targets sequentially, which can capture both high-level semantics and low-level details for crack detection. Compared to DAUnet, which utilizes a dense block for every encoder layer to extract contextual features, our proposed TransMF integrates a Swin-Transformer to capture long-term relations between all visual regions which can extract the richer contextual information.

(2) It can be seen from the PR curve in Figure 4, that the PR curve of TransMF completely wraps the other curves, showing that TransMF is completely better than other

methods on the CRKWH100 [28] dataset. Although it cannot be distinguished from the performance of SegNet and the others on the CrackLS315 [28] dataset, our curve is convex and full, which means our method is better. Precision effectively describes the accuracy of our positive predictions, i.e., all objects that we predicted in a given image. Recall effectively describes the completeness of our positive predictions relative to the ground truth. However, Precision and Recall can be adjusted by changing the value of the classification threshold. Usually, while the classification threshold increase, the Precision will increase and the Recall will decrease. Therefore, comparing methods via only Precision or Recall is not very meaningful and F-Measure is proposed to combine both Precision and Recall into a single measure that captures both properties. Although the Precision of our method is lower than SegNet and HED, both the Recall and the F1 score are optimal, which can prove the superiority of our method.

In addition, we run all methods on the same server with a GeForce RTX 3090 GPU and and a 2.3 GHz E5-2630 CPU. The results of time costs are reported in Table 3, where FPS means frames per second. As the input images are scaled to the same size on two datasets, the time costs of a specific method do not change on different datasets. While the proposed TransMF achieves significant performance improvements, its FPS score does not decrease a lot compared to baseline methods, which means the additional time costs are affordable.

Table 3. Time costs on two datasets.

Dataset	Method	FPS
CrackLS315	HED	18
	Unet	15
	SegNet	14
	DeepCrack	10
	TransMF	12
CRKWH100	HED	18
	Unet	15
	SegNet	14
	DeepCrack	10
	TransMF	12

5.2. Analysis of TransMF Components

In order to demonstrate the effectiveness of using Transformer and the Multi-scale Fusion model in TransMF, we design several variants for a common comparative study introduced as follows:

- TransMF$\neg f$: A variant of TransMF in which the Fusion Module is removed, and only uses the a Conv-Block in an Encoder Module (EM) and Decoder Module (DM).
- TransMF$\neg st$: A variant of TransMF which the Swin-Trans-Encoder Block and Swin-Trans-Decoder Block are removed in the Encoder Module (EM) and Decoder Module (DM).
- TransMF: the full TransMF.

Several variants of TransMF are performed and analyzed as follows, and experimental results are displayed in Table 4, from which we observe and draw the following conclusions:

(1) *Effects of Fusion Module*: From the comparison results of TransMF and TransMF$\neg f$, it can be seen that the Fusion Module plays a great role in feature representation for crack detection. With the help of the Fusion Module (FM), we obtain good features and the impact of noise can be minimized.
(2) *Effects of Transformer part*: We compare TransMF and TransMF$\neg st$, and the result of TransMF is higher than that of TransMF$\neg st$, illustrating the effectiveness of the Swin Transformer, indicating that TransMF can model the long-range dependencies relations of different parts in a crack image.

Table 4. The results of comparison among different variants of TransMF on CrackLS315 and CRKWH100 datasets. The bold means that the best result.

Dataset	Methods	Metrics					
		G	C	I/U	P	R	F1
CrackLS315 [28]	TransMF¬*st*	99.76	74.04	66.59	52.16	48.19	50.1
	TransMF¬*f*	99.75	71.23	65.06	51.48	42.56	46.6
	TransMF	**99.81**	**80.78**	**72.24**	**61.84**	**61.67**	**61.75**
CRKWH100 [28]	TransMF¬*st*	99.83	82.78	75.32	69.21	65.64	67.38
	TransMF¬*f*	99.76	71.45	66.13	57.12	42.98	49.05
	TransMF	**99.85**	**84.08**	**77.37**	**73.76**	**68.22**	**70.88**

5.3. Impacts of the ST Block Layers

In our framework, 4-layer ST blocks are used in both Swin-Trans-Encoder Block and Swin-Trans-Decoder Block. We conduct an experimental study on the number of layers of the ST block denoted as c, and the results are shown in Table 5. Of course, the more ST block layers are set, the better the effect will be. However, for the comprehensive time and efficiency, we select c = 4 in this paper.

Table 5. The results of the number of the BT block layers on three datasets. The bold means that the best result for different block layers.

Dataset	c	Metrics					
		G	C	I/U	P	R	F1
CrackLS315 [28]	c = 1	99.82	81.83	74.52	68.36	63.74	65.97
	c = 2	99.85	81.02	75.83	75.78	62.09	68.25
	c = 3	99.84	83.09	76.52	72.98	66.25	69.45
	c = 4	**99.85**	**84.08**	**77.37**	**73.76**	**68.22**	**70.88**
	c = 5	99.80	79.29	71.37	61.58	58.67	60.09
CRKWH100 [28]	c = 1	99.78	78.17	69.82	57.56	56.45	57.00
	c = 2	99.8	79.49	71.09	60.01	59.08	59.54
	c = 3	99.79	79.02	70.34	57.96	58.14	58.05
	c = 4	99.81	80.78	72.24	61.84	61.67	61.75
	c = 5	**99.84**	**81.13**	**75.21**	**72.84**	**62.33**	**67.18**

5.4. Case Study

We picked a few images, visualized the predicted pictures, and compared different methods. As shown in the Table 6, it can be seen that U-Net [13] and DeepCrack [14] are poor for continuity detection of cracks and cannot capture long dependencies. SegNet [50] and HED [49] are better at capturing continuity, but still not as good as our proposed TransMF, which shows that long-range dependencies relationships are grasped by TransMF. As can be seen from the 4th image in Table 6, there is no noise crack in the image predicted by TransMF but exists in the image predicted by SegNet, which shows the robustness to noise of TransMF.

Table 6. Visualization of original and predicted segmentation images by all the methods.

Original Image	Ground Truth	HED	Unet	SegNet	DeepCrack	TransMF

6. Conclusions

In this paper, we propose a novel crack detection method called *Transformer-based Multi-scale Fusion Model* (TransMF), which detects a crack in form of semantic segmentation. The framework of TransMF includes an Encoder Module (EM), Decoder Module (DM) and Fusion Module (FM), in which the Encoder Module and Decoder Module use multiple convolution blocks and a Swin Transformer block to model the long-range dependencies of different parts in a crack image from a local and global perspective for a better crack image understanding. The output of the Encoder Module and the output of the Decoder Module at different scales are fused in the form of Convolution in the Fusion Module. The output of each layer of the Fusion Module is spliced to alleviate achieve the effect of background noise for the purpose of crack detection. Extensive experiments on three benchmark datasets (CrackLS315, CRKWH100 and DeepCrack) demonstrate that the proposed TransMF in this paper exceeds the best performance at present.

Author Contributions: Conceptualization, X.J. and S.Q.; methodology, X.J.; validation, X.J. and X.Z.; writing—original draft, X.J.; writing—review and editing, X.Z. and S.Q. All authors have read and agreed to the published version of the manuscript.

Funding: This work was supported by the National Natural Science Foundation (NSF) of China (No. U1934209).

Institutional Review Board Statement: Not applicable.

Informed Consent Statement: Not applicable.

Data Availability Statement: Data available in a publicly accessible repository. The data presented in this study are openly available at https://1drv.ms/f/s!AittnGm6vRKLtylBkxVXw5arGn6R (accessed on 1 July 2022).

Conflicts of Interest: The authors declare no conflict of interest.

Abbreviations

Abbreviation	Extension
EM	Encoder Module
DM	Decoder Module
FM	Fusion Module
DL	Deep Learning
AI	Artificial Intelligence
FR	Face Recognition
VLPR	Vehicle License Plate Recognition
CNNs	Convolutional Neural Networks
NLP	Natural Language Processing
CV	Computer Vision
FCN	Fully Convolutional Network
ST	Swin Transformer
G	Global accuracy
C	Class average accuracy
I/U	Mean intersection over Union
P	Precision
R	Recall
F	F-score
PR	Precision-Recall

References

1. Taigman, Y.; Yang, M.; Ranzato, M.; Wolf, L. DeepFace: Closing the Gap to Human-Level Performance in Face Verification. In Proceedings of the 2014 IEEE Conference on Computer Vision and Pattern Recognition, Columbus, OH, USA, 23–28 June 2014; pp. 1701–1708.
2. Silva, S.M.; Jung, C.R. License Plate Detection and Recognition in Unconstrained Scenarios. In Proceedings of the European Conference on Computer Vision, Munich, Germany, 8–14 September 2018; Lecture Notes in Computer Science; Volume 11216, pp. 593–609.
3. Li, T.; Wang, Y.; Hong, R.; Wang, M.; Wu, X. pDisVPL: Probabilistic Discriminative Visual Part Learning for Image Classification. *IEEE Multim.* **2018**, *25*, 34–45. [CrossRef]
4. Li, T.; Meng, Z.; Ni, B.; Shen, J.; Wang, M. Robust geometric ℓ_p-norm feature pooling for image classification and action recognition. *Image Vis. Comput.* **2016**, *55*, 64–76. [CrossRef]
5. Li, T.; Ni, B.; Wu, X.; Gao, Q.; Li, Q.; Sun, D. On random hyper-class random forest for visual classification. *Neurocomputing* **2016**, *172*, 281–289. [CrossRef]
6. Abdel-Qader, I.; Pashaie-Rad, S.; Abudayyeh, O.; Yehia, S. PCA-Based algorithm for unsupervised bridge crack detection. *Adv. Eng. Softw.* **2006**, *37*, 771–778. [CrossRef]
7. Xu, H.; Su, X.; Wang, Y.; Cai, H.; Cui, K.; Chen, X. Automatic Bridge Crack Detection Using a Convolutional Neural Network. *Appl. Sci.* **2019**, *9*, 2867. [CrossRef]
8. Tong, X.; Guo, J.; Ling, Y.; Yin, Z. A new image-based method for concrete bridge bottom crack detection. In Proceedings of the 2011 International Conference on Image Analysis and Signal Processing, Wuhan, China, 21–23 October 2011, pp. 568–571. [CrossRef]
9. Liu, H.; Yang, C.; Li, A.; Ge, Y.; Huang, S.; Feng, X.; Ruan, Z. Deep Domain Adaptation for Pavement Crack Detection. *arXiv* **2021**, arXiv:2111.10101.
10. Zhang, K.; Zhang, Y.; Cheng, H. CrackGAN: Pavement Crack Detection Using Partially Accurate Ground Truths Based on Generative Adversarial Learning. *IEEE Trans. Intell. Transp. Syst.* **2021**, *22*, 1306–1319. [CrossRef]
11. Cao, W.; Liu, Q.; He, Z. Review of Pavement Defect Detection Methods. *IEEE Access* **2020**, *8*, 14531–14544. [CrossRef]
12. Huyan, J.; Li, W.; Tighe, S.; Xu, Z.; Zhai, J. CrackU-net: A novel deep convolutional neural network for pixelwise pavement crack detection. *Struct. Control Health Monit.* **2020**, *27*, e2551. [CrossRef]
13. Ronneberger, O.; Fischer, P.; Brox, T. U-Net: Convolutional Networks for Biomedical Image Segmentation. In Proceedings of the International Conference on Medical Image Computing and Computer-Assisted Intervention, Munich, Germany, 5–9 October 2015; Lecture Notes in Computer Science; Volume 9351, pp. 234–241.
14. Liu, Y.; Yao, J.; Lu, X.; Xie, R.; Li, L. DeepCrack: A deep hierarchical feature learning architecture for crack segmentation. *Neurocomputing* **2019**, *338*, 139–153. [CrossRef]

15. Liu, J.; Yang, X.; Lau, S.; Wang, X.; Luo, S.; Lee, V.C.; Ding, L. Automated pavement crack detection and segmentation based on two-step convolutional neural network. *Comput. Aided Civ. Infrastruct. Eng.* **2020**, *35*, 1291–1305. [CrossRef]
16. Mohan, A.; Poobal, S. Crack detection using image processing: A critical review and analysis. *Alex. Eng. J.* **2017**, *57*, 787–798. [CrossRef]
17. Vaswani, A.; Shazeer, N.; Parmar, N.; Uszkoreit, J.; Jones, L.; Gomez, A.N.; Kaiser, L.; Polosukhin, I. Attention is All you Need. *Adv. Neural Inf. Process. Syst.* **2017**, *30*, 5998–6008.
18. Dosovitskiy, A.; Beyer, L.; Kolesnikov, A.; Weissenborn, D.; Zhai, X.; Unterthiner, T.; Dehghani, M.; Minderer, M.; Heigold, G.; Gelly, S.; et al. An Image is Worth 16x16 Words: Transformers for Image Recognition at Scale. *arXiv* **2021**, arXiv:2010.11929.
19. Liu, Z.; Lin, Y.; Cao, Y.; Hu, H.; Wei, Y.; Zhang, Z.; Lin, S.; Guo, B. Swin Transformer: Hierarchical Vision Transformer using Shifted Windows. In Proceedings of the IEEE/CVF International Conference on Computer Vision, Montreal, BC, Canada, 11–17 October 2021; pp. 9992–10002.
20. Guo, Q.; Qiu, X.; Liu, P.; Shao, Y.; Xue, X.; Zhang, Z. Star-Transformer. NAACL-HLT (1); Association for Computational Linguistics: Minneapolis, MN, USA, 7 June 2019; pp. 1315–1325. Available online: https://aclanthology.org/N19-1133/ (accessed on 2 June 2019)
21. Liu, H.; Miao, X.; Mertz, C.; Xu, C.; Kong, H. CrackFormer: Transformer Network for Fine-Grained Crack Detection. In Proceedings of the IEEE/CVF International Conference on Computer Vision (ICCV), Montreal, BC, Canada, 11–17 October 2021; pp. 3783–3792.
22. Kong, J.; Bian, Y.; Jiang, M. MTT: Multi-Scale Temporal Transformer for Skeleton-Based Action Recognition. *IEEE Signal Process. Lett.* **2022**, *29*, 528–532. [CrossRef]
23. Xiao, Y.; Yuan, Q.; He, J.; Zhang, Q.; Sun, J.; Su, X.; Wu, J.; Zhang, L. Space-time super-resolution for satellite video: A joint framework based on multi-scale spatial-temporal transformer. *Int. J. Appl. Earth Obs. Geoinf.* **2022**, *108*, 102731. [CrossRef]
24. Yuan, W.; Xu, W. MSST-Net: A Multi-Scale Adaptive Network for Building Extraction from Remote Sensing Images Based on Swin Transformer. *Remote. Sens.* **2021**, *13*, 4743. [CrossRef]
25. Jiaji, W.; Liu, Y.F.; Nie, X.; Mo, Y. Deep convolutional neural networks for semantic segmentation of cracks. *Struct. Control. Health Monit.* **2021**, *29*, e2850. [CrossRef]
26. Li, Y.; Han, Z.; Xu, H.; Liu, L.; Li, X.; Zhang, K. YOLOv3-Lite: A Lightweight Crack Detection Network for Aircraft Structure Based on Depthwise Separable Convolutions. *Appl. Sci.* **2019**, *9*, 3781. [CrossRef]
27. Song, W.; Jia, G.; Zhu, H.; Gao, L. Automated Pavement Crack Damage Detection Using Deep Multiscale Convolutional Features. *J. Adv. Transp.* **2020**, *2020*, 1–11. [CrossRef]
28. Zou, Q.; Zhang, Z.; Li, Q.; Qi, X.; Wang, Q.; Wang, S. DeepCrack: Learning Hierarchical Convolutional Features for Crack Detection. *IEEE Trans. Image Process.* **2019**, *28*, 1498–1512. [CrossRef]
29. Mitchell, T.M. *Machine Learning*; McGraw-Hill: New York, NY, USA, 1997.
30. Schulz, H.; Behnke, S. Deep Learning. *KI-Künstliche Intell.* **2012**, *26*. [CrossRef]
31. Valueva, M.; Nagornov, N.; Lyakhov, P.; Valuev, G.; Chervyakov, N. Application of the residue number system to reduce hardware costs of the convolutional neural network implementation. *Math. Comput. Simul.* **2020**, *177*, 232–243. [CrossRef]
32. Chen, H.; Lin, H. An Effective Hybrid Atrous Convolutional Network for Pixel-Level Crack Detection. *IEEE Trans. Instrum. Meas.* **2021**, *70*, 1–12. [CrossRef]
33. Munawar, H.S.; Hammad, A.; Haddad, A.; Soares, C.; Waller, S. Image-Based Crack Detection Methods: A Review. *Infrastructures* **2021**, *6*, 115. [CrossRef]
34. Yao, G.; Sun, Y.; Yang, Y.; Liao, G. Lightweight Neural Network for Real-Time Crack Detection on Concrete Surface in Fog. *Front. Mater.* **2021**, *8*, 517. [CrossRef]
35. Xiang, X.; Wang, Z.; Qiao, Y. An Improved YOLOv5 Crack Detection Method Combined with Transformer. *IEEE Sens. J.* **2022**. [CrossRef]
36. Zhou, Q.; Qu, Z.; Cao, C. Mixed pooling and richer attention feature fusion for crack detection. *Pattern Recognit. Lett.* **2021**, *145*, 96–102. [CrossRef]
37. Qu, Z.; Cao, C.; Liu, L.; Zhou, D.Y. A deeply supervised convolutional neural network for pavement crack detection with multiscale feature fusion. *IEEE Trans. Neural Netw. Learn. Syst.* **2021**. [CrossRef]
38. Li, S.; Zhao, X. Image-Based Concrete Crack Detection Using Convolutional Neural Network and Exhaustive Search Technique. *Adv. Civil Eng.* **2019**, *2019*, 1–12. [CrossRef]
39. Deng, J.; Dong, W.; Socher, R.; Li, L.; Li, K.; Fei-Fei, L. ImageNet: A large-scale hierarchical image database. In Proceedings of the 2009 IEEE Conference on Computer Vision and Pattern Recognition, Miami, FL, USA, 20–25 June 2009; pp. 248–255.
40. Hsiel, Y.A.; Tsai, Y.C.J. Dau-net: Dense attention u-net for pavement crack segmentation. In Proceedings of the 2021 IEEE International Intelligent Transportation Systems Conference (ITSC), Indianapolis, IN, USA, 19–22 September 2021; pp. 2251–2256.
41. Yang, X.; Li, H.; Yu, Y.; Luo, X.; Huang, T.; Yang, X. Automatic Pixel-Level Crack Detection and Measurement Using Fully Convolutional Network. *Comput.-Aided Civ. Infrastruct. Eng.* **2018**, *33*, 1090–1109. [CrossRef]
42. Kheradmandi, N.; Mehranfar, V. A critical review and comparative study on image segmentation-based techniques for pavement crack detection. *Constr. Build. Mater.* **2022**, *321*, 126162. [CrossRef]
43. Dung, C.V.; Anh, L.D. Autonomous concrete crack detection using deep fully convolutional neural network. *Autom. Constr.* **2019**, *99*, 52–58. [CrossRef]

44. Li, S.; Zhao, X.; Zhou, G. Automatic pixel-level multiple damage detection of concrete structure using fully convolutional network. *Comput.-Aided Civ. Infrastruct. Eng.* **2019**, *34*, 616–634. [CrossRef]
45. Zhang, L.; Shen, J.; Zhu, B. A research on an improved Unet-based concrete crack detection algorithm. *Struct. Health Monit.* **2020**, *20*, 1864–1879. [CrossRef]
46. Shokri, P.; Shahbazi, M.; Lichti, D.; Nielsen, J. VISION-BASED APPROACHES FOR QUANTIFYING CRACKS IN CONCRETE STRUCTURES. *ISPRS-Int. Arch. Photogramm. Remote Sens. Spat. Inf. Sci.* **2020**, *XLIII-B2-2020*, 1167–1174. [CrossRef]
47. Fang, J.; Qu, B.; Yuan, Y. Distribution equalization learning mechanism for road crack detection. *Neurocomputing* **2021**, *424*, 193–204. [CrossRef]
48. Kanaeva, I.; Ivanova, J. Road pavement crack detection using deep learning with synthetic data. *IOP Conf. Ser. Mater. Sci. Eng.* **2021**, *1019*, 012036. [CrossRef]
49. Xie, S.; Tu, Z. Holistically-Nested Edge Detection. In Proceedings of the IEEE International Conference on Computer Vision, Santiago, Chile, 7–13 December 2015; pp. 1395–1403.
50. Badrinarayanan, V.; Kendall, A.; Cipolla, R. SegNet: A Deep Convolutional Encoder-Decoder Architecture for Image Segmentation. *IEEE Trans. Pattern Anal. Mach. Intell.* **2017**, *39*, 2481–2495. [CrossRef]

mathematics

MDPI

Article

Semantic Segmentation of UAV Images Based on Transformer Framework with Context Information

Satyawant Kumar, Abhishek Kumar and Dong-Gyu Lee *

Department of Artificial Intelligence, Kyungpook National University, Daegu 41566, Republic of Korea
* Correspondence: dglee@knu.ac.kr

Abstract: With the advances in Unmanned Aerial Vehicles (UAVs) technology, aerial images with huge variations in the appearance of objects and complex backgrounds have opened a new direction of work for researchers. The task of semantic segmentation becomes more challenging when capturing inherent features in the global and local context for UAV images. In this paper, we proposed a transformer-based encoder-decoder architecture to address this issue for the precise segmentation of UAV images. The inherent feature representation of the UAV images is exploited in the encoder network using a self-attention-based transformer framework to capture long-range global contextual information. A Token Spatial Information Fusion (TSIF) module is proposed to take advantage of a convolution mechanism that can capture local details. It fuses the local contextual details about the neighboring pixels with the encoder network and makes semantically rich feature representations. We proposed a decoder network that processes the output of the encoder network for the final semantic level prediction of each pixel. We demonstrate the effectiveness of this architecture on UAVid and Urban Drone datasets, where we achieved mIoU of 61.93% and 73.65%, respectively.

Keywords: semantic segmentation; UAV street scene images; transformer; global and local context

MSC: 68U10; 68T01; 68T07; 68T45

1. Introduction

Semantic segmentation of images, i.e., assigning labels to each pixel, has been widely studied in the field of computer vision. Majorly its applications are in medical imaging [1,2], autonomous driving cars [3–5], satellite image segmentation [6], and point cloud scene segmentation [7]. Due to the rapid development of smart technologies, the application of Unmanned Aerial Vehicles (UAVs), i.e., drones, has significantly increased. UAV devices can capture photos even in remote areas where it is difficult for a human. Aerial images captured by UAV devices contain rich information [8] that can be utilized for different tasks such as traffic density estimation [9], building extraction [10], and flooded area monitoring [11].

Recently, semantic segmentation of UAV images has shown decent performance in a variety of applications [12]. Dutta et al. [13] designed a segmentation framework for UAV images for the early detection of disease in cruciferous crops. Song et al. [14] designed an image fusion-based segmentation network for sunflower lodging recognition using UAV images. Lobo Torres et al. [15] tested Fully Convolutional Network (FCN) based approaches for conducting endangered tree species analyses using UAV urban scene areas. The semantic segmentation of UAV street scene images has opened a new direction of work for researchers [16]. Pixel-level dense prediction results of objects in street scene images are beneficial for land use monitoring. Convolution-based architectures are widely exploited for segmentation in computer vision. The majority of the segmentation models [17–20] adopt FCN-based [21] encoder network and design different decoder architectures. However, the FCN-based encoder backbone results in coarse predictions [22], and the receptive field becomes constant after a certain threshold limit [4]. Due to local receptive fields in Convolutional Neural Networks (CNNs), it maintains local context properly but fails to capture global contexts [23]. For UAV scene segmentation, Lyu et al. [16] constructed a segmentation dataset and designed a segmentation model, which showed satisfactory results for UAV image segmentation. Girisha et al. [24] adopted Long Short-Term Memory (LSTM) or optical flow modules for UAV urban scene segmentation.

UAV images normally contain very complex backgrounds, with lots of variations in object appearance and scale, which poses a significant challenge for semantic segmentation [12]. Even though the existing segmentation frameworks show satisfactory results, including the ones specially designed for UAV scene segmentation, their feature extractor struggles to capture the inherent features of aerial images. Segmenting minority classes, especially small objects such as humans, which have the least number of pixels in the whole image, becomes challenging. For dense prediction tasks on complex UAV images, i.e., semantic segmentation, global and local context information is an important component [22,25]. Considering both, the global and local contextual details can precisely give better performance [8,12,26]. Pixels belonging to the same class but far apart from each other represent the global context, whereas the neighboring pixels of the same class represent the local context. Global and local context modeling is shown in Figure 1. Yellow and red arrows in the figure represent the global and local contextual information modeling.

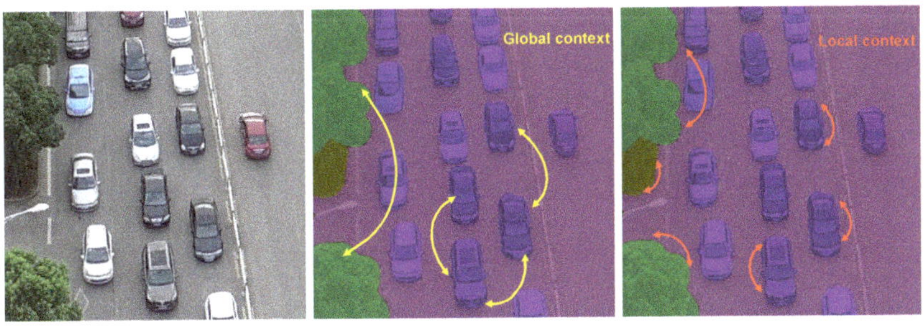

(a) (b) (c)

Figure 1. Illustrating global and local context information for UAV image semantic segmentation. (**a**) Input image. (**b**) Global context modeling. The yellow arrows represent the global contextual information. (**c**) Local context modeling. The red arrows represent the local contextual information.

The focus of this work is to achieve precise semantic segmentation of UAV street scene images. Inspired by the transformer-based design paradigms for computer vision tasks [23,27], an encoder-decoder framework is proposed to address such issues in this work. It incorporates a self-attention-based encoder network, which captures long-range information in the UAV images via maintaining global receptive fields. This allows the network to maintain global contextual details. For modeling low-level contextual details, using the advantage of CNNs in capturing local information, a convolution-based element is introduced in the encoder network, i.e., the Token Spatial Information Fusion (TSIF) module. Capturing local context information lets the network maintain the proper shape and size of the objects in the segmentation results. The output of the powerful self-attention-based encoder network contains semantically very rich information, both global and local contextual details. A decoder network is proposed for final pixel-level predictions, which processes this output information from the encoder network.

In short, the main contributions of this paper are as follows:

1. We propose a new encoder-decoder-based framework for semantic segmentation of UAV street scene images;
2. The encoder network is designed using the transformer-based module to capture global and local context information;

3. A decoder network is constructed to upsample the output of the encoder network to the original size image without losing the semantically rich information;
4. Experiments on UAVid and Urban Drone Dataset (UDD-6) datasets demonstrate that the proposed method outperforms the state-of-the-art methods.

The rest of the paper is presented as follows: Section 2 discusses the related work. In Section 3, we briefly discuss the proposed design. We describe the experimental results in Section 4. Based on our findings, we discuss the advantage of the proposed method in Section 5. At last, in Section 6, we conclude the work of this paper.

2. Related Work

2.1. Semantic Segmentation

In the direction of semantic image segmentation, a Fully Convolutional Network (FCN) [21] is the first work that used Convolutional Neural Networks (CNNs). Following this work, many different methods have been designed to improve its segmentation results. DeconvNet [28] used a progressive upsampling strategy to upsample the coarse output of the FCN. SegNet [29] upsampled a coarse feature map by using max pool indices transferred from the FCN encoder. U-Net [1] used skip connections and introduced contracting and expanding paths. It fused the information from the encoder network to the decoder network during each upsampling stage. GCN [30] and DeepLAbV3+ [17] adopted a dilation rate greater than 1 to increase the strength of the receptive field. DANet [18], CCNet [31], and ISNet [3] used attention-based operations to capture long-range global context details. Li et al. [32] used the Multitask Low-rank Affinity Pursuit (MLAP) method to annotate and segment images. Li et al. [33] used automatic labeling of infra-red images for UAVs using a probabilistic framework.

2.2. Transformer

Transformer-based [34] frameworks have transformed the entire field of Natural Language Processing (NLP). With its huge success in NLP, researchers have also started exploring its application for computer vision tasks. Vision Transformer (ViT) [23] is the first work in this direction, and it used a fully transformer-based design for image classification. After that, many researchers [35–38] followed its work to improve the classification accuracy. DeiT [35] introduced a teacher-student framework to provide easy learning for the network.

ViT split an input image into a sequence of tokens, and the sequence is processed by a set of stacked transformer encoder blocks. It uses a self-attention-based mechanism to maintain the global receptive field, which CNN-based architectures lack [4,23]. After its introduction, many architectures were designed to solve dense prediction tasks such as image segmentation [4,39] and object detection [40,41]. SETR [4] used ViT as an encoder and developed different variants of decoder designs. On top of a ViT-based encoder, Segmenter [42] designed a mask-based decoder network. PVT [27], DPT [43], and Segformer [44] adopted different design choices to generate multi-scale feature representations like CNNs. DPT generated hierarchical feature representation by assembling tokens from different stages of the ViT. PVT and Segformer adopted a framework to progressively shrink the pyramid to output varying scale features. Yuan et al. [45], Xie et al. [44], Wu et al. [46], and Chu et al. [37] adopted different convolution-based variants to fuse positional information.

2.3. Semantic Segmentation of Aerial Images

Due to an increased application of UAV devices, recent semantic segmentation of aerial images [8,25] has given a new research opportunity to researchers. UNetFormer [25] used a ResNet-based encoder module and designed a decoder network using a transformer framework to model image-level and semantic-level details. MFNet [8] employed a framework to maintain low-level details and inter-class discriminative characteristics. UAVFormer [26] used aggregation window-based self-attention modules to model complex features in the UAV scenes. ABCNet [22], CANet [47], and BANet [48] used a dual path approach to capture long-range and fine-grained information. Liu et al. [49] designed a lightweight attention network, which uses spatial and channel attention modules. Iqbal et al. [50] followed a weakly-supervised domain adaption framework for the segmentation of aerial and satellite images. It handles cross-domain discrimination issues between aerial and satellite imagery. Yeung et al. [6] adopted steerable-filter-based and transfer-learning-based paradigms for segmenting satellite images. It addressed the issue of the least availability of labeled data for satellite scenes. Gebrehiwot et al. [51] segmented flooded regions in UAV images, where the flooded water is differentiated from buildings, vegetation, and roads. Ichim et al. [11] used a decision fusion-based strategy to segment the flooded areas and vegetation in UAV scenes. Zhang et al. [52] combined a series of residual U-Net modules for segmenting plants in UAV images. Dutta et al. [13] designed a framework to semantically segment unhealthy leaves in aerial images. ICENet [53] used a positional and channel-wise fusion of attentive features for segmenting ice in rivers. Gevaert et al. [54] used the semantic classification method to manage infrastructural development in informal settlement regions.

3. Proposed Method

3.1. Encoder Network

The encoder network is constructed using a self-attention-based transformer [23] framework. Overall, it consists of an image tokenization module, a linear projection module, transformer encoder modules, and a Token Spatial Information Fusion (TSIF) module. Figure 2a describes an overview of the encoder network. It uses an image as input and splits it into a sequence of tokens using the image tokenization module.

The image tokenization module transforms the two-dimensional input data, i.e., $x \in I^{H \times W \times 3}$ into a sequence of two-dimensional tokens, i.e., $x_t \in I^{S \times (t^2 \cdot 3)}$. (H, W) and (t, t) represent the input image size and the token size, respectively. $S = \frac{HW}{t^2}$ represents the number of tokens coming out from the input image. The linear projection module projects the sequence to a projection dimension, i.e., $x_t \in I^{S \times P}$. P represents the projection dimension. Here, the values of t and P are set to 16 and 1024, respectively.

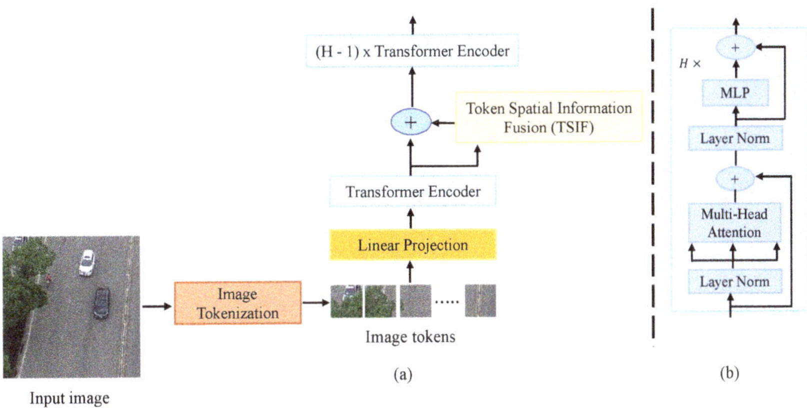

Figure 2. (**a**) Overview of an encoder network design. It consists of linear projection, transformer encoder, and Token Spatial Information Fusion (TSIF) modules. (**b**) Transformer encoder module.

The output of the linear projection module is processed using H number of transformer encoder modules. Each transformer encoder module consists of a Multi-head Self-attention (MHA) block and a Multi-Layer Perceptron (MLP) block. A Layer Normalization (LN) is applied before each block, and a residual connection after each block is applied. Figure 2b demonstrates the overall architecture of the transformer encoder module. Here, H is set to 24.

The collection of multiple Self-Attention (SA) operations makes an MHA block. The input sequence $x_t = I^{S\times P}$ is projected into query (Q), key (K), and value (V):

$$Q \in I^{S\times P}, K \in I^{S\times P}, V \in I^{S\times P}, \tag{1}$$

then the SA operation is performed using Q, K and V vectors as follows:

$$SelfAttention(Q,K,V) = Softmax(\frac{QK^T}{\sqrt{C}})V, \tag{2}$$

feature space of Q, K, and V are split into k times, and the MHA operation is performed in parallel. Here, k denotes the number of heads and is set to 16. The output of each head is concatenated together and projected to the projection dimension. The self-attention-based transformer encoder module gives the ability to incorporate a global receptive field at each stage, and hence supports the network to capture global contextual information [23]. The MLP block consists of two linear layers with a non-linearity function in between them. It performs feature expansion and reduction operations using the layers. The first layer expands the feature space by a factor of e. The second layer restores the expanded dimension back to the original. Here, e represents the feature expansion/reduction ratio. The output of the MLP module is as follows:

$$MLP(x) = (\nabla(xW_1 + b_1))W_2 + b_2, \tag{3}$$

where $W_1 \in I^{P\times L}$ and $W_2 \in I^{L\times P}$ corresponds to the weight of the first and second layers, respectively. P is the projection dimension and L is the expanded dimension. Here, L is set to 4096. The $b_1 \in I^L$ and $b_2 \in I^P$ are the biases corresponding to the first and second layers, respectively. $\nabla(.)$ is the non-linearity function. The overall output of an individual transformer encoder is as follows:

$$y = LN(x + MHA(x)), \tag{4}$$

$$z = LN(y + MLP(y)). \tag{5}$$

The Token Spatial Information Fusion (TSIF) module helps to capture low-level spatial context details about neighboring pixels in image tokens. Since the receptive field of CNNs are local in nature, it can extract local information around the neighboring pixels well [45]. Hence, convolution keeps the ability to capture local context details for dense prediction tasks such as semantic segmentation [44]. TSIF operation can be represented as follows:

$$p' = \psi(Reshape(x)), \tag{6}$$

$$TSIF_{out} = Flatten(p') + x, \tag{7}$$

where ψ is the $R \times R$ convolution operation and it is set to 3 in this work. ψ can also be replaced with other convolution variants as well for fusing the local fine-grained details. Using this design paradigm of the TSIF module also increases the representation power of features.

3.2. Decoder Network

The decoder network consists of four upsampling stages. It takes the output feature map of the powerful transformer-based encoder as input for final segmentation. It uses a gradual upsampling policy to generate the original size feature map as the input image. Before feeding the output of the encoder network to the decoder network, the feature maps are reshaped into a $3D$ representation as follows:

$$G(x_{in}) = P \times \frac{H}{16} \times \frac{W}{16}, \tag{8}$$

where G is the reshape operation, which takes the output feature of the encoder network, i.e., x_{in} as the input. P is the projection dimension and $\frac{H}{16} \times \frac{W}{16}$ represents the output feature resolution of the encoder network. This reshaped $3D$ feature is fed to the decoder network. Figure 3 represents an overview of the decoder network. Each stage consists of bilinear upsampling with a scale factor of 2, followed by a 3×3 convolution operation and a Gaussian Error Linear Units (GELU) activation function. N_c represents the feature channels at each stage and is set to 256. The output feature maps of the last stage are of the same resolution as the original image, i.e., (H, W). The channel dimension of these features are projected to the number of semantic categories, i.e., N_{cls} using a 1×1 convolution operation.

The output feature of the encoder network contains semantically rich information in terms of both global and local context details. This design paradigm of the decoder network generates the segmentation output without losing those details.

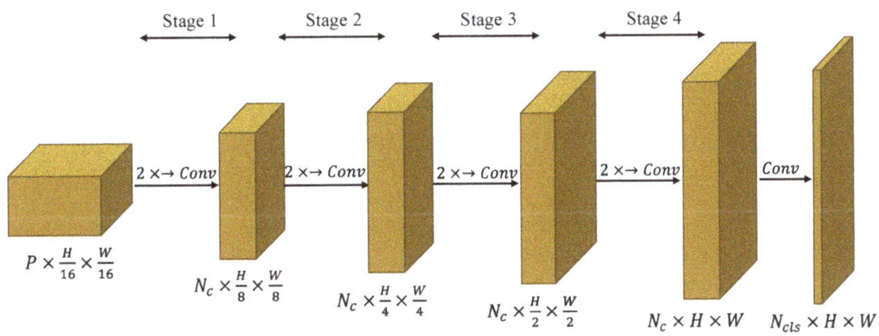

Figure 3. Overview of a decoder network. It consists of four upsampling stages.

4. Experiments

4.1. Dataset Overview

The performance of the proposed method was evaluated on two publicly available Unmanned Aerial Vehicles (UAVs) semantic segmentation datasets; UAVid [16] and Urban Drone Dataset (UDD-6) [55]. The UAVid dataset contains 42 sequences of urban street scene images. Each sequence consists of 10 RGB images of 3840×2160 or 4096×2160 size. Twenty sequences are for training, seven sequences are for validation, and the remaining are for testing. It consists of eight semantic categories; building, road, tree, vegetation, static car, moving car, humans, and clutter. The UDD-6 dataset is collected in multiple cities. It contains 141 RGB images that consist of training and validation sets of 106 and 35 images, respectively. Each image has 3840×2160 or 4096×2160 or 4000×3000 size. It contains six semantic labels; facade, road, vegetation, vehicle, roof, and others.

4.2. Implementation Details

Since it is difficult and computationally expensive to use high-resolution UAV images for training, we split the original image into patches of 512×512 resolution without overlap. The original image size is not divisible by 512, and there will be some extra image regions that will not fit in 512×512 size. For those extra regions, we extract 512×512 size patch with the required overlap. We merge the predictions on each patch into the original size image for evaluation of the metrics. Image attributes are normalized using mean and standard deviation of $(0.4914, 0.4824, 0.4467)$ and $(0.2471, 0.2436, 0.2616)$, respectively. Random horizontal flipping is used for augmentation. Complete experiments are conducted on NVIDIA RTX A6000 GPU, using the PyTorch library. Step learning rate schedule is used with an initial learning rate set to 1×10^{-3} and Stochastic Gradient Descent (SGD) is utilized as an optimizer with a momentum of 0.9 and weight decay of 1×10^{-4} on both the datasets. The network is trained for 120 and 180 epochs on UAVid and UDD-6 datasets respectively, using a batch size of 4. Cross-entropy loss is minimized during training.

4.3. Results on UAVid Dataset

In this subsection, we present the test results using the UAVid dataset. It is an UAV urban scene segmentation dataset, and due to many scale variations, it is very challenging to get high segmentation accuracy. We selected the Dilation Net [56], U-Net [1], MSD [16], ERFNet [57], BiSeNetV2 [58], Fast-SCNN [59], ShelfNet [60], SETR-PUP [4], and Segmenter [42] for comparison. Per class Intersection over Union (IoU) score, Mean IoU (mIoU), and Overall Accuracy (OA) are used as performance metrics. Appendix A.1 describes the evaluation protocol for these metrics. The quantitative results compared with competitive methods are mentioned in Table 1. The highest value of each metric in the table is marked in bold. The proposed framework shows mIoU and OA of 61.93% and 84.49%, respectively. It outperforms other methods at least by 2.25% in mIoU. Per class IoU also shows competitive performance with other methods.

ERFNet and BiSeNetV2 show mIoU of 59.28% and 59.68%, respectively, which is comparable to the performance of the proposed framework with a mIoU of 61.93%. However, the proposed method outperforms Dilation Net, U-Net, MSD, Fast-SCNN, ShelfNet, SETR-PUP, and Segmenter with a decent margin of 13.35%, 3.51%, 4.94%, 15.99%, 14.9%, 7.94%, and 3.18%, respectively, in mIoU. In per-class IoU, the proposed method outperforms Segmenter in five out of eight categories. Humans are the minority class in the whole dataset and also the smallest object to segment. Hence, it is very challenging to segment humans. For the human class, the proposed method shows decent performance, with a mIoU of 22.94%. The proposed method lags ERFNet by 0.2% in OA, but it outperforms by 2.68% in mIoU. It outperforms U-Net, BiSeNetV2, and SETR-PUP by 1.06%, 3.39%, and 4.63%, respectively, in OA.

Table 1. Quantitative comparison of the UAVid test dataset result with competitive methods.

Methods	Class IoU (%)								mIoU (%)	O.A (%)
	Building	Tree	Clutter	Road	Low Veg	Static Car	Moving Car	Human		
Dilation Net [56]	80.70	73.80	45.40	65.10	45.50	24.50	53.60	0.00	48.58	-
U-Net [1]	82.94	77.27	61.80	75.15	62.03	29.98	59.59	18.62	58.42	83.43
MSD [16]	79.80	74.50	57.00	74.00	55.90	32.10	62.90	19.70	56.99	-
ERFNet [57]	**85.58**	**77.87**	**64.50**	77.34	**62.21**	46.13	60.64	0.00	59.28	**84.69**
BiSeNetV2 [58]	81.62	75.97	61.18	77.11	61.30	38.51	**66.36**	15.40	59.68	81.10
Fast-SCNN [59]	75.70	71.50	44.20	61.60	43.40	19.50	51.60	0.00	45.94	-
ShelfNet [60]	76.90	73.20	44.10	61.40	43.40	21.00	52.60	3.60	47.03	-
SETR-PUP [4]	77.77	73.51	55.64	71.62	54.15	26.88	55.89	16.49	53.99	79.86
Segmenter [42]	84.40	76.10	64.20	**79.80**	57.60	34.50	59.20	14.20	58.75	-
Proposed Method	84.67	77.47	63.93	78.44	61.31	**47.66**	59.02	**22.94**	**61.93**	84.49

Qualitative results of the proposed method using the UAVid validation and test datasets are depicted in Figures 4 and 5, respectively. We can see that the proposed approach generates smooth segmentation of UAV images. It captures the global and local contextual information well. Cars are well segmented while maintaining their proper shape and size. In the third and fifth images of Figure 5, small objects such as humans are well segmented.

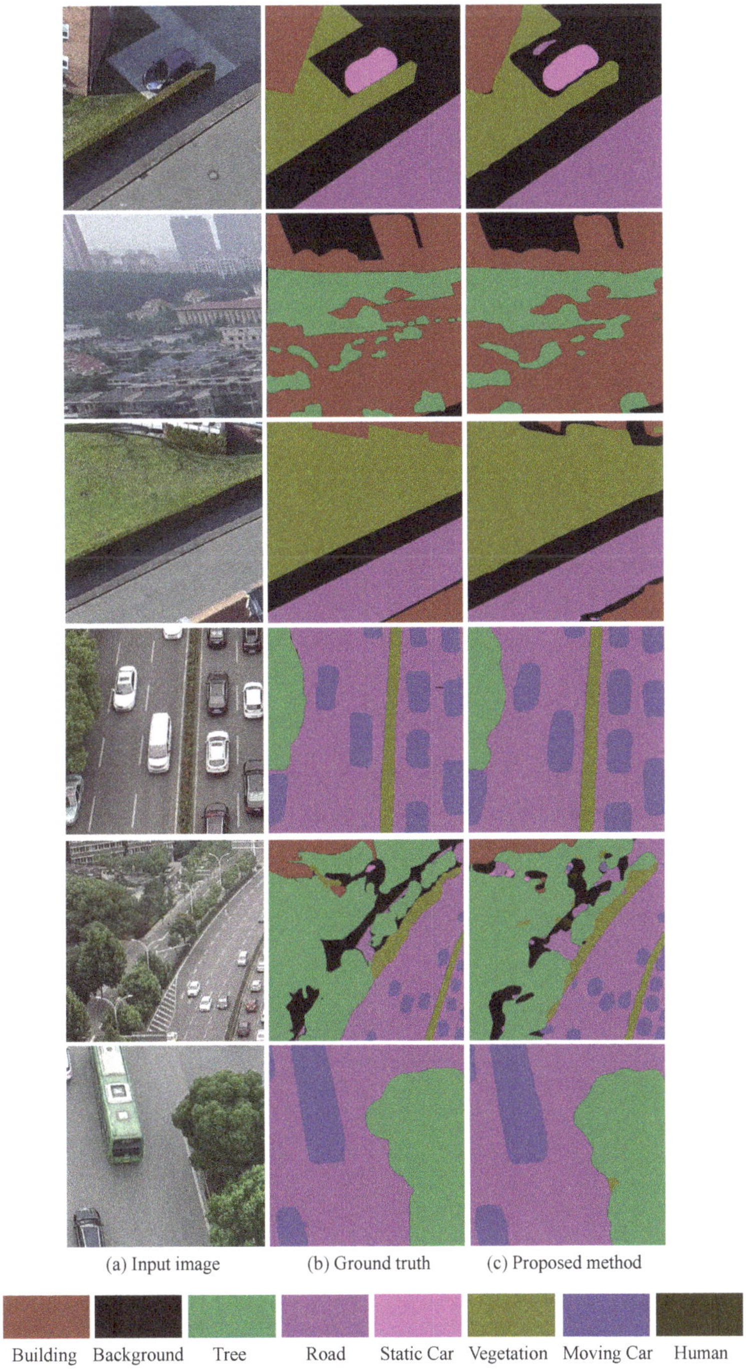

Figure 4. Qualitative prediction results using the UAVid validation dataset.

Figure 5. Qualitative prediction results using the UAVid test dataset.

4.4. Results on UDD-6 Dataset

In this subsection, we present the validation results using the UDD-6 dataset. FCN-8s [21], U-Net [1], GCN [30], ENet [61], ERFNet [57], BiSeNetV2 [58], DeepLab V3+ [17], and SETR-PUP [4] are selected for comparison. Per class IoU, mIoU, mean F1 score, and OA are used as performance metrics. Appendix A.1 describes the evaluation protocol for these metrics. The quantitative results compared with the competitive methods are mentioned in Table 2. The highest value of each metric in the table is marked in bold. The proposed method shows mIoU, mean F1 score, and OA of 73.65%, 84.40%, and 86.98% respectively. It outperforms other methods in most metrics by a significant margin.

Performance of ERFNet and DeepLab V3+ with mIoU of 73.34% and 73.18%, respectively, are comparable with the proposed method with mIoU of 73.65%. Similarly, their OA of 86.91% and 86.90%, respectively, are comparable with the proposed method, with an OA of 86.98%. However, the proposed method outperforms FCN-8s, U-Net, GCN, ENet, BiSeNetV2, and SETR-PUP by 1.88%, 2.81%, 1.07%, 4.21%, 2.43%, and 7.04%, respectively, in mIoU. It also outperforms them in OA by 1.43%, 1.71%, 0.44%, 1.78%, 0.88%, and 3.73%, respectively. The mean F1 score of the proposed method is comparable with the ERFNet. However, it outperforms FCN-8s, U-Net, BiSeNetV2, and SETR-PUP by 1.26%, 1.96%, 1.75%, and 5.15%, respectively.

Qualitative results of the proposed method using the UDD-6 validation dataset are depicted in Figures 6 and 7. It preserves the local and global context details well and produces a fine segmentation output. Red and yellow boxes in Figure 7 represent the local and global contextual details, respectively, in an image. SETR-PUP captures global contexts well but it struggles to capture local details.

Table 2. Quantitative comparison of UDD-6 validation dataset result with competitive methods.

Method	Class IoU (%)						mIoU (%)	Mean F1 (%)	O.A (%)
	Other	Façade	Road	Veg	Vehicle	Roof			
FCN-8s [21]	88.38	67.70	66.12	66.22	83.53	58.65	71.77	83.14	85.55
U-Net [1]	89.34	67.31	65.18	62.56	82.54	58.08	70.84	82.44	85.27
GCN [30]	-	-	-	-	-	-	72.58	-	86.54
ENet [61]	-	-	-	-	-	-	69.44	-	85.20
ERFNet [57]	89.09	**72.28**	67.40	65.37	**86.68**	59.24	73.34	84.17	86.91
BiSeNetV2 [58]	**89.78**	67.99	66.84	58.74	84.44	59.51	71.22	82.65	86.10
DeepLab V3+ [17]	-	-	-	-	-	-	73.18	-	86.90
SETR-PUP [4]	54.58	60.27	63.09	88.19	53.24	80.29	66.61	79.25	83.25
Proposed Method	59.72	71.28	**69.38**	**89.21**	66.16	**86.14**	**73.65**	**84.40**	**86.98**

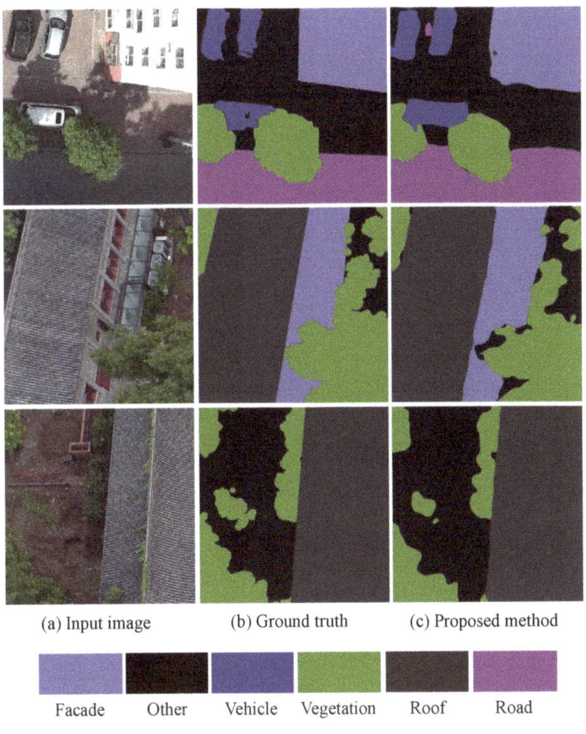

Figure 6. Qualitative prediction results using the UDD-6 validation dataset.

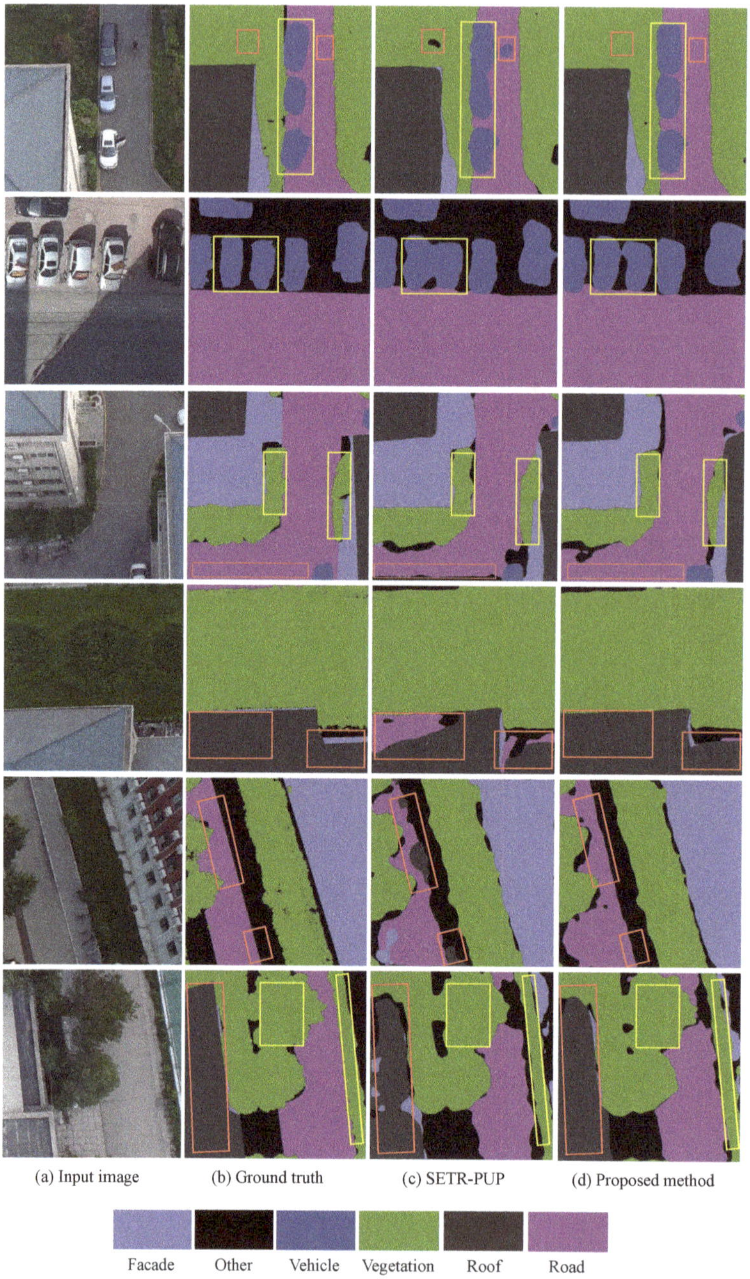

Figure 7. Qualitative prediction results using the UDD-6 validation dataset. The red and yellow boxes represent the local and global context, respectively, in the images.

4.5. Ablation Studies

In this subsection, we discuss the results of the sensitivity test for the adopted approach using the UDD-6 validation dataset. We investigate the effect of different convolution variants for ψ in the TSIF module. We tested 3×3 convolution and 3×3 dilated convolution operations for this. A dilation rate of 2 is used for the dilated convolution. It can be seen from Table 3 that 3 × 3 convolution gives better results. It outperforms the dilated convolution by 0.56%, 0.41%, and 0.006% in mIoU, mean F1 score, and OA, respectively.

Table 3. The effect of different convolution variants for ψ in the TSIF module using the UDD-6 dataset.

ψ	mIoU (%)	Mean F1 (%)	O.A (%)
3 × 3 dilated convolution	73.09	83.99	86.92
3 × 3 convolution	**73.65**	**84.40**	**86.98**

We tested the nearest neighbor and bilinear upsampling policies to study the effect of distinct upsampling operations in the decoder network. It can be seen from Table 4 that the bilinear upsampling approach performs best. It outperforms the nearest neighbor by 0.81%, 0.59%, and 0.81% in mIoU, mean F1 score, and OA, respectively.

Table 4. The effect of a different upsampling policy in the decoder network using the UDD-6 dataset.

Upsample	mIoU (%)	Mean F1 (%)	O.A (%)
Nearest neighbor	72.84	83.81	86.80
Bilinear	**73.65**	**84.40**	**86.98**

The number of feature channels in the decoder network, N_c, is a crucial hyperparameter. We investigate the sensitivity for its two values, 512 and 256. We used a bilinear upsampling operation and 3 × 3 convolution for ψ in the TSIF module for both tests. The test results can be depicted in Table 5. Both the feature channels show very close performance in OA. However, the N_c of 256 shows superior results compared to the 512 in the mIoU and mean F1 score. Overall, it outperforms N_c of 512 by 0.51%, 0.37%, and 0.02% in mIoU, mean F1 score, and OA, respectively.

Table 5. The effect of different feature channels, N_c, in the decoder network using the UDD-6 dataset.

Upsample	ψ	N_c	mIoU (%)	Mean F1 (%)	O.A (%)
Bilinear	3 × 3 convolution	512	73.14	84.03	86.96
Bilinear	3 × 3 convolution	256	**73.65**	**84.40**	**86.98**

5. Discussion

Due to the huge background clutter and variations in aerial images, it poses many challenges for its semantic segmentation. The proposed framework captures the inherent features in a global and local context for UAV images precisely. The qualitative visualization of results shows a smooth segmentation output. The global context about two similar objects in an image such as cars, low vegetation, and trees is well maintained. This can be observed in Figures 4 and 5. The self-attention mechanism in the encoder network captures these long-range details about similar objects. We can also see in Figure 6 that our method can handle global information about cars and vegetation precisely. Similarly, in the first and second rows of Figure 7, global details about the cars are well captured by our method. Long-range vegetation is also well-segmented in the third and sixth rows.

The shape and size of the objects are well preserved, and the boundary information between the two classes is maintained smoothly. This can also be seen in the figures. The Token Spatial Information Fusion (TSIF) module in the encoder network captures these local context details around the neighboring pixels. The roof and facade are smoothly segmented in Figure 6, while preserving the local details. Compared to the SETR-PUP [4], the proposed method gives better results. SETR-PUP struggles to preserve information around the neighboring pixels belonging to the same class. In the fourth and sixth rows of Figure 7, our method segments the roof well. Similarly, in the first and third rows, our method smoothly handles the local context for the vegetation and road categories. These can be seen in the regions marked in red boxes.

The encoder network produces strong feature representation, which is semantically rich in both high and low-level details. The gradual upsampling strategy followed by a convolution operation in the decoder network helps to preserve this rich information, and hence it generates smooth predictions. The quantitative and qualitative findings using the UAVid and UDD-6 datasets show the advantage of the proposed framework in UAV image segmentation.

We performed sensitivity tests for various hyperparameters in our method. As shown in Table 3, the 3×3 convolution for ψ in the TSIF module gives superior results as compared to the dilated convolution. It captures the inherent features of the pixels belonging to the same class in a better way. Similarly, the bilinear upsampling policy in the decoder network gives the best performance. It preserves the overall semantic contextual details precisely for UAV images. A combination of 3×3 convolution for ψ, the bilinear upsampling approach, and the feature channels of 256 in the decoder network generates the best results in segmenting the aerial scenes, as presented in Table 5. Increasing the number of kernels leads to a decrease in performance.

Overall, the proposed design shows competitive performance but it still struggles to segment small objects such as humans. However, when compared to other methods, our method shows decent performance for the human category, but segmenting this category is very challenging. The UAVid and UDD-6 datasets were captured in high-visibility conditions. The performance of the proposed method may degrade for images captured in different weather conditions. The design of an effective framework to handle small objects in UAV scenes, which is also resilient to different weather conditions, can be considered in future work.

6. Conclusions

In this study, we proposed a transformer-based design for the semantic segmentation of UAV street scene images. We used an encoder-decoder framework that captures the inherent features in the global and local context for UAV images. The self-attention-based encoder network captures long-range information, therefore the global context about two similar objects in the image are well maintained. The convolution-based TSIF module fuses local contextual details in the network. This helps the network to segment neighboring pixels while maintaining the proper shape and size of the objects. The decoder network uses semantically rich feature representations from the encoder network for final pixel-level predictions. It generates smooth segmentation with well-preserved boundary information between two classes. We performed a set of ablation studies for the sensitivity test. Overall, the proposed framework shows a competitive result on the two public datasets; UAVid and UDD-6. However, it struggles to segment small objects in complex UAV images. The datasets used in this work were captured in high visibility conditions, so the performance of the framework may degrade for different weather condition images. In future research, we will explore more potential segmentation designs for handling small objects in aerial images, which are also resilient to changing weather conditions.

Author Contributions: Conceptualization, S.K.; methodology, S.K., A.K. and D.-G.L.; software, S.K.; validation, A.K. and D.-G.L.; formal analysis, S.K., A.K. and D.-G.L.; investigation, A.K.; resources, D.-G.L.; data curation, S.K.; writing—original draft preparation, S.K.; writing—review and editing, A.K. and D.-G.L.; visualization, S.K.; supervision, D.-G.L.; project administration, D.-G.L.; funding acquisition, D.-G.L. All authors have read and agreed to the published version of the manuscript.

Funding: This research was funded by the National Research Foundation of Korea (NRF) grant funded by the Korean Government (MSIT) (No.2021R1C1C1012590), (No. NRF-2022R1A4A1023 248), Project BK21 FOUR and the Information Technology Research Center (ITRC) support program supervised by the Institute of Information Communications and Technology Planning and Evaluation (IITP) grant funded by the Korean Government (MSIT) (IITP-2022-2020-0-01808).

Institutional Review Board Statement: Not applicable.

Informed Consent Statement: Not applicable.

Data Availability Statement: The UAVid dataset can be found at https://uavid.nl/ (accessed on 12 December 2022). The Urban Drone (UDD-6) dataset can be found at https://github.com/MarcWong/UDD (accessed on 12 December 2022).

Conflicts of Interest: The authors declare no conflict of interest. The funders had no role in the design of the study; in the collection, analyses, or interpretation of data; in the writing of the manuscript; or in the decision to publish the results.

Appendix A

Appendix A.1. Evaluation Metrics

In this subsection, we describe the metrics used for the evaluation in this work.

Appendix A.1.1. Intersection over Union (IoU)

It is represented as follows:

$$IoU = \frac{True\ Positive}{True\ Positive + False\ Positive + False\ Negative} \tag{A1}$$

Appendix A.1.2. Mean Intersection over Union (mIoU)

It is the mean of the IoU score of all the classes. It can be represented as follows:

$$mIoU = \frac{IoU_1 + IoU_2 + \ldots + IoU_N}{N}, \tag{A2}$$

where N represents the number of classes.

Appendix A.1.3. Mean F1 Score (mean F1)

It is the mean of the F1 score of all the classes. The mathematical expression for the F1 score is as follows:

$$F1\,score = 2 \times \frac{P \times R}{P + R}, \tag{A3}$$

where P and R are mathematically calculated as follows:

$$P = \frac{True\ Positive}{True\ Positive + False\ Positive}, \tag{A4}$$

$$R = \frac{True\ Positive}{True\ Positive + False\ Negative}, \tag{A5}$$

the mean F1 score can be represented as follows:

$$mean\ F1 = \frac{Score_1 + Score_2 + \ldots + Score_N}{N}, \tag{A6}$$

where $Score_1, Score_2, \ldots, Score_N$ denote the $F1$ scores of all the classes, i.e., N.

Appendix A.1.4. Overall Accuracy (OA)

It is represented as follows:

$$OA = \frac{\#.\ Correct\ label\ predictions}{\#.\ Total\ label\ predictions} \tag{A7}$$

References

1. Ronneberger, O.; Fischer, P.; Brox, T. U-net: Convolutional networks for biomedical image segmentation. In Proceedings of the International Conference on Medical Image Computing and Computer-Assisted Intervention, Munich, Germany, 5–9 October 2015; Springer: Berlin/Heidelberg, Germany, 2015; pp. 234–241.
2. Singh, A.; Lall, B.; Panigrahi, B.; Agrawal, A.; Agrawal, A.; Thangakunam, B.; Christopher, D.J. Semantic segmentation of bone structures in chest X-rays including unhealthy radiographs: A robust and accurate approach. *Int. J. Med. Inf.* **2022**, *165*, 104831. [CrossRef] [PubMed]
3. Jin, Z.; Liu, B.; Chu, Q.; Yu, N. ISNet: Integrate image-level and semantic-level context for semantic segmentation. In Proceedings of the IEEE/CVF International Conference on Computer Vision, Montreal, BC, Canada, 11–17 October 2021; pp. 7189–7198.
4. Zheng, S.; Lu, J.; Zhao, H.; Zhu, X.; Luo, Z.; Wang, Y.; Fu, Y.; Feng, J.; Xiang, T.; Torr, P.H.; et al. Rethinking semantic segmentation from a sequence-to-sequence perspective with transformers. In Proceedings of the IEEE/CVF Conference on Computer Vision and Pattern Recognition, Nashville, TN, USA, 20–25 June 2021; pp. 6881–6890.
5. Lee, D.G. Fast Drivable Areas Estimation with Multi-Task Learning for Real-Time Autonomous Driving Assistant. *Appl. Sci.* **2021**, *11*, 10713. [CrossRef]
6. Yeung, H.W.F.; Zhou, M.; Chung, Y.Y.; Moule, G.; Thompson, W.; Ouyang, W.; Cai, W.; Bennamoun, M. Deep-learning-based solution for data deficient satellite image segmentation. *Expert Syst. Appl.* **2022**, *191*, 116210. [CrossRef]
7. Zeng, Z.; Xu, Y.; Xie, Z.; Tang, W.; Wan, J.; Wu, W. LEARD-Net: Semantic segmentation for large-scale point cloud scene. *Int. J. Appl. Earth Obs. Geoinf.* **2022**, *112*, 102953. [CrossRef]
8. Su, Y.; Cheng, J.; Bai, H.; Liu, H.; He, C. Semantic Segmentation of Very-High-Resolution Remote Sensing Images via Deep Multi-Feature Learning. *Remote. Sens.* **2022**, *14*, 533. [CrossRef]
9. Guo, Y.; Wu, C.; Du, B.; Zhang, L. Density Map-based vehicle counting in remote sensing images with limited resolution. *ISPRS J. Photogramm. Remote Sens.* **2022**, *189*, 201–217. [CrossRef]
10. Hossain, M.D.; Chen, D. A hybrid image segmentation method for building extraction from high-resolution RGB images. *ISPRS J. Photogramm. Remote Sens.* **2022**, *192*, 299–314. [CrossRef]
11. Ichim, L.; Popescu, D. Segmentation of vegetation and flood from aerial images based on decision fusion of neural networks. *Remote Sens.* **2020**, *12*, 2490. [CrossRef]
12. Osco, L.P.; Junior, J.M.; Ramos, A.P.M.; de Castro Jorge, L.A.; Fatholahi, S.N.; de Andrade Silva, J.; Matsubara, E.T.; Pistori, H.; Gonçalves, W.N.; Li, J. A review on deep learning in UAV remote sensing. *Int. J. Appl. Earth Obs. Geoinf.* **2021**, *102*, 102456. [CrossRef]
13. Dutta, K.; Talukdar, D.; Bora, S.S. Segmentation of unhealthy leaves in cruciferous crops for early disease detection using vegetative indices and Otsu thresholding of aerial images. *Measurement* **2022**, *189*, 110478. [CrossRef]
14. Song, Z.; Zhang, Z.; Yang, S.; Ding, D.; Ning, J. Identifying sunflower lodging based on image fusion and deep semantic segmentation with UAV remote sensing imaging. *Comput. Electron. Agric.* **2020**, *179*, 105812. [CrossRef]
15. Lobo Torres, D.; Queiroz Feitosa, R.; Nigri Happ, P.; Elena Cué La Rosa, L.; Marcato Junior, J.; Martins, J.; Olã Bressan, P.; Gonçalves, W.N.; Liesenberg, V. Applying fully convolutional architectures for semantic segmentation of a single tree species in urban environment on high resolution UAV optical imagery. *Sensors* **2020**, *20*, 563. [CrossRef] [PubMed]
16. Lyu, Y.; Vosselman, G.; Xia, G.S.; Yilmaz, A.; Yang, M.Y. UAVid: A semantic segmentation dataset for UAV imagery. *ISPRS J. Photogramm. Remote Sens.* **2020**, *165*, 108–119. [CrossRef]
17. Chen, L.C.; Zhu, Y.; Papandreou, G.; Schroff, F.; Adam, H. Encoder-decoder with atrous separable convolution for semantic image segmentation. In Proceedings of the European Conference on Computer Vision (ECCV), Munich, Germany, 8–14 September 2018; pp. 801–818.
18. Fu, J.; Liu, J.; Tian, H.; Li, Y.; Bao, Y.; Fang, Z.; Lu, H. Dual attention network for scene segmentation. In Proceedings of the IEEE/CVF Conference on Computer Vision and Pattern Recognition, Long Beach, CA, USA, 15–20 June 2019; pp. 3146–3154.
19. Yin, M.; Yao, Z.; Cao, Y.; Li, X.; Zhang, Z.; Lin, S.; Hu, H. Disentangled non-local neural networks. In Proceedings of the European Conference on Computer Vision, Glasgow, UK, 23–28 August 2020; Springer: Berlin/Heidelberg, Germany, 2020; pp. 191–207.
20. Lee, D.G.; Kim, Y.K. Joint Semantic Understanding with a Multilevel Branch for Driving Perception. *Appl. Sci.* **2022**, *12*, 2877. [CrossRef]
21. Long, J.; Shelhamer, E.; Darrell, T. Fully convolutional networks for semantic segmentation. In Proceedings of the IEEE Conference on Computer Vision and Pattern Recognition, Boston, MA, USA, 7–12 June 2015; pp. 3431–3440.
22. Li, R.; Zheng, S.; Zhang, C.; Duan, C.; Wang, L.; Atkinson, P.M. ABCNet: Attentive bilateral contextual network for efficient semantic segmentation of Fine-Resolution remotely sensed imagery. *ISPRS J. Photogramm. Remote Sens.* **2021**, *181*, 84–98. [CrossRef]
23. Dosovitskiy, A.; Beyer, L.; Kolesnikov, A.; Weissenborn, D.; Zhai, X.; Unterthiner, T.; Dehghani, M.; Minderer, M.; Heigold, G.; Gelly, S.; et al. An image is worth 16×16 words: Transformers for image recognition at scale. *arXiv* **2020**, arXiv:2010.11929.
24. Girisha, S.; Verma, U.; Pai, M.M.; Pai, R.M. Uvid-net: Enhanced semantic segmentation of uav aerial videos by embedding temporal information. *IEEE J. Sel. Top. Appl. Earth Obs. Remote. Sens.* **2021**, *14*, 4115–4127. [CrossRef]
25. Wang, L.; Li, R.; Zhang, C.; Fang, S.; Duan, C.; Meng, X.; Atkinson, P.M. UNetFormer: A UNet-like transformer for efficient semantic segmentation of remote sensing urban scene imagery. *ISPRS J. Photogramm. Remote Sens.* **2022**, *190*, 196–214. [CrossRef]

26. Yi, S.; Liu, X.; Li, J.; Chen, L. UAVformer: A Composite Transformer Network for Urban Scene Segmentation of UAV Images. *Pattern Recognit.* **2022**, *133*, 109019. [CrossRef]
27. Wang, W.; Xie, E.; Li, X.; Fan, D.P.; Song, K.; Liang, D.; Lu, T.; Luo, P.; Shao, L. Pyramid vision transformer: A versatile backbone for dense prediction without convolutions. In Proceedings of the IEEE/CVF International Conference on Computer Vision, Virtual, 11–17 October 2021; pp. 568–578.
28. Noh, H.; Hong, S.; Han, B. Learning deconvolution network for semantic segmentation. In Proceedings of the IEEE International Conference on Computer Vision, Santiago, Chile, 7–13 December 2015; pp. 1520–1528.
29. Badrinarayanan, V.; Kendall, A.; Cipolla, R. Segnet: A deep convolutional encoder-decoder architecture for image segmentation. *IEEE Trans. Pattern Anal. Mach. Intell.* **2017**, *39*, 2481–2495. [CrossRef]
30. Peng, C.; Zhang, X.; Yu, G.; Luo, G.; Sun, J. Large kernel matters–improve semantic segmentation by global convolutional network. In Proceedings of the IEEE Conference on Computer Vision and Pattern Recognition, Honolulu, HI, USA, 21–26 July 2017; pp. 4353–4361.
31. Huang, Z.; Wang, X.; Huang, L.; Huang, C.; Wei, Y.; Liu, W. Ccnet: Criss-cross attention for semantic segmentation. In Proceedings of the IEEE/CVF International Conference on Computer Vision, Seoul, Republic of Korea, 27 October–2 November 2019; pp. 603–612.
32. Li, T.; Cheng, B.; Ni, B.; Liu, G.; Yan, S. Multitask low-rank affinity graph for image segmentation and image annotation. *ACM Trans. Intell. Syst. Technol. (TIST)* **2016**, *7*, 1–18. [CrossRef]
33. Li, T.; Woo, J.; Kweon, I.S. Probabilistically Semantic Labeling of IR Image for UAV. In Proceedings of the MVA2007 IAPR Conference on Machine Vision Applications, Machine Vision and Application, Tokyo, Japan, 16–18 May 2007.
34. Vaswani, A.; Shazeer, N.; Parmar, N.; Uszkoreit, J.; Jones, L.; Gomez, A.N.; Kaiser, Ł.; Polosukhin, I. Attention is all you need. *Adv. Neural Inf. Process. Syst.* **2017**, *30* .
35. Touvron, H.; Cord, M.; Douze, M.; Massa, F.; Sablayrolles, A.; Jégou, H. Training data-efficient image transformers & distillation through attention. In Proceedings of the International Conference on Machine Learning, PMLR, Virtual, 13–14 August 2021; pp. 10347–10357.
36. Chen, C.F.R.; Fan, Q.; Panda, R. Crossvit: Cross-attention multi-scale vision transformer for image classification. In Proceedings of the IEEE/CVF International Conference on Computer Vision, Virtual, 11–17 October 2021; pp. 357–366.
37. Chu, X.; Tian, Z.; Zhang, B.; Wang, X.; Wei, X.; Xia, H.; Shen, C. Conditional positional encodings for vision transformers. *arXiv* **2021**, arXiv:2102.10882.
38. Yuan, L.; Chen, Y.; Wang, T.; Yu, W.; Shi, Y.; Jiang, Z.H.; Tay, F.E.; Feng, J.; Yan, S. Tokens-to-token vit: Training vision transformers from scratch on imagenet. In Proceedings of the IEEE/CVF International Conference on Computer Vision, Virtual, 11–17 October 2021; pp. 558–567.
39. Zhang, W.; Huang, Z.; Luo, G.; Chen, T.; Wang, X.; Liu, W.; Yu, G.; Shen, C. TopFormer: Token Pyramid Transformer for Mobile Semantic Segmentation. In Proceedings of the IEEE/CVF Conference on Computer Vision and Pattern Recognition, New Orleans, LA, USA, 19–20 June 2022; pp. 12083–12093.
40. Sun, Z.; Cao, S.; Yang, Y.; Kitani, K.M. Rethinking transformer-based set prediction for object detection. In Proceedings of the IEEE/CVF International Conference on Computer Vision, Virtual, 11–17 October 2021; pp. 3611–3620.
41. Carion, N.; Massa, F.; Synnaeve, G.; Usunier, N.; Kirillov, A.; Zagoruyko, S. End-to-end object detection with transformers. In Proceedings of the European Conference on Computer Vision, Glasgow, UK, 23–28 August 2020; Springer: Berlin/Heidelberg, Germany, 2020; pp. 213–229.
42. Strudel, R.; Garcia, R.; Laptev, I.; Schmid, C. Segmenter: Transformer for semantic segmentation. In Proceedings of the IEEE/CVF International Conference on Computer Vision, Virtual, 11–17 October 2021; pp. 7262–7272.
43. Ranftl, R.; Bochkovskiy, A.; Koltun, V. Vision transformers for dense prediction. In Proceedings of the IEEE/CVF International Conference on Computer Vision, Virtual, 11–17 October 2021; pp. 12179–12188.
44. Xie, E.; Wang, W.; Yu, Z.; Anandkumar, A.; Alvarez, J.M.; Luo, P. SegFormer: Simple and efficient design for semantic segmentation with transformers. *Adv. Neural Inf. Process. Syst.* **2021**, *34*, 12077–12090.
45. Yuan, K.; Guo, S.; Liu, Z.; Zhou, A.; Yu, F.; Wu, W. Incorporating convolution designs into visual transformers. In Proceedings of the IEEE/CVF International Conference on Computer Vision, Virtual, 11–17 October 2021; pp. 579–588.
46. Wu, H.; Xiao, B.; Codella, N.; Liu, M.; Dai, X.; Yuan, L.; Zhang, L. Cvt: Introducing convolutions to vision transformers. In Proceedings of the IEEE/CVF International Conference on Computer Vision, Virtual, 11–17 October 2021; pp. 22–31.
47. Yang, M.Y.; Kumaar, S.; Lyu, Y.; Nex, F. Real-time semantic segmentation with context aggregation network. *ISPRS J. Photogramm. Remote Sens.* **2021**, *178*, 124–134. [CrossRef]
48. Wang, L.; Li, R.; Wang, D.; Duan, C.; Wang, T.; Meng, X. Transformer meets convolution: A bilateral awareness network for semantic segmentation of very fine resolution urban scene images. *Remote Sens.* **2021**, *13*, 3065. [CrossRef]
49. Liu, S.; Cheng, J.; Liang, L.; Bai, H.; Dang, W. Light-Weight Semantic Segmentation Network for UAV Remote Sensing Images. *IEEE J. Sel. Top. Appl. Earth Obs. Remote. Sens.* **2021**, *14*, 8287–8296. [CrossRef]
50. Iqbal, J.; Ali, M. Weakly-supervised domain adaptation for built-up region segmentation in aerial and satellite imagery. *ISPRS J. Photogramm. Remote Sens.* **2020**, *167*, 263–275. [CrossRef]
51. Gebrehiwot, A.; Hashemi-Beni, L.; Thompson, G.; Kordjamshidi, P.; Langan, T.E. Deep convolutional neural network for flood extent mapping using unmanned aerial vehicles data. *Sensors* **2019**, *19*, 1486. [CrossRef]

52. Zhang, C.; Atkinson, P.M.; George, C.; Wen, Z.; Diazgranados, M.; Gerard, F. Identifying and mapping individual plants in a highly diverse high-elevation ecosystem using UAV imagery and deep learning. *ISPRS J. Photogramm. Remote Sens.* **2020**, *169*, 280–291. [CrossRef]
53. Zhang, X.; Jin, J.; Lan, Z.; Li, C.; Fan, M.; Wang, Y.; Yu, X.; Zhang, Y. ICENET: A semantic segmentation deep network for river ice by fusing positional and channel-wise attentive features. *Remote Sens.* **2020**, *12*, 221. [CrossRef]
54. Gevaert, C.M.; Persello, C.; Sliuzas, R.; Vosselman, G. Monitoring household upgrading in unplanned settlements with unmanned aerial vehicles. *Int. J. Appl. Earth Obs. Geoinf.* **2020**, *90*, 102117. [CrossRef]
55. Chen, Y.; Wang, Y.; Lu, P.; Chen, Y.; Wang, G. Large-scale structure from motion with semantic constraints of aerial images. In Proceedings of the Chinese Conference on Pattern Recognition and Computer Vision (PRCV), Guangzhou, China, 23–26 November 2018; Springer: Berlin/Heidelberg, Germany, 2018; pp. 347–359.
56. Yu, F.; Koltun, V. Multi-scale context aggregation by dilated convolutions. *arXiv* **2015**, arXiv:1511.07122.
57. Romera, E.; Alvarez, J.M.; Bergasa, L.M.; Arroyo, R. Erfnet: Efficient residual factorized convnet for real-time semantic segmentation. *IEEE Trans. Intell. Transp. Syst.* **2017**, *19*, 263–272. [CrossRef]
58. Yu, C.; Gao, C.; Wang, J.; Yu, G.; Shen, C.; Sang, N. Bisenet v2: Bilateral network with guided aggregation for real-time semantic segmentation. *Int. J. Comp. Vis.* **2021**, *129*, 3051–3068. [CrossRef]
59. Poudel, R.P.; Liwicki, S.; Cipolla, R. Fast-scnn: Fast semantic segmentation network. *arXiv* **2019**, arXiv:1902.04502.
60. Zhuang, J.; Yang, J.; Gu, L.; Dvornek, N. Shelfnet for fast semantic segmentation. In Proceedings of the IEEE/CVF International Conference on Computer Vision Workshops, Seoul, Republic of Korea, 27–28 October 2019.
61. Paszke, A.; Chaurasia, A.; Kim, S.; Culurciello, E. Enet: A deep neural network architecture for real-time semantic segmentation. *arXiv* **2016**, arXiv:1606.02147.

mathematics

MDPI

Article

Deep Multi-Task Learning for an Autoencoder-Regularized Semantic Segmentation of Fundus Retina Images

Ge Jin [1,†], Xu Chen [1] and Long Ying [2,*,†]

1 School of Computer Science and Engineering, Nanjing University of Science and Technology, Nanjing 210094, China
2 School of Computer Science, Nanjing University of Information Science & Technology, Nanjing 210044, China
* Correspondence: lying@nuist.edu.cn or lorin_ying@hotmail.com
† The authors contributed equally to this work.

Abstract: Automated segmentation of retinal blood vessels is necessary for the diagnosis, monitoring, and treatment planning of the disease. Although current U-shaped structure models have achieved outstanding performance, some challenges still emerge due to the nature of this problem and mainstream models. (1) There does not exist an effective framework to obtain and incorporate features with different spatial and semantic information at multiple levels. (2) The fundus retina images coupled with high-quality blood vessel segmentation are relatively rare. (3) The information on edge regions, which are the most difficult parts to segment, has not received adequate attention. In this work, we propose a novel encoder–decoder architecture based on the multi-task learning paradigm to tackle these challenges. The shared image encoder is regularized by conducting the reconstruction task in the VQ-VAE (Vector Quantized Variational AutoEncoder) module branch to improve the generalization ability. Meanwhile, hierarchical representations are generated and integrated to complement the input image. The edge attention module is designed to make the model capture edge-focused feature representations via deep supervision, focusing on the target edge regions that are most difficult to recognize. Extensive evaluations of three publicly accessible datasets demonstrate that the proposed model outperforms the current state-of-the-art methods.

Keywords: retinal vessel segmentation; VQ-VAE; edge attention

MSC: 68U10

1. Introduction

Disruptions to the structure of the retinal blood vessels are common side effects of several disorders. Alterations in the anatomy of the blood vessels in the retina can lead to vascular diseases, such as vascular stenosis, capillary sclerosis, and micro-adenomas, if they go untreated [1]. To improve the prognosis of patients, it is necessary to intervene in the early stage of the disease, and retinal vessel segmentation plays a significant role in the diagnosis of eye-related diseases [2]. Usually, retinal blood vessels are manually segmented by doctors. These morphological data were formerly obtained through eye inspections, which were not only time-consuming and prone to human error but also subjective. Thus, to solve the aforementioned problems, it is necessary to introduce an automatic retinal vessel segmentation method, and this task has attracted numerous research interest [3,4].

In actual application scenarios, automatic retinal vessel segmentation is very challenging for the following reasons. First, the scale and shape of retinal vessels vary greatly. The retinal vessel area occupies 1–20 pixels in the images. As a second point, the semantics of the retinal arteries' anatomy are complex. The optic disc, diseased regions, hemorrhage, and exudates are all sources of potential confusion in retinal fundus imaging. Third, the low contrast between retinal vessels and surrounding tissue makes it difficult for the model to segment targets correctly.

Abundant efforts have been dedicated to tackle the aforementioned challenges. Early research focused on the use of various hand-crafted features to segment retinal blood vessels. Huang et al. [5] created a vessel detection approach and incorporated the measurement findings using Bayesian decision making to provide a confidence value for each blood vessel segment in order to characterize the key properties of retinal vessels. However, the strategy's restricted representation capabilities of the hand-crafted features [6–8] make it ineffective when dealing with very big datasets comprising multiple complex situations.

The dramatic advancements in hardware over the past few years have made deep learning an immediate necessity [9–11]. Ronneberger et al.'s [12] U-Net model has had the largest influence in the area of medical image segmentation. Subsequently, a plethora of ideas was made to enhance performance by incorporating new types of deep supervision [13,14]. The symmetrical U-shaped structure that these models are based on allows for the gradual extraction of contextual information via the continuous link between the convolutional and down-sampling layers. For retinal blood vessel segmentation, U-shape structure-based methods have become the mainstream at present. Researchers tried diverse models [15–19] to preserve local and global semantic information, prevent spatial information loss, tackle varying scales, and segment tiny parts.

Although former U-shaped structure models have achieved outstanding performance in many different scenes, some challenges still need to be handled for the specific retinal blood vessel segmentation task. Challenge (1): Extraction of features from deep stages provides high-level features with rich semantic information but insufficient resolution, while extraction of features from shallow stages yields low-level features with rich spatial details but insufficient global semantic information. Challenge (2): The fundus retina images coupled with precise blood vessel segmentation are relatively rare and hard to access. Because the manual segmentation of the blood vessels is time-consuming and labor-intensive. Moreover, manual annotation is a subjective task, with accuracy impacted by the physician's clinical knowledge and personal bias. Challenge (3): Previous methods did not pay enough attention to the edge information of the target, resulting in low segmentation accuracy of the target edge region. Due to the low contrast and high geometric complexity of the vessel edge, this area is the most difficult part to segment for the retinal blood vessel segmentation task.

In this work, we propose a novel encoder–decoder architecture based on the multi-task learning paradigm to address these challenges and further improve the performance of the vessel segmentation task. To cope with Challenge (1) and Challenge (2), the VQ-VAE (Vector Quantized Variational AutoEncoder) module is incorporated into the U-shaped structure, which can regularize the shared encoding process by reconstructing the input image, elevating the generalization ability of the model when precisely annotated data are relatively rare. Meanwhile, latent feature maps encoding multiple-level semantic information are also generated and fused with the features obtained by the image encoder to further enhance the feature representation. To tackle Challenge (3), an edge attention module is proposed to make the model capture edge-focused feature representations via deep supervision, concerning the target edge regions that are most difficult to recognize. The perception of edge information is enhanced. We have performed comprehensive experiments on DRIVE [20], CHASE-DB1 [21] and STARE [22]. The experimental outcomes demonstrate the proposed method is useful in improving the performance of the model.

To summarize, the contributions and novelty of the present study are highlighted as follows:

1. A novel encoder–decoder architecture based on the multi-task learning paradigm is proposed. The VQ-VAE module branch reconstructs input images to regularize the shared image encoder while generating and integrating hierarchical representations of the input image. This module not only alleviates the challenge caused by limited annotated data but also improves the representation ability of the model.

2. An edge attention module is proposed to learn edge-focused feature representations by deep supervision, which can induce the model to focus on the target edge regions that are most difficult to segment and improve the perception of edge information.
3. Comprehensive experiments are conducted on three public datasets, and experimental results show that our methods can achieve state-of-the-art performance.

The remainder of this study is structured as follows: Section 2 presents the results of the literature review. Section 3 discusses the methodology. The experimental results and analyses are presented in Section 4. Finally, the conclusion is presented in the last section.

2. Related Work

Experts in the field of image processing have devoted more and more attention to the difficulty of segmenting retinal vascular pictures in recent years. Retinal imaging of vascular segmentation is a field that has seen numerous techniques developed. In this article, we provide a taxonomy and comparison of various methods for segmenting the retinal vasculature.

With the successful application of CNN in classification tasks, some researchers subsequently explored its potential for retinal blood vessel segmentation and achieved good performance. Liskowski and Krawiec [23] introduced a six-layer convolutional neural network (CNN) for vascular segmentation in the retina. Before training the model, the training samples were preprocessed with global contrast normalization (GCN) and zero-phase component analysis (ZCA whitening). Samuel et al. [24] proposed a novel network for segmenting retinal blood vessels from retinal fundus images. The method is based on transfer learning with a pre-trained VGG-16 model as its backbone network. Soomro et al. [25] implemented a model for the retinal blood vessel segmentation task. To alleviate visual complexity such as low contrast, uneven lighting, and noise, they applied a morphological operation and principal component analysis (PCA) to preprocess the image. Additionally, a novel post-processing technique was used to eliminate unwanted noise. Wu et al. [26] also applied PCA at the preprocessing stage to reduce the dimension of the input images. The framework was effective overall, but it lacked sophistication due to its lack of small veins and poorly connected blood vessels.

To address the limitations of CNN architectures, Long et al. [27] proposed the fully convolutional networks (FCN) for semantic image segmentation. This model and its variants are widely applied in the field of medical image segmentation. Atli et al. [28] designed an FCN model that up-samples before down-sampling to accommodate both thick and thin blood vessels. To avoid losing contextual information in the training phase, the technique additionally incorporated residual modules. Li et al. [29] built an FCN with skip connections and included active learning. In this case, the proposed model's performance was enhanced through iterative training. In order to avoid the problem of spatial loss of information, Luo et al. [30] developed a size-invariant FCN for retinal blood vessel extraction from retinal images. FCN models have achieved outstanding success in the segmentation of retinal blood vessels. FCN-based retinal vascular segmentation has achieved promising results; however, its predictions often lack crisp boundaries and ignore spatial coherence.

In the field of medical image segmentation, the most commonly used framework is the U-shape based network. It can produce fine segmentation results on small datasets, and further, the local and global semantic information is preserved. Sathananthavathi et al. [31] swapped out the convolutions for Atrous convolutions to broaden the receptive field and, hence, reduce spatial loss of information. The attention gate technique was developed by Li et al. [32] to protect the segmented retinal blood vessels from being masked by irrelevant foreground elements. Similarly, the authors of [33] also used the weighted attention gate approach to filter out irrelevant information. To enhance thin vessel segmentation, Mishra et al. [34] built a basic U-net and used data-aware deep supervision. The average input retinal vascular width was calculated and compared to the effective receptive fields of the different layers to identify the ones that extract vessel features most strongly.

Retinal artery segmentation in real-time using high-resolution images was proposed by Laibacher et al. [35] using a network that makes use of bottleneck modules and bilinear up-sampling to reduce the number of parameters. Adjusting the U-Net architecture with the help of variable receptive fields, Jin et al. [36] were able to decrease vascular missingness due to differences in vessel size, scale, characteristics, and shape in the retina. In [15], Fu et al. introduced a brand new form of network they called Deep Vessel. In order to fully comprehend these multi-level pictorial representations, a multi-layer, deep neural network with a side-output layer was developed. Alom et al. [16] proposed an extension of the U-shape architecture utilizing the power of U-Net, Residual Network, as well as a recurrent convolutional neural network. The authors in [17] combined attention mechanisms and a U-net framework to achieve better results in pancreas image segmentation. CE-Net [18] is able to increase the receptive field and segment smaller blood vessels because it incorporates the residual multi- kernel pooling module and the dense atrous convolution module. For the purpose of segmenting retinal images, Li et al. [37] presented a new approach that is based on a topological vascular tree. To deduce the topological vascular tree from retinal images, the method uses a global graph-based decision with pixel-wide separation and a complete set of node connections. Liu et al. [38] proposed a light-weight network, dubbed as FR-UNet. The model generates the full-resolution representation of features by extending the parallel convolution layer horizontally, and a novel feature fusion module is proposed to aggregate all-scale representations, finally generating the full-resolution representation of features. In the same period, there were two more studies that achieved state-of-the-art results, namely SGL [39] and RV-GAN [40], respectively. The authors of [39] assume that the group truth of the training examples given by clinicians are incomplete and noisy, resulting in a lack of annotations of some vascular fragments. A Study Group Learning (SGL) method is proposed, which includes k-fold cross validation and knowledge distillation, to improve the robustness of the model on noise data, and a learned enhancement map can provide better visualization. A novel Volumetric Memory Network (VMN) is proposed in [41]. The model can automatically segment 3D medical images interactively. First, a user hints at the 2D slice and automatically generates the initial 2D segmentation, then the VMN propagates it to all slices bidirectionally and refines the segmentation. The authors in [42] provided a prototype view of semantic segmentation. A non-parameter scheme based on a non-learning prototype is proposed. The model represents each class as a set of non-learnable prototypes, which only depends on the average characteristics of several training pixels in this class, rather than the previous method to learn the single weight/query vector of each class in a fully parameterized way.

3. Method

The proposed model is described in detail below. First, the overall structure of the whole network in Section 3.1 will be described. The specifics of our proposed methods are then discussed in Sections 3.2 and 3.3.

3.1. Network Architectures Overview

The proposed model is designed based on an asymmetric U-shaped architecture, which consists of the image encoding network, the segmentation decoder and two branches. The backbone network is a modified Resnet-based network, and the workflow of the proposed approach is displayed in Figure 1.

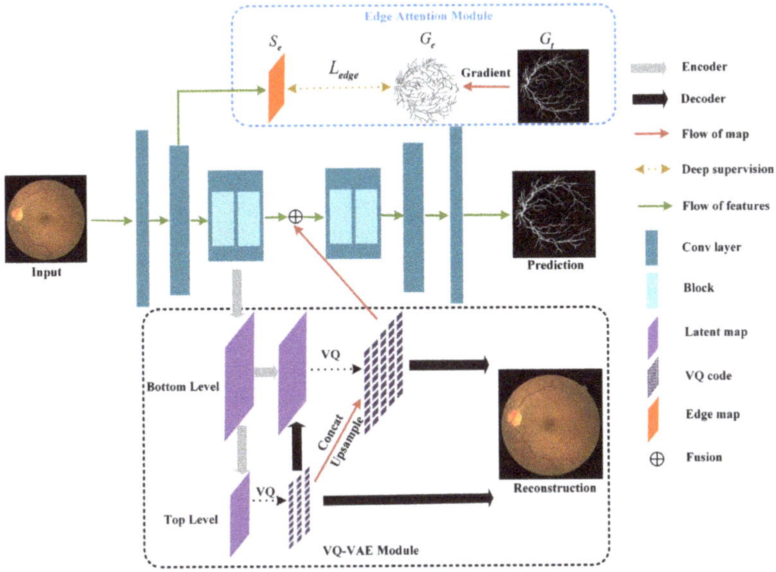

Figure 1. Overview of the proposed model, S_e denotes edge map, G_e denotes edge ground-truth map and G_t denotes ground truth map.

There are two separate branches in the segmentation network, the edge attention module and the VQ-VAE module. Combined with the segmentation decoder, all the branches are trained in a multi-tasking paradigm. First, the retinal blood vessel images are fed into the backbone network. Considering that low-level features retain abundant edge information, the low-level features are fed into the edge attention module. Guided by the gradient of annotated segmentation results, the model can be encouraged to focus on the edge information of the target. Subsequently, the feature maps from the intermediate layer are fed into the VQ-VAE branch to reconstruct the input images and regularize the shared encoding procedure. To further enhance the semantic feature representation, VQ-VAE combines the intermediate feature maps produced by the backbone network with the top-level and bottom-level latent maps produced by VQ-VAE module. The model is trained on three public datasets, i.e., DRIVE, CHASE-DB1 and STARE. Substantial experiments have shown that the proposed approach works.

3.2. Edge Attention Module

Many studies [43–45] have proved that edge information can provide effective constraints in the process of guiding the segmentation of targets. Due to the particularity of retinal fundus images, the edge of vascular tissue is extremely complex and has low contrast with the surrounding background, so the edge of blood vessels is the most difficult to segment. Moreover, the training images of the retinal fundus datasets are very limited, so complex modules may cause overfitting. Unlike [45], we only use the latent features generated from shallow networks and edge ground truth maps, and supervised training is conducted between them to regularize the shared network parameters. This module can improve the sensitivity of the model to edge information by only increasing a very small number of parameters.

It is universally acknowledged that the shallow features in the model contain a lot of low-level information, such as color, texture, and edge information. Therefore, we regularize the shallow shared parameters of the model to induce the model to pay more attention to edge information. The low-level features with the appropriate resolution are fed into the edge attention module to explicitly learn the edge-focused feature representations. Specifically, the low-level features get through a convolution layer and generate edge maps (S_e). Then, we utilize the standard binary cross entropy loss function to measure the difference between the generated edge maps and the edge ground truth maps (G_e) derived from the ground truth images (G_t). The whole workflow is detailed in Figure 1.

$$L_{edge} = -\sum_{x=1}^{w}\sum_{y=1}^{h}[G_e \log(S_e) + (1 - G_e)\log(1 - S_e)] \quad (1)$$

where (x, y) are the coordinates of each pixel in the predicted edge map S_e and edge ground-truth map G_e. The S_e is calculated using the gradient of the ground-truth map G_t. Additionally, w and h denote the width and height of the corresponding map, respectively. The edge attention module can improve the sensitivity of the model to edge information and effectively improve the performance of the model.

3.3. VQ-VAE Module

Training a trustworthy and effective segmentation model requires access to a large number of high-quality annotations. Hand delineation for vascular tissue is often unable to obtain appropriate high-quality annotations for medical image segmentation because it is label-intensive and time-consuming. In order to reduce reliance on annotations and improve generalizability, a modified VQ-VAE module is developed based on the input image reconstruction task. Our module's layout was inspired by the winning entry to the BraTS 2018 challenge, submitted by Andriy et al. [46], who developed a Variational Auto-Encoder (VAE) model that was able to overcome a deficiency in training data. The proposed VQ-VAE module provides input reconstruction guidance to the training process, imposing regularization on the shared encoder to produce representations containing more image-intrinsic spatial and semantic structure patterns. Reconstructing the original images requires a sequence of vector quantized codes. The VQ-VAE produces two layers of latent codes, the first of which reflects broad features such as an object's shape and geometry, while the second represents finer details such as its texture. In addition, the two levels of representation are combined into a single, more accurate one using up-sampling and concatenation methods. To further improve the model's performance, the fused characteristics are then utilized in a subsequent network.

The VQ-VAE can be classified as the VAE family, which has an encoder, code, and decoder. The difference is that the code is not directly generated by the encoder, but is obtained through vector quantization. Using fewer resources, the module can recreate images with higher coherence and quality. While the model's foundation is built on probability, it should nevertheless be able to represent the full range of the true distribution and accommodate various forms of input data. Moreover, the VQ-VAE module can generate high-level and low-level latent code, which, respectively, contain the low-level characters (edge information, colors, textures) and semantic knowledge of the input images. Making full use of this automatically extracted knowledge can effectively improve the feature representation ability of the model. Thus, the aforementioned concerns prompted us to implement the VAE-based branch to enhance the model's feature expression and robustness.

An encoder, decoder, and a shared codebook are all housed in the VQ-VAE branch. To do this, the encoder transforms the data into a set of latent variables, which are then used by the decoder to recover the original data. The distance between the input vector x and the prototype vectors $e_k, k \in 1 \ldots K$ is quantized by the encoder's nonlinear mapping, yielding the quantized output vector $E(x)$. Specifically, K possible vectors in the codebook are generated by replacing each vector $E(x)$ with the index of the nearest prototype vector in the codebook. Finally, the indices are transmitted to the decoder, which still uses another nonlinear function to map them back to the codebook vectors to which they originally corresponded, thus reconstructing the data.

$$Quantize(E(x)) = e_k \ where \ k = \arg\min_j \|E(x) - e_j\| \quad (2)$$

For the VQ-VAE, we use a three-term objective function, as proposed by [47]:

$$L(x, D(e)) = \|x - D(e)\|_2^2 + \|sg[E(x)] - e\|_2^2 + \beta\|sg[e] - E(x)\|_2^2 \tag{3}$$

Quantized code for the training example x is shown by e. The initial component, which indicates the data fidelity term, guarantees accurate reconstructions with small errors. The final two terms are an ingenious addition that brings the encoder's output into line with the codebook's vector space. The second term is utilized in the codebook, where $sg[\cdot]$ means stop gradient. It adjusts the output of the encoder, $E(x)$, to be near to the selected codebook, e. The final term keeps $E(x)$ relatively close to the chosen codebook vector and limits the parameter's variance. In this paper, the β is set to 0.25.

The VQ-VAE module can not only improve the performance of the model but also reduce the dependence of the model on annotations. The reason is that in the process of reconstruction, the encoder implicitly obtains more patterns, while promoting the model to generate more representative features. This module helps the model to consistently achieve good training accuracy for any random initialization and maintains the characteristics generated by the model invariant.

4. Experimental Results

In this section, we detail the experiments of the proposed methodology on three freely available datasets. The available datasets, metrics for measuring progress, and technological issues are briefly outlined before going into the details of the implementation. In addition, studies of ablation are conducted to guarantee that the proposed technique is effective. The experimental findings support the idea that our proposed method is comparable to state-of-the-art models.

4.1. Evaluation Datasets

The proposed retinal vascular segmentation model is evaluated by using data from three publically available databases (DRIVE, STARE, and CHASEDB1). Since FoV masks are not provided by CHASEDB1 and STARE, we built them by ourselves to ensure uniformity across all experiments [48].

- DRIVE: 40 fundus retinal images are included in this dataset. All images were collected by a Canon CR5 nonmydriatic 3CCD camera with a 45-degree field of view (FOV) and cropped from 565 × 584 pixels to 448 × 448 pixels. The dataset contains seven retinal fundus images of diabetes patients. Moreover, the dataset is split into two subsets, that is, training set (20 images) and testing set (20 images).
- CHASEDB1: Each image in this dataset of 28 pictures depicts a vascular patch and has a resolution of 999 × 960 pixels. Fourteen kids' left and right eye retinal fundus images are stored in the database. All images were taken from a 30 degree FOV. The first 20 photos are used as a training set, while the last 8 are utilized as a test set, as stated in [49].
- STARE: In this dataset containing 20 retinal fundus images, half of them have pathological signs. The resolution of the images is 700 × 605. We used 20% of the images as the validation and test sets.

4.2. Evaluation Metric

To evaluate our model more comprehensively, five metrics are introduced for evaluation, including sensitivity (SE), specificity (SP), accuracy (ACC), and the area under the ROC curve (AUC), which are calculated by the following equations:

$$SE = \frac{|TP|}{|TP + FN|} \tag{4}$$

$$SP = \frac{|TN|}{|FP + TN|} \tag{5}$$

$$ACC = \frac{|TP + TN|}{|TP + TN + FN + FP|} \quad (6)$$

True positive (TP) means that the positive sample is correctly classified; false negative (FN) means that the positive sample is wrongly classified as a negative sample; false positive (FP) indicates that the negative samples are wrongly classified as positive samples; true negative (TN) indicates that negative samples are correctly classified as negative samples. In addition, the area under the curve (AUC) of the receiver operating characteristic curve (ROC) is used to evaluate segmentation accuracy based on recall and precision. When a method's area under the curve (AUC) becomes closer to 1, it performs better in segmenting blood vessels.

4.3. Implementation Details

We implemented our network in the Pytorch framework and trained models on an NVIDIA Quadro P5000 GPU with 12 GB memory. Moreover, we utilized the binary cross-entropy loss as the objective function. The Adam optimizer with an initialization learning rate of 1×10^{-3} was applied in the training phase, and the weight decay was set to 0.001. The batch size was set to 2 in the experiments. In order to prevent the gradient from exploding or disappearing during training, we adopted the method proposed by He et al. [50] to initialize the whole network. Moreover, the network was trained for 50 epochs.

Due to the particularity and scarcity of medical image data, some sampling and data augmentation strategies were introduced to prevent overfitting and induce a more generalized network. All three datasets' images were converted into grayscale images and resized to 512×512. Moreover, we conducted uniform normalization on all images, and a 48×48 sliding window with a stride of 6 was introduced to generate patches from vessel images. Then, we conducted horizontal flipping, vertical flipping, and random rotation in the training phase to prevent the model from overfitting and increase the diversity of training samples. In particular, we also used random erase to induce the model to be more sensitive to boundary information. Note that there is no patch extraction operation during the test phase, but full-size images were used as input.

4.4. Segmentation Results

In this work, our model was experimented on three public datasets, including DRIVE, CHASEDB1, and STARE. Results from U-Net [12], DeepVessel [15], R2U-Net [16], AttU-Net [17], CE-Net [18], IterNet [37], SGL [39], and RV-GAN [40] are compared with the proposed method to verify the effectiveness of our method. The outcomes are shown in Table 1.

To quantitatively analyze the experimental results, we perform a statistical comparison based on several important metrics, including SE, SP, ACC, and AUC to evaluate the proposed method and compare it with eight state-of-the-art methods on all three datasets. In addition, we also display the number of parameters of each model in Table 2. As can be seen from Table 1, SGL, RV-GAN, and our method achieved the highest scores on some evaluation metrics, respectively. It shows that our method can achieve comparable performance to state-of-the-art methods. As can be seen in Table 1, the proposed method outperforms most models in four metrics. It achieves a SE of 83.86% in the DRIVE dataset. Some studies [3,39] have verified that higher SE indicates the model is more sensitive to edge information, which further demonstrates that the proposed method has a great ability to focus on microvascular structures. Among the models, RV-GAN as a generative adversarial framework achieves the highest SP, ACC, and AUC on DRIVE and highest SE, and AUC on STARE. The architecture introduces two generators and two multi-scale autoencoding discriminators for better microvessel localization and segmentation. However, due to the complexity of the architecture, it takes a longer time and more computing resources for training to converge the model. The parameters of the network are about 14.8 M, which is about 1.7 times that of our method. Furthermore, the experiments were conducted on the CHASEDB1 dataset, and the comparison results of different methods are shown in the middle of Table 1. The proposed method obtained the highest value on the SP and ACC with 98.65%/97.80% and a comparable AUC of 98.98%, which is good proof of the validity of the proposed method. It is worth mentioning that SGL achieves the highest SE and AUC on CHASEDB1. The authors proposed a Study Group Learning (SGL) framework to improve the generalization ability of the learned model and better address the missing annotation problems in the training set. It applies the cascade method and cross-validation-based pseudo-label generation strategies, which greatly increases model complexity and training time. Like RV-GAN, the number of parameters of SGL is also large, which is 1.8 times of our model. However, the performance of the proposed method is extremely close to SGL and RV-GAN. Last, the performance comparisons on the STARE dataset are summarized at the bottom of Table 1. The proposed method surpasses other state-of-the-art models in terms of SP and ACC. As can be seen in Table 2, although the number of the proposed method parameters is similar to U-Net, R2U-Net, and AttU-Net, it can obtain much better results. In conclusion, compared with state-of-the-art methods, our model can not always obtain the best result, but it can provide a good trade-off between model complexity and segmentation performance.

Table 1. Comparison with state-of-the-art methods on three classical datasets: DRIVE, CHASEDB1, and STARE.

DRIVE Dataset				
Methods	SE (%)	SP (%)	ACC (%)	AUC (%)
U-Net [12]	79.15 ± 0.23	98.08 ± 0.31	96.40 ± 0.13	97.64 ± 0.08
DeepVessel [15]	78.83 ± 0.18	98.13 ± 0.23	96.09 ± 0.12	97.83 ± 0.05
R2U-Net [16]	79.23 ± 0.56	98.03 ± 0.35	96.54 ± 0.07	98.02 ± 0.08
AttU-Net [17]	78.82 ± 0.17	98.48 ± 0.35	96.49 ± 0.19	98.03 ± 0.07
CE-Net [18]	80.15 ± 0.22	98.16 ± 0.19	96.59 ± 0.16	98.11 ± 0.09
IterNet [37]	79.95 ± 0.26	98.26 ± 0.08	96.57 ± 0.17	98.13 ± 0.06
SGL [39]	83.80 ± 0.09	98.34 ± 0.08	97.05 ± 0.13	98.86 ± 0.04
RV-GAN [40]	79.27 ± 0.10	**99.69 ± 0.11**	**97.90 ± 0.15**	**98.87 ± 0.05**
Ours	**83.86 ± 0.13**	98.37 ± 0.28	97.35 ± 0.08	98.82 ± 0.05
CHASEDB1 Dataset				
Method	SE (%)	SP (%)	ACC (%)	AUC (%)
U-Net [12]	76.17 ± 0.86	98.61 ± 0.69	97.16 ± 0.25	97.92 ± 0.15
DeepVessel [15]	75.84 ± 0.54	98.34 ± 0.54	97.18 ± 0.14	97.85 ± 0.13
R2U-Net [16]	81.45 ± 0.71	98.40 ± 0.71	97.21 ± 0.13	98.01 ± 0.07
AttU-Net [17]	77.21 ± 1.01	98.50 ± 0.98	97.26 ± 0.18	98.07 ± 0.06
CE-Net [18]	80.42 ± 0.39	98.39 ± 0.33	97.23 ± 0.36	98.06 ± 0.09
IterNet [37]	79.97 ± 1.55	98.47 ± 1.05	97.31 ± 0.24	98.26 ± 0.12
SGL [39]	**86.90 ± 0.24**	98.43 ± 0.23	97.71 ± 0.19	**99.20 ± 0.08**
RV-GAN [40]	81.99 ± 0.07	98.06 ± 0.13	96.97 ± 0.24	99.14 ± 0.03
Ours	83.29 ± 0.64	**98.65 ± 0.37**	**97.80 ± 0.07**	98.98 ± 0.10
STARE Dataset				
Method	SE (%)	SP (%)	ACC (%)	AUC (%)
U-Net [12]	78.39 ± 1.36	98.71 ± 0.96	96.88 ± 0.48	97.93 ± 0.15
DeepVessel [15]	78.83 ± 0.94	98.14 ± 0.81	97.13 ± 0.41	98.14 ± 0.11
R2U-Net [16]	78.69 ± 0.99	98.62 ± 0.56	96.97 ± 0.33	98.09 ± 0.09
AttU-Net [17]	79.03 ± 1.06	98.56 ± 0.74	97.22 ± 0.45	98.22 ± 0.10
CE-Net [18]	79.16 ± 0.86	98.53 ± 1.11	97.15 ± 0.25	98.17 ± 0.07
IterNet [37]	80.86 ± 0.53	98.46 ± 0.68	97.23 ± 0.36	98.29 ± 0.07
RV-GAN [40]	**83.26 ± 0.27**	98.64 ± 0.37	97.54 ± 0.15	**98.87 ± 0.06**
Ours	81.35 ± 0.85	**98.74 ± 0.48**	**97.54 ± 0.19**	98.84 ± 0.05

Table 2. Parameter comparison with state-of-the-art methods.

Model	U-Net [12]	R2U-Net [16]	AttU-Net [17]	CE-Net [18]	IterNet [37]	SGL [39]	RV-GAN [40]	Ours
Parameters (M)	7.8	8.3	7.2	14.4	8.6	15.5	14.8	8.8

The example segmentation results on three databases are also shown in Figure 2. It can be observed that the proposed method is sensitive to the edge region of the blood vessels with low contrast and has achieved good segmentation results. In particular, we also display the bad segmentation examples in Figure 3. The whole training phase is a multi-task learning process; one task is semantic segmentation, and the other is the reconstruction task. In the experiment, we found that if the number of epochs is set too large, the performance of segmentation will decline significantly, and the entire model is more suited to reconstruction task as it even fails to converge. Thus, the number of epochs is set to 50. To obtain a better view of our model, we also drew the loss curve and ROC curve in Figure 4. As can be observed, the model converges well within 50 epochs.

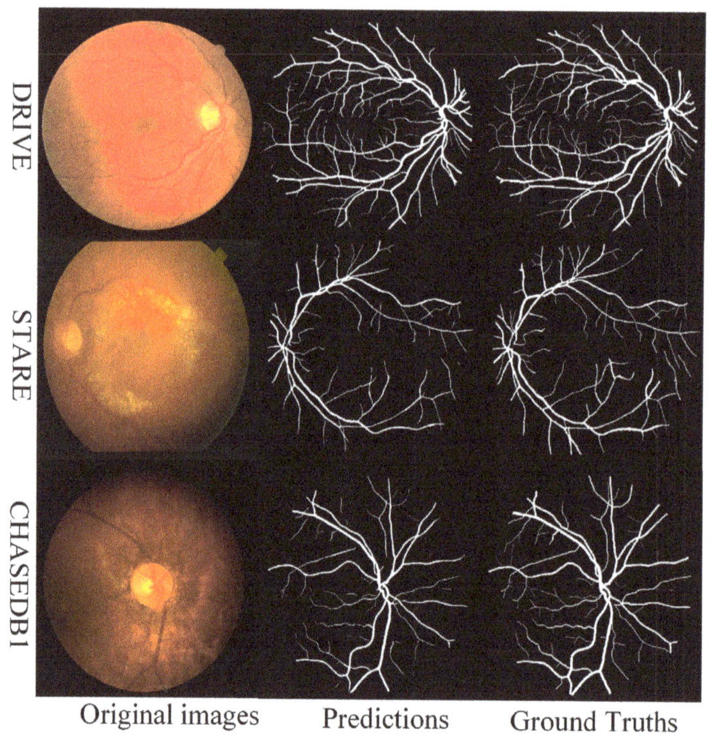

Figure 2. Example segmentation results on three databases.

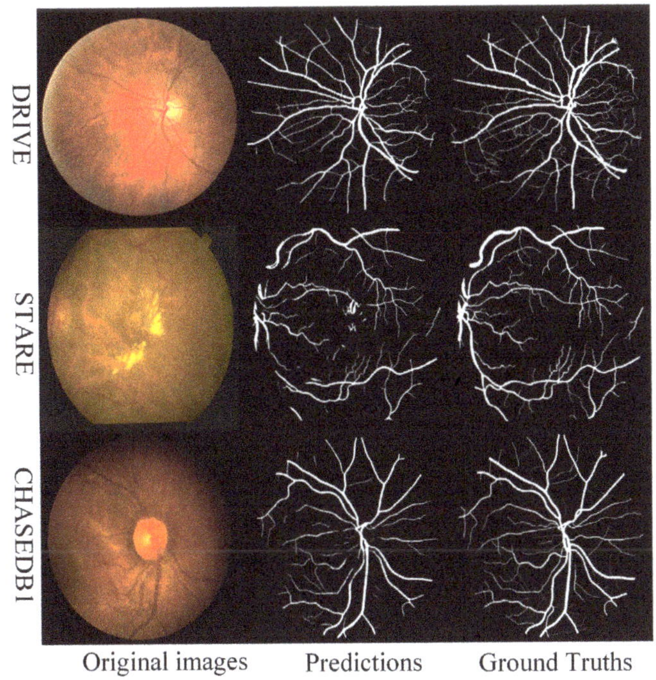

Figure 3. Bad segmentation examples on three databases.

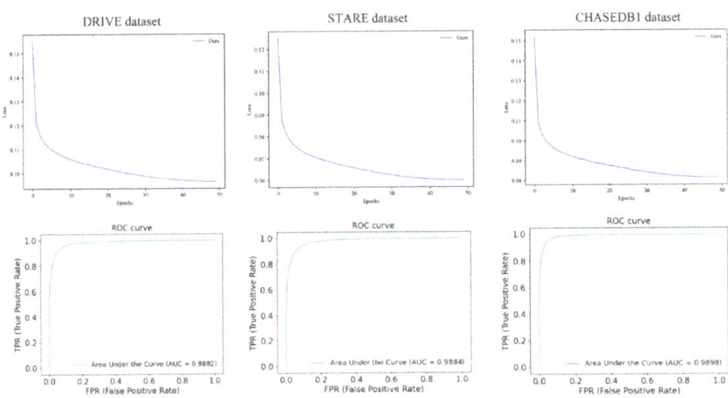

Figure 4. Loss curve and ROC curve on three datasets.

4.5. Ablation Study

In this section, the proposed VQ-VAE module and edge attention module are analyzed in detail. The VQ-VAE module regularizes the encoder parameters in the network while reconstructing the input images. It makes the encoder more robust and can generate features that are more representative. Furthermore, the high and low-level latent features are fused with the intermediate features of the backbone network to enhance the feature representation. Since the low-level features contain rich edge information, we utilize it to generate edge maps and feed it into the edge attention module to explicitly induce the model to learn features that focus on edges. The ablation study validates the proposed methods, and the results are presented in Table 3. The baseline is the backbone network, which removes the VQ-VAE module and the edge attention module. As shown in Table 3, compared with 'Baseline', 'Baseline + VVM' improves the performance from 79.35%/96.16% to 82.31%/97.24% in terms of SE/ACC. Compared with the 'Baseline', the proposed EAM module (referred to as 'Baseline + EAM') increases the SE/ACC by 1.79%/0.71% (from 79.35%/96.16% to 81.14%/96.87%). Finally, we add the VQ-VAE module and edge attention module to the Baseline. The results show that the proposed methods obtain the best results on the three metrics. Many statistical comparisons and component analyses have visual representations in Figure 5. The effectiveness of the proposed modules in segmenting vessels of varying scales, including some miniature vessels that the baseline network cannot handle efficiently, is illustrated with an example from retinal vascular segmentation. In conclusion, the proposed method has the potential to significantly enhance the model's efficiency.

Table 3. Comparison of ablation studies on DRIVE dataset. VVM stands for VQ-VAE module, EAM denotes the eage attention module.

Methods	SE (%)	SP (%)	ACC (%)	AUC (%)
Baseline	79.35 ± 0.09	97.95 ± 0.11	96.16 ± 0.04	97.84 ± 0.03
Baseline + VVM	82.31 ± 0.18	**98.43 ± 0.25**	97.24 ± 0.09	98.55 ± 0.06
Baseline + EAM	81.14 ± 0.15	98.11 ± 0.15	96.87 ± 0.09	98.19 ± 0.04
Baseline + VVM + EAM	**83.86 ± 0.13**	98.37 ± 0.28	**97.35 ± 0.08**	**98.82 ± 0.05**

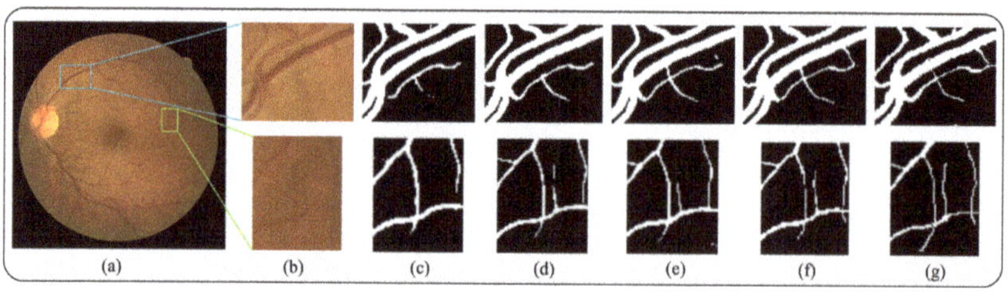

Figure 5. Some typical visual results for different methods in our ablation study on the DRIVE dataset. (**a**) Original image, (**b**) detailed view, (**c**) Baseline, (**d**) Baseline + VVM, (**e**) Baseline + EAM, (**f**) Baseline + VVM + EAM, (**g**) ground truth.

4.6. Effectiveness of the VQ-VAE Module

The VQ-VAE module reconstructs the input images while regularizing the shared parameters of the encoder and generating the high-level features and the low-level features. The reconstruction process induces the model to generate more representative features and enhances the robustness of the model. The two level features and the features generated by the encoder are fused to further improve the feature representation ability of the model. In this section, we mainly conduct experiments to verify that the VQ-VAE module can reduce the dependence of the model on annotations. First, we randomly select half of the training data in the DRIVE dataset as the training set, and the test set remains unchanged. Then, the 'Baseline' and 'Baseline + VVM' are trained on the modified training set and validated on the standard test set, respectively. The results are shown in Table 4. As can be observed, after reducing the training data, all metrics of the baseline network declined significantly. However, the baseline network with the VQ-VAE module still achieves competitive results without significant degradation. It demonstrates that the proposed method can reduce the dependence of the model on the training data and improve its robustness.

Table 4. Statistical comparison of the effectiveness of the VQ-VAE module.

Data amount = Full				
Methods	SE (%)	SP (%)	ACC (%)	AUC (%)
Baseline	79.35 ± 0.09	97.95 ± 0.11	96.16 ± 0.04	97.84 ± 0.03
Data amount = 1/2				
Methods	SE (%)	SP (%)	ACC (%)	AUC (%)
Baseline	74.42 ± 0.39	95.74 ± 0.31	93.78 ± 0.19	95.92 ± 0.08
Baseline + VVM	78.62 ± 0.18	96.75 ± 0.23	95.28 ± 0.12	97.11 ± 0.07

4.7. Limitations

There is a serious class imbalance problem in medical images, especially when the TP class (vessels) is significantly smaller than the TN class (the rest of the image) in the retinal images. The targets we focus on only account for a small part of the whole image, resulting in large regions dominating small regions. Thus, we should pay more attention to the small targets (thin vessel). In addition, the whole framework performs two sub-tasks; one is reconstruction, and the other is semantic segmentation. In the experiment, we found that when the number of epochs increases to a high level, the image segmentation performance will decline rapidly, and the model will pay more attention to the reconstruction sub-task. For this, we display some failure cases in Figure 3. In future work, we should solve the class imbalance problem and make the model training process more stable.

5. Conclusions

In this paper, we present a novel multi-task learning-based network to comprehensively address three challenges that remain in retinal vessel segmentation. The whole network consists of four parts: the image encoding network, the segmentation decoder, the VQ-VAE module, and the edge attention module. The edge attention module is capable of effectively inducing the encoder to capture the edge information of the target and explicitly concern the edge area of the target by deep supervision, which is important for retinal blood vessel segmentation. The VQ-VAE module conducts the input image reconstruction task to regularize the parameters of the encoding network, generating and fusing multi-level spatial and semantic features to incorporate local and global information. It not only improves the model's performance but also helps consistently achieve good training accuracy for any random initialization. Furthermore, the process of regularization can improve the generalization ability and reduce the dependence on sufficient accurate annotated training data. By using three publicly available retinal fundus datasets (DRIVE, CHASEDB1 and START) for in-depth comparative analysis, it is shown that the proposed method can be compared with the state-of-the-art method. We believe the proposed approaches are readily transferable to other medical image segmentation scenarios where few training data and complex anatomical semantics pose significant challenges.

Author Contributions: G.J.: conceptualization, methodology, software, investigation, writing—original draft preparation X.C.: formal analysis, writing—reviewing and editing, validation L.Y.: software, resources, writing—reviewing and editing, formal analysis, conceptualization, investigation, funding acquisition. All authors have read and agreed to the published version of the manuscript.

Funding: This work was supported in part by the National Natural Science Foundation of China under Grant 61902193 and in part by the Priority Academic Program Development of Jiangsu Higher Education Institutions (PAPD).

Data Availability Statement: Not applicable.

Conflicts of Interest: We declare that we have no conflict of interest with each other and with other people or organizations that can inappropriately influence our work. The funders provides software, resources, writing—reviewing and editing, formal analysis, conceptualization, investigation, and the decision to publish the results in this work.

References

1. Zana, F.; Klein, J.C. A multimodal registration algorithm of eye fundus images using vessels detection and Hough transform. *IEEE Trans. Med. Imaging* **1999**, *18*, 419–428. [CrossRef] [PubMed]
2. Sinthanayothin, C. Automated localization of the optic disc, fovea, and retinal blood vessels from digital colour fundus images. *Br. J. Ophthalmal* **1999**, *83*, 231–238.
3. Wu, H.; Wang, W.; Zhong, J.; Lei, B.; Wen, Z.; Qin, J. Scs-net: A scale and context sensitive network for retinal vessel segmentation. *Med. Image Anal.* **2021**, *70*, 102025. [CrossRef] [PubMed]
4. Li, D.; Rahardja, S. BSEResU-Net: An attention-based before-activation residual U-Net for retinal vessel segmentation. *Comput. Methods Programs Biomed.* **2021**, *205*, 106070. [CrossRef]
5. Mo, J.; Zhang, L. Multi-level deep supervised networks for retinal vessel segmentation. *Int. J. Comput. Assist. Radiol. Surg.* **2017**, *12*, 2181–2193. [CrossRef]
6. Nian, F.; Li, T.; Wu, X.; Gao, Q.; Li, F. Efficient near-duplicate image detection with a local-based binary representation. *Multimed. Tools Appl.* **2016**, *75*, 2435–2452. [CrossRef]
7. Li, T.; Yan, S.; Mei, T.; Hua, X.S.; Kweon, I.S. Image decomposition with multilabel context: Algorithms and applications. *IEEE Trans. Image Process.* **2010**, *20*, 2301–2314.
8. Li, T.; Mei, T.; Yan, S.; Kweon, I.S.; Lee, C. Contextual decomposition of multi-label images. In Proceedings of the 2009 IEEE Conference on Computer Vision and Pattern Recognition, Miami, FL, USA, 20–25 June 2009; pp. 2270–2277.
9. Nian, F.; Bao, B.K.; Li, T.; Xu, C. Multi-modal knowledge representation learning via webly-supervised relationships mining. In Proceedings of the 25th ACM International Conference on Multimedia, Mountain View, CA, USA, 23–27 October 2017; pp. 411–419.
10. Zhang, J.; Liu, S.; Yan, H.; Li, T.; Mao, R.; Liu, J. Predicting voxel-level dose distributions for esophageal radiotherapy using densely connected network with dilated convolutions. *Phys. Med. Biol.* **2020**, *65*, 205013. [CrossRef]
11. Jiang, D.; Yan, H.; Chang, N.; Li, T.; Mao, R.; Du, C.; Guo, B.; Liu, J. Convolutional neural network-based dosimetry evaluation of esophageal radiation treatment planning. *Med. Phys.* **2020**, *47*, 4735–4742. [CrossRef]
12. Ronneberger, O.; Fischer, P.; Brox, T. U-net: Convolutional networks for biomedical image segmentation. In *International Conference on Medical Image Computing and Computer-Assisted Intervention*; Springer: Cham, Switzerland, 2015; pp. 234–241.
13. Çiçek, Ö.; Abdulkadir, A.; Lienkamp, S.S.; Brox, T.; Ronneberger, O. 3D U-Net: Learning dense volumetric segmentation from sparse annotation. In *International Conference on Medical Image Computing and Computer-Assisted Intervention*; Springer: Cham, Switzerland, 2016; pp. 424–432.
14. Khened, M.; Kollerathu, V.A.; Krishnamurthi, G. Fully convolutional multi-scale residual DenseNets for cardiac segmentation and automated cardiac diagnosis using ensemble of classifiers. *Med. Image Anal.* **2019**, *51*, 21–45. [CrossRef]
15. Fu, H.; Xu, Y.; Lin, S.; Kee Wong, D.W.; Liu, J. Deepvessel: Retinal vessel segmentation via deep learning and conditional random field. In *International Conference on Medical Image Computing and Computer-Assisted Intervention*; Springer: Cham, Switzerland, 2016; pp. 132–139.
16. Alom, M.Z.; Hasan, M.; Yakopcic, C.; Taha, T.M.; Asari, V.K. Recurrent residual convolutional neural network based on u-net (r2u-net) for medical image segmentation. *arXiv* **2018**, arXiv:1802.06955.
17. Oktay, O.; Schlemper, J.; Folgoc, L.L.; Lee, M.; Heinrich, M.; Misawa, K.; Mori, K.; McDonagh, S.; Hammerla, N.Y.; Kainz, B.; et al. Attention u-net: Learning where to look for the pancreas. *arXiv* **2018**, arXiv:1804.03999.
18. Gu, Z.; Cheng, J.; Fu, H.; Zhou, K.; Hao, H.; Zhao, Y.; Zhang, T.; Gao, S.; Liu, J. Ce-net: Context encoder network for 2d medical image segmentation. *IEEE Trans. Med. Imaging* **2019**, *38*, 2281–2292. [CrossRef] [PubMed]
19. Zhang, J.; Zhang, Y.; Xu, X. Pyramid u-net for retinal vessel segmentation. In Proceedings of the ICASSP 2021–2021 IEEE International Conference on Acoustics, Speech and Signal Processing (ICASSP), Toronto, ON, Canada, 6–11 June 2021; pp. 1125–1129.
20. Staal, J.; Abràmoff, M.D.; Niemeijer, M.; Viergever, M.A.; Van Ginneken, B. Ridge-based vessel segmentation in color images of the retina. *IEEE Trans. Med. Imaging* **2004**, *23*, 501–509. [CrossRef] [PubMed]
21. Owen, C.G.; Rudnicka, A.R.; Mullen, R.; Barman, S.A.; Monekosso, D.; Whincup, P.H.; Ng, J.; Paterson, C. Measuring retinal vessel tortuosity in 10-year-old children: Validation of the computer-assisted image analysis of the retina (CAIAR) program. *Investig. Ophthalmol. Vis. Sci.* **2009**, *50*, 2004–2010. [CrossRef]
22. Hoover, A.; Kouznetsova, V.; Goldbaum, M. Locating blood vessels in retinal images by piecewise threshold probing of a matched filter response. *IEEE Trans. Med. Imaging* **2000**, *19*, 203–210. [CrossRef]
23. Liskowski, P.; Krawiec, K. Segmenting retinal blood vessels with deep neural networks. *IEEE Trans. Med. Imaging* **2016**, *35*, 2369–2380. [CrossRef]
24. Samuel, P.M.; Veeramalai, T. VSSC Net: Vessel specific skip chain convolutional network for blood vessel segmentation. *Comput. Methods Programs Biomed.* **2021**, *198*, 105769. [CrossRef]

25. Soomro, T.A.; Afifi, A.J.; Gao, J.; Hellwich, O.; Khan, M.A.; Paul, M.; Zheng, L. Boosting sensitivity of a retinal vessel segmentation algorithm with convolutional neural network. In Proceedings of the 2017 International Conference on Digital Image Computing: Techniques and Applications (DICTA), Sydney, Australia, 29 November–1 December 2017; pp. 1–8.
26. Wu, A.; Xu, Z.; Gao, M.; Buty, M.; Mollura, D.J. Deep vessel tracking: A generalized probabilistic approach via deep learning. In Proceedings of the 2016 IEEE 13th International Symposium on Biomedical Imaging (ISBI), Prague, Czech Republic, 13–16 April 2016; pp. 1363–1367.
27. Long, J.; Shelhamer, E.; Darrell, T. Fully convolutional networks for semantic segmentation. In Proceedings of the IEEE Conference on Computer Vision and Pattern Recognition, Boston, MA, USA, 7–12 June 2015; pp. 3431–3440.
28. Atli, I.; Gedik, O.S. Sine-Net: A fully convolutional deep learning architecture for retinal blood vessel segmentation. *Eng. Sci. Technol. Int. J.* **2021**, *24*, 271–283. [CrossRef]
29. Li, W.; Zhang, M.; Chen, D. Fundus retinal blood vessel segmentation based on active learning. In Proceedings of the 2020 International Conference on Computer Information and Big Data Applications (CIBDA), Guiyang, China, 17–19 April 2020; pp. 264–268.
30. Luo, Y.; Cheng, H.; Yang, L. Size-invariant fully convolutional neural network for vessel segmentation of digital retinal images. In Proceedings of the 2016 Asia-Pacific Signal and Information Processing Association Annual Summit and Conference (APSIPA), Jeju, Republic of Korea, 13–15 December 2016; pp. 1–7.
31. Sathananthavathi, V.; Indumathi, G. Encoder enhanced atrous (EEA) unet architecture for retinal blood vessel segmentation. *Cogn. Syst. Res.* **2021**, *67*, 84–95.
32. Li, D.; Dharmawan, D.A.; Ng, B.P.; Rahardja, S. Residual u-net for retinal vessel segmentation. In Proceedings of the 2019 IEEE International Conference on Image Processing (ICIP), Taipei, Taiwan, 22–25 September 2019; pp. 1425–1429.
33. Lian, S.; Li, L.; Lian, G.; Xiao, X.; Luo, Z.; Li, S. A global and local enhanced residual u-net for accurate retinal vessel segmentation. *IEEE/ACM Trans. Comput. Biol. Bioinform.* **2019**, *18*, 852–862. [CrossRef] [PubMed]
34. Mishra, S.; Chen, D.Z.; Hu, X.S. A data-aware deep supervised method for retinal vessel segmentation. In Proceedings of the 2020 IEEE 17th International Symposium on Biomedical Imaging (ISBI), Iowa City, IA, USA, 3–7 April 2020; pp. 1254–1257.
35. Laibacher, T.; Weyde, T.; Jalali, S. M2u-net: Effective and efficient retinal vessel segmentation for real-world applications. In Proceedings of the IEEE/CVF Conference on Computer Vision and Pattern Recognition Workshops, Long Beach, CA, USA, 16–17 June 2019.
36. Jin, Q.; Meng, Z.; Pham, T.D.; Chen, Q.; Wei, L.; Su, R. DUNet: A deformable network for retinal vessel segmentation. *Knowl.-Based Syst.* **2019**, *178*, 149–162. [CrossRef]
37. Li, L.; Verma, M.; Nakashima, Y.; Nagahara, H.; Kawasaki, R. Iternet: Retinal image segmentation utilizing structural redundancy in vessel networks. In Proceedings of the IEEE/CVF Winter Conference on Applications of Computer Vision, Snowmass Village, CO, USA, 1–5 March 2020; pp. 3656–3665.
38. Liu, W.; Yang, H.; Tian, T.; Cao, Z.; Pan, X.; Xu, W.; Jin, Y.; Gao, F. Full-Resolution Network and Dual-Threshold Iteration for Retinal Vessel and Coronary Angiograph Segmentation. *IEEE J. Biomed. Health Inform.* **2022**, *26*, 4623–4634. [CrossRef] [PubMed]
39. Zhou, Y.; Yu, H.; Shi, H. Study group learning: Improving retinal vessel segmentation trained with noisy labels. In *International Conference on Medical Image Computing and Computer-Assisted Intervention*; Springer: Cham, Switzerland, 2021; pp. 57–67.
40. Kamran, S.A.; Hossain, K.F.; Tavakkoli, A.; Zuckerbrod, S.L.; Sanders, K.M.; Baker, S.A. RV-GAN: Segmenting retinal vascular structure in fundus photographs using a novel multi-scale generative adversarial network. In *International Conference on Medical Image Computing and Computer-Assisted Intervention*; Springer: Cham, Switzerland, 2021; pp. 34–44.
41. Zhou, T.; Li, L.; Bredell, G.; Li, J.; Unkelbach, J.; Konukoglu, E. Volumetric memory network for interactive medical image segmentation. *Med. Image Anal.* **2023**, *83*, 102599. [CrossRef] [PubMed]
42. Zhou, T.; Wang, W.; Konukoglu, E.; Van Gool, L. Rethinking Semantic Segmentation: A Prototype View. In Proceedings of the IEEE/CVF Conference on Computer Vision and Pattern Recognition, New Orleans, LA, USA, 18–24 June 2022; pp. 2582–2593.
43. Yang, B.; Zhang, X.; Chen, L.; Yang, H.; Gao, Z. Edge guided salient object detection. *Neurocomputing* **2017**, *221*, 60–71. [CrossRef]
44. Wu, Z.; Su, L.; Huang, Q. Stacked cross refinement network for edge-aware salient object detection. In Proceedings of the IEEE/CVF International Conference on Computer Vision, Seoul, Republic of Korea, 27 October–2 November 2019; pp. 7264–7273.
45. Zhou, T.; Li, J.; Wang, S.; Tao, R.; Shen, J. Matnet: Motion-attentive transition network for zero-shot video object segmentation. *IEEE Trans. Image Process.* **2020**, *29*, 8326–8338. [CrossRef]
46. Myronenko, A. 3D MRI brain tumor segmentation using autoencoder regularization. In *International MICCAI Brainlesion Workshop*; Springer: Cham, Switzerland, 2018; pp. 311–320.
47. Razavi, A.; Van den Oord, A.; Vinyals, O. Generating diverse high-fidelity images with vq-vae-2. *Adv. Neural Inf. Process. Syst.* **2019**, *32*, 14866–14876.
48. Wu, Y.; Xia, Y.; Song, Y.; Zhang, Y.; Cai, W. NFN+: A novel network followed network for retinal vessel segmentation. *Neural Netw.* **2020**, *126*, 153–162. [CrossRef]
49. Li, Q.; Feng, B.; Xie, L.; Liang, P.; Zhang, H.; Wang, T. A cross-modality learning approach for vessel segmentation in retinal images. *IEEE Trans. Med. Imaging* **2015**, *35*, 109–118. [CrossRef]
50. He, K.; Zhang, X.; Ren, S.; Sun, J. Delving deep into rectifiers: Surpassing human-level performance on imagenet classification. In Proceedings of the IEEE International Conference on Computer Vision, Santiago, Chile, 7–13 December 2015; pp. 1026–1034.

mathematics

MDPI

Article

Reconstructing a 3D Medical Image from a Few 2D Projections Using a B-Spline-Based Deformable Transformation

Hui Yan * and Jianrong Dai

Department of Radiation Oncology, National Cancer Center/National Clinical Research Center for Cancer/Cancer Hospital, Chinese Academy of Medical Sciences and Peking Union Medical College, Beijing 100021, China

* Correspondence: hui.yan@cicams.ac.cn; Tel.: +86-10-8778-8291

Abstract: (1) Background: There was a need for 3D image reconstruction from a series of 2D projections in medical applications. However, additional exposure to X-ray projections may harm human health. To alleviate it, minimizing the projection numbers is a solution to reduce X-ray exposure, but this would cause significant image noise and artifacts. (2) Purpose: In this study, a method was proposed for the reconstruction of a 3D image from a minimal set of 2D X-ray projections using a B-spline-based deformable transformation. (3) Methods: The inputs of this method were a 3D image which was acquired in previous treatment and used as a prior image and a minimal set of 2D projections which were acquired during the current treatment. The goal was to reconstruct a new 3D image in current treatment from the two inputs. The new 3D image was deformed from the prior image via the displacement matrixes that were interpolated by the B-spline coefficients. The B-spline coefficients were solved with the objective function, which was defined as the mean square error between the reconstructed and the ground-truth projections. In the optimization process the gradient of the objective function was calculated, and the B-spline coefficients were then updated. For the acceleration purpose, the computation of the 2D and 3D image reconstructions and B-spline interpolation were implemented on a graphics processing unit (GPU). (4) Results: When the scan angles were more than 60°, the image quality was significantly improved, and the reconstructed image was comparable to that of the ground-truth image. As the scan angles were less than 30°, the image quality was significantly degraded. The influence of the scan orientation on the image quality was minor. With the application of GPU acceleration, the reconstruction efficiency was improved by hundred times compared to that of the conventional CPU. (5) Conclusions: The proposed method was able to generate a high-quality 3D image using a few 2D projections, which amount to ~ 20% of the total projections required for a standard image. The introduction of the B-spline-interpolated displacement matrix was effective in the suppressing noise in the reconstructed image. This method could significantly reduce the imaging time and the radiation exposure of patients under treatment.

Keywords: image reconstruction; B-spline; deformable; graphics processing unit

MSC: 68U10

1. Introduction

A 3D image, such as computed tomography (CT) or cone-beam CT (CBCT), can be generated from a series of 2D projections acquired in a single X-ray scan. They have been widely used in radiation therapy for target localization [1–4]. CBCT imaging delivers a radiation dose to a large volume of the patient's body and collects the residual dose on the detectors. As the accumulated imaging doses to patients could be significant and increase the risk of secondary cancer induction [5–7], there is a demand for low-dose CBCT with an adequate image quality in clinic. For reducing the imaging dose, two parameters (exposure level and projection number) were needed to be adjusted. However, reducing the exposure level will lead to increased noise in the reconstructed images, while reducing the projection number will violate the Nyquist–Shannon sampling theorem, leading to serious streak artifacts.

To solve these issues, compressed sensing methods based on the total variation (TV) have been developed to improve the image quality of low-dose CT/CBCT [8–12]. Although these methods successfully reduce the noise and streak artifacts, they also tend to over-smooth the edge information. Alternatively, other compressed-sensing-based methods used prior images for low-dose CBCT [13]. In the prior-image-constrained compressed sensing (PICCS) method, prior images were used as an additional constraint to minimize the image's total variation [14]. Adaptive-prior-image-constrained compressed sensing (APICCS) was then proposed to enhance the image quality of PICCS [15,16]. The rigid or deformable registration between the prior image and the reconstructed volume was then incorporated to improve the image quality [17,18]. Moreover, a motion model was introduced to further reduce the scan angle needed for CBCT reconstruction [19–21].

Based on the compressed sensing theory, images can be reconstructed from limited-view and limited-angle projections [22]. However, these methods generally require the sparseness prior of the image, which may be not valid. Based on the deformable transform, images can be reconstructed from prior images [23–27]. Lei et al. proposed a deformable field map method to reconstruct 3D images from limited-angle 2D projections. The missing information was made up of highly correlated prior images. However, due to the high fluctuation of the gradient derived from the objective function, the resulted deformation field map comes with a higher deviation, which could result in the failure of the image transformation [28,29]. To solve this issue, the gradient or deformation field map should be smoothed in a rational way.

Several smoothing methods for deformable transformations can be found in image registration algorithms, including demons registration, viscous fluid registration, B-spline registration and thin-plate splines. Among them, B-spline is the most popular one because of its flexibility and robustness which provide the ability to represent the complex spatial distribution of the data and image in 3D [30,31]. B-spline is used to define the displacement matrixes which map voxels in a moving image to those in a reference image. The individual voxel movement between the two images is parameterized in terms of the uniformly spaced control points that are aligned with the voxel grid, and the displacement vectors are obtained via the interpolation of the control point coefficients using piecewise continuous B-spline basis functions. B-spline interpolation is computationally intensive and requires hours for higher image resolutions [32].

As there are many computation intensity components in CBCT reconstruction, it is more efficient to implement them on a graphics processing unit (GPU) which can handle multiple similar tasks through parallel computation [33]. Its effectiveness was already demonstrated in accelerating image reconstruction tasks, including DRR [34], CBCT [35], 4DCT [36], etc. The integrated GPU-CPU platform can potentially be applied to different medical image applications, such as medical image segmentation and registration [37,38]. Also, GPUs paved the way for various promising real-time and on-line clinical applications, such as tumor motion tracking [39], respiration motion tracking and cardiac motion tracking [40].

In this study, a B-spline-based deformable transformation method was proposed for 3D CBCT reconstructions. Instead of the real-value form of the displacement matrixes in traditional methods, the B-spline coefficients of the displacement matrixes were employed. These coefficients were optimized by minimizing the objective function and finally interpolated the real-value displacement matrixes. For acceleration purposes, the computation of 2D and 3D reconstructions were implemented on a GPU. The proposed method was evaluated through a clinical head-and-neck case and compared with the traditional method. Finally, the influence of the scan angle and scan orientation on the image quality was analyzed, and the advantage of this method was discussed.

2. Methods

2.1. Deformation-Based Reconstruction Method

The traditional method used the real-value displacement matrixes to transform the prior image into the target image. In the following, $V0$ and V are the prior image and target image, and D is the displacement matrix. The transformation from $V0$ to V can be formulated as

$$V = V(D) = V0\left(i + D^x_{ijk}, j + D^y_{ijk}, k + D^z_{ijk}\right), i, j, k = 1, \ldots, n, \tag{1}$$

where $D^x_{ijk}, D^y_{ijk}, D^z_{ijk}$ are the displacements matrixes along x, y, and z axes, respectively. n is the image size, and ijk are the 3D indexes of voxel. V was transformed from $V0$ through trilinear interpolation as described below.

$$\begin{array}{ll}
\bar{i} = \left\lfloor i + D^x_{ijk} \right\rfloor, \bar{j} = \left\lfloor j + D^y_{ijk} \right\rfloor, \bar{k} = \left\lfloor k + D^z_{ijk} \right\rfloor & \\
\hat{i} = i + D^x_{ijk} - i_0, \hat{j} = j + D^y_{ijk} - j_0, \hat{k} = k + D^z_{ijk} - k_0 & \\
u_1 = (1 - \hat{k}) * V0_{\bar{i},\bar{j},\bar{k}} + \hat{k} * V0_{\bar{i},\bar{j},\bar{k}+1}, & u_2 = (1 - \hat{k}) * V0_{\bar{i},\bar{j}+1,\bar{k}} + \hat{k} * V0_{\bar{i},\bar{j}+1,\bar{k}+1} \\
v_1 = (1 - \hat{k}) * V0_{\bar{i}+1,\bar{j},\bar{k}} + \hat{k} * V0_{\bar{i}+1,\bar{j},\bar{k}+1}, & v_2 = (1 - \hat{k}) * V0_{\bar{i}+1,\bar{j}+1,\bar{k}} + \hat{k} * V0_{\bar{i}+1,\bar{j}+1,\bar{k}+1} \\
w_1 = (1 - \hat{j}) * u_1 + \hat{j} * u_2, & w_2 = (1 - \hat{j}) * v_1 + \hat{j} * v_2 \\
V_{ijk} = (1 - \hat{i}) * w_1 + \hat{i} * w_2 &
\end{array} \tag{2}$$

Here, $\bar{i}, \bar{j}, \bar{k}$ are the three-dimensional indices of grid adjacent to the voxel coordinates, and $\hat{i}, \hat{j}, \hat{k}$ are the corresponding fractional parts. (u_1, u_2),(v_1, v_2) and (w_1, w_2) are pairs of weights along three axes.

The fidelity of target image could be guaranteed by approximating its projections to the ground-truth projections. The 2D projections Y can be calculated from V as

$$Y = P(V) = P(V(D)), i, j, k = 1, \ldots, n, \tag{3}$$

where P is the projection operator implemented by ray-tracing algorithm. As there are not enough equations in (3), to solve this ill-posed problem, the regularization term was introduced. Here, the bending energy defined as below was employed to enforce the flatness of D.

$$E(D) = \sum_{k=1}^{n}\sum_{j=1}^{n}\sum_{i=1}^{n}\sum_{m=1}^{3}\left(\left(\frac{\partial D^x_{ijk}}{\partial x}\right)^2 + \left(\frac{\partial D^y_{ijk}}{\partial y}\right)^2 + \left(\frac{\partial D^z_{ijk}}{\partial z}\right)^2\right) \tag{4}$$

The objective function was then established as

$$\min E(D) \quad s.t. \quad \|P(V) - Y\| = 0 \tag{5}$$

This problem could be transformed to an unconstraint problem with a weight μ

$$f(D) = \|P(V) - Y\| + \mu * E(D) \tag{6}$$

The gradient of *f(D)* could be derived as

$$\nabla f(D) = 2P^{-1}(P(V(D) - Y))\nabla V(D) + \mu * \nabla E(D) \tag{7}$$

where P^{-1} is the inverse projection operator which backprojects 2D projections onto 3D volume. $\nabla V(D)$ could be calculated with respect to D along three axes.

$$\begin{aligned}
\frac{\partial V_{ijk}}{\partial D^z_{ijk}} &= \frac{\partial w_1}{\partial D^z_{ijk}} * (1-\hat{i}) + \frac{\partial w_2}{\partial D^z_{ijk}} * \hat{i} \\
&= \left(\frac{\partial u_1}{\partial D^z_{ijk}} * (1-\hat{j}) + \frac{\partial u_2}{\partial D^z_{ijk}} * \hat{j} \right) * (1-\hat{i}) + \left(\frac{\partial v_1}{\partial D^z_{ijk}} * (1-\hat{j}) + \frac{\partial v_2}{\partial D^z_{ijk}} * \hat{j} \right) * \hat{i} \\
&= \begin{pmatrix} \left(-V0_{\bar{i},\bar{j},\bar{k}} + V0_{\bar{i},\bar{j},\bar{k}+1}\right) * (1-\hat{j}) \\ +\left(-V0_{\bar{i},\bar{j}+1,\bar{k}} + V0_{\bar{i},\bar{j}+1,\bar{k}+1}\right) * \hat{j} \end{pmatrix} * (1-\hat{i}) + \begin{pmatrix} \left(-V0_{\bar{i}+1,\bar{j},\bar{k}} + V0_{\bar{i}+1,\bar{j},\bar{k}+1}\right) * (1-\hat{j}) \\ +\left(-V0_{\bar{i}+1,\bar{j}+1,\bar{k}} + V0_{\bar{i}+1,\bar{j}+1,\bar{k}+1}\right) * \hat{j} \end{pmatrix} * \hat{i}
\end{aligned} \tag{8a}$$

$$\frac{\partial V_{ijk}}{\partial D^y_{ijk}} = \frac{\partial w_1}{\partial D^y_{ijk}} * (1-\hat{i}) + \frac{\partial w_2}{\partial D^y_{ijk}} * \hat{i} = (-u_1 + u_2) * (1-\hat{i}) + (-v_1 + v_2) * \hat{i} \tag{8b}$$

$$\frac{\partial V_{ijk}}{\partial D^x_{ijk}} = -w_1 + w_2 \tag{8c}$$

∇E could be calculated with respect to D as below.

$$\begin{aligned}
\frac{\partial E}{\partial D} &= -2(D^x_{i+1,j,k} - D^x_{i,j,k}) + 2(D^x_{i,j,k} - D^x_{i-1,j,k}) - 2(D^x_{i,j+1,k} - D^x_{i,j,k}) \\
&\quad +2(D^x_{i,j,k} - D^x_{i,j-1,k}) - 2(D^x_{i,j,k+1} - D^x_{i,j,k}) + 2(D^x_{i,j,k} - D^x_{i,j,k-1}) \\
&= 12D^x_{i,j,k} - 2D^x_{i+1,j,k} - 2D^x_{i-1,j,k} - 2D^x_{i,j+1,k} - 2D^x_{i,j-1,k} - 2D^x_{i,j,k+1} - 2D^x_{i,j,k-1}
\end{aligned} \tag{9}$$

When both $\nabla V(D)$ and $\nabla E(D)$ were obtained, $\nabla f(D)$ in Equation (7) could be solved.

2.2. B-Spline Interpolation

The uniform cubic B-spline basis functions were employed in this study. The real-value displacement matrix was interpolated from B-spline coefficients. In 3D case, the deformation field at any given voxel was determined with the 64 control points in the immediate vicinity of the voxel's housing tile. B-spline interpolation was performed for each voxel with respect to the 64 control point coefficients as follows

$$D^x_{ijk} = \Phi(I^x) = \sum_{l=0}^{3} \sum_{m=0}^{3} \sum_{n=0}^{3} \beta_l(u)\beta_m(v)\beta_n(w) I^x_{lmn} \tag{10}$$

where $I^x{}_{lmn}$ is the spline coefficient defining the x component of the displacement vector for one of the 64 control points. N_x, N_y and N_z are voxels per region (VPR) defining the distance between control points in terms of voxels in the x, y and z directions, respectively. The volume was, therefore, segmented by the B-spline control point grid into many equal-sized tiles of dimensions $N_x \times N_y \times N_z$. The three-dimensional indices x_t, y_t and z_t of the tile for the voxel at x, y and z was given by $\lfloor i/N_x \rfloor$, $\lfloor j/N_y \rfloor$, $\lfloor k/N_z \rfloor$, respectively. The coordinates of the voxel within its tile were $u = i/N_x - x_t, v = j/N_y - y_t, w = k/N_z - z_t$.

The uniform cubic B-spline basis functions were given by $\beta_l(u)$, $\beta_m(v)$ and $\beta_n(w)$ along the x, y and z axes, respectively.

$$\beta_l(u) = \begin{cases} (1-u)^3/6 : l = 0 \\ (3u^3 - 6u^2 + 4)/6 : l = 1 \\ (-3u^3 - 3u^2 + 3u + 1)/6 : l = 2 \\ u^3/6 : l = 3 \end{cases} \quad \beta_m(v) = \begin{cases} (1-v)^3/6 : m = 0 \\ (3v^3 - 6v^2 + 4)/6 : m = 1 \\ (-3v^3 - 3v^2 + 3v + 1)/6 : m = 2 \\ v^3/6 : m = 3 \end{cases} \quad \beta_n(w) = \begin{cases} (1-w)^3/6 : n = 0 \\ (3w^3 - 6w^2 + 4)/6 : n = 1 \\ (-3w^3 - 3w^2 + 3w + 1)/6 : n = 2 \\ w^3/6 : n = 3 \end{cases}$$

VPR was an important parameter which controlled the approximation quality of B-spline curve for the target image. The fine VPR reduced the approximation error but caused higher computation costs. The coarse VPR increased the approximation error but was more time efficient. The balance between the accuracy and efficiency was investigated in the latter section.

2.3. B-Spline-Based Reconstruction Method

With B-spline-interpolated displacement matrix D, Equations (1) and (3) were reformulated as

$$V = V(\Phi(I)) \text{ and } Y = P(V) = P(V(\Phi(I))) \tag{11a}$$

and the objective function of Equation (5) was updated as

$$\min E(\Phi(I)) \quad s.t. \quad \|P(V(\Phi(I))) - Y\| = 0 \tag{11b}$$

The gradient of the objective function was then expressed as:

$$\nabla f(\Phi(I)) = 2P^{-1}(P(V(\Phi(I))) - Y)\nabla V(\Phi(I)) + \mu * \nabla E(\Phi(I)) \tag{12}$$

The gradient ∇V could be calculated using chain rule as

$$\nabla V(\Phi(I)) = \frac{\partial V}{\partial I} = \frac{\partial V}{\partial \Phi}\frac{\partial \Phi}{\partial I} \tag{13}$$

Combining Equation (2) and Equation (11), $\frac{\partial V}{\partial \Phi}$ could be calculated as

$$\frac{\partial V_{ijk}}{\partial \Phi^x_{ijk}} = -w_1 + w_2 \tag{14a}$$

$$\begin{aligned} \frac{\partial V_{ijk}}{\partial \Phi^y_{ijk}} &= \frac{\partial w_1}{\partial \Phi^y_{ijk}} * (1-\hat{i}) + \frac{\partial w_2}{\partial \Phi^y_{ijk}} * \hat{i} \\ &= (-u_1 + u_2) * (1-\hat{i}) + (-v_1 + v_2) * \hat{i} \end{aligned} \tag{14b}$$

$$\begin{aligned} \frac{\partial V_{ijk}}{\partial \Phi^z_{ijk}} &= \frac{\partial w_1}{\partial \Phi^z_{ijk}} * (1-\hat{i}) + \frac{\partial w_2}{\partial \Phi^z_{ijk}} * \hat{i} \\ &= \left(\frac{\partial u_1}{\partial \Phi^z_{ijk}} * (1-\hat{j}) + \frac{\partial u_2}{\partial \Phi^z_{ijk}} * \hat{j}\right) * (1-\hat{i}) + \left(\frac{\partial v_1}{\partial \Phi^z_{ijk}} * (1-\hat{j}) + \frac{\partial v_2}{\partial \Phi^z_{ijk}} * \hat{j}\right) * \hat{i} \\ &= \begin{pmatrix} \left(-V0_{\bar{i},\bar{j},\bar{k}} + V0_{\bar{i},\bar{j},\bar{k}+1}\right) * (1-\hat{j}) \\ +\left(-V0_{\bar{i},\bar{j}+1,\bar{k}} + V0_{\bar{i},\bar{j}+1,\bar{k}+1}\right) * \hat{j} \end{pmatrix} * (1-\hat{i}) + \begin{pmatrix} \left(-V0_{\bar{i}+1,\bar{j},\bar{k}} + V0_{\bar{i}+1,\bar{j},\bar{k}+1}\right) * (1-\hat{j}) \\ +\left(-V0_{\bar{i}+1,\bar{j}+1,\bar{k}} + V0_{\bar{i}+1,\bar{j}+1,\bar{k}+1}\right) * \hat{j} \end{pmatrix} * \hat{i} \end{aligned} \tag{14c}$$

According to the definition of $\Phi(I)$ in Equation (10), $\frac{\partial \Phi}{\partial I}$ is given by

$$\frac{\partial \Phi}{\partial I} = \sum_{l=0}^{3}\sum_{m=0}^{3}\sum_{n=0}^{3} \beta_l(u)\beta_m(v)\beta_n(w) \tag{15}$$

The bending energy function could also be updated as

$$E(I) = \sum_{k=1}^{n}\sum_{j=1}^{n}\sum_{i=1}^{n}\sum_{m=1}^{3}\left(\left(\frac{\partial \Phi^x_{ijk}}{\partial x}\right)^2 + \left(\frac{\partial \Phi^y_{ijk}}{\partial y}\right)^2 + \left(\frac{\partial \Phi^z_{ijk}}{\partial z}\right)^2\right) \tag{16}$$

and its discrete form is

$$E(I) = \sum_{k=1}^{n}\sum_{j=1}^{n}\sum_{i=1}^{n}\sum_{m=1}^{3}\begin{pmatrix} \left(\Phi^x_{i+1,j,k} - \Phi^x_{i,j,k}\right)^2 + \left(\Phi^x_{i,j,k} - \Phi^x_{i-1,j,k}\right)^2 \\ +\left(\Phi^x_{i,j+1,k} - \Phi^x_{i,j,k}\right)^2 + \left(\Phi^x_{i,j,k} - \Phi^x_{i,j-1,k}\right)^2 \\ +\left(\Phi^x_{i,j,k+1} - \Phi^x_{i,j,k}\right)^2 + \left(\Phi^x_{i,j,k} - \Phi^x_{i,j,k-1}\right)^2 \end{pmatrix} \tag{17}$$

∇E could be calculated using chain rule as

$$\nabla E(\Phi(I)) = \frac{\partial E}{\partial I} = \frac{\partial E}{\partial \Phi}\frac{\partial \Phi}{\partial I} \cdot \frac{\partial E}{\partial \Phi} \tag{18}$$

where

$$\begin{aligned}\frac{\partial E}{\partial \Phi} &= -2(\Phi^x_{i+1,j,k} - \Phi^x_{i,j,k}) + 2(\Phi^x_{i,j,k} - \Phi^x_{i-1,j,k}) - 2(\Phi^x_{i,j+1,k} - \Phi^x_{i,j,k}) \\ &+2(\Phi^x_{i,j,k} - \Phi^x_{i,j-1,k}) - 2(\Phi^x_{i,j,k+1} - \Phi^x_{i,j,k}) + 2(\Phi^x_{i,j,k} - \Phi^x_{i,j,k-1}) \\ &= 12\Phi^x_{i,j,k} - 2\Phi^x_{i+1,j,k} - 2\Phi^x_{i-1,j,k} - 2\Phi^x_{i,j+1,k} - 2\Phi^x_{i,j-1,k} - 2\Phi^x_{i,j,k+1} - 2\Phi^x_{i,j,k-1}\end{aligned} \tag{19}$$

Combining Equations (13) and (15) into Equation (12), $\nabla f(I)$ could be finally obtained as

$$\nabla f(\Phi(I)) = \left[2P^{-1}(P(V) - Y) * \frac{\partial V}{\partial \Phi} + \mu * \frac{\partial E}{\partial \Phi}\right] * \sum_{l=0}^{3}\sum_{m=0}^{3}\sum_{n=0}^{3} \beta_l(u)\beta_m(v)\beta_n(w) \tag{20}$$

2.4. Evaluation

The proposed method was implemented in an iterative manner as shown in Figure 1. Initially, the B-spline coefficients and the displacement matrixes were set to zero. The gradient of the objective function was then calculated, and the B-spline coefficients were updated based on the resulting gradient. After certain iterations, the optimization process converged when the value of ∇f was less than the threshold or the maximum number of iterations reached. The real-value displacement matrixes were interpolated from the optimized B-spline coefficients. Then, the target image was transformed from the prior image via the resulted real-value displacement matrixes. Finally, the approximation errors of B-spline-interpolated displacement matrix and the reconstructed target image were calculated for analysis.

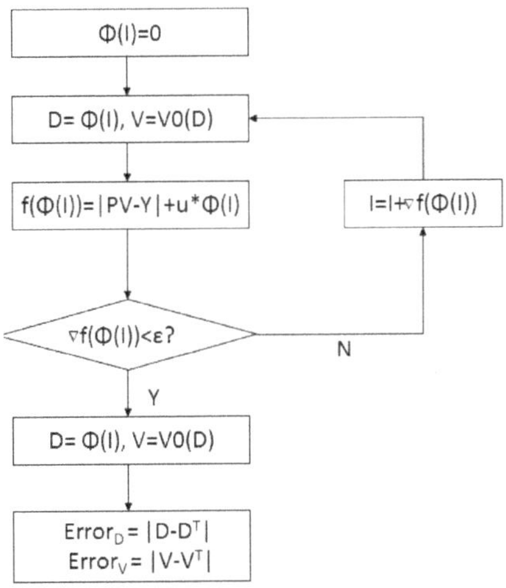

Figure 1. The flowchart of B-spline-based reconstruction method.

To evaluate the similarity between the reconstructed target image (V^R) and the ground-truth target image (V^T), three intensity-based statistical metrics, normalized cross correlation, mutual information and mean absolute percentage error, were employed. Normalized cross correlation (NCC) was defined as

$$NCC\left(X^R, X^T\right) = \frac{(X^R - \mu^R)(X^T - \mu^T)}{\sigma^R \sigma^T} \tag{21}$$

where μ^R and μ^T are means of V^R and V^T and where σ^R and σ^T are standard deviations of V^R and V^T. Mutual information (MI) was defined as

$$MI\left(V^R, V^T\right) = \sum_{x^R \in V^R} \sum_{x^T \in V^T} p\left(x^R, x^T\right) \log_2 \frac{p(x^R, x^T)}{p(x^R)p(x^T)} \tag{22}$$

where $p(x^R)$ and $p(x^T)$ are the normalized histograms of V^R and V^T and where $p(x^R, x^T)$ is the joint histogram of V^R and V^T. In order to calculate the intensity difference between two images, the mean absolute percentage error (MAPE) was defined as

$$MAPE = \frac{1}{n}\sum_{i=1}^{n}\left|\frac{x_i^R - x_i^T}{x_i^T}\right| \tag{23}$$

where $x^R{}_i$ and $x^T{}_i$ are the voxels of images V^R and V^T and where n is the total number of voxels.

The proposed method was examined using a clinical head-and-neck patient. The CBCT image size was 256 × 256 × 256, and the cone-beam projection size was 512 × 384. The full-angle reference CBCT and target CBCT were reconstructed with FDK method using two sets of CB projections that were acquired on two separate days. The CB projections were acquired at every 0.55°. The influence of scan angle (30°, 45°, 60° and 90°) and scan orientation (central angle at 0°, 45° and 90°) were investigated. The accuracy of our method was evaluated by comparing the limited-angle CBCT (target image) to the full-angle CBCT (ground-truth) that was reconstructed with Feldkamp–Davis–Kress (FDK) method. The reconstruction and evaluation codes were built on the open-source platform, Plastimatch, which provides B-spline-based image registration and GPU-based image reconstruction toolkits.

3. Results

The images reconstructed using the proposed and FDK methods on the clinical head-and-neck case is shown in Figure 2. The projections were acquired with a 0° scan orientation and a 60° scan angle. The prior image that was reconstructed using a full-angle scan with the FDK method is shown in Figure 2a. The target image that was reconstructed with the FDK method using a limited-angle scan is shown in Figure 2b. The target image that was reconstructed with the B-spline-based reconstruction method using a limited-angle scan is shown in Figure 2c. As the ground-truth image, the target image that was reconstructed with the FDK method using a full-angle scan is shown in Figure 2d. The similarity between the images in Figure 2c,d was high, which indicated that the proposed method could generate comparable images, using a limited-angle scan, to the ground-truth image, using a full-angle scan.

The images that were reconstructed with the deformation-based reconstruction method as described in Section 2.1 are shown in Figure 3. The projections were acquired with a 0° scan orientation and 30°/45°/60°/90° angles. It was noticed that there was strong noise in the target images that were reconstructed with 30°, 45° and 60° scan angles. The image quality of the reconstructed images became worse as the scan angle decreased. Among the four images, the image that was reconstructed with a 90° scan angle (Figure 3d) showed the best quality and was closer to the ground-truth image (Figure 2d).

The images that were reconstructed with the proposed B-spline-based reconstruction method using a limited-angle scan as described in Section 2.3 are shown in Figure 4. The setting of this reconstruction was the same as the one used in Figure 3. It was noticed that the noise in the images as shown in Figure 4 was greatly suppressed comparing to that in the images in Figure 3. The image quality with the 60° and 90° scan angles was better and was closer to that of the ground-truth image (Figure 2d). The image quality with the 90° scan angle (Figure 4d) was the best but required 50% more projections than that with the 60° scan angle (Figure 4c).

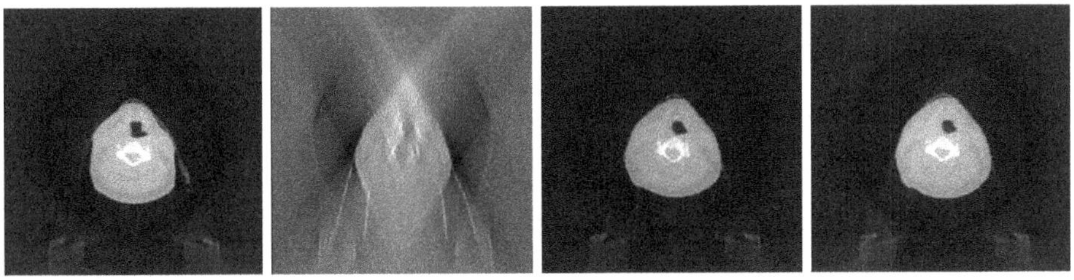

(a) (b) (c) (d)

Figure 2. The comparison between images reconstructed with the different reconstruction methods. (**a**) Prior image acquired reconstructed with FDK method using full-angle scan. (**b**) The target image reconstructed with FDK method using limited-angle scan. (**c**) The target image reconstructed with B-spline-based reconstruction method using limited-angle scan. (**d**) The target image reconstructed with FDK method using full-angle scan.

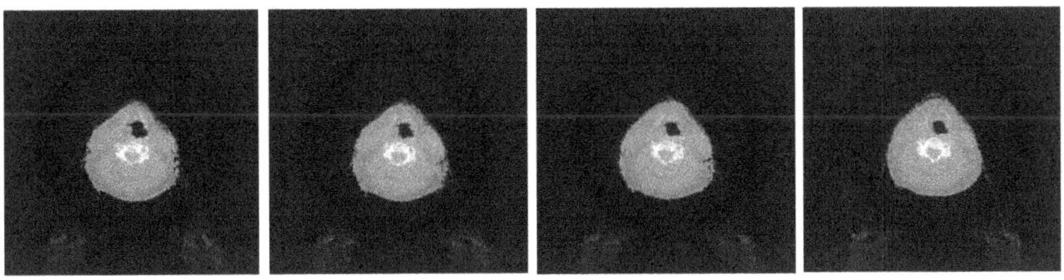

(a) (b) (c) (d)

Figure 3. The images reconstructed with the deformation-based reconstruction method as described in Section 2.1. (**a**) Image reconstructed with 30° scan angle. (**b**) Image reconstructed with 45° scan angle. (**c**) Image reconstructed with 60° scan angle. (**d**) Image reconstructed with 90° scan angle.

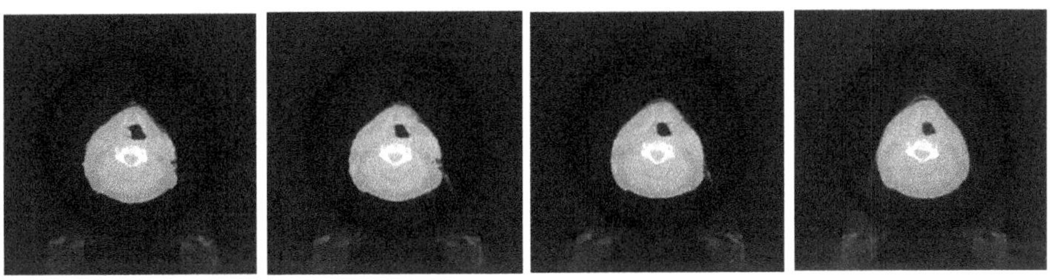

(a) (b) (c) (d)

Figure 4. The images reconstructed with the B-spline-based reconstruction method as described in Section 2.3. (**a**) Image reconstructed with 30° scan angle. (**b**) Image reconstructed with 45° scan angle. (**c**) Image reconstructed with 60° scan angle. (**d**) Image reconstructed with 90° scan angle.

The influence of the scan orientation on the image quality was also investigated. The images that were reconstructed with the FDK method and the proposed method with a 0° scan orientation and a 60° scan angle are shown in Figure 2b,c. The images that were reconstructed with both methods with a 45° scan orientation and a 60° scan angle are shown in Figure 5a,b, while the images that were reconstructed with both methods with a 90° scan orientation and a 60° scan angle are shown in Figure 5c,d. The images as shown in Figure 3a–c that were reconstructed with the FDK method with three scan orientations were significantly different. The images as shown in Figures 2c and 5b,d that were reconstructed with the proposed method with three scan orientations were similar to each other. This indicated that the influence of the scan orientation on the image quality of the reconstructed image was minor.

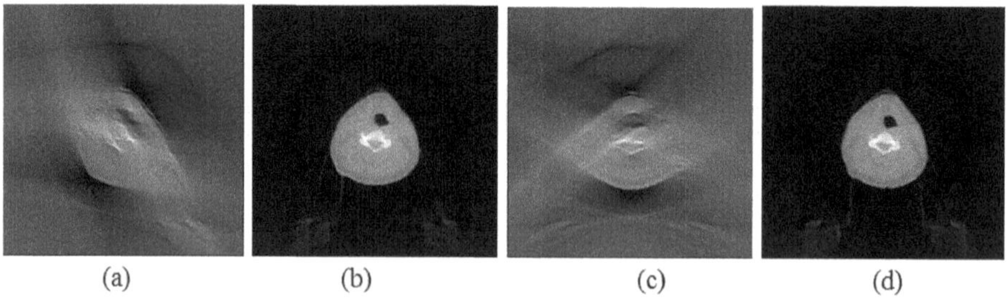

Figure 5. The image reconstructed with different scan orientations with the FDK and proposed methods. (**a**) Image reconstructed with 45° scan orientation with FDK method. (**b**) Image reconstructed with 45° scan orientation with the proposed method. (**c**) Image reconstructed with 90° scan orientation with FDK method. (**d**) Image reconstructed with 90° scan orientation with the proposed method.

The accuracy of the B-spline-interpolated displacement matrix and the reconstructed target image with respect to the different settings of the VPR and scan angles were investigated. In Table 1, the final B-spline-interpolated displacement matrix was compared to the ground-truth displacement matrix which was obtained from the deformable transformation between the prior and ground-truth images. For a combination of the scan angle and VPR, three similarity metrics (NCC, MI and MAPE) were calculated. The result showed that, with a smaller VPR and a larger scan angle, the similarity between the resulted and ground-truth displacement matrixes was higher. In Table 2, the final reconstructed target image was compared to the ground-truth target image. For a combination of the scan angle and VPR, the same three similarity metrics were calculated. The result showed that, with a smaller VPR and a larger scan angle, the similarity between the reconstructed and ground-truth images was higher.

Table 1. The accuracy of the B-spline-interpolated displacement matrix.

Scan Angle	VPR = 60			VPR = 30			VPR = 5		
	NCC	MI	MAPE	NCC	MI	MAPE	NCC	MI	MAPE
30°	0.62	0.72	0.31	0.83	1.21	0.13	0.88	1.31	0.11
60°	0.76	0.99	0.20	0.89	1.25	0.19	0.93	1.33	0.06
90°	0.85	1.08	0.15	0.94	1.29	0.08	0.97	1.37	0.05

Table 2. The accuracy of the reconstructed target image.

Scan Angle	VPR = 60			VPR = 30			VPR = 5		
	NCC	MI	MAPE	NCC	MI	MAPE	NCC	MI	MAPE
30°	0.80	0.91	0.17	0.88	1.31	0.09	0.90	1.33	0.07
60°	0.88	1.22	0.12	0.94	1.51	0.07	0.96	1.55	0.04
90°	0.90	1.28	0.10	0.98	1.58	0.05	0.99	1.65	0.02

The running time on the CPU and GPU platforms were compared in Table 3. The inputs were the 2D projections acquired with the 30° or 60° scan angle and the 3D prior image. The dimensions of the 2D projections were 512 × 384, and the dimensions of the 3D image was 256 × 256 × 256. The output was the 3D image in the dimensions of 256 × 256 × 256. The computation of the 2D and 3D image reconstructions and B-spline coefficients were all accomplished on a GPU. Two popular graphics cards, Nvidia Geforce GTX 1080 and Nvidia Geforce GTX 2080, were tested. The computer was equipped with a Intel Xeon 2609 CPU and a 64GB DRR4 memory. It showed that the running time on a GPU was hundred times faster than that on a traditional CPU.

Table 3. Running time on CPU and GPU for different reconstruction tasks.

Tasks	Reconstruction with 30° Scan Angle			Reconstruction with 60° Scan Angle		
Iterations	CPU	GPU		CPU	GPU	
	Intel Xeon 2609	Nvidia 1080	Nvidia 2080	Intel Xeon 2609	Nvidia 1080	Nvidia 2080
100	11,000s	100s	75s	13,400s	120s	100s
200	19,000s	230s	200s	25,500s	250s	220s

4. Discussion

With a limited-angle scan, the proposed method could reconstruct images comparable to the standard images reconstructed with a full-angle scan. This will significantly reduce the time and dose during multiple data acquisition and would be beneficial for patients under treatment. With the introduction of the B-spline interpolation, the image noise and artifacts were suppressed, and the edge of the anatomical structures was improved. The VPR had a certain effect on the image quality, but it could be minimized with smaller values. With the acceleration of a GPU, the iterative CBCT reconstruction could be mostly accomplished within 10 min. This would make it possible for several clinical scenarios.

There are many factors that could affect the image quality and accuracy of the reconstructed images. Among them, the scan orientation and scan angle are the most important ones. Our experiments showed that the scan orientation had a small influence on the images, but the scan angle had a large influence on the resulting images. When the scan angle was less than 30°, there was strong noise and a larger structure discontinuity in the reconstructed images. A larger scan angle would result in a better image but would take more time for reconstruction computation. Therefore, to balance accuracy and efficiency, a 60° scan angle would be favorable for clinical use.

The introduction of the B-spline interpolation was effective for noise suppression. It could also be feasible in the other types of limited-angle reconstruction methods, such as total-variation-based and optical-flow-based reconstruction methods. In addition, this method could also be used for the reconstruction of 4D-CT and 4D-CBCT with limited-angle projections. In these 4D reconstruction tasks, the 3D volume in one phase could be used as a prior image to predict the 3D volume of another phase. As a large amount of projections is usually required in 4D applications, the reduction of the time and dose resulted by the proposed method on data acquisition would be considerable.

It is also possible to extend this method to the other industrial domains, such as magnetic resonance imaging, radar interferometry, electromagnetism, etc. As these fields differ from medical imaging, it would be important to identify the proper setting and parameters for them. For example, the imaging principle of MRIs would differ from that of CT/CBCTs substantially. The former is generated by detecting the direction of the change of protons in the water, while the latter is generated from the X-ray interaction with the material on its path and finally deposing the residual radiation dose on the detectors. The proper preprocessing and adjustments would be necessary.

5. Conclusions

A new B-spline-based limited-angle reconstruction method was developed and demonstrated its feasibility in reconstructing high-quality images comparable to the standard images. With the introduction of the B-spline interpolation, the image noise was significantly suppressed, and the contour of the anatomical structures was improved. With the GPU acceleration, the limited clinical time of image reconstruction could be greatly alleviated. Potentially, this reconstruction method could be used in the other industrial domains, but proper preprocessing and adjustments would be needed.

Author Contributions: Conception and design: H.Y., Administrative support: J.D. All authors have read and agreed to the published version of the manuscript.

Funding: This work was supported by the Natural Science Foundation of China (No. 11975312) and the Beijing Municipal Natural Science Foundation (7202170).

Conflicts of Interest: The authors have no conflict of interest to declare.

References

1. Nasseh, I.; Al-Rawi, W. Cone Beam Computed Tomography. *Dent. Clin. North Am.* **2018**, *62*, 361–391. [CrossRef] [PubMed]
2. Ruschin, M.; Komljenovic, P.T.; Ansell, S.; Ménard, C.; Bootsma, G.; Cho, Y.B.; Chung, C.; Jaffray, D. Cone beam computed tomography image guidance system for a dedicated intracranial radiosurgery treatment unit. *Int. J. Radiat. Oncol. Biol. Phys.* **2013**, *85*, 243–250. [CrossRef] [PubMed]
3. Létourneau, D.; Wong, J.W.; Oldham, M.; Gulam, M.; Watt, L.; Jaffray, D.A.; Siewerdsen, J.H.; Martinez, A.A. Cone-beam-CT guided radiation therapy: Technical implementation. *Radiother. Oncol.* **2005**, *75*, 279–286. [CrossRef]
4. Efird, J.T.; Jindal, C.; Podder, T.K.; Kang, K.H.; Biswas, T. Cone beam computed tomography-the need for future guidance. *J. Thorac. Dis.* **2022**, *14*, 3681–3683. [CrossRef] [PubMed]
5. Hioki, K.; Araki, F.; Oono, T.; Tomiyama, Y.; Nakaguchi, Y. Monte Carlo-calculated patient organ doses from kV-cone beam CT in image-guided radiation therapy. *Biomed. Phys. Eng. Express* **2015**, *1*, 025203. [CrossRef]
6. Ohno, T.; Araki, F.; Onizuka, R.; Hioki, K.; Tomiyama, Y.; Yamashita, Y. New absorbed dose measurement with cylindrical water phantoms for multidetector CT. *Phys. Med. Biol.* **2015**, *60*, 4517. [CrossRef]
7. Santoso, A.P.; Song, K.H.; Qin, Y.; Gardner, S.J.; Liu, C.; Chetty, I.J.; Movsas, B.; Ajlouni, M.; Wen, N. Evaluation of gantry speed on image quality and imaging dose for 4D cone-beam CT acquisition. *Radiat. Oncol.* **2016**, *11*, 98. [CrossRef]
8. Jia, X.; Lou, Y.; Li, R.; Song, W.Y.; Jiang, S.B. GPU-based fast cone beam CT reconstruction from undersampled and noisy projection data via total variation. *Med. Phys.* **2010**, *37*, 1757–1760. [CrossRef]
9. Sidky, E.Y.; Pan, X. Image reconstruction in circular cone-beam computed tomography by constrained, total-variation minimization. *Phys. Med. Biol.* **2008**, *53*, 4777–4807. [CrossRef]
10. Shouliang, Q.; Teng, Y.; Kang, Y.; Qi, S. A separable quadratic surrogate total variation minimization algorithm for accelerating accurate CT reconstruction from few-views and limited-angle data. *Med. Phys.* **2018**, *45*, 535–548.
11. Song, J.; Liu, Q.H.; Johnson, G.A.; Badea, C.T. Sparseness prior based iterative image reconstruction for retrospectively gated cardiac micro-CT. *Med. Phys.* **2007**, *34*, 4476–4483. [CrossRef] [PubMed]
12. Niu, S.; Gao, Y.; Bian, Z.; Huang, J.; Chen, W.; Yu, G.; Liang, Z.; Ma, J. Sparse-view x-ray CT reconstruction via total generalized variation regularization. *Phys. Med. Biol.* **2014**, *59*, 2997. [CrossRef] [PubMed]
13. Qi, Z.; Chen, G.-H. Extraction of tumor motion trajectories using PICCS-4DCBCT: A validation study. *Med. Phys.* **2011**, *38*, 5530–5538. [CrossRef] [PubMed]
14. Chen, G.-H.; Tang, J.; Leng, S. Prior image constrained compressed sensing (PICCS): A method to accurately reconstruct dynamic CT images from highly undersampled projection data sets. *Med. Phys.* **2008**, *35*, 660–663. [CrossRef] [PubMed]
15. Lee, H.; Xing, L.; Davidi, R.; Li, R.; Qian, J.; Lee, R. Improved compressed sensing-based cone-beam CT reconstruction using adaptive prior image constraints. *Phys. Med. Biol.* **2012**, *57*, 2287. [CrossRef]
16. Huang, J.; Zhang, Y.; Ma, J.; Zeng, D.; Bian, Z.; Niu, S.; Feng, Q.; Liang, Z.; Chen, W. Iterative image reconstruction for sparse-view CT using normal-dose image induced total variation prior. *PLoS ONE* **2013**, *8*, e79709. [CrossRef]
17. Stayman, J.W.; Dang, H.; Ding, Y.; Siewerdsen, J.H. PIRPLE: A penalized-likelihood framework for incorporation of prior images in CT reconstruction. *Phys. Med. Biol.* **2013**, *58*, 7563. [CrossRef]
18. Dang, H.; Wang, A.S.; Sussman, M.S.; Siewerdsen, J.H.; Stayman, J.W. dPIRPLE: A joint estimation framework for deformable registration and penalized likelihood CT image reconstruction using prior images. *Phys. Med. Biol.* **2014**, *59*, 4799. [CrossRef]
19. Ren, L.; Zhang, Y.; Yin, F.F. A limited-angle intrafraction verification (LIVE) system for radiation therapy. *Med Phys.* **2014**, *41*, 020701. [CrossRef]
20. Zhang, Y.; Yin, F.F.; Pan, T.; Vergalasova, I.; Ren, L. Preliminary clinical evaluation of a 4D-CBCT estimation technique using prior information and limited-angle projections. *Radiother. Oncol.* **2015**, *115*, 22–29. [CrossRef]
21. Zhang, Y.; Yin, F.-F.; Zhang, Y.; Ren, L. Reducing scan angle using adaptive prior knowledge for a limited-angle intrafraction verification (LIVE) system for conformal arc radiotherapy. *Phys. Med. Biol.* **2017**, *62*, 3859. [CrossRef] [PubMed]
22. Ertas, M.; Yildirim, I.; Kamasak, M.; Akan, A. Digital breast tomosynthesis image reconstruction using 2D and 3D total variation minimization. *Biomed. Eng.* **2013**, *12*, 112. [CrossRef] [PubMed]
23. Badea, C.T.; Schreibmann, E.; Fox, T. A registration based approach for 4D cardiac micro-CT using combined prospective and retrospective gating. *Med. Phys.* **2008**, *35*, 1170–1179. [CrossRef] [PubMed]
24. Isola, A.A.; Grass, M.; Niessen, W.J. Fully automatic nonrigid registration-based local motion estimation for motion-corrected iterative cardiac CT reconstruction. *Med. Phys.* **2010**, *37*, 1093–1109. [CrossRef]
25. Ehrhardt, J.; Werner, R.; Säring, D.; Frenzel, T.; Lu, W.; Low, D.; Handels, H. An optical flow based method for improved reconstruction of 4D CT data sets acquired during free breathing. *Med. Phys.* **2007**, *34*, 711–721. [CrossRef] [PubMed]

26. Lustig, M.; Donoho, D.; Pauly, J.M. Sparse MRI: The application of compressed sensing for rapid MR imaging. *Magn. Reson. Med.* **2007**, *58*, 1182–1195. [CrossRef] [PubMed]
27. Nie, X.; Saleh, Z.; Kadbi, M.; Zakian, K.; Deasy, J.; Rimner, A.; Li, G. A super-resolution framework for the reconstruction of T2-weighted (T2w) time-resolved (TR) 4DMRI using T1w TR-4DMRI as the guidance. *Med. Phys.* **2020**, *47*, 3091–3102. [CrossRef]
28. Ren, L.; Zhang, J.; Thongphiew, D.; Godfrey, D.J.; Wu, Q.J.; Zhou, S.M.; Yin, F.F. A novel digital tomosynthesis (DTS) reconstruction method using a deformation field map. *Med. Phys.* **2008**, *35*, 3110–3115. [CrossRef]
29. Ren, L.; Chetty, I.J.; Zhang, J.; Jin, J.-Y.; Wu, Q.J.; Yan, H.; Brizel, D.M.; Lee, W.R.; Movsas, B.; Yin, F.-F. Development and clinical evaluation of a three-dimensional cone-beam computed tomography estimation method using a deformation field map. *Int. J. Radiat. Oncol. Biol. Phys.* **2012**, *82*, 1584–1593. [CrossRef]
30. Tustison, N.J.; Avants, B.B. Directly manipulated free-form deformation image registration. *IEEE Trans. Image Process.* **2009**, *18*, 624–635. [CrossRef]
31. Lu, X.; Suo, S.; Liu, H.; Zhang, S. Three-dimensional multimodal image non-rigid registration and fusion in a High Intensity Focused Ultrasound system. *Comput. Aided Surg.* **2012**, *17*, 1–12. [CrossRef] [PubMed]
32. Rohde, G.K.; Aldroubi, A.; Dawant, B.M. The adaptive bases algorithm for intensity-based non-rigid image registration. *IEEE Trans. Med. Imaging* **2003**, *22*, 1470–1479. [CrossRef] [PubMed]
33. Després, P.; Jia, X. A review of GPU-based medical image reconstruction. *Phys. Med.* **2017**, *42*, 76–92. [CrossRef] [PubMed]
34. Dorgham, O.M.; Laycock, S.D.; Fisher, M.H. GPU accelerated generation of digitally reconstructed radiographs for 2-D/3-D image registration. *IEEE Trans. Biomed. Eng.* **2012**, *59*, 2594–2603. [CrossRef]
35. de Molina, C.; Serrano, E.; Garcia-Blas, J.; Carretero, J.; Desco, M.; Abella, M. GPU-accelerated iterative reconstruction for limited-data tomography in CBCT systems. *BMC Bioinform.* **2018**, *15*, 171. [CrossRef] [PubMed]
36. Tian, Z.; Jia, X.; Dong, B.; Lou, Y.; Jiang, S.B. Low-dose 4DCT reconstruction via temporal nonlocal means. *Med. Phys.* **2011**, *38*, 1359–1365. [CrossRef] [PubMed]
37. Satpute, N.; Naseem, R.; Pelanis, E.; Gómez-Luna, J.; Cheikh, F.A.; Elle, O.J.; Olivares, J. GPU acceleration of liver enhancement for tumor segmentation. Comput. *Methods Programs Biomed.* **2020**, *184*, 105285. [CrossRef]
38. Haghighi, B.; DEllingwood, N.; Yin, Y.; Hoffman, E.A.; Lin, C.L. A GPU-based symmetric non-rigid image registration method in human lung. *Med. Biol. Eng. Comput.* **2018**, *56*, 355–371. [CrossRef]
39. Peng, B.; Wang, Y.; Hall, T.J.; Jiang, J. A GPU-Accelerated 3-D Coupled Subsample Estimation Algorithm for Volumetric Breast Strain Elastography. *IEEE Trans. Ultrason. Ferroelectr. Freq. Control.* **2017**, *64*, 694–705. [CrossRef]
40. Lebert, J.; Ravi, N.; Kensah, G.; Christoph, J. Real-Time Optical Mapping of Contracting Cardiac Tissues With GPU-Accelerated Numerical Motion Tracking. *Front. Cardiovasc. Med.* **2022**, *9*, 787627. [CrossRef]

mathematics

MDPI

Article

VRR-Net: Learning Vehicle–Road Relationships for Vehicle Trajectory Prediction on Highways

Tingzhang Zhan [1,2,†], Qieshi Zhang [1,†], Guangxi Chen [2] and Jun Cheng [1,*]

1 CAS Key Laboratory of Human-Machine Intelligence-Synergy Systems, Shenzhen Institute of Advanced Technology, Chinese Academy of Sciences, Shenzhen 518055, China
2 School of Computer and Information Security, Guilin University of Electronic Technology, Guilin 541004, China
* Correspondence: jun.cheng@siat.ac.cn
† These authors contributed equally to this work.

Abstract: Vehicle trajectory prediction is an important decision-making and planning basis for autonomous driving systems that enables them to drive safely and efficiently. To accurately predict vehicle trajectories, the complex representations and dynamic interactions among the elements in a traffic scene are abstracted and modelled. This paper presents vehicle–road relationships net, a deep learning network that extracts features from vehicle–road relationships and models the effects of traffic environments on vehicles. The introduction of geographic highway information and the calculation of spatiotemporal distances with a reference not only unify heterogeneous vehicle–road relationship representations into a time series vector but also reduce the requirement for sensing transient changes in the surrounding area. A hierarchical long short-term memory network extracts environmental features from two perspectives—social interactions and road constraints—and predicts the future trajectories of vehicles by their manoeuvre categories. Accordingly, vehicle–road relationships net fully exploits the contributions of historical trajectories and integrates the effects of road constraints to achieve performance that is comparable to or better than that of state-of-the-art methods on the next-generation simulation dataset.

Keywords: trajectory prediction; spatiotemporal awareness; spatiotemporal graph; vehicle–road relationships

MSC: 68T07

1. Introduction

Vehicle trajectory prediction, an essential component of an automated driving system (ADS), supports planning and decision-making for safe [1,2] and efficient resource allocation [3], especially under highway conditions [4]. In traffic scenarios, vehicles are the most dominant traffic participants and the dynamic obstacles with the greatest impact on traffic safety. If the future trajectories of vehicles are accurately predicted, intelligent systems will have the potential to build safer, more efficient and more comfortable transportation paradigms [5,6].

The trajectories of vehicles in traffic scenes are inextricably linked to the changes in their surroundings [7]. The dynamic interactions among traffic infrastructure elements (e.g., roads and traffic lights) and traffic participants (e.g., vehicles and pedestrians) make up complex and diverse traffic scenarios [8]. The traffic infrastructure constrains the movements of participants who can move freely but are constrained by the infrastructure, and accurate vehicle trajectory prediction in complex traffic environments requires considering environmental constraints and social interactions [9–13]. Ju et al. propose a multilayer architecture called interaction-aware Kalman neural networks (IaKNN), which involves an interaction layer for resolving high-dimensional traffic environmental observations as interaction-aware accelerations, a motion layer for transforming the accelerations to interaction-aware trajectories, and a filter layer for estimating future trajectories with a Kalman filter network [9]. Deo and Trivedi propose an LSTM encoder–decoder model that uses convolutional social pooling to learn inter-dependencies in vehicle motion and outputs a multimodal predictive distribution over future trajectories based on maneuver classes [10]. Guo et al. propose a dual-attention mechanism trajectory prediction method based on long short-term memory encoding that is coupled with the motion trend of the ego vehicle [11]. Chen et al. propose a new model structure, which uses a convolutional social pool to extract general features and uses GAN to extract confidence features of the generated trajectories, enabling the model to generate trajectories that are close to the real trajectories [12]. Malviya and Kala present a multi-behavioural social force-based particle filter to track a group of moving humans from a moving robot using a limited field-of-view monocular camera [13]. Overall, these papers contribute to the development of more accurate and robust trajectory prediction methods for various scenarios, such as complex traffic systems and human–robot interactions. The proposed methods utilise different techniques such as multilayer architecture, convolutional social pooling, dual-attention mechanism, and social heuristics to enhance the accuracy and generalizability of the prediction models.

Two difficulties are currently faced with regard to vehicle trajectory prediction. On the one hand, the combination of the elements in a traffic environment is complex, and current methods are not yet able to reliably cover all elements that have impacts on trajectories [14,15]. On the other hand, on the road, the motions of human-driven vehicles are multimodal [16–19], which means that similar inputs should produce different prediction results. In recent years, the problems concerning the social interactions between vehicles and the modelling of the relationships between vehicles and roads have received attention from researchers, who have proposed many different models and methods aimed at constructing the interactions between the vehicles to be predicted and their surroundings [20–22].

For highway scenarios, vehicle–road relationships (VRR)-Net, a network proposed for predicting vehicle trajectories from a vehicle–road relationship perspective, includes a data preprocessing strategy and an environment modelling framework. First, the input representations of VRR-Net are unified by the idea of serialisation. The relationships between vehicles and environments are mapped to the same representation space, thus extending the feature-capturing advantage of the model for dynamic environments. Specifically, a long short-term memory (LSTM) network with a similar structure separately extracts the interactive features of vehicles with different kinds of environmental elements and is hierarchically organised into a parallel structure. In addition, the social interactions of vehicles are abstracted from the original inputs by a spatiotemporal graph structure, which projects the social interactions into both the temporal and spatial dimensions. In the proposed spatiotemporal graph structure, the movement changes exhibited by the vehicles themselves are described by temporal edges, and the interactions between the vehicles are described by spatial edges. The experimental results show that the temporalised spatiotemporal graph reinforces the social interactions and significantly improves the utilisation of the information embedded in the historical trajectories by the social LSTM encoder.

The contributions of the proposed VRR-Net are summarised as follows.

- A serialised vehicle–road relationship model for highway scenarios is introduced, which integrates the geometry of real highways and the relative positions of vehicles and roads. The serialised model not only preserves the spatiotemporal dependencies between vehicles and roads but also implicitly expresses the manoeuvring interaction behaviours of vehicles that are parallel and perpendicular to the road direction, making the interactions between vehicles and roads more closely related to the motion features of the target vehicle.
- A novel intervehicle interaction model based on a spatiotemporal graph structure is studied; this model abstracts social interaction information at the spatial level and vehicle motion information at the temporal level. In cases where the instantaneous mo-

tions of the observed vehicles are not accessible in real-time, both the local and overall features of vehicle motions in dynamic traffic scenarios can be effectively extracted.

- A novel hierarchical environment encoder module with two LSTM layers is proposed for simultaneously extracting the spatiotemporal features of the interactions of the target vehicle with the road and with the surrounding vehicles. The network integrating vehicle–road and vehicle–vehicle relationships achieves better manoeuvre and trajectory prediction accuracy in highway scenarios than competing approaches.

2. Related Work

The development of trajectory prediction methods has progressed from simple to complex processes that can be outlined in three development stages.

The first-stage approaches try to deduce the future trajectory from only the historical trajectory of the vehicle to be predicted. This approach is intuitive and consistent with vehicle motion patterns. The kinematics-based approach [23–25] achieves superior short-term prediction performance (within 1 s) by extracting physical quantities such as vehicle speeds, constant yaw rates and acceleration values as vehicle motion characteristics [26]. It is worth noting that vehicle manoeuvre categories are used as high-level information that reduces the complexity of the motion model. Methods such as hidden Markov models [27], random forest classifiers [28] and multilayer perceptrons [29] have considered the importance of vehicle manoeuvre categories. However, regardless of this fact, their core ideas start from the vehicle's own motion characteristics only. When the prediction time exceeds 1 s, the associations between future trajectories and physical laws are gradually weakened by the driver's intention, so they cannot produce reliable long-term trajectories [30] to support the planning and decision-making of intelligent systems.

The second-stage approaches build on the previous stage by considering the influence of the social interactions between the vehicles to be predicted and other traffic participants [31]. The methods in [32,33] demonstrated that considering the interactions among surrounding vehicles helps to improve the accuracy of lane-changing behaviour prediction. The effect of this influence on predicting the future trajectories of vehicles is considered significant. Deo and Trivedi [10] proposed a social pooling mechanism to extract the features of the interactions between vehicles based on recurrent neural networks and achieved better long-term trajectory predictions. Guo et al. [11], Giuliari et al. [34] and Yan et al. [35] proposed incorporating attention mechanisms into the field of trajectory prediction so that their model could autonomously select the appropriate trajectory features for prediction when training on massive historical data. Chen et al. [36] constructed a spatiotemporal graph structure for intervehicle relationships and better extracted the spatiotemporal interactions between vehicles.

In the third stage, researchers built on the second stage and started to study the influence of the surrounding traffic infrastructure on the target vehicle [37]. In real traffic scenarios, constraints and controls from traffic infrastructure, such as lane orientations, road boundaries and traffic light scheduling, play important roles in determining the outcome of trajectory prediction. However, it is still difficult to effectively model these complex additions. Trajectron++ [15] and AgentFormer [38] process a high-definition (HD) map into feature vectors via convolutional neural networks, thus giving the networks the ability to perceive their environments. Although the aforementioned methods successfully model the influence of roads on the future trajectories of vehicles using different structures, their feature extraction abilities with respect to environmental influences are still inadequate.

Furthermore, the idea of VectorNet [39], LaneGCN [40] and prediction via graph-based policy (PGP) [21] is to organise the roads contained in the input HD map into a graph structure after segmentation and then use a graph convolutional network (GCN) to extract road features, thereby effectively solving the multimodal trajectory prediction problem in intersection scenes. Although the roads in highway scenarios are relatively simple, with long sections and small turning angles, the constraining effect of roads on vehicle behaviour still cannot be ignored. To comprehensively consider the environmental effects in this scenario and achieve better trajectory prediction accuracy, our study models both the road constraints imposed on vehicles and the social interactions between vehicles. The open next-generation simulation (NGSIM) dataset [41,42] is used to validate the method proposed in this paper for a fair comparison with most existing methods.

3. Hierarchical Model with Spatiotemporal Awareness of Vehicle–Road Relationships

For an arbitrary vehicle at each time stamp on a highway, its future motion is influenced by the environment, including both the road and the surrounding vehicles. The serialised vehicle–road relationships are implemented by a vector transformation of the vehicle trajectory points on the road geometry space, and the vehicle–vehicle relationships are constructed using a spatiotemporal graph structure, including the target vehicle and its surrounding vehicles. Furthermore, the proposed encoder extracts the temporalised features of these two aspects simultaneously using LSTM networks. Therefore, the trajectories output by the decoder are the result of a combination of the local and overall interactions between the vehicle and its driving environment.

3.1. Problem Formulation

A figurative example is given in Figure 1. In this case, the traffic infrastructure is characterised by a relatively fixed location, which acts as a constraint on the movements of traffic participants; the traffic participants are characterised by the ability to move freely but are constrained by the traffic infrastructure. In addition, dynamic social interaction behaviours [9–13] occur among the traffic participants because of their willingness to avoid collisions. Without considering the environmental constraints and social interactions, it is impossible to accurately predict the future trajectories of vehicles in complex traffic environments. Therefore, effectively modelling the constraints and interactions in traffic scenarios is a problem that needs to be focused on for vehicle trajectory prediction.

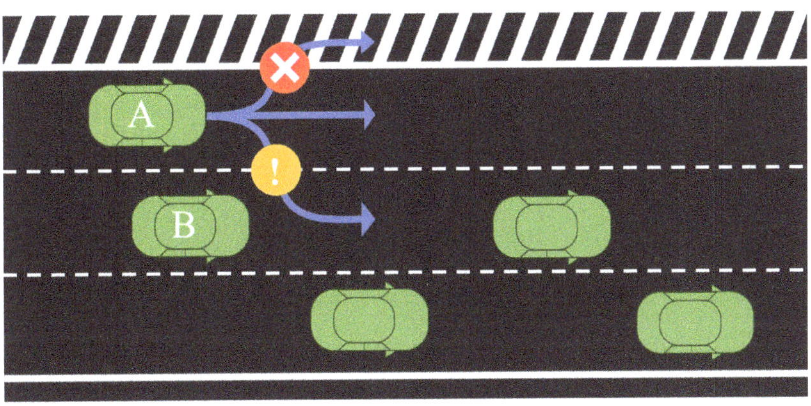

Figure 1. An example of a traffic scenario depicting the relationships between the traffic infrastructure and traffic participants.

At any time step in a freeway traffic scenario, there are two bases for predicting the future trajectory of a target vehicle. The first is based on the spatial relationship between the target vehicle and the road. Highway geometries and attributes (e.g., lane types, lane widths, and lane orientations) limit the future trajectory of the target vehicle in the long term. The second is based on the spatiotemporal interactions between the target vehicle and its surrounding vehicles. Their historical trajectories implicitly influence the future trajectory of the target vehicle as a result of their social interactions.

Both the vehicle trajectories and the geometry of the highway can be represented by combinations of position points. Let $p = (x, y)$ denote the position point in the scene, where $x, y \in \mathbb{R}$ are the lateral and vertical coordinates, respectively.

The road segments of highways are linearly distributed in the road network with a wide road surface, a long distance, less curvature and directional characteristics. We approximate the curved road segments by several straight segments; thus, the road network can be partitioned and represented as a set of straight road segments:

$$RS = \{r_j \mid j = 1, \ldots, m\}, \tag{1}$$

where m is the number of segments obtained from the partition, and each segment $r_j = \left(p_s^{r_j}, p_e^{r_j}\right)$ can be labelled by a start position point $p_s^{r_j} = \left(x_s^{r_j}, y_s^{r_j}\right)$ and an end position point $p_e^{r_j} = \left(x_e^{r_j}, y_e^{r_j}\right)$.

Without loss of generality, let v_0 denote the target vehicle to be predicted, and let $v_1, \ldots, v_n$ denote the n vehicles around v_0. Then, the observed trajectory of each vehicle $v_i (i = 0, 1, \ldots, n)$ is denoted as

$$T^{v_i} = \{p_t^{v_i} \mid t = -H+1, -H+2, \ldots, 0\}, \tag{2}$$

where $H \in \mathbb{N}^+$ is the number of observed historical time steps, and $p_t^{v_i} = (x_t^{v_i}, y_t^{v_i})$ is the position of vehicle v_i at time step t. Correspondingly, the predicted trajectory of target vehicle v_0 in the future is

$$\hat{T} = \{\hat{p}_t \mid t = 1, 2, \ldots, F\}, \tag{3}$$

where $F \in \mathbb{N}^+$ is the number of predicted future time steps, and $\hat{p}_t = (\hat{x}_t, \hat{x}_t)$ is the position of the target vehicle v_0 at time step t. Figure 2 illustrates the architecture of the proposed vehicle trajectory prediction model for learning vehicle-road relationships and vehicle-vehicle relationships in highway scenarios.

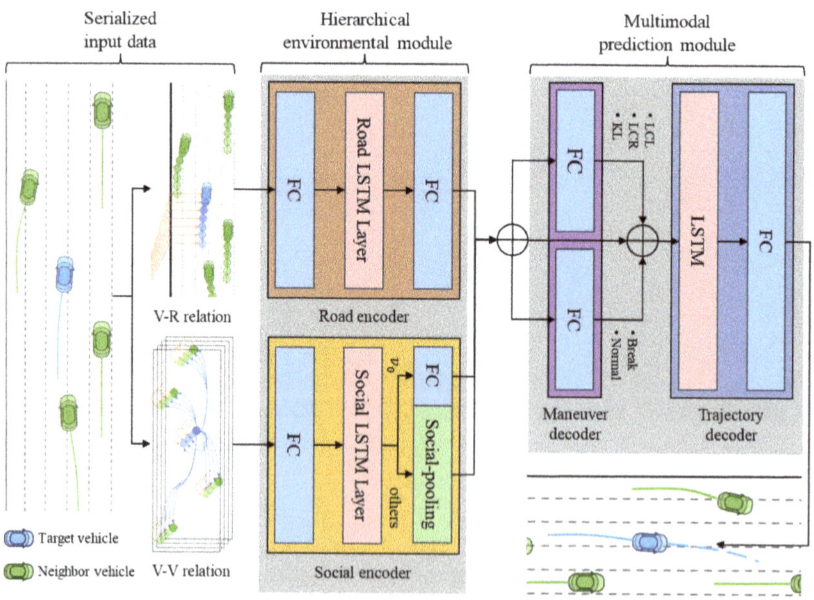

Figure 2. Architecture of the proposed vehicle trajectory prediction model for learning vehicle–road relationships and vehicle–vehicle relationships in highway scenarios.

According to the classifications of manoeuvres mentioned in [10], when a vehicle is driving along a highway, the lateral manoeuvres of the vehicle in the parallel road direction are classified as braking and normal, and the longitudinal manoeuvres of the vehicle in the perpendicular road direction are classified as left lane changes (LCLs), lane keeping (KL) and right lane changes (LCRs). There are six combinations of the results in both directions, which are represented by one-hot codes.

3.2. Serialised Vehicle–Road Relationships

To represent the spatiotemporal relationships between vehicles and roads during the driving procedure, a generalised vehicle trajectory point transformation method is established based on the geometry of road segments.

As shown in Figure 3, given any trajectory point P in the xOy coordinate system, let a vector r denote the segment in which P is located, where $S = p_s^r$ denotes the starting point of r, and $E = p_e^r$ denotes the ending point of r. Then, the projection point P' of P on $\overrightarrow{SE}$ can be represented by the $\overrightarrow{OP'}$ vector as follows:

$$\overrightarrow{OP'} = \overrightarrow{OS} + \frac{\overrightarrow{SP} \cdot \overrightarrow{SE}}{\left|\overrightarrow{SE}\right|^2} \cdot \overrightarrow{SE}. \quad (4)$$

According to Equation (4), the distance from point P to vector r can be expressed as:

$$d(P, r) = \left|\overrightarrow{P'P}\right|, \quad (5)$$

and r denotes the element in road segment RS (as shown in Equation (1)) with the shortest distance $d(P, r)$.

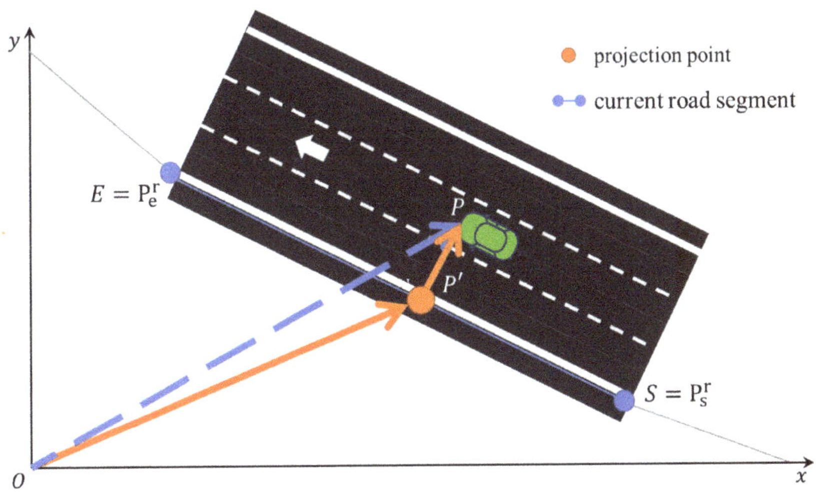

Figure 3. Schematic diagram of the relationships between vehicles and road segments.

In this way, the vector combination with the projection point as the turn is equivalent to the original trajectory points; i.e., they satisfy the following vector relation:

$$\overrightarrow{eq : OP} = \overrightarrow{Op_t^{v_i}{}'} + \overrightarrow{p_t^{v_i}{}' p_t^{v_i}}, \quad (6)$$

where the projection point $\overrightarrow{Op_t^{v_i}{}'}$ reflects the position of the vehicle in the parallel road direction and $\overrightarrow{p_t^{v_i}{}' p_t^{v_i}}$ reflects the position of the vehicle in the perpendicular road direction. Moreover, to eliminate the differences among the representations of points in different coordinate systems, the shift alignment method, with the projection point $p_0^{v_i}{}'$ at the end of the trajectory as the coordinate origin, is applied for vehicle trajectory sequence alignment. Thus, the serialised vehicle–road relationships can be expressed in a form similar to Equation (2) as follows:

$$R^{v_i} = \left\{ (\overrightarrow{p_t^{v_i\prime} p_0^{v_i\prime}}, \overrightarrow{p_t^{v_i\prime} p_t^{v_i}} - \overrightarrow{p_0^{v_i\prime} p_0^{v_i}}) \mid t = -H+1, \ldots, 0 \right\}, \tag{7}$$

where R^{v_i} is the vehicle–road relationship sequence of v_i, $p_t^{v_i}$ and H have the same meanings as in Equation (2), $p_t^{v_i\prime}$ denotes the projection point of $p_t^{v_i}$ on the road segment, and $\overrightarrow{p_t^{v_i\prime} p_t^{v_i}}$ denotes the vector from the projection point to the original trajectory point.

3.3. Spatiotemporal Graph Construction

The historical trajectories of the target vehicle and its surrounding vehicles are used to construct a spatiotemporal graph structure centred on the spatiotemporal location of the predicted object, which highlights the local vehicle motion information and the relative spatiotemporal location relationships of the vehicle interactions while preserving the vehicle motion trends.

As shown in Figure 4, given a set of vehicle history trajectories $\{T^{v_0}, T^{v_1}, \ldots, T^{v_n}\}$ composed of the elements shown in Equation (2), the spatiotemporal graph structure $G = \{V, E_T, E_S\}$ is constructed, where

$$V = \{p_t^{v_i} \mid i \in \{0, \ldots, n\}, t \in \{-H+1, \ldots, 0\}\} \tag{8}$$

denotes the set of vertices composed of the vehicle trajectory points.

$$E_T = \{(p_t^{v_i}, p_{t-1}^{v_i}) \mid i \in \{0, \ldots, n\}, t \in \{-H+2, \ldots, 0\}\} \tag{9}$$

denotes the directed temporal edge from $p_t^{v_i}$ to $p_{t-1}^{v_i}$, which implicitly expresses the local motion information of the same vehicle with the physical meaning of the vehicle velocity.

$$E_S = \{(p_0^{v_0}, p_t^{v_i}) \mid i \in \{0, \ldots, n\}, t \in \{-H+1, \ldots, 0\}\} \tag{10}$$

denotes the directed spatial edge from $p_0^{v_0}$ to $p_t^{v_i}$, which portrays the relationship between the trajectory points at different spatiotemporal locations and the current position of the target vehicle.

In the proposed spatiotemporal graph, the value of each vertex is a positional coordinate such as $p = (x, y)$, so the values of the edges can be represented by vectors such as $\overrightarrow{p_0^{v_0}, p_t^{v_i}}$. In addition, except for the vertex at time step $t = 0$, all the vertices have two entry degrees from a time edge and a space edge. Since the time edges have the physical meaning of velocity, the time edges from $t = -1$ to $t = -2$ are replicated between $t = 0$ and $t = -1$ to unify the incidences of all vertices in the graph, and the new vehicle trajectory is represented by the values of the incidence edges as follows:

$$\begin{aligned} ST = \left\{ (\overrightarrow{p_t^{v_i}, p_{t-1}^{v_i}}, \overrightarrow{p_0^{v_0}, p_{t-1}^{v_i}}) \mid i \in \{0, \ldots, n\} \right\}, \\ t \in \{-H+2, \ldots, 0\} \cup \left\{ (\overrightarrow{p_0^{v_i}, p_{-1}^{v_i}}, \overrightarrow{p_0^{v_0}, p_0^{v_i}}) \mid i \in \{0, \ldots, n\} \right\}, \end{aligned} \tag{11}$$

where ST^{v_i} denotes the temporal representations of the relationships between the vehicles.

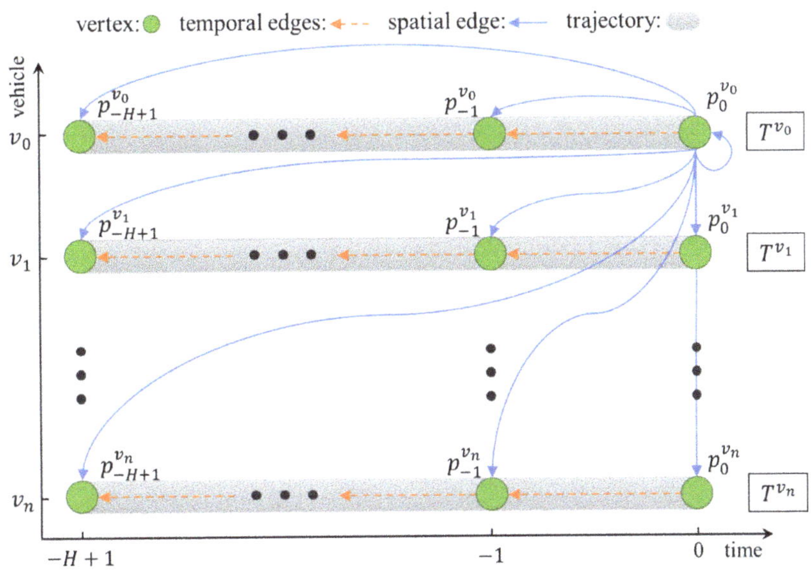

Figure 4. Structure of the spatiotemporal graph constructed using vehicle trajectories.

3.4. Hierarchical Environmental Module

To synthetically model the road and social environment information around the target vehicle, a two-layer LSTM-based architecture is used for separately extracting serialised vehicle–vehicle and vehicle–road interaction features. In highway scenarios, these two features are directly and closely related to the manoeuvring behaviour and future trajectory of the target vehicle.

According to the relationship serialisation methods elaborated on in Sections 3.2 and 3.3, the road LSTM encoder is used to encode a sequence of relationships R^{v_0} between the target vehicle v_0 and the roads, and the social LSTM encoder is used to encode the sequence ST of the relationships between v_0 and its surrounding vehicles $v_1, \ldots, v_n$ based on the spatiotemporal graph. The two LSTM encoders are described in detail below.

- Road LSTM Encoder: For the target vehicle v_0, at each time step t, the vector combination $R_t^{v_0} \in R^{v_0}$ with two-coordinate values, as shown in Equation (7), is embedded into a fixed-length vector f_t^r for the subsequent decoding step.

$$e_t^r = FC\left(R_t^{v_0}, W_r^{emb}\right), \tag{12}$$

$$h_t^r = LSTM\left(h_{t-1}^r, e_t^r, W_r^{lstm}\right), \tag{13}$$

$$f_t^r = FC\left(h_t^r, W_r^{linear}\right), \tag{14}$$

  where $FC(\cdot)$ is a fully connected layer employed as an input embedding function and h_t^r is the hidden state generated by this layer. The capital letter W in this paper denotes the weights of the different network layers, the superscript of each weight indicates its function, and the subscript indicates that it belongs to a specific part of the network.
- Social LSTM Encoder: For the target vehicle v_0 and its surrounding vehicles $v_1, \ldots, v_n$, at each time step t, their edge values $ST_t^{vi} \in ST$ based on the spatiotemporal graph, as

shown in Equation (11), are embedded in fixed-length vectors f_t^v and f_t^s, respectively, for the subsequent decoding process.

$$e_t^{v_i} = FC\left(ST_t^{vi}, W_s^{emb}\right), \quad (15)$$

$$h_t^{v_i} = LSTM\left(h_{t-1}^{v_i}, e_t^{v_i}, W_s^{lstm}\right), \quad (16)$$

$$f_t^v = FC\left(h_t^{v_0}, W_s^{linear}\right), \quad (17)$$

$$f_t^s = CSP\left(\{h_t^{v_1}, \ldots, h_0^{v_n}\}, W_s^{csp}\right), \quad (18)$$

where $h_t^{v_i}$ is the hidden state generated by the social LSTM layer, and $CSP(\cdot)$ is the convolutional social pooling layer proposed in [10].

After passing through the above hierarchical network, the vehicle–road relationship feature f_t^r, the motion feature f_t^v of the target vehicle and the social interaction feature f_t^s are extracted separately from the serialised input data, and then the three features are connected and used as the historical feature f_t output by this module.

3.5. Multimodel Prediction Module

The context vector outputs from the hierarchical environment module are used to decode the manoeuvres and future trajectories of vehicles. Vehicle manoeuvre estimation helps to solve multimodal problems in highway traffic scenarios, leading to more accurate trajectory prediction results.

According to the manoeuvre classification method mentioned in Section 3.1, the lateral and longitudinal manoeuvres are decoded by two fully connected layers with different output sizes and activated by the softmax function as a probability estimate of the target vehicle manoeuvre $\hat{m}$. Furthermore, the predicted manoeuvre loss is calculated by a binary cross-entropy function.

The future trajectory prediction of the target vehicle combines the manoeuvre decoding results and the context vectors output by the hierarchical environment module. A trajectory decoder consisting of an LSTM layer and a fully connected layer is used to output the sequence of predicted trajectories.

$$\hat{h}_t = LSTM\left(\hat{h}_{t-1}, f_t, W_{dec}^{lstm}\right), \quad (19)$$

$$(\mu_{t+1}, \sigma_{t+1}, \rho_{t+1}) = FC\left(\hat{h}_t, W_{dec}^{linear}\right), \quad (20)$$

$$\hat{p}_t \sim N(\mu_t, \Sigma_t), \quad (21)$$

where $\hat{p}_t = (\hat{x}_t^{v0}, \hat{y}_t^{v0})$ is the predicted trajectory coordinate of the target vehicle at time step t, and $N(\cdot)$ is a binary Gaussian distribution function. μ_t, Σ_t are the mean and covariance matrix of the two variables, respectively. Therefore, the loss of predicted trajectories can be calculated by the negative log-likelihood (NLL) error.

4. Experiments

The NGSIM dataset is used to validate the performance of the proposed model, which outperforms the baseline approach and some state-of-the-art methods. Smaller root-mean-square error (RMSE) and NLL error values are achieved for the vehicle trajectory prediction task in freeway traffic scenarios due to the effective features extracted from the serialised vehicle–road and vehicle–vehicle relationships by the hierarchical environment module. In addition, the effectiveness of the vehicle–road geometry relationships and vehicle–vehicle spatiotemporal relationships for manoeuvre and trajectory prediction is demonstrated by ablation experiments.

4.1. Datasets and Model Training

NGSIM is a large open highway vehicle driving dataset that contains real vehicle travel data and corresponding geographic information system (GIS) files for the US-101 and I-80 freeways. On each of the two freeways, the NGSIM authors, the Federal Highway Administration (FHWA) in the USA, selected data collection areas of 500 and 640 m and collected vehicle driving data for 15 min each under light, moderate, and heavy traffic conditions at different times, with a temporal sampling frequency of 10 Hz. As a result, the dataset contains million-scale vehicle location information, and these data are organised into a sequence of vehicle trajectories in temporal order.

The NGSIM dataset consists of samples and is partitioned to be consistent with previous works [10,11,36]. First, the dataset is partitioned into training, validation and test sets at a ratio of 7:1:2 by time period. Second, the length of each trajectory sample is set to 8 s, where the first 3 s are used for observation and the last 5 s are used for supervised labelling. Third, vehicles within 90 feet of the target vehicle in the adjacent lane are treated as surrounding vehicles. If too many vehicles are located within the range (more than 39), e.g., the vehicles are in a congested state, the vehicles that are farthest away are discarded. Finally, for each trajectory point, the amount of data is reduced by using interval sampling, that is, using a sampling rate of 5 Hz. Thus, the observed length of each trajectory is 15 frames, and the predicted length is 25 frames.

In addition, the GIS files in NGSIM provide geometric and attribute information for the study area, where the geometric information is vectorised. As shown in Figure 5, road maps are extracted from this geometric information so that the relationships between vehicles and roads can be described in the same coordinate system. Figure 5a,b show the visualization of the road area and corresponding road lines in two different scenarios, which were used for training and testing our method.

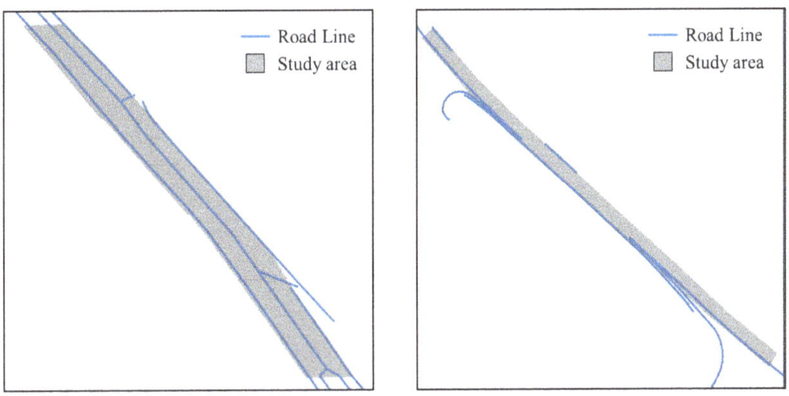

(a) (b)

Figure 5. Highway maps of the study area based on the geometry and attributes contained in the GIS files.

The construction of the VRR-Net model is based on the PyTorch framework. The model is trained with a batch size of 128 and an initial learning rate of 0.001 using the Adam optimiser. In the road encoder and the social encoder, the fully connected layers are activated by a leaky rectified linear unit (Leaky-ReLU) function with an output dimensionality of 32, and the output of the social pooling layer has 80 dimensions. The output dimensions of the LSTM in the encoder and in the trajectory decoder are 64 and 128, respectively.

4.2. Evaluation Metric and Performance Comparison

In evaluations regarding highway vehicle trajectory prediction, the RMSE is widely used, and it is used as evaluation metrics in this paper to conduct a fair comparison and analysis. At each different prediction horizon t, the RMSE is calculated based on the relative errors as follows:

$$RMSE_t = \sqrt{\frac{1}{n}\sum_{i=1}^{n}(|\mathbf{p_t} - \hat{\mathbf{p}}_\mathbf{t}|)^2}, \tag{22}$$

where n is the total number of samples in the test set, and $\mathbf{p_t}$ and $\hat{\mathbf{p}}_\mathbf{t}$ are the ground truth and predicted values of each target vehicle, respectively. Based on the RMSE, the method proposed in this paper outperforms the following baseline methods.

- CS-LSTM [10]: CS-LSTM is an LSTM encoder–decoder-based model, and the proposed convolutional social pool improves the ability of the model to extract intervehicle relationships and output a multimodal predictive distribution based on manoeuvre categories.
- ST-LSTM [36]: ST-LSTM achieves improved prediction performance by using a stacked LSTM encoder–decoder model to process the spatiotemporal graph structure containing vehicle relationships, which directly describes the relationships between the vehicle trajectory points.
- Scale-Net [43]: The Scale-Net utilises an edge-enhanced graph convolutional neural network to solve the dynamic number input problem of the embedding layer, which is decoded by the LSTM encoder; finally, the prediction result is output by a multilayer perceptron.
- Ego-Trand [11]: Guo's method separately uses an attention mechanism for both the temporal and spatial dimensions and constructs an LSTM encoder–decoder structure with a dual-attention mechanism.
- CF-LSTM [44]: CF-LSTM constructs a social force based on a physical approach to learn contextual features using a teacher–student model, which has the effect of reducing the collision rate of the trajectories generated by the LSTM encoder–decoder network.
- MHA-LSTM [45]: MHA-LSTM also uses an attention mechanism to emphasise the importance of the surrounding vehicles, which improves the trajectory prediction performance of the LSTM encoder–decoder network.

In this paper, Table 1 is presented to showcase the accuracy comparison between our proposed methods and recent studies, with the RMSE evaluation metric. The VRR-Net model, which combines vehicle–road relationships and vehicle–vehicle relationships, significantly outperforms other models, such as CS-LSTM, ST-LSTM, and Scale-Net, all of which are similar in size but do not use attention mechanisms, for predicting the trajectories of vehicles from 0 to 5 s in the future. Despite using a graph structure to represent the relationships between vehicles, the VRR-Net model has a 12% relative reduction in prediction error in this timeframe. Compared with the LSTM encoder–decoder models, Ego-Trand and CF-LSTM, which use attention mechanisms, the VRR-Net model achieves comparable results from 0 to 3 s but has an advantage in long-term prediction errors after 3 s. Notably, the advantage of the VRR-Net model over the teacher–student model (CF-LSTM) becomes increasingly apparent in long-term prediction scenarios. The serialised representations of the vehicle–road relationships, coupled with a feature extraction process, enable the VRR-Net model to more comprehensively perceive its environmental context, thereby producing more reliable long-term prediction results. Overall, these results demonstrate that VRR-Net is a promising trajectory prediction model that can achieve superior performance, particularly for long-term prediction tasks in dynamic traffic scenarios.

Table 1. The RMSE performance of the proposed model and the existing advanced models are compared on the NGSIM dataset. The best result is marked in black.

Prediction Horizons (Second)	CS -LSTM [10]	ST -LSTM [36]	Scale -Net [43]	Ego -Trend [11]	CF -LSTM [44]	MHA -LSTM [45]	VRR -Net (Our)
1	0.61	0.51	0.46	0.50	0.55	**0.41**	0.47
2	1.27	1.21	1.16	1.11	1.10	**1.01**	1.08
3	2.09	2.01	1.97	1.78	1.78	**1.74**	1.79
4	3.10	3.01	2.91	2.69	2.73	2.67	**2.65**
5	4.37	4.31	-	3.93	3.82	3.83	**3.71**

4.3. Ablation Studies

The VRR-Net model is decomposed into multiple components, and comparative experiments are conducted to verify the impacts of these different components on the final prediction accuracy. To validate the effectiveness of the spatiotemporal graph-based social encoder, the spatiotemporal graph is deconstructed into the case in which only spatial edges and both spatiotemporal edges are used. The serialised vehicle–road relationships and the road encoder are treated as independent components to verify the effect of the vehicle–road relationships on the trajectory prediction results. Furthermore, the CS-LSTM and ST-LSTM approaches are used as a baseline for comparison purposes, and the experiments are performed on the same NGSIM dataset with the same parameters. Thus, the following three ablation cases are validated:

- VRR-Net without the temporal edges and road encoders;
- VRR-Net without the road encoder;
- VRR-Net.

As shown in Figure 6, the social encoder of VRR-Net is able to capture the social interaction features between vehicles more effectively from the spatiotemporal graph structure, while the VRR-Net model without temporal edges and the road encoder is inferior in performance to the model that encodes both temporal and spatial edges, as well as to the two baseline approaches. The reason for this is that the historical trajectories of the surrounding vehicles are not sufficiently exploited to obtain sufficiently effective features. In contrast, the road encoder further improves the accuracy of trajectory prediction, indicating that the vehicle–road relationships and the road encoder effectively enhance the prediction network's ability to acquire the features of vehicle surroundings.

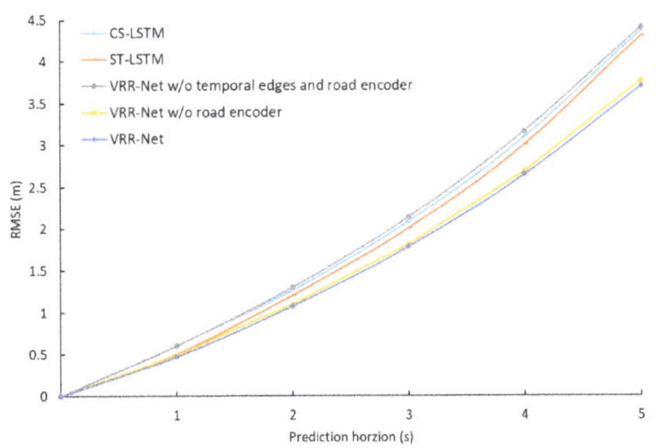

Figure 6. Comparison among the predictions of the three ablated versions of the proposed model under the RMSE loss function, where CS-LSTM and ST-LSTM are the baselines for comparison.

5. Conclusions

The VRR-Net model proposed in this paper integrates the influences of traffic participants and traffic infrastructure to predict vehicles. In terms of input features, VRR-Net only uses vehicle position data to build a spatiotemporal relationship graph, avoiding the use of instantaneous velocities and instantaneous accelerations, which are difficult to obtain in real-time from the surrounding vehicles. This spatiotemporal relationship structure is easy to vectorise and serialise and can effectively extract the environmental features around the vehicle to be predicted. In terms of model structure, VRR-Net adopts a hierarchical design with high scalability. Two parallel LSTM networks are used to address vehicle–road relationships and vehicle–vehicle relationships, and a manoeuvre decoder and a trajectory decoder comprehensively consider both kinds of relationships, thereby further enhancing the model's feature extraction capability for traffic environments. Experimental results obtained on the NGSIM dataset demonstrate that VRR-Net is able to effectively exploit the observed vehicle–road relationships and achieve improved vehicle trajectory prediction performance over that of models that also use LSTM to extract features. Thus, the model's success is attributed to its ability to integrate the spatiotemporal dependencies between vehicles and roads, the intervehicle interaction information, and the social interaction behaviors of traffic participants, which are crucial to predicting vehicle trajectories in complex traffic scenarios. We install four cameras around the vehicle for testing on a highway, and the results show that the proposed method can effectively predict the trajectories around the vehicle. Based on the results, it is evident that the proposed VRR-Net model achieves superior trajectory prediction performance, especially in long-term prediction tasks in dynamic traffic scenarios. However, it is essential to consider the cost of implementing this solution in real-world applications. The VRR-Net model requires additional data processing and feature extraction steps, which may increase the computational cost and complexity of the system. Furthermore, the training process of the VRR-Net model may also require more time and resources than simpler models that do not incorporate attention mechanisms or vehicle–road relationships.

Indeed, other complicated influences are included in real traffic scenarios, in addition to the influences of roads and surrounding vehicles. In future work, we will consider the influences of other traffic infrastructures in high-speed traffic scenarios on vehicle trajectories. Additionally, the generalisation capability and interpretability of the proposed model will be considered in more traffic scenarios. With further research, our future trajectory prediction approach will become more accurate and practically applicable.

Author Contributions: Conceptualization, T.Z. and Q.Z.; methodology, T.Z.; software, T.Z.; validation, T.Z. and Q.Z.; formal analysis, J.C.; investigation, T.Z. and Q.Z.; resources, J.C. and Q.Z.; data curation, G.C.; writing—original draft preparation, T.Z.; writing—review and editing, Q.Z.; visualization, Q.Z.; supervision, G.C. and J.C.; project administration, J.C.; funding acquisition, Q.Z. and J.C. All authors have read and agreed to the published version of the manuscript.

Funding: This research was funded by the National Natural Science Foundation of China (Nos. U21A20487, U1913202), the National Natural Science Foundation of Guangdong Province (No. 2022A1515140119) and Shenzhen Technology Project (Nos. JCYJ20180507182610734, JCYJ20220818101206014).

Institutional Review Board Statement: Not applicable.

Informed Consent Statement: Not applicable.

Data Availability Statement: Not applicable.

Acknowledgments: We acknowledge the support from the National Natural Science Foundation of China (Nos. U21A20487, U1913202), the National Natural Science Foundation of Guangdong Province (No. 2022A1515140119) and Shenzhen Technology Project (Nos. JCYJ20180507182610734, JCYJ20220818101206014).

Conflicts of Interest: The authors declare no conflict of interest.

References

1. Zhang, Q.; Hu, S.; Sun, J.; Chen, Q.A.; Mao, Z.M. On Adversarial Robustness of Trajectory Prediction for Autonomous Vehicles. In Proceedings of the IEEE/CVF Conference on Computer Vision and Pattern Recognition (CVPR), New Orleans, LA, USA, 18–24 June 2022; pp. 15159–15168.
2. Hu, L.; Zhou, X.; Zhang, X.; Wang, F.; Li, Q.; Wu, W. A review on key challenges in intelligent vehicles: Safety and driver-oriented features. *IET Intell. Transp. Syst.* **2021**, *15*, 1093–1105. [CrossRef]
3. Yufang, L.; Jun, Z.; Chen, R.; Xiaoding, L. Prediction of vehicle energy consumption on a planned route based on speed features forecasting. *IET Intell. Transp. Syst.* **2020**, *14*, 511–522. [CrossRef]
4. Izquierdo, R.; Quintanar, A.; Llorca, D.; Daza, I.; Hernandez, N.; Parra, I.; Sotelo, M. Vehicle trajectory prediction on highways using bird eye view representations and deep learning. *Appl. Intell.* **2022**. [CrossRef]
5. Li, S.; Shu, K.; Chen, C.; Cao, D. Planning and Decision-making for Connected Autonomous Vehicles at Road Intersections: A Review. *Chin. J. Mech. Eng.* **2021**, *34*, 133. [CrossRef]
6. Lu, Q.; Kim, K. Autonomous and connected intersection crossing traffic management using discrete-time occupancies trajectory. *Appl. Intell.* **2019**, *49*, 1621–1635. [CrossRef]
7. Singh, D.; Srivastava, R. Graph Neural Network with RNNs based trajectory prediction of dynamic agents for autonomous vehicle. *Appl. Intell.* **2022**. [CrossRef]
8. Fan, X.; Xiang, C.; Gong, L.; He, X.; Qu, Y.; Amirgholipour, S.; Xi, Y.; Nanda, P.; He, X. Deep Learning for Intelligent Traffic Sensing and Prediction: Recent Advances and Future Challenges. *CCF Trans. Pervasive Comput. Interact. (TPCI)* **2020**, *2*, 240–260. [CrossRef]
9. Ju, C.; Wang, Z.; Long, C.; Zhang, X.; Chang, D.E. Interaction-aware Kalman Neural Networks for Trajectory Prediction. In Proceedings of the IEEE Intelligent Vehicles Symposium (IV), Las Vegas, NV, USA, 19 October–13 November 2020; pp. 1793–1800. [CrossRef]
10. Deo, N.; Trivedi, M.M. Convolutional Social Pooling for Vehicle Trajectory Prediction. In Proceedings of the IEEE Conference on Computer Vision and Pattern Recognition Workshops (CVPRW), Salt Lake City, UT, USA, 18–23 June 2018; pp. 1468–1476.
11. Guo, H.; Meng, Q.; Cao, D.; Chen, H.; Liu, J.; Shang, B. Vehicle Trajectory Prediction Method Coupled With Ego Vehicle Motion Trend Under Dual Attention Mechanism. *IEEE Trans. Instrum. Meas. (TIM)* **2022**, *71*, 1–16. [CrossRef]
12. Chen, L.; Zhou, Q.; Cai, Y.; Wang, H.; Li, Y. CAE-GAN: A hybrid model for vehicle trajectory prediction. *IET Intell. Transp. Syst.* **2022**, *16*, 1682–1696r. [CrossRef]
13. Malviya, V.; Kala, R. Trajectory prediction and tracking using a multi-behaviour social particle filter. *Appl. Intell.* **2022**, *52*, 7158–7200. [CrossRef]
14. Gupta, A.; Anpalagan, A.; Guan, L.; Khwaja, A.S. Deep Learning for Object Detection and Scene Perception in Self-Driving Cars: Survey, Challenges, and Open Issues. *Array* **2021**, *10*, 100057. [CrossRef]
15. Salzmann, T.; Ivanovic, B.; Chakravarty, P.; Pavone, M. Trajectron++: Dynamically-Feasible Trajectory Forecasting with Heterogeneous Data. In Proceedings of the European Conference on Computer Vision (ECCV), Glasgow, UK, 23–28 August 2020; pp. 683–700. [CrossRef]
16. Mozaffari, S.; Al-Jarrah, O.Y.; Dianati, M.; Jennings, P.; Mouzakitis, A. Deep Learning-Based Vehicle Behavior Prediction for Autonomous Driving Applications: A Review. *IEEE Trans. Intell. Transp. Syst. (TITS)* **2022**, *23*, 33–47. [CrossRef]
17. Fei, C.; He, X.; Ji, X. Multi-modal vehicle trajectory prediction based on mutual information. *IET Intell. Transp. Syst.* **2020**, *14*, 148–153. [CrossRef]
18. Liu, Y.; Zhang, J.; Fang, L.; Jiang, Q.; Zhou, B. Multimodal motion prediction with stacked transformers. In Proceedings of the IEEE/CVF Conference on Computer Vision and Pattern Recognition (CVPR), Virtually, 19–25 June 2021; pp. 7577–7586. [CrossRef]
19. Li, T.; Yan, S.; Mei, T.; Hua, X.; Kweon, I. Image decomposition with multilabel context: Algorithms and applications. *IEEE Trans. Image Process. (TIP)* **2010**, *20*, 2301–2314. [CrossRef]
20. Bae, I.; Park, J.H.; Jeon, H.G. Non-Probability Sampling Network for Stochastic Human Trajectory Prediction. In Proceedings of the IEEE/CVF Conference on Computer Vision and Pattern Recognition (CVPR), New Orleans, LA, USA, 18–24 June 2022; pp. 6477–6487.
21. Deo, N.; Wolff, E.; Beijbom, O. Multimodal Trajectory Prediction Conditioned on Lane-Graph Traversals. In Proceedings of Machine Learning Research (PMLR), Baltimore, MD, USA, 17–23 July 2022; Volume 164, pp. 203–212.
22. Bahari, M.; Saadatnejad, S.; Rahimi, A.; Shaverdikondori, M.; Shahidzadeh, A.H.; Moosavi-Dezfooli, S.M.; Alahi, A. Vehicle Trajectory Prediction Works, but Not Everywhere. In Proceedings of the IEEE/CVF Conference on Computer Vision and Pattern Recognition (CVPR), New Orleans, LA, USA, 18–24 June 2022; pp. 17123–17133.
23. Barrios, C.; Motai, Y.; Huston, D. Trajectory Estimations Using Smartphones. *IEEE Trans. Ind. Electron.* **2015**, *62*, 7901–7910. [CrossRef]
24. Houenou, A.; Bonnifait, P.; Cherfaoui, V.; Yao, W. Vehicle Trajectory Prediction Based on Motion Model and Maneuver Recognition. In Proceedings of the IEEE/RSJ International Conference on Intelligent Robots and Systems (ICIRS), Tokyo, Japan, 3–7 November 2013; pp. 4363–4369. [CrossRef]
25. Li, B.; Du, H.; Li, W.; Zhang, B. Dynamically integrated spatiotemporal-based trajectory planning and control for autonomous vehicles. *IET Intell. Transp. Syst.* **2018**, *12*, 1271–1282. [CrossRef]

26. Lefèvre, S.; Vasquez, D.; Laugier, C. A Survey on Motion Prediction and Risk Assessment for Intelligent Vehicles. *ROBOMECH J.* **2014**, *1*, 1–14. [CrossRef]
27. He, L.; Zong, C.f.; Wang, C. Driving Intention Recognition and Behavior Prediction Based on a Double-layer hidden Markov Model. *J. Zhejiang Univ. Sci. C* **2012**, *13*, 208–217. [CrossRef]
28. Schlechtriemen, J.; Wirthmueller, F.; Wedel, A.; Breuel, G.; Kuhnert, K.D. When Will It Change the Lane? A Probabilistic Regression Approach for Rarely Occurring Events. In Proceedings of the IEEE Intelligent Vehicles Symposium (IV), Seoul, Republic of Korea, 28 June–1 July 2015; pp. 1373–1379. [CrossRef]
29. Yoon, S.; Kum, D. The multilayer perceptron approach to lateral motion prediction of surrounding vehicles for autonomous vehicles. In Proceedings of the IEEE Intelligent Vehicles Symposium (IV), Gothenburg, Sweden, 19–22 June 2016; pp. 1307–1312. [CrossRef]
30. Girase, H.; Gang, H.; Malla, S.; Li, J.; Kanehara, A.; Mangalam, K.; Choi, C. LOKI: Long Term and Key Intentions for Trajectory Prediction. In Proceedings of the IEEE/CVF International Conference on Computer Vision (ICCV), Montreal, QC, Canada, 10–17 October 2021; pp. 9803–9812. [CrossRef]
31. Li, T.; Cheng, B.; Ni, B.; Liu, G.; Yan, S. Multitask low-rank affinity graph for image segmentation and image annotation. *ACM Trans. Intell. Syst. Technol.* **2016**, *7*, 1–18. [CrossRef]
32. Wang, W.; Qie, T.; Yang, C.; Liu, W.; Xiang, C.; Huang, K. An Intelligent Lane-Changing Behavior Prediction and Decision-Making Strategy for an Autonomous Vehicle. *IEEE Trans. Ind. Electron. (TIE)* **2022**, *69*, 2927–2937. [CrossRef]
33. He, B.; Li, Y. Multi-future Transformer: Learning diverse interaction modes for behaviour prediction in autonomous driving. *IET Intell. Transp. Syst.* **2022**, *16*, 1249–1267. [CrossRef]
34. Giuliari, F.; Hasan, I.; Cristani, M.; Galasso, F. Transformer Networks for Trajectory Forecasting. In Proceedings of the International Conference on Pattern Recognition (ICPR), Montreal, QC, Canada, 10–17 October 2021; pp. 10335–10342. [CrossRef]
35. Yan, J.; Peng, Z.; Yin, H.; Wang, J.; Wang, X.; Shen, Y.; Stechele, W.; Cremers, D. Trajectory prediction for intelligent vehicles using spatial-attention mechanism. *IET Intell. Transp. Syst.* **2020**, *14*, 1855–1863. [CrossRef]
36. Chen, G.X.; Hu, L.; Zhang, Q.S.; Ren, Z.L.; Gao, X.Y.; Cheng, J. ST-LSTM: Spatio-Temporal Graph Based Long Short-Term Memory Network for Vehicle Trajectory Prediction. In Proceedings of the IEEE International Conference on Image Processing (ICIP), Abu Dhabi, United Arab Emirates, 25–28 October 2020; pp. 608–612. [CrossRef]
37. Li, T.; Meng, Z.; Ni, B.; Shen, J.; Wang, M. Robust geometric ℓ_p-norm feature pooling for image classification and action recognition. *Image Vis. Comput.* **2016**, *55*, 64–76. [CrossRef]
38. Yuan, Y.; Weng, X.; Ou, Y.; Kitani, K.M. AgentFormer: Agent-Aware Transformers for Socio-Temporal Multi-Agent Forecasting. In Proceedings of the IEEE/CVF International Conference on Computer Vision (ICCV), Montreal, QC, Canada, 10–17 October 2021; pp. 9813–9823. [CrossRef]
39. Gao, J.; Sun, C.; Zhao, H.; Shen, Y.; Anguelov, D.; Li, C.; Schmid, C. VectorNet: Encoding HD Maps and Agent Dynamics from Vectorized Representation. In Proceedings of the IEEE/CVF Conference on Computer Vision and Pattern Recognition (CVPR), Seattle, WA, USA, 13–19 June 2020; pp. 11525–11533. [CrossRef]
40. Liang, M.; Yang, B.; Hu, R.; Chen, Y.; Liao, R.; Feng, S.; Urtasun, R. Learning lane graph representations for motion forecasting. In Proceedings of the European Conference on Computer Vision (ECCV), Glasgow, UK, 23–28 August 2020; pp. 541–556.
41. Colyar, J.; Halkias, J. US Highway 101 Dataset Federal Highway Administration (FHWA). Technology Report. 2007. Available online: https://www.fhwa.dot.gov/publications/research/operations/07030/ (accessed on 5 March 2023).
42. Colyar, J.; Halkias, J. US Highway 80 dataset Federal Highway Administration (FHWA). Technology Report. 2006. Available online: https://www.fhwa.dot.gov/publications/research/operations/06137/index.cfm (accessed on 5 March 2023).
43. Jeon, H.; Choi, J.; Kum, D. SCALE-Net: Scalable Vehicle Trajectory Prediction Network under Random Number of Interacting Vehicles via Edge-enhanced Graph Convolutional Neural Network. In Proceedings of the IEEE/RSJ International Conference on Intelligent Robots and Systems (IROS), Las Vegas, NV, USA, 24 October 2020–24 January 2021; pp. 2095–2102. [CrossRef]
44. Xie, X.; Zhang, C.; Zhu, Y.; Wu, Y.N.; Zhu, S.C. Congestion-Aware Multi-Agent Trajectory Prediction for Collision Avoidance. In Proceedings of the IEEE International Conference on Robotics and Automation (ICRA), Xi'an, China, 30 May–5 June 2021; pp. 13693–13700. [CrossRef]
45. Messaoud, K.; Yahiaoui, I.; Verroust-Blondet, A.; Nashashibi, F. Attention Based Vehicle Trajectory Prediction. *IEEE Trans. Intell. Veh. (IV)* **2021**, *6*, 175–185. [CrossRef]

mathematics

MDPI

Article

Redesigning Embedding Layers for Queries, Keys, and Values in Cross-Covariance Image Transformers

Jaesin Ahn [1], Jiuk Hong [1], Jeongwoo Ju [2] and Heechul Jung [1,*]

[1] Department of Artificial Intelligence, Kyungpook National University, Daegu 41566, Republic of Korea; ajs0420@knu.ac.kr (J.A.); hong4497@knu.ac.kr (J.H.)
[2] Captos Co., Ltd., Yangsan 50652, Republic of Korea; veryju@captos.co.kr
* Correspondence: heechul@knu.ac.kr

Abstract: There are several attempts in vision transformers to reduce quadratic time complexity to linear time complexity according to increases in the number of tokens. Cross-covariance image transformers (XCiT) are also one of the techniques utilized to address the issue. However, despite these efforts, the increase in token dimensions still results in quadratic growth in time complexity, and the dimension is a key parameter for achieving superior generalization performance. In this paper, a novel method is proposed to improve the generalization performances of XCiT models without increasing token dimensions. We redesigned the embedding layers of queries, keys, and values, such as separate non-linear embedding (SNE), partially-shared non-linear embedding (P-SNE), and fully-shared non-linear embedding (F-SNE). Finally, a proposed structure with different model size settings achieved 71.4%, 77.8%, and 82.1% on ImageNet-1k compared with 69.9%, 77.1%, and 82.0% acquired by the original XCiT models, namely XCiT-N12, XCiT-T12, and XCiT-S12, respectively. Additionally, the proposed model achieved 94.8% in transfer learning experiments, on average, for CIFAR-10, CIFAR-100, Stanford Cars, and STL-10, which is superior to the baseline model of XCiT-S12 (94.5%). In particular, the proposed models demonstrated considerable improvements on the out-of-distribution detection task compared to the original XCiT models.

Keywords: vision transformer; Q/K/V embedding; shared embedding; non-linear embedding; image classification

MSC: 94A08

1. Introduction

Transformer models have attracted considerable research attention as dominant models in deep learning because of their superior performances [1,2]. Transformers were first used in natural language processing (NLP) [1] and are subsequently being widely used as the backbone network for state-of-the-art models [3–5]. Recently, transformers have also been used in the computer vision field. Vision transformers (ViT) [6] exhibit superior generalization performances to that of traditional convolutional neural network (CNN) architectures [6–8].

In standard vision transformers, tokens, which are sequences of cropped image patches extracted from two-dimensional color images, are used. Then, a global self-attention mechanism is applied to extract the relationship among tokens. This procedure can be used to extract information on the long-range relationship among tokens, in contrast to CNNs, in which the local relationship of image pixels is considered. However, this process requires extensive computations that increase quadratically with image resolution [6,9]. To alleviate these inefficiencies, convolutional features have been added explicitly in transformers [10–13]. Another attempt is cross-covariance image transformers (XCiT) [9], which utilize a modified multi-head self-attention (MHSA) technique based on a transposed self-attention mechanism. XCiT considerably reduced time complexity from $O(N^2d)$ to $O(Nd^2)$, where N is the number of tokens and d is the dimension of each token. This implies that the number of tokens is more crucial than the dimension of each token. However, increasing d is also harmful in terms of computational cost (see the original XCiT paper [9]. The XCiT-N12 and XCiT-T12 models in Table 1 of the paper have different d, and the other hyperparameters are identical. GFLOPs for each model do not linearly increase with d. The computational concern of increasing d is not more dominant than N but is also problematic.), and research on resolving the issue is required. To the best of our knowledge, no study has focused on resolving this problem.

Table 1. Corresponding output dimensions of Q, K, and V embedding layers to each model variant are listed below.

Model	Small (S)		Medium (M)		Large (L)	
	d	$d_{q,k,v}$	d	$d_{q,k,v}$	d	$d_{q,k,v}$
SNE	128	64	192	96	384	192
P-SNE	128	96	192	144	384	288
F-SNE-C	128	128	192	192	384	384
F-SNE-C8*	128	186	192	282	384	556
F-SNE-C16*	128	182	192	276	384	544

To resolve this problem, a novel efficient architecture might be developed to ensure linear time complexities in both N and d. In the second method of resolving the problem, the performances of the conventional vision transformer models with small d are maximized. In this paper, instead of presenting a new, efficient architecture design, we try to maximize generalization performances by redesigning the embedding layers for queries (Q), keys (K), and values (V) with fixed d values, which are the same values as in the original XCiT models. We speculate that improved embedding spaces may exist under a fixed dimension of space.

To achieve the goal, we propose three repetitive structures in XCiT models. The structures are simple and can effectively increase generalization performances in XCiT models. First, a two-layer embedding structure with a rectified linear unit activation function (ReLU) is proposed. This method is called a separate non-linear embedding (SNE) method. In contrast to the original embedding in XCiT models, the structure can transform the input data into a non-linear space with activation functions. The second structure is a one-layer shared structure, which is a variant of the first structure. This method is the partially shared non-linear embedding (P-SNE) method. The third structure is a two-layer shared structure with trainable code parameters that can improve the original self-attention mechanism used in conventional transformers. This structure is a fully shared non-linear embedding (F-SNE) model.

Finally, experimental results demonstrate that the proposed method outperforms the original XCiT models in the ImageNet [14] classification task and transfer learning on multiple datasets (i.e., CIFAR-10, CIFAR-100 [15], Stanford Cars [16], and STL-10 [17]). Furthermore, the proposed method outperforms the original XCiT models in the out-of-distribution (OOD) detection task. The contributions of this paper can be summarized as follows:

- We show that two simple and well-known structures, SNE and P-SNE, can improve the generalization ability of XCiT models under the small value of d.
- A novel structure called F-SNE was proposed, which outperforms the original XCiT, SNE, and P-SNE models. The structure is a fully shared model, and a code was adopted to feed different input values to the layers.
- The original XCiT models could not approach the top record among state-of-the-art (SOTA) transformer models in image classification tasks, but the modified XCiT models with the proposed structures are comparable with current SOTA models, such as the Swin [18], CeiT [19], and ViTAE [20] models.

- The high uncertainty prediction capability of the proposed structure, F-SNE, which largely improved the performance of the OOD detection task, was validated.

2. Related Works

We first summarize related works in transformer models as three aspects of architecture, computational cost, and designing embedding layers.

2.1. Architectures

When ViT was first proposed, global self-attention was applied among image tokens to handle long-range information [6]. However, global self-attention requires large-scale pre-training, and its computation quadratically increases according to the input size [8,21]. To address this problem, ViTAE [20], ConViT [22], and LocalViT [23] proposed the use of convolutions besides self-attention to embed both local and global features into the transformer, and T2T-ViT [11] progressively restructured image tokens into reduced-length tokens including local features. Furthermore, Swin transformer [18] utilized windowed attention with a hierarchical architecture to efficiently improve performance.

Few additional approaches to designing embedding layers have been proposed to embed better features in the tokens without increasing dimensionality. CvT [10] utilized convolutional projection for the Q, K, and V embedding of the transformer encoder to take advantage of both the CNN and transformer. In the case of ViP [24], learnable part representations are shared across transformer blocks to make Q, K, or V embeddings. However, linear projection was used to make those embeddings. There are no studies that use fully shared models, such as the proposed F-SNE structure. However, conventional self-attention with linearly projected Q, K, and V embeddings may not sufficiently handle this concern.

2.2. Approaches for Efficient Computational Cost

Current studies on vision transformers mainly focus on not only applying inductive bias to vision transformers but also reducing the computational complexity from quadratic to linear, such as GFNet [25], AFNO [26], and XCiT [9]. These approaches usually have proposed efficient self-attention mechanisms or replaced self-attention with another global operation, such as Fourier transformation. XCiT [9] is one of the representative approaches that focuses on reducing the computational complexity. It introduces cross-covariance attention (XCA) instead of standard self-attention. XCA effectively reduces computation without a large performance gap compared to the baseline. However, XCA has a limitation in that the computation quadratically increases according to the dimensionality of the tokens, which motivates us to find better token embeddings while maintaining dimensionality. However, it does not consider Q, K, and V embedding, which directly affects the attention operation. In contrast to these works, we introduce Q, K, and V embedding techniques to improve the performance of image recognition.

3. Attention Mechanism in Vision Transformer

In this section, we introduce preliminary knowledge about the self-attention and cross-covariance attention mechanisms in vision transformers.

3.1. Self-Attention

Conventional transformers adopt self-attention as the core operation of the network [1,6,27]. In the transformer, the input token X is projected by the linear projection layer W_q, W_k, and W_v to embed Q, K, and V vectors, respectively. Then, the self-attention is operated as follows:

$$SA(Q,K,V) = Softmax\left(\frac{QK^T}{\sqrt{d_k}}\right)V, \tag{1}$$

where $SA(Q, K, V)$ is the output of self-attention, and Q, K, and V are processed by the following linear projection:

$$Q = XW_q, K = XW_k, V = XW_v, \tag{2}$$

on $X \in R^{N \times d}$, $W_q \in R^{d \times d_q}$, $W_k \in R^{d \times d_k}$, $W_v \in R^{d \times d_v}$, where N is the number of tokens and d is the token dimension. This process is typically conducted in a multi-headed manner. When the number of heads is h, $d_q = d_k = d_v = d/h$.

3.2. Cross-Covariance Attention

Cross-covariance attention is a modified self-attention mechanism that can reduce the computational complexity from $O(N^2d)$ to $O(Nd^2)$ [9,28]. XCiT [9] proposed the use of cross-covariance attention instead of standard self-attention, which is widely used in transformer networks, demonstrating its SOTA performance in CV tasks, including in, for example, ImageNet classification, self-supervised learning, and semantic segmentation. They conducted feature dimension self-attention instead of token dimension self-attention, which is used in the standard transformer encoder. By simply transposing Q, K, and V and reversing the order of the dot product, the computational complexity was reduced from quadratic to linear with the number of tokens, N. This transposed feature dimension self-attention can be represented as follows:

$$XCA(Q, K, V) = V \cdot Softmax\left(\frac{\hat{K}^T \hat{Q}}{\tau}\right), \tag{3}$$

where $XCA(Q, K, V)$ is the output of cross-covariance attention and $\hat{Q}$, $\hat{K}$, and τ are the $l2$-normalized Q, K vector, and temperature scaling parameter, respectively. This provides better generalization performances than a traditional self-attention mechanism, and XCiT was adopted as a baseline model to verify the performance of the proposed method.

4. Method

As mentioned in Equation (2), in the conventional embedding method, a linear layer was used for each Q, K, and V. The layer is not shared across the embedding spaces of Q, K, and V. We propose three types of embedding techniques to improve the performance of XCiT, as displayed in Figure 1.

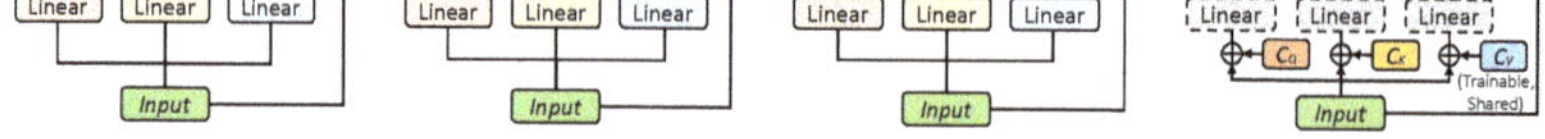

(**a**) Conventional (**b**) SNE (**c**) P-SNE (**d**) F-SNE

Figure 1. Four types of Q, K, and V embedding methods are shown. (**a**) The figure depicts conventional embedding used in the standard transformer encoder. (**b**) Separate non-linear embedding utilizes a two-layer embedding, including non-linearity functions (e.g., ReLU). (**c**) Partially shared non-linear embedding includes a weight-sharing linear layer. The weight-sharing layer is depicted as the gray dotted line block, and it follows after the separated linear layer and ReLU. (**d**) Fully shared non-linear embedding includes two weight-sharing linear layers, also depicted as a gray dotted line, with ReLU. In this case, trainable codes of Q, K, V (C_q, C_k, and C_v) are concatenated to the input tokens.

4.1. Separate Non-Linear Embedding

In contrast to the original XCiT-based models, non-linear transformations were applied to extract Q, K, and V, as follows:

$$\begin{aligned} Q &= \sigma(XW_q^{(1)})W_q^{(2)}, \\ K &= \sigma(XW_k^{(1)})W_k^{(2)}, \\ V &= \sigma(XW_v^{(1)})W_v^{(2)}, \end{aligned} \tag{4}$$

where $W_q^{(1)} \in R^{d \times d_q}$ and $W_q^{(2)} \in R^{d_q \times d}$ represent the weight parameters of the first and second fully connected layers, respectively, and the layers encode the input token as Q. $W_k^{(1)} \in R^{d \times d_k}$ and $W_k^{(2)} \in R^{d_k \times d}$ correspond to K, and $W_v^{(1)} \in R^{d \times d_v}$ and $W_v^{(2)} \in R^{d_v \times d}$ extract V. σ is an activation function. Based on the obtained Q, K, and V, Equation (3) is computed for self-attention.

The layers for the SNE consist of two fully connected layers with an activation function (e.g., ReLU) to conduct a non-linear transformation of input tokens. The non-linear embedding approach exhibits the following advantages. This method could increase the total number of non-linearities of the model. Under a limited number of parameters, the increased number of non-linearities could positively affect generalization. Furthermore, the search space can be expanded to find new combinations of Q, K, and V in non-linear embedding spaces.

4.2. Partially Shared Non-Linear Embedding

P-SNE shares a layer from two fully connected layers in the SNE model. There are two options for which the layer will be selected (i.e., first or second layers). Sharing the first layer is similar to the linear embedding originally used in the XCiT model. The shared first layer produces the same output because the input values are the same. Consequently, we chose the second layer to be shared among Q, K, and V. The shared second layer linearly transforms each activation value extracted from the first non-linear layer. With the shared layer, Q, K, and V can share knowledge on how to build each token.

In general, separate layers of original or SNE structures could result in a problem. In separate layers, even if one of the layers responsible for Q, K, and V extraction does not learn well, the training loss can be minimized. Thus, the network is trained well even if one of the three separate layers for Q, K, and V is not properly updated. However, the phenomenon cannot be shown in the shared layers.

Finally, Q, K, and V in the P-SNE are extracted as follows:

$$\begin{aligned} Q &= \sigma(XW_q^{(1)})W_s^{(2)}, \\ K &= \sigma(XW_k^{(1)})W_s^{(2)}, \\ V &= \sigma(XW_v^{(1)})W_s^{(2)}, \end{aligned} \tag{5}$$

where $W_s^{(2)} \in R^{d_s \times d}$ denotes the weight parameters of the shared second layer when $d_s = d_q = d_k = d_v$. The weight parameters $W_q^{(2)}$, $W_k^{(2)}$, and $W_v^{(2)}$ of the second layer of the SNE were replaced with $W_s^{(2)}$.

4.3. Fully Shared Non-Linear Embedding

For F-SNE, we first integrate the Q, K, and V projection layers $W_q^{(i)}$, $W_k^{(i)}$, and $W_v^{(i)}$ into the shared projection layers $W_s^{(i)}$ for $i = \{1,2\}$, as shown in Figure 1d. Instead of Q, K, and V projection layers that separately transform input token X into Q, K, and V vectors, the shared projection layers transform the input token X into Q, K, and V in the same embedding space.

When fully shared projection layers are used, we adopt codes of C_q, C_k, and C_v. The codes correspond to Q, K, and V embeddings and convert the same inputs into three different vectors. C_q, C_k, and C_v are trainable vectors that are concatenated to the input token X before passing the shared projection layers W_s. Additionally, the same C_q, C_k, and C_v are shared among all the encoders in the transformer. By this sharing, codes converge at the optimal semantic representation of Q, K, and V that exists consistently regardless of the encoder.

Finally, Q, K, and V embeddings by the proposed shared projection layers with codes C_q, C_k, and C_v can be represented as follows:

$$\begin{aligned} Q &= \sigma((X \oplus C_q)W_s^{(1)})W_s^{(2)}, \\ K &= \sigma((X \oplus C_k)W_s^{(1)})W_s^{(2)}, \\ V &= \sigma((X \oplus C_v)W_s^{(1)})W_s^{(2)}, \end{aligned} \tag{6}$$

on $X \in R^{N\times d}$ and $C_q, C_k, C_v \in R^{N\times c}$, where $\oplus$ denotes vector concatenation and c is an arbitrary code size. Here, $C_q, C_k, C_v \in R^{1\times c}$, but these are repeated N times to match the dimension with X. Codes C_q, C_k, and C_v are concurrently computed with the network parameter θ to minimize the loss function as follows:

$$\hat{\theta}, \hat{C}_q, \hat{C}_k, \hat{C}_v = \min_{\theta, C_q, C_k, C_v} \mathcal{L}(D; \theta, C_q, C_k, C_v) \tag{7}$$

where $\mathcal{L}$ is a loss function (e.g., cross-entropy loss). D is the training dataset, and θ denotes the network parameters of the transformer network, including the embedding layers of Q, K, and V (i.e., W_q, W_k, W_v, or W_s). Note that C_q, C_k, C_v, and θ are updated at the same step. A detailed procedure of Equation (7) is implemented as Algorithm 1.

Algorithm 1 F-SNE

Require: D: Training data, θ: Network parameters
Randomly initialize θ, C_q, C_k, C_v
while not done **do**
  Sample batch of data D
  Compute $\mathcal{L}(D; \theta, C_q, C_k, C_v)$ in Equation (7)
  Update θ, C_q, C_k, C_v
end while

5. Experiments and Results

We first introduce the detailed experimental setup and datasets. Then, we evaluate the ImageNet-1k classification performance of the proposed structures according to their scale and conduct brief experiments using distillation. Additionally, we use those models to transfer to the other datasets (i.e., CIFAR-10, CIFAR-100, Stanford Cars, and STL-10). Lastly, we evaluate uncertainty prediction performance through the OOD detection task.

5.1. Experimental Setup

Experiments for the proposed methods were conducted based on XCiT models. In the following sections, the notations XCiT-N12, XCiT-T12, and XCiT-S12 were used to denote XCiT-Nano, XCiT-Tiny, and XCiT-Small models with 12 blocks. We implemented small (S), medium (M), large (L) models based on XCiT-N12, XCiT-T12, and XCiT-S12, respectively. The input image size of the models was fixed at 224×224. The models were trained using a batch size of 4096, 2816, and 1280 for XCiT-N12, XCiT-T12, and XCiT-S12-based models, respectively. For ImageNet training, we trained the model for 400 epochs with an initial learning rate of 5×10^{-4}. For transfer learning, an initial learning rate of 5×10^{-5} was used for 1000 epochs of training. We followed other experimental setups of the XCiT. Overall experiments were conducted on NVIDIA DGX A100 (8 GPUs).

For the Q, K, and V projection layers, dimensions of output tokens depicted in Table 1 were used according to the variants. The starred (*) model is used to compare the proposed method using the same number of parameters as the original XCiT model. Additionally, the shared layers for the F-SNE-Cn-S, F-SNE-Cn-M, and F-SNE-Cn-L models have input dimensions of $(128 + n)$, $(192 + n)$, and $(384 + n)$ to take the input concatenated with the n-dimensional code. Code is a vector of arbitrary code size (e.g., $n = 8, 16, 32, 64$) defined outside the encoder to be shared among encoders. For a fair comparison, we compare the number of parameters and image size as well as the performance in the following sections. In the case of F-SNE, codes were also included in the number of model parameters.

5.2. Dataset

We used ImageNet-1k [14] to train the models from scratch. Then, we used the CIFAR-10, CIFAR-100 [15], Stanford Cars [16], and STL-10 [17] datasets to evaluate transfer learning performance. In the case of an out-of-distribution (OOD) detection task, we used the CIFAR-10 dataset as an in-distribution (ID) and the LSUN-R, LSUN-C [29], iSUN [30], SVHN [31], and DTD [32] datasets as OOD. The detailed information of these datasets is described below.

The ImageNet dataset consists of 1.28 M training images and 50,000 validation images with 1000 categories.

The CIFAR-10 and CIFAR-100 datasets consist of 50,000 training images and 10,000 test images with 10 and 100 categories, respectively.

The Stanford Cars dataset consists of 8144 training images and 8041 test images of 196 categories.

The STL-10 dataset contains 5000 training images and 8000 test images from 10 categories.

The LSUN dataset consists of 10 scene classes and contains around 120,000 to 3,000,000 images for each class. It has 1000 test images for each class. LSUN-R (resize) and LSUN-C (crop) were reconstructed by [33] for OOD detection, so we used these datasets.

The iSUN dataset consists of 6000 training images, 926 validation images, and 2000 test images. We used whole images from this dataset for OOD detection.

The SVHN dataset consists of 73,257 training images and 26,032 test images from 10 digit classes. We randomly selected 10,000 images from test images while uniformly sampling for 10 classes when evaluating OOD detection.

The DTD dataset consists of 5640 texture images from 47 classes. We used whole images of this dataset for OOD detection.

5.3. Imagenet Classification

Tables 2–4 present the ImageNet-1k classification results to compare the proposed method with other models considering the number of parameters. The top-1 accuracies of other models noted in the table originated directly from publications of each model. To investigate the performance of the proposed method, we selected XCiT as a baseline model and modified the Q, K, and V projection layers corresponding to each model variant.

As presented in Table 2, the P-SNE-S model achieved the best score for the below 4M-parameter-constrained models, such as Mobile-Former [34] and PVTv2 [35], improving the accuracy by 1.5% compared to the baseline model.

Table 2. Proposed models were evaluated on ImageNet classification task. The number of parameters was constrained to be below 4 M to be compared to the small (S) models.

Model	Image Size	Param #	Top-1 (%)
Mobile-Former-26M	224 × 224	3.2 M	64.0
Mobile-Former-52M	224 × 224	3.5 M	68.7
XCiT-N12 (baseline)	224 × 224	3.1M	69.9
F-SNE-C16-S (ours)	224 × 224	2.9 M	70.2
PVTv2-B0	224 × 224	3.4 M	70.5
F-SNE-C8-S (ours)	224 × 224	2.9 M	70.6
F-SNE-C16* -S (ours)	224 × 224	3.1 M	70.6
F-SNE-C8* -S (ours)	224 × 224	3.1 M	70.8
SNE-S (ours)	224 × 224	3.1 M	70.9
P-SNE-S (ours)	224 × 224	3.1 M	**71.4**

In the case of a constraint of less than 10M parameters, the P-SNE-M model surpassed the previous SOTA model, CoaT-Lite [36], which recorded 77.5% top-1 accuracy, while improving accuracy by 0.3%. Moreover, the non-linear embedding method (i.e., SNE-M) also improved the classification rates on the ImageNet-1k dataset compared with the baseline model. The results were compared with the other models, including other vision transformers, such as DeiT [8], Swin [18,34], LocalViT [23], PiT [37], ConViT [22], ViP [24], ConT [38], T2T-ViT [11], ResT [39], and CoaT-Lite [36], which used a linear embedding method, in Table 3.

Table 3. Proposed models were evaluated on ImageNet classification task. The number of parameters was constrained to be below 10 M to be compared to the medium (M) models.

Model	Image Size	Param #	Top-1 (%)
ViT-Ti	224 × 224	5.7 M	68.7
T2T-ViT-7	224 × 224	4.3 M	71.7
DeiT-Ti	224 × 224	5.7 M	72.2
LocalViT-T2T	224 × 224	4.3 M	72.5
Mobile-Former-96M	224 × 224	4.6 M	72.8
PiT-Ti	224 × 224	4.9 M	73.0
ConViT-Ti	224 × 224	5.7 M	73.1
GFNet-Ti	224 × 224	7 M	74.6
LocalViT-T	224 × 224	5.9 M	74.8
ConT-Ti	224 × 224	5.8 M	74.9
ViP-Mo	224 × 224	5.3 M	75.1
ViTAE-T	224 × 224	4.8 M	75.3
CeiT-T	224 × 224	6.4 M	76.4
ConT-S	224 × 224	10.1 M	76.5
T2T-ViT-12	224 × 224	6.9 M	76.5
F-SNE-C8-M (ours)	224 × 224	6.3 M	76.8
XCiT-T12 (baseline)	224 × 224	6.7 M	77.1
F-SNE-C16-M (ours)	224 × 224	6.3 M	77.2
ResT-Lite	224 × 224	10.5 M	77.2
Swin-1G	224 × 224	7.3 M	77.3
F-SNE-C16 * -M (ours)	224 × 224	6.7 M	77.4
CoaT-Lite Tiny	224 × 224	5.7 M	77.5
SNE-M (ours)	224 × 224	6.7 M	77.6
F-SNE-C8 * -M (ours)	224 × 224	6.7 M	77.7
P-SNE-M (ours)	224 × 224	6.7 M	**77.8**

While achieving SOTA performances with the parameter constraints (4 M and 10 M), the proposed method also exhibited performances comparable to large models such as PVTv2 [35], CvT [10], GFNet [25], CaiT [40], ViTAE [20], and CeiT [19], as shown in Table 4. In particular, the F-SNE-C16*-L and F-SNE-C32-L models achieved the highest accuracy, which was the same as the previous SOTA model, PVTv2 [35]. As presented in Tables 2–4, the starred (*) models revealed that the performance can be improved by adding parameters to the embedding layers as much as the capacity saved by fully sharing embedding layers.

Table 4. Proposed large (L) models were evaluated on ImageNet classification task.

Model	Image Size	Param #	Top-1 (%)
DeiT-S	224 × 224	22 M	79.8
PVT-S	224 × 224	25 M	79.8
GFNet-S	224 × 224	25 M	80.0
Swin-T	224 × 224	29 M	81.3
T2T-ViT-14	224 × 224	22 M	81.5
GFNet-H-S	224 × 224	32 M	81.5
CvT-13	224 × 224	20 M	81.6
ResT-Base	224 × 224	30 M	81.6
CaiT-XS-24	224 × 224	27 M	81.8
ViP-Ti	224 × 224	32 M	81.9
F-SNE-C8-L (ours)	224 × 224	25 M	81.9
ViTAE-S	224 × 224	24 M	82.0
CeiT-S	224 × 224	24 M	82.0
PVTv2-B2	224 × 224	25 M	82.0
XCiT-S12 (baseline)	224 × 224	26 M	82.0
SNE-L (ours)	224 × 224	26 M	82.0
P-SNE-L (ours)	224 × 224	26 M	82.0
F-SNE-C8* -L (ours)	224 × 224	26M	82.0
F-SNE-C16-L (ours)	224 × 224	25 M	82.0
F-SNE-C64-L (ours)	224 × 224	25 M	82.0
PVTv2-B2-Li	224 × 224	23 M	82.1
F-SNE-C16* -L (ours)	224 × 224	26 M	**82.1**
F-SNE-C32-L (ours)	224 × 224	25 M	**82.1**

5.4. Distillation

We evaluated the performances on the ImageNet classification task using the distillation technique as well. We used RegNetY-16GF [41] as a teacher model to conduct hard distillation as proposed in [8]. Similar to the previous experimental results in [8,9], distillation could improve the performance of each model. Additionally, shared non-linear embedding methods improve the performance of the baseline model, although a separate non-linear embedding method decreased performance. This reminds us of the better properties of the shared embedding methods, which is consistent with the results of the paper. These results are organized in Table 5.

Table 5. Proposed models were evaluated on ImageNet classification with distillation. XCiT performance was obtained from [9]. § indicates the distilled model.

Model	Image Size	Param #	Top-1 (%)
SNE-S§ (ours)	224 × 224	3.1 M	71.5
XCiT-N12§ (baseline)	224 × 224	3.1 M	71.7
F-SNE-C8-S§ (ours)	224 × 224	2.9 M	71.7
P-SNE-S§ (ours)	224 × 224	3.1 M	71.9
F-SNE-C16-S§ (ours)	224 × 224	2.9 M	72.0
F-SNE-C16* -S§ (ours)	224 × 224	3.1 M	72.2
F-SNE-C8* -S§ (ours)	224 × 224	3.1 M	**72.4**

5.5. Transfer Learning

To demonstrate the transferable performances of the proposed method, we conducted transfer learning experiments on CIFAR-10, CIFAR-100, Stanford Cars, and STL-10, as presented in Table 6. All images were resized to 224 × 224 for transfer learning, as in the aforementioned experiments.

As displayed in the average accuracy of Table 6, the proposed method generally improved the performance of the baseline model. In particular, F-SNE-C16*-S, F-SNE-C8-M, and F-SNE-C16*-M achieved the best score under each parameter constraint, below 4M and 10M, despite fewer parameters. Including these best models, on average, F-SNE models showed mostly superior transfer performance for the tiny models compared with other variants. Comparing this model with CeiT (the previous SOTA model) is not a fair comparison because repeated augmentation [42] was not used in the F-SNE models. However, the F-SNE models achieved comparable scores. Fully shared embedding may provide superior generalization capability compared to other variants in the case of tiny model constraints.

The general performance improvement can also be observed in L models, especially F-SNE-C16-L, which achieved the highest accuracy among the SOTA models, such as the T2T-ViT-14, CeiT-S, and XCiT-S12 models. Furthermore, the proposed model achieved accuracies comparable with GFNet-H-B [25] on the CIFAR-100 and Stanford Cars datasets, although it has over twice the number of parameters of the proposed models. This generalization performance may originate from extracting domain-agnostic properties by sharing properties, such as sharing embedding layers between Q, K, and V and sharing codes between blocks.

Table 6. Proposed models were evaluated on transfer learning task as below. All models were pre-trained using the ImageNet-1k dataset. † indicates the results are obtained from the paper. ‡ indicates that the experiment could not be performed because of a lack of source code. ♮ indicates the use of additional data augmentation, specifically repeated augmentation [42].

Model	Image Size	Param #	CIFAR10 (%)	CIFAR100 (%)	Cars (%)	STL10 (%)	Average (%)
XCiT-N12 (baseline)	224 × 224	3.1 M	98.0	85.5	87.9	97.5	92.2
F-SNE-C8-S (ours)	224 × 224	2.9 M	98.1	86.2	89.0	97.8	92.8
F-SNE-C8* -S (ours)	224 × 224	3.1 M	98.3	86.2	89.0	97.8	92.8
SNE-S (ours)	224 × 224	3.1 M	**98.4**	**86.6**	88.9	97.8	92.9
P-SNE-S (ours)	224 × 224	3.1 M	98.2	86.5	88.9	**97.9**	92.9
F-SNE-C16-S (ours)	224 × 224	2.9 M	98.2	86.3	90.2	97.8	93.1
F-SNE-C16* -S (ours)	224 × 224	3.1 M	98.3	86.3	**90.5**	**97.9**	**93.2**
ViTAE-T	224 × 224	4.8 M	97.3 †	86.0 †	89.5 †	– ‡	–
XCiT-T12 (baseline)	224 × 224	6.7 M	98.5	86.7	92.7	98.3	94.0
SNE-M (ours)	224 × 224	6.7 M	98.6	87.2	91.8	98.6	94.0
P-SNE-M (ours)	224 × 224	6.7 M	**98.7**	87.2	91.8	98.6	94.1
F-SNE-C8* -M (ours)	224 × 224	6.7 M	98.5	87.6	92.1	98.3	94.1
F-SNE-C16-M (ours)	224 × 224	6.3 M	98.5	87.2	92.3	**98.7**	94.2
CeiT-T ♮	224 × 224	6.4 M	98.6	87.7	**92.8**	98.3	**94.3**
F-SNE-C8-M (ours)	224 × 224	6.3 M	98.4	**88.0**	92.3	98.6	**94.3**
F-SNE-C16* -M (ours)	224 × 224	6.7 M	98.6	87.8	92.3	98.6	**94.3**
T2T-ViT-14	224 × 224	22 M	97.5 †	88.4 †	–	–	–
ViTAE-S	224 × 224	24 M	98.8 †	**90.8** †	91.4 †	– ‡	–
GFNet-XS	224 × 224	16 M	98.6 †	89.1 †	92.8 †	–	–
GFNet-H-B	224 × 224	54 M	**99.0** †	90.3 †	93.2 †	–	–
F-SNE-C16* -L (ours)	224 × 224	26 M	98.4	87.3	93.2	98.9	94.4
XCiT-S12 (baseline)	224 × 224	26 M	98.6	87.3	**93.3**	98.7	94.5
F-SNE-C64-L (ours)	224 × 224	25 M	98.8	87.7	92.6	99.0	94.5
CeiT-S ♮	224 × 224	24 M	98.9	88.0	92.7	98.9	94.6
SNE-L (ours)	224 × 224	26 M	98.8	87.7	93.2	98.9	94.6
F-SNE-C8* -L (ours)	224 × 224	26 M	98.7	87.6	92.9	**99.3**	94.6
P-SNE-L (ours)	224 × 224	26 M	98.6	88.1	93.1	99.0	94.7
F-SNE-C32-L (ours)	224 × 224	25 M	98.8	88.2	92.9	98.7	94.7
F-SNE-C8-L (ours)	224 × 224	25 M	98.5	88.0	93.1	99.0	94.7
F-SNE-C16-L (ours)	224 × 224	25 M	98.7	88.2	**93.3**	99.1	**94.8**

5.6. Out-of-Distribution Detection

In addition to the evaluation within in-distribution (ID) data, as aforementioned, detecting the input from OOD data is critical to constructing a reliable and generalized model [33]. To demonstrate the generalization performance on OOD datasets, we evaluate the performance of OOD detection according to the procedure proposed by [33,43]. As presented in Table 7, the proposed model improved the OOD detection performances. In particular, the proposed F-SNE models significantly improved performance while achieving 6.9%, 9.84%, and 9.59% lower FPR (at 95% TPR) and 1.97%, 2.87%, and 5.47% higher AUROC compared with the baseline models XCiT-N12, XCiT-T12, and XCiT-S12, respectively. This improvement might be attributed to fully shared embedding layers and shared codes. The shared architecture might embed input data into a smaller manifold and makes tight decision boundaries. Thanks to tight decision boundaries, our F-SNE models accurately distinguish OOD data. This speculation is similar to prior research [44].

Table 7. Proposed models were evaluated on the OOD detection task as below. The models fine-tuned on CIFAR-10, mentioned in Table 6, were used. We considered CIFAR-10 as ID and LSUN-R, LSUN-C, iSUN, SVHN, and DTD as OOD. Scores are averaged for the OOD datasets.

Model	FPR (95% TPR) ↓	Detection Error↓	AUROC↑
XCiT-N12	19.22	11.74	93.66
SNE-S	20.87	12.42	93.25
P-SNE-S	21.87	12.22	93.41
F-SNE-C8-S	13.89	9.11	95.03
F-SNE-C16-S	**12.32**	**8.44**	**95.63**
F-SNE-C32-S	16.01	10.21	93.94
F-SNE-C64-S	14.49	9.06	95.52
XCiT-T12	21.82	12.99	92.70
SNE-M	23.54	13.45	91.10
P-SNE-M	26.59	15.19	90.42
F-SNE-C8-M	20.61	12.56	91.21
F-SNE-C16-M	14.62	9.56	93.95
F-SNE-C32-M	**11.98**	**8.21**	**95.57**
F-SNE-C64-M	16.66	10.71	92.98
XCiT-S12	23.18	13.59	90.73
SNE-L	20.68	12.29	93.02
P-SNE-L	18.72	11.57	93.46
F-SNE-C8-L	17.98	11.15	93.99
F-SNE-C16-L	**13.59**	**8.69**	**96.20**
F-SNE-C32-L	15.67	9.70	94.45
F-SNE-C64-L	18.76	11.61	93.42

6. Ablation Study and Analysis

We analyzed the performances of the proposed structures to determine the best structure and subsequently conducted ablation studies, such as a comparison of shared and unshared code, a code size search in F-SNE, code visualization of F-SNE, and correlation plots of ImageNet and transfer learning performances.

6.1. Which Structure Is the Best?

Among the three proposed structures, the F-SNE structure achieved the highest accuracies, especially in transfer learning tasks. As displayed in Figure 2, each structure of F-SNE coherently surpassed other structures with the corresponding computational cost. The F-SNE structure required a small increase in FLOPs to achieve this improvement but had fewer parameters compared to the XCiT, SNE, and P-SNE structures. According to these results, we can interpret that shared properties of the F-SNE structure have more generalized features within similar expressivity, and this results in the model's ability to be easily adapted to downstream tasks. In addition, we observed that this improvement occurred obviously in smaller structures with limited generalization capacity.

6.2. Sharing or Unsharing Codes in F-SNE

Thanks to the code, the input token can be identified in the F-SNE structure for separately extracting Q, K, and V. In the F-SNE structure, codes C_q, C_k, and C_v are shared among all embedding modules in the transformer model. This sharing can slightly reduce the total number of parameters. In addition, as presented in Table 8, the generalization performance can be improved. Without sharing, the codes could have distinct values across the embedding modules, which could hinder finding the optimal code vectors for Q, K, and V. From this perspective, sharing could be a method for finding the optimal solution.

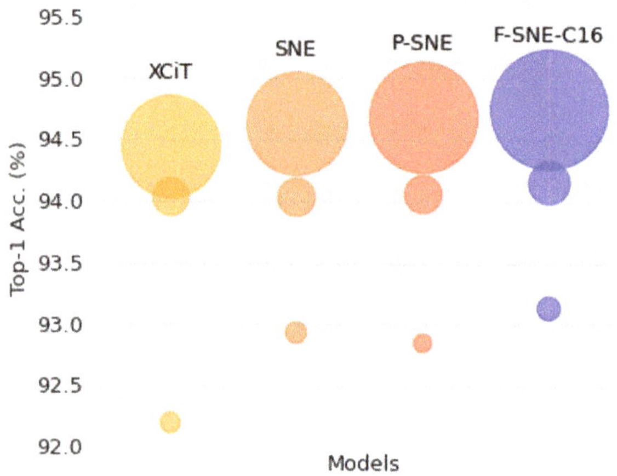

Figure 2. Performances were compared among proposed structures. Averaged top-1 accuracies of transfer learning were used. Circle size corresponds to FLOPs of each structure.

Table 8. The cases of code sharing and unsharing were compared using the ImageNet-1k dataset. The numbers in brackets denote the number of total parameters for each model.

Model	Top-1 (%)
F-SNE-C8-S (Sharing)	**70.82** (2.9 M)
F-SNE-C8-S (W/o Sharing)	70.28 (3.05 M)

6.3. Code Size

Selecting an appropriate code size is critical for using the code C_q, C_k, and C_v in the F-SNE structures. Therefore, we conducted experiments on different code sizes from 8 to 64 to determine an appropriate code size that can provide superior performance. As displayed in Figure 3, a code size of 8 achieved the best accuracy among S models, and a code size of 16 achieved the best accuracy among the M models. A code size of 32 achieved the best accuracy among L models. The M models have an embedding dimension of approximately 1.5 times, and the L models have three times the embedding dimension of the S models, as presented in Table 1. The results can be interpreted to mean that a larger code size is required when the embedding dimension of the model increases.

6.4. C_Q, C_K, and C_V in Different Tasks

The optimal code values were initially found on the ImageNet-1k dataset, and subsequently, the computed code values were used as the initial codes for the downstream tasks. Even if the pre-trained codes were used, the code values might vary according to the tasks because the codes were updated using a back-propagation process using the downstream task dataset.

Figure 4 details the correlation values of codes extracted from each downstream task. Notably, the correlation matrices are similar even if the task is changed. The diagonal elements provide some information on the similarity between the same codes, and non-diagonal elements depict the similarity between different codes. Non-diagonal elements are close to zero, and each code of C_q, C_k, and C_v tends to exhibit orthogonality. These results can be interpreted to indicate that C_q, C_k, and C_v learn their inherent feature to be used as Q, K, and V, regardless of the task; furthermore, the values of the $l2$-norm for each dataset can be obtained, as presented in Table 9. The codes of ImageNet-1k, Stanford Cars, and STL-10 exhibit similar $l2$-norm values, but CIFAR-10 and 100 exhibit distinct $l2$-norm values.

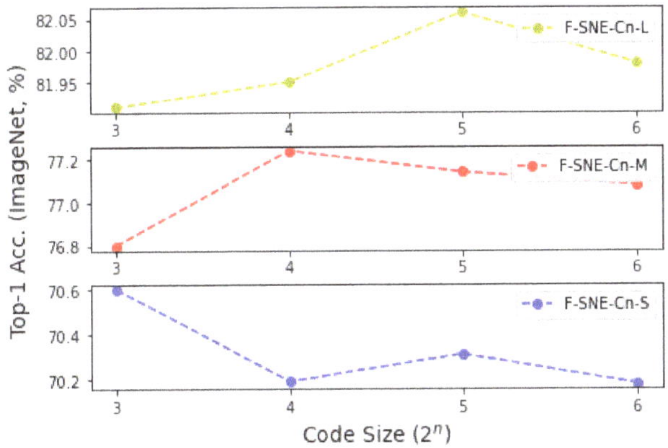

Figure 3. Top-1 accuracies on ImageNet-1k of F-SNE-Cn-S, F-SNE-Cn-M, and F-SNE-Cn-L structures were compared with respect to code sizes from 8 to 64. Results of F-SNE-Cn-S, F-SNE-Cn-M, and F-SNE-Cn-L structures are organized from bottom to top.

Table 9. $l2$-norms of C_q, C_k, and C_v are extracted from F-SNE-C8-S model according to the trained dataset. The codes exhibit similar $l2$-norm values regardless of the dataset.

Dataset	$\|\|C_q\|\|$	$\|\|C_k\|\|$	$\|\|C_v\|\|$
ImageNet	8.86	8.13	8.53
CIFAR-10	9.05	8.34	8.74
CIFAR-100	9.06	8.35	8.77
Cars	8.84	8.13	8.53
STL-10	8.86	8.14	8.56

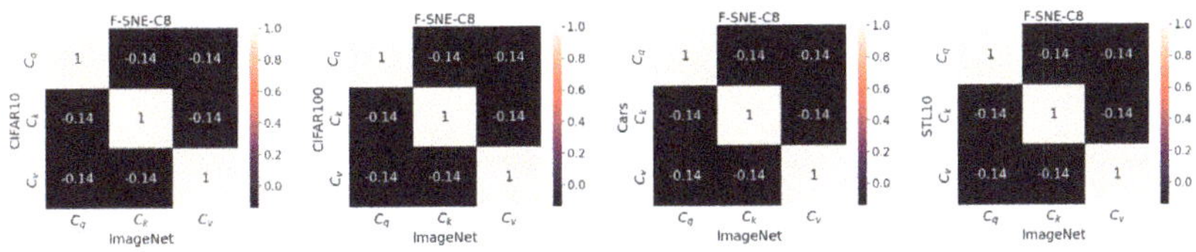

(a) (b) (c) (d)

Figure 4. $l2$-normalized C_q, C_k, and C_v are dot-producted according to the trained datasets. "IMNet", "C10", "C100", and "S10" denote ImageNet, CIFAR-10, CIFAR-100, and STL-10, respectively. C_q, C_k, and C_v are extracted from the F-SNE-C8-S model. (**a**) IMNet-C10. (**b**) IMNet-C100. (**c**) IMNet-Cars. (**d**) IMNet-S10.

6.5. Do Better Imagenet Models Transfer Better?

Generally, better ImageNet models transfer better [45]. An experiment was conducted to verify whether this fact can be applied to our cases. As displayed in Figure 5, a correlation could be observed between performances on ImageNet and on downstream tasks. The correlation tendency is reflected by the domain difference between the upstream and downstream tasks. Thus, the tasks of the CIFAR-10, CIFAR-100, and STL-10 datasets are similar to the task of ImageNet. Therefore, these tasks exhibit high correlations between two tasks. However, correlations are difficult to observe in the Stanford Cars dataset.

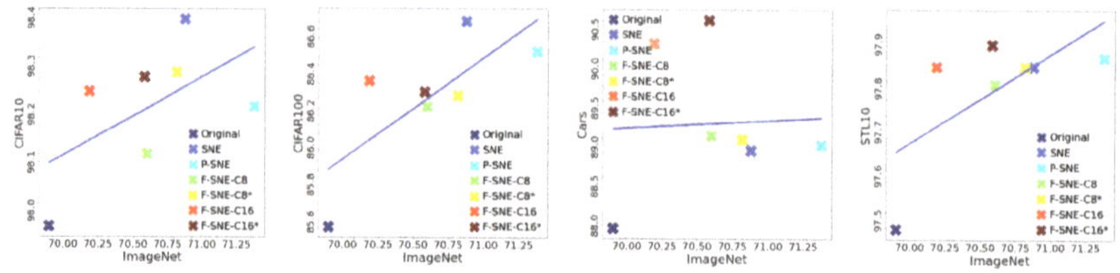

(a) (b) (c) (d)

Figure 5. Correlation between pre-training and transfer learning performances is plotted. S models are used. 'X' markers denote the accuracies of each model, and the blue line denotes the regression slope of the results. In contrast to other correlated plots, the results on the Stanford Cars dataset are not correlated with the results on the ImageNet dataset. Best viewed in color. (**a**) IMNet-C10. (**b**) IMNet-C100. (**c**) IMNet-Cars. (**d**) IMNet-S10.

7. Limitations

This study has several limitations that need to be addressed in future research. (1) While the proposed methods demonstrated significant performance improvements for tiny models, their impact on large models was relatively weak. Further research is required to improve their performances on larger models. (2) The evaluation was limited to classification, transfer learning, and out-of-distribution detection tasks. Future work should demonstrate the performances on other tasks, such as object detection and segmentation. (3) This study focused on supervised learning, but the potential benefits of the proposed methods in the context of self-supervised learning should be investigated. (4) Due to computational resource constraints, the experiments were conducted using ImageNet-1k or smaller datasets. Further evaluation on large-scale datasets is encouraged. (5) This study was unable to clearly interpret the precise function of the shared code. Additional analysis is needed to obtain a deeper understanding of the mechanisms of the proposed methods.

8. Conclusions

We proposed Q, K, and V vector embedding structures for XCiT. In the first embedding structure, two non-linear layers were used to embed the input token into separate non-linear spaces of Q, K, and V. In the second structure, a single layer was shared between the two layers. The results of the experiment revealed that sharing a single layer could improve generalization performance on ImageNet-1k. The third structure shares two layers with the Q, K, and V codes. The codes are trained via a back-propagation algorithm to minimize the loss. The structure can be used for improving the classification rates in several downstream tasks, such as CIFAR-100 and STL-10. Furthermore, the third structure could considerably improve OOD detection performance. Finally, we could improve the XCiT model under the fixed token dimensions using the proposed structures.

For future research, extensive experiments on a variety of vision tasks should be conducted to evaluate the effectiveness of the proposed structures. Moreover, a deeper analysis of the shared code is needed to elucidate its exact role and potential for improvement on larger models and datasets. By addressing these aspects, the proposed structures can be improved in the field of computer vision.

Author Contributions: Conceptualization, J.A. and H.J.; methodology, J.A. and H.J.; software, J.A. and H.J.; validation, J.A.; formal analysis, J.A., J.H., J.J. and H.J.; investigation, J.A.; resources, H.J.; writing—original draft preparation, J.A. and H.J.; writing—review and editing, J.A. and H.J.; visualization, J.A. and J.H.; supervision, H.J.; project administration, H.J.; funding acquisition, H.J. All authors have read and agreed to the published version of the manuscript.

Funding: This research was supported in part by the MSIT (Ministry of Science and ICT), Korea, under the ITRC (Information Technology Research Center) support program (IITP-2021-2020-0-01808) supervised by the IITP (Institute of Information & Communications Technology Planning & Evaluation) and Institute of Information & communications Technology Planning & Evaluation (IITP) grant funded by the Korea government(MSIT) (No.2021-0-02068, Artificial Intelligence Innovation Hub).

Institutional Review Board Statement: Not applicable.

Informed Consent Statement: Not applicable.

Data Availability Statement: The ImageNet-1k dataset can be found at https://www.image-net.org/. The CIFAR-10 and CIFAR-100 datasets can be found at https://www.cs.toronto.edu/~kriz/cifar.html. The Stanford Cars dataset can be found at http://ai.stanford.edu/~jkrause/cars/car_dataset.html. The STL-10 dataset can be found at https://cs.stanford.edu/~acoates/stl10/. The LSUN dataset can be found at https://www.yf.io/p/lsun. The iSUN dataset can be found at https://turkergaze.cs.princeton.edu/. The SVHN dataset can be found at http://ufldl.stanford.edu/housenumbers/. The DTD dataset can be found at https://www.robots.ox.ac.uk/~vgg/data/dtd/ (accessed on 22 March 2023).

Conflicts of Interest: The authors declare no conflict of interest. The funders had no role in the design of the study; in the collection, analyses, or interpretation of data; in the writing of the manuscript; or in the decision to publish the results.

References

1. Vaswani, A.; Shazeer, N.; Parmar, N.; Uszkoreit, J.; Jones, L.; Gomez, A.N.; Kaiser, Ł.; Polosukhin, I. Attention is all you need. In Proceedings of the Advances in Neural Information Processing Systems, Long Beach, CA, USA, 4–9 December 2017; pp. 5998–6008.
2. Devlin, J.; Chang, M.W.; Lee, K.; Toutanova, K. BERT: Pre-training of Deep Bidirectional Transformers for Language Understanding. In *Proceedings of the 2019 Conference of the North American Chapter of the Association for Computational Linguistics: Human Language Technologies, Volume 1 (Long and Short Papers)*; Association for Computational Linguistics: Cedarville, OH, USA, 2018; pp. 4171–4186.
3. Radford, A.; Narasimhan, K.; Salimans, T.; Sutskever, I. Improving Language Understanding by Generative Pre-Training. 2018. Available online: https://www.cs.ubc.ca/~amuham01/LING530/papers/radford2018improving.pdf (accessed on 13 October 2021).
4. Radford, A.; Wu, J.; Child, R.; Luan, D.; Amodei, D.; Sutskever, I. Language models are unsupervised multitask learners. *OpenAI Blog* **2019**, *1*, 9.
5. Brown, T.B.; Mann, B.; Ryder, N.; Subbiah, M.; Kaplan, J.; Dhariwal, P.; Neelakantan, A.; Shyam, P.; Sastry, G.; Askell, A.; et al. Language models are few-shot learners. *arXiv* **2020**, arXiv:2005.14165.
6. Dosovitskiy, A.; Beyer, L.; Kolesnikov, A.; Weissenborn, D.; Zhai, X.; Unterthiner, T.; Dehghani, M.; Minderer, M.; Heigold, G.; Gelly, S.; et al. An image is worth 16x16 words: Transformers for image recognition at scale. *arXiv* **2020**, arXiv:2010.11929.
7. Carion, N.; Massa, F.; Synnaeve, G.; Usunier, N.; Kirillov, A.; Zagoruyko, S. End-to-End Object Detection with Transformers. In Proceedings of the Computer Vision—ECCV 2020; Glasgow, UK, 23–28 August 2020; Springer International Publishing: Cham, Switzerland, 2020; pp. 213–229.
8. Touvron, H.; Cord, M.; Douze, M.; Massa, F.; Sablayrolles, A.; Jégou, H. Training Data-Efficient Image Transformers & Distillation Through Attention. *arXiv* 2020, arXiv:2012.12877.
9. Ali, A.; Touvron, H.; Caron, M.; Bojanowski, P.; Douze, M.; Joulin, A.; Laptev, I.; Neverova, N.; Synnaeve, G.; Verbeek, J.; et al. XCiT: Cross-Covariance Image Transformers. In Proceedings of the Advances in Neural Information Processing Systems, Online, 6–14 December 2021; Ranzato, M., Beygelzimer, A., Dauphin, Y., Liang, P., Vaughan, J.W., Eds.; Curran Associates, Inc.: Red Hook, NY, USA, 2021; Volume 34, pp. 20014–20027.
10. Wu, H.; Xiao, B.; Codella, N.; Liu, M.; Dai, X.; Yuan, L.; Zhang, L. Cvt: Introducing convolutions to vision transformers. *arXiv* **2021**, arXiv:2103.15808.
11. Yuan, L.; Chen, Y.; Wang, T.; Yu, W.; Shi, Y.; Jiang, Z.; Tay, F.E.; Feng, J.; Yan, S. Tokens-to-token vit: Training vision transformers from scratch on imagenet. *arXiv* **2021**, arXiv:2101.11986.
12. Yang, J.; Li, C.; Zhang, P.; Dai, X.; Xiao, B.; Yuan, L.; Gao, J. Focal self-attention for local-global interactions in vision transformers. *arXiv* **2021**, arXiv:2107.00641.
13. Yuan, L.; Hou, Q.; Jiang, Z.; Feng, J.; Yan, S. Volo: Vision outlooker for visual recognition. *arXiv* **2021**, arXiv:2106.13112.
14. Deng, J.; Dong, W.; Socher, R.; Li, L.J.; Li, K.; Fei-Fei, L. ImageNet: A large-scale hierarchical image database. In Proceedings of the 2009 IEEE Conference on Computer Vision and Pattern Recognition, Miami, FL, USA , 20–25 June 2009; pp. 248–255.
15. Krizhevsky, A.; Hinton, G. Learning Multiple Layers of Features from Tiny Images. 2009. Available online: http://www.cs.utoronto.ca/~kriz/learning-features-2009-TR.pdf (accessed on 22 March 2023).
16. Krause, J.; Stark, M.; Deng, J.; Fei-Fei, L. 3d object representations for fine-grained categorization. In Proceedings of the IEEE International Conference on Computer Vision Workshops, Washington, DC, USA, 2–8 December 2013; pp. 554–561.
17. Coates, A.; Ng, A.; Lee, H. An analysis of single-layer networks in unsupervised feature learning. In Proceedings of the Fourteenth International Conference on Artificial Intelligence and Statistics, Fort Lauderdale, FL, USA, 11–13 April 2011; pp. 215–223.
18. Liu, Z.; Lin, Y.; Cao, Y.; Hu, H.; Wei, Y.; Zhang, Z.; Lin, S.; Guo, B. Swin transformer: Hierarchical vision transformer using shifted windows. *arXiv* **2021**, arXiv:2103.14030.
19. Yuan, K.; Guo, S.; Liu, Z.; Zhou, A.; Yu, F.; Wu, W. Incorporating convolution designs into visual transformers. *arXiv* **2021**, arXiv:2103.11816.
20. Xu, Y.; Zhang, Q.; Zhang, J.; Tao, D. ViTAE: Vision Transformer Advanced by Exploring Intrinsic Inductive Bias. *arXiv* **2021**, arXiv:2106.03348.

21. Steiner, A.; Kolesnikov, A.; Zhai, X.; Wightman, R.; Uszkoreit, J.; Beyer, L. How to train your ViT? Data, Augmentation, and Regularization in Vision Transformers. *arXiv* **2021**, arXiv:2106.10270.
22. d'Ascoli, S.; Touvron, H.; Leavitt, M.; Morcos, A.; Biroli, G.; Sagun, L. Convit: Improving vision transformers with soft convolutional inductive biases. *arXiv* **2021**, arXiv:2103.10697.
23. Li, Y.; Zhang, K.; Cao, J.; Timofte, R.; Van Gool, L. Localvit: Bringing locality to vision transformers. *arXiv* **2021**, arXiv:2104.05707.
24. Sun, S.; Yue, X.; Bai, S.; Torr, P. Visual parser: Representing part-whole hierarchies with transformers. *arXiv* **2021**, arXiv:2107.05790.
25. Rao, Y.; Zhao, W.; Zhu, Z.; Lu, J.; Zhou, J. Global filter networks for image classification. *Adv. Neural Inf. Process. Syst.* **2021**, *34*, 980–993.
26. Guibas, J.; Mardani, M.; Li, Z.; Tao, A.; Anandkumar, A.; Catanzaro, B. Efficient Token Mixing for Transformers via Adaptive Fourier Neural Operators. In Proceedings of the International Conference on Learning Representations, Virtual, 3–7 May 2021.
27. Han, K.; Wang, Y.; Chen, H.; Chen, X.; Guo, J.; Liu, Z.; Tang, Y.; Xiao, A.; Xu, C.; Xu, Y.; et al. A survey on vision transformer. *IEEE Trans. Pattern Anal. Mach. Intell.* **2022**, *45*, 87–110. [CrossRef] [PubMed]
28. Khan, S.; Naseer, M.; Hayat, M.; Zamir, S.W.; Khan, F.S.; Shah, M. Transformers in vision: A survey. *ACM Comput. Surv.* **2022**, *54*, 1–41. [CrossRef]
29. Yu, F.; Seff, A.; Zhang, Y.; Song, S.; Funkhouser, T.; Xiao, J. Lsun: Construction of a large-scale image dataset using deep learning with humans in the loop. *arXiv* **2015**, arXiv:1506.03365.
30. Xu, P.; Ehinger, K.A.; Zhang, Y.; Finkelstein, A.; Kulkarni, S.R.; Xiao, J. Turkergaze: Crowdsourcing saliency with webcam based eye tracking. *arXiv* **2015**, arXiv:1504.06755.
31. Netzer, Y.; Wang, T.; Coates, A.; Bissacco, A.; Wu, B.; Ng, A.Y. Reading Digits in Natural Images with Unsupervised Feature Learning. 2011. Available online: http://ufldl.stanford.edu/housenumbers/nips2011_housenumbers.pdf (accessed on 22 March 2023).
32. Cimpoi, M.; Maji, S.; Kokkinos, I.; Mohamed, S.; Vedaldi, A. Describing textures in the wild. In Proceedings of the IEEE Conference on Computer Vision and Pattern Recognition, Columbus, OH, USA, 23–28 June 2014; pp. 3606–3613.
33. Chen, J.; Li, Y.; Wu, X.; Liang, Y.; Jha, S. Robust out-of-distribution detection for neural networks. *arXiv* **2020**, arXiv:2003.09711.
34. Chen, Y.; Dai, X.; Chen, D.; Liu, M.; Dong, X.; Yuan, L.; Liu, Z. Mobile-Former: Bridging MobileNet and Transformer. *arXiv* **2021**, arXiv:2108.05895.
35. Wang, W.; Xie, E.; Li, X.; Fan, D.P.; Song, K.; Liang, D.; Lu, T.; Luo, P.; Shao, L. Pvt v2: Improved baselines with pyramid vision transformer. *Comput. Vis. Media* **2022**, *8*, 415–424. [CrossRef]
36. Xu, W.; Xu, Y.; Chang, T.; Tu, Z. Co-Scale Conv-Attentional Image Transformers. In Proceedings of the IEEE/CVF International Conference on Computer Vision (ICCV), Montreal, QC, Canada, 10–17 October 2021; pp. 9981–9990.
37. Heo, B.; Yun, S.; Han, D.; Chun, S.; Choe, J.; Oh, S.J. Rethinking spatial dimensions of vision transformers. *arXiv* **2021**, arXiv:2103.16302.
38. Yan, H.; Li, Z.; Li, W.; Wang, C.; Wu, M.; Zhang, C. ConTNet: Why not use convolution and transformer at the same time? *arXiv* **2021**, arXiv:2104.13497.
39. Zhang, Q.; Yang, Y.B. ResT: An efficient transformer for visual recognition. *Adv. Neural Inf. Process. Syst.* **2021**, *34*, 15475–15485.
40. Touvron, H.; Cord, M.; Sablayrolles, A.; Synnaeve, G.; Jégou, H. Going Deeper With Image Transformers. In Proceedings of the IEEE/CVF International Conference on Computer Vision (ICCV), Montreal, QC, Canada, 10–17 October 2021; pp. 32–42.
41. Radosavovic, I.; Kosaraju, R.P.; Girshick, R.; He, K.; Dollár, P. Designing network design spaces. In Proceedings of the IEEE/CVF Conference on Computer Vision and Pattern Recognition, Seattle, WA, USA, 14–18 June 2020; pp. 10428–10436.
42. Hoffer, E.; Ben-Nun, T.; Hubara, I.; Giladi, N.; Hoefler, T.; Soudry, D. Augment your batch: Improving generalization through instance repetition. In Proceedings of the IEEE/CVF Conference on Computer Vision and Pattern Recognition, Seattle, WA, USA, 13–19 June 2020; pp. 8129–8138.
43. Hendrycks, D.; Gimpel, K. A baseline for detecting misclassified and out-of-distribution examples in neural networks. *arXiv* **2016**, arXiv:1610.02136.
44. Lee, K.; Lee, H.; Lee, K.; Shin, J. Training confidence-calibrated classifiers for detecting out-of-distribution samples. *arXiv* **2017**, arXiv:1711.09325.
45. Kornblith, S.; Shlens, J.; Le, Q.V. Do better imagenet models transfer better? In Proceedings of the IEEE/CVF Conference on Computer Vision and Pattern Recognition, Long Beach, CA, USA, 15–20 June 2019; pp. 2661–2671.

MDPI AG
Grosspeteranlage 5
4052 Basel
Switzerland
Tel.: +41 61 683 77 34

Mathematics Editorial Office
E-mail: mathematics@mdpi.com
www.mdpi.com/journal/mathematics

www.ingramcontent.com/pod-product-compliance
Lightning Source LLC
Chambersburg PA
CBHW061610220926
51850CB00005B/471
* 9 7 8 3 7 2 5 8 5 7 0 7 4 *